make the familiar new

culture structure power

SELECTED MATERIALS FROM

EXPERIENCE
SOCIOLOGY

David Croteau

—

William Hoynes

LEHIGH CARBON COMMUNITY COLLEGE
SOC 150

Boston   Burr Ridge, IL   Dubuque, IA   New York   San Francisco   St. Louis
Bangkok   Bogotá   Caracas   Lisbon   London   Madrid
Mexico City   Milan   New Delhi   Seoul   Singapore   Sydney   Taipei   Toronto

Selected Materials From Experience Sociology
Lehigh Carbon Community College
SOC 150

This book is a McGraw-Hill Learning Solutions textbook and contains select material from *Experience Sociology*, First Edition by David Croteau and William Hoynes. Copyright © 2013 by The McGraw-Hill Companies, Inc. Reprinted with permission of the publisher. Many custom published texts are modified versions or adaptations of our best-selling textbooks. Some adaptations are printed in black and white to keep prices at a minimum, while others are in color.

1 2 3 4 5 6 7 8 9 0   DIG DIG   14 13 12

ISBN-13: 978-0-07-767008-5
ISBN-10: 0-07-767008-6

Learning Solutions Consultant: Stephanie Corby
Production Editor: Jeni McAtee
Printer/Binder:Digital Impressions
Cover Images © 2012 JupiterImages Corporation

About the AUTHORS

DAVID CROTEAU

earned a B.A. in sociology from Brandeis University and a Ph.D. in sociology from Boston College. Over the years he has taught a diverse range of students at Boston College, Clark University, Keene State College, and the University of Mary Washington. As an associate professor at Virginia Commonwealth University, he taught courses in theory, methods, stratification, movements, and media to both undergraduate and graduate students. He retired early from Virginia Commonwealth University and now uses his sociological training in writing and consulting, as well as teaching.

In addition to various journal articles and book chapters, Professor Croteau is the author of *Politics and the Class Divide,* a finalist for both the C. Wright Mills Award from the Society for the Study of Social Problems and the Transformational Politics Book Award from the American Political Science Association.

WILLIAM HOYNES

earned a B.A. in history and political science from Tufts University and a Ph.D. in sociology from Boston College. He is Professor of Sociology at Vassar College, where he teaches Introductory Sociology as well as courses on media, culture, research methods, and social theory. During his twenty years at Vassar, Professor Hoynes has served as chair of the Sociology Department and director of both the Media Studies Program and the American Culture Program.

In addition to various journal articles and book chapters on public broadcasting in the United States, Professor Hoynes is the author of *Public Television for Sale: Media, the Market, and the Public Sphere,* which was awarded the Goldsmith Book Prize from the Shorenstein Center on Press, Politics and Public Policy at Harvard University's John F. Kennedy School of Government.

CROTEAU and HOYNES are coauthors of *Media/Society: Images, Industries, and Audiences,* which was published in a revised 4th edition in 2011; *The Business of Media: Corporate Media and the Public Interest,* which won the Robert Picard Award for best new book in media economics by the Association for Education in Journalism and Mass Communication; and *By Invitation Only: How the Media Limit Political Debate.* They are also coeditors, with Charlotte Ryan, of *Rhyming Hope and History: Activists, Academics, and Social Movement Scholarship.*

BRIEF CONTENTS

CONTENTS

PART 1
THE SOCIOLOGICAL PERSPECTIVE

1 SOCIOLOGY IN A CHANGING WORLD 2

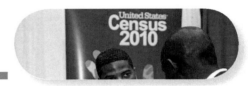

2 UNDERSTANDING THE RESEARCH PROCESS 30

PART 3
THE SOCIAL SELF

6
SOCIALIZATION   134

7
INTERACTION, GROUPS, AND ORGANIZATIONS   160

PART 4
IDENTITY AND INEQUALITY

9
CLASS AND GLOBAL INEQUALITY 218

10
RACE AND ETHNICITY 250

11

GENDER AND SEXUALITY   282

PART 5
SOCIAL INSTITUTIONS
AND SOCIAL ISSUES

13

EDUCATION AND WORK   344

14

MEDIA AND CONSUMPTION 374

16

POLITICS AND THE ECONOMY 434

BOXED FEATURES

THROUGH A SOCIOLOGICAL LENS

IN TRANSITION SECTIONS

SOCIAL CHANGE NOTES

MAPS

Dear Colleagues:

Like all of us who teach sociology, we want to help a diverse range of students grasp the basic concepts of the discipline, see the relevance of those concepts to their everyday lives, and apply what they learn to the world around them. We want students to experience that aha! moment when they see the familiar in a new way and realize that sociology's tools can help them better understand their rapidly changing social world. In other words, we want students to see the world from a sociological perspective and to actively use their sociological imagination. We want them to **experience sociology.**

What's unique about Experience Sociology?

CULTURE. STRUCTURE. POWER. *Experience Sociology* engages students with a clear framework for understanding their world based on three familiar terms at the heart of sociology: **culture, structure,** and **power.** Through the lenses of these three concepts, students learn from their first class to see the world from a sociological perspective and to grasp the significance of sociology for their own lives. For every topic in the book—from the family to the economy to the environment—they learn to recognize the effects of the culture they have been taught, see the structures that constrain or empower them, and notice how power operates at every level of society.

How is theory covered?

Theory has a role in every chapter in *Experience Sociology*. We know how important it is for students not only to be able to apply concepts to their lives, but also to understand and be able to apply sociological theory. With its innovative organization around primary sociological concepts, *Experience Sociology* emphasizes the common ground that informs a basic sociological perspective. But every chapter also addresses the way differing theoretical perspectives illuminate various facets of these key sociological concepts, letting instructors and students go beyond conventional theoretical boundaries and the either-or framing of theoretical perspectives to see how each can contribute to our understanding of the social world.

What's the full Experience?

Experience Sociology is much more than this textbook alone. Incorporating the work of many sociology instructors, it is instead a comprehensive instructional program that combines digital and print resources to promote student learning. Featuring interactive activities and videos tied to learning objectives, and an adaptive diagnostic tool that generates a study plan specifically designed to address students' individual strengths and weaknesses, *Experience Sociology* helps you manage assignments and makes learning and studying more engaging and efficient for your students.

We wrote *Experience Sociology* because we want students to be able to do just that: experience their world differently through the insights of sociology. We hope these resources will help you in introducing your students to the excitement of sociology.

Sincerely,

David Croteau   *William Hoynes*

Make the familiar a new experience for you and your students.

WHY THE 3D GLASSES?

We want students to see their familiar world in a new way. *Experience Sociology* **uses the lenses of culture, structure, and power to empower students to move beyond an individual perspective to gain a sociological perspective.**

make the familiar new

culture structure power

How were you socialized into your society's **culture**?

How do agents of socialization reproduce social **structure**?

How does **power** shape your daily life and your sense of self?

Using the lenses of CULTURE, STRUCTURE, and POWER, *Experience Sociology* **shows students the significance of sociology for their own lives.**

CULTURE, STRUCTURE, and POWER help students explore sociological theory in ways that go beyond conventional theoretical boundaries.

SPOTLIGHT
on social theory

Symbolic interactionism stresses the role of interpersonal interactions in reproducing culture and social structure. Have you ever been in a situation in which you felt at a disadvantage because you lacked the cultural capital to know what behavior was expected of you?

Experience a new classroom dynamic with *LearnSmart*.

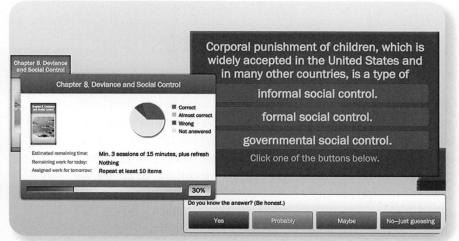

LearnSmart is an adaptive learning system that helps students study efficiently and effectively for greater success. *LearnSmart* intelligently pinpoints concepts students do not understand and maps out personalized study plans that ground students in the fundamentals of sociology, allowing instructors to focus valuable class time on higher-level concepts.

Give students the experience of doing sociology with *Investigate Sociology*.

The engaging, interactive, story-based scenarios in *Investigate Sociology* help students develop their sociological imagination, challenging them to use the lenses of culture, race, class, and gender to delve deeply into significant and timely issues. To complete these scenarios, students study background information, analyze data, conduct interviews, and write up and support their conclusions.

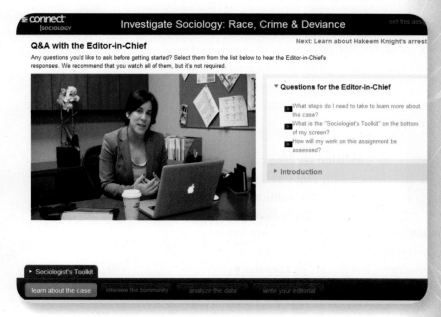

EXPERIENCE SOCIOLOGY includes a variety of boxed features and in-text learning aids to help students appreciate the range of sociology's insights and their relevance to today's fast-changing social world, and to apply sociology's concepts and theories to their own lives.

BOXED FEATURES

Sociology Matters boxes highlight the contributions of sociological research to public policy and to the efforts of public interest organizations, social movements, and others to effect social change.

Sociology Works boxes profile people who studied sociology in college and are now using sociology's insights in diverse work settings. These boxes feature people working in fields such as health care, criminal justice, social work, business, mass media, government, and the military.

Through a Sociological Lens boxes demonstrate how sociology can provide distinctive insights into contemporary social issues. Students can see how sociological research reveals information that can both surprise and empower them in their everyday lives.

Social Change Notes illustrate the ever-evolving nature of our social world. These brief, engaging notes, illustrated with photographs, advertisements, or other images, show students how change has been a constant feature of social life.

In-Transition sections conclude each chapter with a look at the influence of changing social conditions on some aspect of the chapter topic. Examples include the commercialization of deviance, increasing inequality in the United States, the changing nature of organizations, and convergence in gender and sexuality.

IN-TEXT LEARNING AIDS

 Thinking About notes help students connect chapter content to their own experience. These brief notes, found at the bottom of text pages, prompt students to consider how the three core concepts of **culture, structure,** and **power** apply to their own lives and views on issues, thus encouraging students to begin to think sociologically.

Core Concepts Challenge questions encourage students to apply their sociological imagination to what they are learning. Appearing with selected figures, tables, and photographs, these questions prompt students to apply **culture, structure,** and **power** in thinking about an issue as well as to think critically about the graphic, table, or image.

 Spotlight notes prompt students to consider social theories that are discussed within the text. These notes help students use the concepts of culture, structure, and power to apply the theory to their own lives.

EXPERIENCE SOCIOLOGY is available to instructors and students in traditional print

format as well as online within McGraw-Hill's Connect Sociology, an integrated assignment and assessment platform. Connect Sociology's online tools make managing assignments easier for instructors—and make learning and studying more motivating and efficient for students.

⮕ **LearnSmart** This powerful learning system helps students assess their knowledge of course content through a series of adaptive questions, intelligently pinpointing concepts the student does not understand and mapping out a personalized study plan for success.

⮕ *Investigate Sociology* These engaging, interactive, story-based online activities challenge students to delve deeply into issues of race, class, gender, and culture, giving them the experience of *doing* sociology.

⮕ **Integrated eBook** A fully loaded eBook allows students to review *Experience Sociology* anytime and anywhere. They can highlight, take notes, and quickly search for key terms and phrases.

⮕ **Real-time Reports** These printable, exportable reports show how well each student (or section) is performing on each course segment. Instructors can use this feature to spot problem areas *before* they crop up on an exam.

⮕ **Assignable and Assessable Activities** Instructors can easily deliver assignments and tests online, and students can practice skills that fulfill learning objectives at their own pace and on their own schedule.

Teaching and Learning with

TEACHING RESOURCES

- **Instructor's Manual,** written by Nick McRee, The University of Portland, and Sarah Bill Schott, North Central College and Northeastern Illinois University. The Instructor's Manual incorporates tips for both new and experienced instructors and includes learning objectives, brief and detailed chapter outlines, chapter summaries, lecture outlines, lecture ideas, and topics for class discussion.

- **Test Bank,** written by Markéta Cawood, Hopkinsville Community College; Shelly Dutchin, Western Technical College; Erica Hunter, University at Albany; and Karrie Ann Snyder-Carson, Northwestern University. This resource offers 100 multiple-choice and true-or-false questions for each chapter. McGraw-Hill's computerized EZ Test allows instructors to create customized exams using the publisher's supplied test items or instructors' own questions. A version of the test bank is also provided in Microsoft Word files for instructors who prefer that format.

- **PowerPoint Slides.** The selections, which include video resources such as illustrative social scenarios and NBC News segments, can be used as is or modified to meet the needs of individual instructors.

 Design your own ideal course materials with McGraw-Hill's **Create™,** http://www.mcgrawhillcreate.com. Rearrange or omit chapters, combine material from other sources, upload your syllabus or any other content you have written to make the perfect resource for your students. Search thousands of leading McGraw-Hill textbooks to find the best content for your students; then arrange it to fit your teaching style. You can even personalize your book's appearance by selecting the cover and adding your name, school, and course information. When you order a Create book, you receive a complimentary review copy. Get a printed copy in 3 to 5 business days or an electronic copy (e-Comp) via e-mail in about an hour. Register today at **http://www.mcgrawhillcreate.com,** and craft your course resources to match the way you teach.

 McGraw-Hill Campus™ is a new one-stop teaching and learning experience available to users of any learning management system. This institutional service allows faculty and students to enjoy single sign-on (SSO) access to all McGraw-Hill Higher Education materials, including the award-winning McGraw-Hill Connect® platform, from directly within the institution's web site. McGraw-Hill Campus provides faculty with instant access to all McGraw-Hill Higher Education teaching materials (e.g., eTextbooks, test banks, PowerPoint slides, animations and learning objects), allowing them to browse, search, and use any instructor ancillary content in our vast library at no additional cost to instructor or students. Students enjoy SSO access to a variety of free (e.g., quizzes, flash cards, narrated presentations) and subscription-based products (e.g., McGraw-Hill Connect). With this program enabled, faculty and students will never need to create another account to access McGraw-Hill products and services.

EXPERIENCE
SOCIOLOGY

Tegrity Campus is a service that makes class time available around the clock. It automatically captures every lecture in a searchable format for students to review when they study and complete assignments.

With a simple one-click start-and-stop process, you capture all computer screens and corresponding audio. Students replay any part of any class with easy-to-use browser-based viewing on a PC or Mac.

With Tegrity Campus, students quickly recall key moments by using Tegrity Campus's unique search feature, which lets them efficiently find what they need, when they need it, across an entire semester of class recordings.

Help turn all your students' study time into learning moments immediately supported by your lecture.

To learn more about Tegrity, watch a 2-minute Flash demo at **http://tegritycampus.mhhe.com.**

*Visit **coursesmart .com** to purchase registration codes for this exciting product.* CourseSmart offers thousands of the most commonly adopted textbooks across hundreds of courses from a wide variety of higher education publishers. It is the only place for faculty to review and compare the full text of a book online, providing immediate access without the environmental impact of requesting a printed exam copy. At CourseSmart, students can save up to 50 percent off the cost of a printed book, reduce their impact on the environment, and gain access to powerful web tools for learning, including full text search, notes and highlighting, and e-mail tools for sharing notes among classmates. Learn more at **http://www.coursesmart.com.**

ACKNOWLEDGMENTS

Writing *Experience Sociology* has been a multi-year journey for us, a journey we could not have completed without the support of many people along the way. We would like to thank Sherith Pankratz, our initial editor at McGraw-Hill, for encouraging us to begin the project in the first place. Thanks to the many folks at McGraw-Hill who have helped us complete the book. In particular, we benefitted from the hard work of Rhona Robbin, Gina Boedeker, Carla Samodulski, and David Chodoff throughout the writing and editing process. We would also like to thank Steve Debow, president of McGraw-Hill Higher Education's Humanities, Social Science, and Language Division, and Mike Ryan, editor in chief, for their support for the project. Catherine Morris, our project manager, shepherded the project from manuscript to finished product with unfailing good humor. Cassandra Chu oversaw the project's design, Natalia Peschiera oversaw photo research, and Robin Mouat oversaw art. And thanks to Jocelyn Spielberger, Nathan Benjamin, Meghan Campbell, and Laura Ciporen for overseeing *Experience Sociology*'s wealth of digital resources.

Many thanks to our colleagues who have helped us to think about teaching sociology, including Mike Malec and William Gamson at Boston College, Joe Marolla at Virginia Commonwealth University, Steve Lyng at Carthage College, and Eileen Leonard, Bob McAulay, and Marque Miringoff at Vassar College. We appreciate the contributions of our various research assistants, including Meg Burns, Kelly Capehart, Rachel Cerlen, Mollie Sandberg, Jacinthe Sasson-Yenor, and Shawna Seth. More generally, we are grateful to our students, from whom we have learned a great deal about sociology and pedagogy over the past two decades.

Finally, David would like to thank Cecelia Kirkman—again—for everything. William would like to thank his family, Deirdre, Ben, and Nick, for their support, encouragement, and patience throughout the years required to produce this book.

BOARD OF ADVISORS

We would like to thank our board of advisors for their invaluable insights and long-term dedication to this project:

Scott Brooks, University of California-Riverside
Nina Chapman, Golden West College
Susan Cody, Georgia Perimeter College-Dunwoody
Isaac W. Eberstein, Florida State University
Melinda Messineo, Ball State University

ACADEMIC REVIEWERS

Thanks to the following for their thorough and thoughtful evaluations of various portions and drafts of *Experience Sociology*.

Cawo Abdi, University of Minnesota-Minneapolis
Wesley Abercrombie, Midlands Technical College
Doug Adams, University of Arkansas-Fayetteville
Isaac Addai, Lansing Community College
Trudy Anderson, Texas A&M-Kingsville
Robert Aponte, Indiana University-Purdue University-Indianapolis
David Arizmendi, South Texas College
Bryan Auld, Indiana University-Purdue University-Ft. Wayne
Robert Baker, Sandhills Community College
Sergio Banda, Fullerton College
Baishakhi Banerjee Taylor, University of Kentucky-Lexington
Nadine Barrett, University of Central Florida
Joshua Bass, Portland State University
Lance Basting, Chippewa Valley Technical College

John Batsie, Parkland College
James Bazan, Central Piedmont Community College
James Becker, Pulaski Tech College
Joseph Beczak, San Diego City College
Janice Bending, University of Cincinnati-Cincinnati
Claudette Bennett, Howard University
Todd E. Bernhardt, Broward College-Central
Terry Besser, Iowa State University
Gary Bittner, York College of Pennsylvania
Amy Blackstone, University of Maine
Michelle Blake, University of Evansville
Carolyn Bond, Boston University
Karyn Boutin, Massasoit Community College
Christophe Bradley, Indiana University-Purdue University-Ft. Wayne
Judith Brake, Ozarks Technical Community College
John Brenner, York College of Pennsylvania
Helen Brethauer-Gay, Florida A&M University
Daniel Brewster, West Virginia University-Morgantown
David L. Briscoe, University of Arkansas-Little Rock
Rebeca Brittenham, College of Southern Nevada-West Charles
Scott Brooks, University of California-Riverside

Richard Bucher, Baltimore City Community College
Jonathan Bullinger, Camden County College
Mary L. Burns, Michigan State University-East Lansing
Paul Calarco, Hudson Valley Community College
Allison Camelot, Saddleback College
Elaine Cannon, El Camino College
Marketa Cawood, Hopkinsville Community College
Edwin Chambless, El Paso Community College-Valle Verde
Gina Chance, Central New Mexico Community College
Nina Chapman, Golden West College
Adrian Cheatwood, University of Texas-San Antonio
Adrian Chevraux-FitzHugh, Sacramento City College
Andrew Cho, Tacoma Community College
Margaret Choka, Pellissippi State Technical Community College
Bridget Christensen, Southeast Community College
Sue Ciriello, Naugatuck Valley Community College
Rodney Clayton, Central Community College-Hastings
Susan Cody, Georgia Perimeter College-Dunwoody

Charles Combs, Sinclair Community College

Ida Cook, University of Central Florida

Lisa Coole, Massasoit Community College

Mary Kay Cordill, Cape Cod Community College

Linda Cornwell, Bowling Green State University

Carolyn Corrado, State University of New York at Albany

Mary Croissant, Front Range Community College-Fort Collins

Larry Curiel, Cypress College

Cloyis Daughhetee, Arkansas State University

Robert Scott Davis, Treasure Valley Community College

Rhett Davy, North Central Texas College

Susan Day, Texas State University

Rohan De Silva, Milwaukee Area Technical College-Milwaukee

Kelly Dever, University of Florida at Gainesville

Aimee Dickinson, Lorain County Community College

Nancy Dimonte, Farmingdale State College

Greg Donnenwerth, University of Memphis

Joe Donnermeyer, Ohio State University-Columbus

Brian Donovan, University of Kansas-Lawrence

Sue Dowden, El Camino College

Lilli Downes, Polk State College

Michael Dreiling, University of Oregon

Adam Driscoll, University of North Carolina-Charlotte

Susan Dumais, Louisiana State University

Gianna Durso-Finley, Mercer County Community College

Shelly Dutchin, Western Tech College

Isaac W. Eberstein, Florida State University

Samuel Echevarria-Cruz, Austin Community College-Riverside

Martin Edelstein, Baruch College

Sherwood Edwards, College of Dupage

John Ehle, Jr., NOVA Community College-Annandale

Susan Eichenberger, Seton Hill University

Jim Elliott, University of Oregon

David Embrick, Loyola University-Chicago

Graves Enck, University of Memphis

Kevin Ervin, Northern Illinois University

Kathryn Feltey, University of Akron

Catherine Felton, Central Piedmont Community College

Leticia Fernandez, University of Texas at El Paso

Richard Fey, Arizona State University

Lauralee Finley, Florida Atlantic University

Kevin Fitzpatrick, University of Alabama at Birmingham

Dona Fletcher, Sinclair Community College

Martha Flores, El Paso Community College–Valle Verde

Tammie Foltz, Des Moines Area Community College-Boone

Murray Fortner, Tarrant County College Northeast

Tony Foster, Lone Star College-Kingwood

John Gannon, College of Southern Nevada–North Las Vegas

Beverly Gartland, Youngstown State University

David Gay, University of Central Florida

Marie L. Germain, City College-Miami

Steve Glennon, Iowa Western Community College-Council Bluffs

Sergio Gomez, Chaffey College

Kyra Greene, San Diego State University

Mike Greenhouse, Middlesex County College

Sara Grineski, University of Texas at El Paso

Elke Grogg, Ivy Tech Community College of Indiana

Heather Guevara, Portland Community College-Sylvania

Jeffrey Hall, University of Alabama at Birmingham

Bram Hamovitch, Lakeland Community College

Carl Hand, Valdosta State University

Sara Hanna, Oakland Community College-Highland Lakes

Peggy Hargis, Georgia Southern University

Kalynn Heald, Northwest Arkansas Community College

Nina Heckler, University of Alabama at Tuscaloosa

Garrison Henderson, Tarrant County College Southeast

Kimberly Hennessee, Ball State University

Marta T. Henriksen, Central New Mexico Community College

Pablo Hernandez, Lansing Community College

Teresa Hibbert, University of Texas at El Paso

Carmon Weaver Hicks, Ivy Tech Community College of Indiana

Tonya Hilligoss, Sacramento City College

Caroll Hodgson, Rowan-Cabarrus Community College

Donna Holland, Indiana University-Purdue University

Kathleen Holmes, Darton College

Mark Horowitz, University of Texas at Brownsville

Nils Hovik, Lehigh Carbon Community College

Erica Hunter, State University of New York at Albany

Ronald Huskin, Del Mar College

Creed Hyatt, Lehigh Carbon Community College

Peter Iadicola, Indiana University-Purdue University-Ft. Wayne

Denise Ingram, Mercer County Community College

Michael Itagaki, Fullerton College

Jennifer Jackson, Cincinnati State Technical & Community College

Timothy Jacobs, Naugatuck Valley Community College

Laura Jamison, Parkland College

Randy Jarvis, South Texas College

J. Craig Jenkins, Ohio State University-Columbus

Mark Jepson, University of California-Los Angeles

Dennis Johnson, Craven Community College

Jim Jones, Mississippi State University

Ali Kamali, Missouri Western State University

Irwin Kantor, Middlesex County College

Michael Kaune, Saint Francis College

Paul Ketchum, University of Oklahoma-Norman

Steve Keto, Kent State University

William Kimberlin, Laini County Community College

Brian Klocke, State University of New York at Plattsburgh

James Knapp, Southeastern Oklahoma State University

Michelle Knoles, Cowley County Community College

Jamee Kristen, University of Nebraska-Lincoln

Lorien Lake, University of Arizona

Judy Lasker, Lehigh University

Terina Lathe, Central Piedmont Community College

Jodie Lawston, Depaul University

Rebecca Leichtfuss, Moraine Park Tech College

Jason Leiker, Utah State University

Joe Lengermann, University of Maryland-College Park

Troy Lepper, Colorado State University

David Liu, Harrisburg Area Community College

David Locher, Missouri Southern State University

William Lockhart, McLennan Community College

Nicole Loftus, Saddleback College

Royal Loresco, South Texas College

Joleen Loucks, Kutztown University of Pennsylvania

Michael Loukinen, Northern Michigan University

Bradford Lyman, Baltimore City Community College

Jean Lynch-Brandon, Lansing Community College

Joanna Maata, Pennsylvania State University

Anne MacLellan, Community College of Baltimore County-Catonsville

I. Ross Macmillan, University of Minnesota-Minneapolis

Sherry Mader, Western Technical College

M. Wilbrod Madzura, Normandale Community College

Cheryl Maes, University of Nevado-Reno

Lori Maida, Westchester Community College

Farshad Makek-Ahmadi, Naugatuck Valley Community College

Susan Mann, University of New Orleans

Nick Maroules, Illinois State University

Ronald Matson, Wichita State University

Deborah McCarthy, College of Charleston

Dorothy McCawley, University of Florida

Karen McCue, Central New Mexico Community College

Victor McCullum, Triton College

Marian McWhorter, Houston Community College-Central College

Ronald Meneses, University of Florida

Chadwick L. Menning, Ball State University

Melinda Messineo, Ball State University

Janet Michello, LaGuardia Community College

Harvest Moon, University of Texas at Arlington

Mel Moore, University of Northern Colorado

Marcillino Morales, East Los Angeles College

John Morra, Quinnipiac University

Edward Morris, University of Kentucky-Lexington

Kelly Mosel-Talavera, Texas State University-San Marcos

Brian Moss, Oakland Community College-Highland Lakes

Sepandar Mossadeghi, Palm Beach State College-Eissey Camp

Dan Muhwezi, Bulter Community College

Lynn Newhart, Rockford College

Bruce Nicometo, Northwest Arkansas Community College

Claire Nivens-Blower, Cape Cod Community College

Nelda Nix, Community College of Baltimore County-Essex

Cheryl North, Tarrant County College Northeast

Kwaku Obosue-Mensah, Lorain County Community College

Patricia O'Brien, Elgin Community College

Bob O'Neil, Louisiana State University-Baton Rouge

Jacob Oni, Cape Cod Community College

Robert Orrange, Eastern Michigan University

Diane Owsley, Elizabethtown Community College

Bruce Pabian, Delaware Technical Community College-Stanton

Frank Page, University of Utah-Salt Lake City

Chris Papaleonardos, Ohio State University-Columbus

Caroline Parham, Craven Community College

Kevin Payne, Park University-Parkville

Douglas Peck, Stark State

Lisa Pellerin, Ball State University

Jane Penney, Eastfield College

Narayan Persaud, Florida A&M University

Nancy Pietroforte, Rockland Community College

Peggy Preble, Thomas Nelson Community College

Paul C. Price, Pasadena City College

Ariane Prohaska, University of Alabama at Tuscaloosa

Adrian Rapp, Lone Star College-North Harris

Todd Rasner, Hudson Valley Community College

Kent Redding, University of Wisconsin-Milwaukee

Nancy Reeves, Gloucester County College

John Rice, University of North Carolina-Wilmington

Ray Rich, College of Southern Nevada-West Charles

Cecelia Rivers, Northwest Florida State College

Gregg Robinson, Grossmont College

Christine Rodriguez, East Los Angeles College

Fatima Rodriguez, Rutgers University

Robyn Rodriguez, Reedley College

Luis Rodriguez-Abad, University of Texas at Brownsville

Richard Rosell, Westchester Community College

Olga Rowe, Oregon State University

Alan Rudy, Central Michigan University

Amy Ruedisueli, Tidewater Community College

Igor Ryabov, Ohio University-Athens

Charlotte Ryan, University of Massachusetts-Lowell

Ivanka Sabolich, Kent State University

George Saunders, Ball State University

Peter Sawyer, Hudson Valley Community College

David Schall, Milwaukee Area Technical College

Jon Schlenker, University of Maine-Augusta

Rachel Schneider, University of Akron

Andreas Schneider, Texas Tech University

Sarah Bill Schott, North Central College-Naperville

Terri Schrantz, Tarrant County College

Ron Schultz, Gateway Technical College

Jeff Schulz, Central Community College-Grand Island

Megan Seely, Sierra College

Lystra Seenath, Palm Beach State College-Lake Worth

Barbara Seiter, Raritan Valley Community College

Patricia Seitz, Central New Mexico Community College

Charles Selengut, County College of Morris

Monissa Shackleford, Pensacola Junior College

Robert Shelly, Ohio University-Athens

Anson Shupe, Indiana University-Purdue University-Ft. Wayne

Denise Shuster, Owens Community College

Edward Silva, El Paso Community College-Valle Verde

Toni Sims, University of Southwestern Louisiana

Amy Slater, MCC-Blue River Community College

Steven Sloan, Gateway Technical College

Michael Smith, Lakeland Community College

Michelle Smith, Southwestern Illinois College

Karrie Snyder, Northwestern University

Tomecia Sobers, Fayetteville Technical Community College

Stephanie Southworth, Clemson University

Ryan Spohn, Kansas State University

Johnnie Spraggins, University of Texas at San Antonio

Dan Stalder, University of Wisconsin-Whitewater

Rachael Stehle, Cuyahoga Community College Western-Parma

Lawrence Stern, Collin County Community College-Plano

Terrence Stewart, Mott College

Michelle Stewart Thomas, Mt. San Antonio College

Jill Stiemsma, Moraine Park Tech College

Beverly Stiles, Midwestern State University

Randolph Ston, Oakland Community College-Auburn Hills

Michael Stupak, Milwaukee Area Technical College

Holly Suarez, University of North Carolina-Charlotte

Rose Suggett, Southeast Community College

Deborah Sullivan, Arizona State University-Tempe

Richard Sweeny, Modesto Junior College

John Szivos, Mount Wachusett Community College

Margaret Taylor, Greenville Technical College

Sara Thompson, Laredo Community College

Ruth Thompson-Miller, Texas A&M University

Bob Transon, Milwaukee Area Technical College

Tim Tuinstra, Kalamazoo Valley Community College

Toby Vance, El Paso Community College-Valle Verde

Melinda Vandervis, Orange Coast College

Steven Vassar, Minnesota State University-Mankato

Ray Von Robertson, Lamar University

Vu-Duc Vuong, De Anza College

Sally Vyain, Ivy Tech Community College of Indiana

Florence Wakoko, Columbus State University

Glenda D. Walden, University of Colorado-Boulder

Marie L. Wallace, Pima Community College-West

Suzan Waller, Franklin University

Gina Walls, Parkland College

Sheryl Walz, Citrus College

Martha Warburton, University of Texas at Brownsville

Elizabeth Watts Warren, Gordon College

Sandra Way, New Mexico State University-Las Cruces

Sharon Wettengel, Tarrant County College Southeast

Amanda White, St. Louis Community College-Meramec-Kirkwood

Debbie White, Citrus College

Gailynn White, Citrus College

Gordon Whitman, Tidewater Community College-Norfolk

Cindy Whitney, Kansas State University, College of Technology & Aviation

Linda Wicks, Stony Brook University

Cleon Wiggins, Kansas City, Kansas, Community College

Marion Willetts, Illinois State University

L. Sue Williams, Kansas State University

Gerald Williams, Camden County College

Bryan Williamson, Lorain County Community College

Beate Wilson, Western Illinois University

Charles Wilson, Kansas City, Kansas, Community College

Rowan Wolf, Portland Community College-Sylvania

Amy Wong, San Diego State University

Robert E. Wood, Rutgers University

Peter Wood, Eastern Michigan University

Timothy Woods, Manchester Community College

Diane Wysocki, University of Nebraska-Kearney

Pat Yeager, Ivy Tech Community College of Indiana-Evansville

Andrew Ziner, Kutztown University of Pennsylvania

John F. Zipp, University of Akron

SYMPOSIA ATTENDEES

Every year McGraw-Hill conducts several Introductory Sociology symposia for instructors from across the country. These events offer a forum for instructors to exchange ideas and experiences with colleagues they might not have the chance to meet otherwise. They also provide the McGraw-Hill team with invaluable feedback about the needs and challenges of the introductory sociology course, feedback that has contributed both directly and indirectly to *Experience Sociology.*

Doug Adams, University of Arkansas, Fayetteville

Isaac Addai, Lansing Community College

Robert Aponte, Indiana University-Purdue University-Indianapolis

David Arizmendi, South Texas College

Sergio Banda, Fullerton College

Baishakhi Banerjee Taylor, University of Kentucky-Lexington

John Batsie, Parkland College

James Bazan, Central Piedmont Community College

Janice Bending, University of Cincinnati-Cincinnati

Amy Blackstone, University of Maine

Judith Brake, Ozarks Technical Community College

Scott Brooks, University of California at Riverside

Elaine Cannon, El Camino College

Nina Chapman, Golden West College

Margaret Choka, Pellissippi State Technical Community College

Rodney Clayton, Central Community College-Hastings

Susan Cody, Georgia Perimeter College-Dunwoody

Charles Combs, Sinclair Community College

Lisa Coole, Massasoit Community College

Carolyn Corrado, State University of New York at Albany

Larry Curiel, Cypress College

Robert Scott Davis, Treasure Valley Community College

Rohan De Silva, Milwaukee Area Technical College-Milwaukee

Aimee Dickinson, Lorain County Community College

Joe Donnermeyer, Ohio State University-Columbus

Brian Donovan, University of Kansas-Lawrence

Isaac W. Eberstein, Florida State University

Samuel Echevarria-Cruz, Austin Community College-Riverside

John Ehle, Jr., NOVA Community College-Annandale

David Embrick, Loyola University-Chicago

Kathryn Feltey, University of Akron

Tammie Foltz, Des Moines Area Community College-Boone

John Gannon, College of Southern Nevada-North Las Vegas

Sergio Gomez, Chaffey College

Kyra Greene, San Diego State University

Mike Greenhouse, Middlesex County College

Bram Hamovitch, Lakeland Community College

Carl Hand, Valdosta State University

Garrison Henderson, Tarrant County College-Southeast

Peter Iadicola, Indiana University-Purdue University-Ft. Wayne

Laura Jamison, Parkland College

Jim Jones, Mississippi State University

Steve Keto, Kent State University

Brian Klocke, State University of New York at Plattsburgh

Jodie Lawston, Depaul University

Jason Leiker, Utah State University

Joe Lengermann, University of Maryland-College Park

David Liu, Harrisburg Area Community College

David Locher, Missouri Southern State University

Michael Loukinen, Northern Michigan University

Jean Lynch-Brandon, Lansing Community College

Cheryl Maes, University of Nevada-Reno

Lori Maida, Westchester Community College

Farshad Makek-Ahmadi, Naugatuck Valley Community College

Karen McCue, Central New Mexico Community College

Melinda Messineo, Ball State University

Kelly Mosel-Talavera, Texas State University-San Marcos

Sepandar Mossadeghi, Palm Beach State College-Eissey Campus

Cheryl North, Tarrant County College-Northeast

Patricia O'Brien, Elgin Community College

Jacob Oni, Cape Cod Community College

Robert Orrange, Eastern Michigan University

Diane Owsley, KCTCS Elizabethtown Community College

Kevin Payne, Park University-Parkville

Lisa Pellerin, Ball State University

Paul C. Price, Pasadena City College

Richard Rosell, Westchester Community College

Alan Rudy, Central Michigan University

Rachel Schneider, University of Akron

Terri Schrantz, Tarrant County College

Barbara Seiter, Raritan Valley Community College

Michael Smith, Lakeland Community College

Rachael Stehle, Cuyahoga Community College-Western

Lawrence Stern, Collin County Community College-Plano

Michelle Stewart Thomas, Mt. San Antonio College

Rose Suggett, Southeast Community College

Richard Sweeny, Modesto Junior College

Margaret Taylor, Greenville Technical College

Ruth Thompson-Miller, Texas A&M University

Vu-Duc Vuong, De Anza College

Marie L. Wallace, Pima Community College-West

Sheryl Walz, Citrus College

Sharon Wettengel, Tarrant County College-Southeast

Amanda White, St. Louis Community College-Meramec-Kirkwood

L. Sue Williams, Kansas State University

Rowan Wolf, Portland Community College-Sylvania

John F. Zipp, University of Akron

CONNECT REVIEWERS AND CONTRIBUTORS

The following instructors contributed to Connect Sociology with their thoughtful evaluations, their direct creation, or both:

Marketa Cawood, KCTS Hopkinsville Community College

Sue Ciriello, Naugatuck Valley Community College

Susan Cody, Georgia Perimeter College-Dunwoody

Joe Donnermeyer, Ohio State University-Columbus

Gianna Durso-Finley, Mercer County Community College

Shelly Dutchin, Western Technical College

Isaac W. Eberstein, Florida State University

Samuel Echevarria-Cruz, Austin Community College-Riverside

David Embrick, Loyola University-Chicago

Dona Fletcher, Sinclair Community College

Tammie Foltz, Des Moines Area Community College-Boone

Carmon Weaver Hicks, Ivy Tech Community College of Indiana

Erica Hunter, State University of New York at Albany

William Kimberlin, Laini County Community College

Jamee Kristen, University of Nebraska-Lincoln

Terina Lathe, Central Piedmont Community College

Melinda Messineo, Ball State University

Dan Muhwezi, Butler Community College

Lynn Newhart, Rockford College

Douglas Peck, Stark State College

Sarah Bill Schott, North Central College-Naperville

Megan Seely, Sierra College

Karrie Snyder, Northwestern University

Tomecia Sobers, Fayetteville Technical Community College

Margaret Taylor, Greenville Technical College

Marie L. Wallace, Pima Community College-West

Gerald Williams, Camden County College

Pat Yeager, Ivy Tech Community College of Indiana-Evansville

make the familiar new

culture structure power

Sociology in a Changing World

looking **AHEAD**

How can sociology and the sociological perspective help you understand society and your place in it?

How can culture, structure, and power, three core sociological concepts, help you understand sociology's diverse theories?

How can sociology, which emerged in a period of revolutionary change, help you understand your own rapidly changing world?

Every time you turn on a cell phone to make or receive a call, send a text, or surf the Internet, you are connecting with a nearby relay tower and leaving an electronic fingerprint that tells the phone company where you are, what time it is, and to whom (or what) you are connecting. Social scientists mined this data to study the daily movements of 50,000 people for three months. (Out of privacy concerns, the data had been stripped of information that could tie it to specific individuals.)

The result? We are all, it seems, creatures of habit, much more predictable and much less spontaneous than we might like to think. The researchers found that if you know where people have been—whatever their age, sex, or native language and whether they live in a city or in the country—you can accurately predict where they will be, on average, 93 percent of the time. We typically sleep at home (which, for students, might be a dorm room or an apartment), follow a routine in getting ready for and travelling to school or work, drop by the same coffee shop on the way, and spend the day at work or in classes. "Spontaneous individuals," one of the researchers concluded, "are largely absent from the population" (Barabási 2010).

Foursquare—a social networking site that provides a form of location-based advertising—was one of the first companies to exploit the commercial potential of data like these to market to consumers. But the science behind predicting people's movements may also serve such useful public purposes as predicting the spread of disease, designing efficient public transportation systems, and planning for the efficient use of energy.

In revealing "the inherent regularity of human behavior" (Song et al. 2010, 1021), the results of the cell phone tracking study also confirm a central insight of sociology: we live our lives embedded in social structures that we may not be aware of, but that shape our daily activities. ■

The predictability of our daily routines is a simple reminder that patterns of behavior characterize human life more broadly. As people interact with one another, they develop routines that, taken together, create and maintain society. We go to school, go to work, go shopping, date, raise children, vote. These predictable actions maintain the social institutions—family, schools, economy, government—that, in turn, shape our lives.

But humans also have the capacity to change their behavior and, in so doing, to change society. How we create our social world; how we maintain some semblance of social order amid constant change; how the culture, structure, and relations of power that characterize our world help shape our lives; how some people break out of predictable routines to help change the world—these are some of the topics explored in sociology.

This chapter introduces you to sociology, its unique perspective, and its early development as a discipline. It examines some of sociology's diverse theories and the core concepts that unite the field, along with a number of key concerns of sociology—indeed, of all of us—today. We will see how sociology offers us insight into the forces that are shaping our lives and, at the same time, how it helps us to recognize our own capacity to bring about change.

What Is Sociology?

Sociology is *the systematic study of the relationship between individuals and society.* The approach used in sociology can be thought of as a perspective, a way of looking at the world. To take a **sociological perspective** is *to see and understand the connections between individuals and the broader social contexts in which they live.* You can understand your own life—including the forces that have shaped your current daily routines and the options you have in your future—only by considering the broader social contexts within which you live. Your identity (including your race, ethnicity, class, gender, and nationality) as well as the social environment in which you live (including your family, neighborhood, country, culture, and historical period) influence who you are and who you can be. Understanding those connections is at the heart of a sociological perspective.

The Sociological Perspective

American sociologist C. Wright Mills, writing in 1959, provided probably the best-known description of the sociological perspective (or, as he called it, the **sociological imagination**). According to Mills, "The sociological imagination enables us to grasp history and biography and the relations between the two within a society" (p. 6). In other words, our individual

A motorcycle-riding Texan, C. Wright Mills, wrote a classic description of the sociological perspective and a series of books focused on social class and power in the United States (1948, 1952, 1956). He taught at Columbia University from 1946 until 1962, when he died of a heart attack at age forty-five. Mills's critique of the concentration of power in the United States inspired a generation of activists in the 1960s to promote a more inclusive and democratic society, themes that continue to resonate today.

condition (what Mills calls "biography") depends, in part, upon larger forces in society ("history").

Do you live in a prosperous, peaceful society with democratic freedoms or in one where survival is a challenge, violence is a constant threat, and people's basic civil rights are suppressed? Is your mother or father a retail clerk, an auto worker, a school teacher, an engineer, in the military, a business executive, or unemployed? Are you African American, Hispanic, Asian, White? Are you male, female, or transgendered? Are you gay or straight? Are you from a rural community, the suburbs, or a major city? Were you raised as a Christian, a Jew, a Muslim, a Hindu, or a nonbeliever? Although we often like to think of ourselves as rugged individuals responsible for our own lives, characteristics and circumstances like these influence who we are and the options we have. And as Mills (1959) points out, as social conditions change, so do the lives of individuals:

> When a society is industrialized, a peasant becomes a worker; a feudal lord is liquidated or becomes a businessman. When classes rise or fall a man is employed or unemployed; when the rate of investment goes up or down, a man takes new heart or goes broke. When wars happen, an insurance salesman becomes a rocket launcher; a store clerk, a radar man; a wife lives alone; a child grows up without a father. Neither the life of an individual nor the history of a society can be understood without understanding both. (p. 3)

We need only consider the economic downturn of recent years, the wars in Iraq and Afghanistan, the rapid growth of technology, and accompanying social developments to see that Mills's observations are as relevant today as they were more than half a century ago.

Personal choices—especially deciding to volunteer for the armed forces—contributed to this Iraq war veteran's current situation. But those decisions were made in the context of broader social conditions, including economic pressures to earn a living, a culture of popular patriotism, key decisions made by those with political power, and events that transformed international relations. The connections between individual lives and larger social processes are rarely so explicit or so poignant.

However, Mills and other sociologists do not argue that people are simply the passive objects of their social circumstances. Rather, as the sociological perspective reveals, interplay exists between the social conditions that shape our lives and the actions we take as individuals. We don't get to choose the conditions under which we live, the opportunities we enjoy, or the barriers we face, but we do have choices about how we respond to those circumstances, both individually and collectively. Deciding to join the military, have children, attend college, or move to another city are among the many individual decisions a person can make that have a major impact on his or her future. Mills himself was a strong advocate for collective action to strengthen democracy and help to change the difficult and often unequal conditions that face people in society. That idea, too, is as relevant today as ever.

Sociology and Common Sense

You do not have to be a professional sociologist to look at the world from a sociological perspective. Indeed, many popular expressions reflect a kind of common-sense folk wisdom that assumes a sociological perspective. You have probably heard some version of the expression, "You've got to play the cards you're dealt in life." The card game metaphor makes the point that from the beginning, our options in life have been shaped by social conditions that we did not get to pick ourselves. Such factors can heavily influence the opportunity people have for good health, education, material comfort, and overall well-being.

You don't get to choose the cards you are dealt, but you do get to decide how you will play them. For example, you no doubt decided to go to college with the hope that doing so could positively influence your future. Others may have had

the option of attending college but chose not to exercise it. Many more people, of course, never had the option of attending college in the first place; they were dealt a very different hand in life.

The idea that people must play the cards they are dealt in life is consistent with a sociological perspective. But the problem with relying on common-sense folk wisdom to understand the world is that, however insightful it may sometimes be, it can produce a bewildering array of contradictory claims. The maxim about playing the cards you are dealt in life would seem to contradict another popular saying, "Life is what you make of it," which suggests that individuals have total control over their fate. Or perhaps you agree with the maxim, "The apple doesn't fall far from the tree," suggesting that our social origins largely predetermine our character. Without some way of gauging their accuracy, such wildly contradictory claims provide no insight at all.

In addition, an understanding of the world based only on our own individual experience may not be helpful in unfamiliar circumstances. This is especially true in a world in which communications, media, immigration, and international travel are bringing together people of vastly different backgrounds as never before. To operate in such a diverse society we need to understand not only how *we* make sense of the world, but how other people do so as well.

If we are to understand our connection to the social world beyond our own limited experience and be able to sort through competing claims about that world, we need a more systematic way to investigate the patterns of behavior and the processes that make up social life. We need the discipline of sociology.

Sociology as a Discipline

Sociologists combine the sociological perspective with a variety of research methods (discussed in Chapter 2) to study in a systematic way how our actions shape, and are shaped by, broader social forces. Because the sociological perspective can apply to any aspect of people's lives and any social issue, the discipline of sociology addresses an especially broad array of topics, as we will see throughout this book.

Sociology is one of the *social sciences,* a group of research-based disciplines that gather and evaluate evidence in order to study human society. This focus on human society distinguishes the social sciences from the natural sciences, which focus on the physical aspects of nature. In addition to sociology, the social sciences include political science, economics, psychology, and anthropology. Each of these disciplines highlights different aspects of social life.

Take crime, for example. *Political scientists* might study how politicians use the issue of crime in their campaigns. *Economists* might examine the financial impact of crime on society. *Psychologists* might look at the individual features of criminals, perhaps suggesting personality traits associated with certain types of criminal behavior. *Anthropologists* might compare how different societies define crime and respond to it. *Sociologists* emphasize the interrelationship between individuals and larger social forces, as well as the interactions between various social institutions such as government, economy, media, schools,

These children's life chances—their opportunities for good health, education, material comfort, and overall well being—are significantly influenced by the social environment into which they were born. What differences are evident from these photographs? What elements of your social environment influenced your development?

and family. They explore why crime rates vary over time and are often linked to social trends such as changes in the age of the population (since younger people commit crimes at a higher rate than older ones). They examine the role of media in helping to shape people's perception of crime and the criminal justice system through both news coverage and entertainment dramas. They examine the effectiveness of government efforts to reduce crime. Such topics illustrate the broad range of sociological research.

Sociologists have many interests, and the discipline as a whole has many areas of specialization, including medical sociology, sociology of the family, sociology of religion, political sociology, the sociology of race and ethnicity, the sociology of work, the sociology of gender, the sociology of media, and the sociology of social movements. As a result, sociology courses can provide a foundation for further study in any of these fields. As the Sociology Works box on page 8 suggests, the study of sociology can also provide valuable skills for many careers, including some that may seem completely unrelated to sociology itself.

Sociology's Historical and Social Context

Imagine a society in which scientific discoveries reveal more and more about the world, political unrest sparks calls for social change, and economic crises and new technologies transform daily life. You might suspect this was a description of today's United States, but similar upheavals disturbed Europe in the 1800s, which is where and when the formal discipline of sociology first emerged. To better understand the origins of the discipline, we need to consider that historical and social context.

The Rise of Modernity

In the 1700s, European society entered a new historical era, **modernity,** *characterized by the growth of democracy and personal freedom, increased reliance on reason and science to explain*

The Sociology Major and the Job Market

People, culture, social problems, social change—these are all fascinating topics to study and help explain why students often enjoy sociology. However, practical concerns about your future might lead you to ask, "What can I *do* with a degree in sociology?"

The answer is, "Plenty." By majoring in sociology you not only learn to better understand yourself and your world, but you also develop important skills that can prepare you for entry-level positions in a variety of employment settings, including business, education, social services, health care, government, and criminal justice. Sociology can also be an excellent choice for students who plan to go on to graduate school. Majoring in sociology allows you to study a subject area that interests you *and* helps you prepare for your future.

Here are the four key advantages of majoring in sociology:

1. *A sociology degree is flexible.* Because sociology can be applied to virtually any aspect of social life, you can major in sociology with an eye toward your own particular interests. For example, if you are interested in health and medicine, you can take a course in medical sociology; if you are interested in social work, you can take courses related to the social problems you wish to address or the populations you wish to serve. Sociology can help you understand the issues related to your field of interest.

2. *Sociology focuses on the critical use of information.* As part of a liberal arts education, a sociology degree prepares you to find, understand, analyze, use, and communicate information. These fundamental critical-thinking skills apply to an array of work settings and will not become obsolete; they are highly valuable in today's rapidly changing, information-based job market. Since most people change jobs—and even careers—during their lives, mastering such information-based skills is crucial for success. The ability to work with social science data

> Majoring in sociology allows you to study a subject area that interests you *and* helps you prepare for your future.

found in government reports, marketing surveys, and other information sources is particularly important.

3. *Sociology provides insights into diversity.* In our increasingly diverse society, success in many fields of employment requires an understanding of people from different backgrounds. Sociology majors have an advantage in understanding diversity. As a result, they are more likely to work effectively in multicultural workplaces such as schools, hospitals, and businesses as well as in any field in which clients, customers, patients, citizens, or students may be from diverse social backgrounds.

4. *Sociology helps you understand the source of social problems.* Are you interested in a field that addresses social problems, such as social work, criminal justice, or health care? Do you plan to work with community organizations, international aid agencies, or social movements to bring about social change? If so, studying sociology can be particularly relevant. By focusing on the relationship between individuals and their broader social context, sociology helps you to better understand the roots of social problems.

To help you consider how studying sociology could benefit you, we have included a variety of Sociology Works boxes throughout this book that highlight how former sociology students are using the insights of sociology in a variety of fields. If you are considering majoring in sociology, be sure to talk with your instructor, who will be able to tell you about the programs available at your school.

think about it

1. *Do you have any tentative ideas about the kind of work you'd like to do when you complete school? What kinds of classes do you think will help you prepare for the future? Why?*

2. *Take a look at your school's course listings. Do you see any sociology courses that you think you may want to take? What interests you about the topics covered in these courses?*

Many people who have received degrees in sociology, including some who are well known, have made significant contributions to their professional fields. Pictured here, from left to right, are former U.S. president Ronald Reagan, civil rights leader Martin Luther King Jr., and First Lady Michelle Obama.

TABLE 1.1	SOCIOLOGY AND REVOLUTION

SOCIOLOGY AROSE IN THE CONTEXT OF REVOLUTIONARY CHANGE

Cultural Revolution	Political Revolution	Economic and Social Revolution
The rise of scientific thought	American and French revolutions	Industrialization
The declining influence of religion	Uprisings of 1848	Consumer society
The Age of Enlightenment	Growth in democracy and individual rights	Capitalism
		Urbanization

the natural and social worlds, and a shift toward an urban industrial economy. Earlier, during the Middle Ages (roughly 400–1400), religious explanations of the natural and social worlds dominated intellectual life, the land-owning aristocracy and clerical elite dominated political life, and the economy rested on a rural, agricultural base. (Our romanticized images of kings in castles and knights in battle come from this period.) During the transitional Renaissance and Early Modern periods (from roughly the 1400s to the 1600s), scholars laid the foundation of modern science with pioneering works in astronomy, anatomy, and other fields of knowledge; uprisings challenged traditional political authority; and technological advances improved agricultural production.

The rise of modernity in the eighteenth and nineteenth centuries was marked by revolutionary cultural, political, economic, and social change (Table 1.1). The shift from a rural, agricultural economy to an urban industrial economy transformed Europe's social order. At the same time, the new emphasis on reason and science created the conditions needed for the emergence of sociology. Early sociologists sought to understand the dramatic changes they were witnessing and to suggest what might be done to deal with the social problems that resulted from them.

Cultural Revolution: Science and the Enlightenment

During the Middle Ages the Church and its clergy dominated European intellectual life, controlling the era's limited number of books, libraries, and schools. Because religious doctrine formed the basis for acceptable social thought, heretics—those who held beliefs contrary to Church teaching—were often persecuted and even killed for questioning the accepted order. This intellectual climate was not hospitable to the open and free inquiry required for **science,** which *uses logic and the systematic collection of evidence to support knowledge claims.*

The dominance of the Church slowly eroded, however, as scientific research exposed the shortcomings of religious explanations of the natural world. For example, proof that the earth orbited the sun contradicted Church doctrine that the earth was at the center of the universe. Writers and philosophers seized on these advances in the natural sciences to promote the *Enlighten-*

ment, an eighteenth-century intellectual movement that combined a belief in individual freedom and respect for individual rights with the calculated logic of the natural sciences. These Enlightenment thinkers, who were among the first intellectuals independent of the Church, argued that neither the physical nor the social world should be taken on faith. Instead, both should be examined through reason; claims to knowledge should be subject to testing through the collection of evidence, and explanations should be based in natural causes and events. German philosopher Immanuel Kant summed up this revolutionary way of thinking in the motto "Dare to know" (1784/1999).

Political Revolution: The Rise of Democracy

Enlightenment thinkers believed that the open debate of ideas would promote tolerance, individual rights, equality, and democracy. They suggested that applying reason and science to questions of social significance would inevitably advance individual rights and freedom. Enlightenment ideas provided the intellectual basis for both the American (1775–1783) and French (1789–1799) revolutions, as well as for a series of uprisings that swept through Europe in 1848, challenging traditional rulers and promoting democratic ideals. These revolutions stimulated much interest in achieving a more equal society and improved living conditions, but they provoked condemnation from conservatives who saw them as a threat to stability, traditional values, and social order. Thus controversies about the nature and desirability of social order versus social change were among the first topics addressed by early sociologists.

Economic and Social Revolution: Industrial Capitalism and Urbanization

The term *Industrial Revolution* refers to a collection of major developments that transformed rural agricultural societies into urban industrial societies. This process began in Great Britain and spread through Europe and the United States in the nineteenth century.

The rise of modernity introduced rapid social change. Work life shifted from the fields to factories. Home and community life was transformed as people moved from small rural villages to rapidly expanding urban centers. What effect do you think the shift from rural village life based on farming to urban life based on wage labor had on family life?

The practical application of scientific developments, such as the creation of the steam engine, paved the way for **industrialization,** *the use of large-scale machinery for the mass manufacture of consumer goods.* Industrialization required a major investment in factories and mills with complex machinery—such as mechanized looms—at a cost that was often beyond the reach of a single owner. Thus industrialization became linked to the rise of *capitalists,* people who pursued profits by investing in and owning businesses. Mass manufacturing relied on a new type of relationship between workers and owners in which the workers sold their labor for a wage. They used their wages to buy food, clothing, and shelter, unlike rural peasants who produced many of their own material goods and met their basic needs by farming. The result was the birth of both wage labor and *consumerism,* a way of life that depends on the purchase and use of commercial goods and services. These developments fueled the rapid expansion of *capitalism,* an economic system in which the machinery used for production is owned privately,

workers are paid a wage, and markets facilitate the exchange of goods and services.

Economic changes fueled changes in social life. An agrarian economy requires farmers to work and live in rural areas. An industrial economy requires workers to congregate near centralized sites of production. Large-scale mass manufacturing operations were housed in factories and mills, often located along riverbanks to harness water power. As the Industrial Revolution took hold, many people left their rural homes and traveled to newly emerging cities for jobs they hoped would mean a better life. This migration contributed to **urbanization,** *the growth of cities.* Before 1800, more than 90 percent of Europeans lived in rural areas; by the 1890s, more than half lived in cities.

Urban life dramatically changed how people lived. In the agricultural economy of the Middle Ages, peasants worked the fields and lived in tiny rural villages among people mostly like themselves. Children could expect to grow up and live in the village they were born in and to do the same sort of work their parents and grandparents did. In contrast, the modern industrial economy required wage laborers to work the machinery in the factories of rapidly expanding cities. These bustling cities featured considerable diversity and rapid social change, some of which contributed to growing social problems.

Early industrial capitalism was highly productive, but it also created great inequalities, generating tremendous profits for a few wealthy owners from the labor of many overworked and underpaid workers. Disease (linked to poor sanitation), overcrowded and unsafe housing, inadequate transportation, and crime plagued the rapidly growing cities. Excessive inequality and growing social problems caused great concern among political and social thinkers, inspiring calls for reform and igniting revolutionary movements.

The rise of modernity produced rapid and immediately visible changes that showed traditional ways of life were not inevitable; the fate of individuals was tied to broader social changes beyond their control; and human action could transform the world through new ideas, political reform, and technological innovation. Faced with the challenge of understanding these dramatic transformations, social thinkers began applying reason and scientific techniques to study social life systematically and to suggest ways that society might be improved. The resulting ideas became the foundation of sociology.

Foundations of Sociological Thought

Sociology today has its roots in the ideas developed by early sociologists more than a century ago. Some of these thinkers asked profound questions of enduring relevance and are still widely read (Calhoun 2007; Ritzer 2007). Their work on the rapidly changing world of the late eighteenth and early nineteenth centuries continues to provide insight into our own social world today.

Defining the Terrain of Sociology: Comte and Spencer

Auguste Comte (1798–1857) and Herbert Spencer (1820–1903) helped establish the idea that the social world could be the subject of systematic, scientific investigation.

AUGUSTE COMTE: STABILITY AND CHANGE

Auguste Comte, a French intellectual with wide-ranging interests, coined the term *sociology* in the early nineteenth century.

Comte sought to establish sociology as a rigorous science of society—modeled on the natural sciences—that would identify the laws that govern human behavior.

At the core of Comte's new field of study were two fundamental questions about social life: "How and why do societies change?" (social dynamics) and "What is the basis of social stability at a specific historical moment?" (social statics). He was interested in how society had developed from humanity's earliest small-scale bands of hunters and gatherers to his own nineteenth-century European society. He theorized that throughout history societies progressed in a straight line through several stages: the theological (ruled by religion), the metaphysical (ruled by philosophy), and the positivist (ruled by science). For Comte, **positivism,** *a belief that accurate knowledge must be based on the scientific method,* enabled a deeper understanding of human life and was the key to solving persistent social problems.

Comte's efforts to build a science of society were crude by today's standards. Few of his ideas have withstood the test of time, but the focus of his interest—the nature of social stability and social change—continues to be a major concern in sociology.

HERBERT SPENCER: SOCIETY AS A SOCIAL ORGANISM

The British intellectual Herbert Spencer was another early adopter of the term *sociology*. Taking a cue from the biological sciences, Spencer argued that society is a "social organism," much like a human organism. He theorized that, like its biological equivalent, society is made up of separate parts, each with a unique function, that work together to sustain the entire organism. Thus Spencer's theory emphasized the overall structure of society, the functions served by the various elements of society, and the interactions among these elements. Spencer also theorized that when societies evolve, their component parts—and the functions they serve—change as well.

Spencer believed that society progresses as it evolves. Therefore, evolution should be allowed to take place without interference from government. Rather than intervene with reforms in the face of the growing inequality created by unregulated industrial capitalism, Spencer believed in the "survival of the fittest," a phrase he devised before Charles Darwin's work on natural selection and the theory of evolution was published. Spencer's application of the survival of the fittest to human society is today known as *social Darwinism*. Spencer later recanted some of his more extreme views, but in recent years, those who wish to minimize the role of government in social and economic affairs have revived some of Spencer's ideas.

The Key Founders: Marx, Durkheim, and Weber

Spencer and Comte helped to define the terrain of sociology in its earliest years. But the thinkers who are widely seen as the founders of sociology and who set the agenda for the

	Karl Marx	**Emile Durkheim**	**Max Weber**
Biography	1818–1883	1858–1917	1864–1920
	German	French	German
	Writer and activist	Academic	Academic
Key Issues and Key Work	The nature of capitalism	The nature of social solidarity	Decline of tradition
	Conflict and inequality	Shared values and morals	Rationalization of society
	Capital	*Suicide*	*The Protestant Ethic and the Spirit of Capitalism*

next century of sociological theory were Karl Marx, Emile Durkheim, and Max Weber.

KARL MARX: THE EFFECTS OF CAPITALISM

The German-born Karl Marx (1818–1883) is best known as a revolutionary thinker who advocated radical change to advance the interests of workers. Marx combined writing with political activism, and much of his life was spent escaping political repression. Because of his writings, Marx was expelled from France (twice!) and Belgium. In Germany he was arrested, tried, acquitted, and also expelled. Finally, in 1849 he went to London, where he spent the rest of his life in exile. He lived in poverty while he wrote his greatest works, including *Capital,* his comprehensive analysis of the history and dynamics of capitalism.

Marx recognized that industrial capitalism was remarkably productive and thus capable of doing away with hunger and poverty for all. But instead, industrial capitalism was used to produce huge fortunes for a few owners, while leaving workers to labor in dangerous conditions and often live in poverty. In much of his work, Marx sought to explain how and why so much wealth and productivity could coexist with such widespread poverty and misery.

For Marx, the answer could be found in the relationship between capitalists, who owned the means of production, and the laborers, or proletariat, who worked for a wage. The dynamics of capitalism, said Marx, encouraged owners to pay the lowest wages possible because lower labor costs mean higher profits. This dynamic explained the simultaneous creation of enormous fortunes and devastating poverty. Capitalists accumulated great wealth precisely because they were able to exploit the workers who toiled in their factories. This wealth gave owners great power, which they used to control governments and cultural institutions (Marx 1867/1976).

To Marx, conflict between owners and workers was an inevitable feature of capitalism. As a result, he argued that capitalism—like earlier economic forms based on inequality—had within it the seeds of its own destruction. He theorized that the exploitation of workers would eventually become so extreme that wage laborers would rise up and overthrow the capitalist system. In its place, they would adopt *socialism,* a system in which ownership of the major means of production—such as factories, utilities, and railways—is in public, rather than private, hands, and government directs the use of the productive forces of industry for the public good. The goal of socialism would be a society without the extreme inequalities that characterized capitalism. (We explore the nature of capitalism and socialism more closely in Chapter 16.)

Marx's analysis of industrial capitalism was insightful in specifying the connection between wealth and poverty. He accurately predicted that the search for cheap labor would lead to the expansion of capitalism around the globe. He also correctly predicted the growth of labor movements demanding an end to unregulated capitalism. But he failed to appreciate the ability of capitalism to accommodate reform or the important role markets play in stimulating innovation and efficiency. The revolutionary worker movements Marx supported in recently industrialized countries like Great Britain, France, and Germany ultimately reformed, rather than overthrew, capitalism. Meanwhile, the socialist revolutions that did occur, most notably in Russia and China, took place in primarily peasant societies that did not have the capacity to produce an abundance of material goods. Even though the brutal totalitarian states that emerged after these revolutions invoked Marx's name in their official ideology, they bore almost no resemblance to the humanist egalitarian vision that Marx had promoted.

Beyond the specific analysis of capitalism, Marx's work highlighted the importance of power—in this case, economic power and its role in enforcing inequality—as a core concept in sociology. Marx argued that economic power could be used to influence other aspects of social life, including government and cultural institutions, such as schools and the media. Marx's work also stressed the interplay between structure and action that is at the heart of the sociological perspective. "Men make their own history," he wrote, "but they do not make it just as they please; they do not make it under circumstances chosen by themselves, but under circumstances directly found, given and transmitted from the past" (Marx 1852/1978, 595).

The issues Marx explored continue to be important today. Questions about the nature and direction of our economy are among the most significant ones addressed by sociologists. For example, how has globalization changed our economy? How is the most recent economic crisis linked to the dynamics of capitalism? How has the nature of work been changing? How have the labor movement and social welfare programs—both examples of attempts to moderate the excesses of capitalism—affected the lives of workers?

EMILE DURKHEIM: SOCIAL SOLIDARITY

Emile Durkheim (1858–1917), who lived a generation after Marx, was also concerned with understanding social change in the modern world, but Durkheim's life could hardly have been more different from Marx's. The descendent of a long line of rabbinical scholars in France, Durkheim studied to be a rabbi but rejected religion in his teens and became agnostic, believing there was no way to know whether or not God existed. However, he retained a lifelong interest both in the role of religion in social life and in the scientific study of morality.

Durkheim is perhaps the single individual most responsible for establishing sociology as an academic discipline. He held the first academic position in sociology; wrote a book laying out the methods of the discipline, *The Rules of Sociological Method* (Durkheim 1895/1982); and established a well-respected academic journal devoted to the new field.

Like many social thinkers who witness dramatic change, Durkheim was concerned with how to maintain social order. He was particularly interested in the question of **social solidarity,** *the collective bonds that connect individuals.* At the core

of his theory was the proposition that society is held together by shared cultural values. As we explore in more detail in Chapter 3, cultural *norms,* or shared expectations about behavior associated with a society's values and morals, are promoted informally through custom and tradition and are spelled out more systematically in laws. When internalized by individuals, shared values and morals become the foundation for social solidarity.

Durkheim observed that traditional agricultural societies were often tight-knit communities. They shared social bonds across generations because people did the same sort of work, shared a common religion, and followed similar customs. These similar experiences resulted in *mechanical solidarity*—social cohesion based on shared experience and a common identity with limited individuality. As European societies grew and became urbanized and industrialized, however, people increasingly differed from one another. A more complex economy required an increasing **division of labor,** in which *people specialize in different tasks, each requiring specific skills.* As cities developed, a diverse array of people coexisted, often with different religions and cultural traditions. Given this increasing social complexity and diversity, how could social solidarity be maintained?

Durkheim's answer was *organic solidarity,* a new form of social cohesion, characteristic of modern industrial societies, that is based on interdependence. In the tradition of Spencer's "social organism," Durkheim argued that the social glue that holds together modern societies mirrors the way living organisms depend on multiple, specialized components operating in unison. Social cohesion is possible because we are dependent on one another. With its increased division of labor, modern urban industrialized society requires doctors, construction workers, sales clerks, police officers, factory workers, janitors, and thousands of other specialists to keep operating. Durkheim's theory helped to explain why rapid growth and social differentiation in European societies did not lead to the breakdown of social solidarity, but instead produced a new and, Durkheim thought, even stronger form of solidarity that would permit a balance between individuality and a commitment to the group.

Durkheim's work highlights the interplay between social structure and cultural values, especially as they relate to social solidarity. Much of Durkheim's sociological work builds upon this central concern with social solidarity. Indeed in *Suicide,* one of his most influential works and one of the first to show the potential of the sociological perspective combined with systematic research, Durkheim argued that suicide rates could be explained by the strength of the social ties people have with larger social groups (Durkheim 1897/1951). (See the Through a Sociological Lens box on page 14.)

Durkheim also argued that crime and punishment are fundamentally about solidarity (see Chapter 8). Crimes, for

Explaining the Social Basis of Suicide

Why do people intentionally kill themselves? At first glance, suicide seems to be the ultimate example of a private individual act, best explained by psychologists, not sociologists. But sociologist Emile Durkheim broke new ground: he made suicide the subject of the first sociological study to use large-scale data analysis. After examining official government records of suicide cases, Durkheim theorized that certain groups of people are more or less likely to commit suicide because of their relationship to society. This was a fundamental sociological insight.

Durkheim's study, *Suicide,* showed that a sociological perspective could help explain how individuals are affected by the quality of their relationship with larger social groups, even to the extent of taking their own lives. His research revealed, for example, that unmarried adults had higher rates of suicide than married adults, and Protestants had higher rates than Catholics or Jews. Durkheim explained these differences in suicide rates among various groups through an analysis of social *integration,* the strength of social ties that allow people to feel they belong to a group, and social *regulation,* the strength of social norms that control people's behavior. Too much or too little of either would increase the likelihood of suicide. Thus Durkheim identified four types of suicide—egoistic, anomic, altruistic, and fatalistic:

Egoistic suicides result from too little social integration and are committed by people who feel isolated and detached from society. For example, married couples are likely to have a strong bond with one another, whereas divorced, widowed, and unmarried people are more likely to lack a strong social connection; thus suicide rates among these latter groups are higher. Protestants lack the intense communal rituals associated with Catholicism and Judaism, which helps explain their higher rates of suicide. At the other extreme, *altruistic* suicides result from too much social integration, leading individuals to sacrifice themselves for the sake of the collective. For example, during World War II Japan used kamikaze pilots who volunteered to fly suicide missions for their country.

The absence of regulation in the form of social norms and boundaries is also associated with higher suicide rates. *Anomic* suicide often results from a sudden and dramatic change in the level of social regulation, which leaves the individual without any clear rules about how to adapt. These changes can be negative, such as with the death of a spouse or the loss of a job. Ironically, the changes can also be positive, as when entertainers become "overnight successes" and suddenly have access to endless amounts of money and attention. The self-destructive behavior and suicides of many celebrities fit into this category. Conversely, too much regulation can result in *fatalistic* suicide, as in the case of slaves, prisoners, or invalids who see no hope or way to escape the desperate conditions of their lives.

Suicide and Social Integration

	TOO LITTLE	TOO MUCH
Integration	egoistic	altruistic
Regulation	anomic	fatalistic

think about it

1. *Using Durkheim's insights about suicide, consider which of the four types of suicide seems to best apply to suicide bombers who act to advance a cause. Explain your reasoning.*

2. *Based on Durkheim's analysis, what positive steps could be taken to help reduce the risk of suicide for any particular individual?*

Durkheim, are acts that offend the **collective conscience,** or *shared values of a society.* Punishment serves as a means to reinforce social solidarity in the face of such antisocial actions. Without the moral constraints provided by the collective conscience, Durkheim argued, people—and society as a whole—would descend into a chaotic state of **anomie,** or *normlessness, without moral guidance.*

Today, close to a century later, people are still debating the proper role of values and religion in public and private life. How might Durkheim's ideas help explain the resurgence of traditional religious belief? Can the increasing diversity of our society serve as a source of strength, rather than division? How can people maintain healthy social ties in a world where they regularly move from one community to another? How can we affirm people's individuality while maintaining a sense of common identity? As sociologists investigate such twenty-first-century questions, Durkheim's theories continue to be relevant.

MAX WEBER: THE PROTESTANT ETHIC AND THE RATIONALIZATION OF MODERN LIFE

Like Durkheim, German theorist Max Weber (pronounced "VAY-ber") (1864–1920) was also trying to make sense of the shift from traditional to modern society. The son of a high-ranking government bureaucrat, Weber took a series of university positions as a young man, carried out major research projects, and served as a consultant for government agencies. By his mid-thirties, Weber was in a state of exhaustion and suffered a nervous breakdown that left him incapacitated for nearly seven years. When he was able to return to his writing full time, Weber produced his best-known work, *The Protestant Ethic and the Spirit of Capitalism* (Weber 1905/1958).

In *The Protestant Ethic,* Weber argued that culture—in the form of Protestantism—had helped to promote the early development of capitalism in northern Europe. Traditionally, the Catholic Church had encouraged the rejection of worldly affairs and wealth, promising everlasting life to those who were faithful and participated in the Church's defining rituals such as baptism and communion. However, after the Protestant Reformation, some sects—particularly Calvinists—rejected this approach to salvation and instead maintained that people's fate in the afterlife was predetermined before birth and could not be changed by actions they took on earth. But how could a person know whether he or she was going to heaven or hell? Some believers thought that wealth, accumulated through diligent work, was a sign of God's favor, indicating likely salvation. This cultural belief encouraged hard work, investment, and the accumulation of wealth—the essential requirements for success in a capitalist economy. Marx had focused on the economy's role in influencing other aspects of social life—including culture. With *The Protestant Ethic and the Spirit of Capitalism,* Weber argued that cultural beliefs could influence economic development.

As *The Protestant Ethic* illustrates, Weber sometimes tried to understand social action by viewing it from the perspective of the actor, an approach known by the German word *verstehen,* which means "understanding." Understanding why someone behaves the way he or she does also provides insight into the broader culture in which the action is taking place. As we will see, this approach was an important precursor to later sociological theory that focused precisely on how people make meaning of the social world.

Weber also contributed to sociological theory through his effort to explain the shift from traditional to rational action. One of his central theoretical propositions was that, in earlier societies, *tradition*—beliefs and customs often charged with emotional significance that are passed on from generation to generation—primarily influenced the actions of people. However, in newly industrialized capitalist societies, *rationality*—the use of reason and logical calculation to achieve a goal as efficiently as possible—was much more likely to influence people's actions.

Weber argued that the **rationalization of society**—*the long-term historical process by which rationality replaced tradition as the basis for organizing social and economic life*—propelled the social change of his day. The influence of rationalization went beyond individual human action to include broader social institutions. For example, Weber argued that whereas rulers had previously claimed authority based solely on their claim to descent from previous rulers, the authority of government officials now rests increasingly on such rational-legal foundations as elections or specific training and certification. In addition, Weber argued that the principle of rationality was responsible for the formation of bureaucracies within large organizations—government agencies, political parties, industrial companies—that manage economic and political life.

Weber could see that rationalization might be productive for society, since it focused on specifying procedures, training officials, and pursuing efficiency. But he also saw that as rationalization permeated all aspects of social life it would create cold and impersonal societies. Weber believed that bureaucracy was self-perpetuating and becoming the dominant type of social organization. He worried it would constrain human action and imprison us in an "iron cage of bureaucracy."

Ultimately, Weber feared that in modern society humans could engage in meaningful action only in large organizations, in which they were allotted narrowly defined tasks and sacrificed their personal goals to the impersonal goals of the whole. And although he agreed with much of Marx's critique of industrial capitalism, Weber's theory of rationalization led him to predict that postcapitalist societies would not produce the kind of egalitarian future that Marx predicted, but would instead be even more highly rationalized, with more layers of bureaucracy. In this way, Weber was perhaps the most prophetic of the three major founders of sociology. He did not share in the pure optimism for science and rational thought that emerged from the Enlightenment. Instead, he saw the early signs of a dark side to rationality that has now become a cautionary element of contemporary sociological thought.

Weber's sociological theory applies to a wide range of contemporary concerns. Rationalization continues to pervade our lives at home, school, and work in a variety of ways. Do the large lecture halls, high-rise dormitories, and layered bureaucracy of the large university represent the rationalization of higher education? How do the bureaucracies of governments and corporations assist in—and interfere with—the work of those organizations? Are such bureaucracies a threat to our freedom? Weber gives us valuable tools for analyzing the role of rational thought and practice in many areas of our lives.

Recovered Voices: Harriet Martineau, W.E.B. Du Bois, Jane Addams

Because of the prevailing discriminatory attitudes toward women and African Americans during the early years of sociology, a variety of social thinkers were excluded from or marginalized in the academic world. Instead of writing for a strictly academic audience, they wrote for popular publications, authored novels, and spoke out as activists advocating social change. In many ways, they were ahead of their time. Although often at the margins of academic sociology while they were alive, these thinkers are now appreciated more widely for the contributions they made to our understanding of social life. Among these voices are Harriet Martineau, W.E.B. Du Bois, and Jane Addams.

Harriet Martineau

W.E.B. Du Bois, as portrayed on a U.S. postage stamp honoring his social activism

Jane Addams with some of the youngsters who frequented Hull House

Biography	1802–1876	1868–1963	1860–1935
	English	American	American
	Writer and activist	Scholar and activist	Scholar and activist
Key Issues and Work	Gender, slavery, and discrimination	Race and discrimination	Urban social problems
	Society in America	NAACP cofounder	Hull House founder
		The Philadelphia Negro; The Souls of Black Folk; The Crisis magazine	*Hull House Maps and Papers*

HARRIET MARTINEAU: GENDER DISCRIMINATION

Many consider Harriet Martineau (1802–1876), born into an affluent English family, to be the first female sociologist. Her work delved into issues of gender discrimination and slavery that many of the white male sociologists of her time had largely ignored. She also agitated for women's suffrage and the expansion of women's rights in England.

Self-taught and—like other women at the time—excluded from an academic appointment, Martineau began by writing magazine articles and then a series of books on economics and politics that were geared toward the general public rather than an academic audience. Her books were highly successful, making her independently wealthy as well as a literary celebrity. After traveling in the United States for two years, she wrote two books based on her observations, most notably *Society in America* (Martineau 1837/2009), a forceful critique of the failure of the United States to live up to its democratic promise in its treatment of both slaves and women. At this time, she also wrote about the methods of social research in *How to Observe Morals and Manners* (1838/2009). Finally, Martineau made an important contribution to sociology by translating the work of Auguste Comte for English-speaking audiences.

W.E.B. DU BOIS: RACIAL INEQUALITY

W.E.B. Du Bois (pronounced "doo-BOYS") (1868–1963) made important contributions to sociology with his ground-breaking research on race in America as well as with his efforts to promote racial justice. Du Bois, a descendent of African, French, and Dutch ancestors, came from a comfortable middle-class Massachusetts family that provided him with a solid early education and insulated him from the worst effects of racism. When he traveled south to Nashville to study at Fisk University in the 1880s, however, he encountered a rigidly segregated world in which African Americans were frequently the targets of beatings and lynchings. This injustice strengthened his interest in race as a subject of sociological study. In 1895, Du Bois became the first African American to obtain a Ph.D. from Harvard University. He went on to teach sociology and to write a series of studies that elevated race to a place of prominence in sociology. Du Bois published the first sociological study of a black community, *The Philadelphia Negro* (1899), followed by the widely read *The Souls of Black Folk* (1903). Both works explored the complexity of race relations in turn-of-the-century American society.

Throughout his life, Du Bois combined scholarship with activism. He played an important role in the founding of the National Association for the Advancement of Colored People (NAACP), arguably the leading civil rights organization of the twentieth century. He founded—and for a quarter-century edited—the NAACP's influential magazine, *The Crisis,* which is still published today (thecrisismagazine.com). He also nurtured efforts to promote unity among people of African descent worldwide. As an agent of change, he faced opposition from powerful forces. During the Cold War anticommunist hysteria of the 1950s, the U.S. Justice Department accused Du Bois of being an agent of the Soviet Union because of his peace activism and promotion of nuclear disarmament. Although he was acquitted, the FBI continued to harass him and the government revoked his passport. Eventually, he was allowed to travel abroad and he moved to Ghana, where he became a citizen. He died there at the age of 95 on August 27, 1963, the day before the civil rights march on Washington, D.C., where Martin Luther King, Jr., gave his famous "I Have a Dream" speech.

JANE ADDAMS: URBAN SOCIAL PROBLEMS

Jane Addams (1860–1935) is best known as a social reformer and the founder of Hull House, which provided a wide range of social services in the poor immigrant communities of Chicago and served as a model for later similar establishments, known as settlement houses, in other cities. Addams was the first American woman to win the Nobel Peace Prize, awarded to her in 1931 for her longstanding work in building an international women's coalition to promote peace and prevent war. But Addams also made an important contribution to the development of sociology. Her social reform work and her research on social life on the south side of Chicago had a significant influence on the development of urban sociology at the University of Chicago, the home of the first sociology department in the United States.

However, unlike some University of Chicago sociologists, who limited their work to understanding urban life, Addams believed that social theory and research should be linked to action promoting social change. Working to address social problems enabled her to contribute to social reform while developing and testing theories about how society worked. In doing so, she often challenged those in power, advocating for the poor and others at the margins of society.

In *Hull House Maps and Papers* (1895/2007), Addams chronicled life in the immigrant communities around Hull House, producing data that was used to promote reform. In *Democracy and Social Ethics* (1902/2002), she linked democracy with diversity, explaining that a well-functioning democratic society requires an understanding of a wide range of experiences and perspectives, something that early sociology was well equipped to provide. In addition, Addams foreshadowed the development of feminist social theory by critiquing the way male sociologists often based their generalizations about society on men's experiences only. She argued that for researchers to fully understand social problems, they needed to have a sympathetic connection with the people affected by those problems. Her collaboration with poor immigrants informed her sociological understanding that people actively seek to improve their conditions, even when facing great odds in extremely difficult situations.

Although the works of Martineau, Du Bois, Addams, and others may have been underappreciated when they wrote them, those works have since had a significant impact on sociology, encouraging sociologists to pay careful attention to the social complexities of gender, race, class, and power.

Sociology's Diverse Theories

The work of early sociologists served as the source for the development of later sociological theory. In the chapters to come, we consider different theories regarding specific social phenomena. In this section, we examine some of the general approaches to theory that have developed over the years. First, though, we consider what theory is and examine some basic ways that sociological theories vary.

Understanding Theory

The film *Avatar* has sold around $3 billion in movie tickets as of this writing, making it the biggest box office hit in history. Why do you think the film has taken in so much money? Perhaps the story is compelling, the actors superb, or the special effects well worth the price of admission. Or maybe the studio advertised and promoted the film especially well. Or perhaps the film's success is due to the growing number of movie theaters worldwide, which translates into more ticket sales.

Each possible explanation for the financial success of *Avatar* is, in effect, a theory because it tries to explain an observation. Accurate evidence and data—such as *Avatar's* $3 billion in ticket sales—*describes* the world and helps us see "what" has occurred. Theories answer "why?" questions and help *explain* the data or evidence: "Why did this happen?" "Why is this so?" More formally, a **social theory** is *a set of principles and propositions that explains the relationships among social phenomena.* Through their explanations, theories also alert us to the sorts of questions we should be asking in future research.

Of course, sociologists don't just ask about box office hits—although media sociologists would be able to offer some likely explanations for *Avatar's* success. Instead, sociological theorists address broad questions, such as, "Why don't complex societies fall apart?" and "Why do wealth and poverty coexist?" as well as more narrowly defined questions, such as, "Why do some schools succeed while others fail?" or even "Why do students who sit in the back of the class tend to have lower grades than those who sit up front?" When we speak of approaches to sociological theory, therefore, we are referring to broad explanations sociologists have for why society operates the way it does. Although thinking about theory can seem intimidating at first, it actually is fairly straightforward and involves answering the most interesting question of all: Why?

A few other characteristics of theories are important to remember:

■ *A theory is not just a hunch or personal opinion.* It may start off that way—just as our explanations for *Avatar's* success did—but to be useful, theories have to be put to the test to see if they are consistent with the evidence; that's the nature of science. Sociological theory is linked to research and evidence in ways that we explore in Chapter 2.

- ***Theories evolve and are sometimes rejected, leaving the most useful to survive.*** When evidence repeatedly contradicts a theory, the theory is either revised or discarded. The most useful theories are those that endure, some of which we discuss later in this chapter.

- ***Multiple theories often give us a more complete picture than any single one.*** Just as many factors likely contributed to *Avatar*'s success, many factors similarly contribute to most aspects of social life. Considering different theories can alert us to a variety of possible explanations for a social phenomenon and to a range of factors that can contribute to it.

Finally, theories tend to vary along a few key dimensions, which we now consider.

Key Dimensions of Theory

How do professional football teams vary? Some focus on offense, others on defense. Some rely on skilled veteran players, whereas others groom the abilities of younger team members. Some teams get most of their points by running the ball, whereas others generate most of their offense by passing. These are among the key dimensions on which teams vary.

Sociological theories, too, vary along key dimensions, including consensus and conflict, subjective and objective reality, and micro-level and macro-level analyses. Think of each dimension as a continuum rather than an either-or division. Knowing where a theory lies on each continuum can help you understand how it fits into the larger picture of sociological thought.

CONSENSUS AND CONFLICT
Conflict refers to tensions and disputes in society, often resulting from the unequal distribution of scarce resources, which can contribute to social change. *Consensus* refers to solidarity and cooperative interaction, often due to shared values and interests, which can contribute to social stability. Although different theories focus more on one or the other, both consensus and conflict coexist in every society, institution, and organization—indeed, in all social life.

In some instances, conflict can produce certain kinds of consensus (Coser 1956). When countries go to war, a dramatic example of conflict, citizens in each nation often feel a renewed sense of solidarity, which they express through increased patriotism and nationalism. On the other hand, sometimes apparent consensus masks simmering tensions that become evident only when they erupt into full-blown conflict. For example, the ordinary daily routines of some cities have sometimes concealed underlying racial tensions that exploded into broad urban riots sparked by a specific incident.

OBJECTIVE AND SUBJECTIVE REALITY
Objective conditions are the material aspects of social life, including the physical environment, social networks, and social institutions. All of these exist outside of us, and collectively they make up the objective dimension of social life. In contrast, the *subjective dimension* of social life involves the world of ideas, including our sense of self, social norms, values, and belief systems. These all exist "in our head," so to speak, and are part of the cultural aspect of social life.

Both the objective physical world we live in and our subjective interpretations of that world have a significant impact on our lives and our society. For example, we have seen that Marx emphasized the impact of economic life (an objective factor) whereas Weber's theory regarding the Protestant Ethic highlighted the role of cultural beliefs (a subjective factor).

MICRO-LEVEL AND MACRO-LEVEL ANALYSES
The third dimension of sociological theory relates to different levels of analysis—as well as to different levels of society itself. Theories that focus on small scale, usually face-to-face, social interaction are operating at the **micro level of analysis.** ("Micro" means small.) Theories that focus on large-scale social systems and processes such as the economy, politics, and population trends operate at the **macro level of analysis.** ("Macro" means large.) Theories that focus somewhere between very large and very small social phenomena—on organizations or institutions, for example—are using a **meso level of analysis.** ("Meso" means middle.) Often, sociological work focuses on the interaction between these various levels of social life.

Now that you are equipped with a better understanding of what theory is and how theories vary, let's take a closer look at some major theoretical traditions. Since the mid-twentieth century, sociologists have sometimes grouped varied sociological theories into three broad categories: *structural-functionalist theories, conflict theories,* and *symbolic interactionist theories.*

Structural-Functionalist Theories

Structural-functionalist theories *focus on consensus and cooperative interaction in social life, emphasizing how different elements that make up a society's structure contribute to its overall operation.* The roots of this tradition can be found in the work of Spencer and Durkheim. Structural-functionalist theories—often referred to simply as **functionalist theories**—were dominant in the United States in the middle of the twentieth century, when its leading proponent was Talcott Parsons (1902–1979). Parsons saw societies as complex systems made up of interdependent parts—for example, families, courts, schools, the economy—that work together to produce social stability. Because the systems are balanced, they tend to move toward normal states of equilibrium; a change in one part of the system results in a change in another part to compensate. Individuals are integrated into the social structure through culture, especially in the form of shared values. A consensus on basic values results in a moral commitment to society, which helps enable its smooth functioning.

To endure, a social institution must meet a need of the system as a whole; institutions that do not contribute adapt or disappear. Parsons argued that any social organization—whether a small group or a large and diverse society—must perform several key functions to survive, including teaching group members core community values, integrating members into productive participation in social life, defining and attaining community goals, and adapting to a changing environment.

◗ Individuals are embedded within larger social structures that correspond to different levels of sociological analysis. These drummers at the 2008 Beijing Olympics, for example, brought their individual talents to the performance (micro level), but their efforts were coordinated by the organization behind the Beijing Olympics (meso level), which was, in turn, one project of the global International Olympic Committee (macro level).

In an important contribution to functionalist theory, Robert K. Merton (1910–2003) distinguished between **manifest functions,** *the recognized and intended consequences of social phenomena,* and **latent functions,** *their largely unrecognized and unintended consequences.* A manifest function of schools, for example, is to help prepare people for future employment, whereas a latent function is to serve as a dating pool or marriage market. Merton also reminds us that even though some phenomena are persistent, they can be **dysfunctional,** *inhibiting or disrupting the working of a system as a whole.* The persistent overcrowding in many schools, for example, is dysfunctional.

Consider how one might study the family as a social institution using functionalist theories. Families serve a number of functions, including the raising of children (though some societies raise children communally outside of the family and many families do not include children). In recent decades, a changing economy (another part of the social system) and changes in cultural values have contributed to changes in the family, including the rise of two wage-earner families, single-parent families, blended families, and families with same-sex parents. Despite such changes, shared values continue to tell us how to raise children and maintain family life. Families can be dysfunctional, too—for example, by harboring child abuse or domestic violence.

Conflict Theories

Conflict theories *focus on issues of contention, power, and inequality, highlighting the competition for scarce resources.* The roots of this approach can be found in the work of Marx and Weber. Today, work that focuses on class, race, gender, and other forms of inequality is often based in this tradition, drawing on the work of Martineau, Du Bois, Addams, and others. The conflict approach emphasizes that, to meet common needs, people attempt to acquire scarce and valuable resources. These include material goods—such as food, housing, and good jobs—as well as less tangible resources, such as social respect and freedom. Because these resources are often limited, people compete for them, bringing different groups into conflict. Even when conflict is not visible, it is often present but repressed by the dominance of the powerful over the less powerful.

Conflict theories, then, see power at the core of social life. Power enables some people to gain an advantage over others and acquire more resources; more resources, in turn, give them more power. In this ongoing struggle, different groups use culture's values and ideas as weapons to advance their own positions. The dominant culture supports and justifies existing inequalities. Various counter-cultures articulate different values in their challenge to the existing condition.

How would one study the family with conflict theory? Conflict theories explain that the popular image of the "traditional" family of the 1950s, depicting a smoothly functioning social institution marked by consensus about distinct and clearly defined gender roles, was largely a myth. In reality, as we see in Chapter 12, the prevailing male dominance of the period kept women in restricted roles and prevented them from pursuing ambitions they might have had for themselves. The extensive legal, economic, and social inequalities between women and men reflected the different amounts of power each possessed. This inequality had been justified by a dominant culture that viewed men as naturally superior to women. Another problem with the traditional image of a family with one wage earner was that it applied most often to white, middle-class families; poor and working-class women—especially women of color—had long been part of the workforce, and their families operated quite differently. Inequalities continue to exist around family life today, both within families, where power may not be shared evenly, and within broader society, where some forms of family, such as same-sex unions, do not yet have full legal recognition.

Symbolic Interactionist Theories

Symbolic interactionist theories *focus on how people use shared symbols and construct society as a result of their everyday interactions.* Weber's approach of *verstehen,* in which the researcher tries to understand action from the perspective of the actor, laid some groundwork for these theories, as did early work by Georg Simmel (1858–1918), who wrote insightful essays on the dynamics of daily life. However, symbolic interactionist theories were fully developed in the United States, building on work by social psychologists in the early and mid-twentieth century. George Herbert Mead (1863–1931), for example, wrote about how we develop a sense of self through our interaction with others and by self-reflection (see Chapter 6). In his dramaturgical theory, Erving Goffman (1922–1982) showed how social life was very much like a play, with people adopting roles, complete with props and scripts (see Chapter 7).

Symbolic interactionist theories are strongly associated with the subjective and micro-level dimensions of social life. They explain social life by highlighting that the social world is based on interaction between people using cultural symbols, such as words and nonverbal body language. Through interaction, individuals develop a sense of self and create a shared understanding of reality with others. People with more power are typically better able to influence this interpretation of reality. This common interpretation of reality leads to patterns of social interaction within groups that form the basis of social structure. But everyday interaction is also constantly recreating or changing these patterns, so society itself is inherently unstable and constantly in flux. Always under construction, the social world is therefore always capable of change. In this way, the symbolic interactionist theories explain social life by highlighting the active role people take in creating society.

Applied to the family, the symbolic interactionist approach directs our attention to micro-level interactions between family members. As they interact, they develop an understanding of who they are and what their role is within the family. What does it mean to be a "good parent" today? Who will work to earn money? Who will care for children? What responsibility does a child have for an aging parent? Family members must come to some mutual understanding about what is expected from each of them. This shared interpretation of reality produces patterns of behavior that provide a routine structure to family life. But these interpretations and arrangements are not static; they are continuously reexamined and thus subject to change. The changes in family structure over the past half-century illustrate the cumulative effect of individual-level decisions. People in different types of family—including two-parent families, one-parent families, childless couples, families with same-sex parents, and step-families—actively interpret the meaning of "family" and act accordingly.

Feminist Theories and Theoretical Diversity

As we see throughout this book, sociological theory has developed considerably since the mid-twentieth century, when some sociologists grouped the field's varied theories into the categories of functionalist, conflict, and symbolic interactionist perspectives. Newer perspectives often do not fit neatly into these older categories. Among the most important contemporary perspectives is feminist theory. Feminist theories focus on inequality between women and men and could be considered in the tradition of conflict theories. But feminist theories also provide insight into how those inequalities are created and reinforced in daily interactions, placing these insights squarely in the tradition of symbolic interactionism (see Chapter 11).

As with other theoretical traditions, there is no single feminist theory. Instead, a variety of feminist theories emphasize the importance of women's experience, analyze gender inequality, and advocate gender equality (Anderson and Witham 2009; Taylor, Rupp, and Whittier 2008). As we saw earlier in the chapter, feminist ideas from Harriet Martineau, Jane Addams, and others were present during the early years of sociology but were often marginalized in the male-dominated world of academia. The women's movement of the 1960s and 1970s, however, helped create a space for the emergence of feminist scholars who transformed many academic fields, including sociology. Often working across disciplinary boundaries and in newly established women's studies departments, feminist theorists challenged male assumptions about the world and about how social research should be done (Harding 1991; Reinharz 1992).

Historically, men had dominated the analyses of social life and often assumed that their understanding and perspective applied to everyone. Feminist "standpoint theory" rejected this notion, instead emphasizing that all knowledge is constructed from a particular perspective and that women's different experiences need to be included to produce an accurate understanding of social life (Harding 2004; Smith 1974, 1989). In the years that followed, this basic insight was extended to include the recognition that women's experiences vary depending on their class, race, and sexual orientation (Collins 1990; hooks 2000). This understanding has contributed to a wider recognition that the effects of gender, class, race, and sexual orientation intersect in shaping social life (Anderson and Collins 2009; Rothenberg 2009) and that women's lives vary across different societies (Mohanty 2003). Feminist theory has also contributed to a focus on women's bodies as a site of social struggles involving sexuality, beauty norms, violence, reproductive rights, and health (Lorber and Moore 2010). Finally, feminist theory has informed work on men, gender, and sexuality, revealing how our ideas about masculinity are socially constructed (Kimmel and Messner 2009; Pascoe 2007).

In addition, various recent theories—under the umbrella term *postmodernism*—have highlighted how shared meanings and assumptions about the world—a central feature of symbolic interactionist theories—have fragmented, as different groups in society come to understand social reality differently. Meanwhile, rational choice theories have introduced a sort of economic analysis, suggesting that social interaction be understood as exchanges between rational individuals.

One of the great strengths of sociology is that it contains a variety of theories about the workings of social life that reach well beyond the three traditional approaches. But what unites sociology? What is the common ground that enables people using such disparate theories to identify as sociologists? That common ground is the sociological perspective and the core concepts that are at its heart.

Sociology's Common Ground: Culture, Structure, and Power

Diverse sociological theories are united by the core concepts that are central to a sociological perspective, including culture, structure, and power. As we have already seen, these concepts were used extensively by sociology's early thinkers and they have been at the heart of sociology ever since.

To varying degrees, all theoretical approaches rely on sociology's core concepts. For example, functionalism highlights culture's role in providing society with common values, such as love of family. Conflict theory emphasizes how competing groups can manipulate cultural ideas and symbols to their advantage, as when politicians attach the idea of "family values" to their legislative initiatives and suggest opponents are antifamily. Symbolic interactionism emphasizes the process by which individuals create culture, as when people redefine

"family" to incorporate a broader range of relationships. Although these approaches differ in their interpretations and emphases, they all agree that culture is a significant feature of social life worthy of close attention. Similarly, structure and power are important to all sociological theories. Table 1.2 summarizes how these core concepts provide the common ground that links the major approaches to sociological theory.

This section presents a brief overview of sociology's three core concepts. Each concept is later covered in depth in a separate chapter. By learning to use these three concepts to analyze and understand social life, you will succeed in developing a sociological perspective.

Culture

Culture is *the collection of values, beliefs, knowledge, norms, language, behaviors, and material objects shared by a people and socially transmitted from generation to generation.* Culture operates at all levels of society: through everyday interactions between individuals; through organizational norms in schools, businesses, and other groups; and through society-wide

TABLE 1.2	CORE CONCEPTS AND APPROACHES TO SOCIOLOGICAL THEORY		
	Functionalist Theories	**Conflict Theories**	**Symbolic Interactionist Theories**
Key Questions	How is society held together? What function do the parts of society serve?	How is inequality structured in society? How are power relations maintained; how can they be changed?	How do people interpret and understand the social world in their interactions? How do they help shape the reality they experience?
Culture	Culture represents the consensus values and norms of a society into which individuals are socialized.	Conflicting parties use culture to advance their interests. Those in power perpetuate their privilege by socializing people into dominant values and norms. Those who are oppressed develop counter-cultures that challenge the dominant world view.	Through the use of symbols, people create culture based on their interpretation of social reality. They pass on these ideas and values in the socialization process.
Structure	Society is a stable system made up of interconnected structures. People act within structural constraints so that change is typically gradual and temporary, returning societies to a stable equilibrium.	Structure is the social order maintained by dominant groups primarily through coercion and the threat of force. Collective action challenging the existing order is often the source of structural change.	Social structure is produced through recurring individual actions that create a pattern. Structure is inherently unstable and changeable since it must be reproduced continually through individual action.
Power	Power is the ability of a social system to achieve its collective goals. Inequalities between groups serve a positive function in society by motivating the most qualified to fill the most important positions.	Power is often concentrated in the hands of a dominant group that uses it to exploit or oppress others. Inequality is the result of struggle between groups for scarce resources.	Power is rooted in the social relationships between people. Inequality results from the actions of individuals and therefore can be changed.

mechanisms such as the media and religion. At its broadest, culture is a way of life.

We tend to take our own culture for granted since we have internalized its basic customs and assumptions. For example, most of us, most of the time, have a fairly good understanding of what to expect from routine social interactions and what is considered appropriate behavior in those settings. We know when we are expected to be more formal and polite (perhaps with authority figures) and when we can relax and be casual (perhaps with close friends and family). We know that raising a hand to speak when hanging out with friends is unnecessary and that cracking open a beer in class is unwise. These unwritten "rules"—and the ideas about courtesy and respect that inform them—are part of our culture that we have learned.

Consider, for example, the simple matter of where to look when speaking with someone. Most Americans look people in the eye since in American culture direct eye contact signals honesty and forthrightness, whereas avoiding eye contact suggests that one has something to hide. But in some Asian countries, extended direct eye contact is often considered rude and impertinent, whereas averting one's gaze is a sign of deference and respect. Imagine the potential miscommunication if, say, an Asian and an American business executive, unaware of these cultural differences, were assessing each other as potential business partners. The American might think her Asian colleague had something to hide, whereas the Asian executive might think his American colleague was being rude and disrespectful. Understanding the concept of culture helps us interact in a world of diversity and allows us to critically examine beliefs and behaviors we might otherwise view as "natural."

Culture is not "natural" or biologically based because it must be taught and learned through the process of socialization (see Chapter 6). Since people must reproduce culture for it to survive, people can also change culture by adopting new values, beliefs, and behaviors and abandoning older ones. This process of cultural evolution can create conflict as some people seek to hold on to more traditional values and ways of life, while others embrace new ideas and behaviors. As a result, cultural conflicts are common. Clashes in values, beliefs, and ways of life help fuel conflict, sometimes even contributing to warfare. On the other hand, culture is often something to celebrate, and our identity comes, in part, from the elements of culture that we choose to embrace. Our tastes in music, our dress and appearance, our religious beliefs or nonbeliefs, our language, our family's ancestry, among other things, are all cultural features that help to make us who we are.

Culture, therefore, is woven into the fabric of social life and is an essential element of a sociological analysis of society.

Structure

Structure refers to *the recurring patterns of behavior in social life.* These patterns occur at all levels of society, from our daily interactions with others to the global economy. Structures

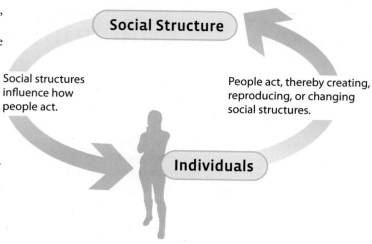

FIGURE 1.1 | THE INTERPLAY BETWEEN PEOPLE AND SOCIAL STRUCTURE

Social structures influence how people act.

People act, thereby creating, reproducing, or changing social structures.

Social Structure

Individuals

range from highly informal patterns, such as where and when we routinely meet up with friends, to much more formal organizations and institutions, such as schools and government.

People create structures to help them accomplish their goals, but, in turn, structures come to constrain what they can do (see Figure 1.1). For example, imagine that you and your friends decide to form a new group to advocate for more parking spaces on campus. In establishing your group, you have to decide things like: Will there be formal leadership positions, such as president and secretary? How will those be chosen? How do you become a member? How will decisions be made? How you answer such questions will determine the structure for your organization. You would hope that the structure you create will help the group function smoothly and promote its goal effectively. But the rules that define the structure will also constrain the behavior of group members because they regulate how members are supposed to behave. As new members join your group, they will experience the rules as an already-existing reality that constrains their actions. They may choose to comply with the rules, thereby reproducing the structure of your group, or work to change them in some way, thereby modifying the structure.

Daily life tends to be ordered by various informal patterns of behavior, or *social structures.* We can talk about "family structure," for example, even though there are no formal organizational by-laws that regulate the behavior of such groups. There are, however, legal standards, social norms, and common practices that establish the "rules" of family life, something we explore later in the book.

Similar to how culture must be reproduced—and can be changed—structures must be reproduced through continuing patterns of behavior or they can be changed through changes in that behavior. History provides examples of how people can act collectively to change social structure. In the nineteenth

thinking about the core concepts
Review the description of sociology's early thinkers. What roles did culture, structure, and power play in their work?

SOCIOLOGY Matters

Sociology and Democracy in Arab Societies

In January 2011, a wave of protests erupted in the Arab world against the region's dictatorial regimes. In Egypt, the most populous Arab country, young people, many of them college students or recent graduates, used Facebook, Twitter, and other social media to coordinate protests against the U.S.-backed regime of Hosni Mubarak, who had ruled with an iron hand since 1981. Labor unions and other groups brought workers out into the streets by the hundreds of thousands. When the military sided with the protesters, the regime was doomed. Though the revolution took many people by surprise, the struggle for democracy in Egypt began decades ago, and in one little-known way, social scientists played a role in it.

Sociologist Saad Eddin Ibrahim is the director of the Ibn Khaldun Center for Development Studies in Cairo, which is named for Abd al-Rahman Ibn Khaldun (1332–1406), who pioneered the formal study of society centuries before the discipline of sociology emerged in the nineteenth century. The center's researchers study and advocate for economic development, democratization, and the strengthening of the agents of civil society—voluntary organizations such as unions, charities, professional associations, and advocacy groups that are neither government nor for-profit businesses. Ibrahim's work led him to conclude that the Arab world would not enjoy peace or widespread prosperity until democracy flourished in the region. As a result, Ibrahim and his colleagues have worked relentlessly for democratic freedom and championed the inclusion of women and minorities in the political process.

A vocal critic of repressive Arab regimes and the U.S. policy of supporting them to promote stability and steady access to Mideast oil, Ibrahim made himself unpopular with the Mubarak government. In 2000, when Mubarak announced elections, Ibrahim and his colleagues said they would conduct independent surveys of voters and publish the results, which threatened to embarrass an unpopular dictator planning a sham election. Ibrahim also explained in a foreign magazine article that he believed Mubarak had no intention of submitting to fair elections and instead was grooming his son to take over the regime as the new president-for-life.

The reaction was swift. The same day the article was published, the Ibn Khaldun Center was looted by State Security guards and Ibrahim and twenty-six of his colleagues were arrested. Ibrahim was convicted and sentenced to seven years' hard labor for "tarnishing" Egypt's image abroad. The imprison-ment drew outcries from human rights organizations, the United Nations, social scientists (including the American Sociological Association), and, eventually, the U.S. government. After three years in isolation, Ibrahim was acquitted of all charges on appeal. He suffered permanent nerve damage in one leg from torture he endured while in prison. A former marathon runner, he needed multiple surgeries before he could walk again, and then only with a cane.

Upon Ibrahim's release, the Ibn Khaldun Center reopened and he and his colleagues resumed their work. In 2007, however, facing a new round of charges, Ibrahim chose to go into exile in the United States rather than risk another prison term. He continued his work on Arab democracy from abroad while his colleagues at the center helped train observers to monitor the polling stations in Egypt's 2010 elections. The fraud they witnessed fed growing public disillusionment that contributed to the 2011 revolution.

As the uprising unfolded, Ibrahim provided analysis of his country's political dynamics in essays for the *Washington Post* and *Wall Street Journal* and in comments in other media throughout the world. When the revolution's success appeared imminent, Ibrahim risked returning to his homeland. Arriving the very day Mubarak resigned, he went immediately to Tahrir Square, the epicenter of the pro-democracy demonstrations. "The spirit in the square was just unbelievable," Ibrahim remembered. "These young people are so empowered. They will never be cowed again by any ruler—at least for a generation."

Like the founders of sociology who were public intellectuals engaged in the political debates of their day, who advised governments on public policy, and who worked with social movements to promote change, Ibrahim and his fellow scholars at Egypt's Ibn Khaldun Center help ensure that, in the Arab world, sociology matters.

think about it

1. *Why can social science research, such as surveying citizens, pose a threat to an autocratic government?*

2. *With the political freedoms they enjoy, do you think young people in the United States feel empowered to help shape the future of their country, as the young people in Egypt did? Why or why not?*

Sources: Goodman (2007); Johnson (2007); Stockman (2011); Ward (2010); Weiss (2011); and the Ibn Khaldun Center for Development Studies (eicds.org).

---

century, six-day workweeks were the norm in industrial societies, and workers usually labored for ten or twelve hours a day. By the early twentieth century, however, a growing number of people joined the labor movement, which promoted the then-radical ideas of an eight-hour workday and a five-day workweek. With great difficulty, labor unions struggled successfully to establish this new standard, thus creating the much-beloved weekend with its two-day reprieve from work. This resulted in a fundamental change in the social structuring of time in our society. (See the Sociology Matters box for an example of the role sociology can play in helping to change social structures today.)

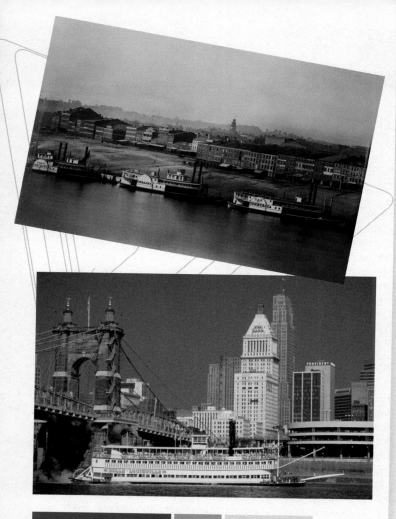

SOCIOLOGY AND CHANGE

Social change influences the lives of individuals and communities alike. These images of the Cincinnati, Ohio waterfront, one a daguerreotype taken in 1848 and the other a photograph taken 150 years later, illustrate the dramatic effects of industrialization, urbanization, and technological change. Both pictures feature paddle-wheeled steamboats, but in one they are a recent technological innovation and a primary form of both commercial and passenger transport. In contrast, the boat in the other—a nostalgic cultural relic of a bygone era—is a tourist attraction.

Power

Power is *the ability to bring about an intended outcome, even when opposed by others.* Power, too, operates at all levels of society, including in families (parents have power over their children), in organizations (managers have power over the people who report to them), and in national and international relations (leaders exercise military and economic power to achieve national goals). Sometimes people *empower* themselves to achieve a goal (as when a student completes a degree to qualify for a particular career). Other times power is used to influence the thinking and behavior of others and even to dominate others. For example, an employer can dictate the rules that employees must follow during work hours.

Power is commonly used to allocate resources (economic power), make rules and decisions (political power), and help to define reality (cultural power). It is thus closely tied to *inequality,* the systematic and unequal distribution of resources among various groups of people. All societies have some form of inequality; it just varies by type and degree. Those who have more economic, political, and cultural resources have a better chance to achieve their goals and overcome hurdles and opposition. In other words, they have more power.

Paying attention to power allows us to see connections and similarities between different forms of inequality, which co-exist and interact. Considering the intersections of race, class, and gender has proven to be especially important in understanding power and inequality.

Culture, structure, and power are not unchanging features of social life; they are part of ongoing social processes. Culture is reproduced and changed through socialization. Structures are created and altered through action. Power can be used to produce or reduce inequalities, which in turn can alter the distribution of power. These dynamics are at the heart of a sociological analysis that recognizes the ever-changing nature of social life.

In Transition

SOCIOLOGY AND CHANGE

Sociology arose over a century and a half ago during a period of transition that marked the emergence of modernity in the eighteenth and nineteenth centuries. Early sociologists, drawing on the core concepts of culture, structure, and power, sought to explain that transition and the social turmoil that often accompanied it. Today, we are living through another period of transition, this time from modernity to an as-yet-uncertain postmodernity, and sociologists are studying the nature and consequences of these changes. By studying sociology yourself, you can better understand these changes, be more equipped to handle them, and perhaps even influence their development.

From Modern to Postmodern Society

Modernity was a period associated with the rise of industrialization, democracy, and science. In contrast, **postmodernity** is *a historical period beginning in the mid-twentieth century characterized by the rise of information-based economies and the fragmentation of political beliefs and ways of knowing.* Because we are in the midst of this transition, it is difficult to summarize neatly what postmodernity will look like or what long-term impact it will have. Nonetheless, we can point to certain features of this transition to the postmodern world. (See Table 1.3.)

Classical theorists were concerned with the rise of an industrial economy; today's sociologists are interested in the relationship between so-called postindustrial economies, in which information-based and service-sector jobs predominate, and the developing industrial economies that now produce the bulk of the world's manufactured goods. Classical sociologists studied the rise of urban life that accompanied industrialization; contemporary sociologists have examined the emergence of suburban life as a new social reality in advanced economies while documenting continued urbanization in the developing world and the growth of "mega-cities." The modern era was marked by a great faith in democratic governments as a means to human progress; in postmodern times, distrust of government and a loss of faith in political ideologies have often led to stalemated conflicts, political disengagement, and widespread cynicism. Finally, classical theorists highlighted the declining influence of religion, the rise of science, and the rationalization

TABLE 1.3	KEY FEATURES OF PREMODERN, MODERN, AND POSTMODERN SOCIETIES		
	Premodern	**Modern**	**Postmodern**
Economy	Agricultural	Industrial	Information based Service oriented
Social Life	Rural	Urban	Suburban Mega-cities
Politics	Religiously sanctioned leaders	Democracy	Disengagement Cynicism
Dominant Culture	Religion	Rationality and science	Fragmented Multicultural

of modern life. Contemporary sociologists have studied our highly fragmented culture, which includes everything from the rise of multiculturalism and rejection of universal truths to a resurgence of fundamentalist religions and reaffirmation of universal truths.

Beyond such broad changes, a number of significant developments are transforming our way of life. These changes are not universal but tend to affect the wealthier societies of the world most. Throughout this book, we use a sociological perspective to better understand these aspects of postmodern society. As you read the list of changes below, consider how they have affected—or will affect—your life:

1. ***The expansion of media and commercial culture.*** In postmodern society, media technologies have dramatically expanded into all aspects of social life, creating new opportunities for communication and new dilemmas. The boundaries between the Internet, television, smart phones, video games, and other media continue to blur, resulting in the all-encompassing and commercialized media environment in which we live. Closely connected to this expansion has been unprecedented growth in advertising and the promotion of consumption. How is the saturation of society by the media influencing social

life? How often do you check or send texts and e-mails? How many advertisements have you seen today? (See, especially, Chapter 14.)

2. ***The threat to the natural environment.*** The ever-increasing production and consumption of consumer goods have taken a serious toll on the environment in the form of resource depletion, pollution, climate change, and an ever-growing accumulation of waste. How can we balance the desire for material comfort with the need to protect diminishing resources? How are environmental changes potentially affecting our health and our way of life? (See Chapter 15.)

3. ***The decline of U.S. cities and the rise of suburbs.*** In the postmodern era, corporations have moved many industrialized manufacturing jobs to developing nations where workers are paid lower wages. As industrial jobs in U.S. cities disappeared, the economic base of major urban areas crumbled, leaving behind unemployment, poverty, and crime in many inner cities. The suburbs, meanwhile, have grown rapidly, permitting more people to own homes in relatively safe and tranquil surroundings. But suburban life has its own problems. It can leave people feeling socially isolated, for example, and require lengthy commutes to work in heavy traffic. How can U.S. cities remain vital in postmodernity? How have the suburbs changed the rhythms of daily life, and what is their effect on people's sense of community? How will the expansion of urban life in developing nations affect those societies? (See Chapter 15.)

4. ***The global economy.*** You need only consider the route traveled by the ingredients of your morning cup of coffee—from the plantations of Brazil, Columbia, or Vietnam to your local coffee shop or grocery store—to realize that we are inextricably part of a global system of production and consumption. The global economy is transforming societies around the world, and the debate over the nature of this change has been an important topic in sociology recently. How does a global economy affect the inequality between rich and poor nations? How has the growth of a global economy affected employment patterns, educational requirements, and family life? (See Chapters 9 and 16.)

5. ***The aging population.*** We are living longer and healthier lives thanks to advances in health information and medical technology. Now society must adjust to the new reality of an aging population. The U.S. Census Bureau (2011) reports that, in 2010, one out of every fifty-six Americans was aged 85 years or older and that, by 2050, one out of every twenty Americans will be that age (U.S. Census

Bureau 2004). How will the need to care for aging parents and grandparents affect future American families? How will social services and the health care system cope with an aging population? (See Chapter 17.)

6. ***The changing family.*** Effective contraception, divorce, blended families, two-wage-earner families, single-parent families, gay marriage, and surrogate parenting, among other developments, have changed the definition of the family and its role in society. How does today's family differ from yesterday's? How have recent social changes affected the nature and function of the family? What is in store for the family in the future? (See Chapter 12.)

7. ***Troubled political institutions.*** In many parts of the world today, the prospect of democracy holds great promise as a substitute for repressive political regimes. But long-established democracies often seem to have their own troubles. Why do some well-established democracies stagnate? What threats challenge the vitality of our democratic institutions? (See Chapter 16.)

8. ***Increased diversity and multiculturalism.*** A recent influx of immigrants has been a catalyst for change as well as conflict in the United States, just as was an earlier wave of immigrants who arrived in the early twentieth century. In addition, the global economy and the relative ease of modern travel have begun to erode the significance of national boundaries. Does the fragmentation and juxtaposition of cultural experiences—in music, food, film, and more—point the way to a new cultural mash-up? Does the presence of such cultural diversity threaten societies with fragmentation? How can the distinct contributions of different cultures be preserved in a world in which cultural traits are increasingly blended? (See Chapters 10 and 14.)

9. ***The changing nature of violence and warfare.*** Powerful and wealthy countries, including the United States, possess advanced weapons that can destroy humanity many times over. Some smaller nations and various nonstate actors have developed low-tech but deadly weapons and tactics. The result is a world bristling with arms, threatened by violence, and locked in political and military stalemates. How can societies reduce violence? What factors contribute to the recent rise in terrorist activity? What is the future of warfare? (See Chapter 16.)

10. ***The changing role of religion.*** To varying degrees, the world's wealthy industrialized nations have become increasingly secular—that is, religion plays a much less significant role in public and daily life in those nations than it once did. But in other parts of the world, religious beliefs continue to inform and drive many aspects of social life.

Because of the increased contact among cultures, differences in religious beliefs now fuel some of the world's major conflicts and some of the most divisive political issues at home. Will secularization continue to expand in the coming years or will religious revivals spread? Can different cultures coexist even with fundamental religious differences? (See Chapter 12.)

The Challenge and Hope of Sociology

Sociology holds great promise. As C. Wright Mills pointed out, it can help us understand the connections between ourselves and the larger social world. In studying society, we learn more about who we are as individuals, why we face the conditions that we do, and how we are connected to others. At its best, sociology promotes an understanding of the social world and our place in it and suggests ways that we might act to improve our lives, our community, and our world.

But sociology comes with some challenges, too. Because it addresses serious problems that face society, it can lead us to some disturbing discoveries about society and ourselves. Issues such as how to care for an aging population, how to balance human needs with environmental concerns, how to address persistent poverty, how to combat racism and sexism, how to respond to extremist violence, and how to accommodate diversity in society are not easy to think about, but they are important and must be faced. Also, looking at our experiences in a broader social context sometimes reveals disconcerting insights about our relative privilege, or lack of it, due to the effects of class, race, gender, sexual orientation, or nationality. Achieving a better understanding of our place in the world's hierarchy of privilege can be enlightening, but also unsettling.

As you will see throughout this book, sociology can force us to move outside our comfort zone and challenge us to think in new ways about assumptions that we take for granted. If we live in relative comfort and freedom, we might find it easy to ignore difficult issues that face society and hope they won't affect us personally. If we are struggling to get by, we might prefer to focus solely on taking care of our private lives, hoping that eventually we can insulate ourselves from economic upheaval, crime, and other social problems. But sociology reminds us that in taking either position we are, by default, helping to reproduce the society in which we live, with all its problems. Whether we realize it or not, whether we like it or not, we are part of the broader social world.

In the face of our changing world, sociology offers hope. It is not a fearful hope that we can somehow manage individually to escape the world's problems. Instead, it is the hopeful realization that societies—and the issues that confront them—are largely created by human beings. That means people working together also have the capacity to change and improve those societies, as well as their own lives. We invite you to take up the challenge to use sociology to better understand the world and your place in it. And we hope that from this understanding, you'll be inspired and better equipped to act—in whatever way you see fit— to make a positive difference in your life and in our rapidly changing world.

Looking Back

1. The sociological perspective is a way of looking at the world that focuses on the relationships between individuals and larger forces in society. Sociology as a discipline couples this perspective with systematic study and research using the methods of social science.

2. The discipline of sociology emerged in the late 1800s, in part as a response to the dramatic economic, political, cultural, and social changes taking place in the modern world.

3. Karl Marx, Emile Durkheim, and Max Weber were the three most influential classical sociological thinkers. Marx is best known for his work on capitalism and on the role of conflict in society. Durkheim's work focused on social solidarity. Weber is best known for his work on the rationalization of society, including the rise of bureaucracy.

4. Because of the sexism and racism of the day, the contributions of other social thinkers such as Harriet Martineau, W.E.B. Du Bois, and Jane Addams were not fully recognized or accepted within the discipline of sociology in their time. However, they made a major contribution, especially in spotlighting issues of gender- and race-based inequality.

5. Sociological theories seek to explain the workings of society by explaining why things happen as they do. These theories vary along three key dimensions: consensus and conflict, subjective and objective reality, and micro-level and macro-level analyses. Diverse theories are sometimes grouped into the functionalist, conflict, and symbolic interactionist approaches.

6. The foundational work in sociology highlighted a number of core concepts that still serve as sociology's common ground. Among these enduring concepts are culture, structure, and power. These concepts are used throughout the book to help analyze social issues and phenomena.

7. Today, sociologists continue to study the social changes taking place as modernity gives way to the postmodern era. In many respects, the postmodern world is distinctly different from the one studied by the classical sociologists. But the enduring core concepts and theoretical insights of those early sociological thinkers—combined with new ideas and theories—can help us better understand our contemporary society. That is the focus of this book.

Critical Thinking: Questions and Activities

1. What is sociology and what is the sociological perspective? How does the sociological perspective apply to your own life?

2. The use of indiscriminate deadly violence against civilians, often referred to as "terrorism," is a topic of intense interest to social scientists. What sorts of issues and questions would someone using a sociological perspective focus on in addressing this topic? What sorts of questions might researchers in other social science disciplines—such as economics, psychology, anthropology, and political science—focus on when considering this phenomenon?

3. What do you see as some of the advantages and disadvantages of the rise of modernity?

4. Of the ten changes in contemporary society listed on pages 25–26, which one do you think is the most significant? Why? What important changes, if any, would you add to the list? Why do you feel they should be included?

5. What cards have you been dealt? Consider, for example, these questions about your childhood: Did you regularly have access to adequate food and clean drinking water? Did you live in a neighborhood that was relatively safe and free of crime? Did you have access to a good education? If you answered no to one or more of these questions, you no doubt had to overcome some hurdles while growing up. If you answered yes to these questions, you have enjoyed privileges that are unavailable to others. Using your sociological imagination, list ten more questions that could help determine whether people have enjoyed access to privileges in their lives.

Key Terms

anomie (p. 14) social normlessness, without moral guidance or standards.

collective conscience (p. 14) the shared values of society.

conflict theories (p. 19) social theories that focus on issues of contention, power, and inequality, highlighting the competition for scarce resources.

culture (p. 21) the collection of values, beliefs, knowledge, norms, language, behaviors, and material objects shared by a people and socially transmitted from generation to generation.

division of labor (p. 13) the way people specialize in different tasks, each requiring specific skills.

dysfunctional (p. 19) inhibiting or disrupting the working of a system as a whole.

functionalist theories (p. 18) see "structural-functionalist theories."

industrialization (p. 10) the use of large-scale machinery for the mass manufacture of consumer goods.

latent function (p. 19) the largely unrecognized and unintended consequences of social phenomena.

macro level of analysis (p. 18) a focus on large-scale social systems and processes such as the economy, politics, and population trends.

manifest functions (p. 19) the recognized and intended consequences of social phenomena.

meso level of analysis (p. 18) a focus somewhere between very large and very small social phenomena—on organizations or institutions, for example.

micro level of analysis (p. 18) a focus on small-scale, usually face-to-face social interaction.

modernity (p. 7) a historical era beginning in the 1700s characterized by the growth of democracy and personal freedom, increased reliance on reason and science to explain the natural and social worlds, and a shift toward an urban industrial economy.

positivism (p. 11) a belief that accurate knowledge must be based on the scientific method.

postmodernity (p. 25) a historical period beginning in the mid-twentieth century characterized by the rise of information-based economies and the fragmentation of political beliefs and ways of knowing.

power (p. 24) the ability to bring about an intended outcome, even when opposed by others.

rationalization of society (p. 15) the long-term historical process by which rationality replaced tradition as the basis for organizing social and economic life.

science (p. 9) a method of inquiry that uses logic and the systematic collection of evidence to support knowledge claims.

social solidarity (p. 13) the collective bonds that connect individuals.

social theory (p. 17) a set of principles and propositions that explains the relationships among social phenomena.

sociological imagination (p. 5) see "sociological perspective."

sociological perspective (p. 5) a view of the social world that focuses on discovering and understanding the connections between individuals and the broader social contexts in which they live; what C. Wright Mills called the *sociological imagination*.

sociology (p. 5) the systematic study of the relationship between individuals and society.

structural-functionalist theories (p. 18) theories that focus on consensus and cooperative interaction in social life, emphasizing how different elements that make up a society's structure contribute to its overall operation. Often referred to simply as "functionalist theories," or "functionalism."

structure (p. 22) the recurring patterns of behavior in social life.

symbolic interactionist theories (p. 19) social theories that focus on how people use shared symbols and construct society as a result of their everyday interactions.

urbanization (p. 10) the growth of cities.

Understanding the Research Process

looking AHEAD

How do social science researchers know what they claim to know?

What special challenges might confront you as a social science researcher?

How can you become a more informed consumer of social science research?

Who is more likely to be killed by a stranger, someone living in a city or someone living in a semirural suburban area? If you are like most people, you would assume—based on news stories, crime shows, and detective novels—that cities are more dangerous and, therefore, urban dwellers are at greater risk. But when researchers examined the evidence, they found that a person living in a semirural suburb was more likely to be killed by a stranger than was a person in a city (Lucy 2003; Lucy and Rabalais 2002).

This finding is so counterintuitive that it might be hard to believe. How, then, do we go about evaluating this claim? The first step in evaluating any claim based on research is to examine and think critically about how the researcher collected and analyzed the data. In this case, a close reading of the study's methods reveals two key factors that contributed to the unexpected findings.

First, the researcher used not only homicide data (the killing by strangers that most people probably think about) but also data from traffic fatalities, which almost always involve strangers. In fact, car accidents cause more than twice as many deaths as do homicides. And the areas with the most traffic fatalities are those where people tend to drive at higher speeds on relatively narrow roads—such as those found in semirural suburbs.

Second, the researchers collected data on the relationship of murder victims to their killers. They found that only about one out of six murders is committed by a stranger; the vast majority of murders are perpetrated by family members, acquaintances, and coworkers. It turns out that the threat that you will be murdered by a stranger is relatively small compared to the threat that someone you know will murder you or that a stranger will kill you in an automobile accident. And you are more likely to die in a traffic accident in semiurban rural areas.

By collecting relevant data about traffic fatalities and about the relationships of murderers and victims and then analyzing those data, the researchers came up with their counterintuitive findings. If you look at the study closely, you can examine the kinds of data collected, the means of collecting them, and the ways the data are analyzed and applied to the hypothesis—and then decide for yourself if the conclusions seem reasonable and valid. This transparency is a central element of the scientific method, which makes use of systematic procedures that can be checked and verified. ■

Sociology, then, is not just a perspective and a discipline. It is also an *activity* that uses the framework of science to ask questions, gather data, and seek answers about the phenomena of the social world, including where we are most at risk of dying at the hands of a stranger (Babbie 2006; Neuman 2005). This activity of sociology can involve not only doing basic research, but also addressing practical problems and communicating with a broad public.

To look at social science research critically and better understand its claims, however, we need to know something about the research process—the focus of this chapter. In particular, this chapter examines the elements of social scientific thinking; explores the role of theory in research; sketches out the major data-gathering techniques; reviews various types of research; provides some critical questions to ask about any social research study, such as the surprising findings discussed in this opening example; and concludes with a glimpse of how research methods are evolving in the twenty-first century.

This chapter gives you some critical thinking tools so that you can become a more informed consumer of social science research. Reading this chapter might also be the first step you take toward conducting a research study of your own in the future.

Social Science as a Way of Knowing

As we saw in Chapter 1, for most of human history, people relied on religious doctrine to interpret both the natural and social worlds. But as the explanatory power of science proved its usefulness, systematic investigation and evaluation of evidence supplanted religion as a way of learning about the natural, or physical, world. Many of us still turn to religion for spiri-

tual guidance, but nearly all of us rely on meteorologists for a weather forecast, medical doctors for health care, and a host of scientists and engineers for everything from repairs to our cars and computers to safe bridges and clean water.

For insights into the social world, we turn today to social scientists. They examine such social phenomena as homelessness, health care, violence against women, public opinion, trends in crime, hiring discrimination, and images of masculinity and femininity in the media and in society. Much of the work sociologists do is **basic research,** *the primary goal of which is to describe some aspect of society and advance our understanding of it.* Some work is **applied research,** *the primary goal of which is to directly address some problem or need.*

Academics typically conduct basic research and publish their findings in journals and books addressed to a scholarly audience. Applied research often takes place outside academia—in social service agencies, businesses, nonprofits, and social change groups, for example—and its results tend to be distributed within the organizations commissioning the study. Each day educators, government officials, business managers, social service providers, health care workers, urban planners, and others rely on the findings of social science research to do their jobs. (See the Sociology Matters box on page 34 for an example of one type of applied research.)

Public sociology is *the effort to bring the findings of both basic and applied sociological research to a broader nonacademic audience.* Sociologists often use the mass media in this effort, writing magazine articles or blogs or contributing op-ed columns to newspapers (Burawoy et al. 2004).

Social science research may not provide us with all the answers we would like, but it can illuminate aspects of society that would otherwise remain unnoticed, and it can help us to avoid common pitfalls in everyday thinking.

The Limits of Everyday Thinking

Growing up, many children are taught to believe in the existence of Santa Claus, a mysterious but jovial character who delivers gifts to good boys and girls during the Christmas holiday. For many of those who celebrate Christmas, Santa plays a central role in the holiday festivities. At some point in childhood, however, believers in Santa have to face the harsh reality that their understanding of this particular part of the social world has been tragically flawed. How could Santa have seemed so real? And how did they go so wrong in sizing up the situation?

These tough lessons of childhood can teach something about the common pitfalls of everyday thinking and the usefulness of scientific investigation. Let's take a look at the series of errors children make in evaluating the truth of the Santa story, errors that we adults need to guard against in our everyday thinking:

■ ***Unquestioned trust in authorities.*** A child who believes in Santa relies on the truth claims of authority figures— parents and other adults. Although we adults are not naïve enough to believe everything we are told, the claims of

Participatory Action Research: Media Coverage of Domestic Violence

Leaders of the Rhode Island Coalition against Domestic Violence had long been frustrated by the way the local press covered their issue, especially domestic murders, which were often featured prominently in the local news. Even reporters with good intentions often wrote stories that helped perpetuate what coalition leaders saw as destructive myths about domestic violence, including the notion that it is caused by substance abuse, that perpetrators are simply "out of control," and that domestic violence is just a private family problem. From their many years of working with survivors of this type of violence, coalition leaders knew that the larger story behind domestic violence tended to be invisible in the news. They felt that if they had a better understanding of how reporters gathered their information, they could work with local journalists to improve their coverage and draw attention to the need for better resources to combat domestic violence.

The coalition partnered with sociologist Charlotte Ryan to develop a study that used *participatory action research,* a form of applied research, to address this problem. In this type of research, community members and sociologists work together to identify the key research questions and design the research project—and sometimes even to carry out the research.

Ryan began by examining local newspaper coverage of twelve domestic violence murders in Rhode Island between 1996 and 1999. In her analysis of eighty-eight articles, Ryan found that the reporters' sources played a key role in shaping the story. Neighbors and on-the-scene witnesses generally emphasized the tragedy of the particular event. Police sources focused on the details of the crime. Only the few reporters who turned to experts in domestic violence—including shelter providers, public health workers, and advocates—included information linking the murders to domestic violence and the need for community resources to deal with it. Ryan concluded: "With a few notable exceptions, the media reinforced the perception that domestic violence murders are isolated family tragedies and did not challenge common myths about domestic violence. In doing so, reporters missed opportunities to broaden the public's understanding of domestic violence, its warning signs and possibilities for prevention and community intervention" (Rhode Island Coalition against Domestic Violence 2000, 5-4).

As part of the research project, the Rhode Island Coalition also conducted a series of conversations with two key groups: local news reporters, to learn how reporters understand their responsibilities and goals; and survivors of domestic violence, to gather their recommendations about how reporters should cover domestic violence stories.

Once all the research was complete, Ryan and the Rhode Island Coalition developed an action strategy based on its key findings. The strategy had two main components. First, Ryan and the coalition produced *Domestic Violence: A Handbook for Journalists* and distributed it to reporters throughout the state (Rhode Island Coalition against Domestic Violence 2000). The handbook provides a wide range of resources, including background information, statistical data on domestic violence, a summary of Ryan's study, and recommendations from survivors of domestic violence. In addition, it gives tips on how to cover domestic violence, identifies "best practices" for crime reporters, and directs them to reliable news sources about this issue. Second, the Rhode Island Coalition began training survivors and advocates about how reporters work so that they could become more effective news sources when communicating with them.

As a result of this collaborative research project, the Rhode Island Coalition is now one of the principal sources for reporters in covering cases of domestic violence in the state. In addition, news coverage has changed in ways that reflect the coalition's emphasis on understanding domestic violence as a social problem, not just a private tragedy.

think about it

1. *Have you read stories about issues related to domestic violence in your local newspaper? If so, has the coverage focused on domestic violence as a private issue or a social problem?*

2. *What might be some of the strengths and weaknesses of participatory action research?*

some authorities can be persuasive. Blindly believing an "authoritative" person or institution (including social scientists!), however, is never a good idea. Intentionally or not, authority figures can be—and often are—wrong. To obtain the most accurate understanding of the world possible, we have to be skeptical about knowledge claims based solely on someone's status as an authority.

■ ***Unquestioned acceptance of "common sense."*** Children inhabit a world in which Santa's existence is reinforced by other believers—their peers. In such a world, the existence of Santa may seem to be common sense since so many others share the belief. But history is full of false ideas that were considered common sense by many people in their time, such as the idea that the world was flat. Common knowledge claims need to be considered with a questioning mind.

- **Unquestioned acceptance of traditional beliefs.** Santa has long been a part of U.S. culture, providing further evidence to a child that he must be real. What else would account for all those Santa decorations, greeting cards, and television specials? Ideas that have withstood the test of time deserve our attention. But beware: just because a belief has been around for a long time doesn't make it true. As with our approach to authorities, we need to temper our respect for tradition with a healthy skepticism that demands knowledge claims be backed by evidence.

- **Generalizations based on personal experience.** Some children have the ultimate evidence: personal experience. They have seen, heard, touched, and even talked to Santa at the local mall. After all, "Seeing is believing." Well, maybe not. In some cases, personal experience can be very useful, but relying on it can also be misleading. We may misunderstand or misinterpret an experience. Or our experiences may not be typical; we may overgeneralize from them. We need broader sources of evidence, especially when we are talking about the social world.

- **Reliance on selective observation.** Using *selective observation,* anyone can find evidence that might appear to confirm the existence of Santa. For example, the milk and cookies left for Santa disappear. A more accurate picture of the world requires us to remain open minded, however, willing to take seriously evidence that contradicts our initial inclinations and to consider alternative explanations for the evidence we have. In other words, we must gather and evaluate evidence systematically to increase the chances that we will reach an accurate conclusion.

- **Biased observation and interpretation.** One final barrier to clear thinking about Santa may be *bias*: a child has a vested interest in believing the story. Who wants to mess with a legend that delivers such generous benefits? In assessing what someone believes, it is helpful to keep in mind the potential interests that this person has in promoting certain ideas. By itself, a person's bias is not a reason to reject a claim, but if someone benefits substantially from interpreting evidence one way or another, we certainly should pay especially close attention to how he or she has gathered and explained the evidence.

Our Santa example may seem trivial, but the problems it illustrates are serious. When adults reach conclusions based solely on a belief in authority, common sense, tradition, personal experience, or selective observation—or when they allow their personal bias to influence their conclusions—they are likely to wind up with a distorted and inaccurate picture of the world. Acting on the basis of such misjudgments can be disastrous for people, public policy, and societies. People can avoid these mistakes by using an approach to knowledge based on social scientific principles, which we discuss next.

" I'm feeling a bit cynical this year. Just bring me cash."
© www.cartoonstock.com

A belief in Santa Claus can be lucrative for children, but it involves some common errors in everyday thinking.

The Elements of Social Science Research

Four key elements distinguish social science research: identifying and understanding patterns in social life, gathering empirical evidence, explaining how the evidence was collected and analyzed, and viewing the resulting research claims as provisional knowledge.

PATTERNS IN SOCIAL LIFE Social science focuses on the patterns in social life—identifiable, repeating patterns in human thought and action. Of course, each human being makes independent decisions, and as a result an individual's behavior is not entirely predictable. On the other hand, social life is not merely a chaotic series of random events. Research shows that there *are* recurring patterns to human perception, behavior, and experience. Social science research largely consists of identifying and understanding these patterns in social life.

For example, social science research can tell us the probability that certain categories of people will or will not vote. Table 2.1 provides some data from the U.S. Census Bureau on the percentage of U.S. citizens aged eighteen years or older who said they voted in the 2008 election.

Do you see the pattern? The older the age group, the more likely its members were to vote. Although there is a slight drop

TABLE 2.1	VOTING IN THE 2008 ELECTION, BY AGE

Age (years)	Percentage Who Voted
18–24	48.5
25–34	57.0
35–44	62.8
45–54	67.4
55–64	71.5
65–74	72.4
75+	67.8
All ages	63.6

Source: U.S. Census Bureau, Current Population Survey, November 2008.

in turnout for those aged seventy-five or older, the overall pattern is clear.

Social scientists use a variety of techniques to describe and measure the patterns in social life. Some of these efforts involve the use of sophisticated statistical techniques. But even a straightforward analysis of the simplest data, such as that presented in Table 2.1, can provide us with insight about the social world.

EMPIRICAL EVIDENCE To describe patterns in social life, sociologists depend on gathering relevant **empirical evidence**—*evidence that can be observed or documented using the human senses.* Empirical evidence can be categorized broadly as quantitative or qualitative. **Quantitative data** are simply *evidence that can be summarized numerically.* Quantitative data are presented in the form of **variables,** *measures that can change (or vary) and thus have different values.* Table 2.1 includes quantitative data with two variables—age and voting. The value for age varies depending on how many years a person has lived; the value for voting varies depending on whether or not a person said he or she voted.

Variables are often categorized as independent or dependent. The **independent variable** is *associated with and/or causes change in the value of the dependent variable.* The **dependent variable** *changes in response to the independent variable.* In our example, age is the independent variable (because it is associated with the likelihood of voting), whereas voting is the dependent variable (because it varies with age). Thus our data show that people are more likely to vote as they get older; voting doesn't make them grow old.

When the independent variable is *associated with* the change in value of the dependent variable, it is known as **correlation,** *a relationship in which change in one variable is connected to change in another variable.* But correlation is not the same as causation. Age is *correlated* with voting, but age doesn't *cause* voting. Instead, age is associated with a variety of factors that influence the likelihood of voting, such as living in a community longer or having a sense that one's vote counts.

As a starting point for quantitative research, researchers often pose a **hypothesis,** *a statement about the relationship between variables that is to be investigated.* In addition to age, for example, we might hypothesize that the more education people have, the more likely they are to vote. Researchers would have to investigate this relationship to either confirm or reject the hypothesis.

Qualitative data are *any kind of evidence that is not numerical in nature, including evidence gathered from interviews, direct observation, and written or visual documents.* Whereas researchers using quantitative data focus on measuring variables, those who use qualitative data usually focus on describing social processes. In presenting qualitative data, researchers often organize their evidence around central themes that have emerged in their study and use direct quotations or vivid descriptions to illustrate their points. For example, to understand why a smaller percentage of people between the ages of 18 and 24 tend to vote than do people in older age groups, you might interview segments of this population. A qualitative approach can provide valuable insights into the specific experiences and attitudes of this group.

To take another example, one study used qualitative data as a tool to evaluate how clients are served by social service agencies. Researchers examined interviews with homeless men and women in Portland, Oregon, that focused on their experiences in shelters and soup kitchens and with other agencies (Hoffman and Coffey 2008). One common theme in the interviews was the experience of being disrespected and treated like children by service providers. One thirty-seven-year-old woman noted that "they treat everyone the same . . . like they are in elementary school," and a twenty-seven-year-old man said that he "tried the Salvation Army program they had up there but I had too much personal pride to be talked down to and to be treated like a child" (pp. 213–14).

Personal stories of this sort, as well as other types of qualitative data, allow researchers to see *how* people experience the social world and how they understand their own experiences. This kind of qualitative data can be extremely important, revealing complexities that statistical data cannot capture. In the study of homelessness, for example, the authors make a compelling case that these personal stories can "help us understand how experiencing a lack of respect and dignity may turn individuals away from services intended to help them" (Hoffman and Coffey 2008, 219), a key lesson in helping social

When sociologists have conducted research among homeless men and women, they have helped local agencies to better understand the experiences and needs of their community's homeless population and to implement more effective services.

service agencies provide more effective and respectful services for the homeless.

Usually a quantitative study allows a researcher to gather information on many different cases but provides a limited amount of information on each case. In contrast, qualitative studies provide a wealth of detail on a relatively small number of cases. Sometimes a sociologist will use a combination of quantitative and qualitative data to get the best of both worlds.

TRANSPARENCY OF METHODS

Social science depends on **transparency,** *the requirement that researchers explain how they collected and analyzed their evidence and how they reached their conclusions.* Transparency allows others to "see" how the research was done by reading a description of the process used in the study. Readers, including scholars, can then critically assess the research and its findings and replicate the study if they wish.

PROVISIONAL KNOWLEDGE
Social science is based on *provisional knowledge*—the idea that all truth claims are tentative and open to revision if new evidence is discovered. According to this approach, we can never be 100 percent certain about our understanding of social phenomena, but we can use systematic analyses to rule out certain claims and identify explanations that are probably true.

The goal of social scientists is to reach tentative conclusions that they can act on, while remaining open to new insights that might be generated by more research. This skeptical attitude means that research findings remain subject to scrutiny and revision as more information becomes known. In this sense, so-

cial science research is an ongoing process: new studies respond to and build on prior research. Table 2.2 provides a short summary of the four key elements of social science research.

The Special Challenges of Social Science

Because social scientists study people and not the physical or natural world, they face a number of challenges that do not generally confront natural scientists:

- *Social researchers are unlikely to be able to control conditions.* In a lab experiment a chemist can control the environment and manipulate a variable such as heat to study its impact on a chemical reaction. But for ethical, legal, and practical reasons, human beings cannot be manipulated at will by a sociological researcher. For example, a sociologist can't set up an experiment in which children are subject to varying levels of abuse to observe the effects.

TABLE 2.2	THE ELEMENTS OF SOCIAL SCIENCE RESEARCH
Identifying and understanding patterns in social life	Scientists seek to identify recurrent patterns in human thought and action.
Gathering empirical evidence	Patterns are identified based on evidence that can be observed or documented using human senses.
Using transparent methods	Researchers need to disclose how they collect and analyze their evidence.
Viewing knowledge as provisional	Social science is based on the idea that truth claims are tentative and open to revision if new evidence is discovered.

RESEARCH AND CHANGE

Sociological research produces provisional knowledge, which is always open to revision in response to social changes or new research findings. For example, Peterson and Berger (1975) made a compelling case that a highly concentrated music industry—with a handful of large companies dominating the production and distribution of music—leads to a lack of diversity in popular music. More than fifteen years later, however, sociologist Paul Lopes (1992) revisited the question of the relationship between concentration in the industry and diversity in popular music and found that musical innovation and variety does not necessarily decline in periods of market concentration. Instead, with large companies releasing music on many different labels, a new open system of music production emerged that allowed the major music producers to control the industry while still fostering musical innovation. Research on diversity in popular music continues. Sociologist Tim Dowd (2004) echoes Lopes's findings, indicating that decentralized production is the key to musical diversity, even when only a few large companies dominate the music industry.

Some sociologists conduct lab experiments on small group interactions but the vast majority of research on large scale social phenomenon takes place through the use of other methods, such as surveys and observation.

- **_Social life cannot be predicted with the certainty of natural laws._** At sea level, raising the temperature of water to 212 degrees Fahrenheit causes it to boil. Assuming the conditions remain the same, the water responds exactly the same way every time the temperature increases. We can never be certain how different people will perceive, interpret, or react to a given situation, however. As a result, in social science there are always exceptions to any rule. We must talk in terms of *rates* of behavior, for example, or the *probability* of something happening. Still, as we have seen, sociologists can describe and explain the *patterns* of perception, behavior, and experience that characterize social life and predict the *likelihood* that certain social phenomena will occur.

- **_Human beings are conscious of being studied, which may change their behavior._** In a classic example, researchers in the 1930s tested various ways to improve the productivity of workers at Western Electric's Hawthorne plant outside of Chicago (Roethlisberger 1939). No matter what changes the researchers initiated—whether they increased or decreased the lighting or lengthened or shortened break times—they discovered that productivity went up. They concluded that the very fact that workers were being observed, rather than the particular changes being tested, contributed to higher productivity. *The fact that human beings will react differently because they know they are in a study has since been referred to as the* **Hawthorne effect.** Although researchers have ways of dealing

One of the ongoing challenges of sociological research is that those who participate in studies know they are being observed, which can alter their behavior or responses accordingly.

In the early twentieth century, more than 25,000 people worked at Western Electric's Hawthorne Works Plant outside Chicago making telephones and phone switching systems. In the early 1930s, researchers seeking to enhance worker productivity found that no matter what various small changes in working conditions they made, productivity at the plant improved. They concluded that workers were responding not to the changed conditions but to being the focus of attention.

with such behavior, the Hawthorne effect is a constant challenge.

The important elements and special challenges of social science research are best seen by examining the actual work of research, a subject to which we now turn.

Doing Research

Two key components, theory and data, act together in social science research. Theory helps us to identify key research questions and to interpret the data that are collected. Data provide the evidence that can support existing theory, lead to changes in theory, contradict a theory, or result in the development of a new theory (Merton 1968a). In this section we explore the role of theory as well as the various types of research techniques used to collect data.

The Roles of Theory

Theory plays several vital roles in social research: (1) it can highlight key questions or issues; (2) it can help explain the data collected; and (3) it can help us see the connections between phenomena that are not immediately apparent.

To illustrate the roles theory plays in social science research, let's consider a classic theory proposed by Arnold van Gennep (1909/1961) in the early twentieth century regarding *rituals*—repeated patterns of behavior performed at specific times, often involving symbols. Recall that the functionalist approach suggests that if something exists in the social world for an extended period of time it must be serving some social function. Van Gennep's more specific theory was that the function of some rituals was to mark a change of social status; he called such rituals *rites of passage*. Van Gennep's theory suggests that rites of passage help to encourage or reinforce certain behavior, affirm common ties through their use of cultural symbols, serve as a communal acknowledgment of the change of status, and provide an outlet for emotions related to the status change.

HIGHLIGHTING KEY QUESTIONS   A researcher can use van Gennep's theory about rites of passage to ask questions about the social world. What are the significant rites of passage today? How do these rituals mark changes in social status? The features that characterize rites of passage can

be found in graduations, weddings, retirement parties, and funerals—each of which marks a significant change in status. High school graduation ceremonies mark the rite of passage from adolescence to young adulthood. They commemorate an accomplishment that society encourages and usually involve symbolic clothing such as robes, mortarboards, and tassels. These events also help channel the many mixed emotions—on the part of graduate and parents alike—that often accompany such a change in social status.

Similarly, when a family member or friend dies we typically follow culturally specific rituals as we mourn and remember. Funerals acknowledge a change of status, provide an outlet for grieving and are laden with culturally significant symbolism, such as the color and types of clothing mourners typically wear. Whatever the specifics of the symbols involved, each rite of passage helps to mark a transition. Van Gennep's theory alerts us to the significance of these rituals.

S P O T L I G H T
on social theory

Functionalism suggests that long-lasting social phenomena serve a useful purpose for society, and van Gennep's theory suggests several useful purposes for rituals. What rituals have been important in your life, and, in retrospect, what purposes did they serve?

EXPLAINING COLLECTED DATA   Theory can help to explain data that have been collected. When James Diego Vigil (1996) studied Chicano street gangs, he learned that a prospective gang member would routinely be attacked and beaten by several gang members at the same time. Vigil argued that this "street baptism" had the practical purpose of revealing a prospective member's fighting skills. But it was also a symbolic ritual that helped to promote gang solidarity and establish an initiate's new identity and status as a member of the gang. Understanding the theory associated with rites of passage helps make sense of this apparently odd behavior.

SEEING CONNECTIONS By moving beyond description and analysis of specific phenomena to a more general or abstract level, theory can help us to see patterns and connections between phenomena that are not immediately apparent. For example, through the theory of rituals as rites of passage we can see the common features of graduations, funerals, and "street baptisms." With a little sociological imagination, you can begin to recognize rites of passage in a wide range of social settings and expand your insights into the various roles they play in social life.

The Theory-Research Dynamic

We've noted that theory helps us to interpret research and research helps us to build theory. To better understand this interactive relationship, let's look at a hypothetical example from the world of sports.

What makes a team successful? Of course, different levels of talent and experience are important, but some sports teams seem to perform better than expected, whereas other teams that are highly talented "on paper" don't live up to expectations. Emile Durkheim's theory of *social solidarity* (see Chapter 1) could provide a starting point for an investigation into this question. Durkheim proposed that any well-functioning social group is held together by shared values. So perhaps bonding is a key to team success.

But does winning help bond the teammates to one another, or do they win because they are already bonded? Theory has helped us to identify a useful concept—social solidarity—and to develop two competing hypotheses about the relationship between solidarity and success in sports. To assess our hypotheses, we need to design a study that will begin to untangle the relationship between solidarity and success. Perhaps we could survey the members of various teams about their values and level of solidarity before a season begins and again after the season concludes. Coupled with the team's performance record, a survey would give us data to assess our competing hypotheses.

We hope that our results will elaborate and clarify our theory, which will lead us (and perhaps other researchers) to conduct further research about the relationship between success and solidarity in any number of organizations, including businesses, schools, or military units. One study will not provide a final

answer to the broader theoretical question about success and solidarity, but each study will provide additional insight into this relationship.

Different theoretical approaches may highlight different aspects of the same social relationship. For example, feminist theorists might suggest that we pay close attention to how gender dynamics might influence group solidarity on sports teams. Do girls or women bond differently on teams than do boys or men? What happens on co-ed teams? Considering a different theoretical approach can lead us to ask yet another set of research questions.

Theory, then, suggests areas of possible research by highlighting key questions, and it helps explain the data collected. In turn, we need data to assess the accuracy of theory. In some cases, research findings lend credence to theories; in others, the data contradict the theory. Either way, we gain a better understanding of the social world when we consider theory and data together.

One instance in which the data did not support the theory involved efforts to reduce heavy episodic drinking, also known as "binge drinking," on college campuses. To encourage students to drink moderately, about half of all four-year college campuses in the United States have adopted a program called "social norms marketing" in recent years. Researchers found that students usually overestimate how much their peers drink, and therefore they often drink more in order to "keep up" with what they perceive to be the norm of the group. Instead of telling students what they should *not* do ("You shouldn't binge drink!"), social norms marketing emphasizes the fact that most students *don't* binge drink. Using flyers, posters, ads, and other venues, college health officials let students know that, for example, "On this campus, 80% of students have fewer than five drinks when they party." By pointing out that the norm on campus is *not* to binge drink, college officials—according to this theory—can persuade more students to moderate their own drinking. However, when Wechsler and his associates (2003) gathered data from 118 college campuses over a four-year period to test

Research has found that social norms marketing, as illustrated by this public service ad, has no significant impact on student behavior, raising questions about its effectiveness.

this theory, they found that campuses using a social norms marketing approach had no significant reduction in student drinking. In this case, the data called into question the theory that underlay social norms marketing.

There is no single correct way to gather evidence for a research study. Instead, sociologists use a variety of **research methods,** *the procedures used by a researcher to collect and analyze data.* Generally they choose whatever method allows them to collect the most appropriate type of data needed to address the questions they are asking. Below we note briefly the most commonly used data collection techniques and illustrate their use with specific examples.

Methods of Collecting Data

The method that a researcher uses to collect data depends to a great degree on what sort of information he or she wants to know. Researchers who are interested in, say, what percentage of students at a particular school voted in the last presidential election (quantitative data) might use surveys and perhaps analysis of existing sources, such as official poll results. Those researchers who wanted to know *why* the students voted the way they did (qualitative data), though, might be more likely to conduct interviews and use focus groups. Other topics might require the researcher to do field research or conduct experiments.

SURVEY RESEARCH Probably the most commonly used technique in sociology is the **survey,** *a data collection technique that involves asking someone a series of questions.* Surveys are popular in part because they are very versatile, are useful for a wide variety of issues, and effectively describe large populations, if appropriate sampling techniques are used (Czaja and Blair 2004).

Survey researchers can use different kinds of questions. Some survey questions are constructed in a *closed-ended* or fixed-response format, which means a respondent must choose from a given set of responses. For example, the Pew Research Center for the People and the Press (2010) gathers data regularly on which media outlets people in the United States turn to for news. The center's 2010 Media Consumption Survey asked more than 3,000 adults a series of questions about how frequently they watch specific television news programs. For each program, respondents were asked to select from four possible responses: *regularly, sometimes, hardly ever,* or *never.* The advantage of closed-ended questions is that the researcher can easily code them for quantitative analysis. According to the Pew Center's 2010 report on news media audiences, 18 percent of respondents watch CNN "regularly," and 50 percent watch the local news "regularly."

However, if you have ever filled out a survey consisting of nothing but closed-ended questions, you might have noticed that sometimes the preselected answers didn't fit what you really wanted to say. Moreover, these types of answers may encourage people to respond in ways that they might not have otherwise. To address such problems, some surveys include *open-ended* questions that do not provide predetermined re-

sponse categories. The Pew Center's media study also includes open-ended questions, such as "About how much time did you spend watching the news or any news programs on TV yesterday?" This type of question allows respondents to give their own estimate—say, 25 minutes or 2 hours—rather than fit their response into a preexisting category. Other news surveys might ask people *why* they watch specific news programs. Such open-ended questions allow for a wider, and perhaps more accurate, range of responses. However, the wide array of answers can be time consuming to record and difficult to summarize and analyze.

Researchers also need to pay careful attention to the way the questions in a survey are worded because even small variations in wording can influence results significantly. The following are just a few of the many problems that can arise when researchers write survey questions:

- **Lack of clarity.** An unclear question can produce inaccurate results. In one infamous example, the well-known Roper polling firm found that 22 percent of people in the United States believed it was possible that the Holocaust never happened, while another 12 percent said they weren't sure (Morin 1994). This startling finding was later revealed to be the result of a poorly worded question: "Does it seem possible or does it seem impossible to you that the Nazi extermination of the Jews never happened?" This awkwardly phrased question required a person affirming the existence of the Holocaust to agree with a double negative: that it was impossible it never happened. The percentage of people expressing doubt dropped to the single digits when the question was later rephrased to read, "Do you doubt that the Holocaust actually happened, or not?"

- **Different definitions.** *Validity* refers to successfully measuring what you intend to measure. For example, one study found that when the Census Bureau asked about the hours that a person worked "last week," most people thought the phrase referred to Monday through Friday. In fact, the question was supposed to include the weekend as well (Polivka and Rothgeb 1993). The researchers discovered that the wording of their question accidentally undermined its validity, since they were measuring something different than what they had intended.

- **Loaded language.** Some "hot button" words and expressions have positive or negative connotations that can influence a survey's results. One study (Rasinski 1989) found that only 23 percent of respondents said too little money was spent on "welfare," but 63 percent said too little money was spent on "assistance to the poor"—essentially the same thing. Clearly, the word *welfare* had a negative connotation.

- **Double-barreled questions.** Each question should be about one topic only. Questions that cover more than one topic are called "double-barreled." A question intended to measure trust and widely used by pollsters for decades reads, "Generally speaking, would you say that most people can be trusted or that you can't be too careful in dealing with people?" Researchers (Miller and Mitamura 2003) showed, however, that this question is really double-barreled: it asks whether or not people can be trusted *and* whether or not you should be careful. It's quite possible to trust people in general but still feel you should be careful in dealing with them. Trust and caution are not the same thing, and the question as originally worded conflates the two concepts.

When you are considering the results from survey research, examine the questions to see if their wording might have influenced the results.

When you interpret survey results, it is also important to know two factors. What is the *population,* the target group a researcher is interested in studying? And who participated in the survey? Researchers refer to this group as the **sample,** or *part of the population that represents the whole.*

Depending on what is being studied, a population might be made up of individual people, institutions, newspaper articles, or a host of other things. Let's say you want to study how students on your campus get news about current events. In this case, you would be interested in the entire student population on your campus. It would be virtually impossible for you to gather data on all the cases in that population—all the students who attend your college. Instead, to conduct high-quality research, you need a good sample that accurately represents the larger population you are studying.

One way to obtain a high-quality sample is to choose it randomly. In a **random sample,** *every element of the population has an equal chance of being chosen.* To draw a random sample, you need a complete list of all the members of the population you want to study. Putting the names of all the students enrolled at your college in a (very large) hat and choosing some of the names would be a random sample, since every student from that population (your college) would have an equal chance of being chosen.

Random samples of adequate size allow researchers to accurately **generalize,** or *describe patterns of behavior of a larger population based on findings from a sample.* Pollsters, for example, are able to make good predictions about the outcome of national elections in the United States by sampling only about 1,200 people. Such polls are not perfect, but they give a close approximation of the views of the target population as a whole. (See the Sociology Works box.)

For many research projects, however, it is not possible to gather a totally random sample. For your hypothetical study of how students on your campus get news about current events, you might decide to walk across campus and give your survey to people you meet "at random." This method will *not* yield a random sample of the students at your college, though, since your selections will be influenced by the area of campus you choose, the time of day you go out, and so forth. In other words, every student at the college will *not* have an equal

chance of being chosen. This method is called a *convenience sample,* a way of choosing study participants based simply on the fact that it is convenient for the researcher. In this case, because you do not know if your sample is representative of all students at the college, you cannot generalize your findings to the population of the campus as a whole.

In between a random sample and a convenience sample is the *quota sample,* in which the researcher tries to achieve a generalizable sample by making sure various groups within the target population are present in representative proportions. The groups typically targeted in a quota sample are those that are relevant for the research question at hand and those that have proven to be significant in other research. For example, if you were studying whether or not students at your school were satisfied with their college experience, you would want your sample to match key features of the student population as a whole, including gender and full- or part-time status. If 60 percent of the students at your college are women, and 25 percent of students attend part time, then your quota sample should match these characteristics. Even though a quota sample is not a true random sample, the more specific your quota system, the more confident you can be that the sample can be generalized to the larger population.

There is one final critical factor in using samples: research studies should report how a sample was generated so that readers can make their own assessment of how well the sample represents the population as a whole.

INTENSIVE INTERVIEWS AND FOCUS GROUPS An **intensive interview** (sometimes known as a "qualitative interview" or "in-depth interview") is *a data gathering technique that uses open-ended questions during somewhat lengthy face-to-face sessions.* These interviews are semistructured, with the interviewer usually using a combination of preplanned questions along with follow-up and clarifying questions that he or she improvises as the session progresses (Rubin and Rubin 2004). Intensive interviews produce more in-depth information from a respondent than a survey provides, but they are very time consuming to conduct. As a result, intensive interview studies generally include a far smaller number of respondents than surveys, commonly fewer than 100 participants, making it more difficult to generalize a researcher's findings to larger populations. One way to expand the number of people involved is to interview them in a *focus group,* made up usually of six to twelve people (Stewart, Shamdasani, and Rook 2006). A moderator asks preplanned and follow-up questions, encourages participation, and helps ensure that no one participant dominates the discussion.

When sociologist Gayle Sulik (2007) set out to explore women's experiences with breast cancer, she designed a study that used intensive interviews as the primary source of data. In

Andrew Kohut and Public Opinion Research

Have you ever wondered who comes up with the polling numbers about elections? One main source of election forecasting and other types of public opinion data is the Pew Research Center, a nonpartisan "fact tank" that provides information on the issues, attitudes, and trends shaping the United States and the world. Since 2004 Andrew Kohut has been president of the center. For Kohut, the study of sociology paved the way for a career spent studying American attitudes and political opinions. His academic training in research methods as a sociology major prepared him for its wider application in the public sphere.

Instead of conducting research as a university professor, Kohut worked at the Gallup Organization, one of the most prestigious polling firms in the country, where he was president for ten years. Kohut then founded several independent research companies that served as precursors to the Pew Research Center, an umbrella organization that is home to seven independent research groups that examine journalism, technology, religion, global attitudes, and social and demographic trends.

Today, Kohut is a well-known commentator about American public opinion. He appears regularly on radio and television and writes essays for the op-ed page of the *New York Times*. In founding the Pew Research Center, he established one of the most reputable sources of information on public opinion in the United States. The center's final survey of likely voters in the 2008 presidential election, released just two days before Election Day, gave Democratic candidate Barack Obama a 52 to 46 percent lead over Republican candidate John McCain, a projection that was almost identical to the actual outcome—a 53 to 46 percent edge for Obama in the popular vote.

Kohut also directs the Pew Research Center's Global Attitudes Project, which conducts public opinion surveys around the world on a wide range of subjects, from the attitudes of the Chinese about their country's economy to the extent of anti-Semitism in Europe to global attitudes about free trade, health care, and the image of the United States. By 2009 the project's survey team had completed more than 200,000 interviews in fifty-five

Andrew Kohut

countries. Conducting public opinion research on a global scale requires researchers to address a variety of challenges: translating their questionnaires into local languages, conducting face-to-face interviews in some nations, and conducting interviews over both landlines and cell phones in others.

As a longtime practitioner of survey research, Kohut knows that the ongoing challenge is to produce "good reliable questioning, representative sampling, high-quality interviewing and thorough analysis of the data." In summing up his ambitions for the projects he directs, Kohut notes: "Our greatest hope is to do a good job of informing the American public about the opinions and trends that are shaping their lives and the world—from politics to the media, to foreign policy, to the major social issues of our time. Our greatest challenge is to tell the story of public opinion fully and with nuance, and at the same time communicate it in a way that is understandable to our audiences" (Kohut n.d.).

> "Our greatest hope is to do a good job of informing the American public about the opinions and trends that are shaping their lives and the world."

think about it

1. *Have you ever responded to a survey—by mail, phone, or online? What did you think of the experience?*

2. *Do you think it is helpful to know the results of public opinion research about current events? Why, or why not?*

3. *For what research project might you want to design your own short survey?*

---

her interviews with sixty breast cancer survivors, Sulik asked the women to provide their "illness narratives"—accounts of the initial diagnosis and how their experience with cancer had influenced their lives; descriptions of their relationships with family members, friends, and doctors; and stories of how they managed during the most difficult times. Sulik found that women experience breast cancer—especially the medical and emotional care they receive—in ways that reflect broad expec-

tations about women's role as caregivers. In particular, women with breast cancer were often remarkably selfless: they tended to be unwilling to ask for help and reluctant to accept help from others. They had to deal with their own fears and pain while trying to help their families cope with the disruption and fear surrounding the illness. The interview format allowed Sulik to gather information that a closed-ended set of questions might not have revealed.

FIELD RESEARCH

As the name suggests, **field research** (sometimes called *ethnography* or *field work*) is *a data collection technique in which the researcher systematically observes some aspect of social life in its natural setting*. In some cases, the researcher tries to remain separate from the activities he or she is studying. In other cases, the researcher engages in *participant observation*, a type of field research in which the researcher both observes and actively takes part in the setting or community being studied. Field researchers talk to the people they observe and develop detailed field notes about what they see and hear—notes that form the foundation of the researcher's analysis (Schatzman and Strauss 1973). One of the key challenges for observational field researchers is gaining access to the setting and being accepted by those they are studying.

As field researchers immerse themselves in the environment they are studying, they become aware of significant questions or issues that deserve closer attention. Mark Fishman worked as a newspaper reporter for seven months in his investigation of how news is made. In a now-classic study, *Manufacturing the News,* Fishman (1980) drew on his field notes from his participant observation as an apprentice reporter to explore how reporters' daily routines—where they look for news and whom they talk to each day—defines the stories that become news.

More recently, researchers conducting observational research at Euronews, a multilingual news channel that broadcasts throughout Europe (Baisnee and Marchetti 2006), found that the demands of producing twenty-four-hour news in seven different languages resulted in a kind of "sedentary journalism," in which journalists produce most of the news without ever leaving their offices. Rather than cover a story on location, the reporters—responding to the norms of round-the-clock news—rely on phone interviews, online and archival research, and the use of video images shot by other journalists.

EXISTING SOURCES

Researchers frequently rely on existing sources, making use of available data and documents rather than collecting new data and evidence. A researcher who conducts **secondary data analysis** *uses data previously collected by other researchers.* Government and private agencies such as the U.S. Census Bureau, the National Opinion Research Center, and Statistics Canada maintain and continually update major data sets, which are made available to researchers wishing to address a variety of research questions. Since such ready-made data sets enable them to skip the time, cost, and effort of gathering original data, many researchers find them an attractive option.

For example, one recent study of the dynamics of friendship that compared data from the 1985 and 2004 General Social Survey found that friendship networks in the United States are changing, with a growing proportion of U.S. adults now experiencing social isolation (McPherson, Smith-Lovin, and Brashears 2006). Between 1985 and 2004, the size of people's core discussion networks declined significantly. That is, U.S. adults had, on average, fewer confidants—people with whom they talked about personally important issues—in 2004 than they did in 1985. In fact, the number of people who reported that they have no confidants at all nearly tripled in the twenty years between the two surveys. The 2004 data indicate that more than half of U.S. adults have no confidants outside of their family. Is this growth in social isolation the experience of a particular generation? How, if at all, do the new forms of online social networking help to create new kinds of friendship networks? These are questions future researchers will want to explore.

Researchers can also analyze various other kinds of existing sources. Historical documents found in libraries and archives are essential to a researcher who is creating a social history. Similarly, mass media content such as a TV reality series or a video game can be an important source of sociological information. **Content analysis** refers to *a variety of techniques that enable researchers to systematically summarize and analyze the content of various forms of communication—written, spoken, or pictorial* (Holsti 1968).

One recent content analysis examined gender portrayals in the world of video games (Dill and Thill 2007). Drawing on a representative sample of images from the top-selling video game magazines—a total of 479 images of game characters from *Electronic Gaming Monthly, PC Gamer, Game Informer, The Official Xbox Magazine, Computer Gaming World* and *GamePro*—the authors found that gender stereotypes are rampant. Sixty percent of female characters were depicted in a sexually suggestive way; almost four in ten of the female characters appeared scantily clad. Less than one percent of male characters were depicted in this way. In addition, more than 80 percent of male characters and more than 60 percent of female characters were portrayed as aggressive—engaged in combat, posing with weapons, wearing armor. Summarizing their findings, Dill and Thill note: "The vision of masculinity video game characters project is that men should be powerful, dominant, and aggressive. The story video game characters tell about femininity is that women should be extreme physical specimens, visions of beauty, objects of men's heterosexual fantasies, and less important than men. An emerging trend, though, is that these sexy, curvaceously thin beauties are also now typically violent" (p. 861). In this study, content analysis gives researchers quantitative data on a popular culture trend that may have broader significance for our society.

EXPERIMENTS

An **experiment** is *a data gathering technique in which the researcher manipulates an independent variable under controlled conditions to determine if change in an independent variable produces change in a dependent variable,*

A recent content analysis of popular video games revealed that they are full of gender stereotypes, with aggressive male characters and sexually suggestive female characters. But many of the female characters are both aggressive and sexualized, including the characters Skarlet and Mileena, from the Mortal Kombat series. What, if anything, do the results of this study suggest about contemporary attitudes about women, violence, and sexuality?

thereby establishing a cause and effect relationship (Campbell and Stanley 1963). In an experiment a researcher compares two groups of subjects: a *control group* and a group that is exposed to some "stimulus" or "treatment." Afterwards, the two groups are compared to evaluate the effects of the treatment. Since researchers need to control the experimental situation, experiments usually must take place in a laboratory setting, rather than in a natural social setting. This requirement greatly limits the types of issues that sociologists can examine using experiments and is one of the reasons experimental research is relatively uncommon in sociology. Still, some sociologists have designed innovative studies that have taken advantage of the benefits of an experimental design in a real-world setting.

For example, an experiment that sociologist Devah Pager (2007) designed to determine the impact of a criminal record on a person's job opportunities made use of actual job interviews with real-world employers. Pager hired and trained two pairs of testers—one pair was White and one pair was African American—and gave them identical backgrounds and resumes, except for one difference. In each pair, one of the testers was given a criminal record and the other was not. She sent the testers out to apply for a total of 350 jobs (the pair of African American testers applied for 200 jobs and the pair of white testers applied for 150 jobs) and waited to see who would be called back for a job interview. The study design was complex, but Pager made sure that the only difference within each pair of job applicants was the criminal record. The independent variable in each pair, then, was a job applicant's criminal record; the dependent variable was whether the applicant would be invited for a job interview. Pager's findings were stark but not unexpected: those applicants with a criminal record were far less likely to get called back for a job interview than their counterparts with no criminal record. Pager's more significant finding was that white job applicants with a criminal record were more likely to get a call back for an interview (17 percent) than were black job applicants with *no* criminal history (14 percent). And black job applicants with a criminal record received a call back only 5 percent of the time. The study's rigorous experimental design applied in a real-world setting, rather than a laboratory, enhances the validity of Pager's research.

Table 2.3 on p. 46 summarizes the most common data collection methods.

Research Ethics

Regardless of which data gathering techniques they use, sociologists are expected to adhere to ethical standards in their research activities. Some standards apply to all types of researchers in the natural and social sciences, such as those forbidding the falsification of data or the misrepresentation of findings. All researchers are also expected to take active steps to help ensure the integrity of their work—for example, by disclosing all sources of funding for the research. But other ethical standards apply to the unique situations that arise when scientists study people.

An important summary of ethical standards for social science research can be found in the professional "Code of Ethics" developed by the American Sociological Association (1999). The code states that the primary goal of ethical guidelines is "the welfare and protection of the individuals and groups with whom sociologists work"—in other words, to ensure that people involved in sociological studies are not harmed in any way. Studies that might be highly stressful or embarrassing, for example, are typically forbidden.

Sociologists are also expected to protect the privacy of their research subjects. In studies providing *anonymity,* subjects remain "nameless" even to the researcher, such as when surveys are returned to a researcher without identifying information. Anonymity is very difficult to achieve, however, since in most studies researchers know who the subjects are. It is more common for researchers to ensure *confidentiality*: the researcher knows each subject's identity but will not make it available to the public in any way. Some studies simply report collective data—on opinions, behavior, or demographic characteristics—and never cite any single individual. A study

TABLE 2.3   MAJOR DATA COLLECTION TECHNIQUES

	Features	Strengths	Weaknesses
Surveys	A series of questions is administered in writing (on paper, via Internet) or verbally (by telephone or in person).	Cost-effective way to get information on a wide range of issues. Results, especially from large random samples, can be generalized.	Closed-response options can be limiting. Data are broad but often not particularly deep.
Interviews and focus groups	Open-ended questions and improvised follow-up questions are asked in relatively lengthy face-to-face interviews that are typically recorded for later analysis.	Allows subjects the freedom to develop detailed responses in their own language; researchers can immediately ask follow-up questions.	Time and labor intensive. Data are rich and deep, but small, nonrandom sample limits generalizability.
Field research	Researchers work in natural settings observing social interactions and ongoing nature of social life.	Less intrusive than direct questioning, resulting in more natural data. Goes beyond what people say to observing what they do.	Very time and labor intensive. Data are rich and deep, but small, nonrandom sample limits generalizability.
Existing sources	Quantitative data are reanalyzed or existing materials, such as media content or historical records, are used.	Convenient and cost-effective. Existing content not affected by researcher's presence.	Data specific to the researcher's question may not be available. No way to know what the people who produced the content were thinking at the time.
Experiments	Researchers use controlled manipulation of social conditions to test hypothesis.	Can isolate specific variable to study.	Typically limited to micro-level questions. Ethical considerations restrict their applicability.

that quotes an individual may use a pseudonym or no name at all or may change some identifying details to ensure confidentiality.

Perhaps the single most important ethical standard in research is the principle of **informed consent,** which means that *subjects in any study must know about the nature of the research project, any potential benefits or risks that they may face, and that they have the right to stop participating at any time, for any reason.* This broad principle goes a long way in protecting human subjects. Because some populations are considered unable to provide informed consent—including those under age eighteen and the mentally ill—special restrictions limit the sorts of research in which they can be involved.

Any college or university that receives funding from the federal government for research involving people must comply with certain rules and regulations aimed at protecting the subjects of the research. One of the most important is that schools must have an Institutional Review Board (IRB) to review proposed research projects and ensure that they comply with ethical standards, thus providing another layer of protection for research participants.

The Research Process: A Student Example

Perhaps the best way to appreciate all the steps in the research process (Figure 2.1) is to use as an example a project appropriate for a student in an introductory sociology class, like you.

Even though this project is simpler in scope than the typical sociological study, the basic research process is the same:

1. ***Choose and explore a general topic.*** A variety of factors, including personal interest, intellectual curiosity, the availability of existing data, and political commitment, could influence the general topic you choose. Perhaps the data on age and voting presented earlier in this chapter piqued your interest, and you find you want to learn more about the behavior of young voters. After choosing young people and voting as your general topic, you explore the existing research to find out what is already known about the voting behavior of this age group. You'll want to look at recent research on this topic so that you can begin to get a handle on the broader theories that help to explain voting attitudes and patterns among young people.

2. ***Identify a specific research question.*** "Young people and voting" is too general a topic. You would need to narrow it down to a specific question of manageable size. For example, you may have noticed that many of your friends did not vote in the last presidential election. At the same time, in your research you may have read the theory that people who vote are also more likely to get involved in other kinds of civic activities. This connection between your own observations and your knowledge of a specific theory might spark a question: What *is* the relationship between voting and volunteer service or charitable work? In posing this research question, you may decide to hypothesize a relation-

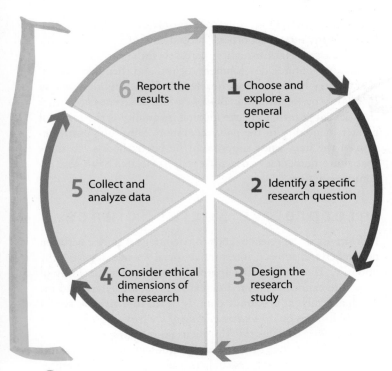

FIGURE 2.1 | THE RESEARCH PROCESS

The research process can be thought of as a cycle because existing research is part of the scholarly literature that researchers consult when they develop and design a new study. When findings from a new study are published, they become part of the research literature that future scholars will review as they develop their own research projects.

ship between two variables: Young people who do service or charitable work are more likely to vote than are young people who do not do such work. This is the hypothesis you would now investigate.

3. **Design the research study and specify the data to be collected.** You now have a question that you must translate into a concrete study. Given your limited resources and time (issues that plague all social researchers!), you decide a survey would be the most efficient way to collect the data you need. To create your survey, you must **operationalize your terms,** that is, *specifically define the variables you are interested in studying.* For example, what qualifies as service or charitable work? Helping family members? Charity work completed to fulfill a requirement for a course? Do respondents have to be engaged in such work now or can they have done it in the past? You must be clear about how you will measure these and all other variables in advance of your study. Once you've clarified your key terms, you'll need to create a *questionnaire,* the specific set of questions that you will ask each person you survey.

At this stage, you must also devise your sampling strategy—that is, determine who will receive your survey. Since this is a small school project, you will likely have to limit your study to students on your own campus. The results of your survey, therefore, will not accurately reflect

the voting behavior of all young people, which limits your ability to generalize your findings. Students on your campus are likely to be different from students elsewhere and will certainly be different from young people who do not attend college. But even for your small study, you need to make sampling decisions: How many students will you select for the study? How will you choose them? In addition, you will need to decide how you want to administer the survey—by mail, by phone, over the Internet, in face-to-face interviews, or any combination of these methods.

4. **Consider ethical dimensions of your research and, if necessary, get approval from your school's Institutional Review Board, or IRB.** You should be sensitive to any ethical issues your research raises. In addition, any research project involving people will likely have to be reviewed by your school's IRB, which will want to make sure, for example, that you are not causing any harm and that all participants will provide informed consent.

5. **Collect, analyze, and interpret the data.** Finally, you are ready to administer your survey. Afterwards, you must enter the resulting data in a computer using a software package that will allow you to analyze this information. Your analysis of the data could range from simple summaries of the responses (for example, 42 percent of respondents voted in the last election) to comparisons between groups (for example, similarities and differences in the amount of charity work done by voters and nonvoters) or more complex analyses of the relationship between the variables. Once your data analysis is complete, you will need to summarize what you have found. The conclusions to be drawn from data are not self-evident, however; data must be interpreted in light of theoretical or substantive questions. How does your evidence apply to the question you raised originally? What have you learned about the relationship between voting and service or charity work? Has your hypothesis been confirmed? Do your findings have any bearing on theories in this field?

6. **Report the results.** The final step involves writing a report of the study. Adhering to the norm of transparency, you will identify your initial research question, explain the process of data collection, present the results, explain what you think these results tell you about your research question, and show how these results fit with previous research and theory on these issues. You might also decide to write a summary of your findings for a broader audience and publish an article in your school's newspaper. Perhaps another researcher will take your study into account when developing his or her own related project, bringing the research process full circle.

Even a simple school project such as this one reveals the complexity of doing research. At every step of the way, you must make decisions that balance the "ideal" project with reality: the limitations under which you are working. Social scientists face similar dilemmas all the time. They do not have unlimited staff, budgets, or time. As a result, research projects always involve compromises. In the best research, though, social scientists find creative ways to gather the data they need to address the question at hand adequately. This process involves both the precision of science and the ingenuity associated with any challenging endeavor.

Now that you have a sense of the general research process, let's take a look at different types of sociological research.

Types of Research

Sociology is a "big tent" discipline that includes a diverse array of approaches to studying the social world. These research approaches can be categorized into three major types summarized in Table 2.4: *positivist, interpretive,* and *critical* social science (Benton 1977; Fletcher 1974; Guba and Lincoln 1994; Ritzer 1975). Because some of the assumptions of these perspectives are mutually exclusive, different researchers tend to emphasize one approach over the other two. However, during their careers, many researchers use two or even all three approaches, depending on the question at hand. Although they vary in some important ways, all three types of research share the basic elements of social science we discussed earlier: their practitioners search for patterns in social life, insist on empirical evidence to support knowledge claims, demand transparency in the methods used to gather and analyze data, and consider knowledge produced by research to be provisional.

In the following sections, we review these three basic approaches—especially with respect to their assumptions about the nature of the social world, their goals, and their view of the role of values in research. We use studies about class and economic inequality to illustrate each type of research.

Positivist Social Science

The most commonly used approach to sociological research is positivism—a term that dates back to Auguste Comte, as you may recall from Chapter 1. **Positivist social science** is *an approach that assumes that the social world, like the natural world, is characterized by laws that can be identified through research and used to predict and control human affairs* (Hoover and Donovan 2007). Researchers using the positivist approach usually look at quantitative data and use the language of variables in their analyses. Positivist social scientists strive for **value-neutrality,** *removing any personal views from the research process.* That is, positivists tend to argue that, with the exception of choosing a topic to study, science should not involve the researcher's values, beliefs, or opinions, and, ideally, social scientists should remain disinterested parties in the research they conduct. To positivist social scientists, a sociologist's job is to study the social world, not try to change it.

One of many examples of positivist research is sociologist Miles Simpson's (1990) examination of the relationship between political democracy and economic inequality. Using existing data from sixty-two countries, Simpson tried to test various theories about why some countries have greater economic inequality than others. Proponents of some economic theories argue that inequality increases in the early stages of a country's economic development, peaks, and then decreases as the country becomes more developed. These theories explain inequality by focusing on *economic* processes. However, other theories suggest that greater income inequality is the result of greater inequality in the *political* system. Simpson's examination of the data lends support to the latter theory. He finds that more democracy in a society is associated with less income inequality.

Interpretive Social Science

If positivist social science tends to encourage distance between researcher and subject, interpretive social science does just the opposite. Those using this approach suggest that the study of social life cannot be limited to features that are external to individuals, such as economic data. Instead, **interpretive social science** focuses on *an understanding of the* meaning *that people ascribe to their social world.* This focus on meaning makes interpretive social science fundamentally different from the natural sciences in the methods researchers use. In particular, interpretive researchers try to empathize with the people they study in order to understand the world from their perspective. This method requires close contact with the people in a study, an approach often traced to Max Weber, who argued for using *verstehen*—a German word that means "to understand"—in social research.

Interpretive researchers usually use qualitative data, often in the form of the words and explanations given by the people they are studying. However, interpretive researchers are not interested simply in how individuals understand social life; they seek to uncover patterns in the ways people make meaning of their social worlds and then describe the form and content of such interpretive patterns. This work does not necessarily promote social change, but often it can promote empathy and understanding for the people being studied.

Interpretive studies tend to deal directly with people's values, beliefs, and opinions because those are an integral part of the social world the researcher is studying. To adhere to the requirement of transparency, interpretive researchers often include a substantive discussion in their published research reports of their relationship with their research subjects. Interpretive researchers share the social science norm that their own personal values, feelings, and opinions should not distort their research findings. However, they also believe that their close connections with the people they are studying can enhance, rather than detract from, the accuracy of a study because their rapport with their subjects means there is less chance that they will misinterpret their findings.

For example, in his pioneering study of a poor urban neighborhood, sociologist William Foote Whyte (1914–2000) spent three years living in "Cornerville" (later revealed to be Boston's North End), spending much of his time with members of a gang of young men he called "the Nortons." Whyte was par-

TABLE 2.4 THREE APPROACHES TO SOCIAL SCIENCE RESEARCH

	Positivist	Interpretive	Critical
Areas of agreement	All three are based on the search for patterns in social life, require empirical evidence to support claims, demand transparency in the methods used to gather and analyze data, and consider knowledge produced by research to be provisional.		
Nature of the social world	Composed of discrete elements that interact in recurring patterns, producing usually stable social systems	Composed of evolving definitions of reality formed in the context of human interaction	Structured by power imbalances that produce conflict and result in social change
Goal of the research	Identify laws in social life to enable prediction and control	Better understand the meaning that the social world holds for others	Better understand how society works to promote social change
The role of values in research	Scientific research should be value-free; researchers should pursue objectivity by maintaining a detached distance from those being studied.	Scientific research should present an accurate portrait of the people being studied, including their values; researchers can gain insight by building relationships with those being studied.	Scientific research inevitably involves a value position that researchers should make explicit; researchers should help promote positive social change.

ticularly close with the gang's leader, Doc, and the two men regularly discussed the community, the corner gang, even the best way to meet people from different sectors of Cornerville society. Whyte's interpretive study, the now-classic *Street Corner Society* (1943/1993), is full of lengthy quotes from Doc, who served as an invaluable neighborhood guide, a sounding board for Whyte's still-developing understanding of the community, and a critical reader of the early drafts of what became Whyte's book.

Critical Social Science

Critical social science is *research carried out explicitly to create knowledge that can be used to bring about social change.* Critical researchers do not focus solely on understanding society; rather, they are interested in understanding society in order to *improve* it in some way. A broad range of sociologists has followed in this tradition. Some invoke a famous line from Karl Marx (1845/1978, 145): "The philosophers have only *interpreted* the world, in various ways; the point, however, is to *change* it."

Critical social science rejects the idea of value neutrality, for which the positivists strive. For the critical researcher, value neutrality is neither possible nor desirable because all science incorporates some value position. Even advocating value neutrality is itself a value-laden position. Critical researchers say the issue is not *whether* values will be a part of their work but rather *which* values will inform research. Critical social science is usually associated broadly with values

that encourage human freedom and social equality. As a result, this approach often addresses issues of power and inequality in society. The fact that critical researchers embrace such values, they argue, does not undermine the credibility of their research. To the contrary, critical social science researchers want to better understand and reveal the dynamics of power in society in the hope of bringing about social change. If such efforts are to be successful, they must be based on an accurate picture of how society works. Thus, although values are at the core of this approach, critical social scientists seek to understand society *as it is* in order to help promote society *as it might be*.

One critical social science study involved living wage campaigns, which try to ensure that the wages paid to workers are high enough to keep them and their families out of poverty. These efforts are usually local, and local economic conditions determine the specifics of each campaign. In the early years of this movement, an activist from the Los Angeles Living Wage Coalition turned to Robert Pollin, an economist, to assess the living wage proposal being considered in that city. Pollin teamed up with Stephanie Luce (1998), a sociologist specializing in labor markets, to produce a study of the proposal. Their goal was to critically assess whether or not the proposal would help low-wage workers and not lead to job losses. As it turned out, their study concluded that the living wage ordinance would help low-wage workers and would not lead to job losses. The researchers didn't stop there, though. They presented their findings to the Los Angeles City Council and helped get the ordinance passed. The two researchers were then approached by other living wage activists from around the country. Recognizing a need, they decided to produce a book that presented their own research on the issue and also examined other existing work.

These three approaches to social science research share some common ground while at the same time allowing for multiple approaches to a single issue, as we explore in the Through a Sociological Lens box on the following page).

Thinking Critically: How to Assess Research

We can't all be experts on research methodology, so it is helpful to have some authorities who monitor the quality of the research for us. The scientific community does this monitoring through the **peer-review process,** *a way in which scholars evaluate research manuscripts before they are published in order to ensure their quality.* When a research article is submitted for publication to a peer-reviewed journal, the editors send the article out to be reviewed anonymously by several other scholars in the field. These scholars provide the editors with their analysis of the strengths and weaknesses of the study. The article will be published only if the reviewers and the editors agree that the study is credible and worthy of consideration. The reviewers do not have to agree with the study's findings; they just have to attest that the question being examined is significant, that the data collected are appropriate and adequate, and that the conclusions reached are warranted. University presses often use a similar process when publishing books.

Although far from perfect, the peer-review process does provide the reader with a certain level of confidence about the basic competence of published research. Many research databases available through libraries allow you to limit your search to works that are published in peer-reviewed journals. You need not dismiss research and evidence published elsewhere, but you may want to give such work a more skeptical look since it has not been subjected to this rigorous review process.

After having surveyed some of the basics of social research in this chapter, you too are now equipped to carry out your own review process of the research that you encounter in both scholarly and popular publications. The ability to think critically about research findings is an important skill to develop that will be relevant to whatever field of study you pursue.

To assess a social scientific study, be sure to ask at least these six questions:

1. *What is the research question?* This is a simple but fundamentally important issue. Be sure the author has clearly identified the specific research question examined in the study.

2. *What is the theory informing the research?* What concepts and perspectives is the researcher emphasizing in this study? What issues might be left out by relying on this theoretical approach?

3. *How are variables operationalized?* When different research studies about the same topic reach different conclusions, it is often because of the way variables are defined and operationalized. One study may define "political participation" as "whether or not someone has voted," whereas another study may define it as "whether or not someone has done any of the following: voted, made a campaign contribution, worked on a campaign, joined a social movement organization, volunteered for a political cause, or taken part in a protest or demonstration." Conclusions about political participation in these two studies are likely to differ considerably because their authors have defined variables differently. When you read a study, be sure you understand what the authors mean by the variables they use.

4. *What is the sample?* Research is almost always based on a sample of a larger population. Different ways of selecting samples of the same population may lead to different results. When reading research, be sure you understand the sample on which the study is based. Is the study based on a single or a few cases, or on a larger sample? Was the sample chosen randomly? Understanding the dynamics of the sample can help you to understand the results of a study.

5. *What are the data?* When reading research, be sure you understand what data have been assembled and analyzed. For example, is the research based on a survey that was designed specifically for this study? When and where did the researcher conduct observational fieldwork? What specific materials are the subjects of a content analysis? It is important to ask such questions when assessing how the author reached his or her conclusions.

6. *Are the conclusions justifiable?* In the final section of most studies, researchers usually interpret their data and explain the significance of the data for the question under consideration. Be sure you understand the claims the authors are making for their work and try to assess whether these claims are justifiable given the data presented in the report.

Asking these questions can help you to think critically about knowledge claims and to be an informed consumer of social scientific research.

Three Ways to Research the Influence of Political Advertisements

We've all been exposed to the onslaught of political advertisements on television and radio at election time. In fact, it seems impossible to escape them. Moreover, these ads are driving up the costs of running for office. A voter might reasonably ask, "Just what is the influence of these political advertisements on elections?" If we were to design a study, however, we would need to specify this deceptively simple research question more carefully. Different research approaches will suggest different research questions. Let's think about how we might hypothetically study this issue using each of the three types of sociological research.

Positivist: If we were using this approach, we would tend to ask a question that explores cause and effect in quantifiable terms: *Does more campaign advertising on radio and television produce more victories in congressional elections?* To answer this question, we would gather data from a sizable sample of contested elections and measure both the amount of campaign advertising for each candidate (in number of minutes on the air or dollars spent on advertising) and the percentage of total votes each candidate received. We would evaluate whether, in fact, candidates who ran more campaign ads were more successful than their counterparts with fewer campaign ads. We would also gather data on other aspects of these campaigns, such as major political endorsements and whether one of the candidates is an incumbent running for reelection, in an effort to rule out other explanations for the variation. This process is called "controlling" for other variables.

Interpretive: If we took this approach in our study, we would look closely at voter behavior, asking a question that gets at their decision-making process: *How do voters use campaign advertisements in deciding on which candidate to support?* Rather than looking at the outcome of elections, this study would focus on the meanings that voters attach to political ads. How do people assess the information in these ads? Do they compare the claims of political ads with what they read in the news or what they know from discussing the election with friends? How do voters respond to the various advertising strategies—including negative ads directed at a candidate's opponent, policy-oriented ads, and ads meant to improve the candidate's image? Do campaign ads motivate people to vote or induce them to stay home? In this study we would examine the influence of political advertisements from the perspective of voters, focusing on how people make sense of this form of political communication.

Critical: In taking a critical approach, we'd want to ask a question about the relationship between advertisements and the money that pays for them: *Do campaign advertisements reflect the interests of major campaign contributors?* Our study would focus on the way political campaigns are financed and the potential relationship between political fundraising and the candidates' policy agenda. Do ads promote the issues that special interest contributors support? Are they silent on controversial issues for which major contributors are often criticized? Who benefits from the vast spending by political campaigns on radio and television ads? As researchers we might emphasize how the findings could contribute to a change in the role of money in politics.

As you can see, researchers working within the three research approaches may start with the same general topic area, but their approaches will lead them to ask very different kinds of questions about political advertising. You may find that each of these studies would be useful, but the stark differences in approach suggest how and why social scientists from different research paradigms often reach a variety of conclusions.

think about it

1. *Which of these hypothetical research projects do you find most compelling?*
2. *Which study would help you to best understand what you define as key questions about political advertising?*

CHANGING TECHNOLOGY AND SOCIAL RESEARCH

W.E.B. Du Bois (1899/1996) spent more than a year conducting his house-to-house survey of African Americans in Philadelphia's Seventh Ward in 1896 and 1897. Around the same time, Emile Durkheim (1897/1951) and his research assistant examined the records of 26,000 suicides to determine each person's age, sex, and marital and parental status. In both cases, the authors completed all their data analysis by hand, painstakingly classifying and calculating everything manually.

Since Du Bois and Durkheim completed their studies, technological changes have helped to transform society, and social research is no exception. The classical thinkers depended mostly on written, qualitative accounts of social life. Early sociologists who collected and analyzed quantitative data had to rely on painstaking hand calculations to present basic statistical information. After World War II, however, academics quickly adopted the first computers to help them record, store, retrieve, and analyze data. These efforts were primitive by today's standards. Often researchers had to transfer hand-recorded data to punch cards—thin cardboard stock about the size of a business envelope on which data was recorded by punching holes with a special machine. The computer then processed large stacks of these cards, aggregating the data and making them available for statistical analysis.

Even these early computers allowed the social researchers to record and manipulate unprecedented amounts of data. However, the data had to be quantitative. As increasingly powerful computers became available, along with advances in statistical analysis, a quantitative revolution took place in the social sciences. By the 1960s, much of the best-known and most prestigious research being published in sociology journals used sophisticated quantitative data and statistical techniques that depended on the use of computers. As researchers began to use personal computers throughout the 1980s and 1990s, software packages that can store and analyze quantitative data, such as SPSS (Statistical Package for the Social Sciences), became a common tool even for those with modest budgets.

Another revolution came about once computers and software programs that could process qualitative data became available. Since the introduction of the tape recorder, qualitative researchers have been able to record interviews, but they then had to transcribe the information for analysis in a laborious process. By the late 1980s, however, computer capacities had expanded so much that it became feasible to store and analyze this qualitative data on computers. The data still had to be transcribed onto a computer, but a new generation of software packages allowed researchers to code their transcripts so that they could instantly retrieve relevant portions later on. Still more advanced computers and software gave researchers the ability to code digital images and sound recordings, as well. Each of these advances has led to new developments in qualitative methods in the social sciences.

Today, computer technologies support almost every form of social research. Researchers use computer-assisted telephone interviewing systems to conduct surveys. A caller reads a prepared script from a computer screen and records respondents' answers directly onto the computer with specially designed software. Increasingly, researchers and polling organizations are using the Internet to collect data through online surveys. Existing data sets—especially collections of survey data on a wide range of topics about people's beliefs and behaviors—are available on the Internet, making them more accessible than ever. Because of the digital revolution, newspapers, magazines, and other forms of media are all available online, making it easier than ever to conduct content analyses of these cultural artifacts. Interviews are now likely to be stored on digital recording devices, which can be easily downloaded onto computers, a cell phone, or an iPad.

As sociologists look for new avenues of research in the twenty-first century, they are certain to take advantage of today's lower-cost video cameras and recording devices, no doubt leading to an increase in multimedia research projects. With more academic journals available on the Internet, research reports are beginning to include sound, photographs, and video along with the written word. More advanced voice-recognition software that allows digitally recorded interviews to be transcribed automatically will greatly reduce the amount of labor for qualitative researchers. As technologies continue to develop and become more powerful, researchers will continue to find ways to put them to use as they investigate the social world.

THINKING SOCIOLOGICALLY ABOUT . . .

The Research Process

- ■ Sociology is an activity that uses the framework of science to ask questions, gather data, and seek answers about the phenomena of the social world.

- ■ There are four key elements of social science research: (1) identifying and understanding patterns in social life; (2) gathering empirical evidence; (3) explaining how the evidence was collected and analyzed; and (4) viewing research claims as provisional knowledge, subject to revision.

- ■ Theory and data act together in social science research. Theory helps us to identify key research questions and to interpret the data that are collected. Data provide the evidence that can support existing theory, lead to changes in theory, contradict a theory, or result in the development of a new theory.

- ■ Sociology includes a diverse array of approaches to studying the social world. These research approaches can be categorized into three major types: *positivist, interpretive,* and *critical* social science.

- ■ Given that we are not all experts on research methodology, it is helpful to have some authorities who monitor the quality of the research, which the scientific community accomplishes through the peer-review process. The ability to think critically about research findings is an important skill to develop that is relevant in a variety of professional fields.

Looking Back

1. Conclusions based solely on a belief in authority, common sense, tradition, personal experience, or selective observation risk being inaccurate.

2. In addition to being a perspective and a discipline, sociology is an activity that involves basic research aimed at a scholarly audience, applied research often directed to some problem or need, as well as public sociology that tries to communicate the findings of both basic and applied research to a general nonacademic audience.

3. Social science research seeks to investigate patterns in social life systematically through the collection of empirical evidence. In doing their research, social scientists are committed to making their methods transparent, and they recognize that their truth claims are provisional.

4. Social science presents special challenges since the subjects being studied—people—are conscious of being studied and may change their behavior in response. In addition, it is difficult to control social life for experimentation or make predictions with certainty because different people can perceive, interpret, and react to a situation differently.

5. Research involves both theory and data. Theory helps us to define research projects and interpret the data we collect. Data provide the evidence that helps us to evaluate and build theory.

6. Research methods are the techniques researchers use to systematically collect and analyze data about the social world. The major methods of data collection are surveys, intensive interviews, field research, and experiments. Some research is based on secondary analysis of already-collected data.

7. Especially because people are involved, social scientists must adhere to basic research ethics that protect subjects from any harm caused by a study.

8. Sociological research generally follows a series of steps that includes exploring a general topic, identifying a specific research question, designing a study, considering the ethical dimensions of the study, collecting and analyzing data, and reporting results.

9. The three approaches to sociological research—positivist, interpretive, and critical—each carry distinct assumptions about the nature of social reality, the goals of research, and the role of values in research.

10. Knowledge of research methods helps us to critically evaluate sociological research.

11. Rapidly changing technology in the past few decades has enabled researchers to collect and analyze ever-increasing amounts of data.

Critical Thinking: Questions and Activities

1. A friend who is a senior in high school tells you, "I'm not going to college. It doesn't make any sense to start off life by taking on all that debt. I saw some financial expert on TV saying you're better off today skipping college and starting a job right away. Look at my uncle; he never went to college and he manages a hotel and does well. Besides, if I don't go to college I won't have to study for SATs, figure out financial aid, or fill out those applications." Has your friend committed any of the errors in everyday thinking described in this chapter? Which ones? Explain.

2. Sometimes two research studies come to different conclusions about the same question. Knowing what you now know about the research process, identify three factors that might explain why two studies of the same issue lead to varying conclusions.

3. Suppose you have agreed to participate in a study of how college students meet potential romantic partners. Would you rather fill out a survey on this topic or participate in an intensive interview? Why? From the perspective of someone participating in a study, what are the advantages and disadvantages of each of these data gathering techniques?

4. Identify a specific research question having to do with a topic of interest to students at your school. Your question might involve, for example, their satisfaction with their educational experience, their future career plans, their use of media, or their favorite classes. Create a short, eight- to twelve-item questionnaire designed to help you better understand that topic. Remember, all the questions should be related to your specific research topic. Make sure to include both closed-ended and open-ended questions. You'll need to be careful and creative as you consider how to ask questions about your topic. Be as clear as you can in writing the questions and choosing the appropriate response categories for the closed-ended questions. Now give the questionnaire to three students and ask them to fill it out. When they are done, ask them if they were confused by any of the questions or if they have any other feedback on the questionnaire. Have the respondents brought up issues you didn't

anticipate? How would you revise your questionnaire based on their feedback?

5. Advertisements frequently refer to research to demonstrate that a product is popular or effective or recommended by experts. Choose a popular magazine and look through the ads for any research-based claims (for example, "Studies show . . ."). When you have found one, evaluate the claim

from a social science perspective. Are data presented to back up any claims? What kind of sample, if any, was used? Is the sample representative of a larger population? Do you agree with the conclusion about the research that the advertisement offers? Can you even evaluate the claim, given the limited information in the ad?

Key Terms

applied research (p. 33) the primary goal of this type of research is to directly address some social problem or need.

basic research (p. 33) the primary goal of this type of research is to describe some aspect of society and advance our understanding of it.

content analysis (p. 44) a variety of techniques that enable researchers to systematically summarize and analyze the content of various forms of communication—written, spoken, or pictorial.

correlation (p. 36) a relationship in which change in one variable is connected to change in another variable.

critical social science (p. 49) research carried out explicitly to create knowledge that can be used to bring about social change.

dependent variable (p. 36) the entity that changes in response to the independent variable.

empirical evidence (p. 36) data that can be observed or documented using the human senses.

experiment (p. 44) a data gathering technique in which the researcher manipulates an independent variable under controlled conditions to determine if change in an independent variable produces change in a dependent variable, thereby establishing a cause-and-effect relationship.

field research (p. 44) a data collection technique in which the researcher systematically observes some aspect of social life in its natural setting.

generalize (p. 42) the ability to describe patterns of behavior of a larger population based on findings from a sample.

Hawthorne effect (p. 38) the fact that human beings will react differently because they know they are in a study.

hypothesis (p. 36) a statement about the relationship between variables that is to be investigated.

independent variable (p. 36) the entity that is associated with and/or causes change in the value of the dependent variable.

informed consent (p. 46) the principle that subjects in any study must know about the nature of the research project, any potential benefits or risks that they may face, and that they have the right to stop participating at any time, for any reason.

intensive interview (p. 42) a data gathering technique that uses open-ended questions during somewhat lengthy face-to-face sessions.

interpretive social science (p. 48) an approach that focuses on understanding the meaning that people ascribe to their social world.

operationalize (p. 47) to define the variables you are interested in studying.

peer-review process (p. 50) a way in which scholars evaluate research manuscripts before they are published in order to ensure their quality.

positivist social science (p. 48) an approach that assumes that the social world, like the natural world, is characterized by laws that can be identified through research and used to predict and control human affairs.

public sociology (p. 33) the effort to bring the findings of both basic and applied sociological research to a broader non-academic audience.

qualitative data (p. 36) any kind of evidence that is not numerical in nature, including evidence gathered from interviews, direct observation, and written or visual documents.

quantitative data (p. 36) evidence that can be summarized numerically.

random sample (p. 42) a sample in which every element of the population has an equal chance of being chosen.

research methods (p. 41) the procedures used by a researcher to collect and analyze data.

sample (p. 42) part of the population a researcher is studying that represents the whole.

secondary data analysis (p. 44) a type of research using data previously collected by other researchers.

survey (p. 41) a data collection technique that involves asking someone a series of questions.

transparency (p. 37) the requirement that researchers explain how they collected and analyzed their evidence and how they reached their conclusions.

value-neutrality (p. 48) the goal of removing any personal views from the research process; part of positivist social science.

variables (p. 36) measures that can change (or vary) and thus have different values.

3

Culture

looking **AHEAD**

What is **culture**, and how can you use the sociological perspective to understand its impact on your life?

How can **culture** both promote consensus and create conflict?

Why is **cultural** diversity increasing today?

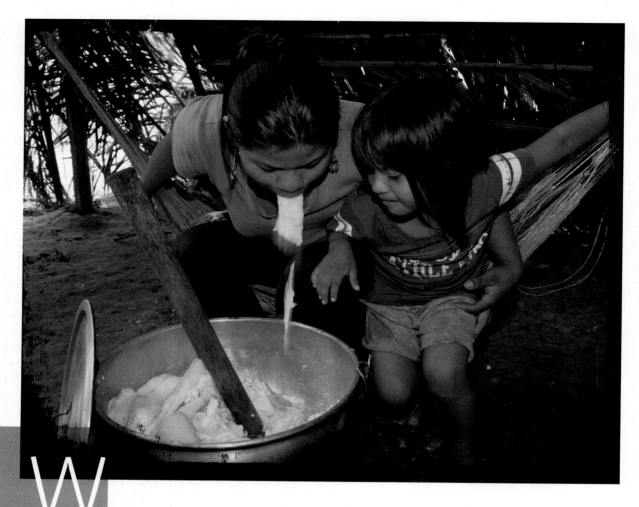

When writer John Wray visited his cousin, an aid worker among the Amazonian Shuar community in a part of Ecuador accessible only by canoe or small plane, he was greeted as an honored guest. His hosts in the village of Pampansa invited Wray to the home of a local community leader, where they would share a bowl of *chicha,* an alcoholic beverage traditionally offered as a friendly greeting to visitors (Wray 2010).

While Wray was honored by the warm welcome and knew that his hosts were offering him a traditional drink as a gesture of friendship, he reports that he would "have given almost anything to escape." That's because in Pampansa, women prepare *chicha* by chewing on fermented yucca root and spitting into a large barrel, where the beverage accumulates before being transferred into a ceramic bowl for drinking.

After Wray's cousin Martin downed his bowlful of *chicha,* which their hosts described proudly as the best in the region, a newly refilled bowl was placed in front of Wray, who paused, wondering how he had ended up in this situation. After all, a year earlier he had visited Martin in a neighboring village and had managed to take only a sip of ceremonial *chicha.* This time, Wray found the *chicha*'s odor overpowering, likening the smell to "an old man's false teeth." Now, out of respect for his hosts, he was faced with guzzling the entire bowl.

In search of a way forward in this unfamiliar—and, for Wray, very unappetizing—situation, Wray recalled something that made the idea of drinking *chicha* more familiar and eased his sense of anxiety. He thought of all the times he had tasted someone else's saliva: "hadn't I tasted spit countless times before? What was *chicha* drinking, after all, but French kissing once removed?" With the inspiration of this familiar activity in mind, Wray quietly gulped down his portion of *chicha*, paying respect to his host's generosity. ■

What we drink and eat, and how we prepare our food, is a familiar—and often vivid—illustration of how culture works. When we are part of a culture, our way of life seems natural, and we take it as a given; we are like fish in water. However, a cultural practice taken for granted by insiders (such as Shuar) may appear to outside observers (such as Wray) as interesting, odd, curious, disturbing, or even threatening.

This chapter explores the central role of culture in social life and its pervasive influence on who we are as human beings. It considers some of the opportunities and challenges posed by our contemporary world, as people of many different cultures interact with increasing frequency and cultural diversity becomes a fact of daily life. As we gain a better understanding of the meaning of culture, we are able not only to analyze its impact on our own lives but also to prepare for a lifetime of interactions with people from cultures other than our own.

Defining Culture

Culture is one of sociology's core concepts. Indeed it is an essential part of the very definition of **society**—*a group of people who live together in a specific territory and share a culture.* Many people associate the word *culture* with museums and symphonies, a connection that is understandable because one definition of the term does involve the "cultivation" of the mind by studying the "best" a society has to offer. In the West, *culture* in this sense generally refers to such attributes as education and refinement in the arts and such artifacts as great works of literature and classical music. For sociologists and anthropologists, however, culture has a much broader, more inclusive meaning. **Culture** is *the collection of values, beliefs, knowledge, norms, language, behaviors, and material objects shared by a people and socially transmitted from generation to generation.* Sometimes culture is simply referred to as a way of life.

Culture must be learned; it is not biologically based. In fact, we can think of culture as all aspects of society that are transmitted socially, rather than biologically. That you may be tall is a biological reality. That you use your height to advantage when you play basketball is a result of cultural influences.

Culture operates at multiple levels, from everyday actions by individuals (micro level), to the norms that operate within an organization such as a school or business (meso level), to the beliefs and practices associated with very large groups of people, including entire societies (macro level). At each level, the elements of culture influence how people live.

At any level, culture can serve as a source of both consensus and conflict in society. Regardless of the size of a particular group, its culture serves as a common ground connecting group members to one another. As we see later in this chapter, however, cultural differences can also contribute to tension and cause clashes among groups within a society and between different societies.

The Elements of Culture

Cultures consist of both material and nonmaterial elements. **Material culture** refers to *the physical objects produced by people in a particular culture, including tools, clothing, toys, works of art, and housing.* **Nonmaterial culture** refers to *the ideas of a culture, including values and beliefs, accumulated knowledge about how to understand and navigate the world, and standards or "norms" about appropriate behavior.* Nonmaterial culture exists in the world of thoughts and ideas; by contrast, material culture is physically real—it can be observed or touched. Collectively, the ideas and practices of a culture make up an entire way of life, affecting how people eat, work, love, think, worship, dress, learn, play, and live.

Because material objects can have symbolic (nonmaterial) meaning, the material and nonmaterial aspects of culture are often interconnected. For example, at the heart of many religions are sacred texts, such as Judaism's Torah, Christianity's Bible, and Islam's Qur'an (or Koran). These writings relate the central beliefs of each faith, thus comprising an essential part of the faith's nonmaterial culture. At the same time, the books themselves are often considered sacred as physical objects, to be treated with great respect as a part of the material culture. The books (Bibles, Qur'ans) are physical objects (material culture), but they also have symbolic (nonmaterial) significance. Thus Islamic detainees at the infamous Guantánamo Bay detention facility have alleged that U.S. interrogators exerted psychological pressure on them by desecrating the Qur'an, stepping on it and even putting it in a toilet, actions that are a grave violation of Islamic cultural norms (Lewis 2005).

Let's consider how the various aspects of culture work together by looking at a much less serious topic: the everyday activity of grooming hair. Most people put at least some thought into what their hair looks like. Whether unkempt or coolly styled, our hair often expresses who we are. Hairstyles also reflect cultural values; we learn what is considered attractive and what meaning different hairstyles convey. We may think we are making purely individual statements when we style our hair, but in fact, as the photographs on page 60 show, we are likely to be influenced heavily by the ideas and practices of our culture.

Often, we are so familiar with our own culture that we have a hard time recognizing its various elements or their significance. If we take a sociological perspective, however, we can

Cultures develop different ideas about what constitutes a desirable appearance. These seem perfectly "normal" from the perspective of those inside a culture but can seem odd from the outside. Which hairstyles appear strange to you? Are there appearance norms in your culture that might seem unusual to outsiders?

see the often hidden ways that cultural ideas and practices help to define our identities and our relationship to various communities. The elements of culture—to which we now turn—are summarized in Table 3.1.

Culture in Our Heads: Values, Beliefs, Knowledge, and Norms

Let's look more closely at the ideas of culture—the particular values, beliefs, knowledge, and norms that lend a culture its unique character. Together, they shape how people think, behave, and view their world.

VALUES: WHAT IS DESIRABLE? A **value** is *a deeply held principle or standard that people use to make judgments about the world, especially in deciding what is desirable or worthwhile.* For example, U.S. culture is highly individualistic. That is, people in the United States generally value individual freedom and autonomy above collective responsibility and commitment to community (Bellah et al. 2007). In contrast, some cultures place much more value on family well-being or some broader collective good than on individual achievement. The Japanese, for instance, emphasize group solidarity and loyalty, and this kind of collective orientation shapes ideas about what it means to be successful (Hofstede 1980; Silver 2002). China, too, has had a strong collective tradition, but recent

TABLE 3.1	ELEMENTS OF CULTURE

Values: Deeply held principles or standards by which people make judgments about the world, especially in terms of what is desirable or worthwhile (for example, wealth equals success, family is important)

Beliefs: Convictions or opinions that people accept as true (for example, my country is good, God exists, the gods exist)

Knowledge: Information, awareness, and understanding that helps people navigate the world (for example, language, mathematics, sociological insight)

Norms: Rules and expectations for "appropriate" behavior (for example, how to dress, what standards of hygiene to maintain)

Behaviors: The actions associated with a group that help to reproduce a distinct way of life (for example "appropriate" sexual practices, the pursuit of formal education)

Objects and artifacts: The physical items that are created and associated with a culture (for example, food, clothing, music)

Symbols: Anything—a sound, a gesture, an image, an object—that represents something else (for example, a handshake, a corporate logo)

Language: An elaborate system of symbols that allows people to communicate with one another in complex ways (for example, English, Spanish, Chinese, American Sign Language)

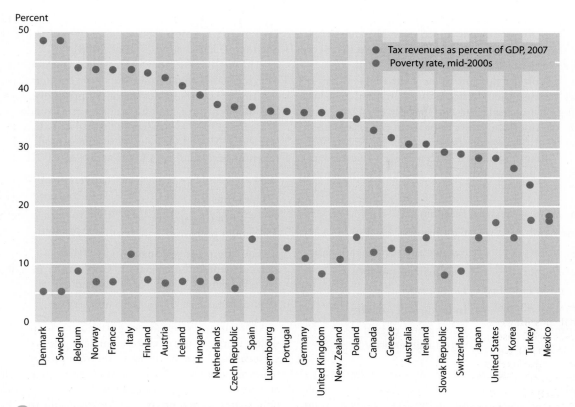

FIGURE 3.1 | RATES OF TAXATION AND POVERTY RATES AMONG INDUSTRIALIZED COUNTRIES
Cultural values are often reflected in public policy, such as taxation. This graph compares poverty rates (the percentage of the population living in poverty, defined as those in households earning less than half the median household income) with taxation rates (as measured by tax revenues as a percentage of gross domestic product, or GDP, which represents the value of all the goods and services produced in a country) for most of the world's industrialized economies. In general, the lower the tax rate, the higher the poverty rate. The United States, with among the lowest tax rates, has one of the highest poverty rates. In contrast, Denmark, with nearly double the tax rate of the United States, has the lowest poverty rate. What might account for the apparent, significant differences in Danish and U.S. cultural attitudes toward taxation and poverty? *Source:* Organization for Economic Cooperation and Development Factbook 2010.

research shows its values in the twenty-first century to be shifting. The Chinese now have a more favorable view of competition than do the Japanese and even, according to the World Values Survey, than do people in the United States (Marsh 2009; World Values Survey 2005–2008).

Values can translate into public policy. For example, the relatively low rate of taxation in the United States reflects more than an aversion to taxes; it reflects popular support for the principle of small government (though major social programs such as Medicare and Social Security have widespread support). However, the relatively low tax rates in the United States also correlate with a relatively high rate of poverty. In contrast, in most other industrialized nations, individualism is less valued, tax rates are much higher, and the poverty rate is far lower. Figure 3.1 shows the relationship between tax rates and poverty rates for thirty industrialized countries.

The link between cultural values and public policy can sometimes have dramatic—even deadly—consequences, as illustrated by the recent experience of Niger, a poor African country beset by periodic food shortages. Niger has long relied on a culture of generosity based on Muslim traditions of charity and communal support to provide for the poor during these shortages (Timberg 2005). Building on this tradition, the government had made a policy of keeping the price of basic food items affordable to help ensure their widespread availability.

In recent years, however, Niger, like many other developing nations, has absorbed Western cultural values emphasizing individualism and deregulated free markets. This cultural change was partly a response to requirements by international institutions, such as the World Bank, that governments eliminate price controls and other market interventions in order to qualify for loans. In Niger, the government abandoned its commitment to price controls. At the same time, the traditional commitment to charity weakened. As Malan Hassane, a local religious leader, commented at the time, "There is nothing like generosity now. Selfishness is gaining ground" (Timberg 2005). When the country suffered a food shortage in 2005, this shift in values from an emphasis on collective responsibility and mutual aid to an emphasis on individual economic success in competitive markets proved disastrous for Niger's poor. Without price controls and without the support of traditional charity, many could not afford even the most basic foods. Facing widespread starvation, the country had to call on international aid organizations for help.

Sociologists are often reluctant to label the major values of a given society because they do not want to imply that values are unchanging or universal. The most widely cited sociological description of American values appears in the classic book *American Society: A Sociological Interpretation* by Robin Williams (1970). Williams identified fifteen basic value orientations as central to post–World War II society in the United States:

Achievement and success	Freedom
Activity and work	Conformity
Moral orientation	Science and secular rationality
Humanitarian mores	Nationalism-patriotism
Efficiency and practicality	Democracy
Progress	Individual personality
Material comfort	Racism and related
Equality	group-superiority

Williams described these value orientations as tendencies and suggested a series of questions to help understand their depth and meaning. For each value on his list—and, we would add, for each value you would include in an updated, twenty-first century list of American values—Williams (1970, 453) would ask a series of questions: "Is it actually an important value in American society? How do we know whether it is or not? Where does it stand in relation to other values? [W]hat groups or subcultures are the main bearers of the value, and what groups or subcultures are indifferent or opposed?" Finally, Williams asks how do the various value systems "work towards or against the integration of the culture as a whole?"

In contrast to Williams, contemporary American sociologists have rarely sought to articulate a list of major American values, but they continue to ask versions of Williams's probing questions about the sociological significance of values. Summarizing recent research on values, sociologist Robert Wuthnow (2008) recognizes that they explain only partially individuals' choices, but he notes that "the influence of values on behavior remained evident in study after study; people with conservative values voted Republican, people with religious values attended religious services, people with altruistic values did volunteer work, and so on" (p. 337). In addition, values change over time, especially during times of broad social change. For example, we may ask how,

if at all, changes in contemporary society, including globalization and the development of new technologies, are influencing our basic values (Gecas 2008).

Although values vary a great deal from culture to culture, research shows that certain values are common across cultures. A series of studies in dozens of countries over two decades by Shalom Schwartz and his colleagues (Davidov et al. 2008; Schwartz 1992, 1994) has identified ten distinct values that are widely shared and generally understood to have a similar meaning across cultures (Schwartz et al. 2001):

Power	Universalism (appreciation of and concern for all humanity)
Achievement	
Hedonism (the seeking of personal pleasure)	Benevolence (generosity and compassion)
Stimulation (the seeking of excitement and personal challenge)	Tradition
	Conformity (the desire to blend in)
Self-direction	Security

Of course, the relative importance of each value on this list differs from culture to culture, and the values do not always coexist easily. It may be difficult, for example, to value power and benevolence or security and stimulation equally. Thus different cultures prioritize values differently, and these differences can be a major source of conflict between cultures. For example, theocratic societies such as Iran or Saudi Arabia, which are ruled or dominated by religious authorities, value tradition and conformity. They often dislike what they perceive to be the values of secular Western democracies, such as self-direction, stimulation, and relative hedonism as exemplified by popular notions of "rugged individualism," the widespread promotion of consumption, and the prevalence of sexualized media content.

That some people place a higher priority on one set of values over another can also be a source of conflict *within* a particular society. Sociologist James Davison Hunter (1991, 1994) has argued that the United States is in the midst of an ongoing **culture war,** *an intense disagreement about core values and moral positions.* According to Hunter, the fault lines of this conflict are readily apparent in venues such as the family, schools, and the arts. For example, debates about same-sex marriage are fundamentally conflicts over the definition of marriage and family. In schools, debates about how to teach American history and sex education are part of broader conflicts about patriotism and sexuality. The arts have long been an arena in which the values of free expression and respect for tradition clash. In 2010, for example, the National Portrait Gallery in Washington, D.C., removed a video from

thinking about culture

What are the value priorities of the community in which you were raised? In Chapter 16 we explore political **culture** in the United States, paying attention to the culturally specific norms and practices in the realm of politics.

MAP 3.1 | THE 2008 ELECTION: RED AND BLUE OR PURPLE?

The map on the left (*A*) shows the results of the 2008 presidential election by state; John McCain won the red states and Barack Obama won the blue states. The map on the right (*B*) represents the results of the 2008 election by county and uses red, blue, and shades of purple to indicate percentages of voters for each candidate. *Source:* Newman (2008).

CORE CONCEPTS CHALLENGE

Which of these maps do you think is a better representation of the election? What do these maps suggest about how divided the political culture *really is in the United States? Did the media's coverage of the 2010 election suggest a country that was more like the map on the left or the right?*

an exhibit of work on sexual differences after a Catholic organization complained that the video's depiction of a crucifix covered with ants was "hate speech" (Trescott 2010). In all such cases, debates can become extraordinarily heated because they are rooted in profound differences in values, and these differences often arouse intense reactions. This culture war is waged primarily at the level of ideas, but occasionally it erupts into acts of violence. For example, gays and lesbians have been targeted for harassment and assault and, in a few cases, extremist antiabortion activists have killed doctors who perform abortions.

Are the differences in how various groups prioritize values in the United States so profound, however, that they truly warrant the label *culture war*? This question has been the subject of much debate among sociologists and other scholars (see, for example, Fiorina 2011; Hunter and Wolfe 2006; McConkey 2001; Thomson 2010). Certainly you will find people with different positions on just about any current social or political issue—from gay marriage and immigration policy to health care reform and the war on terrorism—depending on the values they think are most important. Though people differ in the values they consider most essential, however, they are not necessarily intolerant of other views. Some scholars argue that it is the political elites—politicians seeking to mobilize voters and raise money and political commentators trying to attract audiences and sell books—who highlight differences in values

and encourage polarization and extremism. Ordinary citizens are actually far more ambivalent about their own views and more tolerant of others (Baker 2005; Fiorina 2011; Koch and Steelman 2009).

Journalists who use the familiar shorthand "red state" and "blue state" to describe differences between conservative and liberal regions of the United States encourage the notion of a culture war. Identifying each state as simply red or blue implies that each state is fundamentally conservative or liberal and that the two types of states have little in common with each other. In reality, however, each state includes communities with differing views and values that reflect varying degrees of conservatism and liberalism. A map reflecting the complexity of value preferences in the United States would consist of various shades of purple, rather than stark reds and blues (see Map 3.1).

BELIEFS: WHAT IS TRUE? Whereas a culture's values are usually a set of broad principles, its **beliefs** are *the specific convictions or opinions that its people generally accept as being true.* Our cultural beliefs encourage us to understand fundamental issues in the world in a particular way. Is democracy the best form of government? Should marriage be based on love, or is it primarily an economic arrangement? What constitutes "success" in life? Is violence justifiable in pursuing an important goal? Are all people created equal? Does God

thinking about culture

Why is religion more important in some societies than in others? How does religious **culture** vary? In Chapter 12 we look more closely at the role of religion in society.

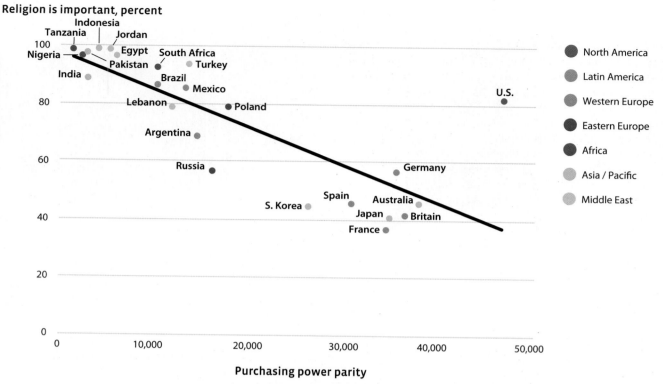

Religion is important, percent

FIGURE 3.2 | THE RELATIONSHIP BETWEEN A NATION'S WEALTH AND THE IMPORTANCE OF RELIGION TO ITS PEOPLE

Poorer countries tend to be more religious, whereas wealthier countries tend to be less so. The United States is an exception to this trend, however. Although it is a very wealthy nation, it is far more religious than its comparative wealth would suggest. More than 80 percent of respondents to this survey said religion was important to them, far higher than in the other wealthy countries in the survey. *Source:* Pew Global Attitudes Project (2008).

exist? The way people answer these questions depends, in part, on their cultural beliefs. What people believe is, in turn, deeply influenced by the culture of which they are a part.

Belief in a god and concern for religion are widespread but more so in some societies than in others. In general, the importance of religion in a culture declines as people become more educated and affluent. As Figure 3.2 shows, however, there is one major exception to this trend: the United States. In a survey of people in twenty-three countries, 82 percent of people in the United States said religion was "important" in their lives, about double the figure for Britain (42 percent), Japan (41 percent), and France (37 percent) (Pew Global Attitudes Project 2008). Such a relatively high level of religiosity helps to explain why debates about abortion, stem cell research, teaching evolution, and gay rights are often more vocal and intense in the United States than in many other industrialized societies. A higher percentage of people in the United States tend to believe in God than in other developed countries, and these religious beliefs influence political debates.

In poor countries, though, religion plays an even more important role in people's lives than it does in the United States. An overwhelming percentage of respondents said religion was "important" in their lives in countries such as Indonesia (99 percent), Tanzania (99 percent), Pakistan (98 percent), and Nigeria (97 percent). Beliefs about God and the importance of religion are central to the culture of these societies.

KNOWLEDGE: HOW DO I GET THINGS DONE?

In the context of culture, **knowledge** is *the range of information, awareness, and understanding that helps us navigate our world.* Sociologists sometimes refer to such knowledge as *cultural capital,* an idea we explore in more detail in Chapter 9, where we consider class-based cultures. People often take for granted the knowledge they have internalized about their own culture. They learn how to speak, read, and write the language; how to dress appropriately for work; and how to behave properly in different situations. To navigate U.S. culture, for example, you have very likely learned how to read a map, how to use a credit card, how to apply to college, how to select items and pay for them in a supermarket, how to practice safe sex, and how to drive a car. In short, you have learned about the sorts of behavior that are rewarded and necessary for success in this culture.

Culture shock is *the experience of being disoriented because of a lack of knowledge about an unfamiliar social situation.* You are most likely to experience culture shock when you are traveling outside of your own country, as John Wray did in the Shuar community in our opening example. In describing a research trip to Kenya, Rachael Irwin (2007) told of her anxiety about riding in a *matatus*—a minibus typically filled well beyond capacity with people and sometimes goats, driving at "breakneck speeds" on poorly maintained roads. Culture shock can also occur within your own country. When someone raised in a small town visits a big city for the first time, or when a person who is not religious spends time in the home of a devoutly religious family, the visitor may suddenly feel out of place.

Cultural knowledge is essential for survival. People from the United States who are traveling in Australia had better know that motorists in that society drive on the left side of the road—otherwise, they are in for an abrupt case of culture shock! Of course, most cultural knowledge is subtler, involving how to act in order to get something done. When you entered college, you probably had to learn about what makes the culture of higher education different from that of high school.

NORMS: WHAT IS APPROPRIATE? Norms

are *a culture's rules and expectations for "appropriate" behavior.* (Behavior that violates the norms of a culture is often labeled as *deviant,* a topic we explore in Chapter 8.) In a sense, norms serve as a bridge between a culture's ideas and its practices since they suggest which practices are appropriate. Norms can tell people what they *should* do as well as what they should *not* do. However, norms are not fixed or rigid. For example, smoking in public places—once a practice taken for granted in our culture—now increasingly violates informal norms and local laws. People are now expected (or required) to buckle their seat belts when they are driving or riding in an automobile. As recently as the 1960s, however, many automobiles did not even have seat belts.

As society changes, culture evolves to address new situations. Nowhere is this process more apparent today than in cyberspace. Norms for those who participate in its various venues—sometimes referred to as "netiquette"—developed rapidly, contributing to an emergent culture among Internet users. Different parts of the Internet each have their own norms. E-mail users learn to use "bcc" (blind carbon copy) when they send out a group email so that they do not reveal the email addresses of their friends or colleagues. At online discussion groups, new users learn to read the FAQ ("frequently asked questions") page before asking questions. Social networking sites such as Facebook strongly discourage "flaming"—posts that attack, insult, or ridicule other users. If you are a regular Internet user, such norms may seem obvious to you now, but they had to be created over time. Like all new users, you had to learn them at some point.

Social norms do not always keep up with technological change, however. In the 1920s, sociologist William Ogburn (1922) coined the term **cultural lag** to describe *the ways that new technological developments often outpace the norms that govern our collective experiences with these new technologies.* For instance, recent developments in digital photography and the proliferation of high-speed Internet access have made it extremely easy for many people to post photos and videos online for wide public viewing. However, the norms that define what is appropriate to make public, how to distribute such images,

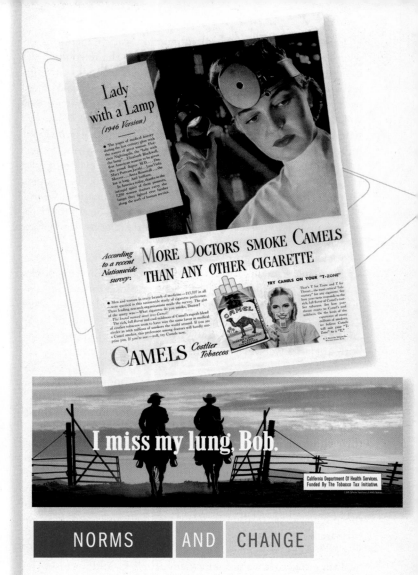

NORMS AND CHANGE

Through most of the twentieth century, cigarette smoking was a widespread and socially respectable activity, well within acceptable norms. Tobacco companies marketed their product aggressively, associating it, as in the Camels ad above, with both sex appeal and, ironically, health. Since confirmation of the health dangers of smoking, an antismoking movement, using public service ads like the one here, has gradually but effectively succeeded in changing the norms regarding smoking, making it an activity that now receives widespread social disapproval.

and what privacy means in this context are still catching up to the technology. Perhaps this concept helps to explain the posting of photos of alcohol-fueled high school parties on Facebook or the "sexting" of nude photos among teenagers. As these examples suggest, cultural definitions of what is—or should be—public and private information are lagging behind the development of the Internet. New norms and behaviors will undoubtedly emerge and solidify as we advance further into the digital age.

Cultural norms for social interaction vary depending on whether the interaction is face-to-face, over the telephone, via e-mail, on social networking sites such as Facebook, through text messaging, or on Twitter. When we interact face-to-face, we use more than words to communicate; we use our tone of voice, hand gestures, and facial expressions, as well. When we send e-mail and text messages, we do not have these additional means of expression, which is why emoticons—symbols such as ;o) or :o(created by text characters—or abbreviations like LOL are so useful in online communication. Also, some topics are not appropriate for certain types of communication. Would e-mailing a friend to ask him to go out for pizza be appropriate, or not? How about breaking off a romantic relationship with a text message?

Society enforces most norms informally. If your cell phone rings during a movie, for example, be prepared for dirty looks from those sitting near you. However, more formal regulations, like a university's code of ethics or the legal system, serve to reinforce particularly significant norms. The study of deviance and crime is linked closely to the study of culture since both are largely about violations of a culture's norms. *Norms that are strictly enforced, with potentially severe penalties for violating them,* are called **mores** (pronounced MORE-ays). Contemporary mores in the United States forbid physical or psychological abuse of one's children, for example. Those who violate such mores face public shame, potential loss of their children, and the possibility of a prison sentence. In contrast, the term **folkways** describes *group habits or customs that are common in a given culture.* Those who violate folkways are not likely to be subject to punishment (Sumner 1906). It may be customary to wear a bathing suit to swim, for example, but those who go swimming in jeans are likely to face only some surprised glances.

Taken together, values, knowledge, beliefs, and norms—the ideas of a culture—help to shape people's orientation toward the world, providing an unwritten guidebook on what to think and how to behave. By studying the ideas of a culture, we focus our attention on how people make sense of their experiences. Understanding what people value, believe, and know and what people define as appropriate and deviant reveals a great deal about the complex workings of society—your own, as well as those of other societies. To communicate the ideas of our culture to one another, however, we need symbols and, in particular, language.

Communicating Culture: Symbols and Language

A **symbol** is *anything—a sound, a gesture, an image, an object—that represents something else.* An image of five interlocking rings represents the Olympic Games. A red light means "stop."

 The flags of Indonesia (*left*) and Poland (*right*) are both horizontal blocks of red and white, the same shapes and colors. But they are distinct flags, with specific meanings to their citizens.

CORE CONCEPTS CHALLENGE

Can you think of other culturally specific symbols that look very similar but have different meanings? Or one symbol that has different meanings to different people?

An upraised forefinger placed on the lips means "quiet." The letters d-o-g together represent the sound "dog," which in English represents a domesticated four-legged creature (which, in turn, represents faithful companionship to many Americans).

The association between a symbol and the thing it represents is arbitrary and culturally defined. The people of Indonesia recognize a banner with a band of red over a band of white as their national flag; turn that banner upside down, however, and you have instead the Polish national flag. In most languages other than English, "dog" is a meaningless sound (and in some cultures the animal itself might more likely represent dinner than companionship). Similarly the same symbol can have different meanings in different cultures. In Mexico, raising your hand with a circle formed by the thumb and forefinger is an obscene gesture; in the United States it represents "OK." A "thumbs-up" gesture has a positive connotation in some societies but is an insult ("Up yours!") in Australia, Russia, Greece, Iraq, and much of Western Africa. In many societies, nodding your head up and down means yes, whereas turning it from left to right means no, but in Bulgaria the opposite is true.

Culture is fundamentally symbolic, and it is through symbols that we communicate and reinforce the elements of our culture to one another and pass them on to our children. As the Through a Sociological Lens box makes clear, cultural symbols in many forms can evoke emotionally powerful associations. However, one form of symbolic communication, language, is our primary vehicle for cultural transmission.

LANGUAGE A **language** is *an elaborate system of symbols that allows people to communicate with one another in complex ways.* Other animals have call systems that allow them to alert each other about their immediate environment—the presence of predators, for example. Human language, in contrast, is unique in its ability to convey information about objects and situations that are not immediately present. With language we can converse about events that happened in the past and plans we are making for the future, and we can even relate stories

thinking about culture
Can you think of an example of a formal code or system of regulations that governs your life? In Chapter 8 we consider systems of social control, as well as the people who deviate from such systems.

How We See Powerful Symbols

Symbols can be a powerful means of representing cultural beliefs, especially in the areas of religion and politics. The meaning we give a particular symbol can vary by culture, however. When the symbol is a potent one, the various meanings can be a source of confusion and sometimes conflict.

One of the most controversial symbols in recent American history has been the "Southern Cross." This flag (left) was never the official flag of the Confederacy, but rather was one of a number of battle flags used by Confederate forces during the Civil War. In the 1940s the Ku Klux Klan adopted the flag, and in the 1950s supporters of racial segregation used the flag as a prominent symbol of their cause. Today, various white supremacist groups still use the flag as their emblem. As a result, for many in the United States the flag symbolizes the fight to maintain slavery as well as recent and contemporary racist movements. For some Southerners, however, the contemporary use of the flag is not racist. To them it represents "heritage not hate."

Sociologist Lori Holyfield and her colleagues (2009) sought to untangle the complex meanings of the confederate flag, noting that previous research indicates that "Confederate symbols accommodate extremely disparate meanings of southern pride and heritage versus white supremacy and racial conflict" (p. 518). They conducted focus group discussions with white college students at a large southern university. After reading aloud a news article about a controversy involving the Confederate flag in Leesburg, Virginia, groups discussed their views of the controversy and opinions of the flag.

The authors heard only rare instances of overt racism in these focus groups. Instead, they found that white students typically sought to downplay the racial meanings associated with the Confederate flag or became defensive and diverted the discussion away from racial issues. In fact, faced with a highly charged symbol, most of these white students had difficulty explaining their own understanding of southern heritage or the meaning of the flag, even as they refused the implication that the flag is a racist symbol.

In analyzing the ways these focus groups largely ignored history and disregarded persistent differences in power and privilege, Holyfield and her colleagues (2009) suggest that, even if unintended, the use of such symbols can convey racist messages. They write, "participants need not approve of uses of the Confederate Flag or racism in order to participate in and perpetuate racist discourses" (p. 525).

The controversy over the Confederate flag is part of a long history of symbols carrying multiple— and sometimes conflicting—meanings. For example, many Christians use the cross, symbolizing the crucifixion of Jesus (below left), as a sign of their faith. But the cross has been used by other, non-Christian cultures, as well. In ancient Egypt the cross (above) was a sign of life. The ancient Greek cross (left)—with vertical and horizontal arms of equal length—represented the four elements: earth, air, fire, and water.

Perhaps the most reviled symbol of the past century is the swastika (right), now forever linked with Nazism. But the swastika is an ancient symbol used in many different cultures. For example, it was a variation on the Christian cross; a Hindu symbol associated with the ferocious goddess, Kali; and a Navajo symbol related to healing rituals.

think about it

1. *What symbols do you encounter in daily life? Are they used in other contexts as well?*

2. *There has been a great deal of debate in recent years about whether statehouses in the South should fly the flag associated with the Confederacy. Where do you stand on this issue? Do you think the flag is simply a symbol of the South's heritage or a symbol of hate?*

---

about imaginary people and occurrences. Language allows us to accumulate and store information, pass it on to one another, and forge a shared history. It is no wonder, then, that efforts to maintain marginalized cultures threatened with extinction often focus on preserving those cultures' languages. Sometimes groups try to revive dying or extinct languages as a form of cultural preservation. For example, members of two Indian nations in Long Island, New York—Shinnecock and Unkechaug—are working with linguists at a local university to document and teach languages last spoken 200 years ago (Cohen 2010).

Sharing a language, however, does not necessarily mean sharing a culture. English, for example, is spoken in many countries worldwide, in some as a first language and in many others as a nearly universal second language, but the people of these countries do not all share a common culture. They usually do, however, speak a particular **dialect** of English. A dialect is *a variant of a language with its own distinctive accent, vocabulary, and in some cases grammatical characteristics.* For example, what Americans call a "stove," the English call a "cooker." Further, a "truck" and an "elevator" in the United States would be called a "lorry" and a "lift" in England.

THE SAPIR-WHORF HYPOTHESIS The principle of *linguistic relativity,* developed by Edward Sapir and Benjamin Whorf and popularly known as the **Sapir-Whorf hypothesis,** *suggests that because of their different cultural content and structure, languages affect how their speakers think and behave.* For example, researchers have found that people more easily identify color differences when they have a language to describe different shades of similar colors (Kay and Kempton 1984). That is, having words to differentiate distinct colors in the red spectrum (including scarlet, crimson, rose, magenta, and maroon) helps us to see those different colors.

This hypothesis is controversial, however. Many scholars believe it overstates the influence of language on thought (Pinker 2007). They point out that, like other aspects of culture, languages adapt to changing circumstances and that speakers absorb or invent new vocabulary for things as they become culturally important.

Nonetheless, language reflects the broader cultural contexts in which it evolved. As a result, *every culture tends to develop unique words, phrases, and expressions that are difficult, if not impossible, to translate into another language.* In that sense, language helps to shape how we see the world. For example, the Mandarin word *guanxi* (pronounced "gwan-shee") translates literally as something like "connection," but it refers to a sort of social currency in traditional Chinese society. People can accumulate *guanxi* by doing good deeds for others or by giving them gifts, and they can "spend" their *guanxi* by asking for favors owed. In a society in which bonds of obligation form a crucial part of social life, such a word has a significant cultural meaning that cannot be translated easily into English (Moore 2004).

LANGUAGE AND SOCIAL INTERACTION As we saw in Chapter 1, the *symbolic interactionist perspective* emphasizes micro-level interactions—people's everyday behaviors—as the building blocks of society. Rather than focusing on large-scale institutions and processes, symbolic interactionists look at how people make sense of the world through the meanings they attach to their own and others' actions. As a result, sociologists working in this tradition are particularly attuned to the importance of the role of symbols and language in human interaction.

For example, through intensive interviews with clinically depressed adults, sociologist David Karp (1996) found that the specific language that they use helps to define their reality. This self-definition in turn shapes the actions people with depression can envision, and ultimately, initiate. Early in their experiences, respondents often did not have an adequate vocabulary for naming their trouble.

By eventually coming to name their condition as "depression," they began to see it in a new light. In naming their experience depression, Karp's respondents developed a new sense of self, which shaped their response to their pain. Their illness identity also influenced how they interacted with family and friends, and helped to break the social isolation that is at the center of the depression experience. They also had to grapple with the exact meaning of this new label, however. One of Karp's interviewees says: "I think of it less as an illness and more something that society defines. That's part of it, but then, it *is* physical. Doesn't that make it an illness? That's a question I ask myself a lot. Depression is a special case because everyone gets depressed. . . . I think that I define it as not an illness. It's a condition. . . . It's something that I can deal with. It's something that I can live with. I don't have to define it as a problem" (Karp 1996, 53). In contrast, other interviewees were comfortable with the definition of depression as "mental illness" and worked to find a "cure"—both distinctly medical ways to define and interpret the situation.

Karp alludes repeatedly to the importance of language throughout his study. He points out that the ideas of "anxiety" and "depression" do not exist in many languages and, therefore, that people who speak those languages cannot use them to define their reality. Even the title of Karp's study—*Speaking of Sadness*—alludes to the importance of language.

SPOTLIGHT on social theory

Consider the experience of the people Karp interviewed. How have you reached a greater understanding of some situation by finding the right name for it, or finding the best way to describe it? How does this relate to the role of language as emphasized by **symbolic interactionists**?

Reproducing Culture: Behavior

In the context of culture, **behaviors** are *the actions associated with a group that help to reproduce a distinct way of life.* When parents remind their children to tuck in their shirt, greet people with a firm handshake, and say "thank you" in response to a gift or an act of kindness, they are helping to encourage a particular set of behaviors considered worthwhile in U.S. culture. These are small matters, but the accumulation of people's many small, everyday actions—at home, at work, at play, at worship—helps distinguish one culture from another.

Behavior also calls attention to the difference between **ideal culture,** *what the members of a culture report to be their values, beliefs, and norms,* and **real culture,** *what they actually do, which may or may not reflect the ideal.* For example, gender equality is an increasingly professed cultural value in American

The Super Bowl is a cultural phenomenon that has as much to do with the extravaganza as it does with football. Major corporations unveil new advertising campaigns during the broadcast, international pop stars perform in choreographed half-time shows, and the U.S. Air Force stages a high-profile flyover just before kick-off each year. Watching the Super Bowl has become an annual ritual for millions of Americans—even those who don't necessarily like football very much.

CORE CONCEPTS CHALLENGE

Put yourself in the shoes of someone from a different culture who watches a football game in the United States for the first time. What would that person make of the game? Might it seem violent, for example? Now, think of how you might react if you were to watch a game you are unfamiliar with, like cricket, a wildly popular sport in much of the rest of the world.

society, but in most two-career households, women do more housework than men (Hook 2010).

Although culture is a social phenomenon, it also permeates the most private and intimate parts of our lives. Take the case of body hair. Do you shave your legs? Your underarms? Your pubic hair? Your head? Your face? In most cases, your answers to those questions are influenced heavily by cultural norms. Since World War I, for example, most women in the United States have shaved their legs and underarms, a behavior that seems "normal" to them. Yet this practice is less common in many European nations (where in some cases it is associated with prostitution), and it is unheard of in other parts of the world. Similarly, men's shaving their faces (but not their underarms or legs) is the norm in much of U.S. society.

Even sexual practices—perhaps the most intimate of all human activity—vary significantly from culture to culture. Cultures differ in their attitudes toward masturbation, premarital sex, homosexuality and bisexuality, prostitution, and other forms of sexual behavior. Even feeling discomfort, awkwardness, or titillation at reading about topics like body hair and sexual practices reflects a culture-laden response. Although advertisers routinely appeal to cultural norms about hair removal to sell products, and sexual imagery permeates the popular media, most people in the United States rarely engage in frank discussion about such topics.

Cultural behavior also encompasses larger scale, organized phenomena such as religious and political rituals (the president's annual state of the union speech), theatrical entertainment (rock concerts), and sports spectaculars (Super Bowl). Indeed, the widespread popularity of the Super Bowl—and the behaviors surrounding it, including those of viewers as well as the athletes and other participants—likely reflects some unique features of U.S. culture that Americans may take for granted but that may well appear odd to someone from a different culture. Thinking sociologically, what is the meaning of such an event for viewers? What might the popularity of the

Super Bowl—even among people who don't like football—tell us about the ideas and values of U.S. culture? In short, understanding culture requires us to examine the complex ways people derive meaning from the cultural behaviors of everyday life. People both create culture and are shaped by it.

Objects: The Artifacts of Culture

Sociologists often refer to the principal elements of material culture as **cultural objects** (also sometimes called "cultural artifacts"), which are *the physical items that are created by and associated with people who share a culture*. Cultural objects are often variations on basic items found in daily life. Consider the many varieties of bread, for instance. Tortillas, baguettes, bagels, and puri bread are cultural objects commonly associated with Mexican, French, Jewish, and Indian cultures, respectively. We live in a culture in which electronic devices of all sorts—such as computers, cell phones, and digital music players—are significant cultural objects.

Cultural objects are found not only in your home, however. Highly prized creations such as works of art or religious icons are also cultural objects. Museums are filled with both ordinary and extraordinary objects that help to tell the story of a particular culture. And the museums themselves, as well as other public buildings, peoples' homes, the streets and highways that connect them, gas stations, water reservoirs, and indeed any aspect of the landscape used or modified by humans—are also cultural objects.

Popular media products—such as books and magazines, films and television programs, songs and photographs—are also cultural objects. Analyzing popular media content often reveals a good deal of information about the culture that produced it at a particular moment in history. At the same time, it can be difficult to see the underlying assumptions embedded in the popular media of one's own culture.

Culture, Ideology, and Power

We have seen how culture helps to define our world, providing models for appropriate attitudes and behavior. How we dress and speak, whom we admire and despise, and how we mourn and mark holidays are all shaped by our immersion in a particular culture. Since people are typically deeply imbedded within their own culture, they usually find it difficult to see its underlying ideas. Sociologists have long paid attention to the assumptions built into any culture, arguing that what people take for granted is one of the keys to recognizing how culture and power are intertwined. One way to understand the meeting of culture and power is to understand ideology.

Ideology is a tricky term that is used in a variety of ways. Sociologists typically define **ideology** as *a system of meaning that helps define and explain the world and that makes value judgments about that world*. Simply put, an ideology is a comprehensive worldview. When we think sociologically about a culture's ideology, we inevitably pay close attention to the most basic assumptions the people living within that culture make, and the consequences of those assumptions.

Within each culture, there is a **dominant ideology,** *a widely held and regularly reinforced set of assumptions that generally support the current social system and serve the interests of authorities*. Even when most people within a culture agree about how the world works, though, most scholars concur that a dominant ideology cannot prevent the emergence of alternative worldviews. Instead, different ideological perspectives, representing different interests with unequal power, engage in a kind of cultural contest. Some ideas and practices are so deeply familiar that most of us have difficulty thinking critically about them or even imagining alternatives.

In considering how culture works through ideology, we need to remember that our commonsense assumptions, the things we take for granted, suggest a particular understanding of the social world, and such assumptions have consequences. In the United States, for example, many people believe that it is simply a matter of common sense that women are better nurturers than men, that education is a route to economic success, and that the United States promotes democracy around the world. When people adopt such commonsense assumptions—as they do with a wide range of ideas—they are also accepting a certain set of beliefs, or an ideology, about the social world.

Similarly, ideology shapes what we define as "natural." We generally think that what is natural is more enduring and stable than what is created by humans. As a result, the structures we define as natural come to be seen as permanent and therefore difficult to challenge. Consider some examples of social relationships that are often seen as natural. Is it natural that some people are rich and others are poor, that most citizens are disconnected from politics, or that people prefer to live in neighborhoods with others of the same racial or ethnic background? If all these situations are simply natural, then we have little reason to be concerned about economic inequality, political apathy, or residential segregation because they are not social

thinking about culture
What is the meaning of World Cup Soccer in U.S. **culture**, and what do you think its prospects are for becoming a media event comparable to the Super Bowl? In Chapter 14 we explore the effect of media on U.S. and global culture.

problems but the natural order of things. What people think of as natural and normal, then, is fundamentally about ideology.

To effectively wield power, those with power within a culture must continually reinforce the idea that certain assumptions are simply "common sense" and "natural" because people's life experiences are likely to lead them to question these assumptions. (In Chapter 5 we explore this link between culture and power, especially as it relates to justifying inequality.) In recent years, for example, widespread cultural assumptions about the definition of marriage have weakened. Gay and lesbian activists demanding the right to same-sex marriage have challenged, sometimes successfully, the longstanding belief that marriage is restricted to a relationship between a man and a woman.

In addition, even in the most repressive societies, some people will not accept the dominant ideology, some people may resist it, and changing historical conditions will undermine certain aspects of it. Ultimately, when we look at ideology from a sociological point of view, we can see the ways that culture is a contested arena that defines our underlying, and often changing, conceptions of the world.

Cultural Diversity

Consider the case of "Billy," described in a manual used to train volunteers with CASA (Court Appointed Special Advocates), a nonprofit network of advocates for abused and neglected children. After making a visit to observe his home environment, a social worker recommended that Billy be kept in foster care (National CASA 2007). She cited the following reasons in her report:

- Billy did not have a space of his own and had to sleep in a room with several other people.

- Billy's mother did not seem to be his primary caregiver, instead letting his grandmother take on that responsibility.

- Billy did not appear to be affectionate with his grandmother; indeed, he seemed intimidated by or even scared of her since he would not look at her directly but instead averted his eyes.

Billy, however, was Native American, and the cultural practices of his tribe explained these supposedly problematic behaviors. In some Native American tribes, for example—as well as in Japanese, Hawaiian, and other cultures—leaving a child alone in his or her own room is considered a form of neglect. Instead, people in these cultures maintain close and continuous contact between a child and other family members, which they see as essential to healthy and loving development. In addition, in some Native American cultures it is perfectly normal for a parent to defer to a grandparent when it comes to child-rearing decisions. Leaving children in the care of grandparents is not considered neglect but a sign of respect for elders in the family. Finally, in averting his eyes, Billy was not showing fear

but rather a traditional sign of respect for his grandmother, with whom he in fact had a close and loving relationship. If the social worker had had a better understanding of Billy's culture, she could have avoided the inappropriate recommendation.

Social tasks—preparing food, creating shelter, raising children, entertaining, governing—are universal in all cultures, but the methods people use to accomplish these tasks vary dramatically. Thus culture is highly diverse, varying not only across time, but also among different societies as well as within a single society. This variation is one of the reasons why "cultural awareness" training is an important part of many professions. Billy's social worker could have benefited from more cultural awareness. For a tragic example of the need for cultural awareness training, see the Sociology Matters box on page 72.

Understanding the diversity across cultures in different societies is more important now than ever before. For much of human history, only a few travelers interacted with people from cultures other than their own. Travel was difficult, expensive, and often dangerous. Today, widespread mobility, a global economy, and technological advances have brought people from many distinct cultures into more frequent and ongoing contact. Mass media—especially television and the Internet—have introduced people to the ideas, images, sounds, and practices of different cultures, even if they don't know the languages people within them speak. As the Sociology Works box on page 73 illustrates, understanding cultural diversity is crucial in today's business world.

To understand the impact of cultural diversity, it is essential to grasp the various types of cultures within our own and other societies, their positions in relation to one another, and how they interact in what has become an increasingly multicultural world.

Dominant Culture, Subcultures, and Countercultures

When we talk about societies—our own or those of other countries—it is common to speak about them as sharing a single culture (for example, "U.S. culture" or "Afghan culture"). To a degree, this is true; societies share basic cultural features. However, societies are large-scale, complex arrangements that inevitably contain internal differences, as well. Competing cultural systems exist even in what appear to be homogeneous societies.

Rather than consisting of a single culture, most societies contain a **dominant culture,** *a culture that permeates the society and that represents the ideas and practices of those in positions of power,* as well as a number of **subcultures,** *cultures associated with smaller groups in the society that have distinct norms, values, and lifestyles that set them apart from the dominant culture.*

Political and educational institutions, major businesses, the mass media, and educational institutions, among others, mostly reflect the dominant culture. For example, until quite recently (and some would argue, still today) the dominant

Cultural Competence and Health Care

Lia Lee was a Hmong child living in California. The Hmong are an ethnic group from the Southeast Asian country of Laos whose culture is rooted in a rural way of life. When Lia was born in a California county hospital, her mother spoke no English, and the medical staff spoke no Hmong. At just three months old, Lia experienced fainting episodes, which doctors attributed to epileptic seizures. Over the next four years, Lia's doctors struggled to control her symptoms by prescribing a dozen different drugs in dosages and combinations that changed more than twenty times.

This dizzying array of treatments would have been confusing to anyone, but Lia's family was especially ill-prepared to understand the process. Illiterate even in their own Hmong language, they were able to follow their doctor's advice only intermittently. Instead, they turned for relief to their culture's familiar religious beliefs about illness. According to that tradition, Lia's fainting spells were caused by the temporary departure of her soul from her body, a condition whose name roughly translates as "the spirit catches you and you fall down." Lia's parents sent away to Thailand for sacred charms to protect her and changed the child's name to fool the evil spirits (Underwood and Adler 2005).

As U.S. society becomes ever more culturally diverse, health care workers are increasingly treating people like Lia and her family, whose beliefs about sickness and health differ dramatically from those of mainstream Western medicine. To treat these patients effectively, health care workers need to pay close attention to their cultural beliefs and traditions. Unfortunately, the Western doctors did not understand the Hmong culture, and Lia's family did not understand the doctors' efforts. As a result, the medical treatment was ineffective. Four years after her initial symptoms, Lia experienced a massive seizure that left her in a vegetative state. She remains in a coma today, well into her twenties.

Lia's story is perhaps an extreme example, but dealing with gaps in communication between patients and health care workers caused by cultural differences is a very real and growing challenge. The federal government, along with several universities, private foundations, and organizations representing health care providers, has launched a variety of public and private initiatives to promote and ensure *cultural competence*—the ability to understand and address the needs of people from different cultures (Rees and Ruiz 2003). For example, some states have enacted regulations that require medical facilities to provide culturally competent care to groups that make up a certain percentage of the community's population. As one key element of this care, facilities are required to make available interpreters fluent in both the language and the cultural traditions of different groups. Organizations such as Resources for Cross Cultural Health Care (diversityrx.org) have stepped up to the challenge. One recent study found that medical interpreters, those who facilitate bilingual communication in hospitals, often act as an essential part of a medical team, becoming informal co-diagnosticians, even though these interpreters do not have formal medical training (Hsieh 2007).

As part of their training, medical students are also learning about the important role of culture in their patients' lives. One book has become required reading in more than 100 medical schools. Titled *The Spirit Catches You and You Fall Down*, it's the tragic story of Lia Lee (Fadiman 1998).

think about it

1. *Have you or your family ever had trouble communicating with a doctor or been uncertain about what is happening at a hospital? If so, do you think cultural differences help explain why?*

2. *How might cultural differences cause problems with communication in school or at work?*

---

culture in the United States was associated with the images, ideas, and values of white, often male, professional middle-class culture. Those in positions of power were disproportionately white, professional men. The cultures of other segments of society were usually not entirely excluded, but they did tend to be marginalized.

White, professional middle-class culture was often the norm from which other cultures deviated. We can see this dominance in action in commonly used phrases such as "the black community" or "working-class literature" or "women's history," each of which signals a deviation from the standard of white, professional men. Rarely, if ever, do we use terms such as "the white community," "middle-class literature," or "men's history" because these are already the unspoken norm in the dominant culture.

Alongside the dominant culture, societies include a number of smaller subcultures with their own distinct cultural traits. For example, Americans in general are enthusiastic about technological advancements, but the Amish—an orthodox Protestant sect living primarily in Pennsylvania and Ohio—reject the use of most modern technology, resulting in a distinct way of life. Skateboarders also form a subculture. They define and

thinking about culture

Do you belong to a particular subculture, or know someone who does?
In Chapter 8 we look at a range of subcultures, exploring how and why subcultures
are often perceived as deviant.

Dean Foster and the Business of Cultural Diversity

As an undergraduate, Dean Foster didn't have a clue what he would do with sociology, but he thought the subject was fascinating. He found especially appealing the basic premise that "we can understand how we work as cultural and social beings and use this understanding to improve our collective lives." When he looks back today and considers the benefits he gained from sociology, his list is extensive: "My professional career, cross-cultural friendships, life goals, and purpose."

Foster is the founder and president of DFA (Dean Foster Associates) Intercultural Global Solutions. DFA helps organizations and businesses working with other cultures around the globe to develop intercultural competencies. Foster spends much of his time travelling to present intercultural seminars, give speeches, and conduct interviews around the world. Describing his work as the "perfect job," Foster notes that "I meet wonderful people from places I only could have dreamed I would visit and work in as a child. I help deal with important cross-cultural challenges in ways that I like to believe change people's lives."

When working internationally, businesses must anticipate and address some common differences among cultures. For example, different cultures have various ideas about time. Some value punctuality; in Germany, Austria, and Switzerland being late is considered a sign of disrespect and incompetence. In the countries of Latin America, by contrast, there is more latitude when it comes to meeting times and deadlines.

In addition, norms governing appropriate relationships between employers and their employees can vary a great deal from one culture to another. In some countries, employees are expected to be deferential to their bosses, avoiding eye contact with them and obeying instructions without comment. In other countries, employees are expected to be candid, although still respectful, with their bosses, giving their input on the task at hand. In all these cases, global businesses must understand the cultural norms within a given society—and convey that understanding to their employees—if they are to communicate and work successfully in international settings.

> "I work with cross-cultural challenges in ways that I like to believe change people's lives."

A cottage industry of diversity training specialists such as Dean Foster—often with backgrounds in sociology, anthropology, and psychology—has emerged in response to the growing need of businesses for cultural awareness in today's global economy. Foster notes, however, that when he was a student, "there was no such field as intercultural training, so there were no internships, mentors, or courses of study." In fact, he first earned a living as a songwriter and folksinger, playing in clubs in New York's Greenwich Village. By the mid-1980s, though, he had used his sociological knowledge to start one of the first intercultural training consultancies.

Dean Foster

Foster's work, he says, forces him "to constantly expect that which cannot be imagined, a testament to the power of culture, and the limits it places on us as cultural beings. I find this is the same kind of challenge that sociology places on us when we try to imagine how is it that we are who we are and behave as we behave. I deal with this question professionally every day."

think about it

1. *When international businesspeople come to the United States, what do you think they need to know about culturally specific work routines that people in this country are likely to take for granted?*

2. *In your travels, have you experienced uncertainty about basic cultural norms? What happened? What did you learn as a result?*

use public spaces in innovative ways, turning roads and sidewalks, steps and hand railings, into a skating space, while developing a distinctive attitude about risk-taking and authority. Since subcultures often highlight their differences from the mainstream, their members often accept, even celebrate, their status as deviant (Gelder 2005).

Members of a subculture, then, share a common identity, whether they are extreme-sports enthusiasts, science fiction fans, or Civil War reenactors. Although subcultures typically do not have a formal membership structure, they usually de-velop a specialized language or style and specific behaviors and objects relevant to their culture. Trekkers—a subculture consisting of fans of the television and movie franchise *Star Trek*—share a language about the fictional Starfleet and a science-fiction version of future space exploration, and they know the various *Star Trek* heroes and villains and the lessons of their multigenerational adventures in great detail. Attending *Star Trek* fan conventions, dressing up as specific *Star Trek* characters; and collecting *Star Trek* memorabilia—even if some of your friends and coworkers think such behavior is

One way people express their connection to a subculture is by purchasing and displaying products that have specific meanings to other members of the subculture. Trekkers—fans of the *Star Trek* television and movie franchise—can purchase a wide range of *Star Trek* merchandise, from uniforms to a living room chair designed to look like Captain Kirk's command chair on the Starship *Enterprise*.

a bit wacky—signals your subcultural connections to other Trekkers.

Work and school organizations can develop their own cultural traits, too. Thus we might speak about the corporate culture at Wal-Mart or the organizational culture at a governmental agency such as NASA. If your school has a significant sports program, take a look around you at the next big game you attend. College athletics—complete with school colors, uniforms, mascots, cheers, and rituals—are part of the distinct cultures of many schools. Special moments in the school's sports history—winning a championship, pulling off a huge upset, a star athlete's choking in a key game—all become part of the lore of that school's culture.

At the micro level, even groups of close friends who live in the same neighborhood can develop a subculture. As they grow up, their common experiences foster similar values and beliefs. They may like the same style of clothing, music, and leisure activities. Over time their shared adventures give them a common history, filled with incidents, terminology, and characters that have little meaning for people outside the group. "Inside" jokes and references help to build a sense of solidarity and belonging.

A subculture that organizes itself in opposition to the dominant culture may be categorized as a **counterculture,** which *champions values and lifestyles distinctly opposed to those of the dominant culture.* Members of countercultures challenge widely held values and attitudes and reject mainstream cultural norms.

In the past half-century, a series of youth-based countercultures have challenged aspects of the dominant culture in U.S. society. For example, young hippies in the 1960s had a distinctive lifestyle and language. They challenged traditional authority by experimenting with recreational drugs, practicing communal living, espousing "free love," and protesting against the Vietnam War. Punks in the 1970s developed their own particular style, including then-atypical piercings and provocative hairstyles, along with a defiant attitude. In recent decades, hip-hop has introduced new music, language, dance, and fashion at the same time that those within hip-hop culture advance a powerful critique of racism and racial discrimination.

Subcultures—including countercultures—often introduce innovation and change to mainstream culture. Features of a subculture that might appear radical or threatening may over time be incorporated into the dominant culture. For example, in U.S. society, tattoos were once found exclusively among various subcultures such as sailors and bikers but have long since moved into the mainstream. Access to birth control, racial intermarriage, equal rights for women, and a host of other social reforms began their life as part of the beliefs and values of political subcultures, only to achieve broad mainstream acceptance eventually. Which aspects of today's subcultures do you think are likely to be incorporated into mainstream culture in your lifetime?

High Culture and Popular Culture

Societies contain not only a dominant culture and various subcultures, but also different cultural expressions that are related to people's position in society. Sociologists have in fact long recognized the relationship between culture and economic inequality. **High culture** refers to *cultural forms associated with elites that are widely recognized as valuable and legitimate.* Examples of high culture include art galleries, the opera, classical music, and literature. Historically, high culture has been the domain of the wealthy and highly educated. Although others may not be formally excluded from these activities, their expense and the specialized knowledge that is often needed to understand and enjoy them can serve to restrict access to those who are able to afford them.

Proponents of high culture may define these cultural forms as the best and most enduring representations of a nation's culture. After all, disciplines that study high culture such as art history and music education are typically part of the high school and college curriculum, and many people associate the very idea of becoming "cultured" with visiting museums or attending the symphony. In contrast, **popular culture** refers to *cultural forms that are widespread and commonly embraced* *within a society.* Popular culture includes such widely accessible forms as television programs, Hollywood films, rock concerts, spectator sports, and amusement parks. To enjoy popular culture, a person generally does not need a substantial amount of money or specialized knowledge.

The distinction between high and popular culture suggests a fundamental conflict. As sociologist Herbert Gans (1999) maintains, "advocates of high culture attack popular culture as a mass culture that has harmful effects on both individuals consuming it and on society as a whole. The users of popular culture fight back mostly by ignoring the critique and rejecting high culture" (pp. 3–4). In the early twenty-first century, however, the distinction between high and popular culture has become blurry. More people, including elites, now consume a diverse mixture of high and popular culture. Various hybrid cultural forms—such as graffiti art exhibited in museums or the pop musician Sting's performing his songs with the Royal Philharmonic Concert Orchestra—mix elements from both types; and many forms of popular culture, including highly rated television programs and best-selling novels, are widely enjoyed by elites as well as other demographic groups. Nevertheless, as Gans points out, the distinction between high and popular culture remains helpful since the cultural choices people make are still influenced significantly by their social standing.

The Commercialization of Culture

Hector is driving to school with the radio playing when one of his favorite songs comes on. He turns up the volume and sings along as the artist praises a certain line of designer clothes. The lyrics are a result of work by Maven Strategies, a company that negotiates deals between major corporate advertisers and hip-hop artists. A corporation will pay the artists to mention its product in their songs. The result? Many rap songs mention brand names of sneakers, watches, vodka, and other products. Although most songs do not include paid advertisements, in 2004—the year Maven Strategies began cutting such deals—product brand names were mentioned almost 1,000 times in the top twenty singles on the *Billboard* charts (Williams 2005). This type of product placement, which continues today, is just one of many ways that *commercialism*—the marketing and sale of products—has become entrenched in contemporary popular culture.

Today, many cultural objects are commodities—products to be bought and sold—and these objects are increasingly produced by corporate conglomerates (Mosco 2009; Schiller 1989; Schor 2004). The stories children learn and the music people listen to are produced and marketed by multinational corporations like Disney and Sony. Corporations now sponsor a broad range of cultural creations, from rock concerts to museum exhibits (Rectanus 2002). From expensive tickets to major events to one-dollar DVD rentals from a kiosk, we spend much of our lives—and many of our dollars—buying cultural products.

This focus on commerce has meant that the language and images of advertising have increasingly entered public and private space, surrounding us with pictures and symbols whose primary purpose is to get us to buy something. Some communities see this as a problem and are fighting back, however. In 2007, new "Clean City" laws went into effect in São Paulo, Brazil—a city of 11 million people—that essentially banned all outdoor advertising. As the president of the city council noted, "What we are aiming for is a complete change of culture [. . .] things were out of hand and the population has made it clear it wants this" (Rohter 2006).

With the ever-growing influence of commercialism, people increasingly tend to measure the value of most cultural objects by their profitability. How many copies of that book or this CD were sold? What was the highest rated television program last week? What were the box office standings for movies released this past weekend? Such concerns reflect a culture in which the dollar sign increasingly denotes "success." As we see throughout this book, especially in Chapter 14, the commercialization of cultural and social life—its packaging, promotion, and sale by major corporations—is an important feature of our changing world, both in the United States and globally.

Multiculturalism

Because so many societies today contain many subcultures and cultural diversity, there is an increasing emphasis on **multiculturalism,** *the recognition, valuing, and protection of the distinct cultures that make up a society.* Rather than assume that all people will adopt the ideas and practices of the dominant culture—a process known as *assimilation*—multicultural societies accept, accommodate, and even celebrate differences in language, religion, customs, dress, traditions, and beliefs. Institutions that acknowledge and accommodate different cultures, such as certain businesses and universities, can also be considered multicultural.

thinking about**culture**
Which policies does your college have that promote multiculturalism?
In Chapter 10, **culture** helps us to understand how various racial and ethnic groups
have interacted in the United States throughout its history.

A multicultural society accommodates various cultural groups. One way such societies cope is by making voting materials, health care information, signs in public places, and other important information available in the languages spoken in the local community.

Because they live in a multicultural society, many people in the United States are exposed regularly to a number of different cultures. Consider the variety of ethnic foods that you can choose from. Major U.S. cities today are likely to have restaurants featuring the food of many different cultures, including Italian, Mexican, Greek, Thai, Chinese, Ethiopian, and Indian cuisine, among others. Fairs and festivals celebrate the food, dress, music, and dances of various cultures. More significantly, in communities that are home to a variety of cultural groups, you are also likely to find institutions associated with these groups, such as temples, mosques, churches, and other places of worship. Businesses such as sari shops and halal butchers sell products not available in mainstream dress shops and grocery stores. Of course, the presence of different cultural groups often means a variety of languages, as well. Today's major cities are often home to people who speak dozens of different languages—and their school systems must cope with this linguistic diversity.

Because of the nature of a multicultural society, a significant number of people within it grow up and live their lives defined by more than one culture. If a student speaks English at school but a different language at home, that bilingual capability is a sure sign that he or she lives in two different cultures at the same time. Some immigrant families straddle the society and culture into which they were born and where they now live (Smith and Gurnizo 1998). Some travel back and forth to their countries of origin; others send money to aid relatives there. Some are even involved in the political affairs of their native countries (Levitt 2004). Television and the Internet help people stay in touch with the news and entertainment culture of their native countries, even while they live in their newly adopted homes. For example, the satellite service Dish Network offers a variety of packages with channels based on countries and regions, such as Africa, China, South Asia, and Israel, and programming in languages such as French, German, Spanish, Italian, Polish, Portuguese, Russian, Japanese, Filipino, Korean, Farsi, Arabic, and Urdo.

People who live in a multicultural society have an extraordinary opportunity to learn about and appreciate the rich diversity of human cultures. Diversity also brings with it challenges and problems, however, as people with different ways of life attempt to coexist. Unfortunately, cultural difference often leads to inequality and conflict as groups with more power oppress, exploit, or otherwise discriminate against those who are different and who have less power. The long, ugly history of religious conflict, ethnic clashes, racist violence, and warfare between nations is one result of this tendency. Therefore, to understand culture more fully, we must inevitably study conflict, relations of power (a topic explored in Chapter 5), and the domination of some groups by others.

CULTURE: CONSENSUS AND CONFLICT

People from the same culture may share the same language, religion, worldview, history, and traditions. When this happens, cultures nurture and promote consensus, cohesiveness, and solidarity through a shared collective identity. However, just as the common bond of culture creates a sense of "us," it can also create a sense of "them"—those outside the culture who are different in some way. Perhaps the outsiders speak a different language, practice a different religion, dress differently, or are from a different social class. Whatever the distinction, as those who share a culture increase the sense that they have a common bond, they often have a tendency to marginalize, belittle, or even demonize "outsiders" who have a different culture.

Cultural conflict is most likely to emerge when values and beliefs differ among different cultures. Contrasting beliefs about religion and clashes over core values have been the source of or justification for many conflicts over the centuries. Unlike questions that can be answered with scientific evidence, disputes about values and beliefs cannot be resolved by appeals to reason. The cultural conflicts that result from these disputes can be intense and ongoing.

One source of cultural conflict is **ethnocentrism,** *the judging of other cultures by the standards of one's own on the assumption that one's own is superior.* Out of ignorance, the social worker mentioned earlier in this chapter was being ethnocentric in judging the Native American family's childrearing practices through the lens of her own culture. Had she known more about how children are brought up in that society, she would have understood that the family had a different approach that could also achieve the goal of raising a healthy child. This family's experience is a relatively mild example, but ethnocentrism can have harsh and even violent consequences if members of one culture act upon a conviction that their ideas,

SPOTLIGHT on social theory

According to **conflict theorists,** more powerful groups within society dominate less powerful ones. Can you think of an example of a powerful group's demonizing or belittling a less powerful group's culture? Why would the powerful group find it advantageous to do so?

The infamously xenophobic Ku Klux Klan, which had several million members during its heyday in the 1920s, appropriated Christian symbolism to promote a white supremacist agenda that asserted the superiority of white Protestants and attacked the supposedly alien influence of black people and most immigrants, including non-Protestant Whites. Today, some Muslim extremists similarly invoke religious symbolism in calling for attacks against perceived threats from the alien cultural influence of nonbelievers. Just as most Christians rejected the Klan, most Muslims reject these extremist views.

values, and way of life are superior to those of another culture. An ethnocentric worldview can be the source of **xenophobia,** *the unreasonable fear and hatred of foreigners or people from other cultures,* which, at its extreme, can result in genocide—the deliberate and systematic destruction of a cultural, racial, or political group. What types of ethnocentrism are most prevalent in the United States today?

Much of the history of colonialism, in which one country conquers or dominates others, is the story of ethnocentrism in action. The Europeans who conquered much of the world from the sixteenth century into the twentieth were confident that their way of life was superior to that of the people whose lands they colonized. They often sought to "civilize" the native peoples, teaching them their language, and converting them to Christianity. As the native peoples resisted, the result was centuries of conflict.

In contrast to ethnocentrism, **cultural relativism** is *the practice of understanding a culture by its own standards.* Cultural relativism does not require adopting or agreeing with the ideas and practices of another culture, but rather making the effort to understand the culture on its own terms and with a willingness to acknowledge it as a viable alternative to one's own. In other words, to practice cultural relativism we need to *understand* a culture, not *judge* it, as, for example, when we seek to learn about religious rituals or family traditions in a different culture.

Studying cultures other than their own (an especially important task in this era of globalization) often requires sociologists to practice cultural relativism so that they can focus their attention on a group's unique values, beliefs, and practices. Such cross-cultural understanding is difficult to achieve; it is hard for any of us to operate outside of the logic of our own culture. At the same time, once we are able to recognize our own values and beliefs—key dimensions of our own culture—

we have taken an important first step toward understanding the experiences of people who live in very different societies.

THE CRITICS OF MULTICULTURALISM Less than two weeks after the attacks on the World Trade Center and the Pentagon on September 11, 2001, President George W. Bush framed the assault in cultural terms by telling Congress and the people of the United States that the members of Al Qaeda, the Islamic fundamentalist group that had claimed responsibility, had attacked because "They hate our freedoms: our freedom of religion, our freedom of speech, our freedom to vote and assemble and disagree with each other" (Bush 2001). That quotation came to symbolize one way of thinking about the ongoing conflict between Western secular societies and Islamic societies. It suggested the conflict was based on fundamentally incompatible cultures.

One of the best-known discussions of this concept of a "culture clash" came from political scientist Samuel Huntington (1993, 1998), who argued that after the end of the Cold War between the United States and the Soviet Union, most new global conflicts would now take place between cultures rather than countries. He went on to describe what he saw as eight basic cultures (which he termed "civilizations") in the world: Western (United States, Australia, and Western Europe), Eastern Orthodox (Russia), Latin American, Islamic, Japanese, Chinese, Hindu (India), and African. These civilizations, he contended, are based on fundamentally different religious and other cultural beliefs. The Islamic world, for example, has few democratic institutions because it does not have a cultural history of separating religious and secular authority, of valuing social pluralism, and of protecting individual rights and civil liberties from the power of the state. In this way, it differs fundamentally from Western civilization. Huntington maintained that as long as globalization results in more frequent contacts between people living in these civilizations, we are doomed to experience more frequent cultural conflict.

There is no doubt that increased contact between vastly different cultures can result in conflict. However, if we analyze Huntington's thesis from a sociological perspective, we can quickly expose some of its shortcomings. For one thing, it oversimplifies the complex mix of cultures around the world and glosses over the enormous variation *within* each of these cultures (Arnason 2001). None of the so-called civilizations Huntington identifies has a single unified culture. As globalization advances and more people, products, and ideas flow across national borders, cultures continue to blend. Also, by focusing exclusively on culture, Huntington's theory ignores the ways that longstanding inequalities in the distribution of privilege and power have helped to fuel global conflict (Evans 1997).

In addition, many different cultures *do* share common values. President Bush recognized these shared values when he told a graduating class at West Point, "The peoples of the Islamic nations want and deserve the same freedoms and opportunities as people in every nation." His earlier quotation about hating freedom targeted the Al Qaeda extremists who attacked the United States. However, violent Islamic extremists do not represent the broader Islamic culture, which encompasses a range of beliefs and values. Indeed, intense debates within Muslim societies regarding democracy, the role of women, and other cultural matters take place every day.

The results of global public opinion surveys show that democracy is widely popular in both Western and Islamic cultures—even though it has yet to flourish in Muslim countries despite 2011's Arab Spring uprisings. However, those same surveys show significant differences in the degree of support for gender equality, social tolerance, and freedom of speech (Inglehart and Norris 2003; Welzel and Inglehart 2010), indicating that the reality is complicated, not just a matter of a simple clash of civilizations or an idealized belief that all societies share a unified set of cultural values.

As we have seen, different cultures within a society can also encounter the problem of incompatible values or beliefs. Feminist political philosopher Susan Okin (1999, 117) argues that "many cultures oppress some of their members, in particular women, and . . . they are often able to socialize these oppressed members so that they accept, without question, their designated cultural status." For example, polygamy, clitoridectomy (the removal of the clitoris) or other forms of genital cutting, and the prearranged marriage of children are all accepted practices within some cultures. What, if anything, should be done when people from such cultures move to Western societies, where those practices are considered violations of individual rights? Should their adoptive countries accept these practices out of respect for different cultural traditions? Or do Western notions of individual freedom, human rights, and gender equality trump these traditional customs? Such questions have been on the front pages of newspapers in Europe. For example, in 2010 the French parliament enacted legislation that prohibits Muslim women from wearing face-covering veils in public

In 2010 the French parliament began to enforce legislation that banned women from wearing face-covering veils in public. Supporters of the legislation argue that traditional religious garb like the face-covering veil violates the norms of secular culture in France and is a sign of the oppression of women. Opponents of the legislation contend that it violates the rights of women to express their religious faith.

CORE CONCEPTS CHALLENGE

Do you think it is appropriate for the French government to ban the veil? Would you be in favor of such a ban in your community? If you were a woman raised in a culture in which wearing a veil is the norm, how would you react to an attempt to force you not to wear it? What reasons might members of a dominant culture use to justify imposing a ban on such clothing?

places, on the grounds that such clothing conflicts with the values of French secular society (Crumley 2009; Erlanger 2010). This issue raises complex questions about incompatible cultural values and practices and challenges us to consider whether it is legitimate to condemn cultural practices we find offensive and whether we can articulate a universal standard of human rights.

Some U.S. critics of multiculturalism are not concerned with such questions because they reject its value entirely. Instead of encouraging people from diverse cultural traditions to coexist peacefully, these critics argue that new immigrants must assimilate into the dominant culture of their adoptive country; otherwise, they maintain, the common ground that is essential to unite a nation will be lost (Huntington 2005; Schmidt 1997). Some of these critics call for teaching Christian values in schools, the adoption of "English-only" laws, an end to bilingual education, and strict limits on immigration, among other measures, to shore up the dominant culture. As we will explore in Chapter 10, these arguments are similar to those made a century ago when new Irish, Russian, Italian, Polish, and other European immigrants arrived in the United States in great numbers. Back then these ethnic cultures were seen as a threat to American values.

SPOTLIGHT
on social theory

Emile Durkheim, whose work was influential for the proponents of **functionalism,** focused on social solidarity—on how cultural values serve to unite people. How do you see this process working today in multicultural societies like that of the United States?

Societies do need common ground—supplied by their cultures—to function successfully, and sociologists since Emile Durkheim have recognized this need. Nevertheless, cultures are also evolving constantly. Think about how global travel, electronic communications, the global economy, and widespread immigration have changed contemporary society. Already contemporary U.S. society has found many ways to accommodate the peaceful coexistence of diverse cultural traditions.

In fact, culture can also be a basis for connection and exchange in ways that help to prevent, or even heal, conflicts. Cross-cultural experiences—from reading the novels, studying the art, or learning about the cuisine of another culture to traveling to other countries, studying new languages, or hosting foreign visitors in your home or school—may provide a bridge that promotes greater understanding and improved relationships across national boundaries. Indeed, throughout history the trend has been in the direction of increased tolerance, accommodation, and appreciation among different cultures.

Cultural Activism

Many people are understandably passionate about cultural issues, which often reflect their deepest concerns. As a result, people from across the political spectrum participate in a wide range of public activities aimed at promoting or contesting culturally specific ideas and practices. In this section, we briefly review three contemporary forms of cultural activism: organizations that promote cultural pride, religious fundamentalism, and anticorporate activism.

CULTURAL PRIDE ORGANIZATIONS

In communities throughout the United States, a variety of civic organizations maintain and promote particular cultures. They provide children with classes about their cultural heritage and sponsor festivals and other events celebrating their traditions. Because New York City is so ethnically diverse, activities celebrating cultural pride take place throughout the city all year long, including the St. Patrick's Day Parade in March, celebrating the experiences of the Irish and Irish Americans; the Puerto Rican Day Parade in June; the West Indian Carnival in September, which celebrates Caribbean cultures and histories; and the Chinese New Year Parade in January or February. The idea of embracing and celebrating one's cultural heritage has become firmly embedded in U.S. society as well as in many other countries.

RELIGIOUS FUNDAMENTALISM

A worldwide resurgence of religious belief among fundamentalists who believe in the literal interpretation of sacred texts such as the Bible

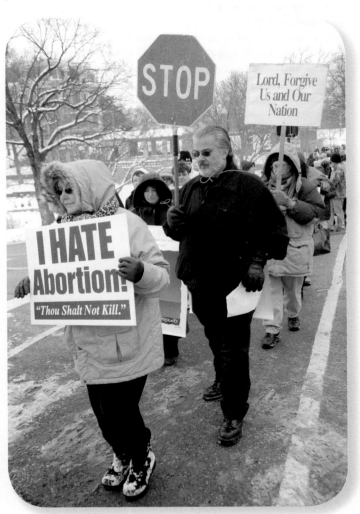

In the past several decades, Christian conservatives have played an increasingly visible role in U.S. politics, often applying their interpretation of biblical teaching to contemporary social issues, such as abortion, and insisting that the United States should be considered a Christian nation. What are some of the potentially positive and negative consequences of intermingling religious faith with political activity?

and the Qur'an, represents another form of cultural activism. Whether at home or abroad, religious fundamentalists are using their faith as the basis for their activism. They criticize the cultural values and practices of Western secular society and develop ways to preserve and promote their own cultural values.

Islamic fundamentalists have challenged the export of Western culture to traditionally Muslim societies. They condemn what they perceive as the hedonism and decadent lifestyles promoted in such cultural products, themes that they say contradict Islamic teachings. They are especially angered by what they see as anti-Islamic media content. Pakistan, for example, ordered Internet providers to block Facebook in 2010 because one of its pages promoted "Everybody Draw Mohammed Day"—an action that violates Islamic beliefs. The ban was lifted once the page was removed. Islamic fundamentalists have turned to strict religious schooling and mass media, especially the Internet, to promote more traditional values and defend them against the onslaught of Western media.

Similarly, in the United States, Christian fundamentalists have fought—unsuccessfully—to eliminate from the mainstream media sexual imagery, violence, positive portrayals of homosexuality, and other content they find objectionable and contrary to their religious teachings. At the same time, these activists promote their religious beliefs through homeschooling, religiously based private schools, religious radio and television broadcasting, and religious books, movies, pop music, and other media content. These efforts have had a significant impact on the political culture of the United States, where religious conservatives are a significant political and cultural force.

ANTICORPORATE ACTIVISM

The role corporations play in shaping culture is a source of contention in many countries. Critics of corporate power in the United States and elsewhere, especially on the political left, engage in yet another form of cultural activism, protesting concentrated media ownership and an unregulated global economy. In the United States, anticorporate cultural activists have established small but vibrant independent media outlets for music, art, news, and other cultural products outside of the mainstream commercial corporate system. Groups such as the Media Foundation, with its signature magazine *Adbusters,* promote a form of activism called "culture jamming," which refashions popular brand images to express a critical message about commercial culture, as in the example shown on this page.

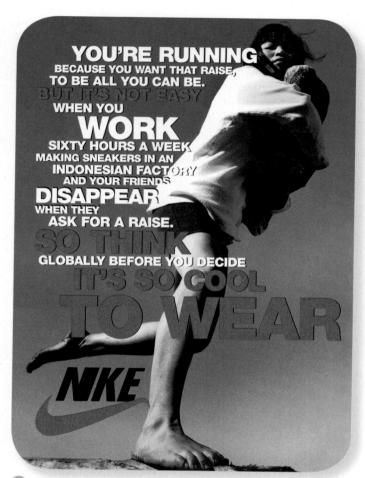

Culture jamming is a form of activism that attaches new and subversive meanings to well-known corporate brands, often rewriting popular advertising campaigns. This example was produced by Adbusters. Complete with the Nike swoosh, it associates the Nike brand with slave labor—a powerful critique of Nike's labor practices.

Whether they are motivated by pride in a culture, by religious belief, or by opposition to corporate power, campaigns by cultural activists often lead to passionate public expression and debate. Although many of the issues taken on by cultural activists receive scant attention in mainstream public policy arenas, this form of activism often produces broad public discussion, testifying to the significance of culture in our everyday lives.

CULTURE AND GLOBALIZATION

Imagine two twenty-something young women discussing their favorite television programs. "I enjoy watching *Divorce Court*," says one. "I love *Friends* and *Martin*," replies the other. "They are so real. . . . They show it how it is" (Miranda 2003). This exchange, overheard a few years ago, would be too ordinary to mention except for one thing: It took place not on Main Street, U.S.A., but rather in a CD shop in Nairobi, Kenya, in east Africa.

Since 1990, television in Kenya has expanded from a single state-run station broadcasting a few hours a day to more than half a dozen channels operating in different parts of the country, some broadcasting twenty-four hours a day. Rarely, however, does the country's rich and diverse mix of local cultures and some thirty indigenous languages figure in the programming on these channels. It is much cheaper to import foreign programs to fill the air time than to produce original programming, so viewers often have no choice but to watch Western—usually U.S.—programming. As a result, a generation of Kenyan youth has grown up watching reruns of old American television series and soap operas.

Some Kenyans worry that this flood of Western media is washing away all that is distinct about their local cultures. As David Makali, director of the Media Institute in Nairobi, puts it, "In Kenya, TV has become a major avenue of cultural promotion, and it is really terrible the way Western culture has taken over. The people are being brainwashed, and we are losing out culturally" (Miranda 2003).

Kenya is hardly alone. Much of the rest of the world has been experiencing a similar media-driven globalization of culture (Crothers 2009). And as in Kenya, media globalization has primarily meant a massive export of Western television, movies, music, and other cultural products to poorer nations that lack the resources or technological infrastructure to support a large media industry of their own. These Western products are often popular, but they also generate resentment as a kind of foreign invasion that is displacing local cultural practices and challenging traditional values and lifeways. In addition, U.S. media products present a limited image that can leave audiences in foreign cultures with misconceptions about American society.

The flood of U.S. media inundating foreign markets may have crested, however. Local media industries have begun competing for local audiences, and new digital media platforms such as YouTube and Facebook are providing new channels of distribution that challenge the dominance of

Satellite dishes bring commercial media products into even the remotest villages across the globe, such as this home in Laos, a country in Southeast Asia. Because it is usually much cheaper to import Western programs than to produce new programming locally, many of the programs that people in poorer countries around the world see are imported from other cultures.

foreign media and offer visibility to local productions that might otherwise be invisible. Locally produced programs, finely attuned to the local culture, tend to be very popular, and local producers have sometimes successfully competed with global media conglomerates by providing alternatives to the homogenized global fare. In Nigeria, for example, popular locally produced films circulate widely on home video, and in much of Latin America *telenovelas* (locally produced romantic serials similar to soap operas) are among the most popular television programs (Akpabio and Mustapha-Lambe 2008; Flew 2007). Such projects are often produced on a shoe-string budget, however, and are unable to match the slick production values Western audiences often expect.

The fusion of different cultural traditions into a new, creative object or idea is as old as art itself. Today, the opportunities for communication among cultures are greater than ever before. However, because of the imbalance between wealthy and poor parts of the globe, affluent countries have been doing most of the talking while hearing very little from other parts of the world. With today's technologies, however, artists in poor countries can feasibly begin to make themselves heard.

■ Culture must be learned and can be thought of as all aspects of society that are transmitted socially, rather than biologically. Culture consists of both nonmaterial and material elements: values, beliefs, knowledge, and norms; symbols and language; behavior and objects.

■ Our own culture can be so familiar to us that we often fail to recognize its various elements or even why it matters. A sociological approach illuminates the often hidden ways that culture helps to define our identities and our relationship to our broader communities.

■ Sociologists have long paid attention to the assumptions built into any culture, arguing that what we take for granted is one of the keys to recognizing how culture and power are intertwined.

■ Culture is highly diverse, varying across time and among different societies as well as within a single society. Unlike other animals whose social organization is instinctual, and therefore virtually identical wherever they are found, humans meet their basic needs by adopting a variety of culture-specific behaviors.

■ Most societies contain a dominant culture, as well as a number of subcultures. These subcultures—including countercultures—often introduce innovation and change to mainstream culture.

■ Living in a multicultural society gives us an opportunity to learn about and appreciate the rich diversity of human cultures. But diversity also brings challenges and problems; cultural differences are often the basis for inequality and conflict.

REVIEW, REFLECT, AND APPLY

Looking Back

1. Culture is an essential part of social life. It must be taught and learned and exists only in the context of groups.

2. The elements of culture include values, beliefs, knowledge, and norms (the ideas of culture); language and other forms of symbolic communication (for transmitting culture); and behaviors and material objects.

3. Within each culture, there is a dominant ideology that generally supports the current social system and serves the interests of authorities.

4. Most societies contain a dominant culture as well as a number of subcultures and countercultures.

5. Multiculturalism refers to the willingness to recognize, value, and protect the distinct cultures that make up a society.

6. Ethnocentrism is the practice of judging another culture by the standards of one's own. In contrast, cultural relativism is the practice of understanding a culture by its own standards.

7. Examples of cultural activism include cultural pride organizations, religious fundamentalism, and anticorporate activism.

8. Media globalization has primarily taken the form of the massive export of Western—primarily U.S.—media products to poorer nations. The flood of U.S. media may have crested, however, as local media industries have begun to take advantage of new digital technologies to compete for local audiences.

Critical Thinking: Questions and Activities

1. Why is "culture" a core concept in sociology? How can the concept of culture help us to understand social life?

2. Why do changes in today's world make it especially important to understand the concept of culture?

3. Imagine that, because of your sociological training, you have been chosen to select the items to be included in a time capsule for your community that will be opened 100 years from now. Assuming the time capsule is about the size of a large suitcase, what cultural artifacts would you choose to represent your "way of life"? Explain why you believe these items are the most important.

4. Suppose you live in a foreign country and know little about the United States. Watch an hour of prime-time television and take careful notes about what you have learned about U.S. society. Were the media images you saw an accurate representation of U.S. society? Why or why not? What lessons about the United States might the export of such cultural products be teaching people in other societies?

Key Terms

behaviors (p. 68) the actions associated with a group that help to reproduce a distinct way of life.

beliefs (p. 63) the specific convictions or opinions that its people generally accept as being true.

counterculture (p. 74) a subculture that champions values and lifestyles distinctly opposed to those of the dominant culture.

cultural lag (p. 65) the ways that new technological developments often outpace the norms that govern our collective experiences with these new technologies.

cultural object (p. 70) a physical item that is created by and associated with people who share a culture.

cultural relativism (p. 77) the practice of understanding a culture by its own standards.

culture (p. 59) the collection of values, beliefs, knowledge, norms, language, behaviors, and material objects shared by a people and socially transmitted from generation to generation.

culture shock (p. 64) the experience of being disoriented because of a lack of knowledge about an unfamiliar social situation.

culture war (p. 62) an intense disagreement about core values and moral positions.

dialect (p. 68) a variant of a language with its own distinctive accent, vocabulary, and in some cases grammatical characteristics.

dominant culture (p. 71) a culture that permeates a society and that represents the ideas and practices of those in positions of power.

dominant ideology (p. 70) a widely held and regularly reinforced set of assumptions that generally support the current social system and serve the interests of authorities.

ethnocentrism (p. 76) the practice of judging another culture by the standards of one's own.

folkways (p. 66) group habits or customs that are common in a given culture.

high culture (p. 74) cultural forms associated with elites that are widely recognized as valuable and legitimate.

ideal culture (p. 68) what the members of a culture report to be their values, beliefs, and norms.

ideology (p. 70) a system of meaning that helps define and explain the world and that makes value judgments about that world.

knowledge (cultural) (p. 64) the range of information, awareness, and understanding that helps us navigate our world.

language (p. 66) an elaborate system of symbols that allows people to communicate with one another in complex ways.

material culture (p. 59) the physical objects produced by people in a particular culture, including tools, clothing, toys, works of art, and housing.

mores (p. 66) norms that are strictly enforced, with potentially severe penalties for violating them.

multiculturalism (p. 75) the recognition, valuing, and protection of the distinct cultures that make up a society.

nonmaterial culture (p. 59) the ideas of a culture, including values and beliefs, accumulated knowledge about how to understand and navigate the world, and standards or "norms" about appropriate behavior.

norms (p. 65) a culture's rules and expectations for "appropriate" behavior.

popular culture (p. 74) cultural forms that are widespread and commonly embraced within a society.

real culture (p. 68) what members of a culture actually do, which may or may not reflect the ideal.

Sapir-Whorf hypothesis (p. 68) the idea that because of their different cultural content and structure, languages affect how their speakers think and behave.

society (p. 59) a group of people who live together in a specific territory and share a culture.

subculture (p. 71) cultures associated with smaller groups in society that have distinct norms, values, and lifestyles setting them apart from the dominant culture.

symbol (p. 66) anything—a sound, a gesture, an image, an object—that represents something else.

value (p. 60) a deeply held principle or standard that people use to make judgments about the world, especially in deciding what is desirable or worthwhile.

xenophobia (p. 77) an unreasonable fear or hatred of foreigners or people of a different culture.

Social Structure

looking AHEAD

How can learning about social **structure** help you see how it operates in your life?

How can your actions and those of others change social **structure**?

As you send a text message on your cell phone or sign an online petition, how does your behavior illustrate the dynamic interplay between **structure** and action?

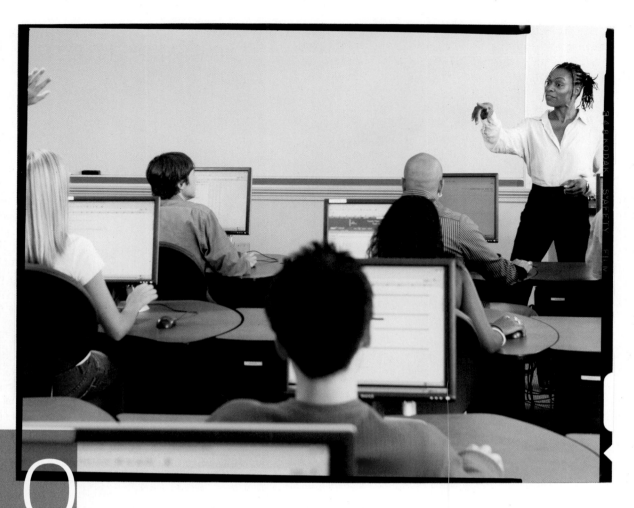

On the first day of a new term, you enter your Introductory Sociology classroom a few minutes early, look around for familiar faces, and wave to a couple of friends. Taking an empty seat that faces the front of the room, you pull a notebook and pen out of your backpack and make small talk with the person next to you.

A few minutes later, a woman enters the classroom carrying a stack of books and papers. She walks to the front, drops her papers on the only desk that faces the back of the classroom, and looks at you and your classmates. You end your conversation and give her your attention. The woman turns to write her name on the blackboard, then faces the class and introduces herself. You sit quietly while she reviews the class schedule and assignments. After a few minutes, you raise your hand and, when called upon by the woman, you ask a question about one of the assignments, which she answers. About forty-five minutes later, the woman finishes speaking—her presentation has lasted for almost the entire period—and dismisses the class. You pack up your gear and head for the door, chatting with your friends as you leave the classroom.

Your first day of class was probably fairly similar to this hypothetical account. Even if you and your classmates had never seen your sociology professor before and were uncertain about what to expect in a sociology class, that first day of class probably went smoothly. But why do occasions such as this one generally follow predictable patterns, even when the people involved have never met?

To put this question a different way, why do people understand the norms, the implicit rules and expectations, of different social settings (classroom, workplace, concert hall, dinner table)? How did you know what to do when you entered the classroom? Why did you sit in a chair facing the front of the room instead of the one facing the back? Why didn't *you* write your name on the blackboard? Why did you stop talking when the woman looked at the class? ■

As you may recall from Chapter 1, a basic insight of sociology is that there are patterns to social life. These *recurring patterns of behavior* make up what sociologists call **social structure.** You knew what to do on the first day of class because you are familiar with the social structure of the classroom. In fact, you probably know it so well that you don't even have to think about it. You sat in one of the chairs facing the front because that's where students sit. And you probably never considered writing your name on the board because you know that such behavior would violate basic expectations of how a classroom operates. In other words, your behavior on that first day of class was constrained by your understanding of the social structure of the classroom.

That same social structure allowed the class to function in the first place. Since students and the professor knew what was expected of them, they were able to accomplish the task at hand. Structure, then, constrains social behavior by putting limits on it, but it also enables social behavior by providing a context within which people can interact. At the same time, you had plenty of room to maneuver within this structure. You chose where to sit and how much, if at all, to pay attention to your instructor, take notes, and ask questions. You could have chosen to violate classroom expectations by arriving late, interrupting the professor, or texting your friends. Although the social structure of the classroom certainly shaped how you behaved, you still had the capacity for **action,** *the ability to operate independent of social constraints,* whether or not such action conformed to classroom expectations.

The concepts of structure and action can help us to understand the dynamic relationship between well-established patterns of behavior and the human capacity to act in new and sometimes unexpected ways. The concept of structure allows us to analyze the patterns and regularities in social life. At the same time, we are not just pawns playing out predetermined roles within the context of social structure. Although social structure shapes our behavior, expectations, and beliefs, it does not fully determine them.

This chapter begins with a discussion of the important concept of structure, including the various levels at which we can analyze social structure. We then turn to a discussion of action, focusing on the ways in which people act in different social contexts. Finally, we conclude the chapter by examining the changing structure of news production in the digital age.

Understanding Social Structure

We all know a great deal about the social structure of the various communities in which we live. As we discuss in Chapter 6, we acquire this knowledge as part of the process of socialization through which we learn our culture's basic norms, values, beliefs, and behaviors. That's why you knew what to do on the first day of class; you knew the basic rules and expectations—the patterns—of the classroom. If you think about it, you can probably begin to define the structure of your family, your neighborhood, your work place, or your school. What are the unspoken agreements about people's obligations and responsibilities, who regularly talks with whom, and how are decisions made? When you can identify these kinds of patterns, you are well on your way to understanding social structure.

Seeing Social Structure

Social structure is invisible—we cannot see it with the naked eye. But with a little knowledge of what to look for, we can map the contours of social structure in different social settings. At the micro level, we might look at the structure of interaction between two people or within small groups. At the meso level, we might look at the structure of an organization such as a school or a business. At the macro level, we might focus on the structure of inequality between developing and industrialized nations. In all these cases, we have two interconnected goals: to describe underlying patterns and to make connections between these patterns and people's actions and beliefs. Thinking sociologically helps you to see both how social structure shapes everyday life as well as how individual actions help to shape social structure.

If we cannot touch it or see it, though, how can we be confident that social structure is real? For one thing, a vast amount of research shows that social life is made up of patterned, routine behaviors. These routines can change, but they tend to be enduring. These more or less predictable routines are the heart of what sociologists call **social institutions,** *the major arenas of social life in which durable routines and patterns of behavior take place.* Social institutions include government, schools, businesses, and religious institutions, among others. We explore these social institutions in Chapters 12–17 of this book.

Thinking about what life would be like without it can help us to "see" social structure. Daily life would be full of uncertainty: you would not know what to expect or how to meet your ordinary human needs for food, clothing, and shelter. When Hurricane Katrina struck New Orleans in August 2005,

---

thinking about structure

Can you see patterns associated with economic inequality, racial discrimination, and sexism when you encounter it? In Chapters 9, 10, and 11, we explore the **structure** of inequality in relation to class, race, and gender.

When the social structure is disrupted, we become keenly aware of its existence. In the aftermath of Hurricane Katrina in late August 2005, residents of New Orleans and nearby areas had to grapple with the absence of clear rules and norms. Some took it upon themselves to create their own rules. Others used their own resources to help rescue neighbors.

the routine patterns of social life in that city were thrown into disarray (Clarke 2006; Lukes 2006). When the levees failed, streets turned into rivers, rooftops became shelter, and residents found that they were refugees in their own city.

During those frightening days, the social structure in the city seemed to collapse temporarily. Tens of thousands of people sought refuge in the New Orleans Superdome and the city's convention center. Because they did not form an established community, the people gathered in these buildings had little shared understanding of how to arrange for privacy and security or how to distribute scarce supplies. The normal patterns of authority were disrupted because officials—including the local police, the mayor of New Orleans, the governor of Louisiana, and the Federal Emergency Management Agency—did not have a clear understanding of what had happened or how to respond. Social norms were suspended: Was stealing food or batteries from a store allowable in an emergency? Was it all right to break in to an empty house for shelter? Even normally mundane patterns of behavior, such as personal hygiene, had to be reinvented as residents struggled to find bathroom facilities, clean water, and clean clothes.

Let's return to the classroom example that opened this chapter. What would school be like if students and teachers were required to start each class from scratch every day? When would you arrive and where would you sit? Who would speak and when would they speak? How would each person prepare for class, and who would lead it? Would there even be any school? Without set patterns of behavior, each day would involve new negotiations about what to do and how to behave, with little time left to accomplish much. Fortunately, most of our day-to-day interactions follow more or less patterned scripts. The total of all these patterns is what we mean by social structure. As the Sociology Works box shows, the ability to understand social structure can be of great practical value, sometimes in unexpected ways.

Creating and Changing Social Structure

We usually experience social structure as solid and unchanging: patterns of everyday life that seem permanent, natural, and inevitable. As *individuals* we cannot change these patterns—you couldn't simply decide that the correct dress code for a formal dinner is a bathing suit. But sociological insight shows that the patterns that make up social structure are *not* natural, unchanging, or inevitable. Instead, they are the result of human action, and humans can therefore change them. People who came before us established these patterns, and by our actions and choices we can help to reproduce—or potentially alter—them.

For example, by attending a conventional class as part of your daily routine, you help to reproduce the current structure of the college classroom. However, when students and teachers experiment with different classroom structures—with, for example, students as co-teachers, small-group learning exercises, or collaborative student-faculty projects—they are taking part in a process that might create new expectations and different patterns of behavior.

In addition, social structures vary over time and from one culture to another. In fact, one of the best ways to understand the structure of a society is to compare it to other societies or other time periods.

The social structure of childcare, for example, differs radically among cultures. Take diapers. Virtually all parents in the United States diaper their newborn babies, changing their diapers several times a day until the children are toilet-trained, commonly between the ages of two and three. Whether they use cloth or disposable diapers, American parents expect babies to wear diapers and consider them to be a necessity. However, most babies in the world do not wear diapers—and they never have. Instead, babies and toddlers commonly go naked from

Brian Reed and the Hunt for Saddam Hussein

Stationed in Iraq from March 2003 to March 2004, where he served as operations officer in the 1st Brigade, 4th Infantry Division, sociologist Brian Reed found a number of ways to apply his sociological training. One of the most dramatic came in December 2003, when Reed used his knowledge of social structure to help plan the military operation that led to the capture of deposed Iraqi leader Saddam Hussein. Reed analyzed the structure of Hussein's social networks, building what he calls "link diagrams" to illustrate the ties among all the people in the network (Hougham 2005; Reed and Segal 2006). Link diagrams are, in essence, visual maps of social structure, emphasizing connections and communications among people. In this case, they led the U.S. military to individuals who ultimately helped them find the former dictator.

Reed believes that the sociological imagination has valuable military applications, and he advocates training in sociology for all military officers. Social structure is a particularly important sociological concept for soldiers to understand. When American soldiers are stationed abroad, in unfamiliar situations, they have little knowledge of the traditions, assumptions, and daily routines of the local population. What these soldiers need, Reed points out, is training in the social structure of the societies where they are deployed so that they can better understand both allies and enemies.

During the Vietnam War, the U.S. military had a very limited understanding of the routines and patterns—the social structure—of Vietnamese society. Hundreds of thousands of U.S. soldiers fought in Vietnam, but most lacked even a rudimentary understanding of Vietnamese language, culture, or history or of the patterns that structure everyday life in Vietnam. More recently, U.S. soldiers in Afghanistan and Iraq have struggled with a similar lack of familiarity with local society. For example, Reed described the challenges in establishing a joint operation by the U.S. military police and the Iraqi national police. Standard U.S. military procedures do not fit daily routines in Iraq, which include frequent calls to prayer and a generally slower pace of life. In these kinds of joint operations, the ability to understand local social structure, Reed has noted, becomes an essential skill.

Knowledge of social structure can also be useful in planning military strategy. During his time in Iraq, Reed used sociological tools to understand the connections among various opposition forces and to determine the social structure of the Iraqi insurgency. In a congressional briefing after his return to the United States, Reed pointed out several ways in which sociological tools were helpful. For example, identifying the structure of insurgent forces gives military commanders practical information on the organization and tendencies of these groups. It also helps commanders make informed predictions about how these forces will respond on the battlefield.

Brian Reed

"Sociology applies to all facets of my profession.... Leadership, relationships, culture, diversity, and social networks are just a handful of relevant topics applicable to me as a professional soldier, and are all areas enhanced by my sociology training."

think about it

1. *How might an understanding of social structure be useful in averting war or other types of conflict?*
2. *In what other contexts would the kind of link diagrams Reed describes be useful?*

---

the waist down or wear open-crotch split pants. The structure of parenting in societies where babies do not wear diapers is different from the structure of parenting in the United States. Meredith Small, who studies cross-cultural parenting practices, explains that children in diaper-less societies are almost always physically connected to a caregiving adult: "With bare bottoms, they ride on the hip or back and it's easy to feel when they need to go" (Small 2005, A23).

To see how social structures vary over time within the same culture, consider gender expectations. The experiences of women and men in the United States in the early twenty-first century are far different from those of the mid-twentieth century. Opportunities for women were significantly more limited at that time than they are today. As recently as the early 1960s, most middle-class American women were expected to marry young, change their last names, have children, and focus their attention on their families and households. Men played a very limited role in childrearing but were expected to support the family. Bank accounts and home deeds were generally issued in the name of the male breadwinner. Childcare centers and parental leave from work were virtually nonexistent. Women who did work outside the home were likely to face significant discrimination in the workplace.

Now fast-forward fifty years to the early twenty-first century. Expectations for both men and women have changed substantially. Although many women work at home to care for children, most women in the United States now work outside the home, and men are likely to play an active role in raising children and doing domestic chores. Women who attend college are likely to share the career ambitions of their male classmates.

In short, the expected patterns of beliefs and behavior associated with gender in the United States (that is, the structure of gender) have changed significantly. What seemed natural and inevitable a generation or two ago now seems artificial and outdated, as we discuss further in Chapter 11.

This change occurred through the cumulative actions of many individuals—sometimes acting by themselves and sometimes acting collectively. Once again we see the dynamic relationship between structure and action: human action creates structure, but that structure then shapes subsequent action. Future action will reaffirm, modify, or radically change existing social structures. Understanding this interplay of structure and action is central to the sociological perspective.

Statuses and Roles: Connecting Everyday Life and Social Structure

Social structure is rooted in the everyday activity of individuals in a society. Sociologists use two key concepts—status and role—to help understand what links people to one another and to the patterns that constitute social structure. For sociologists, **status** refers to *a position in a social system that can be occupied by an individual.* We all occupy various statuses, or social positions. For example, you are a student, and you may also be a daughter or son, a classmate, an employee, a roommate, an athlete, or a musician.

A status can be either ascribed or achieved. **Ascribed statuses** are *those that are assigned to us from birth, regardless of our wishes or abilities.* **Achieved statuses** are *those that we attain voluntarily, to a considerable degree, as the result of our own efforts.* For example, in England at the end of the first decade of the twenty-first century, Prince Charles and his son William both occupied the *ascribed* status of member of the royal family and heir to the throne; in the United States, Barack Obama held the *achieved* status of president. He also occupied the *ascribed* racial status of African American.

In contrast, **roles** are *the sets of expected behaviors associated with particular statuses.* For example, the basic role of someone occupying the student status is to attend class, complete assignments, and show a certain measure of respect for teachers and other students. One reason you know what to do on the first day of class is that you are familiar with the student

role. After all, by the time you enter college, you've had many years to learn it.

To see how structure shapes your behavior and sense of self, think about how easily you adopt specific roles in different social situations. Figure 4.1 illustrates a few common statuses and the groups and social institutions associated with them. Your status as student and the role you are expected to play in this position connects you to the social institution of schools and education. You occupy a variety of statuses in relation to your family—sibling, son or daughter, perhaps parent—and perform a variety of associated roles. As you perform these and other roles, they embed you within social institutions and social structures. The statuses you occupy and the roles you play are your concrete connections to society.

Roles shape your life by clarifying what is expected of you in different contexts. Members of a social group share similar expectations about each member's role so that as individuals interact, their roles are reinforced. To varying degrees, you internalize the components of your roles. Indeed, some roles become so comfortable that you hardly perceive the ways in which they constrain your actions. In fact, roles become part of your sense of self. You would say, "I am a student," not "I play the role of a student."

When you adopt a new role, however, you can be acutely aware of the pressures it places on you. Think about how it feels

FIGURE 4.1 | STATUSES, ROLES, AND INSTITUTIONS
People occupy various statuses and play a variety of different roles that connect them to social groups and larger institutions. What statuses do you occupy and what roles do you play?

to start a job, for example. During the first few days, the expectations associated with your newly occupied status are likely to be unclear or even confusing. Eventually, though, by following instructions, watching other employees, and getting feedback on your own efforts, you learn your role.

The concept of a role explains how an individual's behavior conforms to a general pattern yet is capable of change as a result of social forces. The expectations associated with a role are not rigid, nor do they dictate specific behaviors. The student role, for example, permits a range of behavior. You can probably miss a class once in a while. You might be less attentive in class some days and more obviously engaged on other days. Some students ask a lot of questions whereas others tend to remain silent in class. However, there are limits. If you violate basic norms of the student role by, say, neglecting to do assigned readings or not studying before an exam, you will eventually be unable to perform your role adequately. And if you turn in a plagiarized paper or fail to attend class at all, your behavior may temporarily or even permanently remove you from student status.

Roles change over time, as we saw earlier in the case of gender roles. The parent role has also changed significantly during the past fifty years. If you have grandparents or neighbors in their seventies or eighties, they can tell you what it was like to be parents in the 1960s and 1970s, when many mothers worked in the home. As the number of single-parent households and two-career families has increased, parents have adapted to the changing structure of work. Many working parents now outsource much of the day-to-day caretaking of small children, either in childcare centers, with relatives, or with in-home caregivers. In middle-class families, children's time is often scheduled so heavily that parents find it is part of their role to shuttle their children from one activity to the next. As a result of these changes, the definition of what it means to be a "good parent" and what children, employers, and schools expect from parents has begun to change, as well (Nelson 2010).

Because they connect us to social institutions such as the family, school, and work on a micro level, statuses and roles are key to understanding the way people interact in groups and organizations, and we explore them in more detail in Chapter 7. As the concepts of ascribed and achieved status suggest, however, statuses and roles are also involved in the way structure intersects with power at the micro, meso, and macro levels to produce inequality (for example, compare the status of a corporate CEO to that of a migrant farm worker or the status of a sociology professor to that of a sociology student). For this reason, we visit these concepts again in Chapter 5, on power.

Structure is pervasive throughout social life at the micro, meso, and macro levels. Let's examine each level in turn.

Micro-level Interaction: Finding Patterns

In Chapter 3 we defined *society* as a group of people who live together in a specific territory and share a culture. As the pioneering German sociologist Georg Simmel (1858–1918) explained, those people regularly interact with each other in ways that form patterns. These patterns of interaction endure over time, becoming so routine that they seem to take on their own existence independent of the individuals who create them. For Simmel (1964), these face-to-face, micro-level interactions are the building blocks that shape a society. Two methods sociologists use to examine micro-level social interactions are ethnomethodology and conversation analysis.

Ethnomethodology

Think of your daily routines. With whom do you interact after you wake up in the morning? How do you get to school or work and with whom do you interact on the way? With whom do you interact during your day and in what way? In the evening? Sociologists analyze social structure at the micro level by focusing on the patterns and regularities that emerge from such routine daily activities. Some sociologists contend that we construct social structure on a regular basis, working with others collectively to make sense of the chaotic social world that confronts us every day (Garfinkel 1967). **Ethnomethodology,** *an approach that examines the methods people use to make sense of their daily activities, emphasizes the ways in which we collectively create social structure in our everyday activities.* Ethnomethodologists believe that social structure exists precisely because we are constantly creating it as we construct and reconstruct social order in our daily routines.

Harold Garfinkel (1917–2011) and his colleagues sought to reveal these micro-level social structures through **breaching experiments,** *controlled social situations in which the individuals involved intentionally break social rules, violating basic norms and patterns of behavior.* By breaking rules to which we generally don't pay much attention until they are violated, breaching experiments provide creative and often humorous illustrations of micro-level social structure. For example, Garfinkel once had his students act like visitors rather than family members when they returned to their parents' homes during a school vacation. The students quickly identified underlying patterns of behavior between parents and children as their parents reacted to their children's strange—and surprisingly polite—behavior. In another study, Garfinkel had researchers at a grocery store take items out of other people's shopping carts. When puzzled shoppers confronted them, the researchers responded that it was more convenient simply to take items from another shopper's cart than to search the crowded store shelves. Shoppers were surprised by and sometimes angry at this behavior—expecting an apology as well as an explanation for it—revealing a widespread understanding that items "belong" to a shopper once they've been placed in a cart, even though the shopper has not yet purchased them.

SPOTLIGHT
on social theory

Ethnomethodology emphasizes the daily activity through which we construct and reconstruct social structure. What aspects of your daily life are ruled by patterns of behavior that you simply follow without thinking about them? How might you reveal those patterns?

As these examples show, by violating everyday social norms, breaching experiments expose the unstated social rules that structure countless aspects of social life but that are often visible only when they are broken.

Conversation Analysis

Another micro-level approach to social structure focuses on the ways we talk to one another—the structure of talk. **Conversation analysis** is *a method of analyzing the patterns in face-to-face conversation that produce the smooth, back-and-forth turn-taking of such exchanges.* All talk is organized and ordered—from informal conversations among friends to more formal types of communication, such as a consultation between a doctor and a patient. In other words, conversation has an underlying structure. Even if you are not consciously aware of how talk is organized, you probably adhere to a set of widely shared assumptions about the give-and-take of conversation—assumptions that may differ from one social setting to another.

For example, think about conversations you may have had recently with a family member, one of your professors, and a manager during a job interview. Each conversation no doubt had a different structure. You are so familiar with the structure of talk in different settings that you can quickly shift gears from freewheeling banter with friends to intimate conversation with a romantic partner to classroom discussion mode. You can do this because talk is not a random activity but is instead rooted in a set of patterns—what we call structure—that generally do not have to be articulated.

Sociologists use conversation analysis to examine the underlying structure of social interaction. For example, as you approach a classmate on campus, you might ask a question like "How's it going?" Both of you know, however, that you are not asking for a substantive reply about how your classmate is feeling. Your question is more like a polite greeting. Were you to pause to give a full and honest reply each time an acquaintance asked you, "How's it going?" you would be violating a basic expectation of casual conversation. Of course, in other social settings—at a funeral or in a hospital, for example—the same question becomes a sincere expression of concern, and the questioner expects a full reply. You can navigate these different situations because you and the people you are speaking with know the patterns and expectations of interaction in different social settings.

In an interesting use of conversation analysis, sociologists Steven Clayman and John Heritage (2002) showed that news interviews share a similar structure, even though each program has a different host, guests, audience, and set of topics. No matter what the host and guest talk about, the basic routines and patterns are similar. For example, news interviews follow a specific turn-taking process that is different from everyday conversation. The interviewer asks questions, and the guest is expected to respond to those specific questions. In addition, news interviews are produced for what Clayman and Heritage call "an overhearing audience," and the interview is conducted by a host who maintains a neutral position. Furthermore, the host (interviewer), the guest (interviewee), and the audience are well aware of these patterns and routines. The structure of the news interview constrains the behavior of both interviewer and interviewee and shapes the expectations of their audience.

Patterns of talk are not the same in different social settings. How is the structure of talk different when you are hanging out with your friends compared to when you are conversing with your doctor?

Several years ago, however, Jon Stewart of Comedy Central's *The Daily Show* violated these norms. He turned the tables on Tucker Carlson and Paul Begala, the hosts of the CNN interview show *Crossfire,* when he started asking *them* questions about their program, something guests on a news program rarely do:

PAUL BEGALA: He's either the funniest smart guy on TV or the smartest funnyman. We'll find out which in a minute. But he's certainly an Emmy Award winner, the host of Comedy Central's *Daily Show* and the coauthor of the new mega best-seller *America (The Book): A Citizen's Guide to Democracy Inaction,* at your bookstores everywhere.

Ladies and gentlemen, welcome to the CROSSFIRE Jon Stewart.

JON STEWART: Thank you.

TUCKER CARLSON: Thank you for joining us.

STEWART: Thank you very much. That was very kind of you to say. Can I say something very quickly? Why do we have to fight?

. . .

STEWART: Why do you argue, the two of you?

(LAUGHTER)

STEWART: I hate to see it.

CARLSON: We enjoy it.

STEWART: Let me ask you a question.

CARLSON: Well, let me ask you a question first.

Jon Stewart's memorable appearance on *Crossfire* revealed the hidden structure in the conventions of talk-show interviews. A **convention** is *a practice or technique that is widely used in a particular social setting.* For example, you probably know the conventions associated with a job interview, even if you've never been on one. And you know the conventions associated with standing in a line at a store or fast-food restaurant (even if you find all the waiting frustrating). You quickly learn new conventions as you become connected to new social worlds. If, for example, you were to go to a "speed dating" event—where singles meet and talk with a dozen or more potential dates in quick, five to ten minute conversations—or you were called to testify in a courtroom, you would quickly see how the conventions of talk operate in that particular setting.

Meso-level Social Structure

Conducting breaching experiments and analyzing conversations can reveal a great deal about patterns of behavior among individuals. By shifting our analysis to the meso level, however, we can examine how structure works in organizations.

Jon Stewart's appearance on CNN's series *Crossfire* in October 2004 became a big story because Stewart violated some of the basic rules of the news interview: he criticized the hosts of the show and began asking questions of them.

Organizations and Structure

We all live in and around a vast array of organizations, large and small, from households, schools, and businesses to workplaces, government agencies, and media organizations. The sociological perspective helps us to understand how organizational structure shapes our lives and how our daily activities help us to negotiate, reaffirm, and sometimes revise this structure. **Organizational structure** refers to *the rules and routines, both formal and informal, that shape daily activity within organizations.* If you think about the structures of the different organizations you deal with or know about, you will probably think of the various roles people play in these settings and the norms and expectations of different groups. For example, the structure of your school includes the roles played by administrators, custodial and maintenance staff, professors, and students. Each group has specific norms and expectations associated with a specific role.

Examples of formal rules include codes of conduct and job descriptions. Informal rules and routines include agreements among groups of employees about how best to share office space or computers, the allotment of cooking and cleaning chores among family members, and the regular but unstated ways that students and faculty communicate with one another. As the Through a Sociological Lens box on page 94 shows, one aspect of organizational structure—the way that information flows within the organization—can sometimes be a matter of life or death.

Structure and Communication Within Organizations

By paying attention to organizational structure, we can gain fresh insight into unlikely occurrences. Consider the two space shuttle tragedies: the postlaunch explosion of the shuttle

Looking at Organizational Structure and School Violence

I n 1999 at Columbine High School in Littleton, Colorado, two teenage boys shot and killed twelve students and a teacher and injured more than twenty others before turning their weapons on themselves. Since that deadly incident, school violence has been an issue of national concern. The scale of the attack at Columbine made it, at the time, the worst incident of school violence in American history. But Columbine was only the deadliest of the more than two-dozen school shootings that took place in the United States in the 1990s and early 2000s. In 2007, a twenty-three-year-old student shot and killed two students in a dormitory and thirty more people in a classroom at Virginia Tech before killing himself, an incident even deadlier than Columbine that raised new concerns about guns and violence on college campuses.

As school officials, survivors, and victims' families have struggled to explain such incidents, one question lingers: Why didn't anyone see warning signs that these students were preparing to kill their classmates? After each incident, community members seek to understand how students could commit such terrible crimes.

The concept of organizational structure can help us better understand why those who perpetrate school violence so often escape the notice of school officials until they commit their deadly acts. Sociologist Katherine Newman and her graduate students traveled to two communities that experienced school shootings in the late 1990s—Jonesboro, Arkansas, and West Paducah, Kentucky—where they talked with teachers, parents, and students in the local communities.

In both cases, Newman (2004) found that there were plenty of warning signs that the students who shot their classmates were troubled—including violent writings, threats to classmates, prior disciplinary problems, and mistreatment of animals—but teachers and school officials systematically missed or misread these danger signals. The cause, according to Newman, was a communication problem that she calls "information loss" that resulted from the organizational structure of the schools.

As we have noted, *organizational structure* refers to the routines that shape the daily activity within an organization. Standard routines and practices in schools that promote information loss help to explain why teachers and school officials often do not recognize troubled students. For example, since school officials commonly believe that students transferring or advancing from one school to another should have the chance to make a fresh start, disciplinary records do not follow students from one school to the next. As a result, a middle school principal usually does not share information about a troubled student with a high school principal. Similarly, strict boundaries between school and community generally prevent school officials from learning of disciplinary or criminal incidents that happen outside of school. In addition, teachers in most middle schools and high schools see the students for only about forty-five minutes each day, and few teachers get to know students outside of the classroom. All these factors contribute to a situation in which information about troubled students is fragmented, with any one individual learning only pieces of a larger story.

Given the organizational structure of schools, the depth of a student's alienation and anger often gets lost in the boundaries that limit communication. Therefore, these students commonly go unnoticed until they commit a disruptive and violent act. By determining how the organizational structure of a typical school contributes to information loss about troubled kids, experts can suggest ways to restructure the flow of information so that students with severe emotional problems are less likely to fall through the cracks.

think about it

1. *Do you think that the organizational structure of your high school could produce the kind of information loss Newman uncovered in her research? Explain why or why not.*

2. *What do you think schools and communities can do to share information more fully in an effort to prevent school violence? Is it possible to restructure the flow of information without encroaching on the privacy of students and families?*

Challenger in 1986 and the disintegration during reentry into earth's atmosphere of the shuttle *Columbia* in 2003. In each case, NASA engineers were able to pinpoint the specific technical problem that caused the fatal accident: an o-ring failure for *Challenger* and foam debris for *Columbia*. Identifying the source of the problem is only part of the picture, however. That's because, as sociologist Diane Vaughan (1996, 2003) shows in her meticulous research, NASA engineers were well aware of the technical problems that caused the shuttle accidents. What needs explaining, then, is how and why NASA proceeded with the launch of each of these space shuttles, even though safety problems in both cases were well known.

This issue is far more complex than it may seem initially. Vaughan shows that people in NASA's chain of command adhered to safety rules and followed appropriate procedures as they certified that each shuttle was ready for launch. In both cases, NASA engineers discussed potential hazards and officially defined them as acceptable risks, following standard operating procedure. Instead of looking for rule violations, then, Vaughan explains that we can learn a great deal about the roots of the space shuttle disasters by looking at NASA's organizational structure. In both cases, NASA's complex and hierarchical organization prevented detailed knowledge of the risk from making its way to those ultimately responsible for authorizing the launch.

Instead of an organization that promoted free-flowing communication between the engineers and managers stationed at various locations, Vaughan describes an organization in which people had limited opportunities to voice their concerns, in which it was difficult to contradict one's senior colleagues in public, and in which hunches or other concerns not supported by scientific evidence were excluded from the flight-readiness review process. These factors add up to a pattern that Vaughan labels "structural secrecy," the result of an organizational structure that undermined communication within NASA and effectively concealed the seriousness of known safety problems. In her written comments on the disintegration of *Columbia,* seventeen years after the *Challenger* case she had studied so thoroughly, Vaughan (2003) notes that "the structure of NASA's Shuttle Program blocked the flow of critical information up the hierarchy, so definitions of risk continued unaltered" (p. 197).

More recently, Toyota Motor Corporation made headlines leading to congressional hearings when it ran into difficulty in managing a growing safety problem with the sudden acceleration of some of its car and truck models. As it turned out, this problem was made worse by the company's disjointed organizational structure. Rather than having a single headquarters for all Toyota operations in the United States (the largest market for its vehicles), Toyota requires each U.S. subsidiary to report directly to its global headquarters in Japan. This meant that each U.S. division communicated directly with company leaders in Japan—but not with other Toyota officials in the United States. As a result, the subsidiaries did not share information with each other about the extent of the accelerator problem or confer about potential solutions for it. Limited communication between the U.S. subsidiaries hampered efforts to coordinate a unified response to the initial reports of accelerator problems and delayed comprehensive reporting of the developing problem to government safety regulators. According to Robert Bea, a professor of engineering at the University of California, Berkeley, who studied the Toyota case with his graduate students, Toyota's organizational problems "are similar to those that allowed NASA and the Army Corps of Engineers to ignore structural issues leading to the *Columbia* space shuttle and Hurricane Katrina disasters" (Vartabedian and Bensinger 2010).

The examples of NASA and Toyota demonstrate how organizational structures shape communication patterns and the flow of information. Understanding organizational structure can give us insight into the decision-making process, illuminating the sociological roots of disasters and accidents that we often attribute solely to individual mistakes.

Macro-level Social Structure

At the macro level, we can see social structure in the broad patterns of behavior in a society. At this level of analysis, sociologists often draw on the functionalist perspective to focus especially on how institutions, such as the family, the economy, government, education, and religion, are interrelated. As explained in Chapter 1, this perspective, which dominated American sociological analysis for much of the twentieth century, views society as a set of interdependent structures, each of which makes a specific contribution—serves a function—in maintaining social order.

Structure, Function, and the Interrelationships Among Social Institutions

Sociologists using functional analysis generally assume that social structures have functions that meet the needs of the broader society. For a society to survive, its structures and institutions must continue to meet those needs. At the center of functional analysis is the concept of *equilibrium,* the balance among various structures that maintains social stability. If one part of a society changes, other parts will need to adjust to restore equilibrium.

Functionalists generally focus on broad, macro-level questions, seeking to understand how the various parts of a society work together and what role different structures play in social life (Parsons 1951). Talcott Parsons (1902–1979), one of the leading American sociologists in the middle of the twentieth century and a pioneer of functionalist theory, was particularly interested in questions of **social integration,** that is, *the process by which values and social structures bind people together within a society.*

Consider the functions of work, for example (discussed in detail in Chapter 13). Adults under the age of sixty-five are generally expected to work, either for pay outside the home or doing housework and caring for children inside the home. The economic functions of work are straightforward: jobs provide people with money to pay their bills; at the same time, the labor force produces valuable goods and services for the society as a whole. But what are the social functions of work? What part does work play in reinforcing social integration? How is the structure of work connected to other social institutions—family or education, for example—and how do changes in family structure or educational structure affect the structure of work? These are the kinds of questions that a functional analysis encourages us to explore.

Perhaps you can begin to answer some of these questions yourself. What are the social functions of work? Jobs provide daily routines that lend stability and predictability to life. A person with a job knows what to expect each day. Work also nurtures a sense of responsibility and the ability to get along with others—connecting workers with others in their community. Further, work helps to teach people self-discipline, and working adults are better able to teach their children the values of effort and self-discipline by the example they set than are those who are unemployed. Finally, work helps to define leisure: what would *vacation* mean if you did not have work or school from which to take a break?

Analyzing the structure of work can also give us insight into the way people in a given society experience time. For example, the terms "rush hour" and "prime time television" are meaningful because of their relationship to standard work patterns. City transit authorities schedule more trains and buses at times that are convenient for people whose jobs follow the traditional 9 a.m. to 5 p.m. workday. Prime-time television—the time between 8:00 and 11:00 p.m. during which networks and cable channels schedule the shows they hope will attract the largest audience—is the period when large numbers of the viewing public are at home, having completed the workday. In Europe, August is vacation time, and many people take a break of up to four weeks from work during that month. Since the August holiday is so common, many Europeans are surprised to learn that American employers commonly permit only two weeks

of vacation per year, and often the two weeks cannot be taken consecutively.

Functionalists further point out that because social institutions are interdependent, the equilibrium among them is precarious. As a result, change in one institution will lead to change in others. For example, as the number of jobs that require higher education and training has increased, colleges and universities have expanded to meet the demand. As incomes have stagnated, leaving people struggling to keep up with the cost of living, the number of two-wage-earner families has increased. And because technology has made telecommuting feasible, more and more people work from home rather than travel to an office every day.

SPOTLIGHT
on social theory

Functionalists argue that institutions serve specific functions that help maintain social stability. In the text, we explore some of the social functions of work. Consider some other institution important to you—education, religion, or the family, for example—and evaluate its structural role in reinforcing social integration.

Even a brief inventory of how work has changed within the past few decades, then, raises important questions about interrelated institutions such as family and school. For example, how have high school curriculums changed in response to new technology-oriented jobs and the new skills necessary to qualify for them? How has family life adapted to the changing structure of work? What impact does the lack of work—widespread and persistent unemployment—have on social integration?

William Julius Wilson investigates this last question in his book *When Work Disappears* (1996), a study of the effect of persistent unemployment on poor, urban communities. Using aspects of a functional perspective, he explores what happens to the hopes and dreams of adults and children, to their family life, and to their schools, when the majority of adults in a neighborhood do not have jobs. Wilson argues that the disappearance of jobs is the root cause of chronic poverty, crime, drugs, and gang violence in poor neighborhoods.

Just because a social structure or institution exists, however, doesn't mean that it serves a positive function. Talcott Parsons was criticized widely for his view, typical of the mid-twentieth century, that the traditional separation of gender roles in the family—with the woman as the homemaker and the man as the breadwinner—was functional (Parsons 1949). As feminist theorists have pointed out, rigid gender distinctions constrain both women and men, although in gender-specific ways. For example, traditional gender roles discourage women from contributing to society outside of the home and limit men's ability to take time away from work for parenting responsibilities. Parsons's perspective failed to take into account the negative impact of this structure.

In some cases, therefore, specific structures have negative functions: they are dysfunctional. Other dysfunctional aspects of American society have included slavery and racial dis-

---

thinking about structure
In what ways has your family changed in response to changes in the workplace
or in another institution?

crimination. In parts of the Muslim world, the subjugation of women might be considered dysfunctional in the same way. To analyze how a structure functions in society, therefore, we need to pay attention to who benefits from it and who might be harmed. This sort of approach, as we see in Chapter 5, involves paying attention to issues of power and inequality.

Globalization and the Structure of Work

For many people in the United States, globalization has changed the structure of their work life and their communities dramatically. Perhaps the most significant change has been the decline in manufacturing in the United States. Over the past thirty years, manufacturing jobs have been exported to other countries, closing factories that once offered good-paying jobs, health insurance, and pensions to workers without college educations. The shift of these jobs to lower-wage countries is part of what some analysts call the deindustrialization of America (Bluestone and Harrison 1982; Cowie and Heathcott 2003).

The story of the clothing industry is a good example. A half-century ago, the vast majority of the clothes Americans wore were made in the United States. However, if you take a look at the label in the t-shirt or blouse you are wearing today, you will see that it almost certainly was made outside the United States—in Honduras or Indonesia, for example—by workers who were paid a fraction of what Americans workers expect to be paid. (For a discussion of the return of apparel industry sweatshops in the United States, see the Sociology Matters box on page 98.) Because of low wages, cheap transportation, and improved technology, manufacturers save money by making clothing outside the United States. For similar reasons, many of your possessions—your shoes and accessories, games and electronics, furniture and housewares—were probably made outside the United States.

How has the migration of jobs overseas—a key aspect of globalization—affected the structure of work for U.S. employees? First, of course, it has meant the loss of millions of manufacturing jobs, disrupting longstanding employment patterns. In the late twentieth century, millions of Americans lost their jobs and were forced to find new work, often moving to other cities or states to do so. Unlike many workers in the mid-twentieth century, people could no longer expect to work for the same company or live in the same community that their parents did. Just as important, they could no longer expect to work in the same job or for the same company for their entire adult life.

Second, the loss of these jobs ended a period of stable, long-term employment with good pay and benefits, the work situation for many Americans in the post–World War II period. In its place are newer types of employment—such as retail salespersons, cashiers, food preparers, and waiters (the four largest occupations in the United States in 2009) (U.S. Bureau of Labor Statistics 2010c). Many of these jobs tend to pay lower wages and lack many of the benefits of a manufacturing job, such as health insurance and a retirement plan. As a result, an increasing number of Americans need more than one job to make ends meet.

Third, the loss of manufacturing jobs can have a devastating impact on an entire community. Kathryn Marie Dudley (1997) documented the impact on Kenosha, Wisconsin, when Chrysler closed its automobile assembly plant there and nearly 6,000 people lost their jobs. In her study, Dudley paid special attention to the dilemma faced by workers who had always labored with their hands but who now had to try to compete for jobs that require other types of skills. She also examined the impact of the shutdown on Kenosha's small businesses, civic associations, schools, and places of worship—all of which depended on a stable and prosperous community for customers, volunteers, and congregation members.

Fourth, when a wage earner shifts to lower-paying work, a family is more likely to need two incomes to pay the bills, producing significant strain on life at home. When parents spend more time at work, they have less time for raising children and community activities (Newman 1988).

Beth Rubin (1996, 4) argues that, in addition to changing the nature of work in the United States, globalization has changed the social norms and expectations associated with our jobs. She characterizes this change as a shift in the social contract, the collective understanding about rights and responsibilities—in this case between companies and employees—within society. In manufacturing plants in the 1950s and 1960s, there was an unwritten understanding that if you did your job well, you would likely be employed for life. Employers were responsible for providing wages and benefits that allowed workers to enjoy a decent standard of living. In turn, workers remained loyal to their employers, with families working at the same plant for multiple generations. These norms and expectations have virtually disappeared in today's new economy. Instead, many of today's employees have a grudging understanding that their employment is fleeting and temporary, that flexibility and change are inevitable, and that they must look out for themselves. Loyalty to a company can seem misguided in such a climate. Thus a change in social norms has accompanied the structural change that has characterized the new global economy (Sennett 2000).

How Structures Change: Action

So far in this chapter, we have considered the ways in which social structure operates at every level of our social world and how it shapes our social lives at the micro, meso, and macro

SOCIOLOGY Matters

Working to Eliminate Sweatshop Labor

Clark University sociologist Bob Ross began studying sweatshop labor in the early 1980s, and he published one of the first articles about the reemergence of sweatshop conditions in the garment industry in the United States. In his research, Ross highlighted the growth in New York City sweatshops, in which people worked long hours making clothing for extremely low wages, often in unsafe conditions (Ross and Trachte 1983). But Ross's research was not widely read outside of academic circles.

Fast forward to the 2000s. Bob Ross's research, especially his book *Slaves to Fashion* (2004), is now required reading for a growing student movement concerned about the rise of sweatshop labor. Led by United Students Against Sweatshops (USAS), the anti-sweatshop movement is best known for its "sweat-free campus" campaign, active on more than 200 college campuses, which demands that apparel bearing a college logo (for example, t-shirts, sweatshirts, baseball caps) be produced in factories that pay their workers a living wage.

USAS has partnered with the Workers Rights Consortium to develop tools aimed at encouraging colleges and universities to purchase apparel from manufacturers that respect the rights of their workers. In response to USAS organizing, a wide range of colleges and universities have signed on to the Designated Suppliers Program (DSP), which articulates three key principles for the production of apparel bearing college logos: factories producing the clothing must (1) comply with internationally recognized labor standards, (2) pay workers a living wage, and (3) permit workers to organize a labor union or other employee association. The more than forty schools that participate in the DSP include large state universities such as Ohio State University, the University of Southern California, and Rutgers and small liberal arts colleges such as Macalester College, Smith College, and Ursinus College.

USAS works to pressure more schools to make public commitments to sweatshop-free college apparel and to monitor the compliance of those schools that have already pledged to steer clear of producers that operate sweatshops. In 2010 USAS launched a new campaign—Nike: Just Pay It—that is mobilizing colleges and universities to demand that Nike disburse more than $2 million in severance pay owed to Honduran workers at factories closed abruptly by Nike subcontractors in that country. In response to the USAS campaign, both the University of Wisconsin and Cornell University announced in 2010 that they planned to stop purchasing licensed apparel from Nike.

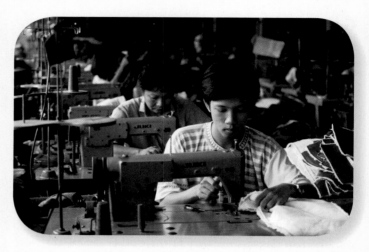

Sweatshops are not just a problem for workers outside the United States. More than 400,000 people in the United States worked under sweatshop conditions in the 1990s; this number dropped to about 250,000 by 2004, as the apparel industry moved more and more jobs offshore. The reason that sweatshops reemerged in the United States in the 1980s, after more than forty years of decline, can be traced to the changing structure of work in the global economy. As unregulated international trade grew, labor unions weakened, and large chain stores in the United States became more prevalent and powerful, sweatshops returned to the United States as a viable way of structuring work.

Sociologist Ross is a frequent speaker at meetings and organizing events for anti-sweatshop groups. Student activists know his talk as a compelling "Sweatshop 101," a sociological perspective that gives his audience a clear introduction to the causes and consequences of contemporary sweatshops.

think about it

1. *Do you know where the apparel that bears your college's or university's logo is made and under what conditions the clothing is produced?*

2. *Would you participate in, or support, the anti-sweatshop movement if you learned that your school sold products made in sweatshops? Why or why not?*

---

levels. However, human beings are not simply products of structure. We think, choose, and act, and even if social structure imposes limits, we always have some capacity for action, as the example of the student anti-sweatshop movement makes clear. Structure and action are in fact two sides of the same coin. As we consider how structure is affected by human action, we need to understand the broader social context, as well.

Types of Action

Max Weber, the pioneering German sociologist whom we met in Chapter 1, defined sociology as the science concerned with understanding social action, that is, human action in social context. Weber was particularly interested in understanding what motivates our actions, and he showed that the goals of human action change across time and culture.

Weber identified three basic types of human action:

- **Traditional action** is *motivated by custom.* Guided by the past, traditional action is anchored by a sense that things have always been done in the same way. Perhaps you have family practices that have been passed on for generations, such as how you celebrate a particular holiday.

- **Affective action** is *guided by emotions and feelings.* When fans tear down the goalposts after their team wins a big college football game, they are guided by their feelings.

- **Rational action** is *motivated by calculations of efficiency.* When people determine their goals and decide how to achieve them, their analysis is a form of rational action. Employees who attempt to act efficiently to help achieve a company's financial goals are guided by this type of action.

Of course, as Weber well knew, human action is complex and is often guided by a combination of these different motivations. But Weber's study of human history led him to believe that modern industrial society is increasingly shaped by rational action. Weber recognized the central role of rational action in the development of modern societies and industrial economies. At the same time, he was concerned that rational action had a tendency to squeeze out other ways of living. A society thoroughly saturated by rational action might be very efficient and highly productive, but Weber worried that it would also be cold and impersonal.

Rational Action: McDonaldization

More recently, the sociologist George Ritzer (2011) has argued that a form of rational action he calls McDonaldization is increasingly organizing our everyday lives (see Table 4.1). According to Ritzer, the effect is to impose the standardized, efficient structure of a fast-food restaurant on all aspects of our lives, including school, work, travel, and leisure. For Ritzer, McDonaldization represents an extreme form of rational action. Just as workers respond to the various timed buzzers and "beeps" in a fast-food kitchen, more and more aspects of our lives are organized by the quest for efficiency. For example, grocery shopping now requires no contact with other people.

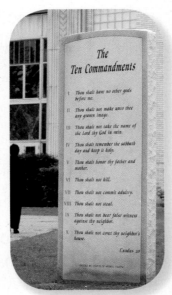

Traditional and rational action are examples of two very different, and sometimes conflicting, understandings of authority. Many people contend that it is appropriate to display representations of the tablet containing the Ten Commandments of the Judeo-Christian tradition, which invokes religion as a traditional authority, near government offices or courthouses. Others believe that courthouses should emphasize rational authority through the rule of law, rather than religion.

You can use a handheld device to scan each item as you put it in the cart, swipe your customer card, place your deli order with a few keystrokes, and pay with your credit card in the self-serve checkout aisle. You can prepare meals by simply pressing a few buttons on your microwave oven. Or you can preplan just about every minute of your vacation, scheduling each activity, tour, meal, and night's sleep as part of a package tour aimed at guaranteeing that you make the most of your time off.

This intense focus on efficiency, however, may lead to unintended consequences. For example, in the name of efficiency we do an increasing amount of unpaid labor—becoming, in effect, our own checkout clerks, bank tellers, gas station attendants, and insurance claims representatives, to name just a few of the tasks we do for ourselves. Simply put, the purpose

TABLE 4.1	RITZER'S FOUR DIMENSIONS OF MC DONALDIZATION
Efficiency	Seeking the best possible method for completing tasks, often by following a series of highly specified, predesigned steps.
Calculability	Emphasizing the quantitative aspects of products and services (focusing on, for example, product size, cost, and time), often characterized by the notion that "more is better."
Predictability	Striving to make products and services the same, regardless of place or time. This process of standardization can be comforting to customers, who know what to expect, but may produce jobs that offer little room for creative thought.
Control	Exercising control over employees and customers by enforcing rigid rules, limiting options, and using new technologies that monitor and regulate behavior.

Source: Ritzer 2011.

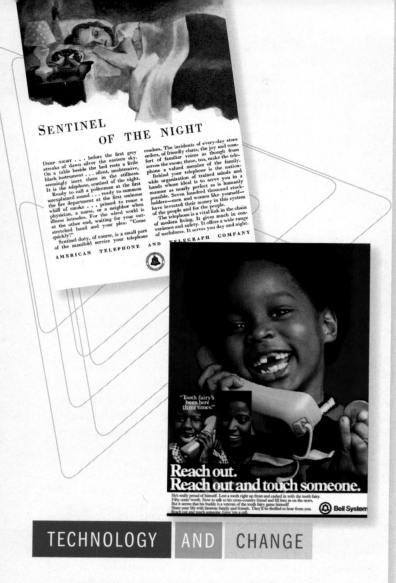

SENTINEL
OF THE NIGHT

AMERICAN TELEPHONE AND TELEGRAPH COMPANY

"Tooth fairy's been here three times!"

Reach out.
Reach out and touch someone.

Bell System

TECHNOLOGY AND CHANGE

As customers started to use the telephone more and more for socializing, telephone companies changed their marketing approach. They stopped emphasizing the practical and emergency uses of the telephone, as in this ad from the 1930s (*top*), and started to stress the ways that talking on the phone can be fun, as in this 1970 advertisement for the Bell Telephone System (*bottom*)

of a fast-food restaurant is to serve inexpensive, great-tasting food quickly. People who eat in fast-food restaurants, however, sometimes have to wait in long lines, pay more money than they anticipate, and find the food to be unappetizing and unhealthful. Workers in fast-food restaurants do jobs that are so routinized and standardized that they have almost no room for independent action. For Ritzer, this disconnect between the allure and experience of the fast-food restaurant is the puzzle

of McDonaldization: how and why can highly rational action produce outcomes that, as Ritzer (1993) puts it, "limit, ultimately compromise, and perhaps even undermine their rationality" (p. 121). Put another way, rational action aims to enhance human experience through a commitment to efficiency and progress. Ritzer suggests that the extreme rational action he calls McDonaldization may be both inefficient and, ultimately, dehumanizing.

McDonaldization is an example of the way human action is shaped by the broader structural patterns of society, in this case the commitment to efficiency in business. The history of phone communication, which we look at next, provides another example of this relationship between action and structure.

Technology and Action: Telephone to Smartphone

The history of phone communication, from the earliest landline devices to today's smartphones, provides a good example of the way human action interacts with evolving technologies to determine the impact of those technologies on social structures. Whatever potential a new technology has, human action—how people use it—is the key to understanding its social significance.

According to Claude Fischer's study *America Calling* (1992) when telephones first became widely available in the early twentieth century, the leaders of the industry marketed them primarily to businesses and stressed their business uses. When phone companies turned their attention to residential users in the 1920s, they marketed the telephone as a practical tool for managing household affairs and for obtaining help in emergencies. The way people used the home telephone, however, was mostly for regular, informal conversations with family and friends. Nonetheless, until some forty years after the introduction of the telephone, marketers continued to stress its practical uses, not its social uses.

Some observers feared that the telephone might undermine local communities, since people could ignore their neighbors and instead build relationships with people who lived far away. This and similar concerns reflect an underlying question: did people use the telephone in ways that changed how they related to their existing friendship structure? The answer, according to Fischer, is no. Instead, people mostly used the telephone in ways that reinforced their existing connections. Telephones made it easier to plan social engagements, though the neighborly practice of "dropping in" unannounced became less common. In addition, telephones certainly made it possible for people to stay in closer contact with their out-of-town relatives.

Cell phones and smartphones have seen a similar evolution. We tend to forget that the mobile phone today, like the telephone in the early twentieth century, is a relatively new technology. In 1990, only 5 million Americans had cell phones; by 2008 the number of users exceeded 270 million (U.S. Census Bureau 2010j). During that period, the cell phone changed

thinking about **structure**

Can you think of other examples in which human *action* determined the purpose of a technological advance?

from an upscale luxury item to a common accessory. As with early landline telephones, the way people use cell phones has changed over time. Like telephones, mobile phones were initially promoted as business tools and as useful in case of emergencies. Over time, however, people began using cell phones for other purposes (and cell phone technology evolved so that the phones could be used for an increasingly broad array of purposes): to talk with friends, send text messages, check sports scores, access the Internet, take pictures, respond to e-mail, listen to music, get driving directions, read the daily newspaper, play games, or watch movies or live sporting events. The list of uses continues to grow.

Cell phones make all of us more accessible to one another. If you keep a cell phone on you, your friends and family can reach you just about anytime and anywhere. As a result, frequent cell phone users probably communicate more regularly with others in their social networks than do those who do not rely on cell phones for everyday communication (Ling 2008). Cell phones also make people more available to bosses and co-workers, blurring the distinction between work time and time off (Wajcman 2008).

Cell phones have also severed the connection between person and place. When you call a person who has a landline, you are calling a particular place. When you call a cell phone, however, you are calling a specific person, but you have no idea where that person might be. In fact, it is common for an initial cell phone greeting to include the question "Where are you?"

Cell phones, therefore, may be contributing to the loss of private time and space in contemporary society, as well as to the loss of a rooted connection to place. Phones ring all around us, wherever we

New friend-tracking software, like Google's Latitude, allows friends to map each other's movements on their cell phone. With this software, you can determine when out-of-town friends are nearby or which local friends are in your neighborhood. As this kind of software becomes more refined, you'll be able to check your cell phone or your Facebook page to see if any of your friends are at the local coffee shop.

Many people, especially teenagers and young adults, communicate by text message more often than they speak on the phone. People rarely send text messages to strangers; instead, most text messages are directed to friends, family, or others on a person's contact list. New communication patterns associated with texting may be different from those typically facilitated by phone conversations.

CORE CONCEPTS CHALLENGE

*Consider **structure** and action in regard to the social dynamics of text messaging. Is texting a substitute for the phone? Does texting make communication with friends and family easier, or is it a way of making new social contacts? Are people using text messaging in new or surprising ways?*

are, and people carry on conversations on public transportation, in cars, on the street, and in other public settings (Freedman 2009). We communicate on the go, and the boundaries between our jobs and our personal lives are increasingly permeable. How we choose to use cell phones contributes to these changes.

At the same time, people use cell phones to help arrange traditional face-to-face contact. You can find friends at a crowded concert or make last-minute dinner plans. With networking software, you can use your cell phone to find out if any of your friends are nearby and leave electronic messages at restaurants or stores that your friends can later retrieve.

Even as people with cell phones use them to talk casually with their friends and family on a regular basis, the social consequences for those without a cell phone may be increasing. If you don't have a cell phone, you are not always accessible, you cannot check in with people on the fly, and you will have a hard time connecting with friends who are delayed by traffic. As cell phones have proliferated, public pay phones have largely disappeared, so people without cell phones have an increasingly difficult time staying in touch. Perhaps two separate forms of social structure are evolving, one based on electronic forms of interaction (e-mail, cell phones, handheld web access) and one that is largely out of the electronic loop.

These two forms of social structure are a global phenomenon, but you may be surprised to learn that Africa is the world's fastest growing cell phone market. By contrast, landline telephones remain comparatively rare throughout Africa, with only one phone line for every thirty-three people on the continent (in contrast, there are more telephone lines than people in the United States). By 2011, Africa had more than 400 million cell phone subscribers, the equivalent of almost half the continent's population (Auletta 2011). In many African countries, there are more than forty cell phone users for every one landline subscriber. (See Map 4.1.)

Cell phones have proliferated in Africa in the 2000s, and mobile phones are far more common than landlines throughout the continent. In Liberia, for example, there are more than 400 mobile phone subscribers for every landline. *Source:* Central Intelligence Agency, *The World Factbook;* calculations by author.

Ratio of mobile phones to landlines

- 1–25 mobile phones for every landline
- 26–50 mobile phones for every landline
- 51–100 mobile phones for every landline
- More than 100 mobile phones per landline

The explosion of cell phone use in Africa surprised the leaders of the telecommunications industry. Since landline telephones were so rare in Africa, industry leaders expected that there would be little interest in, or few resources to pay for, cell phones. But it turns out that demand for the cell phone, even in remote areas, is extraordinary. For most users in Africa, a cell phone is their first telephone, and people are using this technology in new and unexpected ways. For example, farmers in South Africa use their cell phones to learn the current price of fruits and vegetables in the major urban areas, which helps them to negotiate with wholesalers. A fisherwoman living on the Congo River tells customers to call her cell phone when they want to buy fresh fish. She keeps the fish alive on a string in the river and prepares them for sale only after receiving a call. Health care workers in rural areas can use their cell phones to call for an am-

bulance, providing remote health clinics with a real-time connection to more advanced hospitals. Wildlife researchers in Kenya use cell phones to track elephants by placing a cell phone in a waterproof pouch and strapping it around an elephant's neck (LaFraniere 2005; Ngowi 2005). Community health workers in Ghana send regular text messages to expectant parents in remote areas, helping to guide women through their pregnancies by providing advice on prenatal care and nutrition. Innovative electronic banking programs in Kenya, Cameroon, and Tanzania allow people who live in remote areas, far from any bank, to open and manage savings accounts via text message (Kang 2010).

Surely, Africans also use the cell phone to talk with friends and family. As these examples suggest, however, cell phone use is, in many ways, quite different in Africa than it is in the United States.

Cell phone use in the United States and in other countries, like telephone use before it, shows how actions can lead people to interact with their friends in new ways and to try out new patterns of behavior, which may contribute to the development of new structures. In subsequent chapters, we look at new forms of interaction made possible by recent communication technologies such as peer-to-peer networks, blogs, and virtual reality environments. We turn next, however, to a change on a larger scale: a transformation in the structure of the workplace.

⊙❯ The proliferation of cell phones in Africa has been a boon for farmers and small business people, like this market woman in Nairobi, Kenya, allowing them to keep up to date with each other and with wholesalers about market prices.

Workers Respond to Globalization

We have seen how the changing structure of work affects employees in the United States, particularly those who work in manufacturing. And as we have learned from studying the dynamic relationship between structure and action, an analysis of structural change reveals only part of the picture. We also need to pay attention to how people respond to structural change, even when their choices are limited.

As the number of manufacturing jobs in the United States declined during the late twentieth century, what choices or opportunities opened up for displaced workers? The lost industrial jobs should not be romanticized. Factory work was often monotonous, difficult, and dangerous. In one ten-year study, Ruth Milkman (1997) examined a General Motors assembly plant in Linden, New Jersey, where, as part of an effort to compete in the new global economy, the company reorganized work and introduced robots and other technological innovations. The union negotiated a buyout package for workers who wanted to leave. According to Milkman, workers who left, it turned out, were happier than those who stayed. Despite their unstable economic future, most were glad to escape the dreary, demanding work of the assembly line. With the exception of skilled workers who learned how to maintain the new robots, most workers who stayed found that new technologies and management programs made life worse for them. Their jobs became even more monotonous. Their relationships with their supervisors grew worse. Despite some economic uncertainty, most of the workers who left were ultimately able to construct better futures for themselves.

Throughout the United States, as workers lost their manufacturing jobs, some fought plant closings and layoffs, working with labor unions and community groups to try to retain jobs, find new factory owners, or buy the factory themselves. Others returned to school to learn new skills or new careers. Still others sought opportunities by moving away. Some tried to start their own businesses. Others retired earlier than they had anticipated. Facing similar structural conditions, different people made different choices.

In the early twenty-first century, new work patterns are emerging as people negotiate the challenges and opportunities of the global economy. With continuing high levels of long-term unemployment in the United States in the wake of the 2008–2009 recession, and a steep decline in the value of many people's pensions or retirement funds, today's workers are likely to have fewer options than their counterparts did only a decade earlier. The dynamic of structure and action helps us to see the magnitude of the changes, how these changes shape people's opportunities, and how people respond to these changes. One area in which new work patterns are emerging is the news industry.

In Transition

THE CHANGING STRUCTURE OF NEWS PRODUCTION

How do you learn about important events in your community, the nation, or the world? Although word of mouth—conversations with friends and family—is a common source of information, the foundation for much of what we know beyond our immediate experience is the news media. Whether it is an ongoing global story like the war in Afghanistan, a major national event like the 2010 BP oil spill in the Gulf of Mexico, or a local development like the introduction of new municipal zoning policies, the news media often serve as one of our primary sources of information. News reports inform our individual decision-making and provide a common framework for public discussion about current events and issues. From local newspapers to national network television, news media give citizens information they need to be active participants in civic life.

In the digital age, where, when, and how we get our news is undergoing significant change. The younger you are, the less likely you are to rely on the morning newspaper or the evening newscast on television. Instead, you can get your news just about any time on your computer screen or smartphone and, with a little effort, you can access news from around the globe instantly. How we consume news is in the midst of an important transition, but what about the production of news? Is the process of reporting the news also changing in the digital age? As we will see, the organization of news production is also undergoing a major transformation.

How do news organizations decide what is news? The structure of news gathering—that is, the regular routines that editors and journalists follow as they produce the news each day—shapes, to a large degree, what becomes news. Several pioneering sociological studies of daily newsroom activities (Gans 2005; Tuchman 1978) provide insight into the structure of news reporting, the kinds of stories that are most likely to appear in the news, and the kinds that will be largely ignored. At the same time, understanding the structure of news gathering within the traditional news

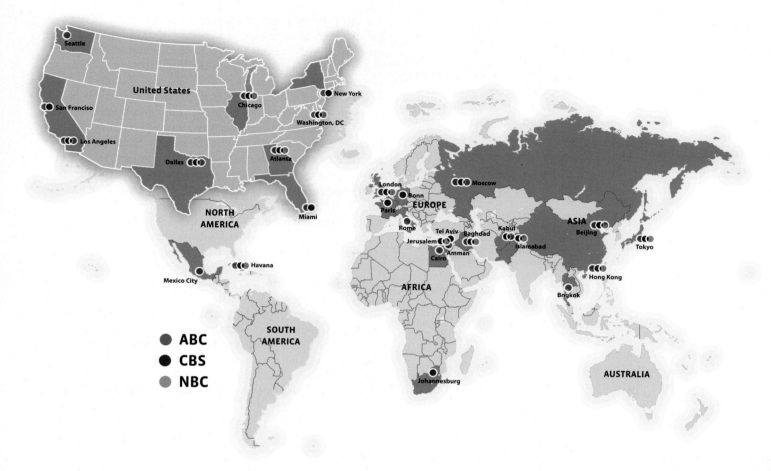

MAP 4.2 | U.S. TELEVISION NETWORK NEWS BUREAUS, 2009

The three television networks maintain news bureaus in a small number of major cities in the United States and other regions of the world—and each of the networks covers a similar group of cities. In large parts of the country and elsewhere, the networks do not have reporters and camera people on-site, looking for news stories. *Source:* Pew Project for Excellence in Journalism (2010).

CORE CONCEPTS CHALLENGE

Given the wide distribution of home video cameras and smartphone cameras in the United States, do you think the **power** *of news bureaus to determine what is news is decreasing? How, if at all, does news change when it comes from bystanders with video cameras rather than professional journalists? How might videos from these outside sources broaden the scope of network news?*

media—television networks, major daily newspapers, and news weeklies—helps us understand how news and the broader media environment are changing in the era of online journalism, YouTube, Facebook, Twitter, and blogging.

Among a news organization's first decisions must be where to look for news. Although some news seems to find reporters—for example, stories that go viral online and cannot be ignored—news organizations need a steady supply of suitable news to fill each day's newspaper or program. Of course, where you look has a significant impact on what you find. Reporters don't just roam the streets, hoping to run across interesting events. Major news outlets have well-developed routines that determine where reporters seek

the news. Sociologist Gaye Tuchman (1978) refers to these routines as the "news net." The news net includes full-time reporters, freelance reporters and writers, wire services like the Associated Press or Reuters that provide news stories to many different news outlets, and stringers who help the organization find news in remote locations (a stringer for a local newspaper may be located on your campus). But the net cannot catch every event that happens: like a fishing net, the news net holds only the bigger stories and lets the smaller ones slip away.

To continue the fishing metaphor, we know that to gather information, news organizations send reporters to strategic locations, just as a fishing boat travels to waters where fish are plentiful. But how do they decide *where* to send reporters? Most major news outlets in the United States maintain bureaus in New York and Washington but not in mid-sized cities like St. Louis or Minneapolis. As for international news, American news outlets are likely to have a news bureau in London or Tokyo, but not in Bangkok or Madrid. As a result, events that happen in and around these predefined important places are more likely to be treated as news. From the outset, then, the way news gathering is organized—where news outlets station their reporters—has a powerful impact on news coverage, just as where the boat travels determines which and how many fish are caught. (See Map 4.2.)

In addition, journalists are assigned to look regularly for news at news beats, which include such official locations as the White House, Capitol Hill, the Supreme Court, city hall, the state house, and local police stations. Reporters cover these beats to generate a steady stream of news, and they do so by developing routines that help them identify the events that are newsworthy. They build relationships with key players and contact these sources regularly to guarantee a steady supply of news.

Like other structures, the organizational structure of the news media is subject to change. For example, fifty years ago many major newspapers assigned reporters to a labor beat, regularly writing about the activities of labor unions and the world of work from the perspective of workers. Today, few papers have a reporter assigned to cover labor. Instead, economic coverage, or business news, focuses on issues of interest to investors and executives. On the other hand, many papers today have an environmental beat, an area unheard of a half-century ago.

In the digital era, the structure of the news media is in the midst of much more profound changes. For example, the reporting cycle of the traditional news—with daily deadlines for newspapers and network television and weekly deadlines for the major newsmagazines—is now outmoded. As cable news channels (CNN, Fox News, MSNBC) and a wide range of online media—including the web sites of traditional news outlets—report and comment on news around the clock, news has moved to a nonstop, twenty-four-hour cycle. In this climate, there is pressure to report news quickly, sometimes before reporters know the full story or the broader context (Kovach and Rosenstiel 1999).

As traditional news media struggle to survive in this fast-paced, information-rich environment, the structure of news gathering and reporting is changing rapidly. In an effort to cut costs and speed up production, news outlets require reporters to write, conduct interviews, take photographs or shoot video, and edit all of this content to facilitate distribution across various media platforms (Klinenberg 2005). For years, including during the recession of 2008 and 2009, news organizations cut their staffs significantly. Fewer journalists remained to produce the news each day, exert-

Most news organizations follow a standard set of daily routines as they identify, gather, and report the news. That's one reason why so many news outlets typically cover the same major stories each day.

ing even more pressure on reporters to do more with less. In this climate, reporters are developing new routines and practices, emphasizing speed and flexibility, consistent with the new economic and technological context (Cottle 2007; Pavlik 2008).

In addition, traditional news now competes with new forms of citizen journalism—news and commentary produced outside the context of a professional news organization. Citizen journalism appears in a variety of media: independent web sites, YouTube or other video-sharing sites, blogs, and social networking sites.

Some of the traditional media have made efforts to incorporate citizen journalism into their own news net. CNN .com's iReport section is full of videos uploaded by users with reports that "are not edited, fact-checked or screened before they post." CNN reporters monitor the iReport site, and some of the user-posted videos ultimately make their way onto CNN. In 2011, during mass pro-democracy protests in Egypt that ultimately forced Hosni Mubarak to resign after three decades as president, the *New York Times* posted reports from Egyptian bloggers and eyewitnesses to the unfolding events on its regularly updated news blog, "The Lede."

Citizen journalism represents a potentially significant change in how news is reported and in how consumers relate to the news. One scholar of online journalism argues that new forms of digital journalism position citizens as "produsers" (Bruns 2005)—part producer and part user of the news—who have a very different relationship to news than do audiences for traditional media. As the structure of news evolves in the digital age, our very definition of "what's news" may also be changing.

In Transition

- Social **structure** refers to recurring patterns of behavior that make social life possible. Understanding social structure helps us to see connections between these patterns and people's actions and beliefs.

- We can see social structure at the micro level (for example, in the structure of talk), the meso level (for example, in organizational structure), or the macro level (for example, in the structure of work).

- Structure constrains behavior by putting limits on it, but it can also enable behavior by providing a context for smooth interaction.

- Even when we are limited by social structure, we always have at least some capacity for *action*. Structure and action are two sides of the same coin; we always need to consider the two in relation to each other.

REVIEW, REFLECT, AND APPLY

Looking Back

1. The sociological perspective helps us to see social structure, the recurring patterns of behavior in social life. Understanding social structure enables us to see the patterns and regularities in social life.

2. People always have the capacity for action, even when their choices are severely limited. Sociology encourages us to examine the dynamic relationship between structure and action by recognizing how social structure shapes, but does not fully determine, our behavior, expectations, and beliefs.

3. We can explore social structure at different levels. At the micro level, we might analyze the structure of daily interactions. For example, our everyday talk and interaction has a structure. We often take for granted our knowledge of this structure of interaction because it seems so natural to us.

4. At the meso level, we might analyze organizational structure. For example, examining organizational structure helps us to understand the complex dynamics involved in the space shuttle *Challenger* and *Columbia* disasters.

5. At the macro level, we focus on broad patterns of behavior, especially the interrelationships of various institutions. For example, sociologists using functional analysis seek to understand how various parts of a society work together and

the roles that different institutions and cultural components play in maintaining social order.

6. With the growth of the global economy, stable patterns of work in the United States changed for many Americans at the end of the twentieth century. The dynamic of structure and action helps us to understand the significance of these changes, how globalization shaped workers' opportunities, and how people responded to these changes.

7. The evolution of phone communication, from the telephone to the smartphone, illustrates people's capacity for action. When the telephone first became available in the United States, it was marketed primarily as a business device. However, most people used the phone for conversation with friends and relatives. Today, the ways in which people choose to use cell phones and smartphones are once again changing some aspects of social life.

8. The organization of news production is changing. News reporters follow a set of daily routines when they gather the news. Analyzing the structure of news gathering helps us to better understand which stories are covered on the evening news and how the news media are changing in the digital age.

Critical Thinking: Questions and Activities

1. How can the concept of structure and its mirror image, action, help us to gain a deeper understanding of social life?

2. Think about the structure of your college classroom. In what ways are the patterns and routines of your classroom similar to those of your high school classes? In what ways are they different? How do the expectations associated with the student or teacher role differ from those you encountered in high school?

3. Identify some of the ways that fast-food restaurants emphasize efficiency, predictability, and an extreme form of rational action. Do you agree with Ritzer's theory of the McDonaldization of society?

4. Various efforts to introduce a videophone—long a standard in science fiction films and television—have been largely unsuccessful. Can structure and action help you to explain why the videophone has never really caught on? Do you think new forms of video chat—including Skype and iChat—will be successful forms of video communication? Why or why not?

5. What are the functions of work? Earning a paycheck may be the most obvious answer, but do our jobs serve other functions, as well? To answer this question, do some research by conducting short interviews with your family and friends about what they get from their jobs. Did the people you interviewed talk about more than their paychecks? If so, what did they say? Try to interview people who have different kinds of jobs or who are in different age groups. Talk with one or two retired people and ask them what they miss— and don't miss—about their jobs.

6. According to popular wisdom, there is no "I" in "team." Using your knowledge of structure and action, think about the differences between an individual sport like tennis, golf, or high jumping, and a team sport like basketball or soccer. How are the patterns of interaction different? How does the structure of the game shape how participants play, or what they are expected to do, or how fans respond to different sports?

Key Terms

achieved status (p. 90) a position in a social system that a person attains voluntarily, to a considerable degree, as the result of his or her own efforts.

action (p. 87) the ability to operate independent of social constraints.

affective action (p. 99) behavior guided by emotions and feelings.

ascribed status (p. 90) a position in a social system, assigned to a person from birth, regardless of his or her wishes.

breaching experiments (p. 91) controlled social situations that intentionally break social rules, violating basic norms and patterns of behavior.

convention (p. 93) a practice or technique that is widely used in a particular social setting.

conversation analysis (p. 92) a method of analyzing the patterns in face-to-face conversation that produce the smooth, back-and-forth turn-taking of such exchanges.

ethnomethodology (p. 91) an approach that examines the methods people use to make sense of their daily activities, empha-

sizing the ways in which we collectively create social structure in our everyday activities.

organizational structure (p. 93) the rules and routines, both formal and informal, that shape daily activity within organizations.

rational action (p. 99) behavior motivated by calculations of efficiency.

roles (p. 90) the sets of expected behaviors associated with particular statuses.

social institutions (p. 87) the major arenas of social life in which durable routines and patterns of behavior take place.

social integration (p. 96) the social structures that bind people together and the values that link people to the broader society.

social structure (p. 87) recurring patterns of behavior.

status (p. 90) a position in a social system that can be occupied by an individual.

traditional action (p. 99) behavior motivated by custom.

5

Power

looking AHEAD

What is **power** and how does it affect your life?

Why do you have more **power** than you might realize?

How is understanding **power** essential for understanding inequality?

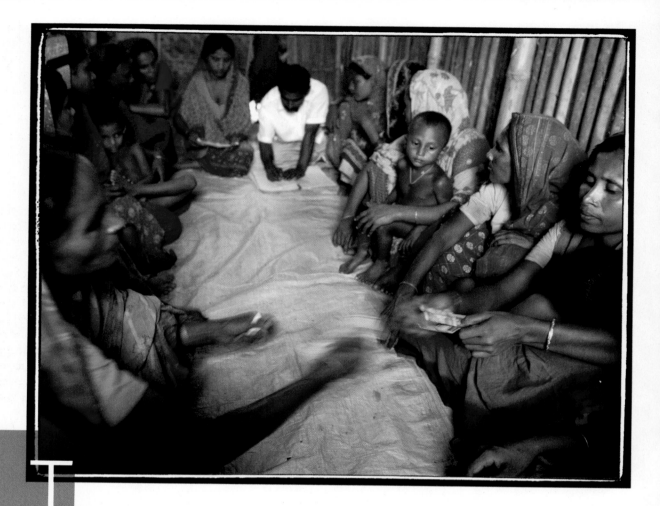

Two decades ago, Munni Akter could barely afford enough food to survive. "I was lost and had no skill to earn," Munni recalls. That's when she managed to get a microloan—just $40—from the Bangladesh Rural Advancement Committee (BRAC). The loan enabled her to begin selling food on the street at a profit. Over the years her business grew. Today Munni runs a small food factory that employs twenty-six workers. She is out of poverty and proudly independent.

Munni Akter is just one of nearly 11 million Bangladeshis who have benefited from microloans, and BRAC is the world's largest nongovernment organization working to reduce poverty. But BRAC is much more than a microlender. The group organizes recipients of microloans into small groups of twenty to thirty people. Group members guarantee each other's loans, provide mutual assistance, and often operate as a springboard for other improvements in their lives. BRAC also operates health care and education programs and teaches women about gender equality and the law so that they can speak up for their rights and resist exploitation.

To spread the message of empowerment, BRAC trains some women as paralegals, or *shebikas* ("helpers" in Sanskrit). These women learn how to handle crises such as rape or domestic abuse as well as to provide other legal services. Over 11,000 *shebikas* now share their knowledge and support with others.

By helping individual women to become empowered and by developing a long-term organizational structure to train a growing number of educators and advocates, the women in these various programs have increased their collective power. That has always been the goal of BRAC's founder and chairperson, Fazle Hasan Abed, who observes, "Poor people are poor because they are powerless. We must organise people for power" (BRAC 2010a, 2010b; Changemakers 2009; Haq 2011). ■

Power is a fundamental sociological concept, affecting every level of society and influencing our daily lives in countless ways. Because power pervades social life, to understand how society works we must consider its role in various social contexts. As noted political philosopher and social critic Bertrand Russell (1938/2004, 4) put it, "the fundamental concept in social science is Power, in the same way in which Energy is the fundamental concept in physics." Power, like energy, takes many forms and is essential in understanding why things happen as they do in society.

The amount of power that we have heavily influences what we can accomplish in life, whether at home, at work, or in our community. People with more resources typically have more power, and those with power can use it to obtain more resources. Power, therefore, is closely linked to social inequality, another fundamental feature of society. Inequality can be based on many different characteristics, including class, race, gender, ethnicity, nationality, sexual orientation, and religious affiliation. But these different forms of inequality have something in common: power and its influence.

In this chapter, we define and examine power and its various characteristics. We look at examples of power in daily life as well as how differences in power affect inequality, and we explore how different types of inequality interact. We conclude by noting how economic power is increasingly translated into political influence through campaign contributions.

Understanding Forms of Power

You know that the United States is a powerful nation and that your boss has more power than you do. But what is "power," exactly? And how can this concept be applied to such different settings as international relations and the workplace? Different approaches to understanding power highlight different aspects of this important concept (Blalock 1989; Gaventa 1982; Lukes 2005; Mann 1986; Poggi 2001; Sharp 1973; Smith 1990; Wartenberg 1990; Wrong 1979).

Defining Power

The word *power* is derived from a Latin word, *potere*, which means "to be able." Max Weber (1922/1978, 926) viewed **power** as *the ability to bring about an intended outcome, even when opposed by others.* Two key components of this definition are the basis for an important distinction: Some sociologists focus on the "ability to bring about an intended outcome," or the "power to" approach, so called because it highlights the capacity to accomplish something. Others focus on the ability to overcome opposition, or the "power over" approach, so called because it highlights the capacity to dominate others (Ng and Bradac 1993). These two aspects of power are not mutually exclusive, and feminist scholars, especially, have worked to integrate both approaches into a comprehensive analysis of power (Allen 2008). Let's consider these aspects of power more closely.

Empowerment: "Power To"

As noted, the "power to" approach emphasizes *the ability to bring about an intended outcome,* highlighting the positive and constructive aspects of power. **Empowerment,** which *increases people's capacity to bring about an intended outcome,* is the focus of much feminist scholarship on power. Social philosopher Virginia Held (1993), for example, argues that power is the capacity to change and empower oneself and others. According to political scientist Nancy Hartsock (1983, 226), the "feminist theory of power" views power as a competence and ability, rather than a form of dominance. Sociologist Patricia Hill Collins (2000) highlights the use of power to resist oppression.

People often discuss power and empowerment in terms of individual effort and achievement. If your goal is to find an interesting, decent-paying job, then acquiring appropriate education and experience can help give you the "power to" accomplish your objective. Empowerment often involves individual enhancement and self-improvement. Individual self-empowerment is the theme of popular self-help books with titles such as *Empowerment: The Art of Creating Your Life as You Want It.*

Empowerment can also involve organizations, communities, and entire categories of people. International development agencies, for example, try to empower poor people by increasing their capacity to care for themselves and their families (Alsop and Heinsohn 2005). The Bangladesh Rural Advancement Committee mentioned at the beginning of this chapter, for example, seeks to empower an oppressed group through a combination of economic assistance and educational programs. Other programs and organizations have also used this combination to produce promising results worldwide. A program in South Africa, for instance, has empowered women to reduce by half the incidence of physical and sexual violence in their community (Kim et al. 2007). Similarly, the women's movement in the United States has helped to empower women, enabling them to gain greater equality in the workplace, more options in their roles at home, better medical care, more equitable access to education, and greater participation in sports. As women have become empowered, they have accomplished these gains without dominating men, making their achievements examples of the "power to" act rather than "power over" others.

The "power to" approach can also apply to social systems such as schools, governments, or even entire societies. American sociologist Talcott Parsons (1960) saw power as the capacity of a social system to achieve collective goals. In the tradition of structural functionalism, Parsons was most interested in the overall operation of societies as social systems. According to his framework, a society is powerful to the extent that it can accomplish its goals. Doing so requires access to resources, among them money and knowledge. Wealthy societies have more resources—and thus are more powerful—than poorer societies (one way that power and inequality are often connected). Powerful societies can maintain a high standard of living for their citizens, ensure self-defense, advance scientific and technological frontiers, and achieve other collective goals. By all these measures, the United States and other wealthy nations are powerful societies, whereas impoverished countries are much less powerful.

Strategies of Empowerment: Educate, Organize, Network

The old saying, "Give a man a fish and you feed him for a day; teach a man to fish and you feed him for a lifetime" expresses the difference between charity and empowerment. A gift provides only temporary relief and fosters a relationship of dependency; a person who is empowered develops an enduring capacity and independence. Whether adopted by an individual, a small group, or a national or an international organization, strategies to increase empowerment generally involve a combination of education, organization, and networking (Dugan 2003).

- **Education** is probably the best-known approach to empowerment. Some teaching philosophies, for example, focus heavily on empowering students rather than simply transmitting facts (Freire 1970). To achieve their goal, people or groups must understand their situation, have a vision of what needs to be done, and obtain the training and skills they need to reach their goal. For some people, a college education can be an important means of learning about their situation and developing the skills necessary for rewarding employment and a more fulfilling life.

- **Organization** involves bringing people together to identify common goals and work to achieve them. Smoothly operating workplaces are well organized, for example, with employees and management cooperating to achieve organizational goals. When communities of disempowered people organize, the neighborhood associations, labor unions, and advocacy groups that result can serve as megaphones

to amplify the concerns of group members and help them to stand up more powerfully to adversaries. The *shebikas* organized through BRAC's Human Rights and Legal Education program, discussed in our chapter opening, show how organization can empower people. As one guide to community organizing notes, "Building a strong, lasting, and staffed organization alters the relations of power. . . . When the organization is strong enough, it will have to be consulted about decisions that affect its members" (Bobo, Kendall, and Max 2001, 12).

- **Networking** involves reaching outside your immediate circle of contacts to find allies. Professional associations in many fields hold conferences and social events to facilitate networking to search for employment or to advance careers. Organizations also network by forming coalitions and other collaborative efforts. In this way, they pool their resources to achieve goals they would be unlikely to accomplish on their own.

Domination: "Power Over"

At all levels of social life, people disagree. For example, a parent grounds a teenager but the teenager resists; a corporation wants to build a toxic waste incinerator near a neighborhood, but the residents object; or one political party proposes legislation that another party opposes. In all these cases, the effort to accomplish something meets opposition and produces conflict. That's why the second part of our definition of power includes the idea of conflict: "the ability to bring about an intended outcome, *even when opposed by others*." This emphasis is called the "power over" approach, since it focuses on overcoming oppo-

This classic graphic illustrates the idea that through organization weaker parties can join forces to take on a more powerful adversary.

sition or dominating others. In one classic definition from political scientist Robert Dahl (1957), power is seen exclusively in terms of domination: "A has power over B to the extent that he can get B to do something that B would not otherwise do" (p. 202).

Domination can occur at any level of society. Forcing children to be brides, as is done in some cultures, reflects both domination at the individual level (the future of a specific young woman is determined by her extended family) as well as inequalities at the societal level (women in such societies lack power in social life). Often macro-level inequalities in power trickle down to affect people's daily lives. At the same time, the personal choices people make have a cumulative impact on broader dynamics of social power, a process captured neatly by the feminist slogan "The personal is political."

The most obvious use of power as a means of domination is in political and economic conflicts, as powerful elites attempt to maintain their advantages over others. We examine such situations more closely later in the chapter, when we explore systems of social inequality.

Strategies to Overcome Opposition: Persuade, Reward, Coerce

Imagine that someone you live with—your roommate, partner, or spouse—has a much lower standard of cleanliness than you do. He or she leaves the sink full of dirty dishes and leaves clothes, papers, and half-eaten food lying around. If you want this person to be neater, you have three options. First, you could try persuasion, which would involve convincing the person to clean up out of fairness, because of health concerns, or to eliminate the growing stench that is putting a damper on your social life. If persuasion didn't work, you could try offering a reward: "If you do your share of the cleaning for a month, I'll pay for us to go out to see a movie." Finally, if all else fails, you could try a threat: "If you don't keep up with your share of the cleaning, you can't live here anymore."

Participants in any conflict, whether minor or serious, have these same three basic options: persuade, reward, or coerce others to get them to comply (Kriesberg 1982, 115).

■ To **persuade** is *to get people's compliance by convincing them of the correctness of your position and goals.* An organization dedicated to combating sexually transmitted diseases, for example, might launch a campaign to educate people about the importance of condoms. Over time, as people hear this message repeatedly, some might begin to alter their behavior. The group has power—it is able to achieve

PLS DNT TXT + DRIVE

A Public Service Announcement brought to you by your school + other drivers

Public service announcements, such as this one discouraging texting while driving, are an example of trying to persuade people to act—or not act—in a certain way.

its goals—to the extent that it can reach and influence people through education. However, this type of power is limited, since it usually cannot overcome stubborn opposition. Also, the use of persuasion is not always forthright or honest. Some actors manipulate, distort, or withhold information to convince others to act in a desired way, such as authoritarian governments that control the media. Citizens in such societies may voluntarily comply with the government's wishes, but the rulers have obtained this compliance by using false, incomplete, or misleading information. Even in open societies, misleading propaganda efforts by governments and powerful corporations can shape the terms of debate about many issues, thereby achieving compliance under false pretenses (Chomsky 1989).

■ A second strategy to overcome opposition is to offer a reward. To **reward** is *to encourage people's compliance by offering a positive incentive.* Rewarding a child with words

PROCLAMATION $5,000.00 REWARD FOR EACH of SEVEN ROBBERS of THE TRAIN at WINSTON, MO., JULY 15, 1881, and THE MURDER of CONDUCTER WESTFALL $5,000.00 ADDITIONAL for ARREST or CAPTURE DEAD OR ALIVE OF JESSE OR FRANK JAMES THIS NOTICE TAKES the PLACE of ALL PREVIOUS REWARD NOTICES. CONTACT SHERIFF, DAVIESS COUNTY, MISSOURI IMMEDIATELY T. T. CRITTENDEN, GOVERNOR STATE OF MISSOURI JULY 26, 1881

Rewarding others is one way to achieve compliance. Why are rewards often used to capture criminals? What rewards—other than cash—can be useful in daily life?

of praise, an athlete with a trophy, or a country with economic or military assistance are all ways to encourage or reinforce desirable behavior.

■ To **coerce** is *to force compliance by threatening, intimidating, pressuring, or harming someone.* Drivers generally obey the speed limit (or something close to it) because they know a speeding ticket can be very expensive. Therefore, the threat of possible punishment has a coercive effect on their behavior. In this case, compliance is a result of *systemic* coercion in which social structures—not just individuals—are in place to deliver a threat.

Reward and coercion are sometimes two sides of the same coin. As a student you may work hard in school, even when you do not enjoy it, because you have been taught that your chances for good employment—with all the accompanying rewards—will be improved significantly if you have a college degree. You also know that receiving failing grades is likely to harm your prospects for graduation and employment—an implicit coercion.

In many cases, coercion is much more sinister, involving threats to people's livelihood, freedom, or physical well-being. In some repressive societies, people who fail to comply with authority can lose their jobs, while those who obey are allowed to pursue successful careers. In the most authoritarian societies, those with power use the most sinister forms of coercion: imprisoning, beating, or killing people who refuse to comply. Because these techniques are inefficient, they are typically used as a last resort. However, through the force of their example, they can have a coercive effect on large numbers of citizens. (Nations, too, use such coercion against their enemies.) Ultimately, though, because force is expensive and can create opposition, people in power cannot rely for long on coercion alone. It is more efficient to have people control their own behavior.

Egyptian police use violence to disperse pro-democracy demonstrators in the country's 2011 revolution. Physical force is typically the last resort in obtaining compliance. As a type of coercion, it is expensive, inefficient, and often ineffective in the long run because it generates anger and resentment.

Power operates in all levels of social life. Many everyday interactions involve power. In this soccer match, a referee uses his authority to intervene in a dispute.

Power in Everyday Life

Power is an essential part of social relationships at every level of social life, including your relationships with your family and friends, your professor, your boss, the police, and the government. Many sociologists, including Max Weber and Karl Marx, focused much of their attention on the operation of power at the macro level of society, examining governmental and economic power. We explore these ideas in more detail later in the chapter.

However, power is also involved in social interactions at the micro level. For example, intimate partner violence is a serious social issue, and rates of physical and sexual abuse are especially high among high school and college students (Straus 2004). Women, in particular, suffer the consequences of this abuse. Intimate partner violence produces a sense of powerlessness in the victim, often leading to depression. A survey of undergraduate women found that the more violence they experience in their relationships, the less powerful and the more depressed they feel (Filson et al. 2010). Perpetrators use violence to assert control and gain power over their partners.

In between macro- and micro-level interactions are the meso-level organizations to which we all belong. Studying power can also help us to understand how such organizations operate.

Power in Small Groups and Organizations

Sociologists who study power in small groups and organizations examine how such groups operate and what roles their leaders play. Many of their insights can be applied to friendship circles, families, and clubs as well as to more formal settings such as schools and workplaces.

thinking about power
How do those who have **power** over your actions and decisions maintain their control?

In one classic formulation, John French and Bertram Raven identified six bases of power in small groups and organizations (French and Raven 1959/2001; Raven 1965). Notice how these power bases overlap with the broader strategies for overcoming opposition we discussed earlier:

- **Reward power** is the control one party has over valued resources that can be used to provide positive incentives. By offering children a weekly allowance, parents can gain power over their behavior.

- **Coercive power** is the ability to punish—for example, by withholding valued resources or by inflicting verbal or physical harm. Police officers can usually generate compliance because they can issue citations, arrest people, or even shoot them if necessary.

- **Legitimate power** is exercised by those who invoke a feeling of obligation; one "ought" to obey, perhaps as a result of shared cultural values or out of respect for someone's formal rank or position in the social structure. You are likely to carry out a boss's order to do a routine task at work; you would ignore a similar order about your private home life.

- **Referent power** is based on feelings of identification, affection, and respect for another person, even if that person does not seek influence over others. A popular colleague in a workplace might have referent power because others look up to her and view her as a model.

- **Expert power** arises from the perception that a person has superior knowledge in a particular area. A lawyer has expert power in legal matters in relation to a client. Expert power is about the perception of knowledge, not necessarily actual knowledge. Someone seen as an authority carries expert power whether or not he has actual expertise. Conversely, a real authority on some topic may not have expert power if others do not recognize that expertise.

- **Informational power** is based on a person's use of facts, data, or other evidence to argue rationally or persuade. A project manager has informational power when she convinces her boss to approve a new product. Those with information can increase their influence by sharing it, withholding it, organizing it effectively, or even manipulating or falsifying it.

These categories can overlap—a leader can withhold a reward as a type of coercion—but the distinctions help us to recognize different sources of power. Also, a person's use of one type of power can affect another. For example, when a manager gives an employee a bad evaluation—a use of coercive power—that action is likely to undermine his or her referent power with that person.

Sociologists and social psychologists have done a great deal of research on the dynamics of small groups, including those associated with power (Forsythe 2010). Researchers have shown that when authorities rely on reward or coercive power, their influence weakens if the amount of resources they control is reduced. However, authorities who have earned respect and are seen as legitimate enjoy group members' loyalty regardless of their ability to reward or coerce. Such loyalty can evaporate, however, if the person in authority acts in ways that group members consider unfair, unethical, or disrespectful (Lammers et al. 2008; Tyler 2005; Tyler and Blader 2003).

Compared to powerful people, those who feel relatively powerless are more likely to use coercion, because they think they have no other means of achieving their aims. Some parents and teachers feel relatively powerless when children seem out of control. These adults are more likely to use coercive threats and punishment than are parents and teachers who feel empowered (Bugental and Lewis 1999).

Authorities generally prefer rewards over coercion because they worry about retaliation (Molm 1997). However, group members often tolerate a coercive leader if the group is successful in achieving its goals (Michener and Lawler 1975), or if they trust the leader (Friedland 1976). If a leader lacks referent power, uses coercion, and asks group members to carry out unpleasant tasks, though, group members are more likely to resist his or her authority (Yukl, Kim, and Falbe 1996). People are also more likely to oppose authorities if they perceive their actions as unjust, view fellow group members as comrades, learn to act together as a group, and believe they have group support when speaking out (Gamson, Fireman, and Rytina 1982).

Power Tactics

How do you try to get your way when dealing with your friends or your boss? **Power tactics** are *the specific strategies people use to influence others in everyday life.* These familiar strategies involve power, though we often do not think of them in those terms. (See Table 5.1.) A child who persists in yelling, "I want it! I want it!" in a store is using a power tactic. A worker who ridicules his or her colleague is using a power tactic. Power tactics vary along three key dimensions (Forsythe 2010, 228):

- **Hard and soft.** Hard tactics are forceful, direct, or harsh. People employing them use economic rewards and other tangible outcomes, and even threats. A cash rebate or a threat to repossess your car is a hard tactic. Soft tactics focus on relationships. People employing soft tactics make use of collaboration and friendship to achieve an aim. A friendly reminder that you need to do some task is a soft tactic.

Tactic	Examples
Appeal	Beg for help; plead with someone to play fair
Bully	Yell; push someone around
Collaborate	Invite someone to help; provide assistance as needed
Complain	Protest to a store manager about poor service; grumble to a professor about an assignment
Criticize	Point out the limitations in a plan; find fault with someone's work
Demand	Ask for a refund; insist on speaking to a supervisor
Discuss	Talk over a situation in a group; come up with a plan of action
Disengage	Walk out in the middle of the argument; give someone the cold shoulder
Evade	Change the subject; don't return phone calls
Inform	Point out the advantages of a plan; note the personal benefits someone will receive
Ingratiate	Flatter; compliment
Inspire	Appeal to a person's loyalty; cheer someone on
Join forces	Find allies to help fight an opponent; agree to approach the boss as a group
Joke	Use humor to help others relax; ridicule opponents
Manipulate	Lie; leave out important details in a report
Negotiate	Offer a deal; offer to compromise
Persist	Refuse to take no for an answer; keep trying
Persuade	Convince someone of the wisdom of a position
Promise	Assure someone that you will follow through with a plan
Punish	Fire someone; ground a child for the week
Put down	Insult someone; disparage a person's abilities
Request	Ask for a favor
Reward	Take someone to lunch as thanks; give someone a promotion
Socialize	Ask about the family; make small talk
Threaten	Warn about taking legal action; warn that you will divulge embarrassing information

Source: Adapted from Forsythe (2010).

- *Rational and nonrational.* Rational tactics appeal to logic and include bargaining and rational persuasion. Many newspaper editorials use rational tactics. Nonrational tactics include emotional appeals, such as when television commercials imply that driving a particular type of car will make you sexy.

- *Unilateral and bilateral.* Unilateral tactics do not require cooperation to initiate; they include demands, orders, or disengagement. Military leaders employ unilateral tactics when they issue orders. Bilateral tactics involve give-and-take, as in negotiations and discussions. When a homeowner and a prospective buyer negotiate a sale price for a house, they use bilateral tactics.

The way power and inequality operate within broader society can influence the dynamics of small groups. For example, women have higher levels of referent power than men

Foucault's Distinctive View of Power

Did you ever think school was like a prison? If so, French sociologist Michel Foucault (1926–1984) would have agreed with you. In *Discipline and Punish* (1975/1995) Foucault explained how modern prisons emerged in the eighteenth century as a humane way of treating criminals, rather than torturing or killing them. Advocates of prison reform argued they would deter crime by more effectively controlling criminals. As it turns out, prisons didn't deter crime, but they did demonstrate a new form of power and social control that involved detailed time schedules, restricting prisoners' physical movement, and observing and evaluating their behavior. These features of prisons were adapted and applied to other new social institutions, including factories, psychiatric hospitals, and modern schools. (We revisit these developments in Chapter 8, on social control.)

Foucault's study of prisons made use of his unique view of power, which has influenced many scholars. Foucault argued that although power can be oppressive and dominating, it can also have a positive effect. He wrote, "We must cease once and for all to describe the effects of power in negative terms: it 'excludes,' it 'represses,' it 'censors,' it 'abstracts,' it 'masks,' it 'conceals.' In fact power produces; it produces reality . . ." (Foucault 1975/1995, 194).

For Foucault, power "produces reality" because it is made up of systems of knowledge that organize, label, and measure the world in distinct ways. For example, science, religion, and business each have an internal logic, unique assumptions, distinct vocabulary, and central ideas. Because a minister or priest views the world in terms of "grace," a scientist in terms of "empirical evidence," or an executive in terms of "profit," each understands the world differently. Each person's ideas and beliefs influence his or her behavior by encouraging some actions and discouraging others.

As knowledge systems—faith in a God, science, or capitalism—become accepted, they become taken-for-granted assumptions about the world and therefore assume enormous power and influence. Those who question or challenge such dominant systems of knowledge are marginalized, ostracized, and even punished. In the end, such systems of knowledge help to control behavior and are therefore forms of power in themselves.

Foucault coined the term *power/knowledge* to show that how we understand and interpret the world both enlightens and restricts us. That's because systems of knowledge order, rank, and make visible various aspects of the world, enabling it to be controlled more effectively. When applied to people, such systems of knowledge serve as mechanisms of social control. New ways of thinking—like the idea for creating the modern prison—are developed into real-world social institutions in which certain types of actions are allowed and encouraged and others are prohibited and discouraged, though resistance is always possible.

Although some people benefit from certain forms of knowledge—clergy have considerable legal power in religiously based societies whereas psychiatrists are influential within our own society—they don't necessarily control the use of that knowledge. That is, individuals don't wield power; instead they navigate through a system of knowledge. In fact, Foucault argued that, rather than people using power, power helps form our sense of self; we are the product of power.

Foucault saw power as dispersed throughout society, rather than being centralized in the hands of small groups or individuals. "Power is everywhere," he wrote (Foucault 1978/1980, 93), "not because it embraces everything but because it comes from everywhere." Power relationships play out in countless local "fields," such as the family, prison, the workplace, a doctor's office, a classroom, and a church. As a consequence, power is fragmented into many different forms. This is why much of Foucault's work was organized around particular subjects, such as prison, sexuality, and madness. Each of these fields has its own power dynamics.

Most powerful of all are the systems of knowledge that cause people to change their behavior willingly, by monitoring their own actions to conform to expectations. Susan Bartky (1990) argues that because of such self-surveillance, many women closely regulate their own bodies through constant dieting, "proper" hair removal, and wearing make-up and fashionable clothing. When carried to extremes, the impact of such disciplinary power can produce eating disorders and other unhealthy behaviors—another form of prison.

think about it

1. *Do you agree with Foucault that power/knowledge helps to control people's behavior? Why or why not?*
2. *Can you think of examples to illustrate Foucault's idea that we regulate ourselves by conforming to social expectations?*

---

do; people typically evaluate women more favorably than men and like them more (Carli 1999). But women who use a direct leadership style are judged more harshly than men, and they have to outperform men to be seen as equally competent. Men have more expert power, and because people generally believe men are more competent than women, men can draw upon this perception as a source of influence. Gender differences are affected by a person's position within the social structure, however; people who are relatively powerful—women or men—report using more direct strategies to influence others than do less powerful individuals. (For a very different take on power, consider the Through a Sociological Lens box.)

The Economic, Political, and Cultural Uses of Power

Think of the people and institutions that have power in our society. What do they do with it? Power is used in many ways, but three of the most important purposes to which it is applied are economic, political, and cultural.

Economic Power: Allocating Resources

Within any group or society, power determines who will receive important resources and how those resources will be used. Within a family, the person who controls spending wields considerable power over other family members, deciding in many cases what food or clothes will be bought, how leisure time will be spent, and where the family will live. Business executives have the power to open new stores, offices, or factories in one place and close them in others. They have the power to hire and lay off workers and to determine their salaries, decisions that can have a profound impact on employees' lives and communities.

Governments at all levels have the power to allocate resources, generating revenue by collecting taxes and fees and then distributing that money through public projects, social programs, military spending, and other policies. Within particular agencies or departments, officials wield power by exercising control over budgets and supplies.

Political Power: Making Rules and Decisions

Power can also be used for political purposes, enabling some people to set the conditions under which others are expected to live. Parents typically set the rules for how a household will function and how children should behave. In a workplace or school, the managers or administrators establish how the group will operate. Setting the rules for how the entire society will operate is the role of government. Politicians and government officials pass laws and establish regulations that organize many aspects of our daily lives. Those with power set the rules, and those without power are expected to follow them.

Cultural Power: Defining Reality

To prepare others to comply with their agenda, those with power define social reality in a particular way and encourage others to agree with their interpretation. Parents, for example, steer their children toward or away from certain types of books, entertainment, or religious instruction. By doing so, they are trying to shape how their children understand and define social reality by influencing their children's values and worldviews. If children internalize their parents' beliefs and values, they are unlikely to challenge or violate the rules set down by parents.

A similar process operates in society at large, as the media and schools shape our worldview. By selecting certain news stories and sources, the news media teach us to view certain topics and people as important and worthy of consideration (local crime stories or celebrities), while marginalizing or ignoring others who are not given routine coverage (advocates for the poor) (Croteau and Hoynes 1994b). Influencing the stories people read, the ideas they consider, and the perspectives to which they are regularly exposed is one way of exercising power in a society (Herman and Chomsky 1988/2002).

Schools exert power by including certain topics and excluding others. Until the middle of the twentieth century, history courses at all levels—elementary school to college—taught American history almost exclusively from the perspective of white, wealthy, straight men. Indeed, U.S. history was virtually equated with this group, since they were the ones who held positions of power in the government, military, and economy. Women of all classes, people of color, the working class, gays

Schools of all sorts shape how children understand the world. Here, boys study in an Islamic religious school or *madrassa*. How did your education help shape your worldview?

and lesbians—the vast majority of the population—were nearly invisible. As these groups have gained power in society, school curriculums have changed, and they now provide a more diverse view of history.

Italian Marxist activist-scholar Antonio Gramsci (1891–1937) argued that the class in power maintains its dominance not simply through the use of force, which is the job of the state's police and military forces, but also through the manipulation of ideas, which it accomplishes primarily through its control of cultural institutions such as the mass media, research and policy institutes ("think-tanks"), and universities. Gramsci (1929–1935/1971) applied the word *hegemony* to this situation. **Hegemony** *exists when those in power have successfully spread their ideas—and marginalized alternative viewpoints—so that their perspectives and interests are accepted widely as being universal and true.* By manipulating ideas, those in power can often manufacture the consent of others. For example, political leaders typically demonize foreign enemies in rallying citizen support for a war. Gramsci argued that hegemony is a tenuous condition that must be actively maintained in the face of constant challenges.

As we see later in this chapter, systems of social inequality are also reinforced by a justifying ideology that oppressed people themselves sometimes internalize. Cultural norms, the legal system, schools, the media, and other social institutions may all play a role in creating and maintaining this ideology.

Economic, political, and cultural powers are based in real-world social institutions, including businesses, government, and religions. At different points in history, each of these has been more influential than the other two. In the West, the power of religious institutions was most important in shaping daily life in the medieval period. By the eighteenth and nineteenth centuries, the rise of the secular nation-state signaled the growing influence of military and political power. In recent decades, economic power, in the form of transnational corporations, has become the most influential, in many cases eclipsing the influence of government (Mann 1986; Poggi 2001).

Power and Social Relationships

Power at all levels of society is rooted in social relationships, and it is limited by the relationships on which it is based. In this section we explore various aspects of these social re-

lationships, including the role of compliance in relationships of power and the importance of disobedience as a strategy for resisting power.

Types of Authority: Traditional, Rational-Legal, and Charismatic

Max Weber (1915/1946b) made an important distinction between legitimate and illegitimate power. **Legitimate power** is *voluntarily accepted by those who are affected.* Weber's idea of legitimate power is sometimes translated as "authority." A religious congregation, for example, might recognize and accept its spiritual leader's right to issue instructions and therefore voluntarily follow his or her wishes. **Illegitimate power** *relies on force or coercion to generate obedience.* A kidnapper or military dictator may be able to cause others to obey orders, but they do not obey willingly. Instead, they comply only because of the threat of violence if they disobey.

Weber (1915/1946b) further specified three types of legitimate power, or authority. The first, **traditional authority,** *has legitimacy because of compliance with well-established cultural practices.* These practices can vary widely, but from Europe's medieval nobility to modern chieftains in countless tribal societies around the globe, traditional leaders are widely perceived as legitimate because they derive their power from longstanding cultural customs that are usually not questioned. The child of a king becomes the next ruler for life because that is the way royalty works; people believe in the tradition. Often religious beliefs help to justify and support traditional authority.

By contrast, **rational-legal authority** *has legitimacy because it is based on established laws, rules, and procedures.* A president or prime minister is elected for a set term through an established process. A university president is hired after the school conducts a formal search and a series of interviews. These individuals gain legitimacy because they were selected through an agreed-upon procedure.

In the classic British movie *Monty Python and the Holy Grail,* an amusing scene sums up the difference between traditional and rational-legal authority. In the scene, Britain's legendary King Arthur encounters some peasants who challenge his legitimacy. The king appeals to traditional authority whereas the peasants insist on a rational-legal process for choosing a leader.

ARTHUR: I am your king!
PEASANT WOMAN: Well, I didn't vote for you.
ARTHUR: You don't vote for kings.

thinking about power
How were you socialized to view those who hold **power** in government?
Those who wield corporate **power**?

119

PEASANT WOMAN: Well, how did you become king then?

ARTHUR: The Lady of the Lake . . . held aloft [the sword] Excalibur from the bosom of the water signifying by Divine Providence that I, Arthur, was to carry Excalibur. That is why I am your king!

PEASANT MAN: Listen—strange women lying in ponds distributing swords is no basis for a system of government. Supreme executive power derives from a mandate from the masses, not from some farcical aquatic ceremony.

ARTHUR: Be quiet!

As these peasants recognize, a rational-legal process requires some transparency and logical justification, whereas tradition is, in effect, self-justifying. Weber argued that with the rise of science, industrialization, and democratic processes, rational-legal forms of authority rapidly replaced traditional ones. The contemporary spread of democratic forms of government around the world continues this trend.

Weber also described a third form of legitimate power. **Charismatic authority** is *power whose legitimacy is derived from the extraordinary personal characteristics of an individual leader, which inspire loyalty and devotion.* Charismatic leadership is usually not transferable. Therefore, this form of authority is typically short lived and episodic. Charismatic leaders can inspire groups of people to act, even though such leaders may possess no formal institutional power. Examples of charismatic leaders include compelling politicians, a motivating team coach or captain, a dynamic celebrity activist, or an inspirational spiritual leader.

The Role of Compliance

Weber based his distinctions between legitimate and illegitimate power on the perceptions of the people obeying the orders, but he did not address *how* those perceptions are created

and, therefore, how different types of leaders sustain their power by maintaining their followers' compliance. To take an extreme example, long-term hostages sometimes identify with their captors and voluntarily follow their wishes, an effect called the *Stockholm Syndrome.* This phenomenon, however, does not transform the abductor's power from illegitimate to legitimate. Instead, it shows compliance is more complicated than it may at first appear.

Power is limited by the social relationships on which it is based. The president of the United States, for example, is powerful only as long as others agree to carry out his commands. If the president orders a military attack or initiates a relief effort, many other people must carry out the commands for these goals to be accomplished. Authoritarian regimes can collapse when a large enough number of citizens refuse to obey their leaders and demonstrate for change—a situation that has occurred many times in history.

On a more mundane level, those with power in everyday life also depend on compliance to maintain their position. Students must agree to complete the paper assigned by their teacher, workers usually comply with the boss's rules, and children consent to their parent's request to finish their chores. In other words, people are not passive objects of the demands of those in power; they can react in a variety of ways, from complying voluntarily to resisting and thereby undermining authority.

The degree of compliance in a social situation is often not apparent at first glance. It takes a sociological understanding of power to see that simmering conflict can lurk just beneath the apparently calm, orderly surface of societies. When compliance is withdrawn, conflict may seem to erupt suddenly and dramatically. For example, in 2011 a series of revolutions and uprisings swept northern Africa and the Middle East in what became known as the Arab Spring. Protests, riots, strikes, and other disruptions can start small and spread rapidly as people decide that they will no longer comply. This type of rebellion is itself another form of power: the power of disobedience.

The three types of authority outlined by Weber can be found in contemporary life. The Pope relies on traditional authority to gain the allegiance of the world's Catholics. A police officer relies on rational-legal authority to carry out her duties. Although she no longer holds public office, Sarah Palin has had a significant impact on U.S. politics through her charismatic authority. What other examples of each type of authority can you think of?

SOCIOLOGY Matters

Promoting the Power of Nonviolence

One of the core sociological insights about power is that it depends on compliance. Consequently, those with little apparent power can use noncompliance, or disobedience, to great effect in bringing about social change. Since this insight comes from sociology, it is no surprise that three of the people most closely associated with the power of disobedience studied sociology in college.

Martin Luther King, Jr. (1929–1968) was a sociology major as an undergraduate. His later activism showed his understanding of how power operates in social relationships and how those who appear powerless can organize to effect change. King's well-known role as a charismatic leader in the civil rights movement began during the bus boycott in Montgomery, Alabama, in 1955–1956, a campaign that relied on disobedience. By refusing to ride the city's buses for over a year and setting up an alternative system of transportation, thousands of African Americans helped end segregation on public transportation. King went on to aid other rights campaigns that relied heavily on *civil disobedience:* nonviolent direct action that violates unjust laws. Using this strategy, activists successfully challenged segregation at lunch counters, department stores, public swimming pools, and many other facilities, and their efforts helped achieve access to voting rights that had previously been denied to African Americans throughout the South.

Although not as well known as Dr. King, Saul Alinsky (1909–1972), who studied sociology as a graduate student, was also highly influential. Among activists he is recognized as the creator of what is often called "Alinsky-style" community organizing. Alinsky transformed his sociological understanding of power into practical applications on behalf of low-income citizens. In Alinsky-style organizing, trained organizers identify and coordinate the efforts of existing neighborhood leaders, who in turn mobilize fellow residents to work on issues they identify as priorities, such as better housing, safer neighborhoods, and stronger schools. In addition to emphasizing the importance of creating strong organizations, Alinsky advocated the use of creative confrontational tactics that rely on disobedience to apply pressure on those in power. He emphasized the importance of operating outside of the experience of your opponent: for example, he organized fun public demonstrations, street theater, and other actions in which community residents could participate, rather than closed-door meetings that those in authority could dominate. In 2008, Alinsky-style community organizing received some unusual popular attention when a one-time community organizer named Barack Obama was elected president.

King and Alinksy focused on developing tactics for civil disobedience in the United States, whereas Gene Sharp (b. 1928) studies and writes about the power of nonviolent social action to bring about change in the face of dictatorship, war, and oppression around the world. Sharp's academic training includes a master's degree in sociology. His classic three-volume work, *The Politics of Nonviolent Action,* sketches out a theory of power based on sociological principles and describes the strategic uses of disobedience. Volume Two chronicles hundreds of nonviolent protest actions, including many forms of communication (petitions, marches, teach-ins), noncooperation (boycotts and strikes), and nonviolent interventions (sit-ins, land seizures, and disclosure of secret information). One little-known action: in 1942, when the German army occupying Poland posted "For Germans Only" signs at cafes and hotels in Warsaw, Polish youth stole the signs and defiantly placed them on the lampposts and trees where Germans had hanged Polish patriots. Sharp's work, now outlined in *From Dictatorship to Democracy* (1993/2010), has been translated into more than thirty languages and made available for free download on the Internet.

Sharp has irritated authoritarian regimes and influenced activists around the globe. As part of an effort to counter calls for more liberal reform and democracy, the Iranian Information Ministry in 2008 began airing a television propaganda message that condemned Sharp as a "theoretician of civil disobedience and velvet revolutions." That was a reference to the fact that many democracy movements in Eastern Europe during the 1980s and 1990s used ideas and tactics found in Sharp's work. The young people who led the Egyptian revolution in 2011 were also influenced by his work, leading the *New York Times* to comment, "For the world's despots, [Sharp's] ideas can be fatal" (Stohlberg 2011).

think about it

1. *How does the concept of power relate to the work of the three people featured in this box?*
2. *Can you think of other situations in which disobedience can be a source of power? If disobedience is so powerful, why isn't it used more often?*

The Power of Disobedience

Since power operates within social relationships, one of the great ironies of social life is that those who think they are powerless often have a great deal of power. History is filled with examples of ordinary people who united and toppled powerful opponents. (The Sociology Matters box discusses several key figures associated with the strategic application of disobedience.)

Workers have united to gain concessions from employers, and women have united to achieve changes in the law and in male-dominated institutions. The nonviolent strategies of the U.S. civil rights movement during the 1950s and 1960s inspired many social movements to fight for the rights of other oppressed groups. The people behind all these movements started out with little or no apparent power to effect change. In the end, however, their collective efforts generated enough power to overcome their oppressors.

Everyone has some power. At a minimum, you always have power over your own actions. James Scott (1987) found that peasants in a Malaysian community could exert some influence over public policies by using "weapons of the weak," including gossip about those in authority, foot-dragging, noncompliance, pilfering, and sabotage. None of these were organized or formal protests, but they enabled relatively powerless peasants to resist domination.

Though it may appear that college students are another group with little power within the institutions they attend, successful student activism has led to changes in college policies and regulations and created new academic programs. During the 1980s, for example, student activism caused many institutions to withdraw their investments in apartheid South Africa. Later, student efforts on behalf of living-wage and anti-sweatshop campaigns led to policy changes regarding pay for campus staff and the way in which schools license and acquire athletic wear. In recent years, students have protested tuition hikes and cuts in funding for education. The success of these efforts demonstrates that students have more power than they often realize.

The success of efforts on behalf of oppressed groups, as well as student activism, demonstrates two simple truths about power. First, when people work together, they increase their own power as individuals to effect change. Second, disobedience is a powerful weapon for those who struggle to effect change. Since power is a social relationship, people ultimately have the power to refuse to comply. They rarely use this power, often out of fear of coercion or force. But when people unite in an act of civil disobedience, they can instigate enormous change. This insight has been a powerful tool for many social movements, which we explore in Chapter 17. Those in power typically resist change promoted by oppressed groups because it threatens the privileges they hold, a topic we turn to now.

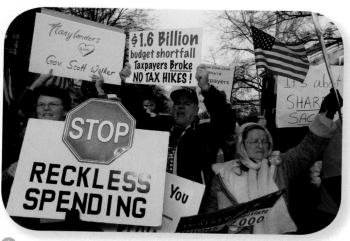

In recent years, a variety of "Tea Party" efforts have protested healthcare reform and what they see as high taxes and excessive government spending. What issues related to power are likely to produce national protests in the coming years?

Power and Privilege

As we cautioned in Chapter 1, viewing the world from a sociological perspective can sometimes make people uncomfortable. Nowhere is that more true than in dealing with the issues of power and privilege, topics that cut across race, class, gender, and other social differences (Johnson 2001). Our interests and perspectives—our existing power relations—affect how we think about power (Lukes 2005). When we learn about the unequal power various groups possess, we realize that, compared to many other people in the world, we enjoy a considerable amount of power and privilege. **Privilege** is *a special advantage or benefit that not everyone enjoys.* The fact that most people go about their daily lives unaware of the privileges they enjoy is, in itself, an indicator of that power.

For example, heterosexuals need not concern themselves with their sexual orientation, since our society's norms, laws, and institutional practices have long been organized to accommodate them. Straight people can get married, obtain employment benefits for their spouses, adopt children, talk openly about their relationships without fear of negative consequences—they can go about their daily lives without thinking about being heterosexual. These are privileges that gays and lesbians often do not have. At the same time, a gay man might be acutely aware of discrimination based on sexual orientation while being unaware of his position of privilege as a white, upper-middle-class male. It is easier to recognize disadvantage than privilege.

The point of recognizing privilege is not to make people feel guilty. Rather, doing so allows us to understand society more accurately by removing the blinders that block our ability to see how power operates. In one way or another, we are all involved in power relations. In our society "race," "gender," "class," and "sexuality" tend to conjure up images of Blacks and Latinos, women, working class and poor people, and lesbians and gays. But studying these topics is not just about studying those with less power. Instead, we study subjects such as gender and sexual orientation to determine how *everyone* in a society is connected through relations of power. In addition, understanding privilege can help us to identify the resources we have available to empower ourselves, assist others, and perhaps reduce inequality.

To understand dynamics of power and privilege, it is often useful to consider the situation of those with less power. Dorothy Smith (1987, 1990) developed **standpoint theory,** which *questions taken-for-granted assumptions about society by looking at it from multiple viewpoints, especially from the perspective of people in subordinate positions.* A "standpoint" is the place from which a person views the world. A person's standpoint is structured by his or her social location, which includes race, class, gender, and sexual orientation.

People with different standpoints see and understand the world differently. For example, when Hurricane Katrina and the subsequent flooding from a faulty levy destroyed large sections of New Orleans and the Gulf Coast in 2005, the federal government's inadequate emergency response efforts left the poor and mostly black residents of this city abandoned (Squires and Hartman 2006). Two-thirds of Blacks believed the government response would have been faster if most of the victims had been white. More than three-quarters of Whites, though, disagreed (Pew Research Center 2005). To varying degrees, we can find similar differences in the perspectives of different groups (men and women, members of different classes) on a variety of issues.

In societies with deep inequalities, groups have differing perspectives. Each of these perspectives is necessarily partial. As a result, considering multiple standpoints, especially of those who have less power, is crucial to gaining a more complete understanding of social life.

Power and Inequality

As we have seen, different groups have varying degrees of power within a society, a situation that inevitably produces **inequality,** *the unequal distribution of resources among groups of people.* All societies have some form of inequality, but its nature and extent vary significantly, because patterns of unequal distribution are not natural, inevitable, or the product of chance. Instead, inequality is socially constructed; it varies according to the culture and social structure of a society.

Social inequality is multidimensional: in other words, different forms of inequality coexist within a society. Max Weber (1915/1946b) argued that society is stratified in terms of class, status, and political power.

Class: Economic Conditions

Everyone has dreamed of winning the lottery at some point because we all know that obtaining a large amount of money can transform a person's life. With it you can buy a beautiful home, a fancy car, premium health care, travel, and other luxury items. You might also use your winnings to buy leisure time, quitting your job and hiring others to cook your meals, clean your home, handle your finances, and so on. Some people have, in effect, already won the lottery simply by being born into wealth. Clearly, one major type of inequality in society is the uneven distribution of money and other economic resources.

A **class** is *a group of people who share a roughly similar economic position and lifestyle.* Karl Marx's analysis of the importance of class was especially influential. As we discussed in Chapter 1, Marx focused on economic inequality and considered how the different classes in capitalist societies relate to each other as they participate in the process of economic production. Marx highlighted the world of work and analyzed classes as groups of people who share a common relationship to the means of production.

In many ways, Max Weber—whose ideas are also discussed in Chapter 1—agreed with Marx that economics is a key to understanding inequality. However, whereas Marx examined the concept of class in terms of work, Weber looked at class in terms of **life chances,** *the opportunities offered by a person's economic position.* For Weber, a class is a group of people who have a similar capacity to earn money, and who consequently share a similar lifestyle. We consider class-based systems of inequality later in this chapter. In Chapter 9, we explore the importance of class in more detail and examine further the differences between Marx's and Weber's approach to this topic. For now, it is enough to know that class is one major type of inequality.

 Housing is one of the clearest examples of economic inequality in the United States. Neighborhoods tend to be segregated based on income levels. As children grow up, they tend to accept the economic standards of their neighborhood as the norm.

CORE CONCEPTS CHALLENGE

What did your neighborhood look like when you were growing up? What would pictures of your street suggest about the class composition of your neighborhood and the relative power of the members of your community?

Status: Prestige

Although Weber and Marx agreed on the importance of class, Weber differed from Marx by arguing that status and political power—two noneconomic factors—were also key to understanding inequality. To Weber, both status and political power could be sources of power independent of a person's class.

Adherents of traditional Marxist thought treated class as the single most important source of inequality, supported by other types of inequality such as those based on race and gender. Weber, though, argued that a person's status—based on his or her social characteristics, such as race, ethnicity, or gender—could have an impact independent of class and therefore should be considered as a distinct form of inequality, not merely a secondary feature of economic inequality.

As we noted in Chapter 4, *status* is a person's position in a social system; it is also the prestige attributed to that individual. Depending on the context, then, status can have two meanings—the position itself or the prestige associated with it. People in their fourth year of high school have the status of a senior, a social position. In addition, seniors enjoy the prestige afforded that social position. A person has a given status because he or she belongs to a community of people who have the same lifestyle, ethnicity, race, ancestry, gender, sexual orientation, education, or occupation. Membership in a status group is usually not formal. Instead, members define some shared feature as important or valuable. Status is, in effect, self-perpetuating. Status groups develop formal and informal rules that designate who belongs. Those who belong may socialize with one another, live in the same neighborhoods, join the same organizations, send their children to the same schools, and marry others within the group.

The members of a status group can sometimes use their membership to gain power over nonmembers. **Social closure** is *the process whereby a status group maximizes its own advantages by restricting access to rewards only to members of the group.* This process can involve subtle or blatant **discrimination,** *treating others unequally based on their background or other personal characteristics.* The white populations in the southern states of the United States before the civil rights era and in South Africa before the 1990s both engaged in social closure to exclude other racial groups from access to voting, education, and other rights and opportunities.

In our society, status and class are often linked; people who belong to higher classes disproportionately come from groups with higher status. However, sometimes people of relatively modest means—respected religious leaders, influential politicians, or admired artists—gain access to high-status communities, even though they have relatively modest incomes. Conversely, people with considerable economic resources sometimes face discrimination and other hurdles because of their status. Middle-class African Americans can face both subtle and blatant harassment and discrimination because of their race (Cose 1995; Feagin and Sikes 1994). This situation has improved significantly in recent years, but in many racially diverse communities, high-status organizations and social circles still tend to be all, or nearly all, white.

Ethnicity and religion, too, have long divided status groups in the United States. At one time, people of Irish ancestry, Jews, and Catholics faced discrimination and were excluded, by rule or by custom, from some neighborhoods, jobs, social clubs, civic associations, and schools. In the nineteenth century, for example, employment ads sometimes specified, "No Irish need apply." For the most part, these groups no longer face such discrimination, but Latinos, Muslims, and other ethnic and religious groups continue to experience discrimination today. Gender and sexual orientation, too, continue to present powerful barriers.

Political Power: Strength Through Organization

In addition to class and status, Weber argued that society is stratified in terms of political power. Weber saw that by creating organizations to advance particular goals, people working together could influence society. He referred to these organizations as "parties," meaning a broad range of political groups, including what we would today call social movements, advocacy groups, and citizens' organizations. As we saw earlier, organizing such groups is one form of empowerment.

Weber saw political power as potentially independent of class and status. For example, lesbian and gay people in the United States who faced status-based discrimination due to their sexual orientation have been able to organize themselves into an influential political force over the past few decades. Although not particularly rich and subject to intense social discrimination, this group has been able to develop political power to improve policies and laws affecting its members' lives. Political organization, then, can serve as a source of power independent of class or status and, as we have seen, can accomplish social change through collective action. But like class and status, political power is distributed unequally in society.

The Intersections of Race, Class, and Gender

As we have seen, Weber argued that social inequality involves class, status, and political power. Similarly, in his work analyzing the black community, sociologist W.E.B. Du Bois, writing early in the twentieth century, highlighted issues of race, class, and nationality. These early works suggested that we should consider many aspects of social life when examining power and inequality.

In recent years, some feminist scholars, including Patricia Hill Collins (2000), have built on this tradition through **intersectionality theory,** which *highlights the connections and interactions between various forms of inequality, especially race, class,*

thinking about **power**
What status groups do you belong to? Do the members of those groups use **power** to maximize their advantages over others?

A woman points approvingly to a racist sign in this photograph from the early 1920s. Although this woman faced the disadvantages of gender inequality, her status as a white person afforded privileges not available to Japanese Americans of either gender.

CORE CONCEPTS CHALLENGE

*How does this photograph illustrate the fact that inequality is multidimensional? How does a person's **culture** teach the kind of attitudes shown in this photo?*

and gender. These theorists recognize the different dimensions of inequality and highlight the interactions that take place between these dimensions. For example, white people as a group enjoy privileges in our society because of their race, but white families trapped in poverty face hurdles because of their class. Meanwhile, within the context of poor white families, men are likely to enjoy privileges not afforded to women.

Focusing on the interaction between power and inequality can help us to gain a deeper understanding of social life in several ways:

- It gives us a more accurate reflection of how we experience the social world. Any person's identity is multifaceted, including his or her race, class, gender, ethnicity, sexual orientation, and nationality. Taking into account all these aspects of identity gives us a better understanding of our own social location.

- Once we recognize that these factors intersect, we can acknowledge that the relative importance of different types of inequality varies depending on the social context and circumstances. Although a Latino man living in poverty may enjoy privileges within his family because of traditional gender inequality, he also faces many disadvantages because he occupies a low position on the class hierarchy and belongs to an ethnic minority.

- We can also see that intersections involve more than simply "adding up" different identities. One aspect of identity can change another. Being wealthy or poor, for example, can change what it means to be male or female.

- When we recognize that race, class, and gender interact, we are better able to avoid overgeneralizing about any one group of people. Patricia Hill Collins (2000, 5–6) notes, "Theories advanced as being universally applicable to women as a group upon closer examination appear greatly limited by the white, middle-class and Western origins of their proponents." For example, the idea that the women's movement of the 1960s and 1970s opened the way for women's participation in the paid workforce needs to be qualified, because significant percentages of poor and working-class women in the United States—especially women of color—were already part of the workforce. By viewing women's increased participation in the paid labor force solely through the lens of gender, we miss the important impact of class and race.

Collins (2000) coined the phrase **matrix of domination** to indicate *the interlocking systems of oppression associated with race, class, and gender.* The metaphor of a matrix suggests more than one dimension and allows for the idea that people can be privileged in some ways and oppressed in others. When one group believes it is superior to another, has the right to dominate the other, and is able to do so, oppression results. Her framework highlights the active domination of weaker groups by those with more power at the individual, group, and institutional levels. Reflecting the core concept of structure, as well as the capacity people have for action, Collins recognizes that these various levels of oppression are also sites for resistance as people use their collective power to achieve autonomy and promote equality.

Collins's matrix approach shows that there are few pure oppressors or victims in society. Most people are privileged on some dimension of inequality and disadvantaged on some other. This is true across different types of stratification systems, which we consider next.

Structured Inequality: Stratification Systems

Societies formalize and institutionalize inequality—including the unequal distribution of power—by developing social structures that perpetuate stratification. **Stratification systems** are made up of *social structures and cultural norms that create and maintain inequality by ranking people into a hierarchy of groups that receive unequal resources.* Over the centuries, various societies have created different types of stratification systems. All stratification systems, however, share three key elements:

1. The unequal distribution of valued *resources*
2. Distinct *groups* that make up society's strata (layers)
3. An *ideology* that explains and justifies inequality

The particular form these elements take in any given society determines the dominant type of stratification system and the distribution of power within the society. We will take a closer look at the elements shared by all stratification systems before we consider some examples.

Unequal Resources

The first element of all stratification systems is the unequal distribution of valued resources. These may include (Grusky 2001, 4):

- *Economic* resources, including money, property, and land
- *Human* resources, such as education, training, and specialized skills
- *Cultural* resources that aid in achieving success, such as knowledge and skills learned through socialization
- *Social* resources, including access to important networks of people
- *Honorific* resources, involving the acquisition of prestige and status
- *Civil* resources, including legal rights involving property, contracts, voting, and speech
- *Political* resources, involving authority in the home, workplace, political arena, or social life

In any stratification system, some resources are distributed more evenly than others. For example, in the United States all citizens have similar legal rights based on the principle of equality under the law, but there are stark differences between rich and poor in terms of economic and human resources. In addition, if a resource is available more readily to one group than to another, that discrepancy can have an impact on another resource. Because the affluent can afford better legal counsel than the poor, the apparent equality of the legal system can be compromised.

Stratified Groups

The second element of all stratification systems is the groups that make up the various strata in society. Stratification based on class, race, and gender is especially widespread and significant, which is why sociologists pay especially close attention to them. However, stratification can also be based on ethnicity, age, religious affiliation, sexual orientation, and disability, among other factors.

The groups within systems of stratification can be based on either an ascribed or an achieved status. As noted in Chapter 4, an *ascribed status* is a position an individual has been assigned in life, regardless of his or her wishes or abilities. Race and sex are examples of ascribed statuses. Stratification systems based primarily on ascribed statuses are said to be closed: they are rigid and impermeable, making it virtually impossible for an individual to move from one stratum to another.

An *achieved status* is a position an individual attains voluntarily, to a considerable degree, as the result of his or her own effort and abilities. College graduates, for example, attain their status due largely to their own efforts. Stratification systems based primarily on achieved statuses are said to be open: it is possible for an individual within such a system to achieve **social mobility,** *movement from one stratum of a stratification system to another.* In systems of class stratification, for example, a person's class status can change as a result of structural changes in the economy, individual ability, education, effort, luck, or other factors. However, a person's achieved statuses are still influenced to varying degrees by social factors beyond his or her control. For example, the family into which you are born can significantly influence your class status.

The various social categories associated with inequality—such as races, ethnicities, classes, and genders—are not natural, inevitable, or biologically based. Instead, the meaning and significance of each category is determined by its cultural context and the social structure—in other words, these categories are socially constructed. They change over time, and they are continually contested, revised, and reinvented. We learn the meaning and significance of these categories for our time and our culture through the socialization process, which we discuss in Chapter 6.

Ideologies That Justify Inequality

The third element of all stratification systems is a related *ideology,* a system of beliefs that helps define and explain the world and justifies the existence of inequality. Those in power produce and promote these ideas to maintain the stratification system, but others sometimes internalize them, as well. In fact, the most efficient way to maintain a system of inequality is to convince most people that the system is fair, inevitable, or both. If the groups within a society believe in the ideology that justifies a stratification system, or if they are cynical about any possibility of changing the system, they are unlikely to challenge it. Consequently, those who struggle to reduce inequality must often debate the ideology that supports it. For example, women's rights advocates have long had to debunk myths about women's biological inferiority.

The three key elements that all stratification systems have in common—unequal resources, distinct groups, and a justifying ideology—vary within different stratification systems. We now take a brief look at several examples of such systems.

Caste Systems: India, Feudal Estates, and Racial Segregation

A **caste system** features *stratification based on various ascribed characteristics determined at birth.* The social stratum—or caste—into which people are born largely determines their life chances, typically affecting their access to education, their work options, where they can live, and whom they can marry. Many agrarian societies have some type of closed caste system, but the best known, by far, is the one found in India, which was outlawed in 1952 but which continues to be practiced informally.

INDIA'S CASTE SYSTEM India's stratification system is traditionally based on the unequal distribution of social honor or respect associated with four major castes, known as *varnas:*

- **Brahmins,** the highest caste, are priests, scholars, and teachers.
- **Kshatriyas,** the second caste, are kings, warriors, and political leaders.
- **Vaisyas,** the third caste, constitute a broad group that includes landowners, merchants, and skilled craftspeople.
- **Sudras,** the fourth caste, includes peasants, servants, and laborers.

Rounding out this complex system are hundreds of sub-caste groups, or *jatis,* typically organized around a single occupation, such as carpenters or barbers and often situated in a particular village or region.

At the lowest stratum of Indian society is a group that exists outside of the *varna* system. Physical contact with members of this lowest grouping is thought to pollute anyone of higher status, so they are often referred to as "untouchables," but they call themselves *Dalits* ("downtrodden"). *Dalits* are often uneducated and typically perform the lowest and least desirable types of labor, such as cleaning public toilets. In addition, *Dalits* are social outcasts who are banned from worshiping with members of the four *varnas.* Consequently, *Dalits* have little power in society.

Membership in a particular caste is determined at birth and cannot be changed. The justifying ideology, derived from both tradition and Hindu religious doctrine, emphasizes the maintenance of caste purity by restricting social contact to members of one's own caste. People are expected to marry within their own caste.

Throughout India's history, the caste system helped maintain social order by clearly defining the rights and responsibilities of those who belonged to various castes. However, resistance and opposition to this system date back thousands of years. After India gained independence from British rule in the mid-twentieth century, it adopted a constitution that eventually outlawed discrimination based on caste. Today the caste system plays only a limited role in India's modern urban life. However, in the country's more traditional rural areas and small towns, the influence of castes remains significant.

FEUDAL ESTATE SYSTEMS During the Middle Ages, European societies were stratified into a castelike system that regulated economic, political, and social life based primarily on the unequal distribution of land. Feudalism, as this system is now known, varied but commonly featured three *estates* that comprised a society's major strata:

- **The nobility.** The nobility, the dominant estate, owned the vast tracts of land upon which the agricultural economy— and their power—was based. Wealthy and powerful nobles lived lives of relative luxury, reaping the benefits of others' labor. An elaborate system of honorific titles, such as *king, queen, duke, earl,* and *baron,* indicated the relative rank

Because of the family into which she was born, this Indian woman is a *Dalit,* or "untouchable." The man in the portrait behind her is Bhimrao Ramiji Amdedkar, a scholar and activist who founded the movement for civil rights for Untouchables, which challenges the ideology underlying this caste system.

and power of each individual within this estate. A person's rank was inherited, and marriage was typically restricted to other members of the nobility. Typically, only the eldest son of a noble could inherit land, so other male children served as military officers, judges, government administrators, or high-ranking members of the Church.

- **The Christian clergy.** As the second estate, the clergy largely served the nobles but had some independence due to their claim of religious authority. They were generally well educated and were themselves divided into an elaborate hierarchy made up of the pope, cardinals, bishops, priests, and other positions. An important role of the clergy was to articulate and enforce the ideology that justified the feudal system. The Church taught that inequality was the will of God and that the poor would receive their reward in heaven rather than on earth. To question inequality, therefore, was to question God's will.
- **Commoners.** The commoners made up the bulk of the population. Typically illiterate, they did not own land but instead lived on and worked the land owned by the nobles. The commoners' labor enriched the nobles but left them living in poor and difficult conditions.

Commoners repeatedly challenged the harsh conditions of the estate system by staging peasant uprisings. Eventually, the power of nobles was curbed with the advent of more democratic political systems and less-rigid class-based economic systems in the eighteenth and nineteenth centuries, as we saw in Chapter 1.

RACIAL SEGREGATION IN THE UNITED STATES The system of racial segregation in the United States, which evolved between the Civil War and the 1960s, can be considered a caste-based stratification system. (It influenced South Africa's apartheid, another caste-based stratification system, beginning in 1948.) The division between Blacks

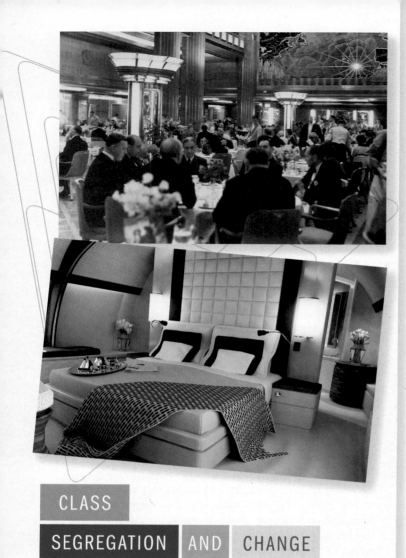

Many forms of public accommodation and transportation are segregated by class. In an earlier era, luxury ocean liners, such as the one illustrated here, served wealthy clientele. In today's faster-paced society, first-class luxury is more likely to be found on private jets, such as the one shown here. Most Americans today are appalled by the racial segregation that once existed in public facilities. Why then is class-based segregation still taken for granted?

and Whites was based on birth and could not be changed. The ideology that justified racial segregation was racism, which those in power supported by invoking tradition, Christian teachings, and pseudo-science. Racial inequality was said to be the foundation of the traditional "southern way of life." Bible stories and passages were used selectively to justify slavery, including the tale that descendents of Noah's son, Ham, were cursed to be slaves (Genesis 9:18–27) and St. Paul's advice that servants accept their lot and obey their masters (Ephesians 6:5–9). So-called scientific classifications of races, based on racist assumptions, also justified racial inequality, as we examine in Chapter 10.

Though it is primarily associated with the southern states, where it was most comprehensive and brutally enforced, racial segregation existed throughout the United States. Blacks faced the most formal and broadest oppression, dating back to a race-based system of slavery. However, other races, ethnicities, and nationalities—most notably Mexican and Chinese Americans—also faced segregation. Whites excluded minorities from many types of employment, and laws restricted their access to education, public transportation, theaters, restaurants, voting, and seats in public office. The legal system supported this unequal treatment. For example, in many communities, deeds to white-owned homes stipulated that they could not be sold to Blacks.

Blacks and other minorities long resisted racial discrimination. The civil rights movement of the 1950s and 1960s successfully challenged the legal foundation for racial segregation. Since then, advocates for social justice have reduced the economic and social impact of racial discrimination, though its impact continues, and informal segregation is still a social reality. We examine various aspects of race and ethnicity in more detail in Chapter 10.

Class Systems: Capitalist and Socialist

Unlike a caste system, in which a person's position is determined by birth, a **class system** features *stratification determined by economic position, which results from a combination of individual achievement and family of birth.* Class systems are more flexible than caste systems and offer more opportunities for social mobility. They are still stratification systems, however; they organize the unequal distribution of resources among distinct groups and are supported by a justifying ideology. We examine classes more closely in Chapter 9. This brief

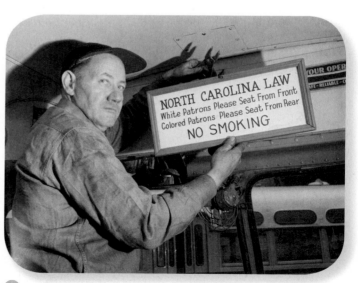

Whites used their power in the United States to create caste-like divisions between Whites and Blacks. Such inequality was challenged successfully when Blacks organized in the civil rights movement to maximize their power.

preview sketches out some of the features of class systems in the two major types of economies, capitalist and socialist.

CLASS IN CAPITALIST SYSTEMS
In the United States and other contemporary capitalist societies, considerable affluence is accompanied by significant class inequality. Economic resources such as income, stocks, real estate, and other forms of property are distributed unevenly, as are education and training. A small upper class of capitalist investors owns a substantial amount of the wealth and thereby wields enormous power. A broad middle class of relatively well-educated workers is employed in jobs that require considerable knowledge and skill and that pay well enough to afford a comfortable existence. A large working class is employed in modest-to-low-paying jobs that require less training and formal education. Those working for low wages and those unable to secure steady employment often live in poverty.

In capitalist class systems, the ideology emphasizes individualism—the idea that success is based on merit, not inherited advantage. The popular idea that "With hard work and determination, you can accomplish whatever you want" is an implicit explanation for inequality: those at the bottom do not work hard, while those at the top do. Inequality is seen as good because it motivates people to work hard to achieve economic success, thereby contributing to the overall affluence of society. As we see in Chapter 9, however, structural factors and barriers beyond an individual's control have a considerable impact on economic success or failure.

Throughout modern history, those below the capitalist class have often resisted inequality; in particular, workers in various countries have organized themselves into labor unions to gain more power and improve their working conditions. As a result, today's capitalist societies vary substantially in the degree to which they are unequal.

CLASS IN SOCIALIST SYSTEMS
The major difference between capitalist and socialist class systems is the nature and degree of government intervention in the economy, a topic we examine in Chapter 16. Capitalist ideology suggests that people should compete in the marketplace free of government interference. In contrast, socialist ideology emphasizes the collective good and economic equality as coordinated by the government. In a socialist system, the government typically owns major industries and taxes wealthy citizens heavily to pay for free or subsidized social programs such as education, health care, housing, and daycare.

Because the state plays such a central role, economic stratification varies across socialist societies, depending on the type of government. State socialism—as found most notably in the former Soviet Union and other communist countries of Eastern Europe before 1991—is characterized by totalitarian governments that typically downplay the existence of inequality. In such systems, political dissent was not tolerated, and those who held political positions (in other words, those who had access to

political resources)—especially membership in the Communist Party and authority in the workplace—were at the highest levels of the stratification system. Thus Communist Party officials had the most power. The key divisions in society were between party leaders, workplace managers, and ordinary workers.

The politically oppressive nature of state socialism, coupled with its inefficiency as an economic system, helped lead to its demise. Today's major socialist societies are quite different. In China, for example, the Communist Party has adopted flexible economic policies, but the central authority still rigidly controls the government-owned companies that carry them out. The party also controls government bodies at all levels of society, including the military, the courts, the media, universities, and religious organizations (McGregor 2010). As a result, China continues to suppress political freedom while incorporating aspects of capitalism into its economy and harboring stark inequalities.

In contrast to state socialism, democratic socialism combines a government accountable to the electorate with an economy that includes considerable state intervention. Found most notably in some Scandinavian countries today, democratic socialism has produced some of the world's most affluent and least unequal countries. These societies tend to cultivate an ideology that values equality and the common good, even if it means putting strict limits on the income and wealth of the country's richest citizens.

Patriarchy

Another type of systemic stratification is based on gender. Women have long been subjected to **patriarchy,** *male domination through social institutions and cultural practices.* Patriarchy can be thought of as a system of stratification since it emphasizes separate and unequal groups (men and women), distributes resources unequally, and justifies this inequality with an ideology that assumes the superiority of men.

Patriarchal arrangements of power are built into many aspects of social life, including the cultural norm that a man should be the "head of household," the idea in some religions that women should play secondary roles, and the continuing underrepresentation of women in positions of political and economic power. Many feminist sociologists focus on understanding women's oppression, how sexism operates, and how women's subordination intersects with other forms of inequality. Consequently, power is an important concept in feminist theory and research (Allen 2000, 2005, 2008; Hartsock 1996; Yeatmann 1997; Young 1992).

As we explore further in Chapter 11, feminist scholars have developed a variety of approaches to understanding the relationships among gender, inequality, and power (Connell 1991; Davis, Leijenaar, and Oldersma 1991; Radtke and Stam 1994). Some argue that women's oppression resulted from the power men had over them and that the liberation of women will challenge and break this power. Socialist-feminists argue that women's oppression was a result of capitalism; women were

---

thinking about power
Do you think success is based on individualism and merit, or are other factors involved?
How does a person's **power** or lack of power fit into the equation?

Kiya Stokes and the Service Workers' Union

When Kiya Stokes enrolled in a sociology course on class and inequality, he had no idea that a few years later he would be on the front lines of the struggle for economic justice. As he studied the sociological perspective, learned about stratification, and read about the contemporary labor movement, he started thinking that maybe he could become a part of the effort to improve workers' lives.

"As an African-American man, I was well aware of the various forms of racial discrimination and oppression that I witnessed and endured," Stokes notes. "Sociology helped broaden my perspectives and showed me in a scientific way that there were other groups within our society that were also victims of various forms of oppression." Learning about the intersections of inequality was not always easy. Stokes admits, "The process was slightly traumatic as I learned not only that there were other oppressed people here but that in different ways I had benefited and participated in their oppression. After I moved past the shame, and empathy, I decided that I needed to do something to make the world a better place."

At the suggestion of his sociology professor, Stokes enrolled in a short training program run by a labor union, and he was hooked. He went on to earn a master's degree in labor studies and then went to work for the Service Employees International Union (SEIU), the nation's largest labor union. After working in Atlanta and Washington, D.C., Stokes is now a research analyst for the union in Los Angeles. He says, "The work that I do helps support campaigns that are designed to increase worker wages, to improve safety standards, and to eventually stamp out poverty."

Reflecting back, Stokes says, "In sociology class I learned a new way to view the world. I learned that we were not just one big happy family here with a predestined lot in life. I saw that

many people *do* work hard and do *not* get adequately compensated for that labor. Others do not do a bit of work but have wealth beyond our wildest imagination. I started questioning other premises and assumptions about the state of the world that most people take for granted. In the end I am certain that without the critical thinking and analytical skills that I learned in sociology class I would not be fighting for working people today."

Kiya Stokes

> "Sociology helped broaden my perspectives and showed me in a scientific way that there were other groups within our society that were also victims of various forms of oppression."

Through his work, Stokes has seen firsthand that when people organize and work together for collective change, they can realize their own power and help promote economic justice. This approach is neatly summed up in the two-word motto of his union: "Stronger Together."

think about it

1. *How are the sociological concepts and ideas introduced in this chapter reflected in Kiya Stokes's story?*

2. *What did Stokes mean by saying that seriously considering inequality was "a slightly traumatic experience" for him? Do you feel the same way about your study of power and social inequality? Why or why not?*

---

exploited as cheap labor in the paid labor force and as unpaid labor at home, helping to sustain male workers. This argument links class and gender inequality.

These examples of stratification systems illustrate some of the many ways that inequality is structured. Although each form of stratification has distinct features, by viewing all of them through the lens of power, we can see many similarities.

Can Inequality Be Reduced?

If all societies have inequality, can it be reduced? The simple answer is yes, although some forms of inequality are easier to combat than others. Interestingly, equality is a fairly new value in human history. Only since the Enlightenment of the eighteenth century has inequality been seen as undesirable. Before that time, it was considered inevitable and often a part of God's will. However, sociology teaches us that inequality is socially constructed and, thus, its nature and extent are neither inevitable nor foreordained. Human action produces inequality, and people can organize to empower themselves and reduce inequality. (The profile in the Sociology Works box illustrates how sociological insights helped to shape one person's decision to fight against economic inequality.)

MONEY, POWER, AND POLITICS

Supreme Court Justice Louis Brandeis famously commented, "We may have democracy, or we may have wealth concentrated in the hands of a few, but we can't have both" (in Lonergan 1941, 42). Brandeis's concern that concentrated economic power can be converted unfairly into political power has resurfaced in recent years as economic inequality has grown (a topic we explore in Chapter 9) and as money has come to play an increasing role in politics. These concerns cut across party lines. As former senators Bob Kerrey (a Nebraska Democrat) and Larry Pressler (a South Dakota Republican) argue, in this age of "wealthy interests" and "big money givers," "confidence in Congress has reached an all-time low in part because Americans perceive that their representatives are primarily accountable to those who fund their campaigns" (Kerrey and Pressler 2010).

Political participation in the United States is unequal and influenced heavily by class, with those at the top having the greatest voice and influence (Schlozman et al. 2005). This disparity is especially true of campaign contributions, which have always played a role in politics. But because of two recent developments, wealthy people have more ability than ever before to translate their economic power into political power, renewing concerns about the danger of which Justice Brandeis warned.

First, the amount of money involved in political campaigns has grown dramatically, making wealthy donors all the more important. For example, after holding steady for decades, the amount candidates spent on presidential campaigns increased dramatically from about $661 million in 2000 to $1.75 billion in 2008 (in 2008 dollars) mostly due to increased reliance on media advertising and sophisticated polling (Figure 5.1). To fund their campaigns, candidates rely primarily on big donors, with less than 1 percent of Americans providing 80 percent of the total funding for the 2008 presidential election (Americans for Campaign Reform 2010). Nearly half (47 percent) of contributions to the 2008 Obama campaign came from just 13,000 donors, each of whom contributed $1,000 or more, whereas only 26 percent came from donors who gave $200 or less. Obama's opponent, John McCain, received an even higher percentage of his contributions (59 percent) from donors giving $1,000

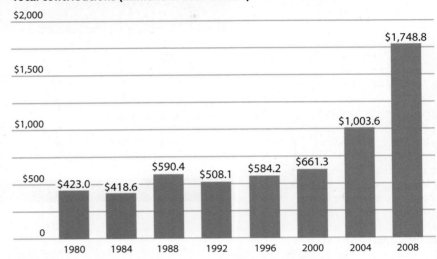

Total contributions (millions of 2008 dollars)

FIGURE 5.1 | TOTAL CONTRIBUTIONS TO PRESIDENTIAL CANDIDATES, 1980–2008 (MILLIONS OF 2008 DOLLARS)

After remaining relatively stable for a quarter-century, the amount of money spent on presidential campaigns has skyrocketed in recent years, with total contributions topping $1.7 billion in 2008. *Source:* Center for Responsive Politics: OpenSecrets.org. Adjusted for inflation by authors.

or more (Malbin 2008). Not surprisingly, large donors come from wealthy households. In 2000, 95 percent of large donors ($1,000 or more) came from the wealthiest 12 percent of households (Schlozman et al. 2005).

Second, much of the money that influences elections does not go directly to campaigns but is instead spent on independent advertising to support or oppose candidates. The potential influence of this kind of indirect funding was exacerbated in 2010 when a divided Supreme Court, citing First Amendment "free speech" concerns, issued a controversial ruling (*Citizens United v. the Federal Election Commission*) that swept away limits on corporate spending in political elections (Liptak 2010). As a result of this decision, a flood of new money entered the process—outside groups spent nearly four times as much on the midterm elections in 2010 than they had in 2006. Led by the biggest contributor, the business community's U.S. Chamber of Commerce, the bulk of this money appears to have come from corporations and their allies, but because such indirect spending does not have to comply with campaign disclosure laws, the source of about half this money was hidden from public view. For example, the second biggest contributor, American Crossroads, was set up by Republican political operatives but is funded primarily by anonymous donors (American Crossroads 2011; Public Citizen 2011; SourceWatch 2011). Thus, although more money is flowing into the electoral process, transparency regarding the source of these funds has declined.

Will citizens organize to curb the power of money in politics? Or, as Justice Brandeis warned, will concentrated economic power erode the health of our democracy? Those questions remain to be answered.

THINKING SOCIOLOGICALLY ABOUT . . .

Power

- **Power** is the capacity to bring about a desired outcome as well as to overcome resistance by others. It operates at all levels of society.

- **Power** can be used to allocate resources (economic), make rules and decisions (political), and help to define reality (cultural).

- **Power** is based on social relationships and requires compliance. Disobedience can be a form of power, since it denies the compliance being sought.

REVIEW, REFLECT, AND APPLY

Looking Back

1. Power includes the ability to bring about a desired outcome ("power to"), as well as the capacity to overcome resistance ("power over"). Education, organization, and networking contribute to empowerment. Compliance may be obtained by persuasion, reward, or coercion.

2. Power operates at all levels of society and can be seen in both everyday situations as well as at the macro level. Power is commonly used to allocate resources (economic), make rules and decisions (political), and help to define reality (cultural)—and thus is closely tied to inequality.

3. Power can be legitimate, accepted voluntarily by those who are affected by it; or illegitimate, relying on coercion to generate obedience. Legitimate power can be based on traditional, rational-legal, or charismatic authority.

4. Power is based on social relationships and requires compliance from others. Disobedience, or noncompliance, can be a form of power, especially for those without access to other forms of power.

5. Considering power and inequality alerts us to the issue of privilege. Understanding relations of power involves understanding various perspectives, including those of people with little power.

6. Inequality is multidimensional and includes stratification based on class (economic conditions), status (prestige), and power (political organization). Intersectionality theory suggests that to understand inequality, we need to consider the ways in which race, class, and gender interact and form what is sometimes referred to as a matrix of domination.

7. All societies have some system of stratification, featuring unequally distributed resources, distinct groups that make up the strata, and an ideology that explains and justifies inequality. Major types of stratification systems include caste systems, class systems, and patriarchy.

8. Economic power can be translated into political power through financial contributions to election campaigns and related advertising efforts.

Critical Thinking: Questions and Activities

1. What are power and inequality, and how are these two concepts related?

2. Do you consider yourself powerful? If you answer yes, what is the source of your power? If your answer is no, what would have to change to increase your power?

3. Identify and describe a common situation in your daily life where you comply with power. Is this a case of legitimate or illegitimate power? Explain.

4. How do various types of inequality intersect in your life? In what ways are you relatively privileged? In what ways do you face disadvantages?

5. Make a list of three people or organizations that you consider to be powerful. Using what you have learned in this chapter, explain what makes each of them powerful. For each, explain how power is rooted in social relationships. Now do the same with three people or organizations that you think are relatively powerless.

Key Terms

caste system (p. 126) stratification based on various ascribed characteristics determined at birth.

charismatic authority (p. 120) power whose legitimacy is derived from the extraordinary personal characteristics of an individual leader, which inspire loyalty and devotion.

class (p. 123) a group of people who share a roughly similar economic position and lifestyle.

class system (p. 128) stratification determined by economic position, which results from a combination of individual achievement and family of birth.

coerce (p. 114) to force people's compliance by threatening, intimidating, pressuring, or harming them.

discrimination (p. 124) treating others unequally based on their background or other personal characteristics.

empowerment (p. 111) an increase in the capacity of people to bring about an intended outcome.

hegemony (p. 119) a condition that exists when those in power have successfully spread their ideas—and marginalized alternative viewpoints—so that their perspectives and interests are accepted widely as being universal and true.

illegitimate power (p. 119) a form of authority that relies on force or coercion to generate obedience.

inequality (p. 123) the unequal distribution of resources among groups of people.

intersectionality theory (p. 124) a perspective that highlights the connections and interactions between various forms of inequality, especially race, class, and gender.

legitimate power (p. 119) authority that is voluntarily accepted by those who are affected.

life chances (p. 123) the opportunities offered by a person's economic position.

matrix of domination (p. 125) the interlocking systems of oppression associated with race, class, and gender.

patriarchy (p. 129) male domination through social institutions and cultural practices.

persuade (p. 113) to obtain people's compliance by convincing them of the correctness of your position and goals.

power (p. 111) the ability to bring about an intended outcome, even when opposed by others.

power tactics (p. 115) the specific strategies people use to influence others in everyday life.

privilege (p. 122) a special advantage or benefit that is not enjoyed by everyone.

rational-legal authority (p. 119) power that has legitimacy because it is based on established laws, rules, and procedures.

reward (p. 113) to encourage people's compliance by offering some compensation as a positive incentive.

social closure (p. 124) the process whereby a status group maximizes its own advantages by restricting access to rewards only to members of the group.

social mobility (p. 126) movement from one stratum of a stratification system to another.

standpoint theory (p. 122) a theory that questions taken-for-granted assumptions about society by looking at it from multiple viewpoints, especially from the perspective of people in subordinate positions.

stratification systems (p. 125) social structures and cultural norms that create and maintain inequality by ranking people into a hierarchy of groups that receive unequal resources.

traditional authority (p. 119) power that has legitimacy because of compliance with well-established cultural practices.

Socialization

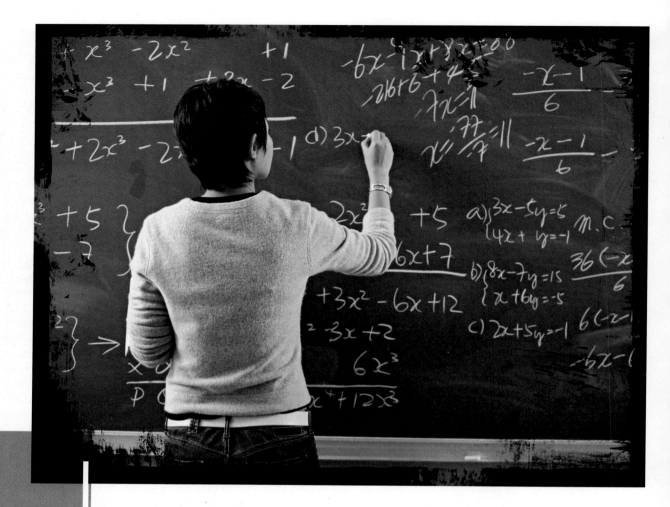

In 1998, sixteen-year-old Melanie Matchett Wood became the first American woman to make the U.S. International Mathematical Olympiad Team. Wood won a silver medal, went on to earn a Ph.D. in math, and is now a leading scholar in her field. Commenting on her Olympiad victory, Wood recalls, "I thought, 'Why am I so surprised?' And then I realized that it was just that I had this image of the people who won this competition—and that image was of boys." The math world included few, if any, female role models (Scharf 2003).

Wood had to overcome cultural norms and expectations that often discourage girls from pursuing high-level math, but she had plenty of support along her way to prominence. Her father, who died when she was just six weeks old, had been a middle school math teacher, and her mother helped keep his memory alive by teaching Melanie math from early childhood. Later, a seventh-grade teacher encouraged Wood's interest in math, inviting her to join the school's MathCounts team. She also found a role model in Zvezdeline Stankova, a woman mathematician with a Harvard Ph.D. who had also been an International Mathematical Olympiad medal winner. Wood notes, "Having a role model like that was a big deal in my life. Previously, I never knew a mathematician that I could look at and think 'in ten years I want to be like that person'" (Gallian 2004). Wood, in her turn, now mentors and supports aspiring women mathematicians.

As Wood understands, the gap between men and women in math achievement in the United States is not a result of innate differences in ability but rather of the powerful cultural lessons boys and girls learn in childhood about gender-appropriate interests and careers. When Wood began mentoring a Princeton undergraduate from Bulgaria, she learned that other cultures teach different lessons. "In her culture, there wasn't an idea that women weren't as good, or even weren't as numerous in math. She hadn't grown up with that" (C. Johnson 2008, A4). ■

Wood's story illustrates the profound power that the cultural messages we absorb from infancy and throughout our lives have to shape what we believe, how we behave, and how we live. But it also illustrates how those messages—in this case, messages about gender, aspirations, and achievement—are subject to challenge and change. **Socialization** is *the process through which people learn their culture's basic norms, values, beliefs, and appropriate behaviors.* Through socialization we learn who we are, what is expected of us, how society operates, and where we stand within our social world. As children we learn the language and symbols of our culture and our social roles as child and sibling. As we grow, we learn new roles, such as friend, student, teammate, employee, lover, spouse, parent, grandparent, and retiree. We also learn and internalize the structure and expectations of the various groups, organizations, and institutions in which we may participate, including families, schools, religious institutions, clubs, sports teams, friendship networks, and workplaces. Through socialization we also forge a sense of self—a sense of who we are as individuals in relation to the people with whom we interact personally as well as to society as a whole. Like Melanie Wood, we can even challenge traditional socialization messages and, in the process, become role models who help to open new possibilities for the next generation.

Reproducing Structure: Agents of Socialization

In transmitting fundamental social norms and role expectations from one generation to another, socialization helps to reproduce social structure and is a key to social stability. Socialization is a dynamic process, however. As social structure changes, the messages imparted through socialization also change.

Because socialization occurs throughout life, it takes place in different ways and in different social contexts, guided by many different **agents of socialization,** or *people and groups who teach us about our culture.* For children, the family is usually far and away the most important agent of socialization. But as children grow up and are exposed to different people and groups, other socializing agents take on increasingly important roles, including school, media, peer groups, the workplace, religion, and total institutions.

Family

Families are the primary agent of early socialization. Within the family most individuals learn basic skills such as how to talk and how to maintain personal hygiene, and they learn important values such as the difference between right and wrong and the proper way to treat other people. "Say 'thank you'." "Respect your elders." "Don't hit your brother." "Always tell the truth." These kinds of instruction teach children the most basic norms, values, beliefs, expectations, and behaviors of their culture.

Families play a crucial role in the early development of a child's sense of identity. Whether or not children learn to see themselves as loved, smart, creative, and strong depends largely on how their families treat them in their early years. Families also influence what nation, ethnicity, race, religion, and class children identify with as they mature. Families are a child's first teachers about appropriate gender roles, which they often signal by the toys and clothing they choose and the chores they assign. As we see in Chapter 11, the process of gender socialization begins at a very young age. Messages full of gender-specific expectations for children about, for example, how to dress and behave are part of a broader process through which girls and boys learn how to act in ways that are promoted as gender appropriate.

Childrearing practices can vary by culture within a society in ways that help reproduce social structure. For example,

 In all cultures, families play a key role in socializing children, especially during the early years. Hygiene, as in this photo of a Nepalese mother washing her child, is only one of the many practices parents teach their children.

CORE CONCEPTS CHALLENGE

What other aspects of their culture do parents in all societies teach their children?

Examining Teenagers' Changing Motivations for Civic Engagement

Why do teens volunteer? When they do, what do they learn about civic involvement? Looking through a sociological lens at how and why teenagers come to join community organizations, do volunteer work, or participate in other community service activities can provide insight into the process of political socialization, especially the cultural values students associate with community activities.

In a study of civic engagement among high school students in Madison, Wisconsin, sociologists Lewis Friedland and Shauna Morimoto (2005) found that young people from a variety of backgrounds are deeply involved in community service activities, even though civic engagement among Americans in general has been declining (Putnam 2000; Skocpol 2003). The sociologists also found that students' motivations for engaging in community service have changed in recent decades. Students used to see service as a value in itself, whereas they now see service primarily as a path to achieving other goals.

In particular, high school students facing an uncertain future think of community service as something they must do to enhance their chances of college admission. According to Friedland and Morimoto, young people experience "higher stress, greater uncertainty, and risk . . . and looser connections among family, friends, and communities" (p. 5) than previous generations. Growing income inequality, rising part-time employment, and an increase in long-term unemployment all reinforce this sense of uncertainty. As a result, since the 1990s high school students have experienced more anxiety about their future than their parents' generation did.

Amidst this uncertainty, Friedland and Morimoto (2005) noted there is "a general awareness among most of the young people we interviewed that their life chances are directly tied to education. Almost all of the young people we interviewed expected (or at least hoped) to better their lives and linked these expectations to college education. And a majority linked their hopes for

college admission to service" (p. 7). The weakening of community ties requires more young people to navigate consequential life decisions with little social support in the form of adult role models, job placement networks, or college alumni connections. Students see a college education as a requirement for a good-paying job and see engaging in community service as one way to improve their chances of being admitted to a good college. This phenomenon, which students refer to as "resume padding," is not confined only to teens at private schools or those seeking admission to elite colleges and universities. Young people of all social classes take this approach to service, regardless of what college they hope to attend.

Teens do not participate in civic life for purely cynical reasons, however. Friedland and Morimoto argue that resume padding is only one motivation for doing volunteer or service work. Other motivations include "altruism, religious belief, and love of politics or volunteerism" (p. 3). Students know that doing community service can make an important contribution, even if they are motivated largely by personal gain. In addition, community service seems likely to teach young people valuable skills that may translate into civic participation later in life.

Friedland and Morimoto's study highlights the complex reasons why young people get involved in civic life, showing how a change in the economic climate has resulted in increased anxiety about college and jobs that, in turn, has changed the meaning of political socialization for many young people.

think about it

1. *Have you ever participated in volunteer or service work in your community? If so, why? If not, why not?*
2. *Do you think the self-interest associated with resume building is inconsistent with the ethic of community service? Why or why not?*

sociologist Melvin Kohn (1977) found that in the United States, working-class parents tend to teach their children to value obedience, the expected attitude for most working-class jobs, whereas middle-class parents encourage their children to value self-direction, the attitude required for the kind of independent thinking expected in many middle-class occupations. These different values, in turn, increase the likelihood that children will end up with the same educational opportunities and in the same kind of work as their parents, thus reproducing the existing structural inequality from one generation to the next. Kohn and his colleagues (1986) found a similar dynamic among families in Poland.

Cross-national research indicates that cultural differences can lead to significantly different parenting styles. For example, family socialization in Malaysia emphasizes obedience and cooperation, values that are consistent with the society's collectivist culture (Keshavarz and Baharudin 2009). This stands in sharp contrast to the emphasis on personal happiness and achievement that is far more common in the United States, particularly in middle-class families. Similarly, Korean American parents focus far more on controlling the behavior of their children than European American parents do. Korean American children see behavioral control efforts as a sign of parental engagement and support, whereas their

European American peers have a negative view of this parenting style (Kim 2005).

School

Daycare, preschool, or kindergarten is many children's first extended experience with people and the world outside of their home. In these settings children learn to interact with other people and adjust to being part of a group. As the agents of socialization most explicitly focused on teaching cultural knowledge, schools prepare children for their later roles in society, providing instruction in a variety of fields, including advanced language skills, mathematics, history, and science. Schools can also socialize students into the politics of getting ahead in life, as the Through a Sociological Lens box explores.

In addition to their formal academic curriculum, schools also convey a **hidden curriculum** consisting of *implicit lessons about how children should behave* (Jackson 1968). These lessons vary depending on the school and often change as children advance in grade levels. However, most U.S. schools teach children to be quiet and attentive, to obey authority, to follow rules, to be respectful of others, and to take pride in their country. Schools in the United States also tend to encourage competition and individual achievement by promoting sports, spelling bees, and honor rolls, among other activities. Schools are also the site for lessons about class and gender, topics we explore in Chapters 9 and 11.

Media

Today's children and teens have been called "Generation M" because of their heavy use of media (Rideout, Foehr, and Roberts 2010). Media play an increasingly significant role in the lives of many young people, especially in industrialized nations. On average, U.S. children between the ages of 8 and 18 spend more than seven and a half hours each day with media outside of school. This is more time than they spend in the classroom and much more time than they spend interacting with their parents. More than 70 percent of U.S. youth now have a television set in their bedrooms, half have a video game console, and one-third have a computer with Internet access in their bedrooms, allowing them to watch TV, play video games, and surf the web without any parental supervision. As a result, media—television, Internet, video games, recorded music, and magazines, for example—are arguably the most influential agents of socialization in contemporary society, a situation that is relatively new.

For most of human history, children learned morals and values from the myths and other stories they heard from their families. Today, children in developed nations receive these lessons from commercial media companies whose primary interest is selling products and socializing young people to be avid consumers. Thus companies such as Disney and Viacom (which owns both Nickelodeon and MTV) now play a central part in introducing children to a set of values, beliefs, norms, and behaviors that promote a consumer lifestyle (Pugh 2009;

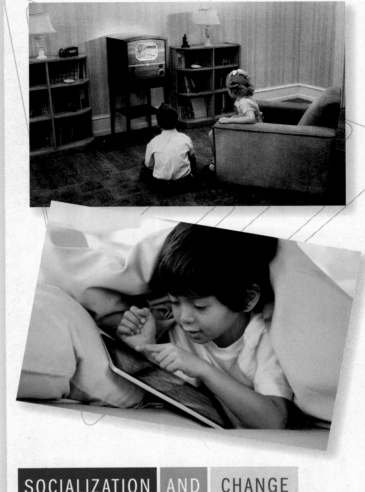

SOCIALIZATION AND CHANGE

Television became a fixture in American households in the 1950s and emerged quickly as a powerful, and sometimes controversial, agent of socialization. Today, online media are increasingly present in the daily lives of children in the United States and around the world. With the rapid development of new handheld devices, what kinds of media will the next generation of children experience?

Schor 2005). Through ads and programming, youth-oriented media help to define popular tastes and desires. For example, MTV's "My Super Sweet 16," a reality-style television series, turned the Sweet 16 parties of wealthy young women into a celebration of high-end teenage consumption, with a companion web site full of ideas and advice for what to wear and how to organize your own Sweet 16 party.

Media have altered the socialization of children in another important way. With television, especially, children for the first time in history have had ready access to the world of adult ideas and situations, even if they cannot read at an adult level. Of particular concern to many parents is the sexually explicit and graphically violent content of some media. Access to media also erodes the significance of physical place: it allows children to "see" the battlefields of foreign wars from their living rooms and increases their access to the intimate lives of adults. In this way the modern boundary between childhood and adulthood that was a staple of the socialization process in the United States has been blurred (Meyrowitz 1985).

The global distribution of U.S. media has increased in recent years, raising important questions about the socializing influence of media. In some countries, media imported from the United States is more popular than locally produced fare. For example, U.S. movies accounted for more than two-thirds of the film audience in Europe in 2009, more than twice the audience share of European films (European Audiovisual Observatory 2010).

Some critics argue that American values are embedded in the media products sold by U.S. corporations. Norms of individualism and consumerism, for example, saturate media exported by the United States and may conflict with traditional values in the nations where such products are consumed. From this perspective, the heavy flow of media from the United States to the rest of the world can erode local cultures and values (Tomlinson 2008). As noted in the discussion of the globalization of culture at the end of Chapter 3, however, the threat may be exaggerated. Some observers argue that the global circulation of U.S.-produced media products does not seem, as some had feared, to be Americanizing global culture.

Nor do globally distributed entertainment products seem to be creating a distinctive global consciousness. Even though hundreds of millions of children and teenagers around the world listen to the same music, play the same games, and watch the same movies, they do not appear to be losing their sense of who they are or where they belong (Ugochukwu 2008).

As a powerful socializing agent, media can make positive contributions to society. At their best, children's media can promote positive values such as honesty, compassion, responsibility, self-respect, and standing up for what you believe in. Media also give people access to a much broader range of news, images, and stories than was available in the past. Media thus allow people to learn more about their society and about the cultures of other people.

Peer Groups

Parents often worry about their children's friends, their **peer group,** *a group of people, usually of comparable age, who share similar interests and social status.* Peer groups can significantly influence people's development and behavior. This is especially true of children and adolescents, whose sense of self is not yet firmly developed and is therefore susceptible to influence by others. As they approach adulthood, adolescents usually become increasingly independent of their families, and during this period peer groups can act as a surrogate family. Peer groups provide young people with the opportunity to experiment with values, beliefs, and behaviors that differ from their

Peer groups can be an important socializing influence on individuals. Members of street gangs, like those pictured on the left, display all the accessories of the subculture they have been taught. They use specialized language, communicate with unique hand gestures, adorn their bodies with gang-related tattoos, often wear special gang colors, and adopt a worldview that places high value on gang membership and loyalty. College fraternities and sororities have similar characteristics. They, too, share special signals and insignia—the Greek letters that identify particular fraternities and sororities—and they encourage group loyalty and mutual assistance.

CORE CONCEPTS CHALLENGE

Peer groups can be powerful socializing agents, strongly influencing the behavior of their members. What is the nature of their **power,** *and how is it exercised?*

parents'. To separate themselves from their families and fit in with peer groups, adolescents commonly change the way they talk, dress, and act, as well as the interests they pursue. This process is not unique to adolescence, however. When adults embark on new jobs and careers or move to new cities or neighborhoods, they often look to members of their new peer groups for clues about social norms and appropriate behaviors. A young couple that moves from the city to the suburbs will have to adopt new norms for social interaction and will probably learn those new norms from a peer group.

There are many different kinds of peer groups. Some are informal, as with groups of friends who choose to spend leisure time together. For teenagers, peer group activities can involve going to the mall or the movies; playing sports or video games; experimenting with cigarettes, alcohol, drug use, and sex; driving around together; or just "hanging out" or texting. Other peer groups exist in more structured environments, as is the case with classmates, teammates, and colleagues at work.

The Workplace

The workplace is one of the most important social settings in which we experience socialization. **Occupational socialization** is *the process of learning the informal norms associated with a type of employment.* As you study, train, or apprentice in a given job category, you are picking up all sorts of cues, large and small, about how to be successful in a given job. For example, skilled tradespeople such as carpenters, plumbers, and electricians not only have to know the technical details of their craft, but they also typically learn the informal rules about how to work with customers, suppliers, and workers from other trades who share the job site. Understanding the expected norms, values, and behaviors of their position can be vital to success in their field.

Socialization into professional occupations—such as medicine and law—is one of the most significant, if often unrecognized, functions of graduate and professional schools. Of course, these schools provide subject-specific information: medical students study anatomy and law students study contracts. But aspiring professionals also learn the often informal, unstated norms of their profession: how to behave as a doctor or lawyer. Doctors, for example, must learn how to wield authority, dress appropriately, and talk with patients. Similarly, lawyers learn how to talk to judges, relate to clients, and deal with conflicts between their clients' interests and their own beliefs. Although some of this material may be touched upon in formal classroom discussions, students pick up most of it informally through socialization.

A classic study of students at Harvard Law School illustrates the powerful effects of occupational socialization into a profession (Granfield 1992; Granfield and Koenig 1990). The researchers found that many of these elite students entered law school intending to practice public interest law, such as by advocating for nonprofit organizations, representing poor clients, and working to prevent government and corporate fraud and abuse. However, during their three years of professional training at Harvard, they switched course. As they became socialized into their profession, many abandoned their commitment to public interest law and embraced the idea of entering a prestigious, high-paying corporate law firm. There, if their senior partners permitted, they might be able to do some *pro bono* (free-of-charge) work for needy clients.

This kind of professional socialization continues over the course of one's career. As people gain experience in a given field, they learn how to relate to younger or less experienced coworkers. If you are promoted, for example, you will have to learn the norms and expectations of your new position, which may include supervising other employees, attending meetings with senior managers, and participating in long-range planning. Your new position may also require you to dress differently, learn a new style of communication, and perhaps change your own family schedule.

Religion

Religion is the socializing agent most explicitly focused on the teaching of values and beliefs. Religious institutions in the past had enormous influence on all aspects of social life, offering social and educational opportunities as well as indoctrination in morality and values. Overall, that influence declined during the twentieth century, but religion still plays a significant role in many people's lives and the U.S. population is far more involved with religion than are residents of most European countries (Putnam and Campbell 2010). In addition, many parents who are not believers or who do not observe their religion often insist that their children obtain religious instruction.

For believers, religion can be an especially potent socializing agent because it often bases its prescriptions on texts such as the Christian Bible or the Muslim Qur'an that most believers consider sacred and some consider infallible. For people who believe that a divinity advocates or forbids certain values, beliefs, and behaviors, religion can supersede other socializing influences. In a society in which material well-being and consumerism are hallmarks of mainstream culture, religious institutions are among the few that promote the serious discussion of nonmaterial values.

In recent decades, religious organizations, especially in the United States, have dramatically expanded their use of mass media, spreading their message through religious-themed news, commentary, and entertainment as well as through the

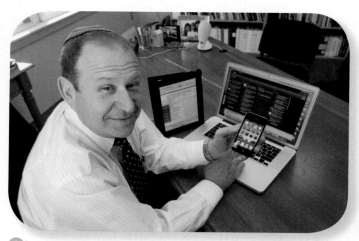

In contemporary life, efforts to promote religious culture have reached beyond traditional services in places of worship to include outreach with high-tech social media and the blending of religion with contemporary marketing. This rabbi gives seminars for others on how congregations can use social media to keep members connected.

more traditional broadcast of religious services. In the United States, evangelical Christian groups have been particularly adept at using books, television, and radio to bring together the socializing influences of religion and media (Blake 2005).

Total Institutions

One unique group of socializing agents are what sociologist Erving Goffman (1961) called **total institutions,** *confining social settings in which an authority regulates all aspects of a person's life.* Goffman identifies five general types of total institutions:

1. Institutions that care for people who are defined as incapable and harmless—for example, orphanages and nursing homes.

2. Institutions set up to care for people who cannot care for themselves but who may represent an unintentional threat to the community—for example, psychiatric hospitals.

3. Institutions set up to protect a community from those whom authorities define as posing a significant danger—for example, prisons and jails, and prisoner-of-war camps.

4. Institutions established to pursue a specific task requiring the total commitment of participants—for example, military barracks and boarding schools.

5. Institutions intended as escapes or retreats from the world—for example, monasteries, convents, and some communes.

Total institutions typically share several key features. All aspects of daily life take place in the same setting under the guidance of the same authority. Members live in groups, and all group members are treated the same and complete the same tasks. Authorities impose a specific schedule, monitoring it through the application of formal rules and regimenting all the activities within the institution.

The closed world of a total institution provides an extreme example of **resocialization,** *the process by which individuals replace old norms and behaviors with new ones as they move from one role or life stage to another.* In total institutions people must submit to a strictly controlled regimen and live in a group with other people in the same condition. Such controlled institutions attempt to reprogram people to avoid past problems (substance abuse, for example), accept current realities (as with seniors adapting to residential elder care facilities), or prepare for future commitments. The U.S. Army, for example, requires new recruits to participate in a ten-week Basic Combat Training course that is intended to socialize civilians into soldiers. At their best, as with high-quality mental health facilities, such institutions can be benevolent means of providing care and helping people prepare for new roles in society. At their worst, as with political concentration camps, they can be coercive and oppressive, designed to destroy the individual will and obtain submission. (The Sociology Works box discusses one example of a total institution.)

Total institutions are not always successful at resocializing all their members. For example, although prisons and psychiatric hospitals control the daily lives of their inmates and can compel inmates to behave in specific ways, the inmates don't always internalize the norms and attitudes being promoted and may not behave in ways consistent with these norms when they are released. This is a matter of concern for those who work in fields such as mental health and juvenile delinquency.

Socialization Through the Life Course

Although socialization is most intense in a person's early years, the agents of socialization discussed in the previous section are active throughout a person's entire lifespan. The **life-course perspective** on socialization *looks at how age, time, and place shape social identities and experiences over a lifetime.* Each stage of life is associated with particular experiences that influence our identity and that require resocialization. Although everyone progresses through various stages of life, those stages and what they mean can differ based on the historical period and culture in which a person lives, as well as on the person's gender, class, and other aspects of personal identity.

thinking about **power**

Total institutions resocialize people subject to their authority. How does the nature of the **power** they use to do this vary in different kinds of total institutions—for example, cloistered religious orders as opposed to prisons?

Kate Corrigan and the Perkins School for the Blind

Kate Corrigan

When Kate Corrigan graduated from The College of the Holy Cross in 2009, she had a B.A. in sociology, was fluent in American Sign Language, and was looking for a job that would allow her to combine those two qualifications. She landed a job as a teaching assistant in the Deafblind Program at Perkins School for the Blind, a residential educational facility in Watertown, Massachusetts, where her sociological background has been a valuable asset.

Corrigan works with twelve to eighteen year olds at Perkins. Since Perkins is a residential school, she spends her time with students in the cottages where they live, rather than in a traditional classroom. Her teaching stresses developing students' communication proficiency, as well as social and daily living skills. As part of the program's focus on negotiating everyday life interactions, Corrigan takes her students on trips to the local community so that they can practice communication in public settings, such as stores and restaurants. Community field trips help students learn independence and how to advocate for themselves in a range of social settings.

Residential schools like Perkins have many of the features of a benevolent total institution. As a former sociology student, Corrigan understands the importance of the program's role in the socialization process. Since her students live at the school year round, the school's educational mission is broader than at the typical middle school or high school. At Perkins, Corrigan notes: "the roles, tasks, and environment typically associated with the home become part of the educational setting." Corrigan often draws upon what she learned in her "Children and Society" class at Holy Cross for insight into the importance of family and school in the lives of children.

During her time at Perkins, Corrigan has applied the sociological perspective to the school's sometimes challenging relationship with local residents. As she points out, "People in the community expect our students to look and behave a certain way because of the institution they represent." These expectations, even when well intentioned, can often impose severe limitations on her students. Corrigan notes, however, that in student-community interactions, "We like to pleasantly surprise people." Still, Corrigan recognizes that the norms within the Perkins community, focused on special needs students, may not always fit smoothly with the norms of the broader community. This understanding of the complexity of the school-community relationship helps Corrigan navigate her interactions with the school's neighbors.

Sociology gave Corrigan more than an understanding of children, schools, and society. Corrigan found sociology exciting because it permitted her to apply what she learned in the classroom to her everyday life. Sociology also gave her valuable research skills that she has applied to several fascinating topics, including the impact of assistive devices on communication among the deaf, the benefits of bilingual education for deaf students, and responses to disabilities among athletes in professional sports.

Corrigan found that sociology helped her ask new questions while also providing a foundation for her pursuit of a career in cultural- and linguistic-based education. In reflecting on her experience as a sociology student, Corrigan offers some helpful advice. "To anyone taking a sociology course for the first time, let the subject inspire you. There are so many avenues with which the subject can be appreciated and applied. Make it your own."

> "Sociology expanded my educational horizons while also giving me the freedom to narrow my focus to exactly what I wanted."

think about it

1. *Why does a residential school qualify as a kind of total institution?*
2. *What "expectations" do you think the public has about Perkins students, and how do you think the students "pleasantly surprise" people? Does your local community have expectations about how students at your school should look or behave?*

The process of change from one life stage to another can involve a shift in a person's responsibilities, living situation, or standing within their community. Moments of transition often involve initiation ceremonies or **rites of passage,** *activities that mark and celebrate a change in a person's social status* (van Gennep 1909/1961). Some of these ceremonies are rooted in religion, such as a confirmation or bar mitzvah, and follow traditions handed down from generation to generation. In the United States, weddings, graduation ceremonies, quinceañeras, and the Marine Corps's final training exercise known as "the Crucible," all mark the entrance into a new stage of life. Different societies have their own culturally specific rites of passage, and outsiders are likely to find some of these unfamiliar. Among the Venda in South Africa, for example, teenage boys and girls go off to separate traditional initiation schools, where older men and women prepare them for sexual relationships with their future spouses. The boys spend up to three months away from their families and undergo male circumcision as the central component of their transition from childhood to adulthood (Lutendo, Maharaj, and Rogan 2008).

Socialization is a never-ending process because people continually adopt new roles and identities. Some of these roles involve advanced preparation.

Anticipatory socialization is *the process by which individuals practice for a future social role by adopting the norms or behaviors associated with a position they have not yet achieved.* For example, children are engaging in anticipatory socialization when they imitate and practice adult roles, playing with dolls to simulate being parents, or playing school to anticipate becoming students or teachers. In later life, young adults might take on internships to see if they want to pursue employment in a certain field, and couples might live together to find out if they are compatible for marriage.

Childhood

The early stages of life, which we label childhood and adolescence, correspond to the period during which infants gradually mature biologically into adults. Interestingly, however, childhood and adolescence are also social constructs; what it means to be a child or teenager varies radically over time and from culture to culture. As a result, the way young people experience this particularly intense period of socialization also varies over time and from culture to culture (Fass and Mason 2000).

Contemporary Western societies tend to view childhood as a natural condition linked to children's physical immaturity. Children are considered innocent, with limited capacities, and in need of intensive care and protection by adults. However, according to Philippe Aries's classic study of the history of family life in Europe, *Centuries of Childhood* (1965), the idea of a distinct childhood period is really a social construction invented in Western society during the sixteenth and seventeenth centuries. Before then, childhood was not distinguished so clearly from adulthood. European paintings of the fifteenth and early sixteenth centuries, for example, often portray children as miniature adults, complete with adult clothing and adult body proportions. Parents introduced their children to the adult world early and abruptly. Given the cramped living quarters of the day, by necessity parents routinely exposed their children to the full range of adult activity; children were served alcohol and sometimes shared the same room as adults having sex. It was common for parents to apprentice their six-year-old children, sending them away from home to live and work. (This practice was imported to colonial America, as well.) Peasant parents might exploit their children as a potentially valuable family resource by renting them out as servants in wealthy homes. Children unable to secure such positions would often roam the streets picking through garbage and searching for anything useful to their families. Few ever attended school.

Several historians have challenged Aries's contention that medieval people had no conception of childhood as a separate stage of life. One, for example, points out that, like children today, medieval children played with toys and engaged in games specifically intended for children (Orme 2003). Another suggests that parents who apprenticed their young children were helping assure that they would have the means to support

Well into the nineteenth century, children in Western society were often seen as economic assets for their families and employed in strenuous jobs in often dangerous conditions. Pictures like the one on the left, showing boys and girls carrying heavy loads of clay, helped spur a successful movement to outlaw child labor in North America and much of Europe. In many poor countries, however, children—like the boy carrying a heavy load of clay at a factory in Cairo, Egypt (*center*)—are still expected to help support their families. On the other hand, the recent Western idea that children need protection and extended schooling is now prevalent in much of the world, as in Taiwan, where the children shown here (*right*) enjoy learning to work with clay in a pottery class.

themselves as adults (Ozment 2001). But scholars agree that the social perception and treatment of children—the meaning of childhood—has evolved over time, just as the expectations of children vary among cultures today.

By the eighteenth century, children in Western society were increasingly seen as innocent, weak, and in need of protection rather than as hardy "little adults." Parents socialized their children to behave differently than adults and often punished transgressions with severe beatings. But children's participation in the adult world continued. Child labor—a term that would not have been used at the time—was common throughout the eighteenth century. Children could fit into tight spaces, so they were favored workers for picking coal in tight mine shafts or cleaning the insides of chimneys. As late as 1890 in the United States, about 1.5 million children between the ages of ten and fifteen were working, many in the nation's bustling factories (American Social History Project 2007).

Only in the early nineteenth century did reformers begin to challenge the idea that children should be employed as laborers. This was part of a broader cultural transformation as, increasingly, Western society defined childhood as a period of life distinct from adulthood. The importance of schooling grew, and the modern-day connection between children and schools was cemented. As a result, children were transformed from being an economic asset—either on the farm or through paid employment in a growing industrial economy—to being an economic burden for whom parents were expected to sacrifice.

In some of the world's poorest nations today, children sometimes continue to live as "little adults." They receive little or no schooling and, by working, begging, or other means, are expected to help support their families.

Adolescence

Adolescence—when youth are nearing physical maturity and are no longer considered children but have not yet taken on the rights or responsibilities of adulthood—was not seen as a distinct period of life until the early twentieth century. Scholars typically tie the rise of adolescence in Western societies to several social developments in the late nineteenth and early twentieth centuries (Chinn 2008; see Figure 6.1):

- Industrialization produced affluence that created a new middle class and enabled middle-class young people to stay out of the full-time workforce, separating them from adult workers.

- Because schooling became an increasingly important requirement for employment, middle-class young people continued their education, completing high school and sometimes even going to college.

- Because they were not working full time, young people had more leisure time and began to be consumers of youth-oriented products, eventually resulting in the formation of a distinct youth subculture.

- The massive increase in immigration created what we might now call a "generation gap" between young people who were socialized into the culture and customs of the new country and their older immigrant parents who had grown up in the old country.

All these factors helped separate young people from adults and helped to make adolescence a distinct period of life.

Much of the turbulence we now associate with adolescence results from the contradiction that exists between culture and biology. Adolescence as a social construction is locked in a battle with puberty as a biological reality. Adolescents are capable of sexual activity and of having children—as they did through most of history—but social norms now typically discourage such behavior. Adolescents are maturing physically and mentally and are capable of working in many different jobs—as they did through most of history—but they are now expected to stay in school and delay their entry into the workforce. Cultural inconsistencies exist, as well. Sex is glorified in media but discouraged by parents and other authorities. Many of the soldiers who serve in the U.S. military are too young to drink alcohol legally. Adolescence, in short, is a period of vexing inconsistencies.

The class differences that played a role in the creation of adolescence continue to play a role in how adolescence unfolds today. Many poor and working-class youth enter the workforce, marry, and start a family at an earlier age than many of their middle-class counterparts. In effect, adolescence is a shorter period for them than it is for middle-class youth. In contrast, middle-class youth are more likely to extend adolescence into their twenties by attending college and then returning home and remaining

---

thinking about structure

A change in social **structure**—the emergence of a new middle class—played a role in the emergence of the currently prevalent view of adolescence as a distinct life stage. How do class differences affect the way different individuals experience adolescence?

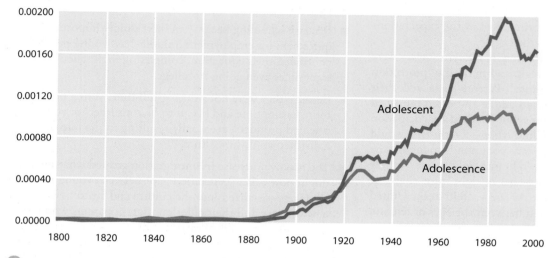

Percent usage in English language books

Adolescent

Adolescence

1800 1820 1840 1860 1880 1900 1920 1940 1960 1980 2000

FIGURE 6.1 | THE EMERGENCE OF ADOLESCENCE

With the emergence of adolescence as a distinct life stage, the terms *adolescent* and *adolescence* became increasingly common in the early twentieth century. This line graph illustrates the dramatic growth in the use of these two terms in American books during the twentieth century, showing a steady rise beginning around 1900. The graph was created by a Google tool that calculates the frequency with which any word or phrase appears in the books that have been scanned into the Google Books database so far.

financially dependent on their parents after college. They may delay starting families or experiment with various types of employment before settling down into a more traditional pattern of adult responsibilities. Some researchers suggest that the result is a new life stage in the United States—emerging adulthood—during which people in their twenties experience greater uncertainty and instability in the development of careers and relationships on the road to adulthood than did previous generations (Henig 2010).

Adulthood

As adults enter different stages of life, they take on new roles and responsibilities for which they learn to adopt appropriate ideas and practices (Elder 2006; Settersten 2002). For many people, adulthood is marked by a variety of milestones that require resocialization. For example, starting your first full-time job means having to adopt a largely new set of attitudes and responsibilities. Similarly, getting married or living with a romantic partner full time requires taking on the role of spouse or partner, requiring further socialization to a new set of challenges. In these and many other cases, we adjust to new roles and relationships as we accumulate experience.

Adult life-course trajectories in the United States became increasingly standardized in the twentieth century, but they varied by gender (MacMillan 2005; Shanahan 2000). A classic study of men born in the United States between 1907 and 1952 identified a sequence of transitions experienced by roughly half to three-quarters of them—completion of high school, entry into first job, marriage, and parenthood (Hogan 1978; Hogan and Astone 1986). However, this typical sequence could be interrupted by various factors, including military service and college. This life course—finish school, get a job, get married, have children—was never a universal experience, but it became a broad cultural ideal and a widespread aspiration among boys and young men of the twentieth century. The life-course sequence for women of the same generation differed from that of their male counterparts. For example, women in the mid- to late-twentieth century were far more likely than men to marry before starting their first job (Marini 1984).

Recent research suggests that the stages of the life course for men and women in recent years are more diverse than they were in previous generations. Still, the most common life-course pattern for men remains work-marriage-parenthood, which may be followed by divorce or unemployment. Women's life-course trajectories are more varied: although many follow the same stages as men, many others experience a gender-specific trajectory of work-marriage-unemployment-parenthood. That period of unemployment reflects the different impact that having children can have on women than men (Jackson and Berkowitz 2005).

Becoming a parent, however, is for many adults—men and women alike—one of the most significant life changes they will experience. Our culture encourages new parents to reorient their lives around the socialization of their children, making a priority of their children's needs and taking on the full burden of responsibility for their care and upbringing. As we saw earlier, this expectation is relatively new in Western society. People learn the dominant parenting norms of their culture through socialization. Most new parents have observed friends or family members with their children, they may have cared for younger siblings or babysat their neighbors' children while growing up, and they may have read advice books. A great deal of what new parents know results from their own childhood socialization, when they absorbed parenting lessons from their own parents—knowledge of which they are not always consciously aware. Many parents are surprised to catch themselves talking to their children with the same tone and language their parents had used with them. As this illustrates, one remarkable feature of the socialization process is that it is often invisible to us.

In 2003, at the age of seventy-two, Canadian runner Ed Whitlock became the first person aged seventy years or older to run a marathon (26.2 miles) in under three hours—an impressive accomplishment at any age. In 2011, at age eighty, he set a new marathon world record for his age group with a time of 3:15:51. His case may be extreme, but as millions of older citizens are living longer and remaining active, they are challenging cultural expectations about "appropriate" behavior for seniors and establishing new norms for living.

cial identity as someone who is no longer young (Karp 2000; Moody 2010).

Retirement is a significant life stage, and those who retire need to learn a whole new set of norms and behaviors. Like other life stages, retirement is socially constructed. Until the creation of Social Security in the 1940s, most people in the United States simply worked as long as they were able. Social Security benefits, Medicare health coverage, and Medicaid long-term-care assistance enabled a much broader group of Americans to stop working when they reached the age of sixty-five, which became the standard retirement age. Now, after decades in which the average age at which Americans retire has been declining, that trend has reversed (see Figure 6.2). A restructured Social Security program delays full benefits for those born in 1960 or later until they are sixty-seven. Among the other reasons Americans are retiring at a later age are increasing life expectancy, inadequate pensions, the need to accumulate more savings for longer retirement periods, emotional and psychological ties to work, and the social

Aging and Retirement

As people move through the stages of adulthood, they experience a continuing set of transitions, including changing or losing a job, getting divorced or remarried, seeing children leave home, caring for an elderly parent, becoming a grandparent, surviving the death of a spouse, and experiencing debilitating mental or physical limitations brought on by old age. As people live through these transitions, they learn the norms and expectations of the new roles they take on.

In the United States, the widespread cultural emphasis on youth can make the social experience of aging a challenge. Although there is no way to stop the aging process, many middle-aged men and women pursue a range of strategies to stay healthy and active as long as possible, including exercising regularly and following a healthy diet. Some pursue the image of youth through cosmetic surgery or other efforts to stave off the effects of aging. In this context, as people continue to grow older, part of the process of aging is negotiating an evolving so-

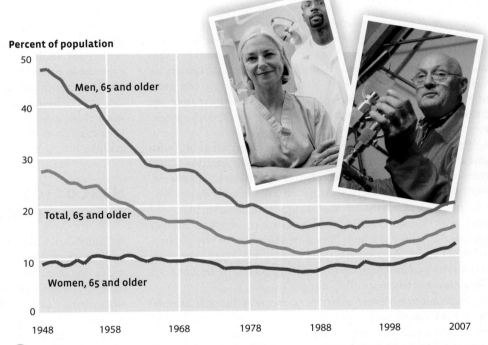

Percent of population

FIGURE 6.2 | LABOR FORCE PARTICIPATION RATE OF WORKERS AGED 65 AND OVER, 1948–2007

From 1948 until 1985, the percentage of men aged sixty-five or over who worked dropped significantly; during this period men were retiring at an earlier age. The percentage of women of that age who worked during this period stayed about the same. However, since 1985 an increasing percentage of both women and men have delayed retirement and continued to work past the age of sixty-five. *Source:* U.S. Department of Labor 2008.

CORE CONCEPTS CHALLENGE

 What does this graph suggest about age, gender, and changes in the structure of the American workforce since 1948?

integration and support provided by regular employment.

In a society in which much of our identity comes from what we *do,* leaving the workforce can be traumatic. Some retirees who have waited years to enjoy their leisure time quickly become bored and fall prey to a sense of isolation (Goldsmith 2004).

Increasingly, retirement is also a financial challenge as people spend more years outside of paid employment because of both longer lifespans and the premature loss of employment. Recent practices at many large corporations mean that longtime employees typically have far less job security than did workers in previous generations (Sennett 2007). Employees in their fifties and early sixties may find themselves targeted for job cuts, pressured to retire before they planned to, or simply pushed out by younger, lower-paid employees, making their work experience unpredictable and effective planning for retirement difficult. Such corporate policies produce a population of the involuntarily retired who lose their jobs at an age when they are unlikely to find comparable full-time work. In the competitive economic environment of the early twenty-first century, age discrimination for workers age fifty and over is becoming increasingly common, affecting the quality of the work experience and increasing the likelihood of premature job loss for aging workers (Roscigno et al. 2007).

For workers who have private retirement accounts with stock investments, the stock market downturn in 2008–2009 created new challenges that also meant delays in retiring. Many men and women in their late fifties and early sixties who had planned carefully for their retirement, accumulating investments that would allow them to retire comfortably in their mid-sixties, absorbed huge losses in the value of their retirement accounts. As a result, more people will work into their late sixties and seventies as they seek to recoup their financial losses, leaving fewer jobs for younger people.

As people enter their elder years, many will confront new challenges. Some will experience the death of a spouse, and others will cope with their own health problems. Still others will remain healthy well into their eighties or nineties but will see their social circles dwindle, as their same-age friends and neighbors move away or die. Among women aged sixty-five or over in the United States, 40 percent live alone, whereas 19 percent of men in this age group live alone (Federal Interagency Forum on Aging-Related Statistics 2010). Given the changes associated with one's elder years, aging can lead to social disconnection and a sense of loneliness (Jylha and Saarenheimo 2010).

In the United States, many senior citizens reach a point at which independent living is no longer viable. Some leave their longtime homes to move in with family members; others re-

locate to specialized elder housing facilities; and still others arrange for in-home eldercare, so that they do not have to move out. Among those over the age of sixty-five, 7 percent of men and 17 percent of women live with relatives other than their spouse. Whereas only about 6 percent of Americans aged sixty-five or older lived in elder housing in 2007, more than 20 percent of those aged eighty-five or older lived in either a long-term care facility or some other form of senior citizen housing (Federal Interagency Forum on Aging-Related Statistics 2010). In all these situations, senior citizens must adjust to new living conditions, facing changes to longstanding living patterns. These changes often involve an increased dependency on others for routine household maintenance such as grocery shopping, food preparation, and laundry.

Elder housing patterns vary across cultures. Where multigenerational family living is typical, aging adults can often remain within their homes, relying on their children and grandchildren for care and support. For example, 70 percent of people aged sixty-five or over in Taiwan live with their adult children, a longstanding pattern of familial caretaking rooted in the Confucian value of respect for elders and a commitment to support one's parents (Chen 2010; Phillips 2000). Research in various cultural contexts suggests that most elders prefer to "age in place," staying at home as long as they can (Costa-Font, Elvira, and Mascarilla-Miro 2009; Sabia 2008).

Historical Events: Marking Generational Identity

An individual's life course isn't just a matter of passing through a sequence of stages. Lives unfold in particular historical and social contexts, and experiencing major historical events can have a transformative effect. The German sociologist Karl Mannheim (1893–1947) (1928/1952) argued that because the shared historical experiences of a group shape its general attitudes and behaviors, the major events that occur during adolescence become key to identifying a specific generation. A recent summary of the research and theory on the significance of major events suggests that our identity is "stamped by the historically significant events and changes" occurring during adolescence and young adulthood (Griffin 2004, 545). Since the Al Qaeda attacks on New York's World Trade Center and the Pentagon were crucial in shaping many people's ideas about the world, people born in the late twentieth century might consider themselves members of the 9/11 generation. Indeed, when American troops killed Osama Bin Laden in 2011, those under age thirty dominated the crowds that assembled to cheer the event (Marcus 2011).

An early effort to study the relationship between a generation's formative events and adult life experiences was Glen Elder's now-classic study *Children of the Great Depression* (1974/1999), which traced the life histories of 167 men and women born in 1920 and 1921, about eight to nine years before the stock market crash that contributed to the Great Depression. Elder shows how the economic crisis challenged traditional gender roles among adults but strengthened gender roles among the children of the era. As more mothers entered the paid labor force, daughters took over many domestic responsibilities while sons gained more independence by working outside the home to help the family. In general, the harsh experience of unexpected economic hardship hurried both boys and girls of that generation into adult activities and identities.

In another study, sociologist Doug McAdam (1989) explored whether youth involvement in a form of high-risk political activity had lifelong consequences. Mississippi Freedom Summer was a 1964 campaign in which mostly white northern students went south to help with voter registration and to support the growing civil rights movement. The campaign made headlines in June 1964 when white supremacists kidnapped and murdered three of the activists. This event set the tone for the summer project, which became a danger-filled and eye-opening experience for the volunteers.

Twenty years after Freedom Summer, McAdam (1989) surveyed more than 200 campaign participants. As a comparison group, he also surveyed more than 100 people who had applied and been accepted to take part in Freedom Summer but had decided not to participate. McAdam found that, in several important respects, the Freedom Summer volunteers were different from those who had dropped out of the project: volunteers were far more involved in political activism, began their careers at a later age, had lower incomes, and were less likely to be married. Although the two groups may have been somewhat different to begin with, the experience of participating in Freedom Summer likely had long-term consequences, and McAdam suggests that this impact was partly the result of a "radical resocialization of those involved" (p. 758). Freedom Summer volunteers left Mississippi with strong political commitments and a strong network of like-minded activists. Often, they pursued their deep political commitments throughout their adult lives. Here we can see how powerful socialization experiences can shape attitudes and priorities and have long-term biographical consequences. Whatever the specifics, historical events provide the context within which our individual socialization takes place.

Culture and Biology: Setting the Stage for Social Life

So far, we have looked at socialization—the way we acquire culture—entirely as a learning process. After all, as Chapter 3 explains, culture is learned, not biologically based. But humans are animals, and like other animals, we have biological constraints and advantages. It is biology that gives us hands capable of making and using our culture's tools; and it is biology that gives us brains capable of developing and learning culture and allowing us to connect with other humans in complex social interactions.

Beyond "Nature Versus Nurture"

If biology makes us capable of culture, what other effects does it have on our behavior? In other words, to what extent does biology, rather than culture, influence who we are and how we behave? This question is the crux of the **nature versus nurture debate,** *a disagreement about the relative importance of biology ("nature") and the social environment ("nurture") in influencing human behavior.* Two positions have occupied the extremes of this debate. One of them, **biological determinism,** *contends that biology, specifically our genetic makeup, almost completely shapes human behavior.* Those who hold this perspective argue that biology explains many types of human action, such as crime, violence, or addiction (Caspi et al. 2002; Jensen et al. 1998). They also sometimes attribute much of the social and economic inequality between groups—especially races, the sexes, and social classes—to innate, biological differences—that is, differences that cannot be changed. (From this point of view, biology, not culture, would explain why more men than women excel at mathematics, making Melanie Wood such a rarity on her Mathematical Olympiad team.)

At the opposite extreme, **social determinism** *contends that culture and the social environment almost completely shape human behavior.* Obviously humans have biological differences, but

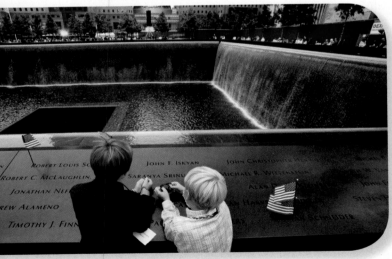

Young people who grew up following the attacks of September 11, 2001, are sometimes referred to as the "9/11 generation" because the events shaped their long-term attitudes about the world. This is especially true of the victims' children, some of whom, like those pictured here during a commemoration at the 9/11 memorial in New York City, were just infants at the time of the tragedy.

Culture is one of the distinguishing features of humans, although some other animals are capable of culture, as well. Chimpanzees learn to place nuts on a stone and break them open using another rock. Humans, however, are capable of vastly more elaborate creativity in the amassing of cultural knowledge, including the invention and use of complicated machinery, such as this combine used to harvest wheat. Both are examples of tools being used to get food, but they are of a radically different order.

these are insignificant compared to the cultural differences that distinguish societies around the world. Humans, in other words, are the highly malleable product of the social learning that occurs during socialization. According to this perspective, most economic and social inequalities—including, say, the unequal accomplishments of men and women in mathematics—result not from innate differences, but instead from the social systems humans create. As a result, although we may never eliminate such inequalities entirely, we can reduce them dramatically. Few scholars today subscribe to either of these extremes. Instead, most now understand that biology and the social environment—nature and nurture—interact in complex ways. Our biology—or more specifically, our genes—represents possibilities; culture and socialization act on those possibilities to make us who we are. (The Sociology Matters box examines the misuse of biology and genetics.)

Genes and Social Interaction

Genes are the basic unit of hereditary information, the mechanism by which we inherit various characteristics from our ancestors. If you have your father's nose or your mother's hair, genes are primarily responsible. Some features of human behavior are also influenced by genes. For example, research suggests that how neurotic, outgoing, open, agreeable, or conscientious you are is due partly to your genes (Guo 2005).

The influence of genes, however, is complicated and subtle (Alper 2002). In most cases, genes represent the potential for particular traits, but how those traits are expressed in a particular person depends on the physical and social environment into which the person is born. If two children have the same gene for height, but one is born into poverty and malnourished while the other is born into affluence and well fed, the poor child will likely grow up to be shorter than will the affluent child.

Similarly, some behaviors also reflect the interaction of genes and the social environment. For example, both abuse in childhood and a particular form of a gene have been associated with antisocial behavior in adult men. However, the social condition appears to trigger the gene's effect. That is, boys who both have the gene and have suffered abuse are the most likely to be antisocial as men. In contrast, boys who have the gene but were not abused and boys who were abused but lack the gene tend not to be antisocial as men (Caspi et al. 2002).

Just as social conditions can trigger a genetically linked effect, they can also help counter it (Shanahan and Hofer 2005). The same gene associated with antisocial behavior in men who were abused as boys is also associated with depression in abused five- to fifteen-year-old children (Kaufman et al. 2004). However, access to consistent social support from family and friends reduces the risk of depression among all children, including those who were abused and have the gene. So, a supportive social environment can promote resiliency in children who are otherwise genetically vulnerable to depression. The social environment, in other words, can not only trigger genes, it can also limit their impact.

Biology matters, but humans are much more than their biology. Rather than determining our fate, biology instead provides us with capacities that allow us to construct our social selves. Virtually all the qualities that make humans distinct—including our sense of self—are a result of social interaction and culture.

Culture, Power, and the Social Self

In a classic work of anthropology, Clyde Kluckhohn (1968) tells the story of meeting a young man in New York City who was utterly bewildered by the American way of life. He spoke

SOCIOLOGY Matters

The Use and Abuse of Biology and Genetics

Sociologists and other social scientists have long been suspicious of efforts to explore the role of biology in social life, and many continue to be so despite advances in the integration of biological and social research. The source of their suspicion is the ghastly history of abuse that has marked attempts to explain society in biological terms.

Slavery, economic inequality, and opposition to social programs that aid the poor have all been justified—and the justifications all later proved wrong—on the grounds that biological differences create insurmountable barriers to equality. These arguments were based on ideology, racist beliefs, and sexist assumptions rather than on scientific evidence. Over time, a preponderance of scientific evidence refuted them, but they live on in popular thinking.

At its worst, belief in the biological destiny of human beings was used to justify disastrous and abhorrent social policies aimed at "improving" the human race. Among these was the Nazis' use of extermination camps and gas chambers to kill six million Jews and millions of other "undesirables" (Black 2003; Muller-Hill 1988). In the United States, misuse of supposedly scientific biological information justified state-level programs that led to the sterilization of more than 65,000 Americans (Bruinius 2006). Attacks on immigrant groups in the nineteenth and early twentieth centuries were based on claims about their supposed biological inferiority. More recently, biological information has been used to link racial inequality to scores on IQ tests. Most social scientists regard these latest abuses as, at best, the result of sloppy science and, at worst, the dressing-up of old racist beliefs in new pseudo-scientific clothes (Devlin et al. 1997; Fischer et al. 1996, Fraser 1995).

Despite this history of abuse, advances in genetics and neuroscience (the study of the brain) have had important sociological implications. Sociologists attempting to integrate these findings with their field have often also had to combat persistent popular misperceptions about the role of genes and other aspects of human biology on human behavior.

In recent decades, for example, the advent of genetic screening has raised hopes about the possibility of developing preventive treatments for certain cancers and inherited conditions such as Huntington disease and cystic fibrosis. But it has also brought the possibility of abuses: suppose that health insurance companies decide not to cover people who are found to carry a gene associated with a particular form of cancer, or that employers reject job applicants who have a genetic link to alcoholism. Troy Duster, a sociologist with deep roots in the quest for social justice, has devoted much of his career to trying to prevent these kinds of misuse of genetic information.

Duster employs a sociological perspective to examine how genetics is being used—and misused—in contemporary science. Before genetic testing was well known, Duster published *Backdoor to Eugenics* (1991/2003), which explored the potential misuse of genetic screening to discriminate against people in the workplace and in other social settings. Duster argued at the time that we need a broad social discussion about the consequences of improved genetic screening.

While recognizing some of the benefits produced by genetic research, Duster cautions that scientists are sometimes too quick to look to genes for answers to what are fundamentally social questions. For example, Duster notes that many diseases, such as cancer and high blood pressure, affect some population groups more than others. However, the biotechnology and pharmaceutical industries, which fund medical research, are interested in producing drugs that address potential biological causes, rather than in examining environmental conditions that may cause or exacerbate serious health problems. Research is directed at identifying genetic susceptibilities that can be treated with drugs rather than at addressing environmental triggers of disease.

Sometimes these concerns about neglecting environmental conditions involve race. Duster notes that, although there is no genetic basis for race (something we explore in Chapter 10), race is a social reality that sometimes has biological implications. For example, the rate of prostate cancer among African American men is much higher than it is for white men, and the National Cancer Institute is looking for a genetic explanation for this difference. Duster points out, however, that black men in Africa and the Caribbean, presumably genetically similar to African American men, have lower prostate cancer rates, suggesting that the cause of the difference is at least as much environmental and social—perhaps the result of diet, stress, or some other factor—as it is genetic (Dreifus 2005).

A sociological approach encourages us to ask hard questions about the interaction of genes and the social environment. At the same time, as new forms of genetic testing develop, sociology helps us to think critically about their social consequences. In recent years, DNA testing has been the subject of much media attention—helping prove the innocence of sometimes long-held prison inmates or to place alleged perpetrators at the scene of a crime, determining paternity, identifying missing children, and connecting biological relatives—and a huge database of genetic information continues to accumulate. Sociology reminds us that we need to place the issue of genetic information in a broader social context, paying careful attention both to its potential benefits and to its possible abuses.

think about it

1. *Why do you think social considerations are deemphasized in a climate that focuses on biological research? What results might this lack of emphasis have?*

2. *How might the misuse of genetic research be avoided or prevented?*

Chinese but not a word of English. His body language—including facial expressions, arm movements, and gait—were all consistent with Chinese norms. His worldview clashed with common American ways of thinking. After a short and alienating time in the United States, he decided to return to China.

This young man was the light-haired, blue-eyed son of American parents from Indiana who had gone to China as missionaries. When they died, the young man was raised by a Chinese family in a remote village. He was socialized into Chinese culture, and his sense of self was inextricably linked to his Chinese upbringing. His social environment was central to his development of a sense of self.

Biology helps set the stage for social life, but our cultural characteristics make us distinct. Our development into fully functioning human beings must be nurtured systematically through ongoing social interaction and socialization.

Humans Without Culture

The importance of socialization and culture to becoming human can be illustrated dramatically with the tragic cases of children raised in isolation. One well-documented case from Ohio in the 1930s involved a child who was given the pseudonym "Isabelle" (Davis 1947). Isabelle's mother was a deaf-mute and unmarried. At the time, so-called illegitimate children faced intense social disapproval, and for this reason the child and the mother were kept secluded in a darkened room, shut off from the rest of their family. Isabelle's first six-and-a-half years were spent in this terrible isolation.

When she was discovered, Isabelle seemed to be mentally incapacitated. She could not speak at all and instead made only a "strange croaking sound." She did not respond normally to sights and sounds. She was fearful and hostile toward strangers, behaving like "a wild animal" (Davis 1947, 436). Specialists began to work with Isabelle, and over time they determined that she could hear and see normally. But she scored almost zero on a verbal test, and a test of her social maturity ranked her at the level of a two-and-a-half-year old.

When given intensive training, Isabelle developed quickly, learning to speak, write, and do basic mathematics. Within two years she had caught up to her peers and had the intellectual development normal for children her age. She went on to function normally in school and took part in activities with children her age. With adequate socialization, the result of systematic training by an expert team that included a speech specialist and a psychologist, Isabelle was able to participate fully in her culture.

A striking large-scale example of the consequences of inadequate socialization emerged during the 1990s. For years, Romania had a state system of poorly run orphanages where more than 100,000 children languished. The children were well fed, clothed, and housed, but they received little stimulation and inadequate attention. After Romania's communist regime fell in late 1989, outside aid agencies took an interest in the or-

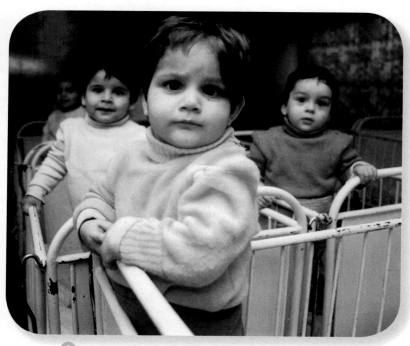

Romanian orphans, such as those in the photo above, were adequately fed, clothed, and housed, but their lack of social interaction and stimulation dramatically stunted their development.

phans and began to promote their placement in foster homes and adoption, though many remained in the orphanages.

Researchers from around the world studied the unfortunate children to learn how inadequate social stimulation had affected their health and to see if they could assist their development. Researchers placed nearly seventy of the children between the ages of six and thirty months in high-quality foster care. For five years, they compared the progress of these children to that of a similar-sized group who remained in the orphanages, as well as to a control group of local children growing up with their own families. Studies that are still ongoing as the children enter adulthood (Parker and Nelson 2005) show that inadequate social stimulation and interaction at an early age produce long-lasting physical and cognitive trauma.

The stress caused by the infants' social deprivation apparently inhibited the production of key growth hormones, an example of how social environment affects biology. The children suffered stunted mental and physical development. Some teenaged orphans had the physical appearance of six year olds. They had IQ scores averaging nearly forty points below normal and high rates of social disorders, including hyperactivity, the inability to form healthy social bonds, and behavior that mimics symptoms of autism, a developmental disorder characterized by impaired social interaction.

When their social environment was improved, the youngest orphans—especially those still less than a year old—made up much of the lost ground in both their physical and mental development, sometimes growing at five times the normal rate while catching up. Stimulation and nurturing support from foster care families, in the form of touching, eye contact, positive verbal reinforcements (cheers, praise, laughing) encouraged the children to thrive and develop. They developed higher IQs and had fewer social problems, such as anxiety and depression, when compared with children who stayed in the orphanages. However, children who had been in the orphanages for a longer period appear to have missed a crucial window for important brain development. A lack of normal social stimulation early on may have taken a long-term biological toll.

The sad tale of isolated children demonstrates how essential socialization is to making us recognizably human. Through social interaction, we develop our capacities, become healthy adults—physically and socially—and, in the process, develop a sense of self.

Reflexivity: Cooley's "Looking Glass Self"

Your **sense of self** is *the collection of thoughts and feelings you have when considering yourself as an object.* Humans are self-conscious beings: we can make ourselves the object of our own thoughts and attention. This capacity for self-reflection is at the heart of the concept of a self, and as we will see, self-reflection emerges only through social interaction.

We are not born with a sense of self; rather we develop it over time as a product of the culture in which we are socialized. In particular, we develop a sense of self through our experience of social interaction. An early American sociologist, Charles Horton Cooley (1864–1929), articulated this point with his concept of the **looking glass self,** *the idea that our sense of self develops as a reflection of the way we think others see us* (1902). (A looking glass is a mirror.)

According to Cooley, our interactions with others involve three steps that, repeated in all our interactions, forge our sense of self:

1. We imagine our image in the eyes of others.

2. We imagine the others making some judgment about us.

3. We experience a feeling as a result of the imagined judgment.

For example, think of a moment when you were either badly embarrassed or very proud of yourself. Why did you feel this way? Was at least part of your emotion based on your perception of how other people were seeing you, as Cooley suggests?

Cooley wrote long before researchers could probe the workings of the human brain. However, as we see later in this chapter, recent findings in brain science are consistent with Cooley's early sociological insights. Our so-called mind-reading skills (our ability to interpret what other people think or feel) and many of our emotional responses—both central to Cooley's model—are built-in brain functions.

As the looking-glass-self idea implies, people's sense of self is determined in relation to their interaction with others and so varies depending on the people with whom they interact. While hanging out with close friends, you feel confident and comfortable, but during a tough job interview, you feel nervous and uncertain. You haven't changed, but the social context and your interaction with others have. Your confidence or nervousness is linked to your perception of others' judgments of you in each of these situations, as well as to the level of significance you attribute to that judgment.

The extent to which people are attuned to the judgment of others can vary dramatically. Some people feel such an excessive concern about what others think of them that it inhibits their behavior. Others seem to care so little about what others think that they are sometimes unapologetically rude. Navigating smoothly through social life generally requires a balanced reaction: taking into account the reactions of others but not letting them dictate your actions. Acquiring this balance is part of socialization.

Spontaneity Versus Social Norms: Mead's "I" and "Me"

Another way of expressing the balance required in developing a healthy self comes from the work of American sociologist George Herbert Mead (1863–1931). Mead argued that the self is made up of what he called the "I" and the "me" (1934/1962). **Mead's "I"** is *the part of the self that is spontaneous, impulsive, creative, and unpredictable.* It is nonreflective and exists only in the present. The instant you start to think about it, you lose that spontaneous self.

Have you ever blurted out something you immediately wished you hadn't said? That was the "I" speaking. When people attribute their actions to instinct or reflexes or acting without thinking, they are referring to Mead's "I." The "I" is also the location of what we often refer to as personality. People with a strong "I" tend to be outgoing, spontaneous, and vivacious. The "I" allows for spontaneous action independent of social conventions. In some cases, it can be the source of resistance to social norms and social control.

To create a healthy self, the "I" must be balanced with what Mead calls the "me." **Mead's "me"** is *the sense of self that has been learned from interaction with others.* When you adhere to social norms—such as when you refrain from saying something for fear of offending someone—the "me" is dominating the "I." When you reflect on the "I," it becomes part of the "me." Socialization involves learning to balance the "I" and the "me."

Social Interaction: Developing a Self

The self is constructed through social interaction as a person matures, both biologically and socially. For example, the capacity to take on the perspective of others begins with the biological maturation that takes place between 9 and 14 months old, when most children become skilled at "gaze monitoring," the ability to follow someone's gaze to see the same thing that person is looking at (Baron-Cohen 1999). This is a child's early attempt to figure out what's going on in another person's head. Building on this ability, children later learn social interaction skills and construct a robust sense of self.

Mead proposed that children advance through four stages of social development:

1. **Pre-play stage.** Through age two children are unable to step fully outside of themselves to view themselves. They cannot completely take the perspective of other people. They may imitate behavior they see, but those acts are not meaningful; they do not fully understand what they are doing.

2. **Play stage.** Beginning at around age three, children begin to be able to take on the role of a single other in a meaningful way. They can step out of themselves, for example, by playing the role of a mom or a dad.

3. **Game stage.** By age six or seven, children learn not only how to play a role but also how to link this role to others' roles. Playing a team sport, for example, involves understanding your role in relation to those of others on the team. This in turn involves learning rules and anticipating the actions of others. At this stage, children can fully imagine how the social world appears to others.

4. **Generalized other.** Finally, as people mature they develop the capacity to consider the **generalized other,** *the values and orientations of their overall community rather than those of specific individuals.* That is, they internalize the values and beliefs of their culture. Being concerned about "what people would think" or simply "knowing right from wrong" are examples of taking into account the generalized other. The generalized other depends on the social context: it varies greatly from culture to culture.

Neurosociology and the Social Brain

Neuroscience is composed of the various fields that study the nervous system, especially the brain. The emerging study of *neurosociology* integrates findings from neuroscience with a sociological analysis of social behavior. From neurosociology we are learning the brain's role in influencing many of the things that make us human, including our unconscious, our emo-

tions, our sense of self, and our ability to interact with others. But we are also learning how social interaction produces physical changes in the brain itself. The brain makes social interaction possible, but it is also itself a product of social interaction. Finally, what we are learning about the way the brain responds to social stimuli is consistent with many of Cooley's and Mead's insights about the importance of social interaction for the development of the self.

The brain is central to social life because it processes stimuli from outside the body. Much of what the brain does—as much as 97 percent (Gazzaniga 1998)—is automatic. Our breathing and pulse, for example, are maintained by the brain even while we sleep. At any given moment, your brain processes much more information from your senses than you are consciously aware of. When you interact with people face to face you are unconsciously picking up information about them from a variety of nonverbal sources such as their body language and tone of voice (Turner 1999, 2000). The facial muscles used in a genuine smile are different from those used in a fake smile, for example, and research shows that most people can recognize the difference and sense a lack of sincerity behind a fake smile (S. Johnson 2004). Such unconsciously perceived signals may account for the "gut feelings" we sometimes have about people we have just met.

The brain helps us "read" people and understand their intentions and behaviors. This task is complex, because social situations are constantly in flux and our assessments must be revised accordingly (Brothers 1997). For example, on a first date, you probably continually try to read your partner's words, actions, and body language to figure out how she or he feels about you. This ability to read other people—an ability central to Cooley's concept of the looking glass self and Mead's ideas about the stages of child development—is sometimes referred to as "mind reading" by neuroscientists (Baron-Cohen 1999). It is partially rooted in the brain through specialized brain cells called mirror neurons that fire whenever you perform an action or experience an emotion. They also fire when you watch someone else perform the same action or convey the same emotion, allowing you to experience what the other person is experiencing.

Emotions are crucial to human communication and behavior, and scientists are beginning to understand how the brain interacts with social cues to control them (Smith and Franks 1999). For example, a crying child is often soothed when picked up by a parent. But why? The child's brain produces opioids—morphine-like molecules—that generate feelings of

thinking about**culture**

Culture shapes our sense of the generalized other. What might be some consequences— large or small—when people with differing views of the generalized other interact, say, in diplomatic negotiations, business deals, or romantic courtships?

comfort. The emotional change is a result of biology, but the biological change is triggered by a social interaction.

That our biological makeup provides positive reinforcements for attachment to others may be one factor in explaining some social behavior, including bonding and trust (Kosfeld et al. 2005). One type of hormone that generates soothing feelings, oxytocin (not to be confused with the painkiller oxycontin) is produced in the context of intense social bonding, including breastfeeding, sexual climax, and falling in love. For humans, connecting with others simply feels good.

As Mead suggests with his concepts of the "I" and "me," learning to balance automatic, often emotion-laden, actions and more considered responses is an important part of developing into an adult and being socialized. Youngsters with relatively little socialization have not yet developed such skills. They respond more automatically than adults through laughing, crying, hitting, and acting out in various ways. Part of the socialization process, which varies by culture, is learning to control our emotional responses so that we do not act impulsively. In effect, we train and strengthen a portion of our brains that regulates our feelings and behavior.

Brain plasticity is the ability of the brain to restructure and reorganize itself, especially as a result of social experiences and learning. When you interact with your environment, you are changing the way your brain is structured or used. Train intensely to become a violinist, and the portion of the brain associated with fingers of the hand that play notes will grow. A person who becomes blind may use the portion of the brain typically devoted to visual information to learn and process Braille.

As we are socialized and learn about our culture, we are also shaping our brains. For example, the left side of the brain is associated with language, logic, and linear thinking, whereas the right side is associated with more holistic and nonlinear reasoning. In a study comparing Australian Aborigine children with Australian children of European descent, sociologist Warren TenHouten (1980, 1999) found that the Aborigine children rely more on the right brain whereas the Euro-Australian children rely more on the left. However, when Aborigine children moved from the Australian outback to Euro-Australian-dominated urban areas, they began to draw more heavily on their left brains. Their need to adapt to a different cultural setting apparently changed the way they used their brains.

Foucault's Regimes of Power

Social interaction and self-reflection are crucial to creating a sense of self. However, the self develops in a particular historical context under certain social and political conditions. As a result, power relations within a society—who holds power and who does not—are important factors in socialization and in the developing sense of self. Your sense of self would be radically different had you been born, say, a peasant serving a noble in medieval Europe, or a native of a nineteenth-century central African country colonized by a European power, or a member of the Saudi royal family. In other words, your sense of self is partially the product of the power relations in your society.

As we saw in Chapter 5, Michel Foucault (1977/1979, 1980) is the social theorist most closely associated with the idea that power shapes our daily life and our sense of self. For Foucault, modern power is embodied in various types of knowledge that are connected to particular social sites, such as schools, hospitals, prisons, and the workplace. The connection of power and knowledge in different social settings produces various "regimes of power" (Callero 2003). For example, psychiatry, medicine, personnel management, education, and criminal justice are all fields in which "experts" use their specialized knowledge in particular settings to monitor, test, categorize, and control others. Thus, Foucault saw power as decentralized within the many social institutions that we encounter in our daily lives. Students, patients, and prisoners, for example, are all monitored by those in power, tested in various ways, and classified so as to fit into a system that categorizes people.

Foucault argued that the very terms and concepts we use to think about our selves do not originate with us but instead are produced and promoted through various regimes of power. Teachers tell us what is good; doctors tell us what is normal. We are socialized to internalize these definitions. We judge ourselves against these standards and work to comply with these expectations. Over time, through socialization, most of us internalize these various forms of social control by becoming, for example, good students, law-abiding citizens, rational thinkers, hard workers, and diligent consumers. By internalizing these standards, we create a self that originates outside our selves. For Foucault there is no "real" self that struggles against powerful external forces. Instead, the self is the product of these various regimes of power.

Understood in this way, culture is not something outside ourselves that we can choose to ignore. Once we are socialized, culture has become a part of who we are; there is no escaping it. It is embedded in how we think and view the world. Imagine the extreme case of a man who decides he wants nothing to do with society and therefore withdraws to some remote location to live off the land in total isolation. Elated by his newfound independence, he shouts to the stars, "Finally, I am free!"—using words and concepts from his culture! His freedom from society is illusory, since he takes with him all that he has learned through socialization. Like this man, we too have made our culture a part of who we are.

ONLINE COMMUNICATION AND IDENTITY

As we have seen, the sense of self develops in a social context. As a result, in today's rapidly changing, increasingly globalized world, the way people are socialized and the way people view themselves is also changing.

In particular, the way we think about ourselves is much more fluid and changeable than it was in eras past. As social roles in many societies have become less rigid and as mass communication has exposed people to a broad and sometimes conflicting set of values and lifestyles, developing an identity has become much more of an intentional, self-conscious act. Rather than being constrained by traditional, rigid expectations, many people are faced with a variety of options. As a result, they must construct answers to many questions: Who am I? What sort of work will I do? Where will I live? Will I have children? What lifestyle will I pursue? Will I follow a set of religious beliefs or be a nonbeliever? Will I be politically active? These and many other aspects of our adult selves are open to various possibilities, but there are limits, of course. In particular, social inequality limits the options of the poor, leaving the relatively affluent to ponder their many options.

Sociologist Sherry Turkle was among the first to recognize that computers could be connected to our sense of identity. In the pre-Internet age, Turkle (1985) found that some young people saw their personal computers as an extension of themselves, a "second self." Later, Turkle (1995) examined the emerging world of online role-playing games, where people could experiment with their identities, moving beyond the limits of real life.

The choices you make in your sense of self are especially evident on the Internet, where your Facebook "wall" or your avatar tell people who you are. Avatars—cartoon-like graphic representations—serve as public faces for otherwise faceless gamers in virtual communities such as Second Life and multiplayer gaming worlds like Worlds of Warcraft. Since gamers can choose among existing avatars or create their own, they actively participate in the construction of their online selves. An online identity need not be constrained by the gamer's biological reality. It can be a different sex, race, age, and appearance.

Recent research indicates some of the possibilities and limits of online identities. For example, one study of virtual sex on Second Life found that people see their online intimate encounters as opportunities to transgress norms and seek out new experiences, even construct secret selves, all without consequences in "first life," one's real life. Second Life encounters are playful and fun, allowing for "unbridled free expression, self-exploration, and transgression," precisely because they aren't real. In fact, real life influences Second Life far more than Second Life bleeds into people's first lives. Second Life reproduces prevailing standards of attractiveness, as almost all avatars embody the same definitions of what it means to be beautiful and sexy (Waskul and Martin 2010).

As a growing number of senior citizens go online, joining virtual communities of age peers such as "Age-net," "Cool Grandma," and "Seniors Daily," researchers have begun to

World of Warcraft is a multiplayer online role-playing game in which thousands of players participate within the online Warcraft universe. Each player creates a distinct online identity in the form of an avatar, with a specific race, class, profession, and reputation—all drawn from a list within the Warcraft world.

explore the ways senior citizens experience online communication. One study suggests that online communities provide valuable support for senior citizens coping with life-course transitions, such as retirement or declining health, by giving them a forum to interact and share their experiences with peers from around the globe and by providing a source of leisure and entertainment. Participation in online communities may help senior citizens to maintain a sense of self during times of transition or even to restore their identity in the wake of painful experiences. Some senior citizens may find that the anonymity of online communities permits them to express emotions that they conceal in real life or to experience new relationships, providing an opportunity for personal growth (Nimrod 2009).

Online communities are also allowing us to make what once was our private self more public. In the past, people drew sharp distinctions between the private self—the aspects of the self shared only with a few close intimates—and the public self—the aspects of the self that were freely ac-cessible to everyone. In recent years, technology has blurred this distinction. Some individuals make what once would have been their private lives freely and publicly available on-line through personal web sites, blogs, pictures, and video.

Finally, online communication has contributed to a general increase in the pace of modern life, which can also alter our sense of self. Turkle (2008) suggests that we now live in an "always-on culture," where the speed and constancy of communication is generating a "rapid response" self, with little time for reflection. In the age of the Blackberry and iPhone, people can be connected to the Internet just about every waking minute. For those who are most plugged-in to the online world, a phone or laptop can feel like an extension of the body—raising questions about the self in the digital age. Turkle (2008) quotes a television producer describing how she felt when her smartphone broke: "When my Palm crashed, it was like a death. It was more than I could handle. I felt as though I had lost my mind" (p. 132).

THINKING SOCIOLOGICALLY ABOUT . . .   Socialization

culture

- Socialization refers to the process through which we learn the basic norms, values, beliefs, and behaviors of our society's culture. As children we learn the language and symbols of our culture and what is expected of us in such social roles as child and sibling. Once we are socialized, culture becomes a part of who we are. It is embedded in how we think and view the world.

- We are not born with a sense of self; rather we develop it over time as a product of the culture in which we are socialized. In particular, we develop a sense of self through our experience of social interaction with others.

structure

- In transmitting fundamental social norms and role expectations from one generation to another, socialization helps to reproduce social structure.

- Changes in social structure typically require new socialization messages to support new structures.

power

- Power relations within a society are important factors in socialization and in the developing sense of self.

- Power shapes our daily life and our sense of self. According to Foucault, our sense of self is produced through various regimes of power connected to particular social sites, such as schools and hospitals. Teachers tell us what is good; doctors tell us what is normal. We are socialized to internalize these definitions and create a self that originates outside our selves.

Looking Back

1. People learn about their culture through the process of socialization. Various agents of socialization—family, school, media, peer groups, the workplace, and religion—play important roles in socializing individuals. One unique group of socializing agents, total institutions, can have an almost all-encompassing influence over their members' lives as they resocialize people, replacing old norms and behaviors with new ones.

2. The life-course perspective views socialization as a lifelong process of learning and adaptation to the new social contexts we encounter over time as we age and relocate. Powerful youth experiences can shape attitudes and priorities that have long-term biographical consequences.

3. Researchers have moved beyond the longstanding nature versus nurture debate to recognize that both biology and the social environment play important roles in shaping human behavior and that biology and the social environment interact in crucial ways.

4. Cooley's looking glass self and Mead's distinction between the "I" and the "me" provide two ways of understanding how our sense of self develops through social interaction and depends on our ability to reflect on our self as an object.

5. The emerging field of neurosociology explores how our brains process information, help us "read" people, and manage emotions. In turn, brains are changed by the nature of our social environment and social interactions.

6. According to Foucault, the very terms and concepts we use to think about our selves do not originate with us but instead are produced and promoted through various regimes of power.

7. In contemporary society our sense of self is increasingly fluid, or changeable, which is often reflected in our online identity.

Critical Thinking: Questions and Activities

1. One aspect of our identity is gender. As a boy or a girl, how were you socialized into learning what was considered culturally appropriate behavior for your gender? Which agents of socialization taught you these cultural norms, and which was the most significant in shaping your sense of self? Explain.

2. Who are you? How does your sense of self reflect the cultural and historical context in which you live?

3. What event do you think has been the most significant part of your generation's political socialization? Explain.

4. What was the nature versus nurture debate, and why do most researchers now reject this framing of the issue? What common ground has replaced this debate? Do you agree with it? Explain.

5. What sociological lessons are we learning from the case of the isolated Romanian orphans?

Key Terms

agents of socialization (p. 137) people and groups who teach us about our culture.

anticipatory socialization (p. 144) the process by which individuals practice for a future social role by adopting the norms or behaviors associated with a position they have not yet achieved.

biological determinism (p. 149) a theory that contends that biology, specifically our genetic makeup, almost completely shapes human behavior.

generalized other (p. 154) the values and orientations of one's overall community rather than those of specific individuals.

hidden curriculum (p. 139) implicit lessons conveyed in school about how children should behave.

life-course perspective (p. 142) looks at how age, time, and place shape social identities and experiences over a lifetime.

looking glass self (p. 153) the idea that our sense of self develops as a reflection of the way we think others see us.

Mead's "I" (p. 153) the part of the self that is spontaneous, impulsive, creative, and unpredictable.

Mead's "me" (p. 153) the sense of self that has been learned from interaction with others.

nature versus nurture debate (p. 149) a disagreement about the relative importance of biology ("nature") and the social environment ("nurture") in influencing human behavior.

occupational socialization (p. 141) the learning of the informal norms associated with a type of employment.

peer group (p. 140) a group of people, usually of comparable age, who share similar interests and social status.

resocialization (p. 142) the process by which individuals replace old norms and behaviors with new ones as they move from one role or life stage to another.

rites of passage (p. 143) activities that mark and celebrate a change in a person's social status.

sense of self (p. 153) the collection of thoughts and feelings you have when considering yourself as an object.

social determinism (p. 149) a theory that contends that culture and the social environment almost completely shape human behavior.

socialization (p. 137) the process through which people learn their culture's basic norms, values, beliefs, and behaviors.

total institution (p. 142) confining social settings in which an authority regulates all aspects of a person's life.

Interaction, Groups, and Organizations

looking AHEAD

How does the **culture** you have been raised in affect your interactions with your friends and family?

How do your everyday activities and those of your friends help create and sustain complex, large-scale social **structures**?

How are your relationships on campus, at work, or in your family affected by who has and who lacks **power**?

I n 2006, Noor was a lonely nineteen-year-old Iraqi caught up in the aftermath of war. A young man from a middle-class family, Noor had hoped to go to college, but because Iraqi campuses were plagued by fighting between Iraq's two major Muslim sects—the majority Shiites and the minority Sunnis—his parents would not let him go. To protect him, they even confined Noor to their home in central Baghdad. As the war waged on, Noor grew badly discouraged, telling an American reporter, "I can't go outside, I can't go to college. If I'm killed, it doesn't even matter because I'm dead right now." Similarly, Sara, a tenth grader, could no longer play basketball at her school, since all after-school sports programs were canceled. Noting that college was no longer in her plans, Sara told the American reporter: "There's no dream for me."

In the midst of war, everyday life can be not only treacherous but also frustrating for civilians as well as soldiers. While American news reports focused on the violence and mounting death tolls, millions of Iraqis like Noor and Sara experienced the quiet desperation that rarely receives news coverage. Like all wars, the one in Iraq destroyed daily routines, shredding the fabric of culture. The war brought rampant unemployment, making survival difficult, and disrupted schooling for millions of girls and boys. Basic goods and services, such as gasoline, electricity, water, and sewage treatment facilities, grew scarce. Widespread sectarian violence, the result of a fierce struggle for power, undermined basic trust in society, making even ordinary social interaction tense and difficult. With the social fabric in tatters and familiar social structures collapsing, people improvised to carve out new ways of living, though these arrangements were fragile at best (Tavernise 2005, 2006). ■

Countries in the midst of war or natural disaster usually have little semblance of normal life. But such cases only emphasize the point that a working society is a marvel. Think about how society typically operates. Each morning, millions of people get up and go about their daily routines. Throughout the day they travel, work, play, and carry on the affairs of daily life. How is all this possible? Sometimes, of course, it is not; daily routines break down, as Noor and Sara experienced in wartime Iraq. Society's structure must be constantly maintained and reproduced: it doesn't happen automatically or inevitably, and its continuation is not guaranteed.

How is this amazing accomplishment achieved? You already know some of the essential elements involved in constructing everyday life. As we consider the dynamics of social interaction and the key characteristics of groups and formal organizations, our core sociological concepts—culture, structure, and power—will help you understand better how we construct everyday life.

We begin at the micro level by examining face-to-face interaction and our shared understanding of social reality (culture) and then by looking more closely at how statuses and roles connect people to one another and to the patterns and routines that are the foundations of social structure. Next we look at networks, groups, and organizations, the specific social ties that form social institutions and the sites where relations of power occur. Finally, we look at the changes in social interaction and organization brought on by the expansion of the Internet.

Culture and Social Interaction

Social life begins with face-to-face interaction. Guided by cultural norms and expectations, we negotiate these micro-level encounters with family members, friends, coworkers, and strangers that are the building blocks of social life. The theoretical tradition of *symbolic interactionism,* introduced in Chapter 1, emphasizes how we make sense of the world by focusing on just these kinds of encounters. Two early-twentieth-century sociological thinkers, Charles Horton Cooley and George Herbert Mead, argued that social interactions were crucial in the development of our sense of self.

Through socialization, we become adept at taking the perspectives of others and determining the intent and meaning of their actions, making this process so much a part of our social interaction that we often forget we are engaged in it. Because it is essential to successful social interaction and to the construction of larger social groups, it is worth taking a closer look at how this process works.

Interaction: Arriving at Common Understandings

As humans, we spend our lives producing symbols. Humans have created languages, such as English or Spanish; we constantly make images, such as the pictures attached to e-mails we send to friends; and we use gestures, such as shaking our heads to mean "no." To interact successfully with others, we need to agree with them about the meaning of these symbols. As we communicate, we rely on the language and knowledge that we share with others to get our meaning across (Blumer 1969/1986).

SHARED LANGUAGE Imagine that you are traveling in a foreign country where you do not speak the local language and the locals don't speak yours. You are separated from your travel group and suddenly find yourself lost in an unfamiliar city. You stop strangers, try to explain that you are lost, and ask for directions. Your efforts are met with quizzical looks as people try to understand what you are asking, and their attempts to help bewilder you. Maybe for the first time, you realize how valuable language is. Without the common ground of shared meaning, social interaction becomes confusing, frustrating, inefficient, even frightening.

Even among those who share a language, however, there are always words or expressions that not everyone will understand, depending on the historical period, the country, or the group or subculture using the word or phrase. If you asked an American youngster to "hop the wag," you would likely get a puzzled look, whereas many British teenagers would immediately recognize this slang phrase as an invitation to skip school. Slang is a common part of subcultures, and slang terms such as *cool, groovy,* or *sweet* often evolve rapidly, fall in and out of favor over a short time, and thus lose their ability—across time or even across groups in the same society—to make interactions meaningful.

When we communicate with people we know, our conversation is often rooted in common references and shared understandings, allowing us to rely on unspoken, taken-for-granted assumptions. In the United States, you might greet a friend by saying, "Hey, what's up?" This extremely vague question is understood to mean something like, "Hello, what are you doing now?" Your friend might respond with another question, asking, "Going to Jimmy's blowout tonight?" Although this question might baffle an outsider, you know that your mutual friend Jimmy is having a party. Because you understand the slang term *blowout,* you know how to respond.

SHARED KNOWLEDGE Language is just one example of how shared understanding facilitates social interaction. The smooth functioning of everyday life depends on what sociologists refer to as **intersubjectivity,** *a common understanding between people about knowledge, reality, or an experience.* Successful interaction requires each person to take the perspective of the other to achieve some common understanding. In this way, social interaction constantly constructs our social world.

While trying to capture our attention, advertisements must also convey meaning. By drawing on a common understanding of social reality, ads can leave many things unstated. Understanding the routines of soccer—and how players typically protect sensitive body parts during a "free kick"—is what makes this advertisement work.

CORE CONCEPTS CHALLENGE

 For this advertisement to make sense, what does the reader need to know that is not explained? Do you think this ad would be effective in all **cultures**? *Why or why not?*

People within a society share knowledge not just of their common language but also of norms and customs, historical references, and other socially useful information that they have learned through socialization (Schutz 1962). In other words, they have a common perspective that enables them to understand how others see the world and allows society to function smoothly. Daily life is full of unspoken, taken-for-granted, and shared interpretations of reality. For example, you have no doubt learned cultural norms for how to conduct yourself in face-to-face interactions, including whether and when to make eye contact, how much personal space to allow, and if and how to greet a person. Do you use a formal greeting? A casual "Hi"? A handshake? A hug? A kiss? All these cultural norms are part of our routine social interactions.

The smooth functioning of everyday life, therefore, is based partially on people's shared understanding of the nature of reality. For example, when you ride public transportation in your home city, you share a common understanding with your fellow passengers and the conductors or drivers about where and how to board, how to pay your fare, and how and where to get off. In a different city or in a foreign country, you would have to figure out all those things, because you would not share a common framework.

Similarly, your enjoyment of any form of entertainment depends on a shared knowledge base. Television comedies like *Family Guy* or *The Colbert Report* assume their audiences will understand their writers' irreverent references to celebrities and politicians, other television programs, and current events. When you "get"—and laugh at—a joke, your enjoyment is rooted in the unspoken assumptions that you share with others. Advertisers, too, often rely on shared views of what is attractive and desirable. That's why logos and slogans can communicate so much about the meaning and identity of specific brands or products.

When you meet and interact with strangers, shared elements of culture form a common ground that facilitates routine interactions. For example, imagine you are purchasing a computer cable at an office products store. As you interact with the checkout clerk, your facial expression, tone of voice, words, and body language all contribute to the brief interaction, during which you and the clerk share basic assumptions about how to proceed (greet each other, exchange money). You don't try to haggle about the price; the clerk doesn't try to give you a hug.

Suppose, however, that you know very little about computer hardware and are trying to find the cable you need to make your printer work. You ask a clerk about the difference between the various cables for sale and—to your shock—she replies by telling you about the differences between ATA, USB, DVI, and an alphabet soup of cables. The clerk's enthusiasm is blinding her to your perspective—you just want her to pick out an inexpensive cable for you. Exasperated, you leave abruptly without buying anything. In this case, you and the clerk failed to achieve intersubjectivity: you never fully agreed on what was needed for this interaction to be successful.

Some failed social interactions can have far more serious consequences than a frustrating trip to the computer store. For example, in 2006 the U.S. commander in charge of day-to-day military operations in Iraq, Lieutenant General Peter Chiarelli, found that some American troops had been their "own worst enemy" because they didn't understand fundamental aspects of Iraqi culture (Rainey 2006). Chiarelli told the story of how U.S. soldiers arrested a Sunni Arab insurgent in his home. In keeping with the emphasis in Iraqi culture on maintaining a man's honor, the suspect asked to be handcuffed outside, out of view of his family. Instead, U.S. troops forced the man to the floor, handcuffed him, and jerked him out the door—in full

SPOTLIGHT on social theory

Symbolic interactionists focus on our day-to-day interactions as the building blocks of social structure. Describe a successful, or unsuccessful, interaction you have recently had with a sales person, school official, or other stranger. What contributed to its success, or what caused the problem?

thinking about **culture**
How would an understanding of Iraqi **culture** help American soldiers in their interactions with these Iraqi citizens? What examples of cultural misunderstandings can you think of?

Having a common culture facilitates ordinary social interactions. In the text we describe a routine interaction with a computer store clerk. Now imagine purchasing food from this street vendor in Egypt. How might the two interactions differ? How might they be similar? What explains these similarities and differences?

view of his family and neighbors. General Chiarelli summed up the incident's consequences in this way: "Every single person in the room, because of this whole concept of honor in this culture, has said, 'To hell with the Americans'." In this case, an interaction based on fundamental cultural misunderstanding had potentially serious consequences.

People who occupy different social positions often see the world from different perspectives. African Americans living in a city center likely see the world differently not only from their white urban neighbors but also very likely from African Americans who live in affluent suburbs. The same dynamics operate on a global scale, as well: people in France or China often have a different vantage point on world events than do residents of the United States. Each group draws upon different stocks of knowledge and experience to understand the social world.

Defining Situations as "Real": The Thomas Theorem

By being socialized in a particular culture we learn to see our world from a particular perspective, and that viewpoint becomes our reality. Sociologists maintain that "reality" is what we learn from our society; in other words, it is socially constructed. Not only do we take our definitions of reality for granted so that we resist seeing society in all of its complexity, but these definitions can also have very real consequences in action. For example, Maps 7.1 and 7.2 (page 166) show two ways of seeing the world—ideas about geography that have affected the way we view the significance and size of various regions and nations. The traditional Mercator projection (Map 7.1), developed in the 1500s, badly distorts the relative sizes of the continents. Also, the orientation of the map—with South

America and Africa on the bottom—is completely arbitrary. The Peters projection (Map 7.2), developed by cartographer Arno Peters in the 1970s, represents the relative sizes of the continents more accurately, though it distorts their shapes. Finally, although we typically (and arbitrarily) represent the North Pole as the top and the South Pole as the bottom on maps and globes, the earth has no top or bottom, so the "inverted" presentation of the Peters projection is just as accurate as the "right side up" Mercator projection.

The early-twentieth-century American sociologist W. I. Thomas (1863–1947) helped to develop our thinking about the need for people to interpret a social situation before they act. During this process, which Thomas (1923) called "the definition of the situation," we consider both our spontaneous interpretation of the circumstances at hand as well as what society has taught us about those circumstances. Our interpretation then influences how we act. Thomas stated his insight, now known as the **Thomas theorem,** this way: *"If men define situations as real, they are real in their consequences"* (Thomas and Thomas 1928, 572). In other words, subjective interpretations of reality have objective effects. If we are to understand how and why human beings act the way they do, we need to pay attention to how they define reality and how that definition, in turn, influences their behavior.

The Thomas theorem helps us to understand how interpretations of a situation shape social interaction on various levels. For example, on the micro level, if a stranger asks for a handout, your definition of the situation is likely to influence whether you give money (see Figure 7.1, page 166). Your interpretation may depend on the way you answer some questions: Is this person down on his or her luck? A victim of a weak economy? A veteran? A substance abuser? Someone who is too lazy to hold a job? Or someone with mental illness? The theorem applies to large institutions, as well. If the government of one nation sees a neighboring country as a military threat, that government may be more likely to invest substantially in weapons. The neighboring country may then misinterpret this investment as a threat instead of a defensive strategy and increase its own investment in weapons, thereby triggering a dangerous arms race. Whether or not these assessments of threat were

MAPS 7.1 AND 7.2 | MAPPING REALITY

The Mercator projection (Map 7.1, left) and the Peters projection (Map 7.2, right) are two-dimensional representations of the three-dimensional globe, though both maps contain distortions. For example, North America appears to be larger than Africa in Map 7.1. Also, the orientation of the map is completely arbitrary. The Peters projection represents the relative sizes of the continents more accurately. For example, it shows Africa (11.7 million square miles) as being larger than North America (9.4 million square miles), and the inverted presentation is actually as accurate as the Mercator projection. However, the Peters map distorts the shapes of the continents, making them appear stretched out. *Source:* radicalcartography.net

CORE CONCEPTS CHALLENGE

→ *Which of these maps appears "right" to you? What role do you think* **culture** *played in your choice?*

accurate, the initial definition of reality can have consequences and shape interpretations of future events.

The Thomas theorem can also help us understand stereotypes, which define individuals as typical examples of whole groups of people. **Stereotypes** are *exaggerated, distorted, or untrue generalizations about categories of people that do not acknowledge individual variation.* Stereotypes are often negative; we have all heard stories and jokes that belittle various ethnic groups. Indeed, stereotypes typically perpetuate unfair negative images of people and have little relationship to who they are, as individuals or as a group. (Some of the possible interpretations noted earlier for the stranger asking for money—especially that the person is a substance abuser or too lazy to work—are common stereotypes about homeless people.) At the

same time, however, you may also be able to think of some "positive" stereotypes, such as the false belief that "All Kenyans are fast runners." Such positive stereotypes also fail to take into account individual variation. Some of the world's best runners are Kenyans, but the vast majority of Kenyans are no more skilled at running than are people from any other society, and top runners come from many parts of the world.

Because they are shared definitions, all stereotypes create a sense of reality, and they can therefore have serious consequences. Television, for example, is full of stereotypes of working-class people, depicting them as unintelligent, lazy, and crude—think of Homer Simpson. Such stereotypes help to justify economic inequality by implying that highly educated professionals are somehow better than working-class folks. The Sociology Matters box examines how using a sociological perspective can challenge stereotypes based on social class and promote social change.

Social scientists often generalize about groups, of course, but their generalizations are usually carefully qualified and based on data. The statement "On average, U.S. citizens have among the highest annual incomes in the world" is not a stereotype, because it is qualified appropriately (that is, with the phrases "on average" and "among the highest annual incomes"), and it can be backed up with data about income levels in different countries. By contrast, the statement "All Americans are rich" is a stereotype, because it paints with an overly broad brush ("All Americans") and ignores the wide variation in income that exists in the United States. It also employs an undefined term, "rich," which people interpret in a variety of ways.

 FIGURE 7.1 | THOMAS THEOREM

If a stranger on the street asks you for money, what do you do? Whether accurate or not, your subjective definition of this situation will likely determine whether you give this person any money.

Subjective definition + = Objective result

SOCIOLOGY Matters

Overcoming Class Stereotypes

▶ Jenny was having lunch with a friend. When the waitress made an error with their order, Jenny's friend commented, "Well, if she was smart, she wouldn't be a waitress."

▶ Terry received an invitation to attend an annual conference of progressive political activists that cost $100 per day, a significant sum for many working people. The invitation noted, "Anybody who does not feel committed enough to pay is not committed enough to participate."

▶ Gilda was a community organizer. A colleague told Gilda that if she would mobilize working-class residents for a meeting on a local issue, he would then step in and negotiate on their behalf. Gilda noted, "He thought of working-class people as props and their voices as sound bites."

These real examples, from readers of a web site called Class Matters, illustrate some of the many ways that poor and working-class people can be stereotyped as unintelligent, uncommitted, or unable to stand up for themselves. The pervasiveness of such stereotypes—sometimes even among middle-class activists who are advocating on behalf of poor and working-class people—makes it difficult for people from different classes to work together to accomplish common goals. Sociological insights can be useful in helping people understand and overcome such stereotypes.

"I think the sociological imagination is really essential to making social change happen," says Betsy Leondar-Wright, a sociologist who grew up in a comfortable upper-middle-class family. Leondar-Wright (2005) has spent years working for a variety of organizations that address issues involving poverty and economic equality. She worked as an organizer in low-income communities and as a coalition builder, working across class, race, and ethnic lines. Her work often involved bringing together people from different backgrounds to address pressing needs such as affordable housing or neighborhood safety. In doing so, she discovered that people had to get past their stereotypes to collaborate successfully.

For example, community organizations based in low-income neighborhoods were frequently staffed by middle-class activists. Too often, activists did not think local residents were capable of leading their own campaigns for neighborhood improvement. "It's easy to fall into stereotypes about people with a particular amount of money or a type of occupation or neighborhood," she writes: "easy and dangerous." Such stereotypes blind people to the more complex realities that exist within any group and choke off potentially creative ideas from local residents.

Leondar-Wright argues that what keeps people from being active in their communities is not a stereotypical lack of intelligence or commitment, but rather a lack of hope. She notes that "most people can't imagine institutional arrangements" that differ from the ones they know. "[A]t one point my job was to knock on doors of low-income tenants to tell them that their housing was in danger of becoming unaffordable after a certain date [because of changes in ownership]. I saw firsthand how most people in their fear jumped immediately to individual solutions: 'My sister is in Tennessee. Maybe she could take us in for a while if we moved there.' The most valuable thing I brought to them was the information that other tenants in other towns had organized and bought their properties and turned them into permanently affordable housing. Three tenant groups I organized now own and run their apartment complexes. My main contribution to their victories was a sense of informed hope. If we want more people to get active, we need to recognize the critical shortage of hope."

Successful community-based organizing efforts like the one in which Leondar-Wright has been involved directly contradict the stereotypes that poor and working-class people cannot make a difference in their communities. In turn, Leondar-Wright believes that the insights of sociology can themselves be a valuable resource in making a difference.

Opening examples copyright © 2011 Betsy Leondar-Wright. www.classmatters .org. Affiliated with Class Action, www.classism.org.

think about it

1. *Do you ever see stereotypes of poor or working-class people on television or in the movies? Explain.*

2. *Have you ever been involved in a group or an organization that included people from different class backgrounds? How do you think class stereotypes influenced the group's dynamics?*

Three Steps to Constructing Social Reality

In their classic work, *The Social Construction of Reality,* Peter Berger and Thomas Luckmann (1966) summarize the process by which people construct reality. As they put it, "Society is a human product. Society is an objective reality. Man is a social product" (p. 61). They label the steps of constructing social reality as externalization, objectivation, and internalization:

1. *Externalization.* People create society through an ongoing process of physical and mental activity. This complex process helps to ensure a stable environment within which we can live. For example, you become friends with another person, spending time together and interacting in ways that create a special relationship.

2. *Objectivation.* Through this process, social arrangements come to seem objectively real; society appears separate from human creation and instead seems "natural," inevitable,

and out of people's control. To continue the example of friendship, your newly formed relationship becomes part of your reality. You call each other "friend" and others recognize your relationship as real.

3. *Internalization.* This is the complex process through which we learn our society's culture and establish our view of the world. Through this process humans come to be influenced by their own creations; they are social products. For example, your friendship influences you: you comply with specific expectations associated with this relationship (such as helping your friend move into a new apartment).

The same three-step process occurs with larger social structures as with micro-level social interactions. People create various structures and social institutions such as families, schools, and governments. They then treat those socially constructed entities as objectively real. Finally, people are influenced by the society they create. With large social structures, which often take decades to develop and solidify, the influence is often felt by later generations. We didn't create our form of government, but it certainly influences our lives. However, the government—like all social institutions—is continually maintained and reproduced through the actions of participants. Political candidates run for office; citizens vote for their preferred candidates (or choose not to vote); and the winning candidate goes to Washington (or the state capital or city hall) to represent his or her constituents. Social order emerges from human action, and it continues to exist only when humans reproduce it through their participation.

Because people are continually constructing society and are, in turn, affected by it, the social world in which we live is always in flux. Anything that humans create they can also change. Thus our definition and understanding of work, families, schooling, and other aspects of society is open to change and evolution.

Social Statuses and Roles

As we have seen, successful social interaction requires some shared understanding through which to create our social reality. But interaction is also shaped by statuses and roles, which provide some of the glue that connects individuals to one another and to the behavioral patterns that constitute social structure. We touched on these ideas in Chapter 4 and examine them in more detail here.

STATUSES A **status,** as we saw in Chapter 4, is *a position in a social system that can be occupied by an individual.* (In a different context, the word *status* is used to indicate honor or prestige.) A **status set** is *the collection of statuses that an individual holds.* For example, you might be a student, an employee, a

parent, a neighbor, a brother or sister, an immigrant, a band member, and a Christian. Each of these positions is a status, and collectively they are your status set. A **status category** refers to *a status that people can hold in common,* such as nurse, father, or New Englander.

Some statuses apply automatically. **Ascribed statuses** are *those that are assigned to us from birth or that we assume later in life regardless of our wishes or abilities.* Your nationality, your sex, your race or ethnicity, and your status as someone's cousin are among the ascribed statuses you might have had at birth. Other ascribed statuses may be assigned later in life, such as teenager, mentally ill person, or widow. In most cases, we cannot change an ascribed status, since it is determined by others.

Achieved statuses, in contrast, are *those that we voluntarily attain, to a considerable degree, as the result of our own efforts.* A person might be the mayor of a city, a doctor, a professional athlete, a criminal, or a spouse—all examples of achieved statuses. You must work, in some way, to acquire an achieved status.

The line between these two types of status is not always clear-cut. Your family may have influenced some of your achieved statuses, such as your choice of religious affiliation or your decision about whether to attend college. You inherited your class status from your parents as an ascribed status, but that status may change in your adult life. You are assigned a nationality at birth, but you might achieve another nationality by becoming a citizen of a second country.

Some statuses can be achieved only by working through formal structures and meeting certain criteria, whereas other statuses are fairly easy to achieve and are open to most people. Lawyers achieve their status through an arduous process that involves completing college, attending and completing law school, and passing a rigorous bar exam. In contrast, basketball fans can achieve that particular status by regularly watching games on television.

In addition, not all statuses are equally important. In U.S. society, the status of cousin, say, has much less significance for most people than the status of college graduate. For many Americans, a cousin is often a relatively distant relative with whom to exchange holiday cards, whereas being a college graduate can be a requirement for a desirable job. In some cultures, though, kinship—even within an extended family—may be an essential status. Extended family ties are typically very strong in Native American communities, for example. In these families, relatives such as cousins often interact on a regular basis and have a sense of mutual obligation to provide economic and social support (Cheshire 2006).

Because statuses are social positions, they exist within hierarchies; as a result, some statuses provide more or less so-

Achieved status

thinking about structure

Humans create, sustain, and change social **structure**. How do your everyday action and interaction help to maintain or change the structure of your community? Of your college?

cial prestige than others. A **status hierarchy** is *a ranking of social positions according to their perceived prestige or honor.* You can probably recognize the status hierarchy within your college: the president and senior administrators hold the positions with the highest prestige, whereas custodial, food service, and clerical workers—all essential for the smooth operation of the school—occupy less prestigious positions. Status is linked to social inequality, because different positions often receive different levels of prestige, power, and, in this case, income. At many college campuses, custodial workers begin their workday before sunrise, receive low pay, and are invisible to many students and faculty. In contrast, college presidents are highly paid and likely to have a formidable presence on campus, with the power to make decisions about college operations.

Many people, regardless of their place in a status hierarchy, have one status that overrides all others. A **master status** is *a social position that is overwhelmingly significant, powerfully influences a person's social experience, and typically overshadows all the other social positions that person may occupy.* Sociologists coined this term to describe the significance of race in the United States in the first half of the twentieth century (Hughes 1945). In the segregated South at that time, race was a master status: it overpowered the importance of other statuses such as education level, religious affiliation, class, gender, and occupation. For example, in the pre–civil rights era, and to a lesser degree today, highly educated African American men were identified primarily by their race, despite their status as skilled professionals or community leaders. For white shopkeepers, police officers, and other people in largely segregated cities, a person's status as a black man was so prominent that it made his other statuses nearly invisible. Even today, as we explore in Chapters 10 and 11, race and gender are among the most visible and most important statuses in U.S. society.

ROLES Whereas statuses are positions in a social system, **roles** are *the sets of expected behaviors that are associated with particular statuses.* As a student, you are expected to go to class, turn in assignments on time, and take part in college activities; at the same time, you have the right to choose your own major and courses and to fair treatment from professors, among others. Those general expectations regarding behavior, duties, and rights that are associated with that role were defined by our

culture before you became a student. You can be somewhat creative in how you carry out a role, but the general rules are well established.

Similarly, the general expectations associated with the parent role in our society are fairly clear. Parents raise their children, are responsible for providing for their basic physical needs, and are expected to give social and emotional support— at least until children leave home as adults. Some parents are unable to fulfill the parent role and are negligent, risking a loss of custody. But there is no single way to fulfill this role effectively, and parents accomplish it in a variety of ways. Some are strict, whereas others emphasize open discussion rather than discipline. Still others try to be friends with their children (and their children's friends) and are a constant presence in their lives. And some parents are so "hands-off" that their children rarely see them.

The roles associated with many statuses are even less formal than that of student or parent. Yet the sets of expectations that come with the role of friend or good neighbor, for example, are still widely recognized. Other roles, such as the one taken on by a person who is ill, are generally understood, as well. In a classic essay, Talcott Parsons (1951) argued that physical illness (the "sick role") has a social side that involves four particular expectations. First, being sick exempts an individual from other role expectations, especially if a doctor has certified the illness. Second, people with an illness are often not held responsible for taking care of themselves; a spouse, parent, or health

SPOTLIGHT on social theory

Talcott Parsons was the leading proponent of the **functionalist perspective,** which stresses how the various elements of society work together. How might playing the sick role, in the way Parsons described, help to reinforce social stability?

➔ Talcott Parsons revealed the widely recognized expectations associated with the "sick role." Like the sick role, other informal roles also involve sets of unstated expectations. Consider, for example, what we might call the "winner role." What expectations exist for this role?

Culture and Social Interaction

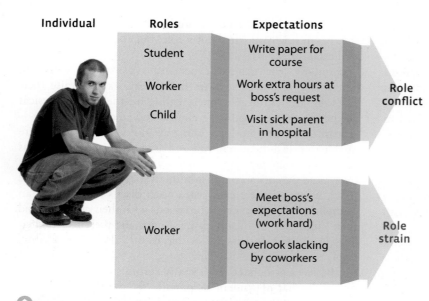

Individual	Roles	Expectations	
	Student	Write paper for course	
	Worker	Work extra hours at boss's request	Role conflict
	Child	Visit sick parent in hospital	
	Worker	Meet boss's expectations (work hard)	Role strain
		Overlook slacking by coworkers	

FIGURE 7.2 | ROLE CONFLICT AND ROLE STRAIN

Because individuals hold many statuses and related roles simultaneously, they often have trouble meeting social expectations successfully. Role conflict occurs when two different roles have incompatible expectations. Role strain occurs when a single role has competing expectations. Have you experienced either role conflict or role strain?

care professional is likely to provide the necessary attention. Third, because illness is socially undesirable, we expect that sick people will want to get better. Fourth, sick people are also expected to make an effort to recover, especially by seeking competent professional help. Sick people who fail to fulfill their role thwart the expectations of others around them. If, for example, you refused to see a doctor after breaking your arm, your parents and friends would probably become increasingly frustrated with you and might even attempt to force you to seek medical help.

We are all constantly juggling the many roles associated with the various statuses we occupy. **Role conflict** occurs *when the expectations associated with different roles clash.* For example, your boss asks you to work extra hours at the café during a particularly busy period, but at the same time, you need to finish a major project for one of your courses. Because there are only so many hours in the day, you must make a choice, and one of your roles—student or worker—is likely to suffer. Parents who must juggle the care of children with the demands of their work are especially prone to such role conflicts. **Role strain,** in contrast, occurs *when the expectations associated with a single role compete with each other.* Teachers experience role strain from the dual responsibility they have both to help and support their students and to evaluate the same students, sometimes with a failing grade (see Figure 7.2).

Roles are crucial in the construction of our everyday lives because they link us to other people. Roles link parents and children, teachers and students, employers and workers, friends, and a host of other statuses. These interconnecting

roles form a network of social relationships that are the basis of social structure.

Dramaturgy: Playing at Social Life

If the idea of people playing roles reminds you of actors performing in a film or play, you are not the first to see this analogy. As William Shakespeare wrote over 400 years ago in his play *As You Like It,* "All the world's a stage, and all the men and women merely players." Today many of us are familiar with role-playing games, such as Dungeons & Dragons, in which each player takes on the key features of a character. Sociologists use this idea as well. **Dramaturgy,** *an approach to the study of social interaction that uses the metaphor of social life as a theater,* is most closely associated with Canadian-born sociologist Erving Goffman. In his well-known work *The Presentation of Self in Everyday Life,* Goffman (1959) drew on some of the elements that make up a theatrical performance to illuminate the nature of social interaction.

ROLE EXPECTATIONS In a play, the playwright largely determines the actor's role. In real life, cultural expectations establish the content of a social role. For example, imagine a lawyer walking into a courtroom dressed in basketball shorts and a t-shirt and greeting the judge by saying, "Hey, buddy." He pulls his papers out of a knapsack and, as the case proceeds, giggles out loud at the opposing attorney's questions and the witnesses' testimony. Such behavior would be absurd, of course, precisely because it violates our expectations about a lawyer's proper "costume" (formal business attire), "props" (briefcase), language (a respectful "your honor"), and emotion (serious). We often take for granted such expectations, but their significance becomes obvious when they are violated.

Appropriate costumes, props, language, and emotions are among the resources actors use to achieve a convincing performance. But an actor must still interpret a role, and there is considerable room for creativity. The same is true with social roles. The expectations associated with any role are socially defined, but individuals who occupy a particular status must actively "play" the role. A lawyer might be folksy and warm in his summation to the jury, for example, or he might be outraged and impassioned. Either behavior could be appropriate to the role.

SPOTLIGHT
on social theory

Dramaturgy is an approach that uses the idea of social life as a kind of theater. Consider a particular role that you play in that theater. How comfortable are you in that role? Do you ever feel the need to separate yourself from the role? Why?

IMPRESSION MANAGEMENT Role playing occurs in the presence of an audience. Actors try to convince the audience that they are "real," that their interpretation of a char-

Focusing on Emotions and the Employee Role

"Thank you for choosing our airline!" "Can I help you find something?" "Would you like to hear our specials for today?" "How may I direct your call?" "I hope your stay with us was a pleasant one!" Health care workers, salespeople, flight attendants, wait staff, customer service representatives, and workers in many other fields are often required to project an emotion to their customers or clients. Usually these jobs require workers to be exceptionally nice; that is, friendly and helpful. They are expected to greet people with a big smile and cheerful small talk, so that the customer or client will feel welcome and relaxed. Bill collectors, on the other hand, need to make people who are delinquent in paying their bills feel uncomfortable; therefore, they are often nastier than natural. Either way, these employees need to express a particular emotion in order to play their role successfully.

Sociologist Arlie Hochschild (1983) developed the idea that certain interactions require us to project an emotion we may not feel—to be nicer or nastier than natural. Viewing these interactions through a sociological lens, she called the effort involved *emotion work,* which, in a classic article (Hochschild 1979), she defined as "the act of trying to change in degree or quality an emotion or feeling" (p. 561). We often engage in emotion work, according to Hochschild, because of *emotion rules,* the "social guidelines that direct how we want to try to feel" (p. 563). When people tell you that you "shouldn't feel guilty," or that you "have the right" to feel angry, they are alerting you to these commonly accepted rules. When emotion rules are applied to a workplace, they amount to what Hochschild has called the "commercialization of human feeling."

As Hochschild's (1983) research shows, however, emotion work can be stressful in a variety of ways. Employees who identify strongly with their jobs, such as social workers, teachers, or nurses, may pour their emotional energy into their work only

Jet Blue flight attendant Steven Slater, tired of smiling and acting friendly to rude passengers, quit his job with a dramatic flourish in 2010 by leaving the plane he was working on through the emergency exit and slide after the plane had landed—becoming a media sensation in the process.

to experience burnout after a few years. Employees who maintain some distance from their employee role may become exhausted by the constant need to express cheerfulness or enthusiasm, even in the face of rudeness or hostility from customers. Employees who succeed in acting the part may feel like they are frauds for not genuinely experiencing the emotions they are expected to feel.

Demands to display specific emotions are most common in service jobs, especially in settings that involve frequent contact with customers. Retail sales clerks, waiters, flight attendants, and childcare workers are all required to show deference to customers. These kinds of jobs are often considered to be "women's work" (even though a sizable number of men hold them) and are devalued as a result. The labeling of emotion work as women's work raises important questions about the connection between workers' characteristics—their gender—and what customers expect from service providers.

Hochschild's influential work called attention to the role of emotion in the workplace and elsewhere. She identified the complex and sometimes negative dynamics involved in emotional labor and spawned two decades of research on the subject (see Wharton 2009). This research now extends well beyond sociology to fields such as management (Anderson, Provis, and Chappel 2003), criminal justice (Tewksbury and Higgins 2006), and applied psychology (Rupp and Spencer 2006).

think about it

1. *Do any of the jobs that you have held involve emotional labor? What was expected of you? Were you comfortable with these expectations?*

2. *Did your emotional labor involve any stress? How did you manage that stress?*

---

acter is authentic. As social actors, we too engage in *impression management:* we try to control the image others have of us through our performance. Sometimes people fully embrace a role and see its performance as an integral part of themselves.

An aspiring concert pianist might enthusiastically immerse herself in her role, wearing a certain type of clothing and hair style and using body language that communicates to her audience that she is already a professional musician. In other situations, though, people attempt to maintain "role distance" by separating themselves from a role as they carry it out. These people want their audience to see the difference between the role they are playing and their "real" selves. A manager who is self-conscious about enforcing discipline, for example, may say, "Look, I hate to do this 'boss' stuff but . . . ."

THE FRONT STAGE AND THE BACK STAGE All actors are familiar with the distinction between the front stage, which the audience can see, and the back stage, which is hidden from view. Actors perform their roles on the front stage, but on the back stage they become themselves again. Social actors also behave differently depending on where they are. The waiter smiling pleasantly at customers may complain bitterly about poor tips among coworkers in the kitchen. The student feigning interest when discussing a course with a professor may later grumble to friends about how boring the class is.

Social Networks

Social networks are *the collections of social ties that connect people to each other.* For many people today, the term conjures up images of Facebook, Twitter, and other Internet sites devoted to connecting people to each other. However, people have always formed social networks, and sociologists have been studying them since long before the rise of the Internet. Strong social ties and networks have traditionally been based on face-to-face interaction, but the Internet offers some distinct advantages for forming and maintaining them.

Online social networking sites rely on new technologies to connect people, opening new opportunities for staying in touch and making it possible to interact with a sizable number of other users. For many, they provide an opportunity to find people with whom they share an interest—in graphic novels, independent films, beach volleyball, or sociology—but whom they are not likely to meet in person. Social networking and other online resources permit people to maintain connections regardless of geographic distance. E-mail helps people maintain contact because it is asynchronous—that is, it doesn't require them to be online at the same time to communicate (Licoppe and Smoreda 2005). E-mail and other technologies also help groups stay in touch, permitting people to broadcast messages to several members of their family, for example, or to an entire network of friends at the same time.

THE NATURE OF NETWORKS Who would be willing to lend you a little money in an emergency? Whom would you ask to be a personal reference on a job application? Whom would you invite to your graduation party? These people are part of your social network. Social connections, such

Pilots highlighted in yellow

- ■ Flight AA #11 – Crashed into WTC North
- ■ Flight AA #77 – Crashed into Pentagon
- ■ Flight UA #93 – Crashed in Pennsylvania
- ■ Flight UA #175 – Crashed into WTC South
- ■ Others

FIGURE 7.3 | VISUALIZING SOCIAL NETWORKS

"Small world" social networks that consist of a small number of people (for example, a family, a workplace, a terrorist network, a board of directors) can be mapped out in a simple diagram like this one, which shows the social network connecting the 9/11 hijackers, who are represented by the color-coded nodes indicating the flight they were on. The dark gray nodes are other people who had direct, or indirect, contact with the hijackers, and the gray lines show reported connections. *Source:* Krebs (2008).

as your friends, can influence who you are and might help you in various situations. Other connections can serve as a link between you and contacts and opportunities in other parts of society. Understanding the patterns of association in social networks helps us understand how people are integrated into society.

The study of social networks tells us a great deal about patterns of social interaction (Scott 2000; Wasserman, Faust, and Iacobucci 1994). Sociologists analyze networks for a number of purposes: to study the social dynamics of a neighborhood, to better understand communication in a workplace, to analyze how HIV/AIDS is spread, or to better understand online social connections. (The social network diagram in Figure 7.3 illustrates the connections among the 9/11 hijackers.) Software programs can help researchers conduct complex network analyses by mapping the linkages among the members of a network. In fact, because of advances in software, computing capacity, and large-scale electronic datasets, sociologists can perform extremely complex network analyses (Watts 2004).

Networks come in many different sizes, and they vary by the strength of their links, by the characteristics of the people involved, by the physical distance between their members, and by the kind of interaction within them, among other characteristics. Network diagrams such as the one shown in Figure 7.3 illustrate the connections among members and their pattern of interaction. As such, they help to reveal the hidden ties (indirect connections) that link people to each other and that illuminate some of the structure of social life.

Social network analysis reveals that our networks are more likely to include people who are like us. According to the principle of **homophily,** *social contact occurs at a higher rate between people who are similar than it does between people who are different* (McPherson et al. 2001). Race, age, religion, and class (including education and occupation) are important characteristics that connect or separate people. As a result, most social networks are much more homogeneous than the population as a whole. Homophily influences what we know about our society, since we are apt to share and reinforce our worldview with others who are like us (Smith-Lovin and McPherson 1993).

For example, friendship networks in the United States are typically characterized by racial homophily (Mouw and Entwisle 2006; Quillian and Campbell 2003). However, students on college campuses may cultivate more robust multiracial and multiethnic friendship networks. Given the degree to which schools and neighborhoods are segregated by race in the United States, college may be the first opportunity many students have for regular interaction with people of various races. White, non-Hispanic college students who have a black, a Latino, or an Asian roommate are more comfortable interacting in racially diverse settings and are more likely to have interracial friendships than are white students who have white roommates. And although white, non-Hispanic college students have far fewer interracial friendships than do black, Latino, or Asian students during their high school years, their proportion of friends of different races increases during the first year of college (Boisjoly et al. 2006; Stearns, Buchmann, and Bonneau 2009).

THE STRENGTH OF NETWORK TIES Some of our networks are made up of close friends or family or others with whom we have strong ties and intimate relationships. Typically, we want to spend time with these people, and the feeling is usually mutual. The stronger our ties are with people, the more likely they are to provide a broad range of support. Most of our social support comes from a relatively small

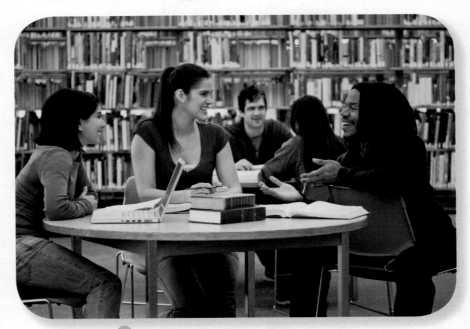

Many students inhabit a more racially diverse friendship network during their college years than they experienced in high school, and this tendency can have a significant influence on the diversity of their subsequent networks as adults.

number of such strong ties (Wellman and Wortley 1990). These close ties can be critical during times of crisis (Hurlbert, Haines, and Beggs 2000). For example, as Hurricane Katrina approached New Orleans in August 2005, residents with strong social networks outside of New Orleans were the first to leave the city, relying on family and close friends for food, shelter, and other assistance. In contrast, people without strong ties to such networks had a more difficult time leaving the city and were typically among the last to evacuate. In the absence of social networks to help with basic necessities such as clothing, food, housing, and transportation, these residents were far more dependent on federal, state, and local government for assistance than were those with strong ties outside the city (Fussell 2006).

Other networks consist of people who have relatively weak ties with one another: coworkers, neighbors, and casual acquaintances. Though they are made up of weak ties, these networks can be helpful, too. In a classic phrase, Granovetter (1973, 1974) argued for "the strength of weak ties." In his review of existing research and in his own study of men in management and the professions, he found that many men were able to obtain better jobs by using their "weak ties" to connect to new opportunities. Members of these networks can often tap into larger social circles than might otherwise be available to them, gaining access to a wider range of social contacts, information, and other resources. Alumni who help college students from their alma mater obtain internships or jobs upon graduation are a good example of this type of interpersonal network in action. Such contacts are often stratified by class;

Culture and Social Interaction

In the Internet era, social networks are changing. Until recently, our primary social networks were rooted in a specific place and were based largely on face-to-face interaction. However, online social interaction means that geographic distance is becoming far less significant; people who regularly interact online are building strong friendship networks with people who may live across the country or on the other side of the globe, and whom they may never meet face-to-face.

students from more prestigious schools enjoy the privilege of alumni contacts who wield considerably more power and influence than do alumni from less prestigious colleges. On the other hand, those with less power in society—including many women, members of racial and ethnic minority groups, and people from impoverished backgrounds—are at a disadvantage because they are largely excluded from powerful social networks.

Formalizing Structure: Groups and Organizations

As we have seen, our social ties are formed through our common culture, our shared interpretation of reality, the statuses and the roles that we assume as we interact with one another, and the social networks in which we participate. Social life involves more than interactions between individuals, however. Throughout society, people interact in patterns that form the basis of small groups, such as families and friendship networks, and larger organizations, such as workplaces and schools. As groups and, especially, organizations are created, social structure becomes more formal, but these structures still involve interactions between individuals.

Groups and organizations are defined by the patterns of participation among their members, and individual membership in groups is maintained through ongoing participation. The relative strength of your connection to your friendship group, whether you interact in person or online, results from the frequency and intensity of your contact with them. If you rarely communicate with your friends, your bond to the group will become weaker. If too many members lose contact, the group itself ceases to exist.

Similarly, for a formal organization to exist, its members must maintain a certain level of interaction, which varies depending on the type and size of the organization. Because schools and workplaces typically require attendance, members of these organizations are more or less forced to interact. Because we spend so many hours of each day in school, at work, or otherwise involved in organized activities, groups and organizations often provide the context for social interaction, and the way they are structured can dramatically affect how that interaction plays out.

Primary and Secondary Social Groups

Social groups are *collections of people who interact regularly with one another and who are aware of their status as a group.* A *crowd* that happens to be in the same place at the same time, such as passengers waiting to board an airplane, is not a group in the sociological sense since the people are gathered for a one-time event and they do not think of themselves as part of some collective entity. Similarly a *category* of people—such as apartment dwellers or people with blue eyes—also are not social groups in the sociological sense. Groups can be informal and can be created, changed, or dissolved with relatively little fanfare. Nevertheless, unlike a crowd or category of people, members of a group often share common interests, values, norms, and expectations.

Sociologists often classify groups according to the nature and intensity of their interaction. **Primary groups** are *made up of people who have regular contact, enduring relationships, and a significant emotional attachment to each other.* A family is one example of a primary group; a collection of close friends who regularly hang out together is another. In both cases group members interact regularly, often spending a great deal of time together, and their connection to the primary group endures over time. Primary group members share a sense of both caring and obligation, even if the relationships among them are not equal (for example, parent and child). Primary groups are especially influential agents of socialization and can have a major impact on a person's life, shaping values and priorities. They often provide important social support.

Secondary groups are *made up of people who interact in a relatively impersonal way, usually to carry out some specific task.* Coworkers at your job or members of a neighborhood watch group are examples of secondary groups. Typically, these groups represent shorter-term or temporary associations, without a significant emotional bond between members. Over time, you will probably join and leave many different secondary groups, and the group will usually emphasize a common task or goal—fighting neighborhood crime, for example—over connections among group members. As a result, secondary groups are not nearly as influential in our lives as primary groups.

It is not always easy to distinguish between primary and secondary groups. Is a high school soccer team, whose members train together year-round and see one another more often than their families during the soccer season, a primary group? Sometimes a primary group can form within a larger secondary group, as when a small group of coworkers develops close relationships. The best way to distinguish between primary and secondary groups is to think about the basis and depth of members' attachment to the group, the sense of mutual obligation, and the amount of influence the group has on members' lives.

Reference Groups

We saw in Chapter 6 that we derive our sense of self in part from taking into account how others likely see and judge us—the "looking glass self." **Reference groups** are *the groups against which we choose to measure ourselves.* A reference group can be a family, a circle of friends, an occupational group, or a community of worship—just about any primary or secondary group.

Reference groups matter because they can influence the choices we make. They are the social groups we take into account as we plan and assess our actions. For example, as you were deciding whether to attend college, you may have considered the following questions: "What will my friends think? Will my family be disappointed if I don't go to college? Will future employers look at my application more positively if I have a degree?" If the answers were contradictory, you needed to decide which reference group was most important to you.

Reference groups can influence our choices even if we do not yet belong to them. Graduate and professional schools, for example, socialize students about the expectations of their chosen profession. Students who have doctors or businesspeople as their reference group will often adopt new habits, ways of thinking, language, behavior, and dress to conform to that group's likely expectations.

Group Size and Social Relationships: Dyads, Triads, and Beyond

According to sociologist Georg Simmel (1964), the size of a group has important effects on internal group dynamics. Consider the characteristics of a *dyad,* a group consisting of just two people (Figure 7.4). Because a dyad can continue to exist only if both participants are committed to it, it is very unstable. Dyads are also the most intense type of social relationships

Two people (dyad) = one relationship

Three people (triad) = three relationships

Four people = six relationships

Five people = ten relationships

Six people = fifteen relationships

FIGURE 7.4 | GROUP SIZE AND SOCIAL RELATIONSHIPS
The size of a group affects the social relationships within it. In small groups, members are likely to interact directly with one another and to see themselves as integral members of the group. As groups become larger, there are many more potential relationships, and the connections between group members tend to be less intense. Think of both a small and a large group to which you belong. Do they fit this general pattern?

because interaction in a dyad is always between two people. Committed sexual relationships and marriages are classic examples of dyads, but best friends or business partners can also exhibit these characteristics.

Group dynamics fundamentally change when a third person is added, creating a *triad*. In a triad, members' attention is divided, since the number of possible interactions increases. As a couple adjusts to a first child or a new friend joins a previously existing dyad, difficulties typically emerge. One parent may feel jealous of the bond between the other parent and a new infant, for example. Two members of the triad may form an alliance in opposition to the third person, sparking tension. When a pair of friends becomes a triad, conflict may arise as two members outvote the third when deciding what to do or where to eat.

Industrial production required the coordination of huge factories, often employing thousands of workers. In this postcard image, taken around 1916, tens of thousands of workers gather in front of a Ford Motor factory in Detroit, Michigan.

Group size also influences social interaction within larger groups. Groups generally become more stable as they get larger because the group can withstand the loss of individual members. However, relationships also become less intense as a group gets larger. Because there is less focus and attention on any one person, members of a larger group typically feel less emotional commitment to one another. Therefore, small groups tend to be intense but unstable, whereas larger groups tend to be more stable but less intense.

Large and small groups also differ in the nature of the social interaction among members. To take a familiar example, the size of a class influences the social interaction within the classroom: how the instructor interacts with each student and with the group as a whole, how students interact with each other, and what kinds of in-class activities work best. You can be anonymous and passive in a lecture hall with 200 students. In a seminar with six students, however, you must participate actively in the discussion.

Organizations and Bureaucracy

More complex and more formal than most groups, **organizations** are *secondary groups that have a degree of formal structure and are formed to accomplish particular tasks*. This broad definition applies to organizations as diverse as your local chess club, the National Rifle Association, Microsoft Corporation, and the United Nations. Although these examples obviously vary enormously in scale, configuration, and purpose, we can learn a great deal about how they operate, and how people behave within them, by studying the structure and culture of organizations, as well as the environments in which they operate.

ORGANIZATIONAL STRUCTURE As with any group, the size of an organization can have a major influence on its structure and operation. Very small organizations can operate with few formal rules, straddling the line between an informal group and a formal organization. But as Elizabeth Long (2003) discovered, even small local women's book clubs come in a variety of forms and with distinct sets of rules. The book clubs Long studied varied in the rules they used to select books, whether they allowed men to join, and how their meetings were run.

Even the smallest organizations require a process for making basic decisions. A small organization such as a neighborhood association may use consensus to reach decisions: all members' views are solicited and every effort is made to reach a general agreement. Such an organization may not need any formal leaders, such as a president or treasurer, but may instead use rotating coordinators to ensure that business gets done.

As organizations grow, however, an informal structure usually proves to be inadequate. A larger organization typically develops a more formal decision-making process and a more elaborate division of labor. As we saw in Chapter 1, Max Weber noted that a shift from traditional to rational action (the *rationalization of society*) was a characteristic of the rise of industrialized society in the nineteenth century. Early industrialists needed to manage ever-larger organizations. Businesses needed to operate factories that employed hundreds or even thousands of workers, producing goods in large quantities that were distributed through a complex transportation network. Paying workers, purchasing raw materials, and shipping goods from the factory—all required the development of complex systems. As new structures and ways of accomplishing tasks became necessary, bureaucracy developed into the dominant organizational structure of the industrial age.

BUREAUCRACY A **bureaucracy** is *a hierarchical administrative system with formal rules and procedures used to manage organizations.* Bureaucracies commonly share key features (Weber 1946):

1. ***A division of labor.*** Because of their size, bureaucracies need specialization; not everyone can do everything. In bureaucracies, people are responsible for narrowly defined tasks.

2. ***A hierarchy of authority and accountability.*** Bureaucracies have a pyramidal structure (see Figure 7.5). With power concentrated at the top of the hierarchy and many bureaucrats at the bottom dividing what little influence they have, authority is highly fragmented, and managers' primary job is to enforce rules and monitor other workers.

3. ***Impersonality.*** Power is located within an office, not in the person who happens to hold that position. People are hired, promoted, fired, or retired, but the bureaucratic structure remains.

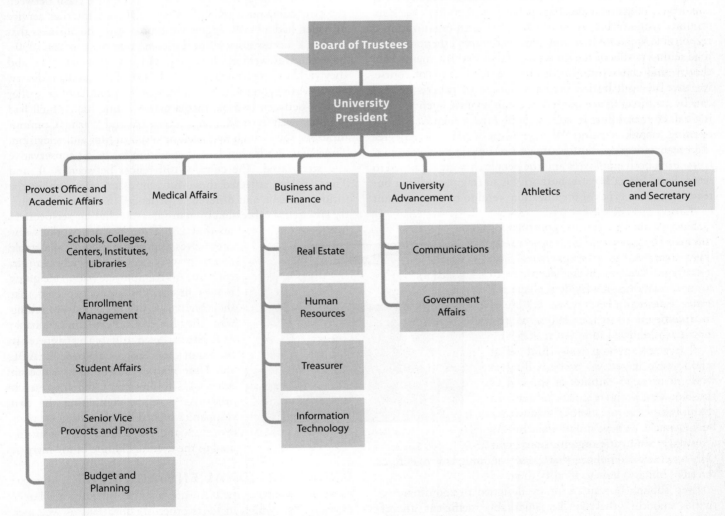

FIGURE 7.5 | FORMAL BUREAUCRATIC STRUCTURE

Like all large organizations, the University of Miami has a formal bureaucratic structure, summarized in this chart. Occupying the positions within its bureaucracy (represented by boxes) are particular individuals who can leave the organization without affecting its structure. Positions in such structures usually carry different amounts of power and prestige and command unequal amounts of resources, with those toward the top having more of all three than those toward the bottom. *Source:* University of Miami website.

CORE CONCEPTS CHALLENGE

Locate a copy of your school's organizational **structure,** *which may be available on its web site. How does your school's structure compare with this one?*

4. Written rules and records. The tasks and duties to be carried out within a bureaucracy are usually written out in formal rules and procedures. Written forms for communicating information and for record-keeping help to ensure consistency.

These four features allow bureaucracies to coordinate the diverse activities of many people. Without them, organizations, especially large ones—from the national government to your favorite retail outlet—would stop functioning. Your college, for example, undoubtedly has a bureaucracy to schedule classes, coordinate student records, manage housing, pay employees, and keep buildings clean and accessible.

As you have probably experienced, however, bureaucracies can have a negative side. If you have ever gotten the "run-around" while trying to figure out who in an organization is responsible for a problem, you have encountered the sometimes maddening results of the division of labor and fragmented authority that characterize most bureaucracies. And, of course, we have all been buried in the avalanche of paperwork that can be required to accomplish a common task such as visiting a doctor, enrolling in college, applying for financial aid, or opening a bank account. All organizations have some degree of bureaucratization, but too much can be counterproductive, frustrating both employees and the people they are supposed to serve. In addition, because authority is so fragmented in a bureaucracy, these types of organizations tend to be very resistant to change.

Since bureaucracies are governed by rules and regulations that apply to everyone, they can be very impersonal, and it can be difficult to make exceptions to accommodate an individual's specific needs. For example, if the workday at your company begins at 9:00 a.m., you may not be allowed to arrive at 9:15 a.m. so that you can drop your child off at school, even if you would be willing to work an extra 15 minutes at the end of the day. Rules and regulations tend to multiply and become more refined within bureaucracies as new situations arise. As a result, bureaucratic organizations typically have detailed policies that specify not only how to enforce the rules but also how to modify them.

Even though bureaucracies are designed to coordinate activities smoothly, they can be remarkably inefficient, and efforts to maximize efficiency often seem to have the opposite effect. For example, customer service phone lines are designed to manage large volumes of calls. Yet customers complain so frequently about not being able to talk to a live human being that a web site has been created that provides frustrated customers of hundreds of companies with guidance on how to get to a live person more immediately (www.gethuman.com).

Although large organizations rely on bureaucratic measures to run smoothly, as the layers of bureaucracy multiply, they often make organizations increasingly unwieldy. Sociolo-

gists seek to understand this complexity, recognizing both the mechanisms designed to coordinate large organizations and the dynamics that can make bureaucracies feel like an exasperating maze. Two factors they look at are an organization's culture and its operating environment.

ORGANIZATIONAL CULTURE Organizations can have distinct cultures that influence how they are organized, the values they espouse, and the way they operate. (For an example of a sociologist who works with different organizational cultures, see the Sociology Works box.) Even organizations involved in very similar activities can have different cultures. For example, the merger between America Online (AOL) and Time Warner in 2000 revealed an enormous culture clash between the two companies (Klein 2003). AOL, an Internet service provider, had a brash, aggressive approach to the business that made it a success story in the dot-com boom years of the 1990s. Its executives were often young, with an informal style, and they viewed their company as the future of the media industry. Time Warner, on the other hand, was the product of an earlier merger between two old-media giants: Time Inc., which had been involved in traditional print media, and Warner Communications Inc., which had been involved in film and television. Time Warner's leaders had a reputation for being conservative and strait-laced. The cultural differences between AOL and Time Warner reflected these different assumptions about the future of media and different experiences in the media industry and found expression in many areas, including perspectives on time. At Time Warner, workers saw themselves as potential "lifers" at a stable company with a good retirement plan. In contrast, AOL employees had made quick money in the 1990s and expected that their big payoff would come from selling what they hoped would become valuable AOL stock. Such differences were only the tip of the iceberg; employees at AOL and Time Warner didn't understand each other and, in some cases, didn't like each other. As a result, combining the two companies proved far more difficult than expected, and the culture clash contributed to the eventual failure of the merger.

ORGANIZATIONAL ENVIRONMENT All organizations, whatever their culture may be, operate in a larger environment, which includes other organizations as well as a variety of conditions that are part of the broader context of a society (Hall and Tolbert 2004). Collectively, *factors that exist outside of the organization but that potentially affect its operation* constitute the **organizational environment.** The strength of the economy, the stability of political rule, demographic factors, other organizations, the legal context, technology, and the cultural environment can all influence the way organizations operate.

Much like individuals, organizations link to other organizations in a network structure in the course of their normal

Mindy Fried and Organizational Change

For Mindy Fried, a sociological perspective is far more than an academic approach. For more than two decades, sociology has informed her work as a family policy analyst in state government, a lobbyist for early childhood services, and most recently as an organizational change consultant.

Fried grew up in a family that loved to observe and analyze people—their relationships, histories, choices, opportunities, and successes and failures—and was drawn to sociology because it connected her longstanding interest in people to what she calls the "big picture." In sociology, Fried "discovered kindred spirits who asked the same kinds of questions that I had about people and their worlds—questions about how people's experiences are framed by their race, gender, age, and ethnicity, questions about how social structures in our society provide answers to how people behave, the opportunities they have, the barriers they encounter."

Describing herself as an "applied sociologist," Fried works as a consultant specializing in organizational change, drawing upon her sociological perspective to help organizations navigate changing contexts. She works with organizations to solve problems, negotiate conflicts, and respond to new challenges and opportunities, using her sociological understanding of interaction and organizational culture (Fried 2008).

Fried works primarily with nonprofit organizations. Through careful observation, she arrives at a sociological understanding of her clients' issues so that she can help them understand and improve their organizations. In a recent project, Fried and her colleagues at Arbor Consulting Partners worked with a university-community partnership focused on improving the health of local residents in a low-income neighborhood. Communication problems—the result of two very different organizational cultures—were hampering the partnership. When Fried came on board, she recognized that improving communication required helping the two groups better understand their differences. Fried conducted interviews, held focus groups with members of both groups, and used participant observation—research methods that allowed her to help "key players develop a deeper understanding of how power, diversity, and agency affected their organizational dynamic." This shared understanding helped to produce more effective communication and a stronger working relationship between the two groups.

As an organizational change consultant, Fried takes the distinctly sociological approach of an "outsider within," someone who is not emotionally involved with the organization, but who makes a commitment to observe, listen, and learn about the various experiences of those who are. Fried explains: "Our status as outsiders within ultimately allows us to interpret multiple perspectives, untangle conflict, and think creatively about how to maximize positive outcomes for an organization."

Mindy Fried

> "Our status as outsiders within ultimately allows us to interpret multiple perspectives, untangle conflict, and think creatively about how to maximize positive outcomes for an organization."

Reflecting on her sociological approach, Fried has no hesitation in describing the value of a sociological perspective. Sociology gives her both a rich understanding of organizational dynamics and the research skills to help her clients build on their strengths and respond to new challenges. But this is only part of the picture. Fried urges students of sociology to "prepare to be challenged because a sociological perspective gives you tools to understand how people's experiences are influenced by social and economic systems that affect our lives as women and men of a certain age or social class or racial/ethnic background. . . . For me, having a sociological perspective on the world is like taking an intellectual once-a-day vitamin pill."

think about it

1. *How might an organizational consultant assist one of the organizations (school, community group, extracurricular club) in which you participate?*

2. *How do you think the perspective of an "outsider within" differs from that of either an insider or an outsider?*

---

operations. Your school, for example, interacts with a variety of other organizations. Government agencies and private corporations provide research grants, businesses sell goods and services on campus, and graduate schools and potential employers receive student transcripts.

The organizational environment also includes the legal context within which organizations operate (Edelman and Suchman 1997). Laws define the nature of some organizations, such as corporations and nonprofit groups. Laws and law enforcement also provide a stable environment within which organizations can operate. Courts enforce contracts and settle disputes. Legal regulations may also restrict organizational behavior. For example, environmental laws limit pollution and antitrust laws prohibit some businesses from growing beyond a certain point.

Technology is another element of the organizational environment. Computers and the Internet have dramatically changed how large organizations function, enabling them to accumulate more data, communicate faster across long distances, and distribute information broadly both internally and externally.

The broader cultural environment also influences how organizations operate. Social norms and role expectations vary across cultures. For example, Chinese managers place a premium on relationships and loyalty, protecting the honor of all members in an organization, and solving problems privately to avoid embarrassing their workers. In addition, Chinese organizations typically feature highly centralized authority, with limited participation in decision making (Nyberg and Jensen 2009). Practicing respect in an organization in the United States might mean treating all organization members equally, whereas in China respect may mean deferring to authority within the organization. Organizations that cross cultural boundaries must accommodate to these differing cultural environments, and they must often adapt to the way power is distributed within an organization.

Power in Groups and Organizations

As we have seen, people in groups and organizations have different amounts of power, and this difference both reflects and reinforces inequality. In addition, groups can exert considerable influence over the actions of individual members, gaining obedience or compliance through various means.

In-Groups and Out-Groups

One way that groups exert control is by including or excluding members through the existence of in- and out-groups. An **in-group** is *a social group with which a person identifies and toward which he or she has positive feelings.* Members of an in-group have a collective sense of "us." An **out-group** is *a social group toward which a person has negative feelings, considering its members to be inferiors, or "them."* We feel a sense of loyalty to other members of our in-group, whether they are fellow environmentalists, soccer fans, or Methodists, and this sense of solidarity is essential to the functioning of society. But camaraderie can easily turn into a sense of superiority over those who are not part of the in-group. For example, people with high-status jobs often build social connections in wealthy neighborhoods and exclusive country clubs. Solidarity within this in-group of the wealthy may be accompanied by negative attitudes toward those less well-off ("they" don't work hard; "they" are not as smart or talented), and may lead the wealthy to exclude others from their neighborhoods and social circles. In- and out-

groups cause tension, rivalry, and even overt conflict between social groups, which often struggle for power as in-groups seek to maintain their perceived superiority.

Conformity: The Asch Experiments

Sociologists have long been interested in how groups promote conformity and elicit obedience from members. Social psychologists have done important studies that reveal the formidable, and often underappreciated, power dynamics that operate within groups.

Imagine, for example, that you have signed up to take a vision test as part of an experiment. The experimenter introduces himself and explains to you and seven other participants that your task is simple. You will be shown pairs of cards, one with three vertical lines of different lengths on it and the other with a single vertical line (see Figure 7.6). You are to identify which of the three lines is the same length as the line on the comparison card and state your response out loud.

The experimenter shows the first and second pairs of cards, and each participant in turn gives the choice that is obviously correct. When your turn comes, you add your response. With the third set, though, you're surprised to hear all the respondents choose what is obviously the wrong answer. When it's your turn to respond, you wonder if they can all be so obviously wrong. Do you stick with your initial answer, or do you change it to conform to what everyone else has said?

Just such a dilemma faced subjects in the classic experiments carried out by Solomon Asch (1952, 1955). What study participants didn't know was that the other "subjects" in the group were confederates (people working with the experimenter). After providing correct answers for the first two rounds, confederates provided incorrect answers for twelve of the next eighteen rounds. Would the "majority effect," as Asch called it, lead the test subject to conform to the group and provide an obviously incorrect response?

Asch found that only a quarter of the respondents gave the correct answer all the time. Three-quarters agreed with at least one wrong answer, though only 5 percent agreed with every

FIGURE 7.6 | ASCH EXPERIMENTS

The Asch experiments suggested that group pressure can generate conformity. Experimental subjects were asked which of the three lines on the right was the same length as the comparison line on the left. When group members who had been prompted beforehand by the experimenter gave wrong answers, some subjects agreed with the obviously incorrect response.

incorrect answer. On average, subjects provided an incorrect response about 37 percent of the time. (Subjects in control groups without confederates easily identified the correct answers.) Asch also found that subjects were more likely to give incorrect answers if the confederates were unanimous in their answers and that the size of the group affected the result. Having only one confederate eliminated the "majority effect," and having three or more produced the full effect.

Asch's experiments included only male college students in an artificial setting and involved only a brief, inconsequential activity. Subsequent research, however, has confirmed the findings: the actions of others often promote conformist behavior. For example, eyewitnesses in criminal cases sometimes change their account of what they saw to conform to contrary information about the crime that they receive later (Wright, Self, and Justice 2000). People seek social approval by going along with the group, and conforming is often part of a broader effort to build and maintain social connections (Cialdini and Goldstein 2004).

Some cultures are more conformist than others. People in the United States and other countries with more individualistic cultures are less inclined to conform than are residents of countries whose cultures are more collectively oriented (Bond and Smith 1996). East Asian cultures, such as in Japan and China, typically define nonconformity in negative terms, whereas Western cultures are more likely to see it in a positive light, viewing nonconformists as unique and their contributions as valuable (Kim and Markus 1999).

Social conditions can also be conducive to conformist behavior, especially in situations characterized by widespread anxiety. In particular, fear about personal safety encourages conformity (Renkema, Stapel, and Van Yperen 2008). The 9/11 attacks produced broad public anxiety in the United States. In the immediate post-9/11 period, fear bred political conformity; citizens proclaimed their national allegiance through public displays of patriotic symbols, and public approval for President George W. Bush's leadership rose sharply.

Groups vary considerably in the amount of influence they have over individual behavior. It may be that people in the United States have become more individualistic and more willing to question authority since Asch conducted his studies in the 1950s. Advertisements routinely encourage people to express themselves and stand out from the crowd. In addition, despite often-powerful group influences, individuals still have the capacity to pursue independent action, whether they are operating within an informal group or a more formal organization.

Obedience:
The Milgram Experiments

In 2010, eighty contestants were recruited for the pilot of a new French reality television game show called *Zone Xtreme*. Contestants signed a contract saying they were willing to adminis-

ter electrical shocks as part of the game. Each contestant was then paired with another contestant named Jean-Paul, who would be challenged with a series of questions while strapped in an electrically wired chair, which was placed in an isolation booth. If Jean-Paul answered a question incorrectly, his partner was told to push a lever to administer an electric shock. As Jean-Paul continued to answer incorrectly, the voltage increased from 20 to 460 volts—a potentially life-threatening jolt. At the lower levels, Jean-Paul was plainly startled by the mild jolts. As the shocks increased in severity, his cries of pain escalated, and he eventually pleaded, "Get me out of here, please! I don't want to play anymore!" But the game show host—a well-known French television personality—encouraged the contestants to continue administering the shocks, and the studio audience goaded them on. After a series of painful cries, Jean-Paul eventually became silent and stopped responding to the highest shock levels, presumably because he was unconscious or dead. Of the eighty contestants, sixty-four played the game all the way to the end, administering the highest voltages despite the pain they were clearly causing (Chazan 2010, Keaten 2010).

As you might have guessed, the "game show" was not real; it was staged as part of a documentary called *The Game of Death*. "Jean-Paul" was an actor, but the eighty contestants and the audience believed the situation was real. This demonstration was modeled loosely on experiments conducted in the United States by Stanley Milgram (a former student of Solomon Asch) in the early 1960s. Milgram's experiments took place in a research lab, where scientists in white lab coats encouraged participants to administer apparently painful—and potentially lethal—electrical shocks, supposedly as part of a study on how punishment affects learning (Milgram 1963, 1965, 1969).

As Milgram's experiments—and the French game show—demonstrate, many of us are socialized to obey authority figures and to comply with social expectations, even when we know such actions are wrong. Although some people in Milgram's experiments did refuse to participate, many others set aside their better judgment and followed orders, ceding power to those in authority. Only when they saw others refusing to take part in the experiment did an overwhelming majority say no—compliance plummeted to just 5 percent when participants were teamed with someone who refused to administer the shocks.

Milgram's experiments were conducted, in part, to better understand why people would go along with atrocities such as the Holocaust, the systematic mass killing of Jews and other people by Nazi Germany during World War II. In the lab, participants often felt uncomfortable, apprehensive, and guilty about the pain they were causing, yet many voluntarily submitted to the man in the white lab coat, whose only power was the perception that he was a legitimate authority figure. A psychologist involved in the updated game-show version of the Milgram experiments suggested that they reveal the "terrifying power of TV" (Chazan 2010).

An overhead shot (*left*) shows the "game show" control panel used in *The Game of Death*. Contestants sat in front of the semicircular panel and were told by the celebrity host to push levers that administered increasingly powerful shocks to a contestant-partner seated in an isolation booth (*right*). Much like the Milgram experiments upon which this demonstration was modeled, most participants followed orders and administered what they believed to be painful—and potentially deadly—shocks.

CORE CONCEPTS CHALLENGE

What gave the game show host the **power** *to get contestants to continue administering the shocks, even when they clearly did not want to do so? Can you think of some real-world situations in which similar power dynamics might operate?*

Because of the potential trauma to participants, Milgram's experiments would not be allowed today. Even the French documentary was highly controversial, with some observers suggesting it manipulated people simply to produce dramatic television—even while it cautioned against the power of television.

Groupthink

Conformity can endanger designated targets of persecution; it can also endanger groups of people working together to achieve a goal. **Groupthink** is *a form of uncritical thinking in which people reinforce a consensus rather than ask serious questions or thoroughly analyze the issue at hand.* The studies that established the importance of groupthink originally focused on elite groups that operated in secrecy as they formulated U.S. foreign policy during the middle of the twentieth century (Janis 1972, 1989). Such groups sometimes produced policy disasters, including the failure to anticipate the Japanese attack on Pearl Harbor at the start of World War II, the failed Bay of Pigs invasion of Cuba in 1961, and the failure to appreciate the capabilities of the North Vietnamese forces during the Vietnam War. In all these cases, U.S. officials made false assumptions about the situation at hand that were reinforced in group discussions until they were eventually exposed as untrue.

People who engage in groupthink ignore evidence or ideas that contradict what they and fellow group members believe. The more group members are alike—the more they share key characteristics such as education, social background, and values—the more likely they are to accept common assumptions about the world rather than ask critical questions about these assumptions. The advisors who developed the Bay of Pigs invasion plan, for example, were the same experts President John F. Kennedy enlisted to assess its likely success. Staunchly opposed to Fidel Castro, Cuba's revolutionary leader, these policymakers ignored his widespread popularity among Cubans and suggested that he could be overthrown by a small army of lightly supplied Cuban exiles who, with limited air cover from the United States could invade Cuba and trigger a spontaneous uprising. The ill-prepared exiles failed quickly, and the successful Cuban defense against the U.S.-backed invasion became a rallying point for Castro supporters, reinforcing his hold on power.

Since they define situations similarly, groupthink participants are more likely to agree on a solution to a problem than to entertain other options that contradict their assumptions. Because they are homogeneous and self-reinforcing, such groups also tend to be shut off from dissenting views and the outside world, making them even more dysfunctional.

Groups that are prone to groupthink minimize internal conflict by encouraging all members to be team players. Group members may conform to steer clear of conflict or avoid appearing foolish, or simply because conforming is easier than challenging the group's assumptions. The result of this conformity, however, can be hasty or irrational decisions.

Leadership, Oligarchy, and Power

As we saw in Chapter 5, power shapes how we allocate resources, make rules and decisions, and define reality. In most organizations, especially workplaces, people struggle constantly over power (Edwards 1982). One important characteristic of any organization, therefore, is its power structure.

In formal bureaucracies, people at each level of the organizational structure have power over those below and are subject to the authority of those above. As bureaucratic organizations expanded in the early twentieth century, sociologists raised questions about their potentially undemocratic impact. German sociologist Robert Michels (1876–1936) (a student of Max Weber) coined the term **iron law of oligarchy** to describe what he saw as *the eventual and inevitable consolidation of power at the top of bureaucratic organizations.* (*Oligarchy* is rule by a powerful few.)

Michels argued that bureaucracies place too much power in the hands of those at the top. Inevitably, these select few misuse their power, which they consolidate through their unique access to information and resources. Once firmly entrenched in power, leaders are cut off from meaningful contact with others in the organization or the general public, rendering them unaccountable for their actions. Meanwhile, those lower down the bureaucratic hierarchy are usually powerless to challenge the oligarchic leaders, though they may disapprove of them; as a result, they tend to be passive.

Despite Michels's fatalistic assessment, bureaucratic inequality can be contested through covert political conflict within organizations, including subtle forms of noncooperation and even sabotage (Morrill, Zald, and Rao 2003). For example, employees sometimes "work to rule," completing only the minimum work required by company regulations, as a way of exercising power from below, a strategy that can dramatically undermine an organization. Sometimes subordinates react so slowly that they effectively prevent the implementation of policies they oppose. In recounting the actions of the Bush administration during the Iraq war, journalist Bob Woodward (2006) described how U.S. military officials refused to share information with British military officials in Iraq, even after

SPOTLIGHT on social theory

Michels's analysis reflects the ideas of **conflict theory**. Have you encountered a situation in which power was concentrated at the top of an organization? How did those below deal with this situation?

President Bush signed a directive expressly authorizing such cooperation. U.S. officials created a separate, classified computer network to shield information from the British military, short-circuiting the presidential directive. The inequality that is typical of hierarchical organizations can also lead workers to engage in overt efforts to change the balance of power—for example, by forming a labor union to protect their interests.

Although most traditional bureaucratic organizations do not operate on democratic principles, some bureaucratic organizations allocate positions in the hierarchy through democratic processes. Civic groups, for example, often elect officials. However, power is still likely to be distributed unequally, since election results place power in the hands of a few members—at least until the next election. More radical ways of distributing power within an organization involve consensus building and collective governance, which can dramatically reduce inequality (Schneiberg et al. 2008). Collective communities (sometimes referred to as communes), in which all members have an equal voice and all decisions are made through deliberative collective discussion, are a familiar example of such organizations. Worker-owned businesses are another example.

Scientific Management and Workplace Control

As we have seen, industrialization led to the first large corporations with bureaucratic organizations in the late nineteenth and early twentieth centuries. There was no illusion of democracy in these bureaucratic workplaces. Owners wanted to control the workplace and limit workers' power to demand better wages or working conditions. A number of industries relied on skilled craft workers, however, many of whom were organized into trade unions. Their knowledge was central to successful production, and therefore they wielded considerable influence over the organization of the workplace and the conditions of their labor.

To consolidate power in the workplace, owners needed to transfer knowledge about the production process from these skilled workers to a small group of managers, while reducing complex jobs to simple tasks that could be done by easily replaceable unskilled and lower paid workers. Such top-down planning and control of production had the added benefit of being extremely efficient, increasing profits (Braverman 1974/1998).

The process of deskilling ordinary workers and increasing workplace efficiency through calculated study became known as **scientific management.** Frederick Taylor (1911) was the leading proponent of scientific management, and the approach is often referred to as Taylorism. Managers would carefully observe workers doing their jobs, noting all the individual steps and measuring the time each step took. Analysts would then examine the collected information to find ways of doing the work more quickly and efficiently. By breaking down complex

thinking about **power**

In bureaucratic organizations, **power** is concentrated in the upper ranks of an organization.
In what ways can the "rank and file" members of an organization exert power? What hurdles do they face in doing so?

Early assembly lines, like this one from a nineteenth-century meatpacking plant, broke down work into small tasks—such as splitting the backbone—for each worker to complete over and over. Each pig or cow, for example, would be worked on by as many as 300 different workers, who each had a specific task to perform in transforming the animal carcass into steak or sausage.

and highly skilled work into simple components, managers could assign each element of the task to a different worker, who would need to know only one simple step.

The classic application of Taylorism was the assembly line. Although famous for its use in the auto industry, assembly line work was first used in Chicago's meatpacking industry. Skilled employees once worked on an entire animal carcass, chopping and slicing the meat into the various cuts. With the application of Taylor's principles, the work was broken down into individual steps, each of which was performed by a separate worker, who could be hired at a lower wage and quickly trained for the monotonous and repetitious job.

Scientific management is not limited to the industrial context within which it was first applied. Today's high-tech workplaces often incorporate many of the Taylorist principles developed a century ago. Management control of the work process is almost universal in today's workplaces. Telemarketers at a call center, for example, typically use a prepared script and follow routine procedures when making phone calls. Managers monitor productivity by using software that records keystrokes on workers' computer keyboards and by occasionally listening in on calls—tactics that recall an earlier era of Taylorism.

Scientific management has its limits today, however. Professional jobs tend to be knowledge based, and workers need to use creativity, collaborate, and respond to rapidly changing markets. The result is a two-tier system of employment, reflecting the class system, in which knowledge workers enjoy considerable autonomy and flexibility, along with high pay, while most other workers are monitored closely, performing routine, repetitious tasks and receiving low pay. We examine the nature of work and the workplace more closely in Chapter 13.

In Transition

ORGANIZATIONS IN A CHANGING WORLD

I n 2006, *Time* magazine declared its "person of the year" to be: you (Grossman 2006). The magazine's editors argued that, because of the Internet, the small contributions of millions of people matter in new ways. The second generation of web sites and software, what is now commonly referred to as Web 2.0, has made everyday users—people like you—into producers of online content.

Technology can be used for a variety of purposes. The same Internet that can mobilize people to donate money to help victims of a disaster can allow an angry fanatic to organize a racist hate group. The same technological capacity that enables people to share diverse views can provide a platform for narcissistic blogs and footage glorifying terrorist acts.

Until the rise of the Internet, formal organizational structures were the norm for carrying out complex, large-scale

tasks. However, new communications technology has made it possible to organize some large-scale efforts without a bureaucratic structure. Instead, groups can create an openly accessible system that enables many people to contribute and participate. For example, the fashion web site Polyvore.com allows users to create, share, and comment on fashion ideas. With more than one million registered users, Polyvore allows members to select items from any online store to build their own fashion "set," which other members comment on, rework, and sometimes post to social networking sites. Polyvore seeks to "democratize fashion" by bringing together a diverse community of amateur designers in a global conversation about style (Jacobs 2010).

The Internet's capacity to bring people from all over the world together to "meet" in the same virtual space makes new forms of organizational structure possible (Harwood and McIntosh 2004; Konieczny 2009). Many organizations now use wikis—web sites consisting of simple online databases that permit all members to create and edit content—to facilitate innovative forms of organizational structure, building trust among employees based on transparency, collaboration, and participatory decision-making. These so-called permanently beta organizations can be more flexible, decentralized, and responsive than large industrial organizations are able to be (Neff and Stark 2004). The long-term viability of these kinds of unstable organizations remains uncertain, however. As organizations grow and mature, they tend to take on the characteristics of bureaucratic organizations.

Other examples of new types of organizations are easy to find. Thousands of people contributed to produce Linux, a popular and free open-source operating system that has challenged Microsoft Windows. Users of Second Life and other virtual worlds create, develop, and take part in this online universe. Thousands of individual merchants sell products on online auction sites, and customers' ratings of these merchants help to steer future patrons away from problematic sellers. Political candidates and activists from all parts of the political spectrum use web sites, forums, e-mail, and other Internet tools for discussion, information sharing, and mobilization.

Of course, not all large-scale efforts lend themselves to fluid forms of organization. Bureaucratic organizations are still likely to typify the mass production of consumer goods—such as cars and home appliances—as well as the delivery of health care and education and the administration of the military, for example. However, the Internet—with its vast communication networks—has provided a means of tapping into the collective intelligence of millions of people in ways that were never before possible. It remains to be seen how such "smart mobs" (Rheingold 2003) might be used to tackle other collective efforts.

THINKING SOCIOLOGICALLY ABOUT . . .

Interaction, Groups, and Organizations

culture

- We are socialized in a particular culture, and we learn to see our world from that culture's perspective. That socially constructed viewpoint becomes reality for us.
- Cultures inform the nature of social roles and the expectations associated with them.
- Organizations often have distinct cultures that influence how they are structured, the values they espouse, and the way they operate.

structure

- Statuses and roles provide some of the glue that connects individuals to one another and to the behavioral patterns that constitute social structure.
- People create groups and organizations, which in turn become more formal social structures.
- After creating these social structures, people treat those socially constructed entities as objectively real, and structures in turn are influenced by the society they create.

power

- People with different statuses often receive differing levels of honor, prestige, power, and income, resulting in inequality.
- Even in small, informal groups, individuals tend to conform to the views of the majority and to obey authority figures.
- In bureaucracies, power is organized hierarchically. People at each level in a hierarchy have power over those below and are subject to the authority of those above. Positions in bureaucracies are starkly unequal.

Looking Back

1. Face-to-face encounters, influenced by cultural norms, are the building blocks of social life. Through our social interactions we come to mutual understandings about reality. How we define reality can have real consequences.

2. People are involved collectively in the social construction of reality. Humans create society, treat it as an objective reality, and then are influenced by the social forces they have created.

3. A particularly important element in social life is social status, the position an individual occupies in the social system; social roles are the cultural expectations associated with a status. Statuses and roles link individuals to larger groups and institutions, helping to create social structure.

4. In sociology, dramaturgy uses the metaphor of a theatrical performance to analyze roles and social interaction.

5. Society consists of links, groupings, and organizations. These include social networks that are formed out of our social ties as well as small-scale primary groups and large formal organizations.

6. The dynamics of groups, large and small, can be analyzed sociologically. For example, in small groups, conformity is an important social dynamic. People who engage in groupthink ignore evidence or ideas that contradict group beliefs.

7. Large organizations rely on bureaucratic structure to operate efficiently, but as the layers of bureaucracy multiply, they make organizations unwieldy and inefficient. The iron law of oligarchy holds that bureaucracies concentrate power in the hands of those at the top.

8. Contemporary developments, especially in technology, have affected how we interact with one another and have led to new types of social networks and to innovative forms of organizational structure.

Critical Thinking: Questions and Activities

1. Write a brief, realistic telephone exchange between two college-age friends. Now rewrite that same exchange, making explicit all the taken-for-granted information that the two speakers share. What type of information was left out of the original version?

2. List all the statuses you currently occupy. Write a brief description of the role expectations associated with three of your statuses. How did you learn about these role expectations? What consequences, if any, are there for deviating from these expectations?

3. Using elements of dramaturgical theory, describe an example of role playing from your own life. Were you successful in your performance? Why or why not?

4. Draw a diagram of the structure of a bureaucratic organization with which you are familiar—for example, a school, workplace, or community group—mapping the lines of authority. Can you explain the logic of the specific organizational structure? Does the organization operate effectively and efficiently? Can you imagine an alternative organizational structure?

5. How has the Internet influenced your social networks? Do you think communication via the Internet is replacing other forms of communication? Why or why not?

Key Terms

achieved status (p. 168) a social position that we voluntarily attain, to a considerable degree, as the result of our own efforts.

ascribed status (p. 168) a social position that is assigned to us from birth or that we assume later in life, regardless of our wishes or abilities.

bureaucracy (p. 177) a hierarchical administrative system with formal rules and procedures used to manage organizations.

dramaturgy (p. 170) an approach to the study of social interaction that uses the metaphor of social life as a theater.

groupthink (p. 182) a form of uncritical thinking in which people reinforce a consensus rather than ask serious questions or thoroughly analyze the issue at hand.

homophily (p. 173) the idea that social contact occurs at a higher rate between people who are similar than it does between people who are different.

in-group (p. 180) a social group with which a person identifies and toward which he or she feels positively; members have a collective sense of "us."

intersubjectivity (p. 163) a common understanding between people about knowledge, reality, or an experience.

iron law of oligarchy (p. 183) the eventual and inevitable consolidation of power at the top of bureaucratic organizations.

master status (p. 169) a social position that is overwhelmingly significant, powerfully influences a person's social experience, and typically overshadows all the other social positions that person may occupy.

organizational environment (p. 178) factors that exist outside the organization but that potentially affect its operation.

organizations (p. 176) secondary groups that have a degree of formal structure and are formed to accomplish particular tasks.

out-group (p. 180) a social group toward which a person feels negatively, considering its members to be inferiors, or "them."

primary groups (p. 175) people who have regular contact, enduring relationships, and a significant emotional attachment to each other.

reference groups (p. 175) the groups against which we choose to measure ourselves.

role conflict (p. 170) the problem that occurs when the expectations associated with different roles clash.

role strain (p. 170) the problem that occurs when the expectations associated with a single role compete with each other.

roles (p. 169) the sets of expected behaviors that are associated with particular statuses.

scientific management (p. 183) the process of deskilling ordinary workers and increasing workplace efficiency through calculated study.

secondary groups (p. 175) people who interact in a relatively impersonal way, usually to carry out some specific task.

social groups (p. 174) collections of people who interact regularly with one another and who are aware of their status as a group.

social networks (p. 172) the collection of social ties that connect people to each other.

status (p. 168) a position in a social system that can be occupied by an individual.

status category (p. 168) a status that people can hold in common.

status hierarchy (p. 169) a ranking of social positions according to their perceived prestige or honor.

status set (p. 168) the collection of statuses that an individual holds.

stereotypes (p. 166) exaggerated, distorted, or untrue generalizations about categories of people that do not acknowledge individual variation.

Thomas theorem (p. 165) the idea that if people define situations as real, they are real in their consequences.

Class and Global Inequality

looking AHEAD

How has class **structure** shaped your family's experiences?

How does **culture** influence how you experience class?

How does economic inequality affect and reflect the **power** of different players in the global economy?

Alfred Lubrano grew up in a working-class family in New York. His father, a bricklayer, helped construct some of the buildings at prestigious Columbia University, which, ironically, Lubrano himself attended. As he notes, "My dad has built lots of places in New York City he can't get into" (Lubrano 2004, 7). Lubrano went on to become a successful reporter, thus entering the middle class. In the process, however, he experienced what he calls "the pain of transition."

Lubrano loved the strong work ethic, lack of pretense, hearty humor, strong family ties, sense of loyalty, and forthright manner that characterized his working-class upbringing, but in countless ways, he didn't fit in. Like his male friends, he lifted weights and played in a neighborhood band, but he didn't share their enthusiasm for customizing cars. Unlike his resourceful father, who knew how to stretch every scarce dollar, he had neither the inclination nor the aptitude to fix household appliances. He cared about college, not Camaros; he didn't fix things, he read books.

But he didn't feel at home at Columbia, either. The mostly upper-middle-class students he met were confident, with a sense of entitlement and belonging that comes from shared experience and expectation. Courtesy of affluent parents, they lived on campus, didn't have to work long hours to pay expenses, graduated without debt, and often had family connections that led to career opportunities. Working-class students like Lubrano lived at home to limit expenses, spent hours working as well as studying, racked up heavy debts, and were on their own finding a job.

Fitting into his new middle-class life after school wasn't easy, either. There were little cultural things: eating Brie instead of Kraft slices; playing squash and racquetball instead of bowling; questioning authorities like doctors rather than being awed by their credentials. And there were big things: he learned to pursue a career, rather than just get a job. His working-class culture was rooted in solidarity with family, neighborhood, church, and union. It was blunt and direct; you spoke your mind and said what you meant. Middle-class culture, in contrast, values individual achievement and success, which can require a self-promotion that many working-class folks find distasteful. And it involves diplomacy and office politics often pursued on the sly; you bite your tongue and tone down your language.

As a result, Lubrano (2004) writes, "I am two people. . . . With one foot in the working class, the other in the middle class, people like me are Straddlers, at home in neither world, living a limbo life" (pp. 1, 8). ■

Alfred Lubrano's story illustrates the importance of class in shaping who we are and how our society operates. As Lubrano (2004) himself puts it,

Class is script, map, and guide. It tells us how to talk, how to dress, how to hold ourselves, how to eat, and how to socialize. It affects whom we marry; where we live; the friends we choose, the jobs we have; the vacations we take; the books we read; the movies we see; the restaurants we pick; how we decide to buy houses, carpets, furniture, and cars; where our kids are educated [. . .] In short, class is nearly everything about you. And it dictates what to expect out of life and what the future should be. (p. 5)

The way we experience class in our everyday lives (at the micro level) is linked to the social structure that helps to perpetuate class inequality (at the macro level). Class, then, is about both personal experience and the broad structures of social inequality. In a global economy, the influence of class and economic inequality encompasses systems that are international in scope. What happens on this world stage can have a dramatic impact on you and your community. For example, the export of good-paying manufacturing jobs over the past few decades has meant many more young Americans decided to attend college to improve their chances of getting a good job. However, U.S. students who graduated from college during the global economic downturn that began in 2008 experienced unexpected difficulty finding jobs.

In Chapter 5, we examined the concept of power and its connection to inequality in society. We considered various forms of stratification and how race, class, and gender intersect to shape people's experience of inequality. In this chapter, we take a closer look at one form of inequality—class—in the United States and consider the broader context of global inequality.

Understanding Class

In Chapter 5, we defined a **class** as *a group of people who share a roughly similar economic position and lifestyle.* Most of us have at least an intuitive understanding of class inequality. We know that being rich or poor shapes a person's life experiences in important ways. The streets of any major U.S. city include both the luxury automobiles of the wealthy and the shopping carts of the homeless. Your community likely has clubs, institutions, and businesses that are stratified by the class of the people who frequent them—everything from exclusive country clubs, fashionable shops, expensive gourmet restaurants, and private schools to bowling alleys, discount superstores, fast-food restaurants, and pawn shops.

Class permeates our popular language. Terms such as "middle class," "blue collar," and "professional" pepper our speech. Many of these terms have their roots in the sociological analysis of class and inequality. That analysis began with the efforts of Karl Marx and Max Weber in the late 1800s and early 1900s to understand the growing inequality and wrenching social changes that accompanied the rise of industrial capitalism. Their ideas, along with those of later sociologists, have given us insight into how class operates.

Marx's Analysis of Class

Karl Marx (1867/1976) based his analysis of class on the idea that if people are to survive, they must meet their basic material needs for food, clothing, and shelter. A society's *economy* is the system by which it meets these and other needs. How an economy is organized affects all other aspects of social life, Marx argued. For example, as we saw in Chapter 1, urbanization, driven by industrialization, changed where people lived as well as how they earned a living and organized their families.

Marx noted that through most of their history, humans lived in nomadic egalitarian societies and fed themselves by foraging for edible wild plants and by hunting. Because these societies produced few surplus goods, they had little economic inequality. However, the emergence of farming about 10,000 years ago enabled societies to live in permanent settlements, develop food surpluses, and accumulate material goods. As wealth increased, inequality also increased. Ever since then, the fundamental economic pattern has been the same: a division between those who own the means of production—the key resources in a particular economy—and those who do not. Marx argued that these groups constitute a society's two major classes, and the dynamics between them account for economic inequality. In agricultural economies, for example, where land is the key resource, the central class division is between

Large paper-making machines dwarf the workers tending them. With the rise of industrialism, capital—needed to finance large manufacturing facilities like this one—became the key economic resource, giving industrial capitalism its name.

landowners and commoners such as peasants, serfs, and share-croppers, who work the land but do not own it. In industrial economies, the key resource is **capital**—*the money to invest in factories, real estate, and other businesses.* In capitalism the basic division is between the **capitalist class** (or *bourgeoisie*), *those who control major capital and own the means of production,* and the **working class** (or *proletariat*), *those who survive on the wages they earn.*

Marx argued that because of their differing interests, the major classes are inevitably in conflict and that this class conflict has been the engine that has driven much of human history. Under capitalism, workers try to maximize their pay and benefits (often by forming labor unions), while owners try to maximize their profits by minimizing the costs of doing business, including labor costs. Thus the working class and the capitalists are locked in an eternal conflict that is part of the very structure of the capitalist system.

Furthermore, capitalists exploit workers, paying them less than the real value of their labor. Eventually, according to Marx, this exploitation would result in an economic crisis, an unsustainable gap between rich and poor, and workers would unite to overthrow the capitalist system. The result, according to Marx, would be *socialism,* an economic arrangement in which the state owns the major means of production on behalf of the workers, thereby abolishing class distinctions based on the ownership of major property.

Marx was aware of other classes, but he did not see them playing a central role in capitalist systems. Small-business owners, for example, whom Marx called the *petite bourgeoisie,* neither generate profit primarily from other people's labor nor earn wages in somebody else's enterprise. Marx argued that over time the large capitalists would swallow up small-business owners. An example today would be local merchants who go bankrupt in the face of competition from big-box chains like Walmart and Home Depot.

Through the late nineteenth and early twentieth centuries, labor struggles in the United States were more violent than in any other industrialized country, with hundreds killed and thousands injured in labor disputes. Today, such violent clashes with police and military troops are more likely to occur in developing countries, where workers struggle for better wages and working conditions. (The photo on the right shows a clash between union members and the police in South Korea.)

CORE CONCEPTS CHALLENGE

What does the often-violent history of labor relations reveal about **power** *in society?*

As capitalism evolved, scholars adjusted Marx's theories to account for new developments, especially the rising importance of the middle class (Dahrendorf 1959; Walker 1979; Wright 1985). For example, in Marx's day, much of the industrial base was owned by families or small groups of capitalists. Since that time, however, public corporations have gained enormous power and influence. Stock in publicly traded companies is owned by tens of thousands of different people and institutions, none of which have direct control over a given company. Instead, authority in the workplace is in the hands of highly paid executives and managers who are part of the upper middle class. As a result, when analyzing class, some scholars focus on the role of authority rather than ownership in the workplace.

Weber's "Life Chances"

Max Weber (1922/1978), working a generation after Marx, differed from him in two major ways. First, rather than focusing exclusively on class inequality and the economy, Weber emphasized the interaction of three dimensions of inequality: class, social status, and political power. For example, political power can limit economic power, as it does when a government regulates corporations or imposes taxes on the wealthy.

Second, Weber differed from Marx in the way he conceptualized class. Whereas Marx saw class in terms of the organization of work, Weber looked at class in terms of **life chances,** *the*

 To order a bottle of fine wine in a gourmet restaurant, a diner not only needs to be able to afford the wine, which can easily cost over $100 a bottle, but also must have some knowledge of grape vintages, the varieties of international cuisine that the wine might accompany, and perhaps even the foreign languages in which the names of wines and their labels are written. All of these reflect cultural aspects of class distinctions.

CORE CONCEPTS CHALLENGE

What other common social interactions reflect aspects of class culture?

likelihood a person has of obtaining valued economic and cultural resources. Essentially, for Weber, a class is a group of people who share a common market situation—that is, they have a similar capacity to earn money and they pursue a similar lifestyle.

Weber's approach to class solves a problem with Marx's analysis. For Marx, a member of the working class is essentially anyone who earns a wage in a workplace that he or she doesn't own. By that definition, a corporate lawyer who earns $200,000 per year and a minimum-wage fast-food worker earning just over $15,000 per year are both members of the working class. Yet the life of a high-paid professional and that of a low-paid service worker are fundamentally different. Weber's focus on life chances allowed him to introduce the idea of a middle class. The members of this class are primarily wage earners and are not capitalists. Their formal education and training, however, provide them with a scarce resource, enabling them to obtain a higher standard of living, with different life chances, than most members of the working class. People in the middle class and those in the working class often differ in everything from the leisure activities they enjoy to their preferences in music and food. In effect, different classes have different cultures.

Is Class Stratification Functional?

For Marx and Weber, class inequality was intertwined with struggles for power in society. In contrast, American functionalists in the mid-twentieth century analyzed economic inequality in terms of the positive good it contributes to society as a whole (Alexander 1985; Merton 1968b). In this view, as expressed in a classic article by Kingsley Davis and Wilbert Moore (1945), stratification helps to "insure that the most important positions are conscientiously filled by the most qualified persons."

To Weber and Marx, class competition produces winners and losers, in part based on how much power each competitor has. In contrast, to functionalists, free competition between individuals for lucrative positions produces a win-win benefit for society. Functionalists argue that for society to survive, well-qualified people must fill important positions. These positions tend to require higher levels of training and often scarce talent. The higher rewards associated with these positions motivate people to train and compete to fill them. Who would undergo the expense and years of education and training required to become a doctor, for example, if a career in medicine provided no greater rewards than a job that required only a high school education? Instead of conflicting classes, then, functionalists see a continuum of occupations offering a variety of rewards and contributing to the survival and smooth functioning of society.

Critics of the functionalist perspective, however, point out that the real world doesn't operate this way (Tumin 1953). Instead, preexisting inequality affects how competitive a person can be, and barriers to mobility often prevent deserving individuals from advancing. In any society that produces a surplus, conflict inevitably emerges over how to distribute that surplus (Lenski 1966). Those who win the conflict can consolidate their power, alter a society's rules and laws, and pass on their advantages to their children. Critics argue that the functionalist analysis fails to account for this kind of enduring inequality and, instead, rationalizes and legitimizes existing inequality. Indeed, in the mid-twentieth century, when functionalists were formulating their approach to stratification, many social groups, including women and African Americans, were effectively barred from competing for society's best-rewarded positions.

Another problem with the functionalist approach to stratification is that it fails to define what is meant by "the most important positions." Who decides what they are? A top movie star can command tens of millions of dollars for a single film, while a teacher may earn a modest salary. Which job is more "important" to society?

Although functionalism proved to be an inadequate explanation of class inequality, it did describe some of the important dynamics of the labor market. Some of its ideas are still popular and, as we will see, are used in promoting education as a means of improving individual life chances.

Class Inequality in the United States

The students at Grove City High School in the working-class suburbs of Columbus, Ohio, were hit hard by budget cuts in the past few years (Garcia 2009). All sports were eliminated, but the cuts didn't stop there. Now there is no marching band, no student government, and no prom. Cuts like this are a reality in poor and working-class communities across the country that can no longer afford to pay for such "luxuries" amidst a deep economic downturn. However, the business of luxuries is booming. In 2011, for example, one seller (ridetoys.com) was offering a gasoline-powered Ferrari Testarossa scale-model car for just over $97,000 for six- to eleven-year-old children of the super-rich. In 2010, popular holiday gifts at Chicago luxury stores included $20,000 men's suits, $16,000 women's crocodile handbags, and $40,000 jewel-encrusted cell phones (Sweeney 2010).

These starkly different realities reflect some of the class inequality in the United States. As we explored in Chapter 5, all stratification systems are characterized by three key elements:

1. The unequal distribution of valuable resources

2. Distinctive groups that make up the various strata in society

3. An ideology, or system of beliefs, that explains and justifies the existence of inequality

Class systems comprise all three of these key elements.

Mapping the Major Classes

The class structure of the United States can be described in various ways (Beeghley 2008; Gilbert 2008; Kerbo 2008; Marger 2007; Zweig 2000). The four-class model used here (see Table 9.1) combines Weber's recognition of people's market situation with Marx's emphasis on the importance of ownership and control. In this model, each class is identified by the primary asset that it controls and contributes to the economy. Of course, the lines between classes are not hard and fast; people move up and down between them and the characteristics of individual members in each class can vary considerably. Nonetheless, the broadly defined class distinctions illustrated in Figure 9.1 and summarized in Table 9.1 can give us insight into the dynamics of inequality in American society.

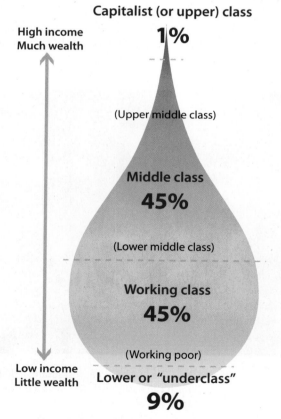

FIGURE 9.1 | A MODEL OF THE U.S. CLASS SYSTEM

The bulk of the U.S. population is about evenly divided between the middle and the working classes. However, a broader range of incomes is found among the middle class, contributing to the elongated shape of this model. The highest incomes in the capitalist class extend far beyond what can be represented here.

TABLE 9.1   MAJOR U.S. SOCIAL CLASSES

	Major economic asset	Occupations	Education	Income level	Wealth
Capitalist (or Upper) Class	Investment capital	The wealthiest often do not work at a job. Some oversee the management of their investments. Some are top corporate executives.	Often college educated, but not necessarily, especially when wealth is inherited.	Top 1 percent of household income (about $368,000 or more). Higher end makes many times more.	Wealth is central. Major holdings in stocks, bonds, real estate, and other investments.
Middle Class Upper ("professional") middle class Lower middle class	Knowledge, expertise	Professionals: engineers, scientists, lawyers, doctors, etc. Other occupations requiring a college degree, such as schoolteacher.	College education is essential to success in this class.	55th–99th percentile (about $55,000–$368,000).	Ranges from limited assets such as a small home and savings to an expensive home, significant savings, and stock and other investments.
Working Class (including the working poor)	Skilled and unskilled labor, including service work	Wide variety, including office workers, factory workers, sales clerks, home health aides, customer service reps, etc.	High school diploma is the norm; technical school common; some college possible—especially when vocationally oriented.	10th–55th percentile (about $12,000–$55,000).	Usually little or no wealth; home is key investment; often in debt.
Underclass (or Lower Class)	None—chronically unemployed	Typically none; sometimes informal economy; public assistance.	Less than a high school diploma is common.	Bottom 9 percent or less (less than $12,000).	No assets; often in debt.

Source: Estimate for income of top one percent is based on Saez (2010). Other income ranges are authors' estimates based on 2009 Current Population Survey household income data, retrieved from www.census.gov/hhes/www/cpstables/032010/hhinc/new06_000.htm.

THE CAPITALIST CLASS: INVESTMENTS AND INHERITED WEALTH   **Wealth** refers to *the value of financial assets such as savings, real estate, stocks, and bonds, minus any outstanding debts.* **Income** is *money received from sources such as wages and salaries as well as from the interest, dividends, and rent generated by wealth.* Most people derive their income primarily from wages and salaries. In contrast, the defining characteristic of the *capitalist class* (or "upper" class) is that its members often generate income primarily through their wealth, rather than through employment.

Some wealthy people have jobs that pay high salaries and bonuses, but generally speaking, the richer people are, the smaller the percentage of their income that comes from employment. Instead, businesses they own generate income for them, stocks produce dividends (profits distributed to shareholders), and real estate yields rental income. For some, management of these investments is their only "job," whereas others hire advisors to manage their wealth and live a life of leisure. The number of families in the United States that are true capitalists is small, perhaps as little as one percent of all households. These families have average incomes of about $1.1 million dollars a year—a few make hundreds of millions—and possess enormous wealth (Piketty and Saez 2010).

Unlike income, wealth accumulates over time and can be passed on from generation to generation. As a result, the concentration of wealth in the United States is much greater than the concentration of income (as we will see), and much of the wealth of the upper class is inherited. In the 2010 *Forbes* magazine list of the nation's wealthiest people, four of the ten richest Americans were siblings who inherited their money from their father—Walmart founder Sam Walton. Even in the midst of an economic downturn, each was worth about $20 billion. One earlier study found that 43 percent of the people on the *Forbes* list were there because of wealth they had inherited. Another 13 percent had inherited a company or wealth worth at least $1 million (United for a Fair

Economy 1996). Your best chance of being part of this class is to be born into it.

THE MIDDLE CLASS: PURSUING THE BENEFITS OF EDUCATION

The **middle class** is *a group that contributes specialized knowledge and expertise to the economy.* To members of the middle class, education and training—usually obtained at college and professional schools—are essential resources. Encompassing roughly 45 percent of the population, the middle class is often subdivided informally into the upper middle class and the lower middle class. Those at the higher end have powerful jobs—often with considerable autonomy—that generate large salaries. Unlike capitalists, members of the upper middle class rely primarily on their salaries for their income, though they may also accumulate stocks and other investments and own expensive homes. Most lawyers, doctors, scientists, engineers, and other professionals fall into this category, as do most business executives.

Lower-middle-class occupations, such as schoolteacher, low-level manager, and social worker, generally offer lower income, fewer benefits, and less autonomy than upper-middle-class jobs. Members of the lower middle class may own their homes and have modest personal savings or retirement accounts but little else. Some lower-middle-class workers—such as teachers and government employees—are heavily unionized, which can help them improve their pay, benefits, and working conditions.

Although upper-class families can ensure their children's financial success by handing down wealth, education cannot be inherited; each generation must learn anew. As a result, middle-class parents are often especially concerned about obtaining the best education for their children so that they can maintain or improve upon their middle-class status.

THE WORKING CLASS: LABOR AND SERVICE

Like the middle class, the working class is broad and diverse, encompassing roughly 45 percent of the population. Whereas members of the middle class are generally engaged in knowledge work and earn a weekly or annual salary, members of the *working class* usually make a product or provide a service and earn hourly wages. The income range for the working class is considerably narrower than the range for the middle class.

All working-class jobs require some skill and knowledge (Rose 2004). However, these jobs can be placed on a continuum, with well-paid skilled trade workers such as mechanics, electricians, and technicians at one end and low-paid, relatively unskilled workers such as home health aides, garment workers, and food service employees at the other end. Skilled trade workers generally need specialized knowledge, but they also work with their hands. Some belong to trade unions that help them get better wages and benefits than their nonunion counterparts. Unskilled workers may only be able to find part time or seasonal employment and—even if they work full time—earn low wages that may not keep a family above the poverty line. These working poor include farm workers, hotel housekeeping staff, home health aides, garment workers, and food service employees. Union members in these occupations tend to enjoy modestly better wages and benefits than their nonunion counterparts, but they still struggle financially.

Historically the term "working class" has evoked images of blue-collar workers in factories and building construction. Although manufacturing jobs are still important, today working-class jobs in the United States—such as daycare provider, food service worker, customer service representative, and retail sales clerk—are increasingly service oriented. Because members of the working class generally earn relatively modest paychecks, working-class families typically have only some savings, and they may own a modest home. Many families have no assets at all, living paycheck to paycheck or struggling with persistent debt. (The Sociology Works box looks at how one sociologist examines issues in the changing workplace.)

THE UNDERCLASS: CHRONIC UNEMPLOYMENT

Sociologists often use the term **underclass** (or *lower class*) to refer to *chronically unemployed people who have no ongoing relationship to the mainstream economy.* Members of the underclass include those only spo-

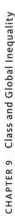

Russ Eckel and the New Workplace

In the 1980s, sociologist Russ Eckel could see that work and the workplace in the United States were in flux. At the same time, Eckel, who had received a Ph.D. in sociology, recognized that employees were rarely included in company discussions about workplace change. Drawing upon his training as a sociologist and his research on automobile workers in the 1980s, Eckel started a consulting group, Nommos, to work with companies and labor unions. The goal was to help employers and employees better understand and manage change in the work setting.

Since founding Nommos, Eckel has worked primarily with major automobile companies—including Ford and General Motors—as they have negotiated a changing global auto industry. In all its consulting projects, Nommos emphasizes the importance of three interrelated elements: (1) bringing employees into the center of the picture so that change is not something "done to" them; (2) listening to and understanding the employee experience; and (3) educating and training workers and giving them meaningful work that allows them to use their skills.

Eckel's newest endeavor, the Millennial Work Project, aims to help organizations understand the skills and expectations of a new generation of workers—young people who have come of age in the era of the global economy and the Internet and who bring a new style and new set of attitudes to work. The Millennial Work Project looks closely at the skills, beliefs, experiences, and hopes of the generation of workers born after 1980 and applies this research to specific workplace problems.

As part of the Millennial Work Project, Nommos contracted with a large university in New England and the union representing clerical and technical workers at that university to help the school and the union understand what young workers value and expect from their work. Through discussions with employees, Eckel found that young workers differ from their counterparts of previous generations in three important respects:

> Young workers do not want work to take over their lives. They have a strong sense of the value of maintaining a life outside of work.

Russ Eckel

> Like previous generations, they want to find jobs that allow them to do meaningful work. Unlike previous generations, however, young workers fully *expect* to have meaningful jobs.

> Employee benefits—including health insurance, vacation time, and, perhaps most important, educational opportunities—are an essential component of job satisfaction for young workers. They recognize the ongoing nature of change in the workplace and are especially concerned about opportunities for continuing education and training throughout their work lives.

Eckel views the Millennial Work Project as a long-term endeavor that will become more important as older workers retire and young workers move up through the ranks. For Nommos, sociology continues to provide valuable tools for helping companies and employees navigate the churning waters and shifting tides of the new economy.

> *Sociology provides valuable tools for helping companies and employees navigate the churning waters and shifting tides of the new economy.*

think about it

1. *How does Eckel's effort to include employees so that workplace change is not simply "done to" them run counter to the usual class-based power differences in the workplace?*

2. *How do workers born after 1980 differ from their counterparts in previous generations? Are some of these differences likely to vary by class? Explain.*

---

radically and briefly employed, those dependent on long-term public assistance, and those who earn money from the informal economy (off-the-books transactions that are not taxed or monitored by the government and can include everything from childcare services and auto repair to begging and drug dealing). A variety of reasons can prevent members of the underclass from finding or retaining regular employment. Their employer may have closed, they may have family responsibilities that prevent them from working, they may lack the skills and education for jobs that are available, or they may have physical disabilities or suffer from mental illnesses or substance abuse. Because they are either unable or unwilling to participate regularly in the mainstream economy, the members of this group typically live in poverty.

Income and Wealth Inequality

The differences among classes reflect substantial inequality in the distribution of income and wealth in the United States. Income levels are usually measured by household rather than individual, because counting the income from multiple wage-earners who live in a single home more accurately reflects people's standard of living. As Figure 9.2 shows, the highest earning 20 percent of American households in 2009 received just over 50 percent of all household income. In contrast, households in the bottom 20 percent received only 3.3 percent of all income. Income inequality has been increasing for decades. The top 5 percent of households have seen their share of income increase by more than 27 percent since 1983, whereas the bottom 80 percent have seen their share of the income pie decline over that time. (The Through a Sociological Lens box on page 229 discusses the intersection of class and race in relation to the growing income inequality among African Americans.)

As Figure 9.3 shows, wealth is even more unequally distributed than income. The wealthiest 20 percent of households, with an average net worth of over $2.2 million, owns 85 percent of the nation's total wealth, leaving just 15 percent for the remaining 80 percent of households. Even within the top 20 percent, wealth ownership is skewed to the top, with the top 1 percent of households owning more than a third of all wealth in the United States. In stark contrast, the bottom 40 percent of households has just 0.2 percent of the wealth. Wealth inequality has been growing more quickly than income inequality. Since 1983, the top 5 percent of households have seen their percentage of wealth more than double, whereas the bottom 40 percent have seen it decline by 62.9 percent (Wolff 2010).

Class Mobility and Class Barriers

Because hierarchical class systems have fewer positions at the top, relatively few people can move up to the highest positions, regardless of talent, dedication, and hard work. As sociologist Jay MacLeod (1995) puts it, "Our society is *structured* to create poverty and extreme economic inequality. . . . This roughly pyramidal structure ensures that even if everyone excels in school and strives ceaselessly for the top, the great majority are automatically bound to be disappointed" (p. 239). Class structure, then, ultimately limits upward mobility and ensures inequality.

Still, class systems are less rigid than caste or feudal systems (see Chapter 5). In a caste system, the caste into which people are born almost completely determines their life chances. In contrast, class systems permit some **class mobility,** *the ability to move from one social class to another.* There are two general types of class mobility: structural and individual. **Structural mobility** occurs because *a shift in available occupations changes*

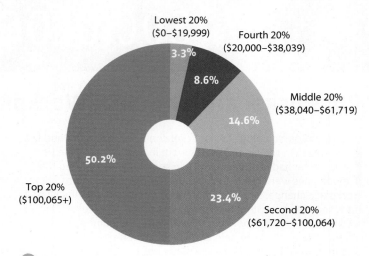

FIGURE 9.2 | THE DISTRIBUTION OF U.S. HOUSEHOLD INCOME, 2009

Source: U.S. Census Bureau (2011a, 2011d)

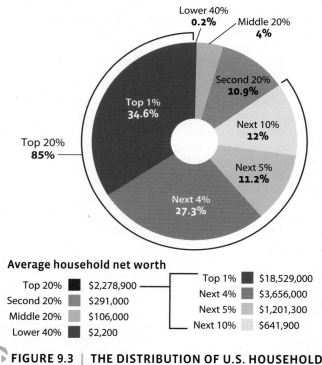

Average household net worth

Top 20%	$2,278,900
Second 20%	$291,000
Middle 20%	$106,000
Lower 40%	$2,200

Top 1%	$18,529,000
Next 4%	$3,656,000
Next 5%	$1,201,300
Next 10%	$641,900

FIGURE 9.3 | THE DISTRIBUTION OF U.S. HOUSEHOLD NET WORTH, 2007

Source: Wolff (2010)

the class system as a whole. For example, in the past several decades the number of relatively high-paying manufacturing jobs has declined, forcing people to find other types of work. Since the fastest growing occupations have been those with low wages (see Table 9.2), many people experienced downward mobility. Workers laid off from an automobile factory that pro-

Examining the Intersection of Race and Class: Growing Income Inequality Among African Americans

Over a hundred years ago, sociologist W.E.B. Du Bois (1903) famously wrote, "The problem of the twentieth century is the problem of the color-line" (p. vii). In the ensuing years, activists targeted segregation and the legal barriers that prevented African Americans and other racial minorities from participating fully in social, economic, and political life. By the latter half of the twentieth century, the strict color line that Du Bois had written about was crumbling, but deeply entrenched class divisions remained.

This shift is embodied in the career of Martin Luther King, Jr. During the often-overlooked last five years of his life, King focused less on racial injustice and more on what he saw as the new social divide in the United States that cut across all races: class. As Michael Eric Dyson (2000) puts it, "King sensed the raging of a more powerful force than he had confronted in all the years of his civil rights struggles: structural economic inequality. . . . King saw that in the struggle to free Northern blacks, race mattered, but class mattered more" (pp. 82–83).

By 1980, sociologist William Julius Wilson confirmed that the life chances of individual Blacks now were influenced more by their class position than by their interaction with Whites. Race was still significant, Wilson (1980) argued, but "in the economic sphere, class has become more important than race in determining black access to privilege and power" (p. 2). Because of class divisions within the black community, he argued, black people no longer share a uniform experience. A more complex social reality has replaced Du Bois's idea of a single "color line," requiring sociologists to examine the interaction of race and class.

Race continues to contribute to social inequality. For example, median family income for Whites in the United States remains about a third higher than it is for Blacks. However, income disparities among black households have grown significantly. As racial barriers fall and new opportunities arise, growing black middle and upper middle classes have emerged. After adjusting for inflation, the number of black households with incomes in the $50,000–$100,000 range has increased by almost 50 percent since 1970, while the number of black households earning more than $100,000 has increased by more than 400 percent (U.S. Census Bureau 2010f).

Not surprisingly, as class differences have increased within the black community, significant cultural differences in corresponding attitudes and values have appeared. In one survey, nearly a third of African Americans said that poor and middle-class Blacks share "only a little" or "no" values in common (Pew Research Center 2007a). Over 60 percent of Blacks felt these values were becoming more different over time. At the same time, over 50 percent of African Americans felt that, overall, the values held by Blacks and Whites were becoming more similar. Nearly four out of ten African Americans in the survey agreed with the statement "Blacks today can no longer be thought of as a single race because the black community is so diverse" (Pew Research Center 2007, 4).

think about it

1. *How does the increasing income disparity among African Americans illustrate how the intersection of various forms of inequality affects life chances?*

2. *What does the African American experience suggest about the relationships between social structure and culture?*

vided good wages and benefits, for example, might have found themselves working instead at big-box stores or fast-food restaurants for much less.

Individual mobility occurs *when a person's class position changes without any change in the larger class structure.* Alfred Lubrano's entry into the middle class, discussed in the chapter opening, is an example of this sort of mobility. Despite the popularity of rags-to-riches stories, however, most children end up with income levels similar to those of their parents (see Table 9.3), and studies suggest that the influence of parents' class on children's futures may be even greater than once thought (Bowles, Gintis, and Groves 2005).

The best way to ensure economic success is to choose your parents wisely. Individual decisions, actions, effort, and ability are not irrelevant, but they always exist within a structural context that shapes the options available. This interplay between individual action and social structure, of course, is precisely the focus of sociological study.

thinking about structure

How have the **structural** conditions into which you were born helped to shape the life options available to you? How have your own choices and actions been influenced by the options available to you?

	Projected Growth in Number of Jobs and Percent Change		2006 Annual Earnings
	Number	**Percent**	
Registered nurses	581,500	22.2	Very high ($51,540+)
Accountants and auditors	279,400	21.7	
Postsecondary teachers	256,900	15.1	
Customer service representatives	399,500	17.7	Low ($21,590 to 32,380)
Office clerks, general	358,700	11.9	
Nursing aides, orderlies, and attendants	276,000	18.9	
Home health aides	460,900	50.0	Very low (under $21,590)
Combined food preparation and serving workers, including fast food	394,300	14.6	
Personal and home care aides	375,800	46.0	
Retail salespersons	374,700	8.4	

Seven of the ten occupations that the U.S. Labor Department projects to grow the most between 2008 and 2018 have *low* or *very low* income levels. None is in the *high* category ($32,390 to $51,530), and only three are in the *very high* category. What might these data suggest for the future of economic inequality in the United States? *Source:* Bureau of Labor Statistics (2009).

The Impact of Class Inequality on Social Life

Class has a concrete impact on daily life. People who share a common class position often share conditions and experiences, such as their state of health, the quality of their education, the type of work they do, their level of political participation, and their lifestyle.

HEALTH   The impact of class on health lasts a lifetime (Chandola, Brunner, and Marmot 2006; Lethbridge-Cejku, Schiller, and Bernadel 2004; Schult and Mullings 2005). Compared to the poor, wealthier people in the United States eat better, enjoy better health care, experience less stress, reside in safer neighborhoods, and live an average of seven years longer. The more education and income you have, the less likely you are to develop—or die from—heart disease, diabetes, strokes, and many forms of cancer.

Your health is partly a result of your individual behavior, but your behavior is also influenced by the structural aspects of class. For example, people with lower incomes are less likely to learn about and adopt healthy eating habits, in part because they are less likely to live near grocery stores that offer fresh fruits and vegetables. Poor and working-class people are also more likely to have highly stressful and insecure jobs over which they have little or no control. Work stress is a major contributing factor to physical illness, including heart disease

and diabetes, and also to mental illness, such as depression. People in higher-paying jobs with a great deal of responsibility may also experience considerable stress, but they generally have more personal control over their work and are more likely to have access to high-quality health care.

EDUCATION   Education is part of what determines your class, but the class into which you are born affects the type of education you are likely to receive. The more money your family has, the better your education is likely to be.

The class gap in education begins with the way public schools in the United States are funded (Kozol 2005). Because school funding is based largely on local property taxes, schools in affluent communities are likely to be better funded than those in poorer communities and better able to provide children with early educational advantages. Affluent families are also better able to afford advantages outside the public school system, including private schools, tutors, and test-preparation courses. Affluent parents who once provided weekly tutoring (for as much as $795 for a single 50-minute session and up to tens of thousands of dollars a year) primarily to help their children prepare for SAT and other standardized tests, now increasingly do so to ensure their children get A's in regular high school courses (Anderson 2011).

The class into which you are born also influences whether or not you pursue higher education as well as the type of higher education you receive. The families of students attending four-

TABLE 9.3   MOBILITY AND FAMILY INCOME

Parents' Family Income	Child's Family Income				
	Bottom 20%	Fourth 20%	Middle 20%	Second 20%	Top 20%
Top 20%	7.3%	11%	18.4%	26%	37.3%
Second 20%	10.7	19.5	19.6	22.9	27.2
Middle 20%	15.3	19.2	25	23.3	17.3
Fourth 20%	24.5	26.2	20.6	16.9	11.8
Bottom 20%	42.3	24.1	16.5	10.8	6.3

Class systems allow for some mobility. However, parents' income level is strongly correlated with the eventual income level of their children—especially at the top and bottom of the income hierarchy. More than a third (37.3 percent) of children whose parents' income level was in the top 20 percent stayed there, six times the rate at which children with parents in the bottom 20 percent rose into the top 20 percent. *Source:* Adapted from Hertz 2005.

CORE CONCEPTS CHALLENGE

Most of us would like to think that where we end up in life is the result of our own effort and ability. But the table suggests that social **structure** *is a major influence, as well. What factors might be contributing to the patterns shown in this table? What does the table suggest about the extent of intergenerational mobility?*

year colleges have always been more affluent than the population as a whole. By 2005, this gap reached the highest level ever recorded. In addition, families of students at private colleges and universities have higher incomes than those at public colleges (Pryor et al. 2007). Also, families with a history of college attendance have role models who can encourage and mentor younger family members to strive for and succeed in college; working-class first-generation college students typically do not enjoy such resources.

Higher education is also highly stratified along class lines (Karabel 2005; Stevens 2007). At the 146 most selective schools in the United States, 74 percent of students come from families in the richest 25 percent of the population, whereas only 3 percent come from the poorest 25 percent (Carnvale and Rose 2004). Despite increased attention to this issue, the nation's top schools have become even less economically diverse in recent years (Kahlenberg 2010b).

There are several reasons for this stratification. First, the cost of selective elite universities can be more than $50,000 a year, making them far out of reach for most students, discouraging those with more modest means from even applying. Second, even when such schools offer substantial financial assistance, their admissions processes favor better-prepared students who have had the early educational advantages that a higher class

position offers. Third, elite schools often give preference to legacy admissions—children of alumni—thereby helping to perpetuate class inequality across generations. Such preferences are estimated to be worth the equivalent of 160 SAT points and increase the chance of admission for legacy children by 20 percent (Espenshade, Chung, and Walling 2004).

Less selective schools are more accessible to those of more modest means, often because of both a lower price tag and looser admissions standards, although students from more affluent families are still overrepresented at these schools. The most diverse schools are two-year community colleges, which come the closest to drawing evenly from across class categories. These schools typically have open enrollment and lower costs. They serve students looking for a two-year degree, students planning on transferring to four-year institutions, and working adults looking to improve their job skills. Many community college students are adults who live at home and work full or part time while they commute to campus. Their college experience differs from that of students at a four-year residential college, an essential life experience for most people in the upper middle class (Leondar-Wright 2005).

In recent years, a growing number of for-profit private education companies such as the University of Phoenix have tailored college degrees to the needs of working adults by emphasizing flexible online classes that focus on job skills. Some of these schools have generated controversy, however, for being exceptionally expensive, failing to deliver marketable skills, and engaging in unethical recruitment practices (Field 2010).

WORK   Your class also affects the experiences you will likely have at work. Working-class jobs tend to be regimented and closely supervised. Working-class employees often must punch a time clock, take breaks and lunch at specific times, and even ask for permission to use the bathroom. Their work is likely to be closely monitored electronically and by supervisors. Overall, they tend to have little or no control over their work, and the work tends to be relatively low paying with limited or no benefits.

By contrast, middle-class workers often enjoy a high degree of autonomy, looser work rules, less supervision, more flexible work hours, and their own office space, and they are sometimes allowed to work from home. Often, middle-class workers supervise working-class employees.

Middle-class employees tend to work at desk jobs in quiet offices with climate-controlled environments on a regular weekday schedule. In contrast, many working-class employees toil in extremes of heat or cold and in exceptionally loud, stressful, and sometimes dirty and dangerous environments. Working-class occupations, such as truck driving, logging, fishing, farming, and ranching, have the highest rates of death and injury on the job. Working-class jobs often involve night shifts or rotating between shifts—all of which can disrupt family life.

Many middle-class jobs—especially upper-middle-class positions—come with much better benefits than most working-class jobs, including private pension plans, medical insurance, generous sick leave, paid vacation, and paid educational leave.

CONSPICUOUS CONSUMPTION AND CHANGE

In the last half of the nineteenth century, industrialization produced a "Gilded Age" dominated by so-called robber barons who controlled key industries. These newly wealthy industrialists often engaged in conspicuous consumption, as in the case of the castle-like Biltmore Estate in Asheville, North Carolina (*top*), which was completed in 1895 for one of the sons of Cornelius Vanderbilt, a shipping and railroad tycoon. Today, some members of the upper middle class have embraced a more modest version of conspicuous consumption, expressed through the "McMansions" (*bottom*) that helped fuel the housing boom—and bust—of the 2000s.

Top-level benefits can include expense accounts, company cars, membership in private clubs, company stock options, and tickets to sporting events.

POLITICS Political participation varies according to class in the United States, leaving those with the highest rates of participation with the most power. There are bigger class dif-

ferences between voters and nonvoters than there are between Republicans and Democrats; the higher a person's income, the more likely that person is to vote (Figure 9.4). The upper middle class and affluent are also most likely to fund political campaigns, either directly or through donations to political action committees (PACs), political parties, and other intermediaries. For example, almost half of the campaign contributions to members of Congress in 2004 came from people with family incomes of at least $250,000 (American National Election Studies 2007). Early donors get a chance to influence which candidates are viable long before a single vote is cast.

LIFESTYLE When you were growing up, did your family have *dinner* or *supper*? Was flying fairly routine for you or did you rarely, if ever, travel by air? Was it taken for granted that you would attend college, or was going to college an unusual accomplishment? Did your parents have an accountant, or did they make use of storefront check-cashing establishments? Such questions have to do with lifestyles, and lifestyles vary by class.

In an early work on class and lifestyles, sociologist Thorstein Veblen (1899/1973) coined the term **conspicuous consumption** to refer to *lavish spending, done to compete for status.* Veblen associated conspicuous consumption with the *nouveau riche* (French for "new rich"); in his day, these were mostly industrialists who had recently acquired their fortunes and often spent lavishly on mansions and other luxury items. Their lifestyle contrasted starkly with that of people who had so-called old money, wealth that had existed for generations. The old-money wealthy generally frowned upon ostentatious displays.

Many class-based status groups recognize members not merely by the amount of money they have but by social factors such as family heritage, race and ethnicity, educational background, and personal behavior. Such groups often develop formal or informal rules that identify who belongs and who does not. Joining an exclusive country club not only may cost thousands of dollars just to apply and thousands more for membership fees, but it also typically requires sponsorship from an existing member, ensuring that only the "right" people are allowed in. More informally, class-based status groups often share a lifestyle because they socialize together, send their children to the same schools, join the same organizations, and marry within exclusive social networks. These behaviors erect barriers of inclusion and exclusion that sometimes involve **classism,** *prejudice or discrimination based on social class.* Membership in a high-status group or low-status group can significantly affect an individual's life chances, including access to education, friendship networks, marriage opportunities, job opportunities, and business and professional contacts.

Poverty

In 2007, twelve-year-old Deamonte Driver died when an infection from an abscessed tooth spread to his brain (Otto 2007). The Maryland boy, who lived in poverty, had no access to dental care, despite being eligible for Medicaid assistance.

thinking about culture
How did the **culture** you experienced growing up reflect your family's class status?

232

Percent of citizens voting by family income

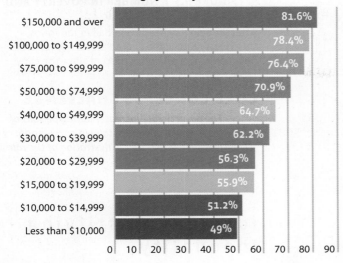

Income	Percent
$150,000 and over	81.6%
$100,000 to $149,999	78.4%
$75,000 to $99,999	76.4%
$50,000 to $74,999	70.9%
$40,000 to $49,999	64.7%
$30,000 to $39,999	62.2%
$20,000 to $29,999	56.3%
$15,000 to $19,999	55.9%
$10,000 to $14,999	51.2%
Less than $10,000	49%

FIGURE 9.4 | REPORTED VOTING BY FAMILY INCOME, 2008

The 2008 presidential election had a 61.6 percent voter turnout rate (McDonald 2010a), the highest in over forty years, but typical class differences in turnout remained. The 2010 nonpresidential election had a 40.3 percent voter turnout rate (McDonald 2010b), with similar class differences. *Source:* U.S. Census Bureau (2009c).

The newspaper story about his death noted that more than two-thirds of the children on Medicaid in Maryland receive no dental care whatsoever—and the situation is worse in other states. Lack of access to dental care, however, is just one of the countless hurdles that poor people face every day (Tyron 2007). Perhaps no group in U.S. society feels the impact of class inequality more acutely than those who live in poverty.

Absolute poverty refers to *a scarcity of resources so severe that it is life-threatening.* Nearly 20 percent of the world's population lives on less than a dollar a day, one indicator of absolute poverty. **Relative poverty** refers to *a lack of the basic resources needed to maintain a standard of living considered acceptable in a particular society.* This form of poverty varies in different societies. Being forced to live without indoor plumbing or running water would certainly be seen as a sign of poverty in U.S. society today, but in some developing nations such conditions are common and do not by themselves necessarily distinguish people as poor.

Poverty is not "natural" or "inevitable." Poverty levels result, at least in part, from government decisions about the allocation of resources. For example, one reason the United States launched the Social Security system in the 1930s was to reduce the high level of poverty among those over age sixty-five. Today this age group has the nation's lowest poverty rate. Similarly, new social programs introduced during the 1960s helped to cut the poverty rate in half between 1960 and 1970 (U.S. Census Bureau 2010f). Nations with similar degrees of wealth have significantly different poverty rates. The poverty rate in the United States is one of the highest among industrialized nations. In 2009 the United States ranked twenty-ninth among the thirty-one member nations of the Organization for Economic Cooperation and Development; only Turkey and Mexico had higher rates. The U.S. poverty rate is more than three times that of Denmark, the country with the lowest poverty rate (OECD 2010). Also, many of the other nations provide more noncash benefits (such as housing, health care, and food), making the impact of poverty less onerous than it is in the United States.

U.S. POVERTY RATES   How do we determine who is poor and calculate the number of poor people? The federal government adopted the method used to determine an acceptable standard of living in the 1960s, when policymakers estimated that poor people spent about one-third of their income on food. Since then, the U.S. **poverty line** has been *a measure of scarcity determined by figuring the cost of a minimal food budget and multiplying it by three.* Each year, the government adjusts poverty thresholds by recalculating the cost of food.

The official measure of poverty now significantly undercounts the poor, in part because people today typically spend one-fifth of their budget on food instead of one-third. Adjusting the poverty calculation by multiplying the cost of food by five would place many more people below the poverty line. In 2010 the Census Bureau (2010g) announced it would begin producing a Supplemental Poverty Measure as an alternative to the older model. This supplemental measure reflects real-world conditions more accurately by factoring in expenses such as housing, childcare, and medical treatment. It may eventually replace the old measure of poverty.

Until then, the government continues to use the outdated measure as the basis for determining the official U.S. **poverty rate,** *the percentage of the population that falls below the poverty line.* In 2010 this rate was 15.1 percent, meaning that more than one out of seven Americans—46.2 million people—lived in poverty (Figure 9.5).

Poverty threshold figures take into account family size, the age of family members, and the number of children in the household. The government counts as income not only wages but also child support and certain public assistance payments, but it excludes noncash benefits such as food stamps and housing subsidies. In 2010 a single parent with one child had to earn $15,030 to stay above the poverty line. However, if that parent worked full time at a minimum wage job ($7.25 an hour in 2010), he or she would earn $14,500, just under the official poverty line.

MISCONCEPTIONS ABOUT POVERTY   The picture that people in the United States have of poverty and the poor is often distorted, sometimes literally. According to one study, African Americans appeared in about 62 percent of the photographs used to illustrate stories about poverty in national newsmagazines and in 65 percent of the images of poor people on television (Gilens 1996). In reality, more than two-thirds of poor people in 2009 were white (68.5 percent) and fewer than a quarter were black (22.8 percent). Children are

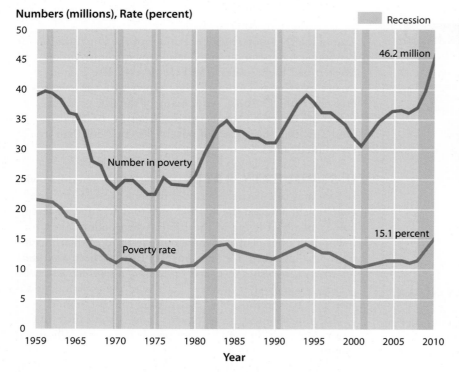

Numbers (millions), Rate (percent)

Recession

46.2 million

Number in poverty

15.1 percent

Poverty rate

1959 1965 1970 1975 1980 1985 1990 1995 2000 2005 2010

Year

 FIGURE 9.5 | NUMBER IN POVERTY AND POVERTY RATE, 1959–2010

After dropping by nearly one-half in the 1960s, the poverty rate in the United States has hovered between 11 percent and 15 percent since the early 1980s. *Source:* U.S. Census Bureau (2011d).

CORE CONCEPTS CHALLENGE

The poverty rate increases during periods of recession (shaded), as it did in 2008–2009. How are such data an illustration of the role of social structure?

Ideology: Justifying Inequality

Growing up, were you told that you could be whatever you wanted to be? That with hard work and perseverance you could accomplish whatever you set your mind to? If so, you were learning an early lesson about ideology.

As we saw in Chapter 5, in the context of stratification, an *ideology* is a system of beliefs that explains and justifies the existence of inequality. An effective ideology helps to legitimize inequality by making it appear natural, inevitable, and acceptable. In the past, belief in "God's will" justified strict systems of inequality. However, in modern societies other ideologies have emerged. If you were raised in the United States, you are probably familiar with these common ideas:

■ Everyone has an equal opportunity to succeed (but is not guaranteed success).

■ Success is based on merit (not on wealth, family ties, or other special statuses).

■ People can achieve success through individual ability and hard work.

Together, these beliefs suggest that class stratification is the outcome of individual characteristics, unimpeded by structural constraints and unaided by group privilege. In other words, success comes from talent and effort; failure results from individual shortcomings. The message of such an ideology is clear: because everyone has an equal chance to succeed, society is fair.

To state these ideas more precisely, the dominant ideology in the United States generally includes the intertwined notions of equal opportunity, meritocracy, and individualism. **Equal opportunity** is *the idea that all people should have the same chance to achieve success.* **Meritocracy** is *a system in which people are rewarded and are able to advance because of their abilities.* These ideas suggest that our stratification system is open and fair. Finally, **individualism** is *a system of beliefs that highlights the importance of the single person over any social group.* Individ-

more likely to be poor than people in any other age group, and more poor people live in rural or suburban areas than in urban areas. In the last half of the twentieth century, class and gender intersected in a **feminization of poverty,** *a trend in which women have come to make up an increasingly large share of the poor.* This trend results largely from the fact that, by 2010, just over half of all poor families were headed by a single woman, about double the rate in 1960 (U.S. Census Bureau 2011a). Other characteristics of the poor are outlined in Table 9.4.

Another myth is that most of the poor remain in poverty for a long time. On the contrary, families and individuals move in or out of poverty from year to year, sometimes repeatedly (Rank and Hirschl 2001). From 2004 through 2007, approximately 31.6 percent of the population fell below the poverty line for at least 2 months, but only 2.2 percent of the population lived in poverty for all 48 months (U.S. Census Bureau 2010f).

Perhaps the biggest misconception about poverty is that people are poor because they are unwilling to work. In fact, about 43 percent of the poor are either too old (over sixty-five) or too young (under eighteen) to work (U.S. Census Bureau 2011a). In addition, the poverty rate increases during periods of recession and declines when the economy improves, indicating that structural factors beyond individuals' control are a major cause of poverty. In reality, people live in poverty for many reasons. Some are born into it; others become poor as a result of job loss, divorce, the cost of a debilitating illness, or the addition of a child. People of sound mind rarely choose voluntarily to live in poverty. One reason for misconceptions about the causes and prevalence of poverty is ideology.

TABLE 9.4 — THE POOR IN THE UNITED STATES, 2009

RACE AND ETHNICITY

Most poor people are White. Of the 43.6 million poor:

- 68.5% are white (including white Hispanics)
- 42.4% are white non-Hispanics
- 23.1% are black
- 28.7% are Hispanic (of any race)
- 3.7% are Asian

The poverty rate is highest among Blacks and Hispanics.

- Black, 27.4%
- Hispanic (of any race), 26.6%
- Asian, 12.1%
- White, 13%
- White (non-Hispanic), 9.9%

AGE

The poor are disproportionately children. Of the 46.2 million poor:

- Over one-third (35.5%) are children under the age of 18 (16.4 million)
- 7.6% are at least 65 years old (3.5 million)

One out of five children live in poverty (22%)—the highest poverty rate; the lowest poverty rate is found among the elderly (9%); for adults aged 18 to 64, the rate is 13.7%.

FAMILY AND GENDER

Half of poor families are headed by single mothers. Of the 8.8 million poor families:

- 51.5% (4.7 million) have a single female householder
- 39% (3.6 million) have a married couple
- 8.7% (888,000) have a single male householder

WORK

Many poor adults work. Of the 31.4 million poor people aged 16 years or older:

- 8.3% work full time, year-round
- 25.7% work less than full time, year-round
- 66% did not work at least one week during the year

LOCATION

Poor people are found in both urban and suburban areas in similar numbers. Of the 46.2 million poor people:

- 19.5 million (42.4%) are in urban areas
- 18.9 million (40.8%) are in suburban areas
- 7.9 million (17%) are in rural areas

The poverty rate in rural and urban areas is similar:

- 19.7% in urban areas
- 11.8% in suburban areas
- 16.5% in rural areas

Source: U.S. Census Bureau (2011a)

---

ualism is associated with personal rights and freedoms as well as personal responsibility and self-reliance. The idea of pulling yourself up by your bootstraps and the notion of the self-made man are popular expressions of individualism.

Ideologies help justify the advantages of those in power, and they are also crucial for maintaining social control; otherwise, subordinate groups would more readily challenge structural inequality. People who suffer the consequences of economic inequality sometimes believe the dominant ideology and blame themselves for their predicament. Many, however, see through these ideological myths but do not have the power to challenge or change the system of inequality. Although few people actually believe that class inequality results from merit and individual effort alone (Smith and Kluegel 1986), holding on to the promises offered by the dominant ideology can be a source of hope that things will one day improve.

Instead of relying on ideological myths, sociologists have studied how economic inequality really works and found that factors other than merit and individual effort heavily influence the likelihood of our success or failure.

Culture, Structure, and Class Reproduction

Why does class inequality persist? To begin with, families and schools socialize people to adopt beliefs, behaviors, and outlooks consistent with their class, thus reproducing the culture of that class. Public policy also helps to reinforce class inequality.

Cultural Capital

To explain the reproduction of classes, French sociologist Pierre Bourdieu (1930–2002) built upon Weber's attention to culture and lifestyles. For Bourdieu, people reproduce classes across generations by passing on to young people not only money but also cultural assets. To describe these assets, Bourdieu coined the term **cultural capital,** which *consists of various types of knowledge, skills, and other cultural resources.* Different forms of cultural capital are valuable within different social contexts. Bourdieu contended that young people are socialized differently depending on their family's class and that they learn class-based tastes, behaviors, and attitudes that distinguish them from people in other classes. As in other examples of socialization, people internalize these lessons, and the associated tastes, behaviors, and attitudes come to seem natural to them. These internalized lessons

SPOTLIGHT on social theory

Symbolic interactionism stresses the role of interpersonal interactions in reproducing culture and social structure. Have you ever been in a situation in which you felt at a disadvantage because you lacked the cultural capital to know what behavior was expected of you?

can help steer young people toward class positions similar to those of their parents. Bourdieu was especially interested in how everyday consumption—our choice of food, music, fashion, and leisure—marked class-based differences.

Bourdieu (1986) notes that cultural capital interacts with economic capital and with **social capital,** *relationships that are potentially economically valuable resulting from membership in a group.* For example, it is not enough to want to sail as a pastime; you need to have the economic capital to pursue such an expensive leisure activity. Similarly, knowing powerful, wealthy, or influential people—having social capital—can assist you in getting into high-status schools, companies, and professions.

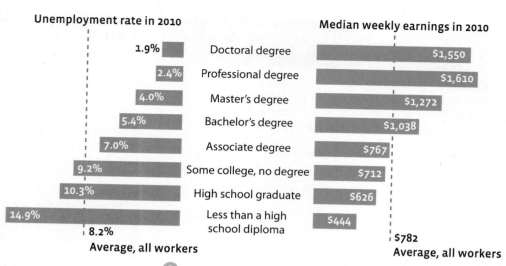

Unemployment rate in 2010

Doctoral degree	1.9%
Professional degree	2.4%
Master's degree	4.0%
Bachelor's degree	5.4%
Associate degree	7.0%
Some college, no degree	9.2%
High school graduate	10.3%
Less than a high school diploma	14.9%

8.2% **Average, all workers**

Median weekly earnings in 2010

Doctoral degree	$1,550
Professional degree	$1,610
Master's degree	$1,272
Bachelor's degree	$1,038
Associate degree	$767
Some college, no degree	$712
High school graduate	$626
Less than a high school diploma	$444

$782 **Average, all workers**

FIGURE 9.6 | UNEMPLOYMENT AND EARNINGS BY EDUCATIONAL ATTAINMENT

Source: Bureau of Labor Statistics (2010b).

Families: Training Children

Applying Bourdieu's framework to the contemporary United States, Annette Lareau (2003) studied the socialization of children in black and white middle-class and working-class families. She found that children of the same social class—regardless of race—have much more in common than children of the same race who belong to different social classes. Lareau speculates that, as the children she studied grow up, race is likely to become a more significant factor.

In her study, Lareau distinguished between two types of childrearing. Parents who practice *concerted cultivation* actively assess their children's skills, interests, and behaviors. They arrange play dates; organize sports; provide music lessons, tutoring, and museum visits; engage children somewhat like "little adults"; and ask their children about their opinions, feelings, and thoughts. This approach to childrearing is especially prominent in middle-class families, regardless of race.

In contrast, working-class families tend to rely on what Lareau calls the *accomplishment of natural growth.* They focus on providing basic necessities and on creating opportunities for children to spend time at home, playing informally with peers, siblings, and other relatives. These parents also maintain a clear distinction between adults and children and are more inclined to tell their children what to do than to reason with them.

Each approach to childrearing offers advantages and disadvantages that, in the end, help to reproduce class inequality. The constant challenges middle-class children face, and the frequent social interactions they encounter with a variety of people, socialize them to interact effectively with people in many different middle-class settings. However, their hectic schedules leave them little time to simply enjoy being with their families. By contrast, working-class children develop more independence and self-reliance, but they experience a more limited range of activities, leaving them less familiar and comfortable with different social settings.

Schools: Individual Mobility and Class Reproduction

One purpose of schools, and higher education in particular, is preparing people for employment. In doing so, schools can provide individuals with a chance at social mobility while, paradoxically, helping to reproduce class inequality for society as whole.

EDUCATION PAYS The role of education in helping individuals to compete for good-paying jobs is well known and well documented. Figure 9.6 shows that higher educational attainment is associated with lower unemployment and higher wages. More variation exists within each category of educational attainment than these average numbers suggest, however. For example, income levels for people with a bachelor's degree vary significantly depending on their major and the type of school from which they graduated. Still, on the whole, the more education you have, the more likely you are to be employed and well paid.

Education can help individuals compete, but it does not change the class structure. As we saw earlier in the chapter, structural factors—including how public schools are funded and the high cost of higher education—create barriers to quality education that contribute to unequal educational outcomes. In addition, schools sort students by class. In high school, middle-class students are steered into college-prep courses emphasizing independent thinking and self-direction, which prepare them to move on to higher education and middle-class

SPOTLIGHT on social theory

How would **functionalist** theory explain the relationship between education and earnings? Do you think this theory adequately explains the levels of income of different people you know?

life. Working-class students are more likely to be channeled into classes that emphasize the importance of following rules and obeying authorities, thereby preparing them for working-class jobs. In this way, although schools serve employers and the capitalist system by providing appropriately trained workers, they help to reproduce class distinctions in society (Bowles and Gintis 1976).

REWARDING CULTURAL CAPITAL Culture also plays a role in how schools reproduce inequality. Schools are generally organized to value the cultural capital of the higher classes and reward students accordingly. Since more affluent students already possess that sort of cultural capital, the academic playing field is tilted in their favor, increasing the odds they will achieve academic success. Working-class students are at a disadvantage when trying to meet the middle-class expectations of the school environment and often feel alienated. As a result, they can rebel, refuse to conform to academic expectations, and inadvertently help recreate their status in the working class (Willis 1977).

Jay MacLeod (1995) studied young, low-income black and white men in Boston, focusing specifically on the role of aspiration in their lives. The youth MacLeod studied related to their schoolwork quite differently based on their differing aspirations. MacLeod found that the young white men he studied had a fairly pessimistic outlook on their future. They saw their schooling as irrelevant and their prospects as lower than those of their parents because of the loss of good-paying working-class jobs. On the other hand, the young black men he studied were more optimistic, because they measured their prospects against the more repressive history of discrimination faced by African Americans in the past. They hoped their efforts in school would pay off, and they expected diligence in the workplace to be rewarded with increased responsibilities, promotions, and pay raises. However, aspiration by itself cannot overcome structural barriers. When MacLeod followed up with these black men seven years later, he found most ended up in dead-end jobs, like their white peers. Most now tempered their belief in the openness of American society but often blamed themselves for their failure.

All of your hard work will soon pay off.

SCHOOLS AND IDEOLOGY When the students MacLeod studied blamed themselves for their failure, they were reflecting another influential role that schools play in reproducing class: ideology. Schools can strengthen class inequality by helping to justify it and by reinforcing the idea that failure results from individual shortcomings, not structural biases.

We are so accustomed to accepting the connection between education and unequal rewards that we rarely see data such as those in Figure 9.6 as unfair. Instead, we usually understand them as a reflection of a generally fair system of meritocracy that rewards those who have ability, work hard, and make smart choices about their chosen field of study. In such an analysis, we tend to ignore the structural and cultural forces that work in favor of students from affluent backgrounds and against students from more modest backgrounds.

Public Policy and Inequality

Beyond the role of culture, economic inequality is caused in part by—and can be reduced through—government social policies. These policies tend to follow two different approaches.

One approach aims to create more *equal outcomes* by reducing the gap between the rich and poor. One way of accomplishing this is to provide everyone with some basic public goods, such as health care and free education, which reduces the impact of income differences. Another way is to raise the floor (raise wages for those in low-income positions) and lower the ceiling (increase taxes on the highest income-earners). This ensures a living wage for those doing necessary but lower-paying work while limiting inequality that results from extremely high incomes. Government intervention of this sort produces less inequality.

The second approach focuses on encouraging *equal opportunity* by creating a more level playing field on which people compete for scarce good jobs. This is usually done by supporting more education as the means to individual mobility, thereby promoting fairer competition. This limits government intervention but results in more inequality.

U.S. society and government policy have mostly favored the equal opportunity approach over the equal outcomes approach, encouraging more education while accepting higher levels of inequality. As a result, the percentage of Americans over age twenty-five with at least a four-year college degree nearly tripled between 1970 and 2009, from about 11 percent to 30 percent (U.S. Census Bureau 2010m), but during the same period economic inequality *increased* significantly. More education for more people did not reduce inequality because it did not change the overall class structure nor did it change the rewards associated with different types of employment. Instead, the United States has more economic inequality than is found in other industrialized nations. Those countries, in contrast, have placed higher value on reducing economic inequality and enacted different economic policies.

To give one example, the United States is the only advanced economy in the world that does not guarantee workers any paid vacation, whereas some countries mandate over thirty days of paid vacation annually (Figure 9.7). Without the protection of federal mandates, U.S. workers in the private sector must rely on individual employers to provide paid vacations and holidays. As a result, nearly one out of four workers gets no paid vacation time at all. Private-sector employees get an average of nine paid vacation days a year—less than half the number mandated in most other wealthy countries—and six paid holidays, also less than in most other wealthy countries (Ray and Schmitt 2007).

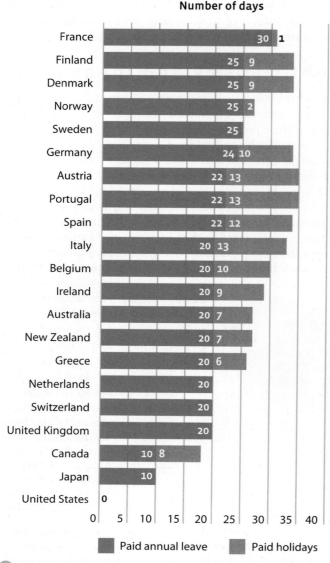

Number of days

Country	Paid annual leave	Paid holidays
France	30	1
Finland	25	9
Denmark	25	9
Norway	25	2
Sweden	25	
Germany	24	10
Austria	22	13
Portugal	22	13
Spain	22	12
Italy	20	13
Belgium	20	10
Ireland	20	9
Australia	20	7
New Zealand	20	7
Greece	20	6
Netherlands	20	
Switzerland	20	
United Kingdom	20	
Canada	10	8
Japan	10	
United States	0	

■ Paid annual leave ■ Paid holidays

FIGURE 9.7 | MANDATED PAID VACATION DAYS AND HOLIDAYS IN TWENTY DEVELOPED COUNTRIES

The United States is the only developed country that does not mandate a minimum number of paid vacation days and holidays for its workers. *Source:* Ray and Schmitt (2007).

WAGES AND LABOR LAWS Raising the wage floor helps to reduce inequality, and the most direct way to raise low-income wages is to legislate a minimum wage. Because the federal minimum wage is not adjusted for inflation, its real value has fluctuated since it was first implemented in 1938. It peaked at $8.71 in 1968 (in 2009 dollars), was allowed to reach a nearly sixty-year low by 2007, and was increased to $7.25 an hour by 2009 (Shierholz 2009). Given the relatively low federal minimum wage, some states implement their own, higher, minimum.

Labor laws that enable workers to form unions without fear of being fired can also help ensure higher wages and better benefits. Union members in the United States earn, on average, about 14 percent more in wages than nonunion workers (after controlling for experience, education, region, industry, occupation, and marital status). Measured against comparable nonunion workers, the rate of union members with health insurance is 28 percent higher; the rate with pensions is 54 percent higher; and union members enjoy 26 percent more vacation time (Mishel, Bernstein, and Shierholz 2009).

Current labor laws make it very difficult for workers to join a union, while making it relatively safe for private employers to try to get rid of unions ("union busting") or to prevent workers from forming them (Compa 2004; Levitt 1993; Logan 2006; Mehta and Theodore 2005). In 2010, only 6.9 percent of private-sector workers belonged to a union. Public-sector (government) employees have been less likely to face union-busting tactics and are five times as likely (36.2 percent) as private-sector workers to belong to a union (U.S. Bureau of Labor Statistics 2011a). In recent years, though, some state legislatures—typically citing budgetary concerns—have curtailed or eliminated the rights of public-sector unions to bargain collectively. This trend, illustrated dramatically by a lengthy conflict in Wisconsin in 2011, expanded to the public sector the attack on unions that had long characterized the private sector. Polls, however, indicate greater disapproval than approval of these attempts to curtail public-sector unions (Keeter 2011). Partly as a consequence of the low rate of unionization in the United States, many U.S. workers have relatively low wages and benefits compared to workers in other industrialized countries. (The Sociology Matters box examines how sociologists have studied the challenges facing workers' organizing efforts.)

TAXES If the minimum wage raises the floor to reduce inequality, then imposing higher taxes on the wealthy lowers the ceiling. But compared to a half-century ago, the wealthy today enjoy substantially lower taxes whereas taxes on middle-income families are higher than they were (Johnston 2003, 2007). In a system of **progressive taxation,** *those with higher incomes pay a higher tax rate.* Throughout the 1950s the U.S. federal tax rate on personal income beyond the first $400,000 for married couples filing jointly was more than 90 percent (Figure 9.8)—a highly progressive rate aimed at limiting the extremes of income inequality. However, that rate was slashed in the 1980s and today it stands at 35 percent. The tax rate on capital gains—income earned from investments mainly by those in the highest income brackets—has similarly been cut by more than half since the mid-1970s. In contrast, the top tax rate for median family incomes rose substantially in the late 1960s and 1970s, and although it dropped again in the 1980s, it remains higher today than it was in 1955 (Tax Policy Center 2011a).

Well-known billionaire investor Warren Buffett has criticized this system, noting that because capital gains are taxed at a lower rate than wages, the tax rate on his income is nearly half that of his secretary (Bawden 2007). In late 2010, he argued that taxes should be cut for most Americans, "But I think that people at the high end—people like myself—should be paying a lot more in taxes. We have it better than we've ever had it" (Ovide 2010).

American workers pay more in taxes than they used to in part because corporations pay less. One congressional study found that, by taking advantage of tax loopholes, nearly two-thirds of

Why David Sometimes Wins: Organizing Workers

Workers in the United States face an uphill battle in organizing. On paper, they have the right to join a labor union to pursue good wages, benefits, and working conditions. In reality, though, labor laws are stacked against them while giving employers an unfair advantage, according to the international human rights group Human Rights Watch (Compa 2004). For example, employers can legally launch aggressive pressure campaigns against employees attempting to organize, including holding mandatory meetings at which workers are often threatened with dire consequences if they join a union. Employers are even allowed to permanently replace workers who strike over wages and working conditions. Employers also often illegally fire workers who try to organize a union, exploiting a slow and ineffectual legal process that can tie up worker complaints about labor law violations for months or even years, reaching resolutions long after a union election is held (Compa 2004).

Such laws and procedures contribute to a relatively weak labor union movement in the United States compared to many other industrialized countries. Union weakness is a factor that contributes to higher poverty rates and greater economic inequality, and is one of the key reasons why many U.S. workers do not have the sorts of wages and benefits that workers in other nations enjoy.

Sociologists have been studying the organizing efforts of workers and identifying their most effective organizing strategies. For example, Jennifer Chun (2009) showed how low-wage service workers in both the United States and Korea have gained wide community support by focusing on broad and culturally resonant issues of social justice rather than on narrow workplace disputes. After studying California organizing campaigns in the janitorial services, residential construction, railroad transportation, and apparel industries, Ruth Milkman (2006) found that, contrary to conventional wisdom, organizing campaigns were more likely to fail from inadequate funds than from employer opposition and were more likely to be successful if run in a "top-down" fashion by labor leaders (rather than from below by rank-and-file workers). She also found that immigrant workers were sometimes more effective at organizing than native workers because they have a stronger sense of group solidarity resulting, in part, from their experience with labor and political struggles in their native countries. Moon-Kie Jung (2006), who analyzed the efforts of Hawaii's agricultural workers to organize over a fifty-year period, found that by explicitly embracing diversity—even reserving certain union positions for representatives from different racial and ethnic groups—workers successfully countered employers' efforts to keep them divided along ethnic lines by repeatedly bringing in new workers from different countries.

Sociologist Marshall Ganz draws on his own experience as a labor organizer in his work in labor studies. In the 1960s, Ganz dropped out of college to work with the United Farm Workers, best known for its charismatic leader Cesar Chavez. Ganz eventually became the union's head of organizing, helping direct one of the most famous labor struggles in U.S. history. He later returned to school, got a Ph.D. in sociology and began teaching at Harvard University about organizing and leadership strategies. In 2008, Barack Obama's presidential campaign tapped his expertise, making him a key advisor for the training of the campaign's field organizers.

In 2009, Ganz wrote *Why David Sometimes Wins*, a sociological analysis of his experiences with the United Farm Workers whose title invokes the biblical struggle of an underdog against a giant. Ganz (2009) argues that the success of the farm workers developed from diverse leadership teams—in terms of factors such as ethnicity and gender—with ties to different social networks. They built the union's strategic capacity—doing the most with what resources they had—through an ongoing process of experimentation, learning, and adaptation that involved taking risks, evaluating results, and implementing changes in strategy. In this way, ordinary workers built an organizational structure that had the power to influence employers with much greater resources. When such strategies were later abandoned, he argues, the union's effectiveness declined.

The odds are still stacked against workers, but such nuanced sociological studies have provided organizers with a range of insights to improve the effectiveness of their work. Some sociologists argue that a revitalized and more effective labor movement is essential to reducing economic inequality (Clawson 2003).

think about it

1. *What role do culture, structure, and power play in these sociological analyses of union organizing?*

2. *How might a stronger labor movement in the United States affect political decision-making, as well as the conditions of workers?*

U.S. companies and 68 percent of foreign companies pay no income tax at all (Government Accountability Office 2008). For example, forty-six of the biggest U.S. corporations paid no income tax in 2003, including Walt Disney, Reebok, Time Warner, Marriott International, AT&T, and Boeing (McIntyre and Nguyen 2004). The government has made up the difference by increasing the payroll taxes on workers (also known as FICA—Federal Insurance Contributions Act), which pay for Medicare and Social Security. Payroll taxes are a form of **regressive taxation** since they *disproportionately affect those with lower incomes.* For example, as of 2010, federal law exempted income above $106,800 per year from the Social Security payroll tax.

Taxing the inheritance of large estates has traditionally been another way to help reduce the concentration of wealth. When the first-ever U.S. billionaire, oil tycoon John D. Rockefeller, died in 1937, his children paid a 70 percent estate tax on most of his fortune they inherited, leaving them and their offspring with enough money to remain among the nation's wealthiest

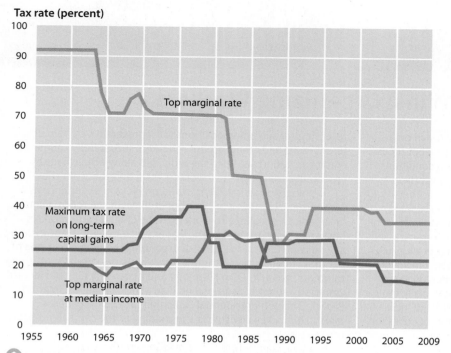

Tax rate (percent)

Top marginal rate

Maximum tax rate on long-term capital gains

Top marginal rate at median income

FIGURE 9.8 | FEDERAL TAX RATES, 1955–2009

Source: Tax Policy Center.

people to this day. The situation was different when oil industry billionaire Dan Duncan died in 2010. This time, because of dramatic changes in U.S. tax policy, Duncan's four children inherited his $9 billion fortune tax-free, making Duncan the first billionaire ever to pass on his estate without paying a single dollar in estate taxes (Collins and Pizzigati 2010).

PUBLIC ASSISTANCE   Public policy also affects economic inequality through the administration of public assistance programs. **Public assistance** *includes either tax credits or actual payments and benefits provided to citizens by the government.* Welfare for the poor is the best-known form of public assistance. It includes cash payments, food stamps, childcare, and housing subsidies. Since major welfare reform took effect in the mid-1990s, the focus of welfare benefits has shifted from direct cash payments to programs that promote work, such as job training and childcare.

Contrary to popular perception, however, most public assistance goes to people in the middle and working classes—not the poor. If you are attending a state college or university, for example, you are benefiting from public assistance, because the cost of your education is subsidized by taxpayers. Perhaps the most important form of middle-class public assistance is the home mortgage tax deduction, which allows homeowners to deduct the interest on a loan of up to $1 million used to purchase or improve a home; the larger the price tag on the home, the larger the government tax break. Consequently, about 80 percent of

home mortgage tax benefits go to the top 20 percent of households in terms of income. In 2008 the mortgage interest tax deduction program cost the federal government about $100 billion, three times the amount spent on all public housing and low-income housing subsidies combined (Blau and Abramowitz 2007; Timiraos 2009).

The public assistance provided to corporations, sometimes referred to as "corporate welfare," is also many times more generous than the assistance given to the poor. Corporations—and indirectly the shareholders who own them—receive billions in this kind of assistance in the form of direct subsidies and tax breaks and the free or low-cost use of public resources such as forests. For example, in 2006 the federal government paid $21 billion in direct subsidies to agricultural concerns—many of which are large, profitable agribusiness corporations. Of that money, 66 percent went to the richest 10 percent of recipients (Slivinski 2007). States and localities, too, often compete to attract businesses by slashing taxes, paying for infrastructure, subsidizing utilities, and providing other incentives, all at taxpayer expense. In 2008 and 2009 the federal government spent hundreds of billions of dollars bailing out large banks after they teetered on the brink of collapse, largely due to irresponsible lending practices, threatening the broader economy. Though some of these loans were repaid, the bailouts cost taxpayers many billions of dollars and were the biggest example of corporate welfare in U.S. history (Kiel 2011; SourceWatch 2010).

The use of public resources to aid the middle and upper classes is the outcome of a political process. Those with the most political power write the rules, and they tend to write them for their own benefit. As we will see, political power also plays a role in global inequality.

Power and Global Inequality

In 2010, as its stock price surged, Apple surpassed Microsoft for the first time as the world's most valuable high-tech company, likely bringing smiles to the faces of its investors (Helft and Vance 2010). But in China, workers who assemble many Apple products, including the popular iPhone and iPad, were not celebrating the good news. Instead, ten of them committed suicide in the first five months of the year, most by jumping off the balconies of company-built dormitories next to their mas-

thinking about power

How do the social policies that the government enacts, such as tax policy, reflect the relative **power** of different segments of society?

MAP 9.1 | A GLOBAL VIEW OF PER-CAPITA INCOME LEVELS

This map is based on 2008 per-capita income (average income per person). Per-capita income in low-income countries is $975 per year or less; in lower-middle-income countries, $976–$3,855; in upper-middle-income countries, $3,856–$11,905; and in high-income countries, $11,906 or more. *Source:* The World Bank

CORE CONCEPTS CHALLENGE

What does this map suggest about the relationship between a nation's wealth and its global political **power?** *How might a nation's wealth influence its power? How might its political and military power influence its wealth?*

sive factory complex in Shenzhen (BBC 2010a, 2010b). The workers were employed by Taiwan-based Foxconn Technology, the world's largest assembler of computers and handheld electronic devices, which contracts with Apple and other high-tech companies. Foxconn employees work six days a week for entry-level pay of $132 a month. They typically put in ten- to twelve-hour workdays and are routinely expected to work overtime. They are forbidden to talk during their shifts and are subjected to what workers refer to as military-style discipline, leading one worker to tell reporters, "It's like a prison." Yet Foxconn is considered to be one of the better places to work. Conditions in many other Chinese factories are much worse.

The rash of suicides attracted embarrassing media coverage until government authorities ordered the Chinese press to tone down its coverage. After the Western media picked up the story and companies that contract with Foxconn expressed concern, the company instituted a 20 percent pay raise to improve morale and installed nets around its dormitories to foil suicide attempts.

Similar tales of bleak working conditions lurk behind many of the consumer electronics and other brand-name goods that dominate today's global economy. The economic inequality

that we have explored in the United States has parallels in other countries, and inequality *within* individual countries exists side-by-side with **global inequality,** *the differences in wealth and power among the countries of the world.* The economic systems of individual countries are increasingly interconnected, and to understand economic inequality in any one country, including the United States, we must consider that country's place in the global economic structure.

Categorizing National Economies

Researchers and others commonly use the terms *developed, developing,* and *underdeveloped* to summarize a country's level of industrial and technological development. A country at a higher level of development generally produces more goods. As a result, its people have a higher material standard of living than those in less-developed countries.

Analysts sometimes use more nuanced categorizations of national economies. For example, Map 9.1 sorts the world's countries into four income levels, according to an analysis by

Power and Global Inequality

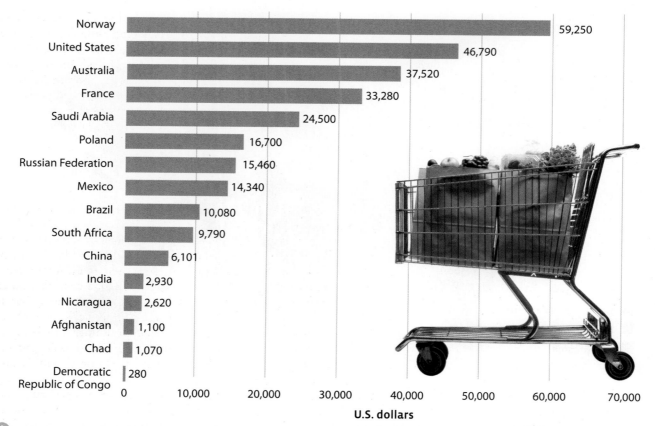

FIGURE 9.9 | PER-CAPITA PURCHASING POWER IN U.S. DOLLARS FOR SELECTED COUNTRIES, 2008

This graph illustrates, on average, how much a person from each country could purchase in a year in 2008. Data are in 2010 U.S. dollars and take into account the relative cost of goods and services in different countries. *Source:* The World Bank, World Development Indicators.

the World Bank. Widespread poverty in much of Africa and southern Asia make these among the poorest places on Earth, whereas the United States, Canada, the nations of Europe, Japan, and Australia are among the world's wealthiest countries.

We can get a more concrete idea of what high and low incomes mean on a global scale by considering *purchasing power,* the average value of the goods and services people in a country can purchase in a year. As Figure 9.9 shows, purchasing power ranges from nearly $60,000 per person per year in Norway to just $280 in the Democratic Republic of the Congo.

The global distribution of income is extremely unequal (see Figure 9.10):

■ The average income of the top 20 percent of the world's population—which includes nearly all U.S. citizens—is about *fifty times* the average income of the bottom 20 percent.

■ More than 50 percent of the world's income goes to the richest 10 percent of the world's population, and nearly 75 percent goes to the richest 20 percent.

■ Just 1.5 percent of the world's income goes to the poorest 20 percent of the population, and only 5 percent goes to

the poorest 40 percent—roughly 2.5 billion people—who live on less than $2 a day.

■ The world's 500 richest *individuals* have a combined income greater than the world's poorest 416 *million* people (UN Development Programme 2005).

The Impact of Global Inequality

As we saw earlier in this chapter, your class status within the United States has implications for your health, education, and lifestyle. Similarly, a country's income level typically corresponds to a variety of social indicators, resulting in starkly unequal social conditions around the world:

■ *Life expectancy and health.* Poverty kills. On average, life expectancy for people in the world's poorest nations is about thirty years less than it is for people in wealthy nations. Poor countries have high rates of infant mortality, and people die at an early age from malnourishment, pneumonia, malaria, diarrhea, and HIV/AIDS. Around 10 million children under age five die each year of under-

CHAPTER 9   Class and Global Inequality

242

World income distributed by population quintiles, 2007

Richest 20%	82.8% of income
Second 20%	9.9 % of income
Middle 20%	4.2% of income
Fourth 20%	2.1% of income
Poorest 20%	1.0% of income

FIGURE 9.10 | GLOBAL INCOME DISTRIBUTION

Source: Ortiz and Cummins (2011).

nutrition and related causes; these comprise 30 percent of all childhood deaths (Commission on Social Determinants of Health 2008; World Health Organization 2004).

■ *Housing.* About a third of the world's urban population—more than a billion people—live in slums—housing that lacks durability, sufficient living area, access to clean water and sanitation, and secure occupancy rights (UN Human Settlements Programme 2003a, 2003b). The rural poor in developing nations migrate to urban areas for jobs and schooling, often only to find grinding poverty and disease amidst vast city slums.

■ *Education.* Most people in many poor countries are illiterate. Adult literacy rates in Afghanistan (18 percent), Mali (26 percent), and Niger (29 percent)—among the world's lowest—reflect the deep poverty of such countries, where schooling is often not free and children must work from a very early age (World Bank 2011).

Over the past half-century, the number of people living in absolute poverty has decreased, largely due to the dramatic economic growth in China and India, which together account for about 40 percent of the world's population. However, in other parts of the world, particularly sub-Saharan Africa, poverty persists, and the number of people living in poverty has increased significantly (United Nations 2005).

These global changes have had a direct impact on the United States. Because China and other countries with growing economies use more resources, oil and food prices have increased worldwide. The shift of manufacturing to developing nations has reduced employment in U.S. factories, while contributing to a massive trade deficit as the United States imports more foreign goods. In addition, poverty, despair, and inequality contribute to instability and conflict in various parts of the world, situations that have in some cases led to the involvement of U.S. military troops.

Inequality Within Countries

Inequality exists in every country, produced in part by the kinds of public policy decisions we discussed earlier in this chapter. Map 9.2 illustrates the varying levels of income inequality around the world. The highest levels are found in Central and South America and southern Africa. In these areas, a small elite controls limited resources, while most people live in poverty. In many highly unequal countries, the ruling and business elites use agreements with foreign corporations and governments to maintain their wealth and power at the expense of the nation's poor and working classes. In this way, inequality within nations is connected to global inequality.

Wealthy nations such as France and Sweden generally have comparatively low levels of economic inequality because of high taxes on the wealthy, generous minimum wages, and other policies that reduce inequality. The exception is the United States, the most unequal wealthy country in the world. In societies with the least amount of inequality, moderate and low-income groups tend to have much more power than they do in the United States. Compared to U.S. citizens, people in countries such as Norway and Canada are more likely to be organized into labor unions, to vote, and to have the option of voting for a political party that represents labor or the working class. In many respects, therefore, the nature and extent of inequality depends on the balance of power in a society.

Explaining Global Inequality

Global inequality has many causes. For example, different countries have different climates and different amounts of natural resources, both of which undoubtedly contribute to their degree of affluence or poverty. In addition, most sociologists acknowledge two major *social* causes of global inequality: culture and power.

MAP 9.2 | WITHIN-COUNTRY INCOME INEQUALITY

This map shows the degree of economic inequality within each country, based on family income. *Source:* www.siteatlas.com

Culture and Global Inequality: Modernization Theory

Through most of human history, people possessed relatively few material goods, so economic inequality was limited. However, as we saw in Chapter 1, industrialization transformed northern European societies, both destroying traditional ways of life and creating unprecedented material abundance. However, not all countries experienced this change. **Modernization theory** *attributes global inequality to cultural differences between countries.* According to this theory, some societies resisted industrialization, preferring to retain traditional ways of life rather than adopt disruptive new technologies. Maintaining family and community relationships, the agricultural economy, and traditional religious beliefs were more important than adopting new means to produce greater material abundance. The result was a growing economic gap between industrialized nations and the developing world that was rooted in these different cultural values and orientations.

Power and Global Inequality: Dependency Theory

Many sociologists argue that today's global inequality is rooted in a much less benign process than cultural differences. Their alternative, **dependency theory,** *attributes global inequality to the exploitation of weaker, poor nations by wealthy, more powerful ones.* This theory locates the origin of growing global inequality in the increased exploration, travel, and trade that began

roughly 500 years ago—long before industrialization. As European explorers ventured to Africa, the Western Hemisphere, and East Asia, they clashed with indigenous peoples, subjugated them, established colonies, and gained control of their natural resources and labor. Rather than voluntarily opting out of development, poor countries were prevented from developing by powerful colonizers who became wealthy by exploiting their natural resources and cheap labor. Typically, colonial powers would import raw materials from colonies and turn them into valuable manufactured goods. With slavery, colonial powers took West Africans to labor in American plantations, enriching the colonial nations while impoverishing the colonies.

Colonialism and Neocolonialism

In the modern era, roughly since 1500, the fates of nations have been deeply intertwined in global struggles over resources. The most obvious type of global struggle was **colonialism,** *the use of military, political, and economic power by one society to dominate the people of another society, usually for economic benefit.* From the 1500s through the 1900s, European powers used their military might to subjugate other peoples across the globe. According to a famous saying, the sun never set on the British

Empire because its colonial holdings were spread out across the world. The use of the English language in many parts of the world today is, in part, a legacy of this colonial subjugation. Africa, India, North America, much of South America, and other areas of the world were all conquered by colonial powers.

Colonial powers typically exerted direct political control over their colonies or established puppet governments while engaging in military occupation and establishing cultural dominance. Most important, colonial powers usually sought to extract the natural resources from their colonies and exploit the labor available there.

Most colonies resisted their colonial occupiers. By the latter half of the twentieth century, independence movements had successfully lifted the military yoke of colonial rule. However, these new nations often struggled to overcome their colonial past, which had stripped them of vast resources, left them ill prepared to develop modern economic systems, and often institutionalized a culture of political corruption. Some observers argue that colonialism has been replaced by **neocolonialism,** *a system of economic domination of poorer nations by wealthier ones without formal political control or military occupation.* In a neocolonial situation, former colonies continue to depend on wealthier nations for capital investment and technical expertise, giving these wealthier countries enormous influence over their development. In addition, former colonies often experience civil wars and political infighting as different factions struggle for control of resources, adding yet another hurdle to economic development (United Nations 2005).

World Systems Analysis

Another approach to global inequality, **world systems analysis** *focuses on the interdependence among the countries in a single global economic system.* Sociologist Immanual Wallerstein (1974, 1979) sees the poverty of some countries as connected directly to the wealth of others. He sorts countries into one of three primary groups, depending on their relationship to the global economy:

- ■ *Core nations* include the United States, Canada, Japan, and the European countries. These, the world's wealthiest countries, are at the center of the global economy. Most core nations benefited from colonialism and continue to dominate the global economy through multinational corporations and global financial institutions.
- ■ *Periphery nations* include many countries in Africa, Latin America, and parts of Asia. These are the world's poorest and least powerful countries, at the fringe of the global economy. They participate in the global economy by providing natural resources and cheap labor for the transnational corporations while also serving as markets for some goods.

- ■ *Semi-periphery nations* include China, India, Mexico, and Pakistan. These middle-income nations are better integrated with the economies of core countries than are the periphery nations and often have a stronger domestic industrial base.

With modern communications and transportation, capital from core nations can move easily around the globe. Poorer countries are often dependent on this foreign investment to fund their economic development. They frequently compete against one another to attract foreign investment by offering low or no taxes, minimal environmental regulations, and a low-cost, nonunion labor force.

Typically based in core nations, multinational corporations look to cut costs and boost profits by shifting production to semi-periphery nations. This allows them to take advantage of low-wage labor and lax environmental regulation and to avoid paying some taxes in core nations. In doing so, they create jobs and stimulate the local economies in these poor countries.

This local economic development is often temporary, however. For example, in the 1990s—especially after the passage of the North American Free Trade Agreement (NAFTA)—some U.S. corporations moved manufacturing jobs to Mexico, which helped devastate some "rust belt" communities in the United States but helped Mexican workers, whose average manufacturing wage rose to $2.08 an hour. But these gains were short lived: many companies soon began the process over again by moving production to China, where manufacturing workers were earning an average of just 61 cents an hour (Ferriss 2003).

This is an example of the *race to the bottom,* the process of poorer nations competing for foreign investment by sacrificing wages, tax revenue, worker safety, and environmental standards. The race to the bottom can keep periphery and semi-periphery nations poor while channeling profits back to investors in core countries. If workers in these poor countries organize into unions to improve their conditions—as workers once did in wealthier nations—or if national governments insist on high-quality environmental standards, corporate investors can simply move to a new country that offers more favorable incentives. The existing rules for the global economy—rules that favor the free flow of capital—are coordinated through the world's global financial institutions.

Global Financial Institutions

In recent decades, global financial organizations have had an enormous influence on the economic and social policies of poor countries (Kaplinsky 2007). The three major players in global finance are the World Bank, which provides poor countries with investments and loans for development; the

International Monetary Fund (IMF), which provides financial and technical assistance to promote economic growth; and the World Trade Organization, which administers trade practices between countries. Although all three organizations ostensibly aim to promote development in and provide aid to poorer nations, many critics contend that they are key vehicles through which core nations and multinational corporations dominate poorer countries.

For example, critics contend that the conditions the World Bank sets for loans—known as *structural adjustment programs*—actually benefit foreign investors rather than the poor countries and in fact lead to increased poverty. In some cases, to receive assistance from the World Bank and IMF, countries have been required to shift from producing essential food crops for do-mestic use, such as corn and beans, to cash crops intended for export, such as coffee and cotton, thereby worsening hunger locally. These organizations have also insisted that governments slash vital social service spending in order to repay foreign loans, sometimes with disastrous results for the health and education of the local population.

In recent years, activists from around the world have organized to promote basic labor and environmental standards and to advocate debt forgiveness. Activists have used education, the promotion of "fair trade" goods whose production meets basic labor and environmental standards, and street protests at the meetings of global financial institutions to advance their cause. Their advocacy has led to more public scrutiny of these institutions as well as some reforms (Stiglitz and Charlton 2007).

In Transition

U.S. INEQUALITY IN GLOBAL CONTEXT

Economic inequality in the United States has long been closely connected to the global economy, and this close relationship has produced starkly different results in two recent periods. From 1945 to 1975, the U.S. economy experienced enormous growth. The economic infrastructure of most industrialized countries had been damaged or destroyed by World War II. With virtually no competition, U.S. manufacturers dominated much of the global marketplace. Plenty of well-paid working-class jobs were available in automobile plants, the steel industry, and other types of manufacturing. Strong labor unions fought for better working conditions and wages, and the benefits of this economic growth were spread across all income levels (see Figure 9.11).

By the 1970s, though, global economic conditions had changed. U.S. companies failed to invest adequately in newer technologies such as smaller, more fuel-efficient automobiles and were caught off-guard by newly emerging global competition. To stay competitive, corporations based in the United States began exporting many of the high-paying manufacturing jobs that had provided economic security for

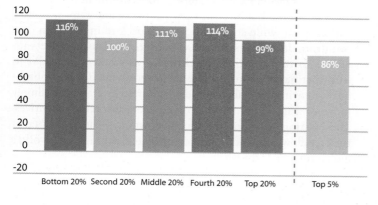

Change in real family income 1947–1979

- Bottom 20%: 116%
- Second 20%: 100%
- Middle 20%: 111%
- Fourth 20%: 114%
- Top 20%: 99%
- Top 5%: 86%

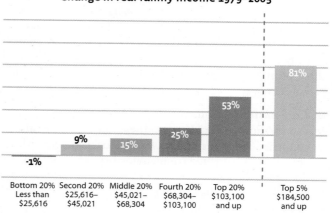

Change in real family income 1979–2005

- Bottom 20% (Less than $25,616): -1%
- Second 20% ($25,616–$45,021): 9%
- Middle 20% ($45,021–$68,304): 15%
- Fourth 20% ($68,304–$103,100): 25%
- Top 20% ($103,100 and up): 53%
- Top 5% ($184,500 and up): 81%

FIGURE 9.11 | CHANGE IN REAL FAMILY INCOME, 1947–1979 AND 1979–2005

In the decades after World War II, the benefits of economic growth were spread evenly, and families at all income levels enjoyed significant increases in their income. In recent decades, however, those with already high incomes have seen the biggest gains; most people have experienced more modest gains or no gains at all. *Sources:* Economic Policy Institute (1994); U.S. Census Bureau, Income, Table F-3.

working- and middle-class Americans to poor nations that offered lower wages, fewer labor and environmental regulations, and, often, repressive governments that maintained political stability and made labor organizing difficult or impossible. The result was **deindustrialization,** *the process by which investment in the nation's manufacturing capacity decreased,* devastating the economies of many communities, especially in the midwest and northeast. The export of good-paying, working-class jobs often left middle-income workers scrambling for jobs with lower wages, while increased corporate profits translated into higher incomes for affluent stockholders. The result was increased inequality.

The economy continued to grow, but now, as Figure 9.11 shows, the benefits went disproportionately to those already making higher incomes. From 1979 to 2005, the income growth of the richest people remained high, while people at lower income levels had much lower growth or none at all. Working-class and lower-middle-class workers have actually fared worse than Figure 9.11 suggests, because in the past few decades more families have become two-income households. In a historic shift in family structure, both husband and wife in most families today work outside the home to improve, or just maintain, their standard of living (Levy

1998). In the future—especially in the wake of the most recent financial crisis—many families will probably see their incomes decrease.

What all this means is that the gap between rich and poor has expanded significantly, and income inequality in the United States today is greater than at any time since the Great Depression of the 1930s. This growing inequality has a profound effect both on family structure and on social structure as a whole. For example, because of stagnant wages, parents in many families work longer hours or take on a second job; as a result, they have less time to care for their children, volunteer in their communities, or become politically active. As employer-provided benefits have declined, millions of Americans have found themselves without health insurance, leading to some reform of the system in 2010. During this period of increasing inequality, many families have also taken on a growing amount of personal debt. This trend, as well as a decline in personal savings, contributed to the economic crisis that began in 2008. This latest crisis is still reverberating around the globe, and its impact on the global economy will influence both U.S. and global inequality for years to come.

THINKING SOCIOLOGICALLY ABOUT . . .

Class and Global Inequality

culture

■ Class is not just about money: it includes a major cultural component that is passed on through socialization, especially through the family and schools.

■ Different societies have different cultural values that place more or less emphasis on limiting economic inequality.

structure

■ Individual action is important in determining your class position, but it always takes place within a structural context that shapes the options available to you.

■ The structure of the global economy helps to shape the opportunities and living conditions of people around the globe.

power

■ Because of their different levels of material and cultural resources, people from different classes have different levels of power in society.

■ Wealthy, industrialized nations have considerably more power than poor or developing countries. Multinational corporations based in wealthy countries, along with global financial institutions, have considerable power to influence the global economy.

Looking Back

1. Class is a system of stratification involving both economic and cultural resources. Marx explored class based on the relationship workers had to the means of production, whereas Weber emphasized people's life chances. Functionalists argued that economic stratification makes a useful contribution to the social order.

2. The U.S. class system includes the capitalist (upper) class, middle class, working class, and underclass. Considerable income inequality exists in the United States, and wealth is even more heavily concentrated at the top.

3. Class systems accommodate mobility; however, the class a person's family belongs to heavily influences the class to which he or she will belong as an adult. The impact of class on daily life can be seen in health, education, work, politics, and lifestyle.

4. Poverty can be defined in either absolute or relative terms. After declining sharply in the 1960s, U.S. poverty rates have remained relatively stable.

5. In the United States, class inequality is supported by an accompanying ideology that emphasizes equal opportunity, merit, and individual effort.

6. Class must be reproduced from generation to generation. Each class possesses cultural capital, which families and schools play an important role in reproducing.

7. Global inequality refers to the differences in wealth and power among countries. These differences affect health and life expectancy, housing, education, and many other conditions of daily life. Public policy influences the degree of within-country inequality found in different nations.

8. Modernization theory suggests that the vast gap between rich and poor nations is the result of cultural differences. Dependency theory explains global inequality by focusing on colonialism and neocolonialism. World systems analysis highlights the interdependence among countries, showing how domination of poorer countries by wealthy ones continues today. Some critics argue that this domination is achieved, in part, through global financial institutions.

9. The United States enjoyed economic domination in the post–World War II years, the benefits of which were spread evenly across people at all income levels. Since the 1970s, however, economic inequality has grown in the United States as the benefits of a more competitive global economy have gone disproportionately to those with higher incomes.

Critical Thinking: Questions and Activities

1. What is your family's class? In what ways has class helped to shape your life? What privileges, if any, did you enjoy because of your family's class position? What barriers, if any, did you face? Were you taught some version of the ideas of equal opportunity, meritocracy, and individualism? What is the relationship between your family's class position and the ideology you learned?

2. Are you a first-generation college student? If so, has the experience exposed any class issues for you and your family? (Do you recognize some of the issues Alfred Lubrano raises in the opening of this chapter?) If not, what aspect of your family's cultural capital were you able to draw on in planning for and attending college?

3. Given what you now know, how would you explain why people are rich or poor? How do human action and structural forces figure in your explanations?

4. Do you think economic globalization has, on balance, been a positive development or a negative one? Explain.

5. The Walton family, of Walmart fame, has inherited a vast fortune generated from selling low-priced consumer goods to low-wage workers. Most of these products are manufactured abroad. Apply your understanding of deindustrialization and the global economy to explain the dramatic success of Walmart and stores like it.

Key Terms

absolute poverty (p. 233) a scarcity of resources so severe that it is life-threatening.

capital (p. 222) money to invest in factories, real estate, and other businesses.

capitalist class (p. 222) (or bourgeoisie), those who control major capital and own the means of production.

class (p. 221) a group of people who share a roughly similar economic position and lifestyle.

class mobility (p. 228) the ability to move from one social class to another.

classism (p. 232) prejudice or discrimination based on social class.

colonialism (p. 244) the use of military, political, and economic power by one society to dominate the people of another society, usually for economic benefit.

conspicuous consumption (p. 232) lavish spending, done to compete for status with others.

cultural capital (p. 235) various types of knowledge, skills, and other cultural resources.

deindustrialization (p. 247) the process by which investment in the nation's manufacturing capacity decreased.

dependency theory (p. 244) a theory that attributes global inequality to the exploitation of weaker, poor nations by wealthy, more powerful ones.

equal opportunity (p. 234) the idea that all people should have the same chance to achieve success.

feminization of poverty (p. 234) a trend in which women made up an increasingly large share of the poor.

global inequality (p. 241) the differences in wealth and power among the countries of the world.

income (p. 225) money received from sources such as wages, interest on savings, and dividends from stocks and bonds.

individual mobility (p. 229) a change in a person's class position that occurs without any change in the larger class structure.

individualism (p. 234) a system of beliefs that highlights the importance of the single person over any social group.

life chances (p. 223) the likelihood a person has of obtaining valued economic and cultural resources.

meritocracy (p. 234) the notion that people are rewarded and are able to advance because of their abilities.

middle class (p. 226) a group that is distinctive for its contribution of specialized knowledge and expertise to the economy.

modernization theory (p. 244) a theory that attributes global inequality to cultural differences between countries.

neocolonialism (p. 245) a system of economic domination of poorer nations by wealthier ones without the use of formal political control or military occupation.

poverty line (U.S.) (p. 233) a measure of scarcity determined by figuring the cost of a minimal food budget and multiplying it by three.

poverty rate (p. 233) the percentage of the population that falls below the poverty line.

progressive taxation (p. 238) tax policy in which those with higher incomes pay a higher rate.

public assistance (p. 240) either tax credits or actual payments and benefits provided to citizens by the government.

regressive taxation (p. 239) taxes that disproportionately affect those with lower incomes.

relative poverty (p. 233) situation that exists when people do not have the basic resources to maintain a standard of living considered acceptable in their society.

social capital (p. 236) relationships that are potentially economically valuable resulting from membership in a group.

structural mobility (p. 228) a change in class position that occurs when a shift in available occupations changes the class system as a whole.

underclass (p. 226) chronically unemployed people who have no ongoing relationship to the mainstream economy.

wealth (p. 225) financial assets, such as savings, real estate, and stocks.

working class (p. 222) (or proletariat), those who survive on the wages they earn.

world systems analysis (p. 245) an approach that focuses on the interdependence among the countries that make up a single global economic system.

Race and Ethnicity

looking **AHEAD**

How does culture define your race?

How do individuals and institutional structures perpetuate racial and ethnic inequality?

How do majority and minority groups reflect inequalities in power?

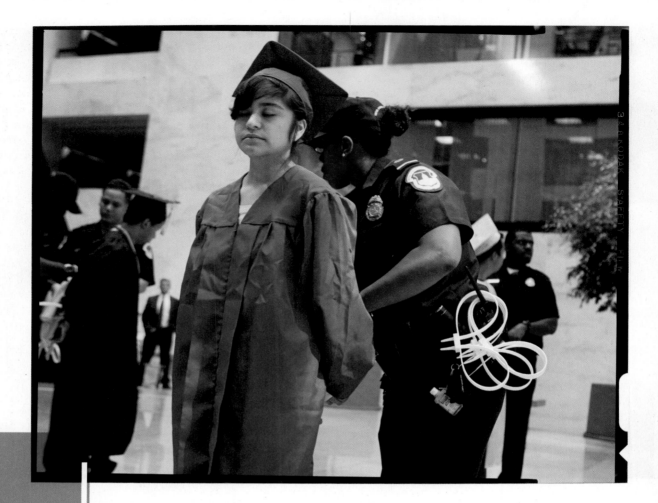

In the summer of 2010, Diana Martinez, an eighteen-year-old student and the Mexican-born daughter of undocumented immigrants, stood quietly in a cap and gown—symbolizing her academic status—while a Washington, D.C., police officer handcuffed her. She and other undocumented students were being arrested for disorderly conduct for participating in a sit-in coordinated by United We Dream, a coalition of immigrant youth groups. The demonstrators were calling for the passage of legislation that would allow immigrant children who served in the military or completed college to qualify for U.S. citizenship, thus fulfilling a lifelong dream (Bahrampour 2010).

The nation's undocumented immigrants typically avoid the public spotlight, always aware that their illegal status could lead to arrest and deportation. In publicly announcing their undocumented status, Martinez and her fellow demonstrators were thus doing what would have been unthinkable to their parents. Their act of defiance in pursuit of citizenship might be a sign of things to come.

Immigration—and especially unauthorized immigration—divides people in the United States, especially along ethnic lines. One poll found that whereas 62 percent of non-Hispanics thought illegal immigration was a "serious crime," only 24 percent of Hispanics did. The same poll found that 60 percent of non-Hispanics felt that illegal immigrants were mostly a drain on society, whereas only 21 percent of Hispanics thought so (AP-Univision 2010).

Frustration with the federal government's failure to control illegal immigration has led some states and localities to act on their own. A controversial law passed in Arizona in 2010, for example, made it a state crime to be in the country illegally, required legal immigrants to carry paperwork proving their status, and instructed Arizona police to question anyone they "reasonably suspect" of being undocumented. Some supporters of immigration restrictions have links to racist organizations (Potok 2007), but most argue that their concerns have nothing to do with race or ethnicity and reflect only a desire to curb *illegal* immigration. In fact, according to one poll, along with an overwhelming percentage of Hispanics (86 percent), a majority of non-Hispanics (56 percent) support providing a legal way for undocumented immigrants to become U.S. citizens (AP-Univision 2010). That is the outcome for which Diana Martinez is hoping. ■

Debates about immigration and citizenship are as old as the country itself. Even before the United States existed, the arrival of Europeans in a land already populated by many native societies sparked conflict between people of different races and ethnicities. As we will see, neither race nor ethnicity is rooted in biological fact; both are cultural creations. But these cultural ideas have real-world consequences; they affect patterns of action—social structure—and they contribute to persistent inequalities in power and resources among racial and ethnic groups. In many ways, the social history of the United States is intertwined with the history of ideas about race and ethnicity, including debates about who is entitled to citizenship and equal rights.

Today, whether or not we realize it, whether or not we want them to be, race and ethnicity are parts of our identity, influencing our lives and the way people interact with us. To better understand ourselves and our increasingly diverse society, we need to grapple with the impact that race and ethnicity have had on our history and the role they continue to play today.

The Role of Culture: Inventing Ethnicity and Race

Many societies, including the United States, classify people in terms of *race* and *ethnicity*. **Ethnicity** refers to a *shared cultural heritage, often deriving from a common ancestry and homeland.* That cultural heritage can include, among other things, common language, traditions, customs, symbols, and distinctive foods and music. Ethnicities are social constructions that exist only to the extent that people embrace them or have them imposed by others. People are constantly reinventing and redefining ethnic identities, which can make them fluid and murky.

In the United States, the ethnic label *Hispanic* applies to people who come from Spanish-speaking countries or whose

ancestors did. Many people who fit that description, however, reject the label because it lumps many cultures together. Instead, some people prefer the term *Latino* (male) or *Latina* (female) to specify a heritage from Latin America. Many prefer to identify with their specific ancestry as, for example, Mexican Americans (or Chicanos), Puerto Ricans, Cuban Americans, or Colombians. Similarly, some people of European ancestry in the United States identify with their ethnic roots, for example, calling themselves Polish Americans or Italian Americans. Others identify themselves as simply *American,* in the process creating yet another ethnicity.

In contrast to ethnicity, a **race** is *a category of people widely perceived as sharing socially significant physical characteristics such as skin color.* Ethnicity can be confused with race, since the two can overlap. For example, in the United States, many people mistakenly think of Hispanic as a "race" equivalent to "white," "black," or "Asian." In fact, the homelands from which Hispanics come are inhabited by people of Native American, African, European, and Asian origin. As a result, Hispanics may be of any race, though most identify as white.

Race as a Social Construction

If you walk into a room full of people, you can usually tell just by looking who is white, Asian, or black. Isn't race, then, a biological reality? Although it is based on physical characteristics and thus reflects biological variation, race, like ethnicity, is a social construction (Mukhopadhyay, Henze, and Moses 2007). Races exist only to the extent that people use physical characteristics to assign one another to social categories, but those categories do not represent biologically meaningful divisions in the human species.

For example, most important biological differences among people—differences that affect health, longevity, susceptibility to disease, and so on—are invisible and do not play any role in the definition of racial categories. These differences include things like blood types or the presence of genetic markers that predispose people to certain diseases. In addition, people are arbitrarily selective in the visible physical characteristics they do use to define racial categories. In the United States, for example, they largely ignore eye color and hair color when making racial distinctions, focusing instead on skin color (see the top photos on p. 254). Finally, no clear dividing line distinguishes one racial group from another. Physical variation occurs along a continuum, making it impossible to categorize humans neatly into a few distinct racial categories. (See the photo collage on the bottom of p. 254.) For example, much more physical variation exists among Whites than exists between Whites and any other racial category; some people classified as white even have darker skin than some people classified as black.

In short, when it comes to race, we don't see many physical differences that matter, we ignore many differences we can see, and we classify people into supposedly sharply bounded categories when in fact the members of those categories have continuously overlapping physical characteristics.

People make racial distinctions in part by paying attention selectively to some physical variations while largely ignoring others. Why are the different skin tones in these men more socially significant than their different hair color? What does this selective attention suggest about the arbitrary nature of race?

In reality, there is only a single human race with no subcategories or subspecies. All humans share a common ancestral lineage that evolved in Africa about 100,000–200,000 years ago (Mukhopadhyay, Henze, and Moses 2007). As a result, no biological feature or cluster of features clearly distinguishes one category of humans racially from any other. To understand what this common origin means in terms of the socially constructed nature of race, consider the physical feature most closely identified with racial differences in the United States: skin color.

Skin color is determined mostly by varying amounts of a pigment called melanin. Humans are vulnerable to the harmful effects of intense sunlight, which include an increased probability of having a child with birth defects for women and reduced fertility for men. Melanin—and the dark skin associated with it—protects against these adverse effects, but it also reduces the skin's ability to produce the essential nutrient vitamin D from sunlight. As a result, dark skin provides an evolutionary advantage in sunlight-intense tropical environments, whereas lighter skin provides an evolutionary advantage in re-

Human physical variation is too subtle and diverse to be captured accurately by a handful of racial or ethnic classifications.

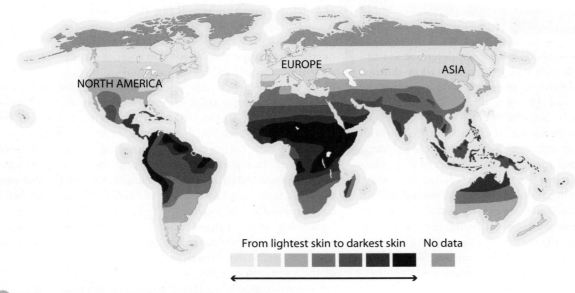

MAP 10.1 | GLOBAL DISTRIBUTION OF SKIN TONE

Skin tone is roughly distributed along the earth's latitudes so that, for example, people in parts of Mexico, northern Africa, and portions of China all share similar skin tones, even though they are commonly classified as belonging to different racial groups. *Source:* Jablonski and Chaplin (2002).

gions of less intense sunlight (Jablonski and Chaplin 2002). As humans across many generations migrated and adapted to different geographic regions, they developed a range of skin tones that vary more or less continuously from dark to light between regions of intense sunlight and those of less intense sunlight (Map 10.1) (Jablonski and Chaplin 2002).

In addition, skin tone is not consistently connected to other physical features such as hair type or nose shape. Dark- or light-skinned people can have all types of hair, noses, and other physical attributes. Skin tone, in other words, is not a fixed biological attribute of any one race. To understand how it became linked with race in the popular imagination, we have to look to social factors—cultural beliefs, social structures, and power relationships—not to biology.

Pseudo-Science and Race

The term *race* took on its popular contemporary connotations in the eighteenth century, when European scientists began systematically to name and classify the plants and animals of the natural world. When they turned their attention to humanity, however, ethnocentric assumptions of European superiority reduced their efforts to pseudo-science (Smedley 2007).

For example, the Swedish naturalist Carolus Linnaeus (1707–1778), who laid the foundation for the biological classification system still in use today, invented four subspecies of

Early pseudo-scientific classification schemes perpetuated racist beliefs. This image is from an 1857 book titled *Indigenous Races of the Earth* by physician Josiah Nott and Egyptologist George Gliddon. It suggests white biological superiority, with Blacks somewhere in between Whites and chimpanzees.

Homo sapiens, attributing to each not only physical traits but also judgmental character traits. White-skinned *Europeanus,* described as creative and governed by laws, was at the top. The other three were copper-skinned *Americanus,* described as stubborn, easily angered, and governed by customs; sallow-skinned (yellowish) *Asiaticus,* described as greedy and governed by opinions; and dark-skinned *Africanus,* described as lazy, negligent, and governed only by impulse (Smedley 2007). This classification laid the groundwork for "scientific" justifications of **racism,** *the belief that one race is inherently superior to another.*

Later writers developed variations on this sort of racist classification system. These schemes often contradicted each other, proposing a widely varying number of "races," each based on different physical types and accompanying social characteristics. Whites, for example, were often divided into subgroups that purported to reflect the superiority of northern Europeans—labeled in various schemes as "Teutonic" or "Nordic"—over such other Whites as "Celtics," "Semitics," and "Mediterraneans" (Smedley 2007).

From today's perspective, the rationale used to justify these racial classification systems seems arbitrary and even bizarre. For example, in the nineteenth century, German anatomist and anthropologist Johann Blumenbach (1752–1840), apparently after admiring the symmetry of a particularly well-preserved skull from the Caucasus Mountains (located between Russia and Turkey), concluded that it must have been Caucasians whom God had created in his own image. Other races, he decided, had degenerated physically and morally from God's vision because they had moved and adapted to new environments. Thus, religion and folk belief, couched in pseudo-scientific language, combined to give us the term *Caucasian,* still in common use as a synonym for "White" (Mukhopadhyay, Henze, and Moses 2007).

These arbitrary and conflicting classification systems went hand in hand with a belief in **racial essentialism**—*the idea that supposedly natural and immutable differences separated the races.* Whites who created the classification systems lived in societies with the power to enforce these ideas. Cultural notions of racial essentialism were used to justify white supremacy, slavery, and the European colonial domination of other peoples.

Race and Ethnicity Over Time and Across Cultures

Because races and ethnicities are cultural creations rather than biological facts, the definition and significance of racial and ethnic groups varies from culture to culture and changes over time. In nineteenth-century China, people drew distinctions based on body hair rather than skin tone. To them, extensive facial hair marked European missionaries as uncivi-

lized barbarians (Mukhopadhyay, Henze, and Moses 2007). In many parts of the world, ethnicity is more important than race; people are much more concerned about one another's tribe, clan, or ethnic affiliation than about skin color or other physical characteristics (Cornell and Hartmann 2007).

In countries where race does matter, definitions of race—and the standards for assigning people to one race or another—vary enormously. In the United States, sexual encounters between white owners and black slaves were common, and in the nineteenth century people of mixed race were often called "Mulattos." In the early twentieth century, however, Whites began changing state laws so that racial categories became mutually exclusive, and in the case of mixed ancestry, the Black status prevailed. For example, Virginia passed the "Racial Integrity Act" in 1924 mandating that all newborns be classified as either white or colored, with colored including those with *any* black or Native American ancestry. During the first half of the twentieth century, versions of this so-called one-drop rule—one drop of black blood makes a person black—were adopted by state legislatures throughout much of the South and Midwest (Murray 1997).

In recent years, however, the United States has returned to acknowledging mixed-race status. Since 2000, the U.S. Census

8. Is Person 1 of Hispanic, Latino, or Spanish origin?

☐ **No**, not of Hispanic, Latino, or Spanish origin
☐ Yes, Mexican, Mexican Am., Chicano
☐ Yes, Puerto Rican
☐ Yes, Cuban
☐ Yes, another Hispanic, Latino, or Spanish origin — *Print origin, for example, Argentinean, Colombian, Dominican, Nicaraguan, Salvadoran, Spaniard, and so on.* ⟋

9. What is Person 1's race?   Mark ☒ *one or more boxes.*

☐ White
☐ Black, African Am., or Negro
☐ American Indian or Alaska Native — *Print name of enrolled or principal tribe.* ⟋

☐ Asian Indian   ☐ Japanese   ☐ Native Hawaiian
☐ Chinese   ☐ Korean   ☐ Guamanian or Chamorro
☐ Filipino   ☐ Vietnamese   ☐ Samoan
☐ Other Asian — *Print race, for example, Hmong, Laotian, Thai, Pakistani, Cambodian, and so on.* ⟋   ☐ Other Pacific Islander — *Print race, for example, Fijian, Tongan, and so on.* ⟋

☐ Some other race — *Print race.* ⟋

FIGURE 10.1 | RACE, ETHNICITY, AND THE U.S. CENSUS
The U.S. Census includes questions about race and Hispanic origin. The categories included in these questions reflect the unique social history of the United States. *Source:* U.S. Census Bureau.

Bureau (2011c, 2011e) has allowed people the option of indicating a mixed racial heritage, and by 2010 more than 9 million people—about 3 percent of the population—reported being of two or more races (see Figure 10.1). Some people with mixed-race backgrounds, though, still choose to identify with a single race. When President Obama filled out his 2010 census form, he identified himself only as black, although his mother was white (Roberts and Baker 2010).

The countries of Latin America and the Caribbean have long had a variety of categories for people of mixed descent—including mixtures of European, African, and Indian—and physical appearance carries much less social significance in the region than it does in the United States. For example, the legacy of slavery in Brazil endured in the ranking of people by racial cat-

egory. However, in Brazil these categories were never codified legally. In addition, intermarriage and sexual relations among indigenous peoples, Africans, and Europeans were much more commonly accepted than in the United States. Brazilians now have dozens of racial categories based on differences in a variety of physical features, including hair, lips, eyes, and noses, as well as skin color. As a result, siblings from the same family can fall into different racial categories. Also, in Brazil the presence of any white ancestor helps to determine a person's classification, and over half of Brazilians fall into the broad category of "white" (which is broken down into many smaller subcategories). However, many white Brazilians would be perceived as black if they traveled to the United States (Kephart 2003). For a look at various systems of racial and ethnic classification, see Figure 10.2.

Australia 2001 Census

Are you of Aboriginal or Torres Strait Islander origin?
If you are of both Aboriginal and Torres Strait Islander origin, mark both 'Yes' boxes.

☐ No
☐ Yes, Aboriginal
☐ Yes, Torres Strait Islander

What is your ancestry? Provide more than one if necessary.

☐ English
☐ Irish
☐ Italian
☐ German
☐ Greek
☐ Chinese
☐ Australian
☐ Other

England 2001 Census
What is your ethnic group?
A) White
☐ British
☐ Irish
☐ Any other white background

B) Mixed
☐ White and Black Caribbean
☐ White and Black African
☐ White and Asian
☐ Any other Mixed background

C) Asian or Asian British
☐ Indian
☐ Pakistani
☐ Bangleshi
☐ Any other Asian background

D) Black or Black British
☐ Caribbean
☐ African
☐ Any other black background

E) Chinese/other ethnic group
☐ Chinese
☐ Any other

Brazil 2000 Census

Choose your race:
☐ White - branca
☐ Black - peta
☐ Yellow - amaréta
☐ Brown - parda
☐ Native, aboriginal - indigena
☐ Undeclared

Bulgaria 2001 Census

What is your ethnic group?
☐ Bulgarian
☐ Turkish
☐ Gypsies
☐ Other

Canada 2001 Census

Are you an aboriginal person, that is, North American Indian, Métis or Inuit (Eskimo)? If "Yes", check the box(s) that describe(s) you now.

☐ No, > Continue with the next question
☐ Yes, North American Indian
☐ Yes, Métis
☐ Yes, Inuit (Eskimo)

Are you a member of an Indian Band/First Nation?
☐ No
☐ Yes, member of an Indian Band/First Nation

Are you a Treaty Indian or a Registered Indian as defined by the Indian Act of Canada?
☐ No
☐ Yes, Treaty Indian or a Registered Indian

Mexico 2000 Census

Are you Náhuatl, Mayan, Zapoteco, Mixteco or of another indigenous group?

☐ Yes
☐ No

South Africa 2001 Census

How would you describe yourself in terms of population group?

☐ Black African
☐ Coloured
☐ Indian or Asian
☐ White
☐ Other

FIGURE 10.2 | RACE AND ETHNICITY ACROSS CULTURES

Because race and ethnicity are social constructions, they vary by culture. Different countries use different classification systems in their census collection. If you moved to another country, your race or ethnicity might change. Source: American Anthropological Association (2011).

For many years, white people were the assumed norm when manufacturers created "flesh"-colored products such as adhesive bandages. Today, reflecting changes in the culture, manufacturers are more likely to recognize a diversity of skin tones, as with these "multicultural" crayons.

Structure and Power Among Racial and Ethnic Groups

By identifying certain cultural or physical traits as socially significant, people create a social reality that influences how they behave with one another. In other words, "seeing" others in terms of race, ethnicity, and other social categories (such as religion, age, and sexual orientation) can affect how we act toward them and help to legitimize social inequality based on those categories. Let's look at some of these dynamics.

Minority and Majority Groups

In any given society, people often think of its members who are of different races and ethnicities in terms of majority and minority groups. A **minority group** is *a collection of people who suffer disadvantages and have less power because of identifiable physical or cultural characteristics.* In contrast, a **majority group** is *a collection of people who enjoy privileges and have more access to power because of identifiable physical or cultural characteristics.* Sociologists do not use these terms in a literal sense. A minority group need not be an actual minority of the population, and a majority group need not be an actual majority. In South Africa under the white supremacist apartheid regime, for example, the black population held the minority status even though they far outnumbered Whites.

Although the status of individual members of a minority can vary widely, *as a group,* compared to the majority group, minorities tend to have lower incomes, less education, less political influence, and poorer health. Conversely, individual members of a majority group may not wield great power or have access to great resources, but, *as a group,* majorities dominate society. In addition to greater resources, the majority group also has the power to create and enforce the labels used to designate minority groups.

Members of minority groups tend to be conscious of their status and aware of the hurdles and barriers they face in society. To navigate a majority-dominated society successfully, they must learn how the majority group operates. In contrast, majority-group members often take their status for granted and are unaware of their relative privilege. They typically do not need to learn about minority cultures to be successful within a society their group dominates.

Patterns of Majority-Minority Interaction

The relationship between majority and minority groups in a society can range from benign to destructive. In some cases, members of a minority group might find acceptance and equal standing with the majority group, whereas in other situations a minority group may be subjected to widespread prejudice and discrimination. To have **prejudice** means *to "pre-judge" someone or some group negatively based on inadequate information.* These judgments are often based on **stereotypes,** *exaggerated, distorted, or untrue generalizations about categories of people that do not acknowledge individual variation.* Stereotypes can be either negative or positive; examples of positive stereotypes are the Asian math whiz and the African American sports star. Prejudice is limited to beliefs and attitudes that individuals hold but may not act on. When prejudice is joined to action, however, it leads to **discrimination,** *unequal treatment that gives advantages to one group of people over another without justifiable cause.*

The patterns of interaction among majority and minority groups can take a variety of forms, sometimes straddling more than one category. In a society that embraces **pluralism,** *dis-*

tinct ethnic and racial groups coexist on equal terms and have equal social standing. Members of these groups recognize and maintain their differences, but the differences have no significant impact on anyone's political, social, or economic standing. Switzerland is a successful pluralistic society. The Swiss Confederation—Switzerland's official name—unites four cultures, each with its own regions and its own official language: German, French, Italian, or Romansch (based on Latin).

Amalgamation is *the process by which a majority and a minority group blend or mix to form a new group.* This is typically accomplished through intermarriage over the course of several generations. For example, Mexican society today is primarily an amalgamation of Indian and Spanish cultures that have blended to create what is now a distinctly Mexican identity.

Assimilation is *the process by which members of a minority group come to adopt the culture of the majority group.* As we will see, the experience of many white European ethnic groups in the United States has been one of assimilation; ethnic groups largely abandoned their distinct cultures and were absorbed into the nation's dominant culture. The assimilation experience is often partially voluntary, as minority group members emulate the dominant culture, and partially coerced as majority-group members require others to conform to their cultural expectations.

Segregation involves *keeping distinct social groups physically and socially separate and unequal.* In the United States, segregation is most associated with the oppression of African Americans, especially in the South after the Civil War and before the civil rights movement.

Genocide is *the systematic killing of a group of people, based on their race, ethnicity, nationality, or religion.* Typically, genocide involves a majority group seeking to exterminate a minority group. The deliberate killing of Jews and others by the Nazi regime in Germany and other European countries during World War II is the most infamous example of genocide, but not the first and, unfortunately, not the last (Kiernan 2007).

Minority Group Responses to Discrimination

Minority groups can respond to majority-group domination in a variety of ways:

- **Withdrawal** involves physically escaping the worst oppression. As we will see, the Great Migration of African Americans out of the South to the North and Midwest in the early and mid-twentieth century is one example of this strategy. Other examples include the formation of racial and ethnic enclaves in urban areas: places with names like Germantown, Little Italy, and Chinatown.

- **Passing** involves blending in with the dominant group. White ethnics in the United States often changed their names on arrival to better blend into the dominant Anglo-Saxon culture. Germans with the name "Schmidt" would change it to "Smith," for example. Today many recent immigrants from Vietnam, China, India, and elsewhere similarly adopt names that are more familiar to native-born Americans and easier for them to spell and pronounce. Passing can also occur when people in a minority group take advantage of physical similarities to the members of the majority group, as when light-skinned Blacks conceal their race or even change their hair to appear more "white."

- **Code-switching**—a term coined by sociologist Elijah Anderson (1999)—refers to the strategy of complying with the social expectations of the majority by creating a "front-stage" self-presentation while maintaining a different more comfortable and authentic "back-stage" identity. Code-switching may involve dressing "white" or using "white" English at work or school, while retaining a more comfortable mother tongue, ethnic slang, and ethnic dress at home.

- **Resistance** involves actively asserting oneself—either individually or collectively—in defiance of majority discrimination. The many civil rights struggles that have characterized U.S. history are examples of this strategy.

The Origins of Racial and Ethnic Diversity in the United States

In the United States, ideas about race and ethnicity are rooted in the country's history—the European conquest of native peoples, the immigration of Europeans, the enslavement of Africans, and the recruitment of Asian laborers.

Native Peoples

In 1492, before Europeans established their first permanent settlements in the Western Hemisphere, an estimated 50 million people lived in North and South America, about 5 million of them in what is today the United States and Canada (Taylor 2001). When Europeans arrived, the Aztec capital of Tenochtitlán had a quarter of a million inhabitants—five times the size of London at the time (Gonzalez 2000). Native peoples formed hundreds of different societies with unique languages, religions, forms of government, and cultural traditions. These ranged from the Inuit, who lived in nomadic bands in what is today the Canadian Arctic, to the powerful urban civilizations of the Aztec and Maya in what is today Mexico and the Inca in what is today Peru.

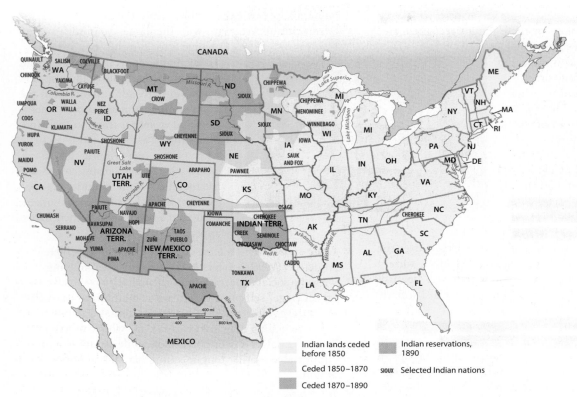

MAP 10.2 | NATIVE AMERICAN LOSS OF TERRITORY FROM BEFORE 1850 TO 1890

By 1890, conquest and expansion had confined most of the Native American population to a series of reservations, transforming North America from a land controlled by dozens of different native societies to one dominated by white European Americans. *Source:* Davidson et al. (2011).

Indian lands ceded before 1850

Ceded 1850–1870

Ceded 1870–1890

Indian reservations, 1890

SIOUX Selected Indian nations

The European invasion that began with Christopher Columbus's first voyage in 1492 had a devastating effect on native peoples. At any given place, within a decade after contact with Europeans, the native population typically fell to about half its precontact numbers, and within fifty years to just one tenth (Taylor 2001). Most of this devastation was caused by disease. The native peoples had no immunity to the many infections the Europeans brought with them, including smallpox, measles, tuberculosis, and the bubonic plague, and they succumbed to them in huge numbers. Like many European settlers, early Massachusetts founder John Winthrop interpreted the widespread deaths as a sign that God was "making room" for the colonists and "hath hereby cleared our title to this place" (in Takaki 2008, 40).

Of those who survived disease, many were killed as European powers, vying for control of the Americas, steadily dispossessed native peoples of their land and autonomy. By just before the American Revolution in 1776, the British and French controlled much of what became the United States and Canada. The Spanish were the dominant power in what is now the southwestern United States, Mexico, and much of Latin and South America, whereas the Portuguese controlled what is now Brazil.

After it achieved independence from Britain, the United States continued to subjugate and uproot the native populations of North America as it expanded westward. Its tactics included political deception, blatant treaty violations, forcible removal, and military conquest. By 1890, the country's Native American population had been reduced to less than 250,000 (Gibson and Jung 2002) who were confined largely to reserva-

tions that represented only a tiny fraction of the lands their ancestors had once occupied (Map 10.2). The U.S. government, which managed these reservations, sometimes seized Native American children and sent them to boarding schools where they were taught English and encouraged to adopt Christianity and abandon their own language and culture.

Native peoples struggled to maintain their cultural identity despite this invasion, and they have had an enduring and continuing impact on post-conquest societies, especially in places with the densest precontact populations, such as Mexico, Guatemala, Ecuador, Peru, and Bolivia.

Hispanics or Latinos

In the first half of the 1500s, various Spanish explorers traveled through what is today the southern half of the United States, claiming the region for Spain as they went. These expeditions—which took place decades before the 1607 founding of the first British colony at Jamestown, Virginia—gave names to many geographical features in the United States and established some of its earliest European settlements, including St. Augustine in Florida and Santa Fe in New Mexico (Gonzalez 2000).

Spanish control of areas that became Mexico, Puerto Rico, Cuba, and other nations of Central and South America laid the foundation for ethnic combinations that we now define as Hispanic or Latino.

MEXICAN AMERICANS Mexican Americans are the largest Latino group in the United States, partly because when Mexico gained its independence from Spain in 1821, it

LINCOLN INSTITUTION
INDIAN DEPARTMENT.

One way to dominate a population is to eradicate its culture. Native American boarding schools, typically run by Christian missionaries, taught native children to adopt European ways of life and abandon their own language, religion, traditions, and styles of dress.

included what are today the states of Texas, New Mexico, Arizona, California, Nevada, Utah, and part of Colorado. In the 1820s, thousands of white U.S. citizens illegally crossed the Mexican border into the sparsely populated region of Téjas—present-day Texas. By 1835, U.S. citizens in the region outnumbered Mexicans by five to one. A year later they launched an insurrection that ended with the creation of the Republic of Texas. Its president, Sam Houston, declared in his inaugural address that the newly created republic reflected "glory on the Anglo-Saxon race" (Montejano 1987; Takaki 2008, 158).

In 1845 the United States annexed Texas, and an ensuing border dispute provided the justification for the Mexican-American War (1846–1848). By the end of the war, the United States seized nearly half of Mexico, including what is now California and the U.S. southwest, fulfilling the common belief in Manifest Destiny, which asserted that white Americans had a divinely ordained right and duty to occupy the continent from coast to coast (Horsman 1981).

The Treaty of Guadalupe Hidalgo that concluded the war in 1848 granted U.S. citizenship to about 80,000 formerly Mexican citizens who now found themselves living within the United States. Overnight, they had become, as Mexican American leader Pablo de la Guerra, later put it, "foreigners in their own land" (Takaki 2008, 165). In California, the discovery of gold that same year triggered a massive influx of Anglos—white English speakers—making Mexican Americans a minority there. Ironically, the newly arrived Whites often saw the native Mexicans as "foreign" competitors for their land claims.

As they gained political power, Anglos began changing the laws already biased in favor of Whites to give themselves further advantages at the expense of the native Mexican population, creating a de facto racial caste system. Throughout the Southwest, Mexican Americans faced the same segregation

as African Americans. They were excluded from many restaurants and other public facilities, and their children attended segregated schools intended to prepare them to be farm workers, not to help them get ahead. White-controlled courts also rejected the titles many Mexican Americans held to land, thus helping Anglos gain control of most of the Southwest. Deprived of land, many Mexican Americans worked for Anglos in mining, railroad construction, and ranching and farming, earning lower wages than their white counterparts (Montejano 1987). Both stoking and exploiting this racial and ethnic conflict, employers were able to blunt efforts by Mexican Americans and other workers to organize unions and strike for better conditions (Roediger 1999).

Some Mexican citizens, meanwhile, fled the political turmoil of the 1910 Mexican Revolution and headed north across the U.S. border in search of security and work. But then, when work dried up during the Great Depression of the 1930s, 400,000 Mexicans—including many U.S.-born citizens—were sent back to Mexico, sometimes forcibly. Just a few years later, though, labor shortages that followed the outbreak of World War II prompted the U.S. government to recruit 200,000 Mexican laborers to work temporarily in the United States through the *bracero* program (from *brazos* for arms). Since then, agriculture in the Southwest has remained dependent on the labor of migrant Mexican and Mexican-American farm workers. The low pay and difficult conditions of this work sparked many labor disputes, which increased in the 1960s and 1970s with the rise of the United Farm Workers union led by César Chávez and Dolores Huerta.

PUERTO RICANS Puerto Ricans, the second largest Latino group in the United States, are also linked to U.S. expansion. The United States invaded and occupied Puerto Rico during the Spanish-American War of 1898, transforming the island from a Spanish colony to a U.S. colony. In the ensuing decades, U.S. sugar companies acquired vast tracts of land on the island, displacing small growers and prompting sometimes violent labor clashes. Many agricultural workers fled to the U.S. mainland in search of better opportunities. In 1917, Puerto Ricans became U.S. citizens and, in 1947, Puerto Rico became a commonwealth with the right to elect its own

Understanding Whiteness

In a classic essay, Peggy McIntosh (1988) notes that Whites are often taught to recognize the disadvantages that minorities face but not the advantages they enjoy as Whites. She describes some of the dozens of ways that she benefits from white privilege in her daily life. When she shops, for example, she doesn't experience the suspicion and harassment to which minorities are often subjected. Minorities are often judged individually as if they represented their entire community: If they excel, they are a credit to the community; if they behave questionably, it's because of the deficiencies of their community. As a white person, McIntosh does not bear this burden. Cumulatively, these and similar advantages constitute an "invisible package of unearned assets," as McIntosh calls it, that reflects the dominant position of the white majority in the United States.

McIntosh's essay is one example of the study of whiteness. People often think of race in terms of minorities. But white majorities in the European colonies created the modern idea of "race" during the eighteenth century, and to understand "race" we must understand whiteness and its connection to power and inequality.

Although he is best known for writing about the condition of black Americans, African American sociologist and activist W.E.B. Du Bois (1935/1998) recognized the importance of whiteness a century ago. Although American society as a whole was divided by class, he noted, the working class was divided further along racial lines. White workers might be poorly paid, but they were "compensated in part by a sort of public and psychological wage. They were given public deference and titles of courtesy because they were white" (p. 700). They, like white people of all classes, could attend public functions and enjoy public parks. They were served by a white police force, by a court system staffed by white jurists, and by white elected officials, and they had access to the best schools, which were reserved for them. Ironically, however, by embracing these race-based privileges, white workers lost the opportunity to organize with black workers to improve conditions for all of them.

Du Bois was writing at a very different moment in history than ours, of course, but sociologists have used his basic sociological insights to inform their current analysis of race, particularly on the nature of whiteness (Rothenberg 2004). Sociologists engaged in "whiteness studies" examine both the historical roots and the contemporary processes associated with whiteness and white privilege. The questions they explore (some of which are discussed in this chapter) include: How did diverse ethnic groups once considered fundamentally different become lumped together as "Whites"? How have the U.S. political, legal, and economic systems been structured to give advantages to Whites? Does white privilege endure, and, if so, what forms does it take? How can Whites help to combat racism and its legacy?

The point is not to blame today's Whites for the history of racial injustice. Instead, whiteness studies help us better understand that history of injustice, to recognize its continuing legacy today, and to use those insights to work toward a more just society.

think about it

1. *Has your education about race included consideration of what it means to be "white?"*
2. *How does the study of whiteness illustrate the sociological insight that power is a social relationship?*

---

governor. Although it otherwise remains subject to U.S. law, it has only a nonvoting delegate to Congress and its residents cannot vote for president. Puerto Ricans are divided about the island's future political status. Some support the current arrangement, some favor gaining U.S. statehood, and some advocate independence (Takaki 2008).

CUBAN AMERICANS The Spanish colony of Cuba, unlike Puerto Rico, gained formal independence after the Spanish-American War. However, it remained subject to U.S. military and economic intervention and suffered from political instability. In 1959, Fidel Castro led a revolution to overthrow the Cuban dictator Fulgencio Batista and instituted radical economic reform, eventually aligning his nation with the Soviet Union and communist bloc nations. Castro's reforms were popular among many of the country's poor, but not among the more affluent middle and upper classes, many of whom fled to the United States, forming the core of today's Cuban American community.

WASPs and White Ethnic Groups

The colonies founded by Great Britain on the east coast of North America were what became the early United States, and for many years the descendents of colonial-era immigrants from Great Britain—White Anglo-Saxon Protestants, or WASPS—were the country's most powerful ethnic group. Other white ethnic groups arrived in large numbers during the nineteenth and twentieth centuries.

WHITE ANGLO-SAXON PROTESTANTS The WASP label combines race, ethnicity, and religion. It refers mostly to people of English ancestry but also includes those of Scottish and Welsh ancestry. It excludes Whites from other parts of Europe as well as Catholics and Jews. (The Through a Sociological Lens box explores the study of whiteness.)

WASPs were not a single unified group. Religious rivalries and class divisions made life better for some than for others. However, as the first immigrants to what was to become the United States, WASPs were able to develop and control the country's emerging government, business, and religious institutions. They thus amassed enormous power and avoided the sorts of discrimination that later immigrants would have to overcome. In the early years of the United States, WASPs typically believed in white racial superiority—often calling themselves the Anglo-Saxon race—and created laws to exclude non-Whites from the new nation.

The monopoly on power that WASPs maintained through much of U.S. history loosened considerably by the middle of the twentieth century. The influence of this group endures, however, on much of U.S. culture, most noticeably in the use of English as the country's dominant language and the standing of Protestant Christianity as the country's largest religious affiliation.

WHITE ETHNIC GROUPS The first major wave of European immigrants who were not WASPs arrived in the early and mid-nineteenth century. After their English landlords evicted them to make way for more grazing lands for cattle and sheep, many impoverished Irish tenant farmers were left dependent on potatoes for survival. When blight devastated the potato crop in Ireland in 1845, hundreds of thousands of Irish tenant farmers fled to the United States. At around the same time, large numbers of Germans arrived, as well.

Many WASPs at first denied these and other European newcomers equal racial standing with themselves, referring to them instead as "Celtic" (Irish, Welsh, Scots), "Alpine" (German, Norwegian, Swedish, and other central European), and "Mediterranean" (Italian, Spanish, Greek, and other southern European). But as the new groups gained some power, they rejected these separate designations and claimed the mantle of racial superiority together with WASPs as part of a broadened "white" race (Mukhopadhyay, Henze, and Moses 2007).

The history of the Irish in America illustrates this process (Ignatiev 1996). The Irish had white skin, but they were Catholic, not Protestant, and many spoke Gaelic (Irish) rather than English. As a result, many WASPs considered the Irish a different race and discriminated against them as they did against black people, though never subjecting the Irish to the systematic legal discrimination Blacks faced. Often poor and unskilled, the Irish commonly lived in the same neighborhoods as free Blacks in northern cities and were often referred to as "white Negroes." Common stereotypes portrayed them as happy, lazy, and stupid with a penchant for drink, dance, and music—stereotypes that were also associated with Blacks.

In time, the Irish learned English and took steps to differentiate themselves from black people, establishing their own

Along with Italians, Jews, Greeks, and others, Irish immigrants were among those not considered "white" in the nineteenth century and subject to discrimination. Common complaints were that new immigrants didn't speak English, had unfamiliar religious beliefs, had strange cultural practices, had too many children, engaged in crime and excessive drinking, and took away jobs from established Americans. How do such criticisms compare to today's discussions about immigration?

churches and schools and forming their own social organizations. Although they had earlier supported the abolition of slavery, they gained political power by associating themselves with the Democratic Party, which at that time supported slavery. As a result, the Irish eventually came to be perceived as "Whites" in American society—an option not available to darker-skinned people of African or Asian descent.

The second—and largest—wave of white ethnic immigrants arrived between 1890 and 1924. During that span, 20 million people came to the United States, most of them from southern and eastern Europe, including Italians, Poles, and Jews. Driven by poverty or political repression and drawn by the demand for labor in a rapidly industrializing United States, they were often met with resentment, prejudice, discrimination in housing and employment, and, sometimes, outright violence (Daniels 1997).

thinking about culture

Can you think of ways in which the WASP influence on **culture** has affected you? Consider common words you use, values you have, and the history you were taught in school.

Anti-immigrant sentiment increased after World War I (1914–1918), resulting in the Immigration Act of 1924. This law slashed total immigration to 150,000 a year (excepting immigration from the Western Hemisphere) and dramatically reduced the percentage of foreign-born people in the United States for the next forty years. The legislation effectively ended Asian immigration because it prohibited immigration by "aliens ineligible to citizenship" and naturalization was limited to Whites only. It also slashed immigration from southern and eastern Europe through a severely restrictive quota system (Daniels 1997).

African Americans

Unique among the diverse racial and ethnic groups that make up the U.S. population, most African Americans are descended from people forcibly removed from their homeland, sent here against their will, and subjected to a lifetime of coerced labor. This experience is reflected in the distinctively North American idea of race that European colonists created to justify an economic system based on the slave labor of Africans. Before the American experience, slavery existed mostly independent of race. Greeks and Romans kept slaves with pale skin just like themselves, while some dark-skinned Africans captured and enslaved dark-skinned members of other African tribes. In what became the United States, however, a new notion of race was invented piecemeal, over a series of decades, and eventually used to justify a race-based slave system that was the foundation of the agricultural economy of the day, especially in the American South (Johnson and Smith 1999; Smedley 2007). This process so influenced the uniquely American notions of race—and the interaction between race and class in the United States—that it warrants close attention.

INDENTURED SERVITUDE Race-based slavery emerged only after a labor system based on white indentured servitude failed. When English colonists settled the region that later became the United States, they needed workers to build settlements and raise crops. Especially during the early and mid-1600s, colonists relied primarily on the labor of indentured servants. These poor Whites, mostly Britons and Germans, contracted to work for a period of four to seven years in exchange for trans-Atlantic passage and sometimes "freedom dues"—which might include food, clothes, a gun, and, most important, land—upon completion of their contract. Some came voluntarily; others—including homeless children, convicts, beggars, and others considered by British officials to be social undesirables—were shipped forcibly. The work was brutal and the conditions harsh, and many indentured servants died before gaining their freedom. In many ways, they were essentially slaves: they were bought and sold

as property, served at the whim of their employers, and were often chained and beaten. Unlike slaves, however, they suffered only temporary servitude; slavery was lifelong (Jordan and Walsh 2008).

Indentured servitude declined eventually, however. As word of the harsh conditions spread, fewer people volunteered to indenture themselves. Unrest grew among indentured servants who had been cheated of their freedom dues, and in 1676, white and black servants joined black slaves in Bacon's Rebellion in Virginia, frightening wealthy colonial officials. To maintain their authority, powerful Whites used race to keep poor Whites from joining forces with poor Blacks and slaves (Johnson and Smith 1999; Horton and Horton 2005).

SLAVERY AS AN ECONOMIC INSTITUTION In the early 1600s, Africans were only a small part of the colonial work force. At first, many were treated similarly to white indentured servants. They lived with white servants; had similar legal rights, including the right to sign contracts; and were even able to travel to some extent. As the supply of indentured servants dwindled, however, white planters began to rely increasingly on the labor of black African slaves.

The enslaved Africans were the victims of an economic system that linked England, West Africa, and England's American colonies in a three-stage pattern of trade. In the first stage, English goods were shipped to West Africa and traded for Africans who had been kidnapped by fellow Africans and sold to European slavers. Packed into ships under horrific conditions, up to 20 million captives suffered the second stage, the infamous middle passage from Africa to the Americas that only half would survive. In the Americas, they were exchanged for raw materials such as tobacco, rice, and cotton. Finally, the raw materials were shipped to England and exchanged for finished goods, beginning the cycle again (Johnson and Smith 1999; Horton and Horton 2006).

THE RACIALIZATION OF SLAVERY As the importance of slave labor grew, the ideology justifying it changed. At first, colonists claimed that as non-Christians, Africans were unworthy of freedom. In a few cases, African slaves successfully sued for their freedom after converting to Christianity. By the end of the 1600s, however, with slaves increasingly converting to Christianity, religious differences no longer provided a convincing rationale for enslaving Africans and their descendants (Johnson and Smith 1999; Horton and Horton 2006). Instead, Whites now drew on pseudo-science and, ironically, biblical scripture to claim that black Africans were a different and inferior human subspecies fit only to serve the superior white race (Smedley 2007).

At the same time, wealthy Southern landowners used their political clout to strip slaves of any legal rights and to define

This man's back shows the scars left from brutal whippings he received as a slave in the American South.

 This idealized image of George Washington, painted in 1853, shows the nation's first president on his Mount Vernon plantation among his slaves. Like other large landowners of the time, Washington depended on slave labor to run his home and to generate his wealth by working his plantation.

CORE CONCEPTS CHALLENGE

What cultural beliefs about the nature of slavery does this painting promote? Who do you think is the intended audience for a picture like this?

slave status legally in racial terms. In 1705 the Virginia Assembly for the first time passed laws designating slaves as property. Slave rebellions in the following years provoked increasingly restrictive laws, including laws making it illegal for slaves to learn to read (Johnson and Smith 1999; Horton and Horton 2006).

SLAVERY AND AFFLUENCE Race-based slavery, justified by an ideology that viewed Africans as less than human, underlay the growing wealth of the new colonial elites and not just in the South. Members of a white planter aristocracy owned large estates and benefitted directly from the labor of their many slaves. George Washington, among the wealthiest colonists of his day, owned more than 300 slaves. But even the northern colonies—not directly dependent on plantation agriculture—benefited from slavery. Merchants, shipbuilders, metal smiths, rum distillers, sawmill operators, and many others all profited directly or indirectly from the slave trade (Johnson and Smith 1999; Horton and Horton 2006).

Slaves lived under varied conditions, but their labor was always coerced, and the coercion was backed by force, often applied barbarically. White masters also often took it as their prerogative to rape their female slaves, and the offspring of these encounters were legally slaves at birth. Slaves resisted their oppression in various ways, from avoiding work, to escaping, to joining rebellions (Johnson and Smith 1999; Horton and Horton 2006).

SLAVERY'S LEGACY While Thomas Jefferson was writing "All men are created equal" in the Declaration of Independence, a slave in the next room was on call to attend to his every need. In 1776, some Whites recognized that slavery was unjust and spoke out against it, but they were few. Slavery persisted for nearly a hundred years in the newly independent United States until it was outlawed by the Thirteenth Amendment to the U.S. Constitution in the wake of the Civil War (1861–1865). The legacy of slavery endured, however, with the imposition of legalized (*de jure*) racial segregation in the South and segregation in fact (*de facto*), if not by law, in much of the rest of the country. Under the South's so-called Jim Crow laws, all aspects of life, including housing, employment, education, and political participation, were structured along racial lines, ensuring that Blacks and Whites would remain separate and unequal.

Racial segregation was enforced through violence and terror. Between 1882 and 1968, for example, white mobs lynched and killed an estimated 4,742 Blacks (and many members of other ethnic minorities, as well) (Allen et al. 2000). During the Great Migration of the early and middle twentieth century, many African Americans—some two million by 1930—fled the repressive South in search of economic opportunity in the urban North (Takiki 2008).

African Americans had long challenged their subordinate status under Jim Crow, and in the 1950s these efforts coalesced and intensified in the civil rights movement. By the mid-1960s,

A group of white people in Indiana pose proudly for a photo after a lynching in 1930. Lynchings of this sort, often of alleged criminals, were conducted in broad daylight with the consent of local authorities. Some were treated as community events with a carnival atmosphere. Photos like this one—sometimes including children—were regularly taken to commemorate the occasion, and copies of these gruesome pictures were then sold as postcards.

this landmark movement had succeeded in dismantling legal segregation and begun to significantly change the country's entrenched culture of racism.

Asian Americans

The experiences of African slaves in the plantation economy were unique. However, throughout U.S. history, race and ethnicity have been used repeatedly to divide workers for the benefit of the powerful. Early Asian Americans experienced this phenomenon as well.

CHINESE AMERICANS Early Chinese immigrants to the United States fled the violence of Britain's "Opium Wars," political turmoil resulting from peasant rebellions, and harsh economic conditions. The hope of finding possible riches in the California Gold Rush of 1849 motivated the earliest Chinese to immigrate. More came between 1863 and 1869—recruited to displace higher-paid Irish workers—to build the transcontinental railroad, a massive, sometimes brutally dangerous, labor-intensive project. After the railroad was completed, some Chinese workers moved to cities, most notably San Francisco, while others played a prominent role in California's emerging agricultural economy (Takaki 2008).

The Chinese were particularly vulnerable to discrimination because, as non-Whites, they were ineligible for U.S. citizenship. California, for example, targeted them with a special tax on foreign miners who were not going to become citizens. Over the years, white workers grew increasingly resentful of Chinese workers, often blaming them for taking their jobs and driving down wages. In the 1870s, Irish American politician Dennis Kearney rose to prominence in California with the slogan "The Chinese must go!" and led violent attacks on Chinese workers. In the early 1890s, unemployed white workers rioted throughout California, beating and sometimes shooting Chinese immigrants and shipping them out of town in freight cars in what the Chinese would come to call the "driving out" (Takaki 2008). Anti-Chinese feeling culminated in the Chinese Exclusion Act of 1882—the first U.S. law to prohibit immigration on the basis of a specific nationality—effectively ending Chinese immigration for a decade (Takaki 2008).

In the face of this hostility, Chinese immigrants already in the country often had to develop their own businesses and rely on their own community for support. Chinese laundries—which were inexpensive to start up—became a staple of many western cities, and urban "Chinatowns" emerged as the center of Chinese social and economic life.

JAPANESE, KOREAN, AND FILIPINO AMERICANS Japanese, Koreans, and Filipinos have distinct cultures and sometimes conflicting histories, but they share some common experiences in the United States. In the late nineteenth and early twentieth centuries, some 200,000 Japanese, along with others from countries including China, Korea, and the Philippines, were recruited to work on sugar-cane plantations in Hawaii, which was annexed as a U.S. territory

A group gathers behind the barbed wire fence of an internment camp in California around 1942. Camps like these kept Japanese Americans confined for the duration of World War II.

in 1898. Plantation owners expected that this ethnic diversity would keep their workforce divided and vulnerable to exploitation. In 1919, however, the workers united in a successful strike and formed the Hawaii Laborers' Association, Hawaii's first interethnic union (Jung 2006, Takaki 2008). From Hawaii, some Japanese, Korean, and Filipino immigrants went on to the mainland, most of them to work on farms in California. The Asian Exclusion Act, part of the Immigration Act of 1924, however, brought Asian immigration to a virtual stop.

In what was perhaps the most dramatically racist act against an Asian group in the country's history, the U.S. government interned nearly 120,000 Japanese Americans—two-thirds of them U.S. born—for the duration of World War II. In the wake of Japan's attack on Pearl Harbor in December 1941, the government uprooted entire families and sent them to camps in often remote and desolate areas of the country. Although the United States was at war with Germany and Italy as well as Japan, no such measures were taken against white Americans with German or Italian ancestry. In 1988 the U.S. government paid survivors of the camps $20,000 each in reparations and apologized for what it called a "grave injustice," admitting that the internments were done "without adequate security reasons" and "were motivated largely by racial prejudice, wartime hysteria, and a failure of political leadership" [Public Law 100-383 (1988)].

Diversity Today

As a result of the civil rights movement and immigration, U.S. society is one of the most racially and ethnically diverse societies in the world.

The Civil Rights Revolution

During the 1950s and 1960s, the struggle for social justice known as the civil rights movement succeeded in dismantling legal discrimination for the first time in U.S. history and fostered a culture of tolerance that made racial and ethnic prejudice broadly unacceptable. Sometimes working through interracial and interethnic coalitions, previously marginalized groups celebrated their distinct cultures, gained some political power, and challenged discriminatory practices. Changes in immigration law that Congress enacted in the 1960s contributed further to the new diversity that has marked the United States ever since.

Racial and Ethnic Groups Today

Although the United States as a whole is diverse, that diversity varies significantly from region to region. According to the U.S. Census Bureau (2009a), different ancestries predominate in each of the four major regions of the country. In the Northeast, Irish ancestry is the most common (17 percent), whereas African American ancestry is most common in the South

TABLE 10.1	SUMMARY OF MAJOR RACIAL AND ETHNIC GROUPS IN THE UNITED STATES, 2010
Racial/Ethnic Group	**Percentage Within Population**
White (any ethnicity)	72.4%
Non-Hispanic white	63.7
Latino/Hispanic (any race)	16.3
Black or African American	12.6
Asian	4.8
American Indian or Alaska Native	0.9
Native Hawaiian and Pacific Islander	0.2

Source: U.S. Census Bureau (2011c, 2011e, 2010h).

(19 percent), German in the Midwest (29.3 percent), and Mexican in the West (23.4 percent).

WHITE AMERICANS At 72.4 percent of the population, white people of many different ancestries continue to be by far the largest racial group in U.S. society. Non-Hispanic Whites account for 63.7 percent of the population (see Table 10.1). Whites are found in substantial numbers throughout the country, with especially heavy concentrations in parts of the Midwest and northern New England. In 2010, only Hawaii, New Mexico, California, and Texas (as well as the District of Columbia) were "majority minority" states with a non-Hispanic white population of less than 50 percent. In contrast, about half of the states were at least 75 percent white and non-Hispanic (U.S. Census Bureau 2011c, 2011e).

HISPANICS OR LATINOS Latinos are the largest and fastest-growing minority group in the United States. Numbering 50.5 million in 2010, they make up 16.3 percent of the U.S. population and are expected to be nearly one-quarter of the U.S. population by 2050. Nearly 53 percent identify themselves as white only, 2.5 percent as black or African American only, and 6 percent as two or more races; and 36.7 percent report being of "some other race," likely treating Hispanic as a racial rather than ethnic category (U.S. Census Bureau 2011c, 2011e). Latinos are concentrated in the Southwest and West (reflecting the annexation of these areas from Mexico), in Florida (where Cuban Americans are concentrated), and in the New York metropolitan area.

AFRICAN AMERICANS African Americans number nearly 39 million. At about 12.6 percent of the U.S. population, they are the nation's largest racial minority. Most African Americans live in the South, but they are also a major presence in cities of the northeast and northern Midwest. In addition, recent immigrants are diversifying the African American community, especially in major metropolitan areas. In 2007, nearly 8 percent of those who reported their race as only black were foreign born, compared with just 1 percent in 1960 (U.S. Census Bureau 2011c, 2011e, 2010h).

ASIAN AMERICANS Asian Americans today account for 4.8 percent of the population in the United States. Chinese, Indian, and Filipinos are today's largest Asian subgroups. Those in the second largest subgroup—from India—are relatively recent arrivals. Filipinos are the third largest subgroup. In addition, many Koreans and Vietnamese immigrated to the United States in the wake of the Korean War and the Vietnam War. Asian Americans are mostly located on the West coast, in major Hawaiian urban centers, and in the New York region (U.S. Census Bureau 2011c, 2011e).

Asian Americans are found at every class level, but on average they have both higher incomes and more education than members of other racial and ethnic groups, including Whites. As a result, they are often perceived to be a "model minority," a label that overlooks the diversity within the Asian community and disregards the discrimination Asians have endured during much of American history. It can also place unfair pressure on Asian youth to live up to a stereotypical ideal.

NATIVE AMERICANS In 2010, 1.7 percent of the U.S. population (over 5.2 million people) reported their race as American Indian or Alaska Native, either alone (0.9 percent) or in combination with another race (0.7). Of these, 3.1 million identified as exclusively Native American and the rest identified as multiracial (U.S. Census Bureau 2011c, 2011e). As with other groups, most native peoples identify with a particular tribal heritage—such as Cherokee, Iroquois, or Navajo—more than with such generic, outsider-imposed terms as "Indian," "Native Peoples," or "Native American."

Not until the passage of the Indian Citizenship Act of 1924 were Native Americans granted the unlimited right to American citizenship. Before then, they had only limited access to citizenship that usually required them to give up tribal membership. Citizens or not, poverty and bleak prospects drove many to move away from reservations and into the white-dominated society. In the 1960s and 1970s, though, Native Americans organized to revive their traditional cultures and gain wider recognition of the injustices committed against them. In 1976 the Supreme Court ruled that states do not have the right to regulate activities on Indian reservations, opening the way for the establishment of the casinos and other gambling operations that have provided economic opportunity for some tribes.

ARAB AMERICANS The Arab world consists of more than twenty culturally varied Arabic-speaking countries. As a result, Arab Americans are a diverse ethnic group whose members, like those of other ethnic groups, often identify more with their specific ancestral homelands than with a broader ethnic label. The three largest Arab American subgroups are those who report ancestry from Lebanon (30 percent), Egypt (11.7 percent), and Syria (9.5 percent) (U.S. Census Bureau 2009a). Often highly educated, Arab Americans hold both bachelor's and graduate degrees at nearly double the rate of Americans as a whole, and their median household income is slightly higher than the U.S. national median (Arab American Institute 2010).

In the United States, many people confuse the ethnic label "Arab" with the religious label "Muslim." In fact, more than 80 percent of the world's Muslims live *outside* the Arab world, mostly in sub-Saharan Africa, Southeast Asia, and the Far East. Furthermore, one out of ten people in the Arab world is not Muslim (Kayyali 2007). Among Arab Americans, between 50 percent and 63 percent are Christian, whereas between 24 percent and 50 percent are Muslim (Kayyali). Just 0.55 percent of the U.S. population, or about 1.7 million people, claim Arab ancestry (U.S. Census Bureau 2009a). However, because many Christians with Arab ancestry do not self-identify as Arabs, the actual number of Arab Americans may be much higher, perhaps 3.5 million (Arab American Institute 2010).

The earliest Arab immigrants, mostly Lebanese Christians, began arriving in the 1880s. Among more recent immigrants, Muslims predominate. In a striking example of the social construction of race, in 1915, George Dow, a Syrian immigrant living in segregated South Carolina, successfully argued in court that Syrians were white and therefore eligible for citizenship under the existing immigration laws, which limited citizenship to "free white persons" (Naff 1985). The U.S. Census Bureau ever since has counted Arab Americans as white. However, some Arab Americans petitioned the Census Bureau, unsuccessfully, to make "Arab" a separate racial category on the 2010 census (Ashmawey 2010).

Since the September 11, 2001, attacks by Muslim extremists, many Arab Americans, particularly Muslims, have found themselves demonized and subjected to discrimination and violence. Half of American Muslims report that it has been more difficult to be Muslim in the United States since the attacks (Pew Research Center 2007).

Immigration in the Post– Civil Rights Era

In the post–civil rights era, two developments coincided to produce a significant change in immigration patterns. First, global migration increased dramatically, with people from poorer countries seeking economic opportunity in the world's wealthy countries. Second, the Immigration and Nationality Act of 1965, passed in the midst of the civil rights revolution,

Percentage of foreign-born population by region of origin

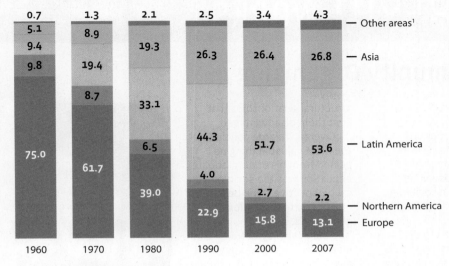

	1960	1970	1980	1990	2000	2007	
Other areas[1]	0.7	1.3	2.1	2.5	3.4	4.3	— Other areas[1]
Asia	5.1 / 9.4	8.9	19.3	26.3	26.4	26.8	— Asia
	9.8	19.4 / 8.7	33.1				
Latin America	75.0	61.7	6.5	44.3	51.7	53.6	— Latin America
Northern America			39.0 / 4.0		2.7	2.2	— Northern America
Europe				22.9	15.8	13.1	— Europe

¹ Other areas include Africa and Oceania.

↩ **FIGURE 10.3 | FOREIGN-BORN POPULATION SINCE 1960**

Changes in immigration law enacted in the 1960s eliminated preferences for European immigrants, contributing to a shift toward greater immigration from Latin American and Asian countries. *Source:* U.S. Census Bureau (2010h).

eliminated the discriminatory national quotas that had favored immigrants from northern and western Europe. Instead, the act put in place a system that favored family members of U.S. citizens, skilled workers, and political refugees. New immigrants started arriving from more regions than before, and as a result, the percentage of foreign-born people in the United States from Latin America and Asia, especially, increased significantly, whereas the percentage of foreign-born people from Europe declined (see Figure 10.3).

Significantly, the 1965 legislation allowed naturalized immigrants to sponsor an unlimited number of family members as new immigrants. Once naturalized, these family members could in turn sponsor more family members, a process sometimes called "chain immigration." An unintended consequence of this provision was to increase overall immigration to unprecedented levels, raising the foreign born as a percentage of the country's population to levels approaching those of the 1920s (see Figure 10.4). By 2008, about one out of eight people in the United States was born elsewhere. Because recent immigrants tend to have a higher birthrate than native-born Americans, the result will significantly affect the racial and ethnic composition of the United States in the coming decades (Lee and Bean 2004). (The Sociology Works box on page 270 explores a sociology major's work with immigrant tenants.)

Transnational Migrants

Unlike earlier immigrants, who often sought to assimilate into the dominant society and typically had limited contact with their homelands, many of today's immigrants are **transnational migrants** who *retain strong personal, cultural, and economic ties to both their country of birth and their newly*

 The increase in unauthorized immigration has generated considerable controversy.

CORE CONCEPTS CHALLENGE

Some people advocate limiting immigration, stricter enforcement of immigration laws, and a clampdown on the borders. Others argue for continuing high levels of legal immigration and contend that unauthorized immigrants should have more access to citizenship. What role do **culture** *and* **power** *play in these conflicts?*

Diversity Today

269

SOCIOLOGY WORKS

Mikey Velarde and Community Organizing

When Mikey Velarde began college, he intended to study cognitive science. He had no idea that a few years later he would be helping to organize a tenants' meeting in New York City's East Harlem as part of his new job as a community organizer. But, motivated by a growing desire to understand—and challenge—racial and ethnic inequalities, Velarde switched from cognitive science to a major in sociology. He graduated with a bachelor's degree and now works primarily with immigrant tenants to help them secure dignified housing in the face of plans for urban development that threaten to displace low-income residents. Velarde has learned a broad array of skills as he works to support local community activists in myriad ways. He knocks on doors to build support networks and to staff meetings of the local tenant association; he organizes community protests; he corresponds with journalists; and he conducts research on housing code violations.

Velarde helps to organize local tenants' associations and to support the development of local leaders within these organizations. He sees the formation of these community-based organizations serving a dual purpose: they contribute to a broader social justice movement and help to deliver specific, immediate benefits to local tenants.

As an undergraduate, Velarde took a range of sociology courses that emphasized questions about the relationship between power and inequality with a specific focus on the experiences and perspectives of oppressed groups. These classes deepened and broadened his knowledge of the dynamic intersection of race, class, gender, sexuality, and nationality in contemporary U.S. society.

Just about every day Velarde is reminded of the relevance of sociology to his work and the lives of the people he serves. He recalls, for example, how, during a discussion at a community meeting, tenants began to grasp the connections among racial inequality, poor housing conditions, and city policies. The fragile housing situation in their neighborhood, they concluded, was more than an isolated phenomenon, but rather an expression of structural relationships that kept them disadvantaged.

Overall, Velarde concludes, the most valuable thing he gained from his undergraduate education was the sociological perspective. "The best and most basic tool sociology has given me is, as Mills put it, a 'sociological imagination'." Ultimately, he says, sociology "has given me a language to critique and contest unjust social arrangements. I am reminded even in the most difficult times that these very arrangements are within the reach of social actors." For community organizer Mikey Velarde, sociology encourages hope in the capacity of human beings to recognize—and challenge—injustice.

Mikey Velarde

> "Ultimately, he says, sociology 'has given me a language to critique and contest unjust social arrangements'."

Velarde has combined his personal experience as a Chicano from El Paso, Texas with the insights he gained from sociology to cultivate a sociological imagination that he brings to bear on his efforts to help the residents of East Harlem improve their lives. He urges others to similarly bring the sociological imagination to bear on their own goals and circumstances. His advice? "Connect to the material from your own social location and life experience."

think about it

1. *What relationship does Mikey Velarde see between sociology and his work in East Harlem?*

2. *How does the sociological perspective encourage Velarde's optimism about our capacity to challenge injustice?*

---

adopted home (Gibson 1988; Portes and Rumbaut 2001). Many recent immigrants have access to inexpensive telephone and Internet services that can provide instantaneous communication with family at home. They can travel to their homeland more easily and can stay abreast of home country news and entertainment on satellite television and the Internet. Transnational migrants often make *remittances*—money transfers to relatives back home—which make up a significant share of the national economies of most Central American countries, the Philippines, Pakistan, Egypt, and other nations (Vertovec 2009). Recognizing these trends, some countries—such as the Philippines—make it easy for migrants to retain their citizenship even as they become citizens in their new homeland. These emerging models of citizenship are likely to become more common, promoting economic advancement and social integration without full cultural accommodation.

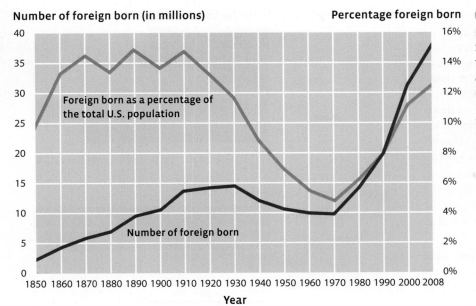

Number of foreign born (in millions)

Percentage foreign born

Foreign born as a percentage of the total U.S. population

Number of foreign born

Year

◀ FIGURE 10.4 | FOREIGN-BORN POPULATION WITHIN THE UNITED STATES, 1850 TO 2008

The *number* of people in the United States born elsewhere has reached unprecedented levels (purple line, left axis), but the *percentage* of the U.S. population that is foreign born is still less today than it was in the late 1800s and early 1900s (orange line, right axis). Source: U.S. Census Bureau (2010h).

Unauthorized Immigration

The surge in immigration that began in the 1960s has been followed by a political backlash similar to the one that followed the earlier surge that began in the late nineteenth century. As before, critics worry that increasing the number of immigrants from different cultures will potentially "disunite" the country (Schlesinger 1998). Unlike before, however, the focus of today's backlash is unauthorized immigrants.

Because these immigrants are by definition "unauthorized" (they are also called "illegal" or "undocumented"), determining their exact number is impossible. The Department of Homeland Security estimates that 10.8 million of them were in the United States in 2010—about a million fewer than three years earlier, a decrease that is likely due to the downturn in the economy. Over 60 percent entered the United States before 2000, and nearly two-thirds (62 percent) are from Mexico. Nearly half live in California (24 percent), Texas (16 percent), or Florida (7 percent) (Hoefer, Rytina, and Baker 2011). They are employed mostly in agriculture, construction, and service occupations.

Several factors have contributed to the increase in undocumented immigrants. First, many Mexicans were recruited as legal temporary workers under the *bracero* program that began in the 1940s. When the program ended in 1964, many stayed in the United States without documentation (Durand, Massey, and Zenteno 2001). Second, the North American Free Trade Agreement (NAFTA) took effect in 1994, eliminating barriers to cross-border trade and investment and undermining broad sectors of the Mexican economy. In particular, many small-scale Mexican farms failed in the face of competition from government-subsidized U.S. agricultural products. As a result, displaced Mexican workers sought opportunities in the United States (Portes 2002). Finally, U.S. employers play a significant role in recruiting immigrant laborers, including undocu-

mented workers, especially in agricultural and meat processing facilities (Rodriguez 2004).

Culture, Structure, and Power: Explaining Ethnic and Racial Inequality

Why has U.S. history been so marked by racial and ethnic inequality? And why has inequality persisted, as we will see, in a society in which discrimination is outlawed? To answer these questions we need to look through the lens of sociological theories about culture, structure, and power at both the legacy of past racial discrimination as well as the new forms of discrimination that have emerged since the civil rights era. These theories address the attitudes and behavior of individuals as well as processes that take place within institutions and society as a whole.

Enduring Inequality

Since the civil rights era, minority groups in the United States have made remarkable progress, but most continue to experience discrimination.

■ ***Housing.*** Numerous studies show that racial discrimination is a significant factor in the continuing stark racial and ethnic segregation of the nation's neighborhoods (Squires,

Friedman and Saidat 2002; U.S. Department of Housing and Urban Development 2005).

- **Education.** Although their achievement is comparable in the early school years, Blacks lag behind Whites on many education measures by the time they reach middle school. Teachers in black-majority districts have less experience and are more likely to be teaching outside their area of expertise than are teachers in white-majority districts (Jones 2007). Similar gaps affect other minorities, as well.

- **Health care.** Racial minorities and Hispanics tend to receive a lower standard of health care than do non-Hispanic Whites, even after controlling for key factors such as income and insurance (Institute of Medicine 2003).

- **Media.** Stereotypical portrayals of racial and ethnic minorities have a long history in the media and are not entirely a relic of the past (Entman and Rojecki 2001; Gray 2004).

- **Economics.** Blacks and Hispanics are about three times more likely to be poor than are non-Hispanic Whites. The median income for non-Hispanic white households is about 40 percent greater than it is for black households and about 30 percent greater than for Hispanic households. Blacks have only about one-tenth the wealth of Whites (U.S. Census Bureau 2010f; Oliver and Shapiro 2006).

In these and many other ways, racial and ethnic inequality continues to characterize U.S. society, as shown in Figure 10.5.

The Legacy of Past Discrimination: The Black-White Wealth Gap

Imagine a long-distance foot race in which some competitors are shackled with leg irons at the start, while others can run freely. Partway through the race, a judge instructs the runners to stop where they are and orders the leg irons removed. The race then continues, but even though all competitors are now allowed to run freely, the gap between frontrunners and those who had been shackled continues to affect the outcome.

This analogy reflects the dilemma facing society in dealing with the legacy of racism. Sociological research shows that people's life chances are affected dramatically by the families into which they are born. So even those who have not experienced discriminatory practices directly can still indirectly inherit either the privileges or disadvantages they create. One of the clearest examples of this legacy is the black-white wealth gap.

As we saw in Chapter 9, income refers to money a person receives over a set period of time. Wealth, though, is what people own, including savings, real estate, stocks and bonds, and other investments. The median income of Blacks is about

Median family income (in thousands of dollars)

Percentage living in poverty

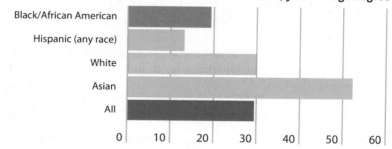

Percentage of those aged 25 or older with at least a 4-year college degree

FIGURE 10.5 | RACIAL AND ETHNIC INEQUALITY

A half-century after the civil rights movement, a number of measures indicate the persistence of racial and ethnic inequality in the United States today. Source: U.S. Census Bureau (2011a, 2011d, 2011e).

CORE CONCEPTS CHALLENGE

How do the group disparities illustrated here reflect the relationship of race and ethnicity to American social structure?

60 percent that of Whites, but the median wealth of Blacks is only about 10 percent that of Whites. Even when we compare only college graduates, Whites have four times as much wealth as Blacks (Oliver and Shapiro 2006).

The massive gap in wealth reflects the persistence of past inequalities from generation to generation. Imagine two young people, both hired fresh out of college to work for the same company at exactly the same salary. Their incomes are equal. However, if only one of them comes from a family with some financial assets, her wealth may be significantly higher. Her parents might have paid for her college education and car and may help pay for a first house, thus reducing or eliminating her mortgage payments. Upon her parents' death, she may inherit real estate, stocks, or other financial investments, allowing her to pass on similar advantages to her children. The other young graduate, enjoying none of these advantages, has more limited options despite his equal salary.

The sort of cumulative, intergenerational impact of wealth inequality illustrated by this example affects everyone, regardless of race. Even though most Whites are not wealthy—and some Blacks have considerable wealth—Whites have never had to face the race-specific barriers created by what sociologists Melvin Oliver and Thomas Shapiro (2006) call the **racialization of the state,** *the implementation of government and private-sector policies that discriminated against minorities and provided Whites with numerous advantages.* These policies included the following:

- The legalization and enforcement of slavery
- Laws that barred Blacks and other minorities from owning property
- Local ordinances that barred Blacks from entering certain occupations
- Regulations that prevented Blacks from selling to Whites, making it nearly impossible for Blacks to compete with white-owned businesses
- Segregated and unequal schooling that ensured unequal opportunities in the job market based on race
- Biased federal home loan programs that steered money to the rapidly growing white suburbs after World War II
- Biased bank loan practices that required black applicants to meet more stringent mortgage criteria than white applicants and continued long after the end of legal segregation

Although these circumstances no longer exist, they made it far more difficult for Blacks than Whites to accumulate wealth and pass it on to their children, a legacy whose impact continues to be felt today.

One lesson of contemporary research, then, is that racial and ethnic inequality continues today because the discrimination of the past still matters. One attempt to overcome this legacy involves **affirmative action,** *a variety of policies and programs that aim to avoid discrimination and redress past discrimination through the active recruitment of qualified minorities for jobs, promotions, and educational opportunities.* One debate over affirmative action is explored in the Sociology Matters box on page 274.

Individual Attitudes and Behaviors: Prejudice and Discrimination

Social-psychological theories that focus on individual attitudes and behaviors can help us understand how people come to adopt their views about inequality. As we noted in Chapter 7, people often define themselves as a member of an *in-group* and feel negatively toward members of an *out-group.* Racism creates an in-out group distinction based on a usually negative stereotype. According to the Thomas theorem (also discussed in Chapter 7), social characteristics that are defined as real have real consequences. Thus a widely accepted stereotype can become the basis for prejudicial attitudes toward the members of an out group.

Stereotypes and prejudice are limited to beliefs and attitudes, but discrimination, as we have seen, involves actions and behaviors (Pettigrew and Taylor 2000). Racial discrimination, for example, involves actions that help maintain the domination of one race over others based on the dominant group's belief in the subordinate group's inferiority (Wilson 1973). As such, discrimination is generally limited to those who have the power to act in ways that hinder others. Those who are relatively powerless may have prejudices of their own, but they generally lack the resources or ability to turn those prejudices into effective discriminatory action. In this sense, discrimination can be thought of as prejudice plus power.

Institutional Discrimination: Structural Barriers to Equality

Individuals can discriminate—for example, a small business owner might refuse to hire members of a different racial or ethnic group. However, racial and ethnic inequality is typically produced and reinforced through institutional discrimination, not just individual action. **Institutional discrimination** *results from the structural organization, policies, and procedures of social institutions such as the government, businesses, and schools.* Institutional discrimination is especially powerful, since it affects large numbers of people. It is especially difficult to change, since it is not associated with any one individual but rather is a generalized feature of an institutional bureaucracy.

In some cases, institutional discrimination is intentional, as with Jim Crow laws in the pre–civil rights era South. In many cases, though, policies and practices that are not themselves overtly or intentionally discriminatory can have a discriminatory impact. For example, the hiring practices of many workplaces rely heavily on informal word-of-mouth communication. When those workplaces are nearly all white, the result can be institutional discrimination toward racial and ethnic minorities who do not have access to these informal channels of communication.

Theories of Prejudice and Discrimination: Culture and Group Interests

Sociological explanations for prejudice and discrimination tend to fall into one of two theoretical traditions, those emphasizing culture and those emphasizing group interests. Much

thinking about **structure**

The **structure** of an organization can contribute to institutional discrimination. How can an institution's structure help prevent discrimination?

SOCIOLOGY Matters

Race, Class, and the Affirmative Action Debate on Campus

If education is to serve as a fair mechanism for individual social mobility, it must be equally accessible to all qualified students. Historically, college and university administrators limited or barred the admission of racial and ethnic minorities while giving wealthy white children of alumni preferential treatment (Kahlenberg 2010a; Karabel 2005; Stevens 2007). Since the 1960s, race-based affirmative action has been used to help overcome the effects of this discrimination and promote more racially diverse campuses. In recent years, however, court decisions have limited race-based affirmative action, and some states have prohibited its use altogether. Meanwhile, some scholars and policymakers have been using sociological insights to suggest new ways to maintain diversity and promote fair access to higher education.

One major sociological criticism of race-based affirmative action programs is that they are blind to the way race intersects with class to affect who benefits from them. Perhaps the most comprehensive study of the subject suggests that the greatest beneficiaries are minorities from middle- and upper-class backgrounds (Bowen and Bok 1998). The programs can also benefit recent minority immigrants, even though they have not suffered the effects of American racism's historical legacy. Meanwhile, affirmative action provides no benefit to poor and working-class Whites disadvantaged by attending weak schools in low-income school districts.

Consequently, some analysts argue for a shift from race-based to class-based affirmative action, thereby assisting students to overcome educational disadvantages, regardless of race (Kahlenberg 1997, 2010b). They argue that well-designed class-based programs will continue to benefit racial and ethnic minorities because minorities are disproportionately represented among the poor and working class. At the same time, however, class-based programs would also benefit white students of modest means, thus overcoming the political objection faced by race-based programs that they unfairly exclude disadvantaged Whites.

If they are to be fair, however, class-based affirmative action programs must take into account the sociological insight that the wealth gap between races is much greater than the income gap. Relying solely on family income as a measure of class would likely harm some racial and ethnic minorities because it would mask the effect of this legacy of racial discrimination. One possible solution would be to define class broadly enough to capture factors beyond income that can influence early educational quality, such as school-district income levels, parents' education level, and family wealth.

Sociologists have also pointed out that one of the principal tools colleges use to evaluate students for admission—scores on standardized tests such as the SAT and ACT—is inherently unfair. The tests are supposed to be an unbiased measure of a student's individual ability, but they turn out to be weak predictors of later academic success. Competitive colleges nonetheless rely heavily on them, giving the appearance that admission decisions are based solely on merit. In fact, these tests give an advantage to affluent students who typically score higher than less affluent students, thanks to well-funded schools, expensive test-taking tutoring, and a home environment that promotes college-related cultural capital. In fact, some sociologists argue that overemphasis on standardized test scores, to the neglect of other indicators of ability such as class ranking, is precisely what puts both racial minorities and lower-income students of all races at a disadvantage. If such tests were a less important part of the decision, the admissions gap between the races and classes would be greatly reduced (Alon 2009; Alon and Tienda 2007).

In the coming years, sociological insights about race and class will continue to help inform the debate over affirmative action and contribute to the development of policies that try to create a fairer system of higher education.

think about it

1. *Overall, do you think affirmative action based on race has been useful? Why or why not?*

2. *Do you agree with advocates who now suggest shifting to class-based affirmative action? Why or why not?*

---

sociological work on the subject, however, combines elements of each approach.

LEARNING PREJUDICE THROUGH CULTURE

Cultural explanations focus on the way familiarity breeds comfort whereas unfamiliarity often produces anxiety or fear. Our socialization has made it easy for us to interact with people who look and behave like us because they are familiar and predictable. By contrast, interacting with people who look different or whose behavior is unfamiliar and therefore unpredictable, can make us uncomfortable.

As children grow up, their socialization often encourages them to form attachments with those in their own group, people like themselves, while often learning negative stereotypes about out-group members, people less like themselves. Some research suggests that youngsters learn stereotypes and develop prejudices as early as age three, often before fully comprehending their meaning or significance (Aboud 1988). Later in life, the mass media can perpetuate negative stereotypes with entertainment that presents such stock characters as the Asian martial-arts expert, the black criminal, the Arab terrorist, or the exotic Asian sex symbol (Wilson, Gutierrez, and Chao 2003).

According to Gordon Allport's (1954) *contact hypothesis,* contact between members of different groups will reduce prejudice *if* the contact is sustained, involves groups with equal status who share common goals, and is sanctioned by authorities. Those are difficult conditions to meet, but college campuses often qualify. For example, one study found that white students randomly assigned a minority roommate had more contact and were more comfortable with members of other races than white students who were assigned a white roommate (Boisjoly et al. 2006). However, without a structure to encourage interaction, diversity on campus does not necessarily translate into increased interracial or interethnic contact.

DISCRIMINATING TO GAIN ADVANTAGE

Group-interest explanations of prejudice and discrimination focus on the way groups compete with one another for scarce and valuable resources such as jobs or desirable housing. Such competition can lead to conflict and to discrimination by one group against another as a means of gaining an advantage over them. As we saw, discrimination often seems to increase in difficult economic periods as competition for scarce resources increases.

Split labor market theory *argues that ethnic and racial conflicts often emerge when two racial or ethnic groups compete for the same jobs.* According to this theory, employers, higher-paid workers, and lower-paid workers form three groups with separate and competing interests (Bonacich 1972, 1976; Gordon, Edwards, and Reich 1982). Employers recruit lower-paid workers to maximize their profits, thereby creating conflict between higher-paid workers and the lower-paid workers who are replacing them. As we have seen, employers often encouraged immigration as a source of inexpensive labor, sometimes stoking racial and ethnic divisions among workers to prevent them from organizing for better wages and working conditions. In the short term, discrimination against minorities also served the interest of higher-paid workers—often Whites, in the context of American history—because it prevented minorities from competing with them for desirable jobs. In the long term, however, these divisions weakened the negotiating power of all workers.

More generally, members of one group can see those of another as a threat, especially when facing difficult circumstances. A **scapegoat** is *an individual or a group of people falsely blamed for a negative situation.* When people are frustrated by their inability to overcome difficulties, they sometimes seek simplistic explanations for their troubles in the form of a scapegoat. In the wake of World War I, for example, Germany faced enormously complex economic and political difficulties, but the Nazis scapegoated Jews and other minorities, blaming them for all the nation's problems. In the United States, Blacks, Irish, Jews, communists, immigrants, and Muslims, among many others, have all been targeted as scapegoats at different times (Hardisty 1999).

Discrimination in the Post–Civil Rights Era: Hidden, Implicit, and Color-Blind

Continuing racial and ethnic inequality in the post–civil rights era has prompted sociologists to conduct new research and develop new theories to explain how discrimination operates in a society in which it is often illegal and covert (Quillian 2006).

HIDDEN PREJUDICE

Robert Merton (1949) recognized long ago that people who were not prejudiced could engage in discriminatory behaviors to conform to biased social norms. Some Whites in the segregated South, for example, acquiesced to the dominant culture even though they personally rejected its racist assumptions. Similarly prejudiced people may keep silent about their attitudes when the dominant norms condemn them but still engage in discriminatory behavior. Indeed, recent research suggests that, in some cases, norms promoting racial and ethnic equality in the post–civil rights era have not eliminated racism but rather have driven it underground, transforming overt prejudices into covert ones.

For example, some people refrain from racist talk or action in public but give vent to racial or ethnic stereotypes when among friends and family. In one study, over a thousand students from a variety of colleges and universities kept journals recording their social interactions for several weeks during the 2002–2003 academic year (Picca and Feagin 2007). The journals of the more than 600 white students in the study showed them to be nearly always polite to their black peers, avoiding racially offensive language in public "front-stage" situations. However, in "back-stage," white-only settings, students reported the frequent use of the word "nigger" and other racial epithets to refer to Blacks. Some students reported feeling uncomfortable about the racist language but lacked the courage to object. In their journals, the white students also commonly referred to Blacks in terms of racial

---

SPOTLIGHT on social theory

Split labor market theory is in the tradition of **conflict theory.** Have you worked in or seen a workplace in which higher-paid workers and lower-paid workers were divided along ethnic or racial lines?

SPOTLIGHT on social theory

As part of the symbolic **interactionist** tradition, **dramaturgical theory** draws attention to the differences between front-stage and back-stage behaviors. Are research findings that racist back-stage behavior is relatively common among college students, whereas front-stage behavior is noticeably free of such actions, consistent with your own experiences?

---

thinking about power

People in authority have often used scapegoats as a means of gaining or maintaining their **power** over others. Can you think of an example of the use of this tactic, from your own life or from recent history?

stereotypes, describing them as lazy, criminally inclined, and oversexed. The results suggest that, even fifty years after the civil rights movement, these stereotypes and prejudices remain deeply entrenched and widely prevalent.

Hidden prejudices can also lead people who deny they are motivated by any personal prejudice to engage in discriminatory practices. White employers, for example, may justify their acknowledged reluctance to hire Blacks by citing the prevalence of crime in black communities. Ironically, some managers admit to steering clear of hiring Blacks precisely because of the public sanctions against racial discrimination: they fear a discrimination lawsuit if an African American employee needs to be fired (Wilson 1997).

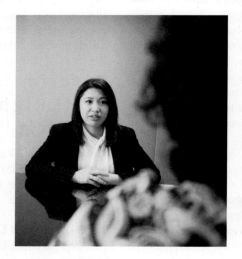

IMPLICIT BIAS   In 1926, Emory Bogardus published a study of the *social distance* between groups, based on a nationwide survey of college students. To measure social distance, he asked students how closely they were willing to interact with the members of certain other groups. Being willing to marry someone from a group, for example, indicated very little social distance, whereas wanting to bar members of a group from the country indicated great social distance. Bogardus—and later other researchers—repeated the survey over the years, refining the measures and expanding the sample to include the general population, not just college students (Bogardus 1967). The results show decreasing social distance over time, indicating a reduction in racial and ethnic prejudice. There are exceptions, though. In the wake of the September 11, 2001, terrorist attacks, for example, the acceptance of Muslims and Arabs declined (Parrillo and Donoghue 2005).

As researchers learn more about how the brain works, however, they are finding that some biases may be more implicit—existing at the subconscious level—than overt and at a conscious level where they can be measured in surveys. Recent research suggests that we learn prejudices at a deep, unconscious level and respond to people with lightning-fast assessments that are beyond rational evaluation (Vedantam 2005). In our conscious activities, we can control our behaviors and overcome implicit biases, but this restraint is cognitively challenging and requires additional effort (Richeson et al. 2003). At the unconscious level, we may be acting on well-known stereotypes and deeply held prejudices.

Social psychologist Mahzarin Banaji and her colleagues have devised a series of implicit association tests (IAT) that measure unconscious biases by tapping into fast, unexamined responses. (You can take some of these tests yourself online at https://implicit.harvard.edu.) These researchers have found that most respondents show an unconscious preference for people like themselves, regardless of their stated beliefs. Even when people who feel and say they are not biased are tested, in most cases the results indicate they actually have unconscious biases based on race, ethnicity, sexual orientation, and class as well as other categories. These tests have their critics (Blanton and Jaccard 2008), but, if confirmed by further research, they may demonstrate that implicit bias is one source of enduring prejudice and discrimination in contemporary society.

Racial discrimination persists in many areas of social life, whether because of prejudice, hidden racism, or implicit bias. One method sociologists use to measure discrimination is the *field audit* (Quillian 2006). In typical field audits, researchers pair people from different races or ethnic groups who are otherwise similar on all characteristics that might affect the study's outcome. They then send each member of the pair into social situations in which they may encounter discrimination, such as renting an apartment or applying for a job. Using this method repeatedly, researchers have documented persistent racial discrimination in housing (Turner and Ross 2005) and hiring (Altonji and Blank 1999). One study even found discrimination based on no more than the name on otherwise comparable resumes mailed in response to ads for jobs. Resumes for people with white-sounding names, such as Emily and Greg, were 50 percent more likely to get a callback than were those for people with black-sounding names, such as Lakisha and Jamal (Bertrand and Mullainathan 2004). Another study found that employers were much more likely to hire a white person with a criminal record than a black person with a criminal record (Pager 2003). Yet another study found that doctors recommended different treatments for people of different races who came to them with identical symptoms (Shulman et al. 1999).

THE NEW RACISM   Sociologists often refer to today's persistent racism as *the new racism,* and they describe its dynamics with a variety of approaches that have a variety of labels, including "symbolic racism" (Kinder and Sanders 1996), "laissez-faire racism" (Bobo, Kluegel, and Smith 1997), "color-blind racism" (Bonilla Silva 2001, 2009), and "modern racism" (McConahay 1986). Although their analyses vary somewhat, these approaches agree on two points:

- Prejudice and discrimination persist in contemporary social life.
- The ways in which prejudice and discrimination manifest themselves have changed in the post–civil rights era.

For example, in a significant shift from earlier attitudes, many Americans today advocate race neutrality and a "color-blind" society. But ideas that once might have been progressive and antiracist can reinforce existing racial inequality in a different historical era. **Color-blind racism** is *the promotion of race neutrality when it actually helps to maintain existing racial and* *ethnic inequality.* It reveals itself in the rejection of efforts to reduce racial and ethnic inequality on the grounds that those efforts violate a color-blind approach to society and may even constitute reverse racism.

Some who advocate color-blind policies are likely using race neutrality as a cover for prejudiced views, understanding that overt racism is no longer acceptable in our society. However, color-blind approaches are not inherently prejudicial, and some advocates of this view genuinely believe that race neutrality is the best route to racial justice. The result is a complex mix of racial and nonracial beliefs that in combination—intentionally or not—can help perpetuate racial inequality.

How do those who believe that racism is no longer a significant hurdle in our supposedly post-racial society explain the continuing inequality among racial and ethnic groups in U.S. society? Some simply deny that inequality and discrimination exist, despite the vast body of social science research showing that it does. Some point to cultural differences to account for this variation and, in particular, to the success of Asian Americans as evidence that racial and ethnic discrimination no longer holds back social advancement. Some have argued that enduring racial inequality simply reflects the natural outcome of competition between groups with inherently differ-

ent abilities. Richard Herrnstein and Charles Murray (1996), for instance, claimed that differences in scores on intelligence tests (IQ scores) reflect innate and unchangeable differences between the races. Critics have pointed out the inadequacies of such studies, which ignore the impact of environment on IQ scores (Fischer et al. 1996). They argue that efforts to measure differences in intelligence are repackaged racist ideas that hark back to the ugly history of racist pseudo-science.

Critics of color-blind policies argue that to pretend that race no longer matters is to overlook the legacy of racism and the persistence of prejudice and discrimination. As U.S. Supreme Court Justice Harry Blackmun famously said in defending the use of affirmative action, "In order to get beyond racism, we must first take account of race."

In the nineteenth century, a civil war led to the end of slavery in the United States. In the twentieth century, the civil rights movement led to the end of racial segregation and legal discrimination. In both cases, social change came only after intense controversy and prolonged conflict. Just as those struggles were contentious in their day, so too are the efforts to understand inequality and advance racial and ethnic justice in a post–civil rights society.

In Transition

MULTIRACIAL AND MULTIETHNIC IDENTITIES

As part of his stand-up act a few years ago, comedian Chris Rock would raise a question about the success of golf great Tiger Woods and popular rapper Eminem. "What's happening in America," he would ask in astonishment, "when the best golfer is black and the best rapper is white?" This line always got a laugh, but it also exposes enduring racial stereotypes. Tiger Woods's father had a mix of African American, Chinese, and Native American ancestry, and his mother had a mix of Thai, Chinese, and Dutch. Yet in the United States, Tiger Woods is still often seen simply as black.

Woods's complex ancestry highlights the growth of multiracial and multiethnic identities. As marriages across racial and ethnic lines increase, people with these new identities are likely to play a larger role in tomorrow's world. It has long been common for people to identify with multiple ethnicities, saying, for example "I'm Irish on my father's side and Russian on my mother's." Today, however, multiethnic identities include an ever-larger range of ethnicities from all parts of the world.

As immigration and intermarriage increase, so do the number of people with multiracial identities. At least one in every twenty Americans under the age of eighteen is now multiracial, and some analysts expect that proportion to rise to one in five by 2050 (Lee and Bean 2004). In the 2010 census, 9 million Americans (3 percent of the population) identified themselves as being of two or more races, although this number is an undercount since those who answer "multiracial" are classified as "some other race" (U.S. Census Bureau 2011c, 2011e). In addition, cultural norms still encourage people in the United States to identify with only one race. For example, in the 2010 census, only 7.4 percent of Blacks indicated they had a multiracial background, even though the U.S. Census Bureau estimates that at least 75 percent of black Americans have a multiracial ancestry. As multiracial identities become more socially accepted, however, we are likely to see a significant increase in the percentage of people who embrace them, the latest development in our evolving conception of race and ethnicity.

Percent

FIGURE 10.6 | INTERMARRIAGE RATES OF NEWLYWEDS, 2008

Asians are the most likely to marry someone of a different race or ethnicity. Whites are the least likely to do so. *Note:* "Newlyweds" refers to people who got married in the 12 months before the survey. All groups (other than Hispanic) are non-Hispanic single races. *Source:* Passel, Wang, and Taylor, 2010

Rising intermarriage is one sign that the boundaries between some racial and ethnic groups have become less rigid. Intermarriage between members of different white ethnic groups was rare a hundred years ago but is now so common that only about 20 percent of Whites have a spouse with the same ethnicity, and such unions are no longer even categorized as interethnic (Lee and Bean 2004). Interracial marriage was still outlawed in fifteen states when the Supreme Court declared such statutes unconstitutional in 1967. Today, though, about one out of

seven marriages in the United States unites either people of different races or Hispanics and non-Hispanics, a rate that has doubled between 1980 and 2008 and increased sixfold since 1960 (Passel, Wang, and Taylor 2010). (See Figure 10.6.)

Only one in nine Whites is in an interracial or interethnic marriage. In contrast, nearly a third of Asian Americans and a quarter of Hispanics are married to someone of another race or ethnicity, usually non-Hispanic Whites. More than two-thirds of Native Americans marry someone who is not Native American (Lee and Bean 2004). Intermarriage by Whites has doubled since 1980 and tripled for Blacks but has remained fairly steady for Hispanics and Asians, probably because a growing number of Asians and Hispanics are available as potential partners as their percentages of the population increase (Passel, Wang, and Taylor 2010). Intermarriage rates also vary by gender within racial and ethnic groups. Among Whites and Hispanics, intermarriage rates are about equal for men and women. However, the intermarriage rate for black men (22 percent) is more than twice as high as it is for black women (8.9 percent), whereas Asian women (39.5 percent) intermarry at twice the rate of Asian men (19.5 percent). Younger people and native-born adults are more likely to marry outside their racial or ethnic group than are older people and immigrants, suggesting intermarriage will likely increase in the coming years as the taboo against it fades and recent immigrants become more established (Passel, Wang, and Taylor 2010).

As the trend toward intermarriage continues, it promises to alter the nature of racial and ethnic relations in the United States, making it easier for members of minority groups to cross boundaries in employment, housing, and marriage. Perhaps it will even diminish the social significance of racial and ethnic categories altogether.

Race and Ethnicity

culture

- Race and ethnicity are social constructs whose definitions change over time and vary across cultures.

- Social norms about race and ethnicity—both racist and antiracist—are learned through the process of socialization.

structure

- Interpretations of race and ethnicity influence patterns of social interaction.

- The policies and practices of social institutions can both reflect racist beliefs and perpetuate racial and ethnic inequality.

- Groups, from slaves to the activists of the civil rights movement and later, have resisted racial discrimination, sometimes producing long-lasting changes in the social structure.

power

- Racial and ethnic inequality reflects differences in power within society.

- Powerful groups have historically justified their privileges on the basis of their supposed racial or ethnic superiority.

- The post–civil rights era has seen both enduring racial and ethnic inequality as well as new relations of power, reflecting the increasing diversity of society.

Looking Back

1. Race is not a biological reality, but rather a social construct whose origin lies in eighteenth- and nineteenth-century pseudo-science. Ethnicity is also a social construct that, like race, has been interpreted differently in different cultures and in various historical periods.

2. Grouping people into different races and ethnicities sets up majority-minority group dynamics that become a part of the social structure and reflect inequalities in power.

3. The social history of the United States resulted in unique ideas and practices concerning race and ethnicity. In particular, Whites used ideas about race and racial superiority to justify slavery and adopt laws that enshrined racial inequality.

4. Native societies were decimated by the arrival of European colonizers. Spanish colonists, the ancestors of today's Hispanics, took control of what is now the southwestern United States. White Anglo-Saxon Protestants settled primarily on the east coast and rapidly expanded their landholdings westward. African slaves were imported in growing numbers as labor for an agrarian economy. In the nineteenth century, Asian laborers—especially Chinese—were recruited to work on railroads and in other industries.

5. Rising immigration from throughout Europe in the nineteenth and early twentieth centuries increased ethnic diversity. Some groups—including Jews, the Irish, and Italians—were not considered "white" until they gradually assimilated.

6. The civil rights movement helped transform society, making racial and ethnic discrimination illegal and promoting tolerance. One consequence was a change in immigration laws that opened the way to new diversity. Recent immigrants, who come mostly from Asia and Latin America rather than Europe, are substantially changing the racial and ethnic makeup of the country.

7. Despite the gains of the civil rights movement, racial and ethnic inequalities endure, reflecting racism's historical legacy as well as contemporary practices. Racial prejudice and discrimination operate at different levels of social life, involving individual attitudes and behaviors and the structural barriers created by institutions. Prejudice and discrimination can be fueled by cultural differences or by the pursuit of group interests. In a post–civil rights society, prejudice and discrimination can be hidden, implicit, or produced by support for color-blind policies.

8. One consequence of our increasing diversity is the growth of multiethnic and multiracial identities, in part the result of an increase in interracial marriage.

Critical Thinking: Questions and Activities

1. A friend asks, "Are you blind? Of course race exists!" Explain to your friend why race is, in fact, a social construction, rather than a biological fact.

2. How did you first learn about race and ethnicity? Did this early socialization include the perpetuation of stereotypes? Explain. What socializing forces later influenced your understanding of these issues?

3. Is the social history of race and ethnicity in the United States summarized here consistent with what you learned in high school? If not, how is it different?

4. How do you think changing demographics in the United States will influence other aspects of life fifty years from now?

5. Do you think racial attitudes today among people under age thirty differ significantly from those held by older people? Why or why not? (How could you find out for sure?) What factors do you think contributed to this situation?

Key Terms

affirmative action (p. 273) a variety of policies and programs that aim to avoid discrimination and redress past discrimination through the active recruitment of qualified minorities for jobs, promotions, and educational opportunities.

amalgamation (p. 259) the process by which a majority and a minority group blend or mix to form a new group.

assimilation (p. 259) the process by which members of a minority group come to adopt the culture of the majority group.

color-blind racism (p. 276) a form of bias in which the promotion of race neutrality helps to maintain existing racial and ethnic inequality.

discrimination (p. 258) unequal treatment that gives advantages to one group of people over another without justifiable cause.

ethnicity (p. 253) shared cultural heritage often deriving from a common ancestry and homeland.

genocide (p. 259) the systematic killing of a group of people, based on their race, ethnicity, nationality, or religion.

institutional discrimination (p. 273) unequal treatment that results from the structural organization, policies, and procedures of social institutions such as the government, businesses, and schools.

majority group (p. 258) a collection of people who enjoy privileges and have more access to power because of identifiable physical or cultural characteristics.

minority group (p. 258) a collection of people who suffer disadvantages and have less power because of identifiable physical or cultural characteristics.

pluralism (p. 258) a situation in which distinct ethnic and racial groups coexist on equal terms and have equal social standing.

prejudice (p. 258) to "pre-judge" someone or some group negatively based on inadequate information.

race (p. 253) a category of people widely perceived as sharing socially significant physical characteristics such as skin color.

racial essentialism (p. 256) the idea that supposedly natural and immutable differences separate the races.

racialization of the state (p. 273) the implementation of government and private-sector policies that discriminated against minorities and provided Whites with numerous advantages.

racism (p. 256) the belief that one race is inherently superior to another.

scapegoat (p. 275) an individual or a group of people falsely blamed for a negative situation.

segregation (p. 259) keeping distinct social groups physically and socially separate and unequal.

split labor market theory (p. 275) the theory that ethnic and racial conflicts often emerge when two racial or ethnic groups compete for the same jobs.

stereotypes (p. 258) exaggerated, distorted, or untrue generalizations about categories of people that do not acknowledge individual variation.

transnational migrants (p. 269) immigrants who retain strong personal, cultural, and economic ties to both their country of birth and their newly adopted home.

11

Gender and Sexuality

looking AHEAD

How has **culture** influenced your understanding of gender roles and sexuality?

How are your ideas about gender and sexuality reinforced through social **structures** such as your family or your school?

Are differences in **power** in your family or friendships the result of inequalities based on gender and sexual orientation?

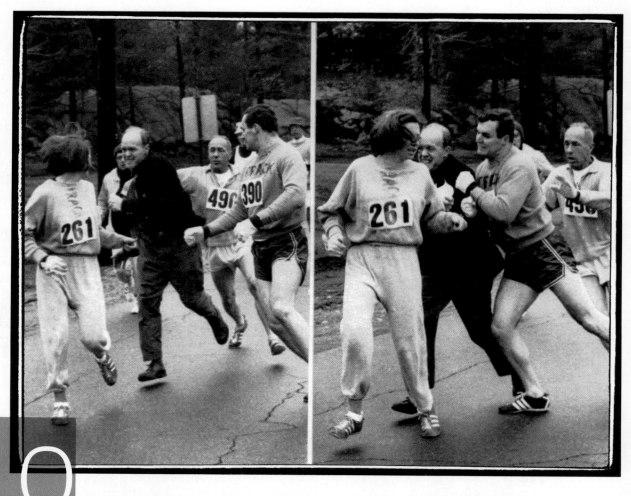

On April 19, 1967, a twenty-year-old student named Kathrine Switzer was running the Boston Marathon when a truck carrying press photographers and race officials drove by slowly. One of the officials, Jock Semple, was stunned when he noticed Switzer. Jumping off the vehicle and yelling, "Get the hell out of my race!" Semple lunged at the young runner and tried to rip off her official race number. He missed the number but grabbed the back of Switzer's sweatshirt, momentarily preventing her from advancing. Switzer's boyfriend, who was also running, shoved the race official, allowing Switzer to escape and finish the race.

What had Switzer done to evoke such an angry outburst? She had dared to run a marathon at a time when women were banned from competing in such events. A year earlier, Roberta Gibb had become the first woman to finish the Boston Marathon, but she had to run unofficially, and she even had to hide in the bushes near the start so that race officials would not spot her. Switzer managed to obtain an official number by registering under a gender-neutral name, K. V. Switzer (Switzer 2007).

At the time, the men who organized long-distance road races in the United States used their power to ban women from competing in marathons for what they argued were biologically obvious reasons: women were simply too frail to complete the grueling 26.2-mile event safely. Conventional wisdom held that even if some women could finish the race, doing so would likely cause physiological damage, perhaps even preventing them from having children. Women could not compete officially in U.S. marathons until 1971 or in an Olympic marathon until 1984.

Today, hundreds of thousands of women run in marathons each year. Their safe participation shows that what was widely considered biological reality just a few decades ago was, in fact, a social construction—a part of the structure of sports produced by the power of men that created needless social barriers for women. ■

In this chapter, we examine the idea of gender and consider how people mistake socially constructed differences as natural. We look at how cultural norms are reinforced or modified in daily life and within social structures, and how artificial distinctions between women and men contribute to gender inequality. In addition, we consider similar issues of social construction as they apply to human sexuality. We also look at how people have organized to challenge inequality based on gender and sexuality.

Biology and Culture: Sex and Gender

In everyday life, you often see the terms *sex* and *gender* treated as if they meant the same thing. For example, a questionnaire might ask for your "gender," expecting you to indicate either "male" or "female." Sociologists distinguish between sex and gender, however, to highlight the difference between biology and culture (Stoller 1968).

Sex is *the biological distinction between females and males.* In contrast, **gender** refers to *the socially constructed cultural expectations associated with women and men.* Biology makes us male or female; culture teaches us to be men or women. To take two simple examples, most females have the physical capacity to give birth to children, but males do not. This ability is a sex difference. In our culture, women are free to wear dresses in daily life, but men are generally discouraged from doing so. This restriction is a gender difference. It is based on culture and has nothing to do with biology.

The distinctions between sex and gender are not always so clear-cut. Scholars debate the influence of biologically based sex differences on social behavior. However, much of what our culture associates with *sex* differences are, in fact, socially produced *gender* differences. For example, when Kathrine Switzer ran in the 1967 Boston Marathon, the women's world record in the marathon—from competitions outside the United States—was 3:19:33, while the men's record was 2:12:00. Some men pointed to this 67-minute gap as evidence that women were biologically unfit for the difficult race. As of 2011, however, women runners had narrowed the gap to less than twelve minutes: 2:15:25 for women and 2:03:59 for men. Clearly, social factors, not biological ones, were responsible for most of the gap between women's and men's performance in the past. In sports, as in many other areas of life, we can mistakenly attach biological explanations to what are primarily social factors. To help unravel the relationship between sex and gender, let's examine each more closely.

The Biology of Sex

A person's sex is determined at conception when the mother's ovum (or egg cell) contributes an X chromosome to the embryo and the father's sperm contributes either an X or a Y chromosome. An XX combination produces a female; an XY combination a male. Chromosomes help determine physical development, including distinctions between the sexes. *Primary sex characteristics,* including the genitals and reproductive organs, are sex differences that are directly involved in reproduction. *Secondary sex characteristics,* including wider hips and breast development in females and more extensive body hair and increased muscle mass in the upper body in males, are not directly involved in reproduction.

Sex differences can be grouped loosely into two categories: absolute differences and differences of degree. Absolute sex differences include those related to reproduction. Only females menstruate, ovulate, become pregnant, and breastfeed their babies; only males can impregnate females. Other differences, though, are of degree. Both men and women possess the same hormones, for example, but in different amounts.

Most individuals are clearly biologically female or male. But some people are **intersexual**—*individuals born with ambiguous reproductive or sexual anatomy.* Intersexual people have some ambiguity in their genitals, chromosomes, gonads (female ovaries or males testes), or hormones. Being intersexual can include conditions such as having external female genitals but internal testes, an additional chromosome (XXY), or hormonal irregularities that at puberty produce secondary sex characteristics associated with the other sex. Because of the range of conditions involved, experts disagree about who and how many people qualify as intersexual, with one study estimating between 0.2 percent and 1.7 percent of the population (Blackless et al. 2000).

The Limits of Biology

Imagine that researchers devise a project to investigate whether the ability to walk in high-heeled shoes is biologically based. They choose a random sample of women and men, have them strap on some heels, and record the results. Lo and behold, it turns out that, on average, women perform significantly better than men. The researchers might suggest that these results are likely due to biological differences between the sexes in body mass, balance, and coordination.

Actually, the ability they are measuring has been learned with practice—as anyone proficient in walking in heels can tell you. With some effort, it's entirely possible for men to develop this skill, but in our culture they are not encouraged to acquire it. Socialization, not biology, produced the difference.

In fact, studies show an overwhelming number of similarities in the psychology and abilities of women and men, with more variation occurring within each sex than between the two (Hyde 2005). Yet the popular media often highlight misinterpretations and pseudo-science regarding supposedly innate differences between the sexes. For example, a once-popular book touting that "men are from Mars and women

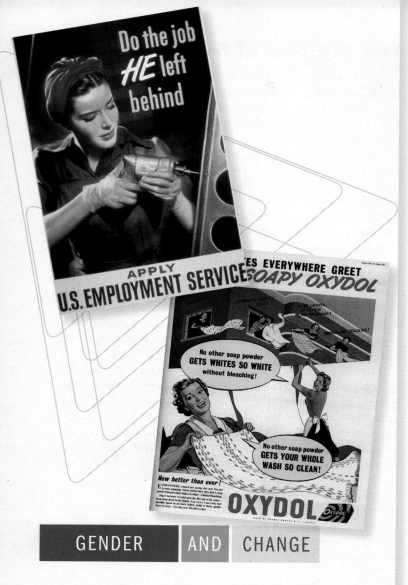

GENDER AND CHANGE

Cultures promote appropriate gender roles through the images presented in mass media. Over time, these images can reveal the socially constructed nature of gender. With millions of men fighting in World War II, government propaganda efforts (as in the poster, top, from 1943) promoted the idea that women are capable of taking up traditionally male occupations. Just a few years later, however, television and advertising (bottom) were once again highlighting traditional domestic roles for women. If a historian from the future looked back at today's ads, what would she or he learn about gender in our society?

from Venus" (Gray 2004) simply treats cultural stereotypes—such as women are passive while men are active—as innate differences, without adequately considering the role of gender socialization in producing them. We can recognize the falseness of such claims in an outrageous example such as our hypothetical study of walking with high heels, but more subtle real-world studies can be misleading.

For example, men often outperform women in tasks that require subjects to use visualization and mentally manipulate

objects. Researchers sometimes attribute such superior performance to innate differences that developed during evolution and cite these results as a reason why men dominate some scientific fields such as engineering. An understanding of how gender influences human development, however, provides us with a different perspective on this research.

In one study, researchers briefly showed subjects a grid that contained two dozen identical objects and one object that was different (Feng, Spence, and Pratt 2007). The subjects had to determine the location of the odd object quickly. Consistent with the idea that they have evolved better spatial abilities, men succeeded in the task 68 percent of the time, whereas women succeeded only 55 percent of the time, a statistically significant difference. However, after some of the subjects spent ten hours playing a video game that involved shooting at a target (a game popular with boys, less so with girls), the difference between the sexes disappeared upon retesting both at once and five months later. A difference in skill that researchers and others could have misinterpreted as the result of innate physiological differences instead turned out to be easily influenced—and erased—by environmental conditions, in this case, access to and practice with video games.

There *are* actual differences in the architecture of male and female brains. In the coming years we will likely learn more about these differences and how men and women use their brains in different ways to get the same job done. As we saw in Chapter 6, though, the human brain has a remarkable ability—known as brain plasticity—to restructure and reorganize itself in response to social experiences and learning. As we will see, expectations about gender create different social experiences for women and men from the moment of birth. Just as the gender gap in marathon performance was due largely to culture, not biology, so are many of the differences measured by today's research. If we want to understand the social life of women and men, then, we need to look beyond biology to gender and its social construction.

Gender as a Social Construction

Almost all the differences we associate with men and women are culturally produced, not biologically based. From infancy, we are taught our culture's expectations regarding gender, we develop identities that are based on those expectations, and we view the world through the lens of gender expectations that we usually take for granted. For example, if you got into a taxi cab with a female driver, you would probably take note; without even thinking about it, you most likely expect a man to drive a taxi. Similarly, you might be surprised to encounter a male dental hygienist or daycare provider.

If we look at how notions of gender differ over time and across cultures, we can see the powerful influence of culture.

GENDER IN A DIFFERENT TIME
Throughout the history of the United States, activists have challenged widely accepted ideas about gender and, over time, changed

how people think. In 1848, participants at a ground-breaking women's rights convention in Seneca Falls, New York, pointed out some of the oppressive political, legal, educational, and economic conditions that women faced. In a document modeled after the Declaration of Independence, these activists produced an inventory of grievances that included the fact that women could not vote, had no legal or property rights and could be abused by their husbands at will, were excluded from most occupations and professions, and were prevented from obtaining a college education. "The history of mankind," they concluded, "is a history of repeated injuries and usurpations on the part of man toward woman, having in direct object the establishment of an absolute tyranny over her" (Stanton 1889, 70–71).

The activists at Seneca Falls were an important part of the women's movement that ultimately changed the way most people in our society view gender. Eventually, their efforts helped to win the vote for women with the passage of the Nineteenth Amendment to the Constitution in 1920. In hindsight, we can see the biases behind the gender claims that dominated nineteenth-century America, even as we recognize their persistence in some parts of contemporary society.

GENDER IN A DIFFERENT CULTURE Blatant and comprehensive discrimination against women continues in many parts of the world, illustrating how ideas about gender vary not only across time but also across cultures. In Saudi Arabia, for example, a close ally of the United States, women play no official role in government or politics, have few social rights, and are not treated as equal members of society (U.S. Department of State 2004). Although women make up 58 percent of university students, the types of work they can perform are restricted, and they comprise only 15 percent of the workforce. They are expected to remain at home caring for husband and family. By law and custom, schools, workplaces, and transportation are segregated by sex, and women cannot attend most public events unless a close male relative accompanies them. Saudi women generally cannot drive, appear in public with their heads uncovered, travel abroad, receive an identity card, or be admitted to a hospital for treatment without permission from a male relative or guardian. A woman cannot conduct financial transactions (even if she owns a business) without deputizing a male relative as her representative. In the court system in Saudi Arabia, which is based on Islamic law, the testimony of a woman is given half the weight of the testimony of a man.

Many of these gender practices contrast sharply with contemporary Western values, but they are similar to those in the United States a century and a half ago, when the activists at Seneca Falls produced their inventory of grievances. Despite strong restrictions on political protest, some Saudi women have dared to challenge their treatment publicly; however, there are no ongoing women's rights organizations in the country.

Gender Identities and Transgender People

As these examples of difference over time and across cultures show, gender is a social construction that originates in culture but that becomes a part of a person's sense of self. **Gender identity** is *a person's identification as a woman, a man, or some combination of the two.* Most males learn to identify as men; most females learn to identify as women. (Some cultures recognize three or four genders; see the Through a Sociological Lens box on page 288.) We explore this process in more detail later in this chapter.

Gender identity is largely learned; however, it remains unclear whether, and to what degree, biology—especially prenatal hormones—might influence the development of gender identity. This is another example of the current recognition that both biology and culture play a role in human development, although much work remains to be done to specify this relationship (Fausto-Sterling 2000). Broad consensus exists among researchers that biology does not *determine* gender identity, however.

Gender expression is *the communication of a person's gender identity to others, through behavior, clothing, hairstyle, and other means.* Since gender is different from sex, gender identity and gender expression are not necessarily consistent with biology. The differentiation between sex and gender is central to the idea of transgender identity. **Transgender people** are *individuals who identify with a gender different from the one*

Many colleges and universities have taken the lead in creating gender-neutral environments. As of 2007, nearly 150 such institutions have added gender identity and gender expression to their nondiscrimination policies; 141 have some gender-neutral bathrooms that are open to both women and men; and 30 have gender-neutral housing, where roommates are of the same gender but not necessarily the same sex (Jaschik 2007).

thinking about culture

Ideas about gender vary by **culture**. Have you experienced a culture or subculture in which some gender norms differed from those commonly found in the dominant U.S. culture?

Examining the Case of Two-Spirits

Brian Rainforth (left) and Raven E. Heavy Runner are pictured at a 2006 gathering of two-spirits in Montana (Leeland 2006). Though from different tribes—Rainforth is Klamath, Heavy Runner is Blackfeet—these men are part of a common tradition of two-spirits that goes back many generations and includes We'wha of the Zuni tribe, pictured on the right in an 1886 photo.

In 1886, anthropologist Matilda Coxe Stevenson (one of the country's first female social scientists) toured Washington, D.C., with We'wha, a representative of the New Mexican Zuni tribe. The newspapers covered We'wha's visit. She was photographed, demonstrated Zuni weaving techniques on the National Mall, and even met with then-president Grover Cleveland. Although We'wha was six feet tall and had distinctly male physical features, Americans understood her to be a woman. What her audiences didn't realize was that We'wha was a biological male but her culture considered her to belong to a third gender, neither male nor female (Roscoe 1992).

Our society is used to dividing men and women into two distinct genders. However, many cultures see more than two genders, allowing for a blending of characteristics. For example, well over 100 Native American cultures have recognized a gender that is now commonly known as "two-spirit" (Gilley 2006; Jacobs, Thomas and Lang 1997). Although they may be physiologically male or female, two-spirits such as We'wha take on some of the social roles generally associated with the other sex.

Historically, most two-spirits were males who dressed in women's clothes and did work associated with women, such as handcrafts, cooking, and childrearing. They adopted, in effect, a third gender. A smaller number of tribes recognized two-spirit females who took on roles associated with men, including hunting, warfare, and tribal leadership. Some tribes considered female two-spirits to be a fourth gender distinct from male two-spirits.

Social roles, not sexuality, defined two-spirits. However, homosexuality and bisexuality were common among both male and female two-spirits, with two-spirits sometimes marrying someone of the same sex who was not a two-spirit.

The treatment two-spirits received within their cultures varied widely, ranging from reverence to scorn. Sometimes they held a high social status. Mystical or healing powers were attributed to them, or they played important pragmatic roles, such as mediating disputes between women and men. In some cultures, two-spirits were not particularly distinct from others except for their adoption of cross-gender roles. In other cultures, however, two-spirits were marginalized and might be excluded from many tribal activities.

European Americans failed to understand—and were perhaps threatened by—the role of two-spirits, since this category contradicted their strict two-gender culture. They labeled such people pejoratively as *berdache,* a word whose origin is connected with male prostitution, which is inaccurate and offensive to most native people. The word for people who had both female and male gender characteristics was different in various tribal languages, but since the early 1990s the Ojibwa term *two-spirits* has been widely adopted. Today, some two-spirits people meet in annual gatherings to affirm their unique identities (Leeland 2006).

think about it

1. *How do two-spirits illustrate the socially constructed nature of gender?*

2. *What are the advantages and disadvantages of recognizing more than two genders in a culture?*

associated with their sex. Some transgender people report that they feel trapped in a body of the opposite sex. Some wear the clothes and hairstyles of the gender with which they identify and adopt the vocal pitch, speech patterns, posture, and body language associated with that gender. Being transgender is not necessarily connected to sexual orientation, nor is it the same as being a *transvestite,* a person of one sex who dresses in clothing associated with the other sex.

Some transgender people become **transsexuals,** *people who have sex reassignment surgery to change their physical appearance.* Such surgery alters their genitalia and is usually accompanied by hormone treatments that promote secondary sex characteristics, such as breasts for women and facial hair for men. Though it is not biologically possible to change a person's sex—for example, males who undergo sex change operations cannot bear children, and they still have XY chromosomes—surgery and hormone treatments can make a person's body more consistent with the gender with which he or she identifies.

Masculinities

As we have seen, ideas about gender vary over time and across cultures. Even within U.S. society today, people often have different ideas about what it means to be a woman or a man, depending on their class, race, and other social characteristics.

The women's movement has long promoted the idea that there is no single way to be a woman; many femininities exist. Similarly, although a broad dominant definition of *masculinity*—the properties and characteristics associated with men—pervades society, various subcultures have differing social norms and expectations for "masculine" behavior and attitudes. Researchers talk about Latino masculinity, gay masculinity, working-class masculinity, and so on. Furthermore, even within these subgroups, ideas about masculinity can vary.

Instead of a single interpretation of masculinity, the intersection of gender with race and class creates a variety of masculinities (Connell 2005). Working-class men, especially those involved in manual labor, often have a sense of masculinity that values group solidarity, physical strength and toughness, and resistance to those in authority. By contrast, middle-class men often value self-reliance, individual ability, and mental proficiency (Tolson 1977). A male college student from a working-class or poor background may be acutely aware of these differences since his college education is preparing him for a middle-class social world that is different from that experienced by his father and other male relatives and friends.

A person's race and ethnicity also influence his or her experience of gender. African Americans of both sexes, for example, are more likely than Whites to be critical of gender inequality, to recognize that it is socially produced, and to support social action to reduce it (Kane 2000). Those who experience racial or ethnic inequality and discrimination (or both) tend to become more aware of the degree and social origins of gender

These people are all biologically male and culturally men. However, differences in culture, age, race, and class—among other characteristics—help to produce a variety of masculinities. Being a man means different things in different contexts.

inequality. Meanwhile, Hispanics typically favor more traditional gender roles, with a greater degree of separation between genders, than do either white or African American men. However, evidence indicates that differences among racial and ethnic groups regarding gender have been declining over time, which suggests that ideas about gender are converging (Kane 2000).

Gender Distinctions and Power

Traditionally, men have set up so-called masculine characteristics in opposition to feminine characteristics, often claiming masculine qualities as superior to and more desirable than feminine characteristics, thereby promoting **sexism,** *the ideology that one sex is superior to the other.* Boys learn to be boys, in large part, by learning *not* to behave like girls. Boys are often warned that "big boys don't cry" (presumably unlike girls) and criticized for throwing or running "like a girl." A culture that encourages boys to be different from girls limits the options available to boys and teaches them that characteristics associated with girls are undesirable. This attitude is probably part of the reason gay men are so often subject to abuse from straight men; according to traditional gender norms they are seen as not adequately masculine and are associated with inferior feminine qualities.

Like race and class, gender involves social relationships and power dynamics between groups of people, in this case women and men. In a society in which gender signals both difference and male superiority, men will have considerably more power than women. Men perpetuate this domination by treating culturally produced gender differences as if they were unchangeable sex differences. We examine such gender inequality in more detail later in this chapter.

Socialization in Structural Context

Since it is not biologically based, gender must be taught through socialization. To a considerable degree, men and women behave the way they do because they are conforming to the cultural expectations about gender they have learned.

EVERY GIRL EVERY BOY

FOR EVERY GIRL WHO IS TIRED OF ACTING WEAK WHEN SHE IS STRONG, THERE IS A BOY TIRED OF APPEARING STRONG WHEN HE FEELS VULNERABLE. FOR EVERY BOY WHO IS BURDENED WITH EXPECTATION EVERYTHING, TIRED OF PEOPLE HER INTELLIGENCE. WHO IS TIRED OF OVER-SENSITIVE, WHO FEARS TO BE FOR EVERY BOY COMPETITION IS TO PROVE HIS THERE IS A GIRL UNFEMININE FOR EVERY GIRL HER E-Z-BAKE BOY WHO WISHES EVERY BOY TO LET ADVERTISING DICTATE HIS DESIRES, THERE IS A GIRL FACING THE AD INDUSTRY'S ATTACKS ON HER SELF-ESTEEM. FOR EVERY GIRL WHO TAKES A STEP TOWARD HER LIBERATION, THERE IS A BOY WHO FINDS THE WAY TO FREEDOM A LITTLE EASIER. THE CONSTANT OF KNOWING THERE IS A GIRL NOT TRUSTING FOR EVERY GIRL BEING CALLED THERE IS A BOY GENTLE, TO WEEP. FOR WHOM THE ONLY WAY MASCULINITY, WHO IS CALLED WHEN SHE COMPETES. WHO THROWS OUT OVEN, THERE IS A TO FIND ONE. FOR STRUGGLING NOT

Based on a poem by Nancy R. Smith, this poster highlights the parallel impact that gender expectations have on girls and boys. Gender distinctions limit the options available to both sexes.

Like other social constructions, gender is not fixed; our ideas about gender are reproduced or modified as we interact with other people every day. However, we are not free to reinvent gender without consequences because our interactions take place within social structures such as the family, school, and work that enforce certain gender expectations. These structures can impose negative sanctions, or punishments, on those who violate gender expectations, while rewarding those who conform. In this section, we consider how these interactions work.

Learning Gender: Socialization and Gender Roles

As we discussed in Chapter 7, sociologists define roles as the sets of expectations that are associated with different social positions. The roles you occupy do not exist in isolation; instead, a role gives you a part to play in social life, complete with expectations governing proper behavior, appearance, language, and attitudes. A **gender role** is *a set of social expectations regarding behavior and attitudes based on a person's sex.* Men and women are equally capable of folding laundry or changing the oil in a car. But in heterosexual couples, women usually do the laundry whereas men do auto maintenance—or at least bring the car to the garage. The fact that some couples share or reverse these assignments highlights their arbitrary nature.

Traditional advice to "be a man" or "act like a lady" is loaded with social expectations that reflect our culture's beliefs about gender. In fact, gender roles help to shape our identity by influencing a wide range of characteristics, including the following:

- *Appearance.* What clothing, hair styles, jewelry, and makeup are appropriate?
- *Activities.* Who knits or sews? Who uses power tools? Who initiates a date?
- *Behaviors and emotions.* Who is expected to be nurturing and expressive? Who is expected to be tough and stoic?
- *Aspirations.* What kind of future should a man or woman want or expect? What job? What role in the family?

When socialization is effective, people want to be female or male as defined by their culture, and they perceive this learned

Because gender must be reproduced it can also be modified. Parents who use children's books that challenge traditional gender roles are exposing children to alternative ideas about gender. Growing up, were you exposed to traditional gender socialization, or did you receive nontraditional messages, as well?

desire to be both normal and natural. A child who violates these expectations is often chastised, sometimes by being labeled a tomboy or sissy.

"Doing Gender": Social Interaction and Power

How are gender roles created? How are they perpetuated or changed? In a classic article, Candace West and Don Zimmerman (1987) argued that gender is constantly being created—and potentially altered—through the process of **"doing gender,"** *creating gender through interactions in particular social settings.* Thus ideas about gender may be contested and changed, both in our individual interactions and in institutional settings.

INDIVIDUAL INTERACTIONS Two students who don't know each other walk toward a campus building. When they get to the entrance, the male student darts forward and opens the door for the female student, who smiles, says "Thanks," and walks in. He nods and says, "No problem." What just occurred? Perhaps the male student was flirting or was raised to be a polite "gentleman" and hold doors open for women (though not for men). The student is behaving according to the expectations he has learned through socialization.

However, in terms of "doing gender" what just happened is one of the countless tiny—often trivial—ways that gender is recreated in daily life. Whether the gesture was a sign of courteous respect or was based on a largely unconscious assumption that women are the weaker sex and need help from men, it marks a traditional gender difference. (It's unlikely that the

woman would have darted ahead to open the door for the male student.) Over time, such actions reinforce the notion that gender differences are natural. In this sense, gender is not who we are but rather what we do.

People "do gender" in a variety of situations. How does a married or cohabitating heterosexual couple decide how to divide their household chores? Who does the cooking or the dishes? Who takes out the garbage or unclogs the drain? The answers to such questions often reflect different levels of power in personal relationships—and sometimes women are the ones with more power at home. One study asked straight couples whether the man or woman is most responsible for making four decisions: What couples do together on weekends, who manages household finances, who decides about big purchases for the home, and who most often decides what to watch on television. In 26 percent of cases, men made the decision in more areas than women; 31 percent of couples split decision-making responsibilities equally; and in 43 percent of couples, women made more decisions than men (Morin and Cohn 2008).

In making daily decisions, couples constantly negotiate and create gender, sometimes redefining its meaning. For example, when men take on equal or primary responsibility for childcare, they can develop the close emotional and nurturing behaviors popularly associated with mothers, thus redefining the meaning of gender to incorporate the father's caregiving role (Coltrane 1989).

SPOTLIGHT
on social theory

In the tradition of **symbolic interactionism,** "doing gender" is a part of **feminist theory** that highlights the ability of actors to create social reality in daily life. How have you acted in ways that reinforced traditional gender roles recently? How have you acted in ways that redefine their meaning?

INTERACTIONS WITHIN INSTITUTIONS Within their families, schools, and workplaces, people use their power to enforce social expectations, making it easier for all of us to conform to gender roles than to defy them. Family members, teachers and classmates, and colleagues tend to praise and encourage conformity, thus reinforcing it. Men and women who challenge or reject established gender roles, though, are likely to encounter criticism and sanctions. Thus gender is not only taught through socialization and recreated daily in individual interactions; it is also enforced within the context of social structures and institutions.

For example, Karen Davies (2003) shadowed nurses and doctors in Sweden as they did their daily work and later conducted in-depth interviews with them about their experiences. Despite a recent influx of women doctors, she found an assumption of male dominance throughout the institutional culture of hospitals and the broader professional culture of medicine that shapes the way people experience gender on the job and influences how doctors and nurses interact.

The deeply contradictory messages about the role of mothers within U.S. culture illustrate how class and gender intersect for women. Middle- and working-class women who work outside the home are often criticized for not staying at home with their children. On the other hand, public assistance policies, such as Temporary Assistance for Needy Families (TANF), explicitly require poor women to leave their children for work, school, or job training.

CORE CONCEPTS CHALLENGE

How do these contrasting standards for people of different classes reflect differences in **power** between the classes?

 Parents often construct a gendered environment for their babies well before infants even know what the toys, images, and colors in their nursery represent. Here hearts, flowers, and the "feminine" color pink dominate this designer nursery, which is clearly intended for a girl.

CORE CONCEPTS CHALLENGE

How do nursery designs reflect our **culture's** gender expectations? What might a stereotypical boy's nursery look like? What lessons are infants taught through the creation of such environments? In what other ways do we affirm gender at a young age?

Davies found that male doctors were more accustomed than female doctors to being in a dominant position in relation to nurses. One female nurse, noting that she was more willing to follow a male doctor's orders, commented that, "The male doctor is usually more authoritarian . . . . [I]f he says to me, 'Go and take that patient's blood pressure,' then I go and do it. I don't stop and think about it, whereas with a woman I might have thought that she could go and do it herself" (Davies 2003, 731). Female doctors, too, recognized this gender difference. One said, "I find it difficult to ask for help with things I could do myself—yesterday I hesitated in asking an assistant nurse to clean the floor when an incontinent woman wet herself—I mean it's preposterous to imagine that I should clean the floor and be late for my out-patients—and yet all the same . . . it's hard asking another woman for help with the dirty work" (p. 731).

Gender contributed to differences in power relations, too. After working together for a time, female nurses were more likely to seek to establish a collaborative relationship with female doctors than with male doctors. In turn, female doctors were more likely to see nurses as part of a team that worked together to decide on the best care for patients. In contrast, male doctors often overlooked or ignored the insights of experienced nurses, arguing that since the doctor is responsible for the final decision, he should make it on his own. It is likely that similar situations exist in hospitals in the United States. Hospitals are just one example of places where "doing gender" happens in daily life and social structure influences power relations between men and women.

Gender and the Family

Of all the social environments we encounter, the family probably has the most influence on our understanding of gender—an impact that starts from the moment we are born.

GENDER SOCIALIZATION FROM BIRTH Upon learning of a woman's pregnancy or the birth of a child, many people immediately ask, "Is it a boy or a girl?" From the earliest moments of life, then, adults view infants through the lens of gender and treat newborns differently depending on their sex, thus beginning the gender socialization process.

As more than thirty years' worth of research has documented, gender socialization occurs almost from the moment a baby is born. Since the early research studies, however, gender norms have evolved, and so have parents' expectations and behaviors. For example, a classic study from the mid-1970s found that parents, especially fathers, engaged in significant gender stereotyping (Rubin, Provenzano, and Luria 1974). When asked, fathers were more likely than mothers to rate their newborn girls as softer, weaker, and more delicate than boys. Both parents described their daughters as little, beautiful, pretty, and cute and their sons as big. A similar study, done over twenty years later, found that although these gender stereotypes still existed, they had become less intense. In addition, the gap between the gender stereotyping of fathers and mothers was gone (Karraker, Vogel, and Lake 1995).

Parents and others reinforce gender in infants in a variety of routine ways, such as with greeting cards and gifts containing messages and images that fit with gender stereotypes (for example, blue for boys, pink for girls) (Bridges 1993).

GENDER SOCIALIZATION THROUGHOUT CHILDHOOD   Early lessons about gender continue as a child grows up. One study placed mothers and their six-, nine-, or fourteen-month-old babies on the floor with toys and examined the interaction between them (Clearfield and Nelson 2006). The researchers found no difference between the behavior of female and male babies. However, even before the children were able to speak, mothers were already asking more questions of their daughters than of their sons, thereby encouraging verbal development. Mothers also interacted more with their daughters, often comforting and hugging them, while leaving their sons to explore independently.

By the time their children are eighteen months old, parents routinely encourage them to play with gender-stereotyped toys. Parents give their children more praise and other forms of feedback and encouragement when they engage in gender-traditional activities, such as boys playing with trucks, than when they engage in cross-gendered activities, such as boys playing with dolls (Caldera, Huston, and O'Brien 1989; Caldera and Sciaraffa 1998). Throughout childhood girls and boys are treated differently. Their clothes, chores, play, and sports all carry gendered messages. In the earliest years of their lives, children have already been subjected to intense and near-constant affirmation of the expectations society has for their gender, and they begin to respond accordingly.

Teaching Gender in School

The first regular experience most children have outside of their families is with school. Gender socialization here begins at a very early age and continues throughout a child's education.

Karin Martin (1998) found that preschools help children develop a gendered identity by altering how they relate to their own bodies. Their generally relaxed movement and free activity on the playground contrasts with the more formal discipline and proper behavior they are taught once they are inside the school building: waiting in line, raising their hands, sitting still in neatly organized rows of desks, and following many other rules and procedures. These lessons are different for boys and girls, however. Martin found that teachers reprimanded girls more often for not behaving formally but allowed boys to be more disruptive and to behave more informally by sitting in relaxed positions and engaging in freer play than girls. Girls were told to be quiet three times as often as boys were, even though boys were frequently much noisier. Even the clothes parents chose for their children signaled differences in self-discipline. Many girls wore dresses, which limited their ability to move freely and left them vulnerable to potentially embarrassing ex-

As youngsters, girls and boys play easily together at games such as soccer. However, even at such a young age they are being taught about the differences between the genders, and soon most will resist playing with members of the other sex. Did this happen to you?

posure. Thus the bodies of young children are conditioned to conform to gendered expectations.

As children grow older, school continues to foster and reinforce gender differences, often through choice of curriculum. In high school, girls not planning on going to college often train for traditionally female professions such as cosmetology and secretarial work, whereas boys are more likely to take courses in traditionally male trades such as auto mechanics and welding. As we see later in this chapter, gendered curriculum distinctions continue in college.

As awareness of gender issues increases, families and schools are adopting more flexible attitudes about gender. At some schools, teachers line children up by shoe color instead of by sex, and boys who choose to wear skirts to school are allowed to do so. Some schools make it a policy to support whatever choice children make regarding their gender (Brown 2006).

Gender Lessons From Peers

As young people become sexually active, develop an adult persona, and become independent of the family, regular interaction with peers—friends and classmates who are usually of the same general age and, often, of the same sex—reinforces and expands on the lessons about gender they have learned from their family and schools. Peer groups can have a positive impact on a person's self-esteem and result in long-lasting friendships. They also tend to reproduce dominant gender norms.

thinking about **structure**

In many ways, the **structure** of school reinforces what children have learned about gender in their families. What did your school's structure teach you about gender? In what ways did your school reinforce or challenge gender stereotypes?

Gender socialization can be a positive influence. Same-sex friends can bond and provide mutual support, even while reinforcing some traditional gender norms. What positive experiences resulted from your same-sex peers? How did they reinforce gender norms?

As boys become men, for example, they often bond with other young men, forming relationships that promote the dominant masculine identity of their culture (Connell 2000; Kimmel 1996). Our society often encourages young men to belong to sports teams, fraternities, the military, and other primarily male groups. Though this peer socialization can offer mutual support, it also can pass on to new members the sexist ideas and behaviors the group's culture accepts and promotes, such as sexual jokes that degrade women and attitudes that are dismissive of their intelligence and disrespectful of their abilities. Michele Adams and Scott Coltrane (2005) note that, "Full initiation into such groups usually involves some type of woman- and/or gay-bashing activity that accentuates the boundary between male and not male, masculinity and femininity, heterosexuality and homosexuality" (p. 238).

Peer socialization can exaggerate and reinforce gender distinctions by encouraging a person to develop a sense of self that is connected to a group of people of the same gender—and disconnected from the other gender. Young men can adopt an air of detachment or an exaggerated posture of toughness while denigrating signs of weakness or emotionality they supposedly detect in others. Young women often concentrate on their own physical appearance—including norms regulating clothing, weight, hairstyles, and makeup—while policing that of their peers. Both women and men often adopt the norms for appearance promoted in the media.

Media and Gender

Media portrayals of gender in television shows, movies, music videos, as well as the news can signal appropriate or acceptable behavior and attitudes, especially to young men and women. Sometimes media images and portrayals can challenge traditional gender roles, but often they repackage cultural stereotypes.

In the news, women make up a small percentage of sources. For example, over a twenty-year period, studies of the long-running and prestigious *NewsHour* on public television have found that women made up a small, though increasing, percentage of the guests: just 13 percent by 1990 (Croteau and Hoynes 1994a), 18 percent by 2006 (Rendall and Hollar 2006), and 20 percent by 2010 (Rendall and Morel 2010). Women are also underrepresented among the staff of news organizations, where male supervisors outnumber women almost two to one (American Society of Newspaper Editors 2011).

Entertainment media of all sorts often help reinforce gender stereotypes: television ads feature happy homemakers obsessed with cleaning, entertainment programs often show career-dominated men and love-sick women, video games highlight women as eye-candy and men as heroic warriors, and Internet pornography treats women as sexual objects (Gauntlett 2002; Gill 2007).

The gender images provided by the media are more than just meaningless entertainment. Photographs of rail-thin, airbrushed models present unrealistic standards of beauty for women to aspire to. Nevertheless, after viewing images of models in magazine advertisements for just three minutes, women reported being more dissatisfied with their own bodies—regardless of their own weight, height, or age (Hamilton, Mintz, and Kaschubeck-West 2007). Idealized images of men in the media highlight muscular bodies and youthfulness. One study showed that although men are cynical about such photographs, they believe the images show the "ideal" male body

 Idealized images of women have long been a staple of media content. But idealized—and airbrushed—images of male bodies create unrealistic standards for men, too.

CORE CONCEPTS CHALLENGE

Do you think such advertising helps reproduce gender stereotypes in our **culture** *or are they harmless? Whatever their effect, do you think the impact of idealized images in advertising and other media is different for men and women? Why or why not?*

that women appreciate. Younger men, especially, acknowledge that such images constantly remind them that their own bodies may not match up to the ideal. Perhaps that is why few men of any age report being satisfied with their own bodies (Pompper, Soto, and Piel 2007).

Culture, Power, and Gender Inequality

As we all learn about gender through socialization and then help reproduce gender roles by "doing gender" in our daily lives, we become part of the way gender is structured in society. This structure reflects differences in power between men and women. As a result, every social institution is marked by substantial gender inequality. **Gender stratification** refers to *the systematic and unequal distribution of power and resources in society between women and men.* Though the United States has made significant progress in overcoming gender inequality over the past century, men continue to dominate positions of power (see Figure 11.1). In this section, we consider the origins of inequality between women and men and then review some examples of gender inequality in the United States.

Sex and the Origins of Patriarchy

Patriarchy refers to *a social system dominated by men.* In a patriarchal society men hold most of the powerful political and economic positions and benefit from cultural expectations that limit the role and influence of women. Patriarchal societies have existed around the globe and throughout history. In contrast, no clear example of a **matriarchy**—*a social system dominated by women*—is known to have ever existed (Eller 2001; Motz 1997).

Why has patriarchy been so pervasive? This question has no single answer, but sociologist Joan Huber (2007) argues that male dominance was due largely to sex differences, especially women's role in carrying, bearing, and breastfeeding children. Throughout human evolution, the vast majority of women were either pregnant or lactating through most of their adult lives. Although pregnancy had a significant impact on women, lactation may have had an even greater effect.

Until the modern era, infants and toddlers were totally dependent on their mothers for sustenance because the food consumed by older humans was too difficult for them to chew and digest. Mothers needed to breastfeed their infants frequently—about every fifteen minutes during the day (and less frequently at night) for the first two years, then with less frequency for an additional two years. Such frequent breastfeeding over an extended period limited the types of activities in which mothers could engage. This limitation may have had minimal impact in early hunting and gathering cultures, which show only limited gender stratification. However, about 10,000 years ago,

	Men	Women
Fortune 500 CEOs	94%	6%
Fortune 500 Board of Directors	84%	15.7%
Fortune 500 Executive Officers	86%	14.4%
U.S. Senate	83%	17%
U.S. House of Representatives	83.6%	16.4%
State Governors	88%	12%
Mayors of 100 Largest Cities	92%	8%
State Legislatures	76%	23.6%
U.S. College Presidents	77%	23%

 FIGURE 11.1 | GENDER STRATIFICATION IN LEADERSHIP POSITIONS

Men continue to dominate the leadership positions in business, government, and higher education. *Source:* Catalyst (2010).

CORE CONCEPTS CHALLENGE

*How do the data presented here challenge the idea that women and men now have equal **power** in society? Do you expect such numbers to change significantly during your lifetime? Why or why not?*

as many human groups began practicing agriculture and raising animals for food, men could control the newly developed food surplus and dominate social and political life more easily than women could, thus increasing their power (Collins et al. 1993). Their generally larger physical size, greater strength, and exemption from pregnancy and lactation also enabled men to use violence—or the threat of violence—to obtain obedience from women. This physical domination likely contributed to the emergence of patriarchal societies across the planet.

Culture Trumps Biology

Biology may go a long way in explaining the *origins* of patriarchy. But the ability of humans to alter the social environment has accelerated exponentially in just a couple of centuries, undermining the significance of sex differences. Today, machinery often replaces the need for physical strength. Medication can moderate the impact of menstruation. Couples can prevent pregnancy by using effective birth control, or terminate a pregnancy through safe abortion. Women can become pregnant through artificial insemination, and emerging biotechnologies will likely create more options for reproduction. Once a baby is born, mothers can manage breastfeeding with the use of a breast pump, or supplement or replace it with other foods and nutrients.

Such cultural interventions are quite recent. Women did not begin to abandon old-style, near-continuous lactation until the late nineteenth or early twentieth century. The emergence of the germ theory of disease led to safer public drinking water and ways to prepare food for infants, which enabled women to breastfeed less frequently and to use bottle-feeding as an alternative (Huber 2007). As a result of such cultural innovations, the sex differences between women and men became less significant. Once men had accumulated power in society, however, they tended to resist sharing it with women, producing gender-based inequality that continues today.

Work and Education

In the United States, women still earn only about 80 percent of what men do, making the workplace one of the best-known examples of gender discrimination. If we could wipe out workplace discrimination, however, the wage gap between women and men would be reduced somewhat, but it wouldn't be eliminated. By some estimates, factors other than direct workplace discrimination explain at least three-quarters of the wage gap (Dey and Hill 2007). Taking a comprehensive sociological approach to this issue can help us to see the many different factors that contribute to this inequality, including the role of education.

EDUCATION, MAJORS, AND OCCUPATIONS

Traditionally, men have surpassed women in educational achievement, with many colleges and universities even barring women from enrollment well into the twentieth century. In recent decades, however, women have caught up and are surpassing men in terms of education. Overall, men still hold more advanced college degrees than do women (see Figure 11.2), but this discrepancy is a legacy of the past. In 2009, among young adults aged 25 to 29 years, 35 percent of women but only 27 percent of men possessed a bachelor's degree or higher—and the gap is growing (U.S. Census Bureau 2010d). In the 2008–2009 academic year, women earned a slight majority (50.4 percent) of the doctorates during that period, as well as 60 percent of master's degrees (Bell 2010).

In 2009, workers with a high school diploma earned, on average, $30,627 per year, those with a bachelor's degree $56,665, and those with advanced or professional degrees $85,818 (U.S. Census Bureau 2010c). As women continue to outpace men in educational achievement, the overall wage gap between the sexes should continue to decline.

Although women and men currently have similar access to education, the fields of study they choose to ma-

	Men		Women
Doctorate	1.7%		0.9%
Professional	2%		1.2%
Master's degree	7.3%		7.9%
Bachelor's degree	19%		19%
Associate's degree	7.9%		10%
Some college (no degree)	16.8%		17.3%
High school diploma	31.4%		30.8%
Less than high school	13.8%		12.9%

FIGURE 11.2 | U.S. EDUCATIONAL ATTAINMENT, 25 YEARS AND OLDER, BY SEX

In recent years, women have outnumbered men on college campuses, closing the gap in educational attainment. *Source:* U.S. Census Bureau (2010); authors' calculations.

jor in and the professions they pursue are still often segregated along gender lines, likely reflecting early gender socialization. Women earn the majority of bachelor's degrees in relatively low-paying fields such as education, psychology, and the health professions—three traditionally female fields—whereas men earn more degrees in relatively high-paying—and traditionally male—fields such as engineering, mathematics, and the physical sciences (Dey and Hill 2007). (The Sociology Matters box on page 298 shows how sociology has helped inform efforts to encourage women to become engineers.) These differences between women's and men's choices of college major contribute to the wage gap. Even in fields that do not require a college degree, women tend to cluster in low-paying service and retail jobs (see Table 11.1).

In 2010, sixteen of the top twenty occupations for women had median earnings (half earned more, half earned less) below the overall men's median of $824 a week. The median weekly earnings of women who were full-time wage and salary workers were $669, or 81.2 percent of men's earnings.

WORKFORCE PARTICIPATION
In the mid-twentieth century, about one out of three women—disproportionately members of the working class—were employed outside the home. Today, about 60 percent of women (and just over 70 percent of men) are in the paid labor force (U.S. Bureau of Labor Statistics 2011b). This change has happened for a variety of

TABLE 11.1   TWENTY LEADING OCCUPATIONS OF EMPLOYED WOMEN, 2010

Occupation	Women Employed (thousands)	Men and Women Employed (thousands)	Percent Women	Women's Median Weekly Earnings
Total, 16 years and older (all employed women)	65,638	139,064	47.2	$669
Secretaries and administrative assistants	2,962	3,082	96.1	657
Registered nurses	2,590	2,843	91.1	1,039
Elementary and middle school teachers	2,301	2,813	81.8	931
Cashiers	2,291	3,109	73.7	366
Retail salespersons	1,705	3,286	51.9	421
Nursing, psychiatric, and home health aides	1,700	1,928	88.2	427
Waiters and waitresses	1,470	2,067	71.1	381
First-line supervisors/managers of retail sales workers	1,375	3,132	43.9	578
Customer service representatives	1,263	1,896	66.6	586
Maids and housekeeping cleaners	1,252	1,407	89.0	376
Receptionists and information clerks	1,187	1,281	92.7	529
Childcare workers	1,181	1,247	94.7	398
Bookkeeping, accounting, and auditing clerks	1,179	1,297	90.9	628
First-line supervisors/managers of office and administrative support	1,035	1,507	68.7	726
Managers, all others	1,014	2,898	35.0	1,045
Accountants and auditors	989	1,646	60.1	953
Teacher assistants	893	966	92.4	485
Personal and home care aides	838	973	86.1	405
Office clerks, general	837	994	84.2	597
Cooks	790	1,951	40.5	381

Source: U.S. Department of Labor, Women's Bureau.

reasons. Effective and convenient birth control in the form of "the Pill"—introduced in the early 1960s—enabled women to control the timing and number of pregnancies; as a result, they needed to spend less time raising children and could devote more time to paid employment. At roughly the same time, the women's movement helped change cultural norms and the legal environment in ways that made working outside the home more feasible for women. Because wages for male workers have remained stagnant over the last thirty years, many families have needed the additional income that employed women could offer to maintain or improve their lifestyle.

Women and men have different work patterns, however, which contributes to the wage gap. These patterns reflect the enduring power of gender norms that assign women the primary responsibility for raising children (Budig and England 2001; Kreider and Elliott 2009; Waldfogel 1997). Women are more likely than men to use family leave, to work part time, or to leave the workforce altogether to care for children. Nearly one out of four mothers (23 percent) leaves the workforce, and another 17 percent work only part time. In contrast, only one out of 100 fathers leaves the workforce, and only 2 percent work part time. Fathers typically rely on women—either spouses or paid childcare workers—to care for their children.

Mothers who return to work after raising their children have lost experience and seniority in relation to their male counterparts, one of the reasons that women who do not have

Using Sociological Insight to Encourage Women Engineers

When Naomi Chesler, now a distinguished professor of biomedical engineering at the University of Wisconsin–Madison, took an aptitude test in high school, she learned that her talents in math and science would suit her well for engineering. This profession—one of the highest paid occupations—is dominated by men. Confident in her abilities, however, Chesler majored in engineering as an undergraduate, earned her Ph.D. in medical engineering, and obtained a university position. As a young faculty member she was mentored in a program that encouraged individual competition and placed obstacles in her path on the assumption that overcoming such challenges would help produce success. Despite her love for the field and her ability to excel at it, she found this traditional, hierarchical, and masculine approach less than satisfying (Maurer 2009).

She began talking with her father, Mark Chesler, a sociologist who has researched race and gender discrimination in higher education, about how she might take gender differences into account to create a different kind of mentoring program for female junior engineering faculty. Drawing upon sociological research, the Cheslers realized that because of different socialization, women and men often have different learning styles, and these differences were not being accommodated in traditional mentoring programs. For example, many women prefer collaborative and interactive ways of learning, rather than the isolated and individualistic style that dominates engineering departments. This mismatch in learning styles was one factor that was causing female students to drop out of engineering.

As a result of their collaboration, the Cheslers developed a model for mentoring young women engineers that used a supportive and collaborative approach, rather than emphasizing aggressive individual competition. The medical engineer and the sociologist teamed up to write an article that encouraged "multiple mentoring" from numerous sources rather than a reliance on one mentor, mutually supportive "peer mentoring" to deemphasize hierarchical relationships, and "collective mentoring" that puts responsibility for effective mentoring on an entire department or organization rather than on the individual mentee (Chesler and Chesler 2002). They also emphasized the need for organizational change, not just individual efforts, to help ensure success. Naomi Chesler has repeatedly put this sociologically informed model into action, and it has helped her to establish award-winning mentoring programs.

At an event sponsored by the Boston chapter of the Society of Women Engineers, high school girls learn about electrical engineering by working in teams to "reverse engineer" some computer equipment—dismantling it to analyze how it is constructed.

Whereas the Cheslers' program helps retain women in engineering, the Society for Women Engineers (SWE) promotes mentoring as a way to encourage girls to enter the field in the first place. SWE targets girls in elementary and high school with programs that encourage collaborative hands-on engineering activities, celebrate the accomplishments of women engineers, and introduce girls to engineers and engineering college students who can serve as role models. By intervening in girls' early socialization, SWE hopes to encourage more girls to become the engineers of the future.

Mentoring is just one way to help overcome the gender gap in high-paid professions. But when built upon a sociological understanding of gender, such programs can make a difference.

think about it

1. *What sociological insights about gender informed the creation of the mentoring programs mentioned here?*

2. *Have you ever been involved in a mentoring program? If so, what impact did it have on you? If not, in what aspect of your life might such a program have helped you?*

Without the labor of women at home—both the unpaid labor of wives and the low-paid labor of service workers—most highly paid male corporate executives would be unable to work long hours to achieve personal success in their fields. How else do women who work in the home contribute to the success of men?

Gender prejudice often occurs at the subconscious level, and it colors how people view and evaluate each other's work, contributing to discrimination (Barres 2006; Valian 1999). In professional environments, coworkers and supervisors are more likely to see men as competent and logical and women as unreliable and emotional, and over time these skewed perceptions influence the way they evaluate their fellow employees. Cultural norms also promote discrimination in the workplace by discouraging women from having greater success than their husbands or from focusing on career advancement rather than raising a family. Lack of encouragement coupled with negative perceptions can undermine women's self-confidence and reduce their ambitions. These differences in ambition or competitiveness are then misread as innate, rather than culturally created (Fels 2005).

The wage gap is just one example of the multifaceted impact of gender. Gender inequality is pervasive throughout society, including in the family, politics, the media, and religion, and power disparities are also reflected in sexual harassment and violence against women.

Home and Family

During the past few decades, the lives of women and men have changed significantly. More women today spend more hours doing paid labor outside the home than in the past. But in one classic study, Arlie Hochschild and Anne Machung (1989) found that as growing numbers of women worked at full-time jobs, they still came home to a **second shift**—*the phenomenon of employed women still having primary responsibility for housework and childcare.* In households with two wage-earners, heterosexual couples still viewed the man's position as the primary career, while the woman's job was often seen as supplemental. Whereas men might "help" with the housework, women worked outside the home to "help" pay the bills.

More recent research shows that women have cut in half the number of hours they spend on housework, while men have doubled the number of hours they spend doing it. Cross-national research in industrialized countries suggests that the higher a woman's education and income, the more her husband takes part in housework and childcare (Davis and Greenstein 2004; Stapinski 1998). Still, women spend more hours than men doing housework, regardless of whether or not they work or have children.

At first glance, how a couple divides household chores would seem to be purely a matter of individual choice. However, Mikiko Fuwa (2004), in her study of twenty-two advanced industrial nations, found that the level of gender inequality in a society is likely to influence how couples negotiate the division of household chores, illustrating the influence of social structure on personal decisions. In societies with relatively more gender inequality—including Japan and Italy—women tend to earn a lower percentage of what their husbands do, and the

children earn more than women who do. Ten years after college graduation, women work fewer hours (44 per week) than men (49 per week), even when they are employed full time, a disparity that reflects both the different types of positions men and women tend to hold and the larger burden of family responsibilities women assume. Couples are more likely to relocate because of a man's career, a change that usually advances the man's career and interrupts the woman's. In part because of these differences in labor force participation, the pay gap between women and men—even within the same field—widens as workers get older.

DISCRIMINATION AND THE GLASS CEILING

Although factors outside the workplace contribute to the wage gap in important ways, workplace discrimination is also a reality for many women. One result of this discrimination is the **glass ceiling,** *the often invisible barrier created by individual and institutional sexism that prevents qualified women from advancing to high levels of leadership and management.* More men than women hold managerial positions, but social scientists debate how systematic this gap is and whether it occurs primarily at higher levels of management or throughout the management structure (Baxter and Wright 2000; Yamagata et al. 1997). At the upper levels of corporate management, the relative absence of women is startling. In 2009, about one out of eight *Fortune* 500 companies—the 500 largest companies in the United States—listed no women among their corporate officers. This group included such well-known companies as Dick's Sporting Goods, Dollar General, Hershey, Hertz, and General Dynamics. None of the *Fortune* 500 companies had a team of corporate officers made up of at least 50 percent women (Catalyst 2007).

thinking about culture

Cultural norms regarding gender have a powerful effect on the behavior of men and women in the workforce and on their careers. What kinds of norms influence men? What effect do these norms have—both positive and negative—on their careers?

parent who earns less is more likely to give up a job and stay at home to care for children. In countries with more gender equality—including Canada and the United States—women earn higher wages and have greater opportunity for career advancement. As a result, women's earnings are closer to those of men, making their time in the workforce more valuable to the household and giving women more power in negotiating the division of housework. In these relatively egalitarian countries, cultural values encourage men and women to share domestic responsibilities, thus promoting more micro-level equality. Fuwa's study suggests that macro-level gender inequality must be addressed before micro-level changes can be fully implemented.

Political Power

The degree to which women have been marginalized in the halls of political power is symbolized by the bathrooms in the U.S. Capitol. A restroom for female senators was not installed until 1992 (Taley 2006). Female members of the House of Representatives did not get their own restroom until 2011. More important, as of the 2011–2012 Congress, women held just 17 of the 100 Senate seats (17 percent) and just 72 of the 435 seats in the House of Representatives (16.4 percent) (Center for American Women and Politics 2011).

Around the world, women accounted for just 19.1 percent of the members of all national legislative bodies in 2010 (see Table 11.2). In 1995 the UN Economic and Social Council adopted a goal of 30 percent representation for women in each country's legislative body (Elson and Keklik 2003). By July 31, 2011, however, only twenty-six countries had met the goal, many of them through legislated or voluntarily quotas. The percentage of women in the U.S. Congress is well below the UN goal, and as of mid-2011, the United States ranked 68th. The absence of women in positions of political power means women are underrepresented in the groups that are responsible for creating public policy, passing laws, directing resources, and setting political priorities.

Religion and Gender

Because the world's religions are numerous and varied, it is difficult to generalize about gender roles. However, the world's largest religions—including forms of Judaism, Islam, Buddhism, Hinduism, and Christianity—severely restrict the role of women in rituals and in institutional governance. In most cases, sacred texts in these religions personify God and the major prophets and disciples as male. Religious writings and teachings are often used to justify male domination in social life. For example, the Christian Bible notes that "wives should submit to their husbands in everything" (Ephesians 5:24), while the Qur'an (4.34) instructs that if wives are not obedient, men may "admonish them, and leave them alone in the sleeping-places and beat them." However, as with other

| TABLE 11.2 | COUNTRIES WITH THE HIGHEST AND LOWEST PERCENTAGES OF WOMEN IN NATIONAL LEGISLATIVE BODIES, 2011 |

Highest Percentage of Women		Lowest Percentage of Women	
1. Rwanda	56.3	1. Belize	0
2. Andorra	53.6	2. Micronesia	0
3. Sweden	45.0	3. Nauru	0
4. South Africa	44.5	4. Oman	0
5. Cuba	43.2	5. Palau	0
6. Iceland	42.9	6. Qatar	0
7. Finland	42.5	7. Saudi Arabia	0
8. Norway	39.6	8. Solomon Islands	0
9. Belgium	39.3	9. Tuvalu	0
10. Netherlands	39.3	10. Yemen	0.3

Note: The United States was 68th out of the 187 countries ranked.
Source: Inter-Parliamentary Union (2011)

religious beliefs, religious leaders reinterpret doctrines of faith regarding gender relations to reflect changing cultural values in the society at large. Thus, as gender equality has become a mainstream value, many religions are beginning to affirm the role of women in their sacred traditions. For example, there are women rabbis, and some Protestant denominations have women pastors or priests.

Sexual Harassment

Another form of gender discrimination is **sexual harassment**, *unwelcome sexual advances, requests for sexual favors, and other verbal or physical harassment of a sexual nature* (U.S. Equal Employment Opportunity Commission 2010). Harassment can take place anywhere: at work, on campus, or in the community. Most cases of sexual harassment are committed by men against women, but the perpetrator and victim can be of either gender.

Some harassment involves the abuse of power. The clearest cases are *quid pro quo* ("this for that") harassment, which involves a proposed exchange of some benefit, or withholding of some sanction, for sexual favors: Sleep with me and I'll raise your salary; refuse and you're fired. Such cases are clearly abuses of authority and blatantly illegal. Other cases involve severe or pervasive sexual harassment that creates a hostile work environment, including inappropriate sexual jokes, sexually

thinking about structure

How do cross-national comparisons of gender inequality illustrate that macro-level social structure can influence micro-level decisions, such as the division of housework?

explicit e-mails or screen-savers, pornography, sexual cartoons, or unwanted verbal comments or physical contact. Typically, for such cases to be prosecuted, the offensive behavior must continue after a victim has lodged a complaint.

The legal standard for the creation of a hostile work environment—that a "reasonable person" in the same or similar circumstances would find the situation offensive—is not easy to meet, since there are many gray areas where reasonable people can disagree. In fact, some sexual harassment is unintentional. One person may think he or she is saying something funny or complimentary, but a colleague is offended—a good example of the failure to achieve intersubjectivity, as discussed in Chapter 7.

Violence Against Women

Abuse of power, which is sometimes involved in sexual harassment, takes another, extreme form in violence against women. As in other relations that involve power, violence against women is both a consequence and a cause of inequality. Men carry out this violence on an individual level as well as in more organized and systematic ways.

DOMESTIC VIOLENCE AND SEXUAL ASSAULT

For much of history, violence against women in the home was widely accepted. In the United States, men had the legal right to assault their wives physically as recently as the late 1800s. Even today, other societies tolerate domestic violence. In many countries, though, feminist activists have been successful in changing cultural norms, legal standards, and law enforcement practices regarding domestic violence. In the United States, domestic violence is now widely recognized as a major social problem and is treated as a crime.

The U.S. Department of Justice (2008) defines **domestic violence** as "*a pattern of abusive behavior in any relationship that is used by one partner to gain or maintain power and control over another intimate partner.*" (The term *intimate partner violence* is also commonly used.) Such abuse may include physical, sexual, psychological, emotional, and economic components. According to the Department of Justice, it includes "any behaviors that intimidate, manipulate, humiliate, isolate, frighten, terrorize, coerce, threaten, blame, hurt, injure, or wound someone."

About 85 percent of intimate partner violence is directed at women, making women about seven times as likely as men to be the targets of such violence. Although some women do perpetrate abuse against men, such abuse is milder than that aimed at women, and female victims are far more likely than male victims to say they are afraid and to suffer serious injury. Intimate partner violence makes up about 20 percent of all nonfatal violent crime directed at women, and it causes about 30 percent of all murders in which the victim is a woman. It comprises only 3 percent of nonfatal violent crime directed at men and 4 percent of male murders (U.S. Department of Justice 2008). The nature of domestic violence against men is different, as well. Women often become violent in self-defense, or they exploit an opportunity to retaliate violently against an

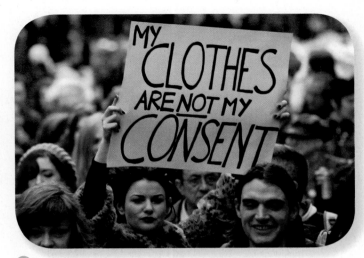

People concerned about violence against women have recently organized provocatively titled "slut walks" to counter the attitude that women provoke violence against themselves by how they choose to appear. This attitude blames the victims for the crime committed against them and implicitly absolves the male perpetrators of responsibility.

CORE CONCEPTS CHALLENGE

What does the prevalence of violence against women, both in and outside the home, indicate about **power** *and gender in our society?*

abuser—such as when a man passes out from drinking excessively (Belknap and Melton 2005).

Rape overlaps with domestic violence, since some domestic violence involves sexual assault. One major study found that only about 16.7 percent of female victims were raped by a stranger. Instead, most rapes (which sometimes involved multiple attackers) were by an acquaintance (27.3 percent), a spouse or an ex-spouse (20.2 percent), a relative other than a husband (22.4 percent), a date or former date (21.5 percent), or a current or former cohabitating partner (45 percent). About one out of six women in the United States has been the victim of rape (14.8 percent) or attempted rape (2.8 percent) at some point in her life (Tjaden and Thoennes 2000, 2006).

When men are taught, through socialization, to denigrate women and feel a sense of entitlement toward them, domestic violence can be a result. However, in the United States, changing cultural values that reject violence against women and better prosecution of perpetrators appear to be having a significant impact. Between 1993 and 2005, the rate of nonfatal intimate partner assaults plummeted by 60 percent, whereas the number of intimate partner homicide victims in that period dropped by 25 percent (Catalano 2007).

Internationally, however, the situation is not as promising. Although reliable data on violence against women in many countries are difficult to obtain, the World Health Organization (WHO) interviewed over 24,000 women in fifteen culturally diverse settings in ten countries to obtain comparable data.

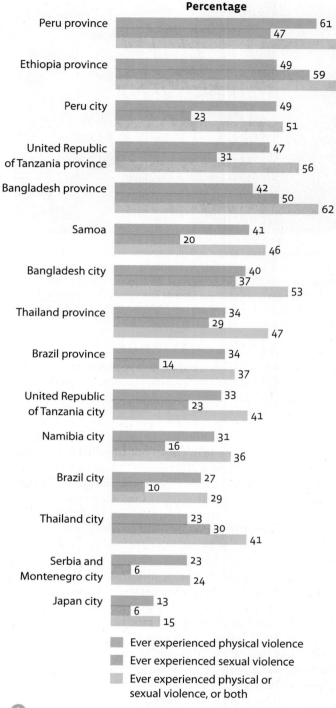

Percentage

Peru province: 61, 47, 69
Ethiopia province: 49, 59, 71
Peru city: 49, 23, 51
United Republic of Tanzania province: 47, 31, 56
Bangladesh province: 42, 50, 62
Samoa: 41, 20, 46
Bangladesh city: 40, 37, 53
Thailand province: 34, 29, 47
Brazil province: 34, 14, 37
United Republic of Tanzania city: 33, 23, 41
Namibia city: 31, 16, 36
Brazil city: 27, 10, 29
Thailand city: 23, 30, 41
Serbia and Montenegro city: 23, 6, 24
Japan city: 13, 6, 15

■ Ever experienced physical violence
■ Ever experienced sexual violence
■ Ever experienced physical or sexual violence, or both

FIGURE 11.3 | VIOLENCE AGAINST WOMEN BY CULTURE

Male violence against women is not natural or innate; it varies by culture. Rural women in Ethiopia, for example, are nearly five times as likely to have experienced physical or sexual violence as urban women in Japan. *Source:* World Health Organization (2005a).

WHO's work confirms that domestic violence varies significantly by culture (see Figure 11.3). For example, 71 percent of women in rural Ethiopia reported having been the victim of sexual or physical assault at one time, compared to 15 percent of women in a Japanese city. The WHO (2005) report notes that "Domestic violence . . . continues to be frighteningly common and to be accepted as 'normal' within too many societies" (p. vii). (The Sociology Works box examines one sociology major's work with recent immigrants for gender justice.)

STATE VIOLENCE AGAINST WOMEN We usually think of violence against women in terms of crimes committed by individuals, but governments are also implicated in this type of crime (Barstow 2001). Some governments willfully ignore sexual assault by failing to pass or enforce laws against it. In times of war, governments and military groups have organized and carried out systematic violence against women, including sexual slavery, in which women are forced to serve as prostitutes for soldiers.

Military groups have also used mass rape to terrorize civilian populations. Soldiers often murder the rape victims afterward. In 1994, for example, men raped as many as 500,000 women in Rwanda as part of that central African country's genocidal civil war. During the violence in Croatia and Bosnia-Herzegovina in southeastern Europe, in the early 1990s, the number of rape victims was as high as 60,000. Since 1998, a variety of war crimes against women, including rape, abduction, and sexual slavery, have been recognized as grave violations of international law and have been subject to prosecution in international courts (UN Development Fund for Women 2007).

HUMAN TRAFFICKING AND GLOBALIZATION Another form of organized violence against women involves human trafficking, in which criminal networks recruit, entrap, and transport individuals, holding them against their will for either sexual exploitation or forced labor. Such activities have increased significantly as globalization has made travel and immigration easier. Though precise numbers are impossible to obtain, experts estimate that at any given time at least 2.5 million people from over 125 countries are victims of human trafficking. About 80 percent of the victims of this modern-day slavery are poor women and girls (half under age eighteen). Criminals lure women and girls with the promise of legitimate jobs, but nearly 90 percent of them are forced into prostitution (UN Office on Drugs and Crime 2006). Although the crime is widely recognized, little has been done so far to effectively combat it.

GENITAL CUTTING *Female genital cutting* is an umbrella term covering a variety of procedures that involve the partial or total removal of the external female genitalia. The most common form involves the removal of the clitoris and the labia minora, a procedure that traditional circumcisers or medical personnel often perform without anesthetic any time from infancy through adolescence. Some cultures use the practice to encourage virginity until marriage and fidelity afterward. Others use it as an initiation rite to a community of adult women. Still others perform the procedure in the mistaken belief that it has hygienic benefits or enhances fertility. Whatever the reason, an estimated 100 million to 140 million women have

Mona Moayad and Gender Justice

After earning her undergraduate degree in sociology from the University of Texas at Austin, Mona Moayad received a couple of job offers in Washington, D.C., one from the Federal Trade Commission, which oversees consumer protection and competition issues, the other from the little-known Tahirih Justice Center (2011), which describes itself as a "nonprofit organization that works to protect immigrant women and girls from gender-based violence through legal services, advocacy, and public education programs." Choosing the small nonprofit over the big federal agency, Moayad took an important step toward a career promoting social justice.

As a paralegal in immigration and family law at the center, Moayad worked with women and girls who had been victims of gender-based persecution. Her day-to-day work included conducting intake meetings for those seeking services, preparing and presenting case summaries, preparing complaints for a variety of family law cases, and interviewing clients to help them complete immigration forms. The center's programs include providing *pro bono* (free) legal services to immigrant women who had fled their home countries to escape torture, rape, human trafficking, forced marriage, domestic abuse, female genital cutting, and crimes committed against them in the name of family honor or because they had become widows.

Moayad's training in sociology proved useful for this demanding work. "Sociology gave me the framework to understand why direct legal services are so important and necessary to empower disadvantaged communities," she notes. "Studying social stratification gave me a clearer understanding of what challenges my clients were facing: characteristics of the 'working poor,' the wage gap between women and men, institutionalized racism that is deeply woven into every aspect of society which limited my clients' abilities to move up the 'social ladder' and have access to more opportunities for themselves and for their children. This knowledge gave me the context to understand where my clients were coming from and gave me the stats to defend and advocate for my clients." Moayad used her sociology degree and experience at the Tahirih Justice Center as stepping stones to law school, earning a law degree from the City University of New York (CUNY) School of Law in pursuit of a career as an activist lawyer.

Mona Moayad

Looking back on her education in sociology, Moayad notes, "The two most useful courses I took were 'Social Movements' and 'Social Stratification.' Social movements provided my first exposure to the history of systemic changes in the United States through the unification of diverse peoples. Social stratification gave me the foundation to understand the intersection of gender, race, and class in American society and how our current institutions further entrench social inequalities by limiting access to opportunities for economic mobility."

Although her mother also has a degree in sociology, and is, as Moayad puts it, "very passionate about the subject," Moayad says, "[I] had no idea I would major in sociology" and did not decide to do so until after she took introductory sociology in her second year of college. "I was fascinated by sociology; it helped me understand what was going on in the world around me in every aspect."

"Sociology has given me a heightened awareness about the inequalities that exist within society. It has given me the framework to understand the deficiencies of the legal system and why—although insufficient—reform legal work is necessary in order to bring about change in society."

> "Sociology gave me the framework to understand why direct legal services are so important and necessary to empower disadvantaged communities."

think about it

1. *How are power and inequality central to Moayad's work?*

2. *Have you ever thought of using a degree in sociology as a stepping stone to law school or other professional training? What type of training might you be interested in and how could sociology help prepare you for it?*

---

undergone some form of genital cutting (World Health Organization 2010).

Although it has long been an accepted part of some cultures and religious practices, especially in Africa, many human rights advocates consider genital cutting to be a form of orga-

nized violence against women, and some women from the cultures that condone it have organized to stop the practice. Some female genital cutting interferes with sexual pleasure, and some procedures can interfere with urination and contribute to complications during childbirth (World Health Organization

2010). Whereas male circumcision—the removal of the fore-skin from the penis—is also prominent in some cultures, its purpose and significance differ starkly from female genital cutting. In particular, male circumcision has no significant effect on sexual functioning, is not performed to inhibit sexual activity, and may help the man reduce his chance of HIV infection (World Health Organization 2007b).

As genital cutting illustrates, sexuality is another area related to gender in which cultural differences result in many variations.

Sexuality

Sexuality refers to *a person's sexual desires, behaviors, and identity.* Like gender, sexuality is related to biologically based sex characteristics but is also a social construction. Sexuality is about much more than biological reproduction. As a social behavior, sexuality is heavily influenced by norms and expectations that vary by culture and change over time. In discussing sexuality, then, we need to consider both biology and culture.

Biology, Culture, and Sexuality

There are two basic ways to approach human sexuality. On the one hand, we can look at humans as highly evolved animals for whom sex is simply a "natural" biological activity necessary for reproduction, as it is for other animals. Hormones help fuel a sex drive that enables human beings to reproduce successfully—perhaps *too* successfully, since population growth strains the planet's resources. In this vein, some people invoke "nature" to make judgments about what is "normal" sexual activity, and some observers condemn homosexuality as "unnatural" because it cannot result in conception. However, contrary to common belief, other nonhuman primates—our closest animal cousins who are social beings and have relatively large brains and facial features similar to humans—engage in a variety of sexual activities, some of which have nothing to do with reproduction. Bonobo chimpanzees (also known as pygmy chimps), for example, use sex as play, to mark an end to an argument, to help form a friendship, to trade for food, and more. Since bonobos often engage in homosexual sex, oral sex, or sex with juveniles, their sexual behavior is not only for procreation. Therefore, even in nature, sex includes a broad range of practices with a variety of purposes.

On the other hand, human behavior is the product of culture as well as biology, and in this sense, human sexuality isn't so much "natural" as it is a set of socially regulated practices that vary across cultures and over time. Religious belief—which

often includes ideas about right and wrong expressions of sexuality—has been one way of communicating cultural norms about sexuality. For example, the use of birth control was forbidden by all Protestant denominations until 1930 and is still considered sinful by the Catholic Church today. The Church also condemns masturbation and homosexuality (Jutte 2008).

Cultures typically have a variety of norms and expectations regarding sexuality. At what age is sexual activity appropriate? Is sex with a first cousin acceptable? Is sex outside of marriage acceptable? Is monogamy—commitment to a single sexual partner—necessary? Different cultures answer these questions differently. However, all cultures have some form of **incest taboo,** *a norm restricting sexual relations between certain relatives.* Since reproduction between close relatives increases the risk that offspring will be born with harmful physical or mental effects, incest taboos reduce this risk. Incest taboos also promote social integration by encouraging people to reach beyond their immediate family for a sexual partner and reduce conflict within the family by marking boundaries that restrict competition for sexual partners. Other taboos, such as age restrictions, protect vulnerable children not yet mature enough to consent to sexual activity.

As with other aspects of human social life, sociologists understand that sexuality is the result of both nature and nurture; it has a biological basis but varies culturally. As such, it is another aspect of our lives that is socially constructed.

Sexuality as a Social Construction

The bedroom may seem like the last place that would be submitted to a sociological analysis. But sociology applies not only to our public actions but also to the most personal and private aspects of our lives. Sex reflects a culture's collective norms.

Culture heavily influences when, how often, where, with whom, and how humans have sex (Kimmel 2007). Researchers have documented a variety of sexual customs around the world. A passionate kiss on the lips frequently initiates a sexual encounter in U.S. culture. But the Thonga of Mozambique and Siriono of Bolivia, among others, find such kissing to be repulsive because of the possibility of exchanging saliva; mouths are intended to be used for food. The Zande people of central Africa typically have sex several times a night but, in contrast, the Yapese people of the Pacific Islands typically have sex only about once a month. In some cultures, sexual intercourse always occurs outside so as not to "contaminate" the living quarters; in others it always happens indoors. Oral sex is a staple of sexual encounters in some cultures but is absent from others. Men typically initiate sex in many cultures, whereas women typically do so in others.

Because all these sexual behaviors and more are considered "normal" in their cultural context, there clearly is no single understanding of human sexuality. Amidst all these variations in sexual behavior, humans manage to reproduce, express love, form strong social bonds, experience pleasure, and simply have fun.

Changing Norms: The Sexual Revolution in the United States

To get a sense of the social construction of sexuality, consider how sexual attitudes, behaviors, and norms have evolved in the United States. In a major cultural shift, the past century has seen an increasing willingness to discuss sexuality openly and a greater emphasis on individual freedom and personal choice in matters of sexuality.

Through much of the twentieth century, sexuality was closely controlled by restrictive social norms. Morality and religion preached that the only appropriate use of sex was to start a family. Reflecting the inequality of the day, women were subjected to a double standard: premarital sex by men was commonly tolerated, whereas women were expected to remain virgins until marriage. Because women didn't have easy access to effective birth control or safe legal abortions, and unmarried mothers were subjected to severe social stigma, female abstinence before marriage was a practical necessity.

By the mid-twentieth century, however, a number of factors helped to change sexual attitudes and behaviors in the United States, creating what came to be called the sexual revolution:

- In 1948, Alfred Kinsey and his colleagues helped spark serious public discussion of sexuality when they published the first of two books on male and female sexuality (Kinsey, Pomeroy, and Martin 1948/1998; Kinsey et al. 1953/1998). Though crude by today's standards, the work used a social scientific approach to explore what had largely been taboo subjects, including homosexuality. Their findings suggested that many people were more open to a variety of sexual experiences than was often acknowledged. Such work was significant, since sexuality was typically considered a private matter not to be discussed in public, and most people lacked even basic sexual information to a degree that is difficult to imagine today.

- The vibrant youth culture of the post–World War II baby boom generation during the latter 1950s and 1960s rebelled against many social conventions, including restrictive sexual norms. Students living away from home in rapidly growing residential college campuses encountered a social environment that enabled sexual experimentation. By the late 1960s, some members of this youth subculture were advocating the wholesale rejection of sexual conventions and promoting sexuality for pleasure, not just procreation.

- The introduction of the Pill in 1960 helped to make such sexual freedom possible. Oral contraceptives made it easier for women to control if and when they had children.

- A broader women's movement decried the sexual double standard and affirmed the right of women to control their own bodies and enjoy their sexuality.

This new freedom was not without consequences. As people engaged in more frequent sex with a greater number of partners, the frequency of sexually transmitted diseases and teen pregnancies rose in the 1970s, which helped spark a backlash against the sexual revolution. Social conservatives advocated a return to "family values," including a revival of earlier norms regarding sexuality and gender roles. Debates over these cultural values continue to this day, but most aspects of the sexual revolution have long since moved into the cultural mainstream, influencing the expression of our sexual identities.

Sexual Identities

Queer theory argues that sexual identities are socially constructed, evolve, and can change during a person's life (Seidman 1996). **Sexual identity** (or sexual orientation) refers to *our sense of self as it relates to the type of sexual attraction we have for others.* In our society, there are four basic sexual identity groups (summarized in Figure 11.4):

- **Heterosexuals** are *attracted to people of a different sex.*
- **Homosexuals** are *attracted to people of the same sex.*
- **Bisexuals** are *attracted to people of both sexes.*
- **Asexual** people *experience no sexual attraction for anyone.*

Although it remains an area of debate, growing evidence suggests that sexual identity is rooted in biology but influenced by culture. The American Academy of Pediatrics offers its clinicians advice that is typical of this growing consensus: "Sexual orientation probably is not determined by any one factor but by a combination of genetic, hormonal, and environmental influences" (Frankowski 2004, 1828).

Sexuality is a sensitive and private topic, and many people are guarded about discussing it. It is therefore impossible to ascertain whether what people *say* in surveys about their sex lives is accurate. Also, given the continuum of attitudes and behaviors that marks sexuality, classifying people into distinct categories can be difficult and misleading. For example, most people who report having engaged in same-sex activities at some point in their lives do not identify as gay, lesbian, or

| | Degree of Opposite-Sex Attraction | |
	High	Low
Degree of Same-Sex Attraction — High	Bisexual	Homosexual
Degree of Same-Sex Attraction — Low	Heterosexual	Asexual

FIGURE 11.4 | SEXUAL IDENTITIES

bisexual (Herbenick et al. 2010; Laumann et al. 2000). Thus the percentage of the population that falls within each type of sexual identity is a matter of debate.

More recently, the U.S. Census Bureau has begun to collect data on same-sex couples and the gay, lesbian, and bisexual population in the United States. Based on these and other surveys, one analysis found that 9 million people—3.5 percent of the adult U.S. population—identified themselves as lesbian, gay, bisexual, or transgender (Gates 2011). In 2009, there were 581,300 same-sex couples in the United States, a number that is likely to increase as the social stigma and threat of discrimination associated with homosexuality and same-sex relationships decreases (Gates 2010).

Inventing Heterosexuals and Homosexuals

Just as culture influences how people understand sexual behavior, it also influences how we understand sexual identity. In fact, the very idea of linking identity to sexuality—of identifying as "straight," "gay," or "bi"—is a relatively recent social invention.

All forms of sexual behaviors have existed throughout human history. Some forms of homosexual activity were a routine part of social life in some societies, as we saw from the example of the two-spirits earlier in this chapter. Perhaps most famously, homosexuality was prevalent in ancient Greek culture, and the word *lesbian* is derived from the island of Lesbos, home of the ancient Greek poet Sappho, who wrote her love poems for women and girls.

However, through most of human history, sexual behavior and what we now call sexual identity have been separated. In earlier times, engaging in heterosexual or homosexual activity didn't necessarily mean a person was regarded as a heterosexual or a homosexual. Not until early scientific efforts to categorize human sexual behavior in the mid-nineteenth century was the notion of "homosexuals" as a distinct category of people created to contrast with "heterosexuals."

In *The History of Sexuality*, Michel Foucault (1978/1980) argued that in the mid-nineteenth century, in part because of the increasingly diverse and rapidly growing populations concentrated in recently industrialized cities, scientists undertook new efforts to study sexual behaviors. For the first time, sexuality—which had always been a part of daily life—was scrutinized and analyzed. In the process of studying sexual behaviors, researchers began classifying them into distinct categories—including "normal" and "deviant." Increased knowledge about sexual practices led to efforts by those in power to restrict

them. Governments began trying to regulate and control these newly labeled deviant practices. For example, they enacted sodomy laws banning practices associated with homosexuality (though performed by many heterosexuals, as well), such as anal intercourse and oral sex. By the end of the nineteenth century, Western societies treated someone who engaged in homosexual activity as a member of a new and distinct social category: homosexuals.

In the latter half of the twentieth century, however, skepticism about the strict separation of sexualities and efforts to enforce it increased. As early as 1948, Kinsey suggested that, rather than belonging to one of two distinct categories, men's sexuality fell along a continuum, with many men experiencing both heterosexual and homosexual feelings and behaviors to varying degrees. Many researchers have confirmed Kinsey's findings, though popular culture often still views "gay" and "straight" as sharply divided and mutually exclusive identities.

Bisexuality and Asexuality

Are you gay or straight? As noted, our culture generally insists on dichotomous—either-or—sexual identities. But what if your answer to that question is "both" or "neither"?

Being *bisexual* means having a sexual identity based on attraction to both women and men. People in various cultures have long engaged in sexual activity with people of both sexes, but the notion of bisexuality as a distinct identity emerged in the nineteenth century. The term *bisexual* was not commonly used until the mid-twentieth century.

Being *asexual* means lacking sexual attraction to either gender. This identity, too, violates our culture's expected norms about sexuality. Asexual people are not celibate; they typically don't choose to refrain from sex, resist sexual urges, fail to find a sexual partner, or have moral or religious objections to sex. Instead, asexuals—who make up about one percent of the population, according to the limited research available on the subject—are simply not sexually attracted to anyone (Bogaert 2004).

Sexual Identities and Inequality

Cultures have widely divergent views about lesbian, gay, bisexual, and transgender people (LGBT). **Heterosexism,** *a set of attitudes and behavior that indicates an assumption that everyone is heterosexual,* is common. Assuming a female friend is referring to a man when she mentions a date is an example of heterosexism. People with heterosexist attitudes don't neces-

thinking about **power**

Once scientists categorized people as homosexual or heterosexual, governments sought to use their **power** to control people with sexual identities they considered deviant. In what ways do governments still use power to control people's sexual identity?

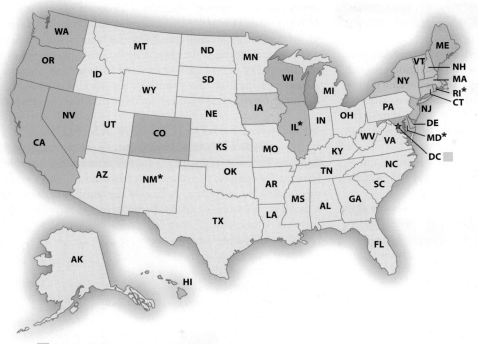

MAP 11.1 | SAME-SEX MARRIAGE AND RELATIONSHIP RECOGNITION LAWS, 2011

As of 2011, licenses for same-sex marriages or civil unions are issued in Connecticut, Iowa, Massachusetts, New Hampshire, New Jersey, New York, Vermont, and Washington, DC. Most states, though, continue to ban same-sex marriage. *Source:* National Gay and Lesbian Task Force (2011).

CORE CONCEPTS CHALLENGE

*How does the legal **structure** in various states create barriers for same-sex couples? Does legally recognizing same-sex marriage create barriers for heterosexual couples? Explain.*

States with full marriage equality
Massachusetts (2004); Connecticut (2008); Iowa (2009); Vermont (2009); New Hampshire (2010); District of Columbia (2010); New York (2011)

States with broad relationship recognition laws
civil unions: Vermont (2000); New Jersey (2007); Illinois (2011); Rhode Island (2011); Delaware (2012); Hawaii (2012)
domestic partnerships: California (2005); Oregon (2008); Washington (2008); Nevada (2009)

States with limited relationship recognition laws
designated beneficiaries: Colorado (2009)
domestic partnerships: Maine (2004); Maryland (2008); Wisconsin (2009)

* States that recognize same-sex marriages performed in other states
Rhode Island (2007); Maryland (2010); New Mexico (2011); Illinois (2011)

sarily have negative feelings toward LGBT people; they simply overlook their existence. In contrast, **homophobia** is *the disapproval and fear of LGBT people*. Homophobia is often the source of hostility and discrimination.

Discrimination against lesbian, gay, bisexual, and transgender people is pervasive, though some movement toward more equality is evident. Homophobic laws and customs have blatantly discriminated against LGBT people, often forcing them to stay "in the closet." The American Psychiatric Association labeled homosexuality a "mental disorder" until the mid-1970s. Sodomy laws were used almost exclusively to target gay men until the U.S. Supreme Court ruled them unconstitutional in 2003 (American Civil Liberties Union 2010; Human Rights Campaign 2010).

Because federal legislation does not bar discrimination against LGBT people in employment, in the absence of state protections, it is legal to fire or refuse to hire people simply because they are gay, bisexual, or transgender. Some states, though, have adopted employment protection laws prohibiting such actions. In some ways, the private sector has been ahead of government in recognizing LGBT rights in the workplace. For example, as of 2010, 89 percent of *Fortune* 500 companies prohibited discrimination on the basis of sexual orientation and 57 percent offered domestic partner health insurance benefits to LGBT employees (Human Rights Campaign 2011a).

Same-sex marriage is legal in several countries, including Canada, Belgium, the Netherlands, South Africa, and Spain, whereas various forms of civil unions are legal in at least fifteen other countries. However, since 1996 the U.S. government has defined marriage as a legal union between one man and one woman (Public Law No. 104-199), and most states continue to bar same-sex marriages, limiting the legal rights of gay and lesbian partners (Map 11.1). As yet, LGBT parents have no consistent legal standing across the states. Child custody, visitation, and adoption rights are just some of the issues still being debated and resolved in various legal venues.

Homosexuals were banned from military service until 1993, when a compromise "don't ask, don't tell" policy (designed by sociologist Charles Moskos) permitted gays and lesbians to serve as long as they did not openly disclose their sexual identity. Since that time, though, an increasing majority of the public has supported allowing gays to serve openly (Pew Research Center 2010b). A 2010 Defense Department study found that only 30 percent of military personnel thought repeal of "don't ask, don't tell" would have a negative effect (U.S. Department of Defense 2010). In 2010, a federal court found this policy unconstitutional, prompting congressional action later that year that finally overturned the ban.

Homophobic beliefs are often rooted in religious doctrine, but there is no consensus among the world's religions regarding the status of LGBT people. Indeed, debates about homosexuality, the role of gays in each faith, and the blessing of same-sex unions have deeply divided some denominations. The Episcopal Church in the United States was deeply divided in recent years over the ordination of an openly gay bishop, for example. Intolerance can be extreme. In a few Muslim countries, including Iran and Yemen, homosexuality is still punishable by death.

More informally, our culture still contains homophobia. For many young people, *gay* is a synonym for lame or stupid. "Gay bashing" ranges from well-known insulting slang terms—such as *fag* or *dyke*—to hate crimes such as harassment, assault, and even murder. Such harassment sometimes leads to suicides, especially by beleaguered gay teens (Dvorak 2010).

In one particularly horrendous period of persecution, German Nazis arrested and beat tens of thousands of gay men—sometimes castrating them—and used them as forced laborers in concentration camps. Once imprisoned, they were forced to wear pink triangles, which activists have since recast as a powerful symbol of the LGBT movement.

Challenging Inequality Based on Gender and Sexual Identity

A half-century ago, a chapter such as this one simply would not have appeared in a sociology textbook. In an example of how human action can change cultures and social structures, however, feminists and LGBT activists have helped to modify political, legal, and cultural reality as well as the scholarly agenda. This section briefly explores some of these efforts.

Gender in Sociology

As we saw in Chapter 1, most early mainstream sociologists ignored issues of gender and sexuality, reflecting the sexist views of the societies in which they were working (Kandal 1988). The "founding fathers" of sociology in the nineteenth and early twentieth centuries often based their generalizations about society on the experiences of heterosexual men. Women writing sociological works at the time were mostly excluded from formal academic positions. As a result, gender played a marginal role in early conventional sociology.

One exception was a critical theory of gender stratification developed by Friedrich Engels, a close collaborator of Karl Marx. Engels (1884/1972) tied gender stratification to the rise of private property and class. Although he made gender secondary in importance to class, Engels at least recognized gender inequality as unjust and saw the intersection of class and gender stratification. As a result of his work, the emancipation of women was a goal of many socialist political movements.

GENDER STRATIFICATION AS FUNCTIONAL

By the middle of the twentieth century, Talcott Parsons was one of a number of sociologists who wrote about "sex roles." Parsons recognized the role strain involved in being a woman in middle-class America, especially the tension between being a mother and working in paid employment. However, reflecting his functionalist theoretical orientation, Parsons accepted uncritically the idea that the specialization of sex roles served a useful function in society.

According to Parsons, paid labor serves an *instrumental* function because it is task oriented, with short-term, impersonal interactions, while the family serves the *expressive* functions involved in stable, long-term, personal relationships. With work separated from home life, men specialized in instrumental functions, whereas women focused on the expressive tasks of nurturing children and caring for husbands. Parsons seemed to assume that women and men voluntarily accepted this state of affairs and embraced the values associated with it. For Parsons, this clear separation of sex roles reduced competition between husband and wife for status in the family. "If both were equally in competition for occupational status, there might indeed be a very serious strain on the solidarity of the family unit," Parsons wrote (1940/1954, 79). He argued that the useful functions provided by sex role segregation helped to explain why "the feminist movement has had such difficulty in breaking it down" (p. 80). In the 1960s and 1970s, the women's movement challenged these assumptions.

SPOTLIGHT on social theory

Parsons's **functionalist** approach to gender rationalized inequality between the sexes. Do you agree that specialized roles for each sex can serve a positive function? How might such specialization be dysfunctional for society?

FEMINIST SCHOLARSHIP Objecting to the functionalists' assumptions, feminist scholars pointed out that there was no reason why individuals could not perform *both* instrumental and expressive tasks, or if these tasks were to be separated, why men had to be limited to instrumental and women to expressive. They also pointed out that functionalist arguments ignored reality: first, a significant portion of women—overwhelmingly members of the working class—were already in the labor force, and second, Parsons's model of family life was limited to a particular middle-class version that was dominant in the United States in the middle of the twentieth century. Since that time, feminist scholarship has influenced every subfield in the discipline (Chafetz 1999). This chapter reflects many insights from feminist scholars.

Women's Activism

Feminism is *a philosophy that advocates social, political, and economic equality for women and men.* Activism on behalf of women's equality has been a constant force in the modern world, but various periods of especially intense activism are commonly identified as "waves." *First-wave feminism* took place mainly in the United States and the United Kingdom during the late nineteenth and early twentieth centuries, when activists working on behalf of women's political and social rights won the right to vote for women. The Seneca Falls convention mentioned earlier in this chapter is from this era, as are such noted feminist leaders as Susan B. Anthony and Elizabeth Cady Stanton. The activists of this period had broad goals beyond winning the right to vote, including eliminating discriminatory laws, increasing access to higher education, and working to make birth control more readily available.

Second-wave feminism refers to the period of intense activism during the 1960s and 1970s, when activists tackled issues related to gender inequality, including discrimination in the workplace and in education, gender stereotypes in popular culture, restrictive gender roles, reproductive rights, and sexual freedom. During this era well-known activists such as Betty Friedan, the author of *The Feminine Mystique* (a book that helped inspire a revival of interest in women's rights), helped form the National Organization for Women (NOW), and Gloria Steinem, another important activist, founded *Ms. Magazine* as a platform for feminist ideas.

Third-wave feminism refers to activism beginning in the 1990s, though some feminist scholars and activists view this period as a continuation of second-wave feminism. Activism today promotes female self-empowerment and sexual self-esteem, gives special attention to race and class diversity within women's experiences, and often includes a playful subversion of popular culture. For example, third-wave feminists combated the patronizing use of the word *girl* to refer to women by reclaiming it as "grrl power," a confident affirmation of women's strength.

LGBT Activism

Sexual identity and gender identity are not just private issues; they are also public and political concerns. During the past half-century, social activism has made the public increasingly aware of issues affecting LGBT people (Clendinen and Nagourney 1999; Miller 2006). On June 28, 1969, the New York City police raided a gay bar called the Stonewall Inn, as they had done many times before. This time, however, patrons refused to go quietly to jail, and while the police waited for patrol wagons, a crowd gathered outside the bar and began heckling and then attacking the officers. The spontaneous demonstration that followed was repeated on subsequent nights in what has become known as the Stonewall Riots, a defining moment for the LGBT community and a symbolic turning point in the history of social movements. After years of being forced to hide from police harassment, gay people took to the streets to demand their rights.

Stonewall primarily involved white, gay men. Since then, a diverse gay rights movement has emerged, taking on a broad range of issues, including supporting LGBT people of color; combating hate crimes; supporting teens who face bullying, harassment, and estrangement from their families; mobilizing people of faith to support LGBT rights; assisting aging gay couples who face unique financial challenges as a result of their not being allowed to marry; combating discriminatory laws and practices in civilian society and the military; working for equality in the workplace; and helping same-sex parents. College campuses have been especially active in cultivating LGBT activism and developing movement leaders. Over the years, activists have shifted the nation's culture and laws toward considerably more equality for the LGBT community, though much remains to be done.

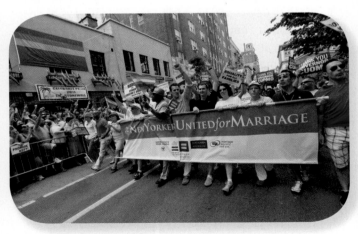

In 1969, gays and lesbians were forced to live almost entirely "in the closet," and public gay rights activism was so rare that the clash (left) between police and gay men outside of New York's Stonewall Inn became iconic. Today, many LGBT people live openly and LGBT activism is common, including the movement to recognize same-sex marriage. On the right, supporters of gay marriage march past the Stonewall Inn to celebrate the enactment of New York's gay marriage law in 2011.

CONVERGENCE IN GENDER AND SEXUALITY

As we have seen, ideas about gender and sexuality are changing constantly. In recent years, one ongoing change has been that women and men have become more similar in both gender and sexuality.

Gender Convergence

Gender convergence is *a trend toward increasing similarity in how women and men live.* This convergence varies depending on social context, much like gender itself. Some women in booming developing countries, for example, are experiencing increased economic opportunities and independence for the first time, newfound freedom that is allowing them to carve out new gender roles in otherwise traditional societies. Those most affected are middle-class, educated women who have the chance to defer marriage and motherhood while pursuing careers in fields such as business and technology. In India, for example, a growing population of young, single women has chosen to live independently, rather than staying at their parents' house or getting married. Although Indian women marry young compared to their Western counterparts, the average age at which they marry has risen slightly, with college-educated women putting off marriage the longest. Although arranged marriages are still common and traditional gender roles still deeply entrenched, new economic realities are enabling some women to pursue careers and lifestyles once limited to men (Sengupta 2007).

In wealthy developed countries, traditional ways of dividing responsibility between work and family are becoming less common and gender roles less rigid (Fischer et al. 2007; Lang and Risman 2007). As we have seen, women and men participate in the labor force at rates that are converging. As a result, they now have increasingly similar attitudes toward the best way to allocate their time: both women and men report they want to strike a balance between work and family life.

In particular, younger men and women in wealthy societies are increasingly taking on similar roles. Younger fathers spend more time doing childcare than their own fathers did (Gerson 1987). College students of both sexes have similar aspirations to pursue advanced degrees and careers, have similar attitudes about the appropriate role of women in society, provide similar answers to a variety of questions about personal values (including about the desire to raise a family), and hold comparable opinions about some social and political issues (Astin 1998).

Sexual Convergence

Over the past few decades, gender convergence has gradually changed the sexual double standard between men and women, especially among younger people. The age at which women and men become sexually active, their number of sexual partners, and their attitudes toward sexuality have become more similar. One phase of this convergence occurred in the wake of the sexual revolution of the 1960s and 1970s, when girls became more sexually active at an earlier age, thereby behaving more like boys. A second phase began in the 1990s, when boys began delaying the age of their first sexual activity, thereby behaving more like girls.

Risman and Schwartz (2002) suggest that the traditionally large gap between the rate of girls' and boys' sexual activity before the sexual revolution meant that a few sexually active girls were having relations with a larger number of boys. Gender norms of the time discouraged sexual activity on the part of "good girls," leaving boys to pursue sex with "bad girls," who were ostracized as "sluts." As gender norms changed, girls' sexual activity has become more accepted and widespread. Consequently, boys' early sexual activities are now more likely to be in the context of an ongoing relationship with a girlfriend rather than a fleeting encounter with a "bad girl." Sex in such ongoing relationships is more likely to be safe and responsible, contributing to some positive trends. In recent years, the rates of sexually transmitted diseases, teen pregnancies, and abortions have all declined, suggesting that teens are being more sexually responsible.

Gender and Sexuality

culture

- Gender refers to the socially constructed cultural expectations associated with men and women. Different cultures produce different gender norms.

- From infancy, we are socialized into our culture's gender expectations, develop gendered identities, and view the world through the lens of gender expectations that we usually take for granted.

- Sexuality also varies by culture, and different cultures have different norms regarding sexual identities that must be taught through socialization.

structure

- Gender is built into social structure, as when social institutions enforce gender expectations.

- Gender must constantly be maintained and recreated—actions that sociologists call "doing gender." Gender roles and identities are fragile and may be contested and changed.

- Social structures often reflect expectations regarding sexuality, as when the legal system is tailored to heterosexual couples.

power

- In every society, differences in power between men and women have resulted in social institutions with considerable gender inequality.

- Inequality based on sexuality also reflects differences in power in society.

- Feminists and LGBT activists have organized, using their collective power to promote change.

Looking Back

1. *Sex* refers to the biological characteristics that distinguish females and males. *Gender* refers to the socially constructed expectations associated with women and men. Transgender people, who identify with a gender not typically associated with their sex, illustrate the difference between sex and gender.

2. Much of what our society attributes to sex is, in fact, gender. Notions of gender vary over time and across cultures. Gender is taught through socialization, and "doing gender" refers to daily interactions in a variety of social settings that involve the reinforcement or modification of gender.

3. Gender inequality and stratification are part of the structure of society. Sex differences likely played an important role in the establishment of patriarchy, whereas cultural developments have radically reduced the importance of sex in relation to gender.

4. Gender inequality can be found in all the major social institutions, including the workplace, family, media, politics, and religion. Individual or organized violence against women is one way male power is used to dominate women.

5. Norms about sexuality and sexual identity are culturally produced, resulting in wide variations. In Western society, the invention of distinct sexual orientations is a relatively recent phenomenon. Sexual minorities are often subject to discrimination.

6. Feminist efforts have helped to create more equality between women and men. Activism has also helped to reduce discrimination against LGBT people. Gender and sexual convergence have occurred in many areas of social life, as standards become more similar for men and women.

Critical Thinking: Questions and Activities

1. Both gender and race have socially constructed characteristics that are mistakenly attributed to biology. Using a sociological perspective, describe how else race and gender are similar. How are they different?

2. Take note of how the words *sex* and *gender* are used to refer to women and men in popular media and other places. Can you find examples in which the word *gender* is being used to mean biological differences?

3. What do you think are the major differences, if any, between how gender affects your life and how it affected the lives of your parents?

4. Where do you see the most entrenched forms of gender inequality? Why has this particular area been so resistant to change?

5. How were you socialized to understand different sexual identities? Did this socialization include homophobic biases?

Key Terms

asexual (p. 305) people who experience no sexual attraction for anyone.

bisexual (p. 305) people who are attracted to others of both sexes.

doing gender (p. 291) creating gender through interactions in particular social settings.

domestic violence (or intimate partner violence) (p. 301) a pattern of abusive behavior in any relationship that is used by one partner to gain or maintain power and control over another intimate partner.

feminism (p. 309) a philosophy that advocates social, political, and economic equality for women and men.

gender (p. 285) the socially constructed cultural expectations associated with women and men.

gender convergence (p. 310) a trend toward increasing similarity in how women and men live.

gender expression (p. 287) the way a person communicates gender identity to others, through behavior, clothing, hairstyle, and other means.

gender identity (p. 287) a person's identification as a woman, a man, or some combination of the two.

gender role (p. 290) a set of social expectations regarding behavior and attitudes based on a person's sex.

gender stratification (p. 295) the systematic and unequal distribution of power and resources in society between women and men.

glass ceiling (p. 299) the often invisible barrier created by individual and institutional sexism that prevents qualified women from advancing to higher levels of leadership and management.

heterosexism (p. 306) attitudes and behavior that indicate an assumption that everyone is heterosexual.

heterosexual (p. 305) people who are attracted to people of a different sex.

homophobia (p. 307) the disapproval and fear of LGBT people.

homosexual (p. 305) people who are attracted to people of the same sex.

incest taboo (p. 304) a norm restricting sexual relations between certain relatives.

intersexual people (p. 285) individuals born with ambiguous reproductive or sexual anatomy.

matriarchy (p. 295) a social system dominated by women.

patriarchy (p. 295) a social system dominated by men.

second shift (p. 299) the phenomenon of employed women still having primary responsibility for housework and childcare.

sex (p. 285) the biological distinction between females and males.

sexism (p. 290) the ideology that one sex is superior to the other.

sexual harassment (p. 300) unwelcome sexual advances, requests for sexual favors, and other verbal or physical harassment of a sexual nature.

sexual identity (or **orientation**) (p. 305) our sense of self as it relates to the type of sexual attraction we have for others.

sexuality (p. 304) a person's sexual desires, behaviors, and identity.

transgender people (p. 287) individuals who identify with a gender different from the one associated with their sex.

transsexuals (p. 289) people who have sex reassignment surgery to change their physical appearance.

Education and Work

looking AHEAD

How—and what—have schools taught you about the social norms and values of your culture?

Do schools provide a structure that promotes social equality—or do they reinforce social inequality?

How does power operate in workplaces such as those where you have had experience?

When Claudia Crisostomo's three children—six, nine, and ten years old—arrive home from school each day, their mother is heading out to her job at a uniform laundry. Because her shift begins at 3:00 p.m., and she returns home late in the evening, she is not able to help her children with homework or read to them before bedtime. Nor is she able to go to evening events at the school, attend after-school meetings with teachers, or take her kids to the doctor or dentist. The Crisostomos live in Newburgh, New York, a small city about sixty miles north of New York City, where public transportation is limited. Consequently, getting to important events and appointments—such as school assemblies and doctor visits—usually requires an expensive taxi ride.

Because Ms. Crisostomo, a Mexican immigrant, does not speak or read English with confidence, she feels disconnected from her kids' school experiences and has a hard time advocating for her children with school officials and medical professionals. Although educators stress that parental involvement is a key factor in helping kids to succeed in school, Ms. Crisostomo has neither the kind of work schedule nor the facility with English needed to get involved with her children's school (Berger 2006). ■

I n immigrant communities across the United States, the Crisostomos' experience is a familiar one. Countless immigrant parents work evening hours, and even when they can take part in school activities, they often are uncomfortable navigating the school environment. Yet the education their kids are getting in that environment is a crucial factor in helping them achieve a better quality of life than the parents themselves enjoy. Education and work are closely interconnected, as one of the aims of education is to teach individuals the knowledge and skills they will need to get jobs and lead a happy, productive life.

In this chapter we look at these two intertwined social institutions: education and work. We consider their roles and functions in society, their structure, and their relationship to social equality and inequality. We emphasize the various social and cultural factors that shape people's school and workplace experiences.

Education and Schooling

Education is a word you know well. If you are reading this book, you are probably pursuing a college education. The news is full of stories about education, politicians often talk about the importance of education, and potential employers ask job candidates about their education. Sociologists define **education** as *the social institution through which individuals acquire knowledge and skills and learn cultural norms and values.* Education is vital to the transmission of basic cultural knowledge from one generation to the next, including traditions and an understanding of history. Education also imparts knowledge and skills related to specific jobs and household management.

The learning associated with education occurs in different settings beyond schools. For example, learning takes place at home, on the playground, and at work involving parents, friends and neighbors, and employers. However, the sociological study of education focuses foremost on schools, which are the primary arena of formal education, and on **schooling,** *organized instruction by trained teachers.*

Schooling is an important part of social life throughout the world. Most countries emphasize the value of schooling and invest in organized instruction for their citizens. Three key indicators highlight the widespread belief in the importance of schooling (Brint 2006). First, young people throughout the developed world, and in much of the developing world, spend a great deal of their childhood in school (see Table 13.1). In the United States, children typically attend school six hours a day for about 180 days each year. Children in some countries go to school for more than 200 days each year; Japanese children, for example, attend school for at least 210 days each year (Wray 2008).

Second, most wealthy nations make a substantial investment in schooling by financing a system of formal education. A key

TABLE 13.1 AGE RANGE AT WHICH 90 PERCENT OF THE POPULATION IS ENROLLED IN SCHOOL, SELECT COUNTRIES

Country	Age Range (years)
Belgium	3–17
Brazil	7–16
Chile	6–16
England	4–16
France	3–17
Germany	4–17
Israel	5–17
Italy	3–15
Japan	4–17
Korea	6–17
New Zealand	4–15
Norway	4–17
Spain	3–16
Sweden	3–18
Turkey	7–12
United States	6–16

Source: Organization for Economic Cooperation and Development.

reason is that political participation and economic growth depend, in part, on schooling to teach citizenship and job skills. Perhaps the most fundamental of these skills is **literacy,** *the ability to read and write.* As Map 13.1 illustrates, literacy rates vary throughout the world. Adult literacy is near universal (99 percent) in developed countries, and literacy has increased substantially in developing countries in recent decades, rising to 81 percent of adults in 2010 (UN Development Programme 2010). In the United States and throughout most of the developed world, government funds help to finance schools from elementary schools through colleges and universities. Developing countries typically have fewer resources to invest in schools, but spending on formal education is still often a very high priority. The Education for All Global Monitoring Report (2010) cites limited financial resources as one of the primary obstacles to improving education, estimating that education spending will have to double to make a basic education, including adult literacy, universally accessible in low-income countries.

Third, a large number of adults have jobs in education, working as teachers, support staff, and administrators in schools

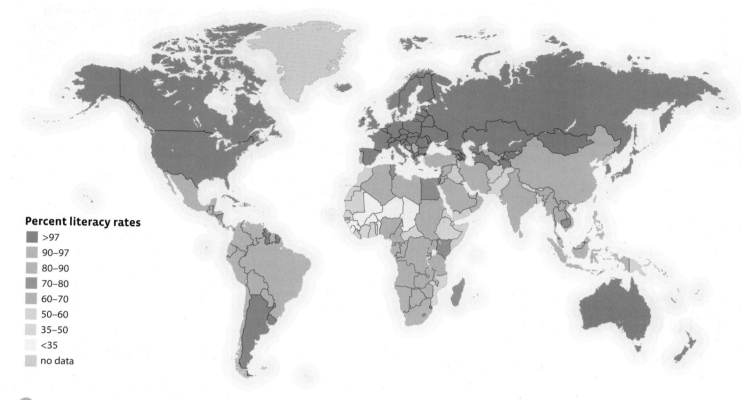

Percent literacy rates
- >97
- 90–97
- 80–90
- 70–80
- 60–70
- 50–60
- 35–50
- <35
- no data

MAP 13.1 | LITERACY RATES AROUND THE WORLD

National literacy rates vary considerably. Literacy exceeds 97 percent in North America, Australia, and most of Europe, but literacy rates are significantly lower in most of Africa, Asia, and South America. *Source:* UN Human Development Programme (2009).

and school offices. Schools are a major employer in the United States. In 2008, there were more than 2 million elementary and middle school teachers, more than 500,000 high school teachers, and more than 600,000 school administrators (U.S. Census Bureau 2008), with hundreds of thousands of others employed in schools as teaching assistants, librarians, custodians, and food service workers, among many different occupations. Similarly, from preschools to universities, schools are a major employer throughout the world.

Education in the United States: A Brief Social History

Until the nineteenth century, most children in the United States did not attend school. Instead, children typically worked in the household, on the farm, or as wage laborers. Some children received an education in a specific trade by serving an apprenticeship. Formal education, though available, was offered almost exclusively to upper-class children, who attended private schools and private universities.

Leaders of the American Revolution, notably Thomas Jefferson, advocated the development of a public elementary school system as a way to unify the new nation and promote active citizenship and democratic self-government. Yet in the late 1700s and early 1800s, education in the United States remained a patchwork of schools with minimal government funding and limited enrollment. Women, African Americans, and Native Americans were largely excluded (Urban and Wagoner 2009).

Public schools—"common schools" at the time—did not emerge until the early 1830s, when educational reformers in the Northeast argued for the development of free taxpayer-supported schools that would be accessible to all children. With the United States amidst a transformation from a rural and agrarian society to one shaped by industrialization, urbanization, and an influx of new immigrants, advocates of common schools emphasized the civic value of education. During this period of social change, according to historian William J. Reese (2005), "schools were expected to strengthen the moral character of children, reinvigorate the work ethic, spread civic and republican values, and along the way teach a common curriculum to ensure a literate and unified public" (p. 3).

After the Civil War, school enrollment increased and common schools expanded dramatically. In 1870, 57 percent of five to eighteen year olds were enrolled in school. By the turn of the century, there were more than 250,000 public schools in the United States, and 72 percent of children were attending school (Reese 2005). Starting with Massachusetts in 1852, states began enacting compulsory attendance laws in the middle of the nineteenth century. By 1918, all forty-eight states had laws requiring children to attend school, usually through eighth grade—and the foundation of our contemporary system of universal compulsory education was established.

Public education continued to expand in the first half of the twentieth century as a high school education became increasingly common. Between 1900 and 1950, the school year lengthened from an average of 144 days to 178 days, and total public school enrollment climbed from 15.5 to 25.7 million students (Reese 2005). Local governments increasingly invested in schools, which were becoming the largest public expenditure in many communities. Then, as now, schools were the focus of public scrutiny and became an arena for debate and controversy over the substance of the curriculum, teaching methods, academic standards, the goals of education, and, more generally, the place of education in society.

The Functions of Schooling

What are schools for? This question is deceptively complex and cannot be answered adequately with the obvious response, "Schools are a place to learn."

SPOTLIGHT
on social theory

A **functionalist** perspective emphasizes the role of education in society. Do you think the functions of schooling are changing in the twenty-first century?

In exploring the various dimensions of this not-so-simple question, a sociological perspective directs us to consider the functions of schooling. We identify seven fundamental functions of contemporary schools:

1. *Transfer of knowledge.* Schools are a vital site where children and teenagers acquire knowledge defined as important by previous generations, including subjects from history and literature to math and science.

2. *Job preparation.* Schools do more than transfer general knowledge. They also play an important role in teaching job skills. Most schools help prepare future workers. Many high schools, colleges, and adult education programs emphasize specific job-related skills.

3. *Occupational sorting.* In preparing young people for future jobs, schooling helps to sort people into different kinds of jobs. Not all schools are the same. Some schools emphasize specific trades, giving students skills in, say, plumbing or auto repair, whereas other schools focus on college preparation and send many graduates off to college and, subsequently, graduate school.

4. *Childcare.* Schools are responsible for children for the bulk of the work day and thus serve as a major source of childcare for working parents. Some of the demand for a longer school day and an extended school year comes from those in need of the kind of full-time childcare that schools provide.

5. *Social integration.* Schools give children common cultural references that help to build social solidarity. Schools

are often valuable community-building institutions that connect children and adults in the shared activity of teaching and learning. Schools often emphasize local and national history, helping to reinforce a sense of community and national identity.

6. *Change and innovation.* In bringing students and faculty together to study and learn, schools are a site from which new ideas and practices emerge. Schools are a major source of technological innovation, and schools can be a source of ideas that stimulate economic, political, and cultural change.

7. *Socialization.* Schools serve as a powerful agent of socialization, teaching lessons that extend well beyond the subject-specific curriculum. Contemporary schools often adopt an explicit socialization role, integrating into the school day educational activities about issues such as diversity, health, sexuality, and drug and violence prevention.

In the sections that follow, we explore many of these functions of education.

Education, Culture, and Socialization

There is widespread consensus that schools should teach the "three Rs"—reading, writing, and arithmetic—but what else do schools teach? As you will see in this section, schools provide lessons that extend well beyond specific academic knowledge and skills.

The Hidden Curriculum

Much of the socialization that happens in schools takes place outside the formal subject-matter curriculum. In the early twentieth century, Emile Durkheim (1925/1961) coined the term **moral education** to describe *the role of schools in teaching children the central values and beliefs of their society.* For Durkheim and many later sociologists, schools play a vital part in instructing children about their culture's core values.

Schools, for example, teach children lessons about the value of hard work, discipline, obedience to authorities, being on time, following the rules, and the consequences of misbehaving. In addition, typical evaluation systems teach kids about inequality (some students receive higher grades than others), and the school's structure teaches about hierarchy (the chain of command in schools, leading up to the principal). Sociologists refer to these implicit teachings as the **hidden curriculum,** or *the lessons students learn simply by attending school, in contrast to the lessons from the formal subject-specific curriculum.*

In recent years, politicians and parents have increasingly demanded that schools instruct children about core values

thinking about **culture**

The ethnic diversity of the U.S. school population has increased in recent years. Did your high school stick to teaching traditional lessons about U.S. **culture**—or did it take into account the cultural values of recent immigrants?

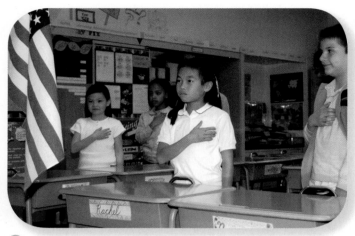

In this classroom scene, schoolchildren are saying the Pledge of Allegiance to start the school day.

CORE CONCEPTS CHALLENGE

What are public schools teaching when the Pledge of Allegiance is a part of the school's daily routine? How are the values of U.S. **culture** reflected in the messages conveyed in the Pledge?

and appropriate behavior. In many communities, schools are expected to help solve social problems by educating children about violence, sex, drugs, intolerance, health, nutrition, and basic civility. As a result, a new cast of school employees—among them, student assistance counselors, violence prevention coordinators, health educators, and diversity trainers—is becoming increasingly important on the public school stage.

Students also learn a great deal about national identity during the school day. Public schools in the United States adhere to a relatively standard set of patriotic rituals that identify both the school and its population as American. For example, many public school students recite the Pledge of Allegiance each day and participate in school assemblies to recognize national holidays such as Veterans Day and Memorial Day. One study suggests that the rapid spread of American public schools since the nineteenth century was part of a broader process of nation building in which the school became the central arena for forging national solidarity and preparing future generations to be engaged citizens (Meyer et al. 1979).

Schools also transmit fundamental social values connected to religious definitions of

national identity. Consider how the Pledge of Allegiance, in referring to "one nation under God" (a phrase inserted in 1954), emphasizes a religious basis for American identity. In contrast, public schools in France present a far more secular version of national identity, and religious displays are illegal in French public schools. Consequently—and controversially—Muslim girls are not permitted to wear headscarves in France's public schools.

Socialization Messages in Schools

Schools teach about behavior and values in both formal instruction and informal interactions between students and school officials. Brint and his colleagues (2001) identified five ways in which socialization messages are disseminated in U.S. primary schools:

1. Teacher-initiated interactions with students
2. Everyday classroom routines
3. Student participation in schoolwide activities and programs
4. Visual displays and oral rituals in public spaces
5. Subject matter in the formal curriculum

The authors found that the content of socialization messages outside the formal curriculum consists largely of traditional lessons about appropriate behavior. For example, most teacher-initiated interactions with students stress the importance of orderliness and effort, as when a teacher reminds students to "listen quietly when someone else is speaking" and to "finish on time." Broader, schoolwide activities are likely to emphasize the values of participation and respect and include conflict resolution programs and public recognition of students for positive contributions. Public spaces typically transmit messages that highlight the importance of obeying school rules and re-

A Muslim girl in France arrives at school, where she must remove her headscarf before classes. What kinds of religious displays have you seen at schools in your community? Should they be permitted? Why or why not?

specting authority—say, by means of a poster that reminds students to act responsibly or by requiring students' silence during the principal's morning announcements.

Brint (2006) identifies three dimensions by which schools evaluate students, producing specific language for describing students who conform to their socialization messages:

1. **Behavior conformity.** Daily life in schools is full of informal instruction on proper behavior. For example, you must raise your hand and wait to be called on before speaking, and you must request permission to use the bathroom. School authorities call students who follow these rules "well disciplined."

2. **Moral conformity.** Schools train students to internalize values about what is moral, right, or proper (see the Through a Sociological Lens box on page 352). Teachers and school officials commonly emphasize the importance of "honesty, tolerance, courage, hard work, or fairness . . . [and] may also assign reading materials that illustrate the consequences of not being guided by these moral virtues" (Brint 2006, 134). Students who appear to conform to these moral standards are generally regarded as "good" students.

3. **Cultural conformity.** Schools also instruct students on what Brint calls "approved styles and outlooks"—culturally desirable behaviors and perspectives. These are likely to vary significantly by school setting. For example, large urban public schools may teach students how to get along in complex, rule-based organizations by completing assignments precisely as instructed by the teacher. In contrast, elite private schools are far more likely to encourage students to demonstrate their creative thinking by producing quirky projects that may even question the assumptions of a given assignment. Brint notes that those who conform to cultural styles are perceived to be "well adjusted" to the cultural expectations of their specific school environment.

Mixed Messages About Socialization

The values that schools teach are a dynamic mix of old and new. They reflect both the schools' traditional interest in an orderly, achievement-oriented environment and wider, more recent social trends that encourage tolerance and respect for diversity. For example, formal instruction—including that in textbooks, assignments, and in-class lessons—now often emphasizes respect for cultural diversity and the importance of inclusiveness.

Sometimes conflicts arise within the community—or, more broadly, in the nation—about the mix of old and new messages. Educational historian Jonathan Zimmerman's *Whose America?* (2002) examines a series of longstanding conflicts over what public schools should teach about history, religion, and sexuality. Zimmerman shows that these conflicts are rooted in such deeply held beliefs that there seems to be little room for compromise or even discussion. For example, debates about prayer in school, demands to include creationist theories in science classes as an alternative to Darwin's theory of evolu-

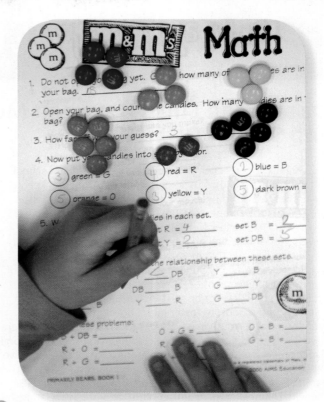

These elementary school students are learning math with the help of M&M's. Some teachers see this practice as a way to engage students in school, making math fun—and perhaps rewarding, too. When teachers use popular products like brand-name candy and pizza as rewards, what are students learning beyond addition and fractions?

tion, and disagreements over whether and what to teach about sex and sexuality pit different worldviews, values, and understandings of morality against one another.

The point is that socialization in schools reflects specific historical and social circumstances. Disagreements about the values children should learn have therefore made American public schools a site of ongoing political conflict.

Beyond their role as agents of socialization, schools are commonly seen as engines of social mobility and economic opportunity. In the next section, we look at how sociologists describe and interpret the relationship between education and opportunity.

Educational Structure and Inequality

Education is the great equalizer. If you want to get ahead in the world, the best route to success is through education, right? This is the official story, and it reflects the important

Tracing the Links Between Moral Authority and School Discipline

A high school teacher before returning to graduate school to study sociology, sociologist Richard Arum was keenly aware of the complex problems facing public schools. As Arum (2003) reports in the preface to his book *Judging School Discipline,* he taught in an urban public school system where disorder and violence were common.

Arum recognized that most of the research literature and news media coverage of public schools focused on measures of educational achievement—test scores, dropout rates, college admissions statistics. For his part, Arum was concerned about the ability of a school "to foster moral development and successfully socialize youth in its charge" (p. viii). His interests were influenced by social theorist Emile Durkheim's writings on moral education, by the longstanding public concern about ineffective school discipline, and by the increasing burdens schools must bear in an age when adults spend more time at work—and less time with their children. Arum set out to explore the relationship between school discipline and what he saw as a crisis in moral authority in U.S. schools. *How* have public schools lost their moral authority, Arum wondered?

To focus his investigation, Arum turned his attention to the courts, specifically probing how court decisions might have contributed to a "decline in moral authority and the erosion of effective disciplinary practices in American public schools" (p. 4). Arum examined court data, along with data on thousands of schools from four national surveys that had studied school disciplinary practices, student and teacher perceptions of school discipline, and educational achievement. Arum and his graduate students used a computerized legal archive to identify more than 6,000 relevant state and federal court cases that involved questions of school discipline, and they employed a series of statistical techniques to analyze the patterns in these cases.

Arum's analysis showed that some states had pro-school judicial climates (in which courts were more likely to rule in favor of schools) whereas other states had "pro-student" court climates (in which courts were more likely to rule in favor of students). He sought to identify whether these differing court climates affected how teachers and students act in school. He found that in pro-school judicial climates, teachers felt they had more classroom control and greater support for rule enforcement from their principals. In contrast, in pro-student climates, court rulings helped to undermine the legitimacy of school disciplinary practices because of the ever-present threat of lawsuits from parents and students.

Applying his sociological training, Arum relied on Durkheim's view of schools' role in moral education to interpret these re-

sults. He noted that although pro-student court rulings were important in educating students about the core democratic rights of free expression and due process, these pro-student rulings also had significant unintended consequences. In particular, Arum argues that pro-student court decisions have been part of a broader weakening of the school as a respected institution and of the teacher as a legitimate authority—two shifts that make it much more difficult for schools and teachers to do their jobs of educating and socializing young people. Arum argues that his research suggests that courts and state legislatures need to expand the discretion and legal protections granted to teachers and school administrators so that they can develop effective disciplinary practices that will maintain order in schools—and be perceived by students and parents as legitimate.

think about it

1. *Do you think schools should focus on moral development, rather than just academic achievement? Explain.*

2. *Arum argues that schools have lost their "moral authority" and have experienced a decline in "effective disciplinary practices." Do you agree? Was this your experience in high school?*

---

relationship between achievement in school and career opportunities for adults. But education is not a simple equalizer. Not all people have the same educational opportunities, and research suggests that although schools sometimes reduce in-

equality, they also sometimes reinforce it. In this section, we examine the ways schools sort people into different kinds of jobs, often perpetuating existing inequalities, and we probe the issue of why school structure matters for students and teachers.

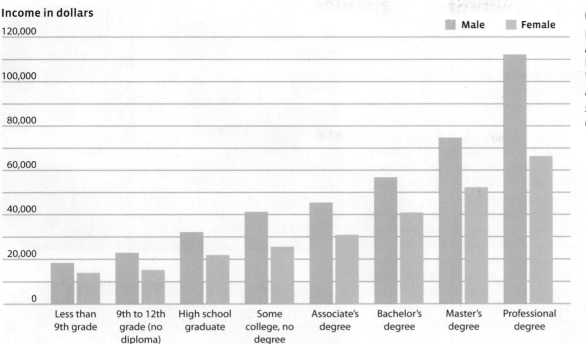

Income in dollars

Education and Income

As Figure 13.1 shows, one thing is clear: those with more education, on average, make more money. At each educational level, average income rises substantially for both men and women. In 2009, individuals with a bachelor's degree had an average income almost three times higher than those who had not completed high school.

There are exceptions to this link between education and income. You may have a neighbor who never went to college but has a very high income as a building contractor. Or you may know someone who completed graduate school but struggles on the salary of a part-time teacher. Despite such examples, the education-income link is well established and quite strong. As a general rule, the more education you have, the higher your income will be as an adult.

Education and Social Mobility

Education helps an individual get a better job with greater rewards. It also substantially increases an individual's chance of upward social mobility. The benefits of schooling may affect subsequent generations, as well. One recent study tracked the educational achievement of three generations over a thirty-year period and found that when women from disadvantaged backgrounds have the opportunity to attend college, their future children are more likely than the children of their peers who did not attend college to be successful in school and ultimately to complete college themselves (Attewell et al. 2007). However, only about one-quarter of adults in the United States have completed college; by 2009, 27.5 percent of U.S. adults aged 25 and over had a bachelor's or graduate degree (see Figure 13.2).

Although school achievement is a route to occupational success, the relationship among education, social mobility, and economic advancement is complex. As we saw earlier in this book, systems of stratification are made up of structural positions, the rewards associated with each position, and the people who occupy these positions. Education can help an individual to advance within a stratified, unequal system, but it does little or nothing to reduce structural inequality itself.

Suppose, for example, that we could give every working adult in the United States a college education. Would everyone

FIGURE 13.2 | EDUCATIONAL ATTAINMENT, U.S. ADULTS AGED 25 AND OVER, 2005–2009

Source: U.S. Census Bureau (2009b).

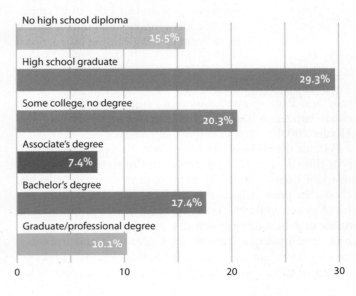

Educational Structure and Inequality

then advance to a better job? The answer is no for a couple of reasons.

First, the value of a college education would plummet, because a college degree would no longer be scarce. Indeed, consider that a college degree is valuable precisely *because* some people do not have one. As college degrees become increasingly common, graduate or specialized professional degrees become more necessary for career advancement. Second, even if everyone had a college degree, some people would still have to collect garbage, serve coffee, clean streets, and work as cashiers. There will always be a need for low-skill jobs that do not require higher education. Changing the workforce's level of education will not change this structural reality.

What *would* reduce economic inequality, though, would be to change the rewards associated with different positions, perhaps by increasing wages at the bottom and raising taxes on top income earners. In other words, to reduce economic inequality, we need to pay attention to issues such as wages and taxes, not just education. Proving the point, in the United States today, a larger percentage of the population than ever has a college degree, yet economic inequality hovers at an all-time high.

How Schools Reinforce Social and Economic Inequality

Ironically, the schools themselves—the very institutions that society counts on to pave the way to opportunity and equality—reinforce social and economic inequality. They do so through various means, some of which are unintended. **Social reproduction theory** *explores the ways that schools help to reproduce systems of inequality.* Social reproduction theorists argue that social and economic inequalities are built into the experience of schooling and the curriculum and inevitably result in unequal educational opportunities.

ACCESS TO RESOURCES In August 2010, the new Newton North High School in Newton, Massachusetts, opened its doors to student and teacher raves. This state-of-the-art complex houses two theaters, a student cafe, an Olympic-size swimming pool, tennis courts, indoor and outdoor tracks, and a climbing wall, in addition to 119 gleaming instructional areas. The price tag? $197.5 million (Thomas 2010). Meanwhile, a few miles away in budget-strapped Boston, thousands of public high school students take classes in run-down old buildings. Poor sports facilities and insufficient gear put the schools' student athletes at a disadvantage on the playing field (Hohler 2009).

Perhaps the clearest reason that schools reproduce inequality is their dramatically unequal access to financial resources. Jonathan Kozol's (1991, 2005) account of daily life in public schools in poor neighborhoods features heartbreaking stories of young children trying to do their best in crumbling, unsafe school buildings with overcrowded, windowless classrooms and inadequate textbooks. Under such circumstances,

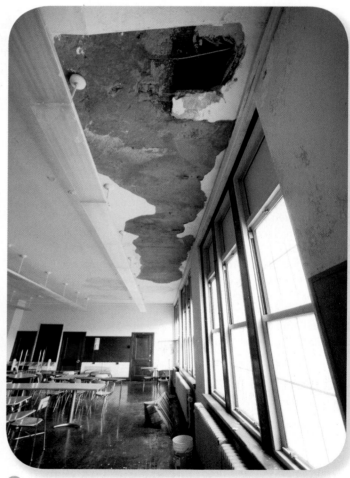

Learning environments can vary widely from one school district to another. Some schools in well-off communities, such as Newton North High School in Newton, Massachusetts, have state-of-the-art facilities (top). In some poor districts, however, schooling takes place in dilapidated—and often unsafe—buildings (bottom). How might differences in school facilities have an impact on educational opportunities for students?

academic achievement can be extremely difficult, and graduation rates in many urban school districts are remarkably low, as Figure 13.3 illustrates.

The money that could improve such deplorable conditions is scarce because public schools are funded primarily from local property taxes, so poor communities, by definition, have far fewer resources for their schools than wealthier communities. Given these realities, children in well-off neighborhoods (like Newton) are far more likely to attend schools that spend more money on teachers, counselors, computers, laboratories, educational materials, buildings, and playgrounds than schools in poorer districts (like many in Boston). From the starting gate, then, we have public schools that—because they reflect existing variations in the wealth of school districts—provide unequal opportunities (see the Sociology Matters box on page 356).

The inequality of public schools' financial resources is only the tip of the iceberg. Beyond this factor, some well-off families have the resources to send their children to elite private day schools or boarding schools. Here students not only receive educational advantages but also prepare for future power—making beneficial social connections, building up their self-esteem, and getting encouragement to see themselves as the leaders of tomorrow (Cookson and Persell 1985). Untold numbers of other children, including those whose families lack the financial means for such privileged learning, do not have access to such educational opportunities.

In addition, even as access to higher education continues to expand, the high cost of college and the enormous debt incurred by many families who struggle to afford college (see Table 13.2) mean that educational inequality persists from kindergarten *through college.* And the quality of a college education can vary significantly, as well, with more affluent and better-prepared students benefiting disproportionately from the nation's best colleges and universities (see Figure 13.4 on page 357).

SORTING BY CLASS School districts differ in far more subtle ways than just in their monetary resources. In their classic work *Schooling in Capitalist America,* Samuel Bowles and Herbert Gintis (1976) argued that a key function of schools is to mold future workers. Thus, they said, part of schools' job is to sort students by class, preparing them for different kinds of jobs.

A primary way that schools sort by class, according to Bowles and Gintis, is by teaching students class-specific lessons about authority. For instance, students in working-class communities are more likely to be taught about the importance

High school graduation rates

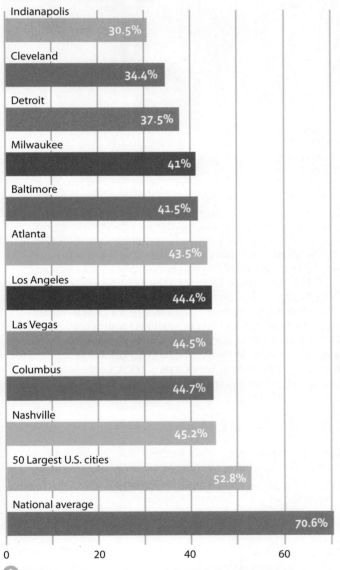

FIGURE 13.3 | LOWEST HIGH SCHOOL GRADUATION RATES AMONG THE 50 LARGEST U.S. CITIES

Source: Original data from *Cities in Crisis 2009: Closing the Graduation Gap,* Editorial Projects in Education Research Center (April 2009).

| TABLE 13.2 | COLLEGE COST AND STUDENT DEBT, 2008 |

Type of College	Average Price, Full-Time Students	Percentage of Students Graduating With Debt	Average Debt for Graduating Seniors
Public four-year	$18,900	62%	$20,200
Private, nonprofit	$35,500	72%	$27,650
Private, for-profit	$28,600	96%	$33,050

Sources: National Center for Education Statistics (2010); The Project on Student Debt (2010).

SOCIOLOGY Matters

Challenging the Structure of School Financing

The public school system in Syosset, New York, a wealthy community in Long Island, offers students an incredibly rich curriculum: courses in seven foreign languages as well as American Sign Language, almost thirty advanced placement (AP) classes, and a nationally recognized arts education program. Public school students in Ilion, New York, an economically depressed community in upstate New York, by contrast, have far fewer curricular opportunities: courses in only one foreign language (Spanish), just four AP classes, and a financial situation that makes it difficult to purchase necessary equipment for science classes (*New York Times* 2011b).

For Cassie Schwerner, program director at the Schott Foundation for Public Education, sociology provided a framework for thinking about how to challenge these educational inequities. In the 1980s and 1990s, Schwerner assisted school reform advocate Jonathan Kozol on his award-winning book *Savage Inequalities*. Kozol's book contrasts the conditions between schools in poor neighborhoods and those in more affluent areas.

Working with Kozol gave Schwerner a close-up view of what's wrong with our public education system and showed her that the structure of school financing is a primary problem. Schwerner turned to her sociology background to map a route for equalizing school financing. In graduate school she had studied a variety of organized social change efforts, looking at how advocates work with media to define social issues and how activists build coalitions. Schwerner's doctoral dissertation, "Sing a Song of Justice," examined initiatives to build multicultural organizations for social change. Schwerner paid particular attention to the complex relationships among race and class differences.

Since she joined the Schott Foundation in 1997, Schwerner has worked to organize and fund the Fair Funding Initiative, which seeks to bring racial and fiscal equity to public schools in New York state. She was a prominent participant in the Campaign for Fiscal Equity (CFE), a grassroots New York City organization dedicated to ensuring that adequate resources and opportunities are available for all schoolchildren, regardless of their place of residence or their parents' income.

The CFE went to court to challenge New York state's school financing, arguing that the current system was unfair and inadequate and led to schools that could not properly serve students in poorer communities. The problems were especially acute in New York City, where more than 85 percent of the students are African Americans, Latinos, or other racial or ethnic minorities. Schwerner, building on her sociological background and her

research on coalition building, guided the CFE in forging alliances among community, school, and parent organizations and helped to organize the funding community to support the reform campaign.

In 2006, after a protracted court battle, New York state agreed to a settlement of $11 billion for new school construction. Then in 2007, the state legislature voted to enact a major increase in state aid to public schools, along with other reforms, such as smaller class sizes and initiatives to improve teacher quality. Throughout this multiyear campaign, Schwerner and the Schott Foundation supported the CFE financially and strategically.

In 2007 the Schott Foundation received a Critical Impact Award from the Council on Foundations for its work with the CFE. The award recognizes "those who truly make a difference [and] . . . enhance the common good." Schott was recognized for its effort to reform New York City's public schools, working to restructure the school finance system to guarantee a basic education for all students.

think about it

1. *In what tangible ways might the New York City public schools improve as a result of the state legislature's 2007 reforms?*

2. *What challenges and obstacles do you think are likely to remain after the school reforms are implemented? Why?*

---

of obedience and following directions. This emphasis prepares them for working at the lower levels of an organization, in jobs that encourage compliance and often permit little autonomy. In contrast, children from more privileged communities generally attend high schools (and, later, colleges) that encourage creativity, innovation, and independent-mindedness. This edu-

cational focus trains students to deal with authority in ways that are more suited to future managers and executives.

Teaching styles and subject-matter curricula are also likely to vary according to students' class status. Rigidly structured, discipline-oriented instructional methods—such as those featuring military-style boot-camp principles and a curriculum

...affluent communities with high tax revenues that produce...

...get good-paying jobs that allow them to buy homes in...

...well-funded schools that provide high quality education for...

...well-prepared students who go on to good colleges and...

...poor communities with low tax revenues that produce...

...get low-paying jobs that force them to live in...

...poorly funded schools that often provide weak education for...

...poorly prepared students who usually don't go to college and...

▲ FIGURE 13.4 | HOW EDUCATION REPRODUCES SOCIAL AND ECONOMIC INEQUALITY

focused exclusively on preparation for end-of-year state tests—are increasingly common in schools that serve students from poor communities. In contrast, teaching methods that emphasize collaborative exploration and self-discovery are found far more often in wealthy public school districts and selective private schools. Furthermore, public schools in working-class and poor communities are far more likely to feature vocational and technical classes, whereas public schools in higher-income communities are more likely to include arts education, a wider range of academic subject areas beyond the state-mandated core classes, and opportunities to pursue college-level courses.

CREDENTIALING Universities, colleges, and professional schools play a vital role in what sociologists call **credentialing,** *the process whereby individuals with advanced educational degrees and formal certificates monopolize access to the most rewarding jobs.* According to sociologist Randall Collins (1979), educational certification is so important for future career opportunities that the United States is in effect a "creden-

tial society." This state of affairs helps to explain the often-intense competition for limited slots in select colleges and universities and why degree holders are quick to highlight their recognized credentials. Inequality is built into the credentialing system because the value of educational credentials stems to some degree from limited access to these credentials.

CULTURAL CAPITAL People across the various levels of a society have unequal access to cultural resources, and schools respond to—and help to reproduce—these differences. As we saw in Chapter 9, **cultural capital** refers to *various types of knowledge, skills, and other cultural resources.* Sociologists recognize that high-status groups use knowledge, taste, preferences, and styles to signal their status and to exclude others from their social circles (Bourdieu and Passeron 1977). For example, knowledge of classical music or fine art, opportunities for study abroad, and experience with diverse cuisines are forms of cultural capital. Such knowledge, experiences, and tastes provide people with advantages in high-status social networks, whether on the job, in school, or in more informal settings. Cultural capital can serve as both a ticket to enter high-status groups and a sign of one's membership.

Cultural capital gives students advantages in school. It prepares them to fit in with others, to understand what schools expect from successful students, and to use their cultural knowledge for higher grades. Furthermore, sociologists have shown that *parents'* cultural capital can have a significant impact on their children's educational opportunities and experiences. Kaufman and Gabler's (2004) study of the college admissions process in the United States found that the cultural activities of parents help to explain which students ultimately attend elite colleges. Specifically, students with parents who visit art museums regularly are far more likely to attend an elite college than students whose parents do not, even when the students themselves are not regular museum-goers. Parents not only transmit their cultural capital to their daughters and sons, but also use it to help their children secure future membership in advantaged groups.

Parental cultural capital—or lack of it—can also significantly shape younger children's early educational experiences. Adrian Blackledge (2001) found that immigrant Bangladeshi mothers in England did not have the appropriate forms of cultural capital to help their children with schoolwork, even though the mothers were concerned about their children's education. These women worked hard to teach their children Bengali, the language of their home country, but did not have sufficient command of English to help with their kids' homework. As a result, the moms could not live up to teachers' expectations for appropriate parental involvement, and school officials concluded that they were not committed to their children's education. In Blackledge's view, these mothers had the "wrong" kind of cultural capital—knowledge of Bengali but not English—to the detriment of their children's current educational experiences and future job opportunities.

Contemporary education experts stress the importance of parents' involvement with teachers and officials at their children's schools. Lareau and Weininger (2003), for example, argue that middle-class parents have real advantages over working-class parents in fulfilling educators' expectations in this regard. Specifically, middle-class parents have forms of cultural capital that make it far easier for them to engage actively with educators and are far more likely to be comfortable with educational jargon. Further, these parents display a sense of entitlement and a confidence that they can advocate strongly for their children. Such attitudes are far less common among working-class parents.

Lareau and Weininger contrast the experiences of two families—the Marshalls, a middle-class African American family living in a wealthy suburban community, and the Carrolls, a poor African American family living in a public housing project—to highlight the significance of cultural capital in school settings. Although the parents in both families believed that they should connect with their children's schools to encourage their kids' academic success, they were not equally equipped to do so. The mother of ten-year-old Tara Carroll was not familiar with common educational jargon and was often unsure of what school officials expected of parents. When Tara's mother interacted with teachers and school administrators, she was more inclined to defer to their authority than to challenge it by actively advocating for her child. In contrast, ten-year-old Stacey Marshall's parents did not hesitate to intervene on Stacey's behalf. The Marshalls not only asserted the legitimacy of advocacy with school officials to promote their child's interests, but also trained Stacey on how best to advocate for herself. Lareau and Weininger argue that these distinctive approaches to school reflect—and help to reproduce—differences in cultural capital.

RACIAL SEGREGATION
In 1954 the U.S. Supreme Court ruled in *Brown v. Board of Education* that **racial school segregation,** *the separation of students into exclusively white and exclusively black public schools,* was unconstitutional. The Court declared, "In the field of public education, the doctrine of 'separate but equal' has no place. Separate educational facilities are inherently unequal."

More than a half-century later, however, U.S. public schools are still remarkably segregated (see Map 13.2). After desegre-

gation efforts during the 1960s and 1970s, a process of *resegregation* began in the late 1980s that continued into the early 2000s. By the 2003–2004 school year, approximately three-quarters (73 percent) of black students attended schools with a student body made up primarily of minority students. More than one-third (38 percent) of black students attended schools where 90 percent to 100 percent of students were racial minorities (Orfield and Lee 2006). These numbers show that racial segregation in schools in the early 2000s was nearly as extreme as it had been in the 1960s.

Why did resegregation happen? Research shows that racial segregation in schools results in large part from residential segregation and is associated closely with concentrations of poverty. Since neighborhoods are typically segregated by race, local schools often reflect these patterns, as well. In addition, the rise of charter schools, magnet schools, and other "school choice" programs (discussed later in this chapter) appears to have magnified racial segregation because white families are far more likely to take their children out of multiracial neighborhood schools when they find other options.

The quality of education at segregated schools—and its impact on achievement—is also an issue. According to Gary Orfield, the leading scholar of contemporary school segregation, racially segregated schools "have less qualified, less experienced teachers, lower levels of peer group competition, more limited curricula taught at less challenging levels, more serious health problems, much more turnover of enrollment, and many other factors that seriously affect academic achievement" (Orfield and Lee, 2006, 29). One study of college freshman found that even the most successful students from racially segregated schools—those who went on to attend highly selective colleges and universities—were less prepared, both academically and socially, for college life than were similar students from racially integrated schools (Massey and Fischer 2006).

The effects of segregated schools are likely to extend beyond issues of academic achievement. For example, a recent study found that minority students in racially segregated schools are far more likely, as adults, to spend time in prison or jail than are their counterparts at integrated schools, and the incarceration rate for black students in segregated schools has increased over time (LaFree and Arum 2006).

Even so, some research suggests that, under certain circumstances, there may be some benefits to racially segregated schools. One study found that in schools with predominantly minority students *and predominantly minority teachers,* students were more optimistic about their post–high school educational opportunities and future job prospects and had more positive attitudes about teachers and schools than did minority students in predominantly white schools (Goldsmith 2004). Although such positive attitudes do not erase the school achievement gap between minority and white students, they do promote the confidence needed for academic success.

Similarly, historically black colleges and universities—including Howard University, Morehouse College, Spelman

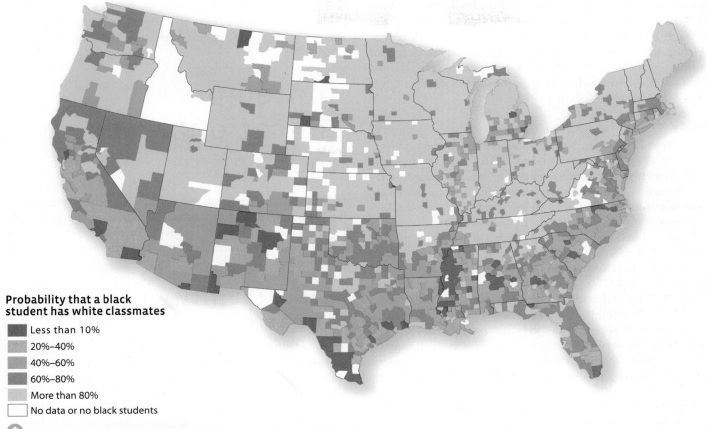

**Probability that a black
student has white classmates**

- Less than 10%
- 20%–40%
- 40%–60%
- 60%–80%
- More than 80%
- No data or no black students

MAP 13.2 | RACIAL SEGREGATION IN U.S. SCHOOLS, 2000
In the most racially segregated school districts, shown in orange, there is a less than 10 percent probability that black and white children will share the same classroom. *Source:* Elizabeth Anderson and Jeffrey Jones, "Racial segregation in education: Black/white school segregation, 2000." Map adapted from the *New York Times*, April 2, 2000, p. A5. Retrieved from The Geography of Race in the United States web site, http://www.umich.edu/~lawrace/schoolsegregation1.htm. Courtesy of Elizabeth Anderson, University of Michigan.

College, and Tuskegee University, among more than 100 such schools—have served for generations as sources of educational opportunity for African Americans when they were excluded from many private and public colleges and universities. Even today, when many colleges and universities actively pursue a diverse student body, historically black colleges and universities offer African American students a learning environment that supports confidence building and academic achievement and that establishes social networks for subsequent job opportunities (Brown and Davis 2001).

Schools as Complex Organizations

Schools are complex organizations that are shaped by policies and rules, their own organizational histories, and powerful social forces. To understand what happens in schools, why, and with what consequences, we need to consider how the size and organizational structure of schools influence the educational process.

SCHOOL SIZE In one study, education scholars Valerie Lee and Julia Smith (1995) distinguished between schools organized as a bureaucracy and those organized as a community, and they show that these two structural forms are related to school size. Large schools are typically bureaucratic organizations structured along traditional, hierarchical lines, with teachers reporting to administrators. They usually have a uniform curriculum, and information is sent home to parents about how best to help their children. In contrast, small schools are more likely to have a communal organization that gives teachers time to plan lessons together, emphasizes curricular flexibility and cooperative learning, and actively involves parents.

Does school size affect students' level of achievement and engagement? School size *does* matter. In their study of high

thinking about **structure**
Why might students engage more, and learn more, if they attend a school with a communal
structure? What structure did your grade school and high school have,
and how did that structure affect your learning?

school sophomores, Lee and Smith (1995) found that students in smaller schools with a communal structure learn more and are more tuned in to their courses. But a communal organizational structure is far easier to implement in small schools than large ones. The lesson for school reformers might be that small schools make meaningful organizational restructuring a real possibility.

TRACKING   Many schools adopt formal or informal structures of **tracking,** *placing students into different curricular paths intended to accommodate varying levels of academic work.* Tracking systems allow schools to manage students with widely varying skills and interests. Sometimes these tracks are rigid, with some students on a college-prep track and others on a vocational or jobs-skills track. In other situations, the tracks are informal and involve various courses labeled as remedial, general, advanced, AP, or honors.

Tracking was a common feature of U.S. high schools through the mid-1960s. But concerns arose that tracking was an obstacle to social mobility—that tracks locked students into a particular path from an early grade and limited future educational and work opportunities for those not on a college-prep track. Given these concerns, most U.S. high schools eliminated or substantially modified their tracking procedures between 1965 and 1975, according to Sam Lucas (1999). Lucas found, however, that even when the tracking barriers were removed and students were permitted to take a wider range of classes in high school, course placement was not based on prior achievement in a subject area. Instead, parents from economically advantaged families, who had more information about curricular choices, acted to have their children placed in more advanced courses. Thus, although in some schools formal tracking systems may be a thing of the past, informal curricular tracks, reinforced by class and educational differences among parents, remain an organizational reality.

Researchers have examined how the informal tracking structure that persists in U.S. high schools might affect academic achievement. In general, they have found that students in "higher" tracks learn more than students with similar abilities in "lower" tracks. Carbonaro (2005) examined the relationship between school structure (the learning opportunities in each curricular track) and student action (the degree of student effort) with an eye to understanding how both structure and action shape academic achievement. He found that action—in this case, student effort—matters. Those who work harder learn more and are more successful, as measured by grades and test scores.

However, the tracking structure itself remains a significant factor in shaping both effort and learning. Students in higher tracks generally put more effort into their school work than do students in lower tracks. Even when students in lower-track classes apply a great deal of effort, they still learn less than comparable students in higher-track classes. In other words, effort matters, but the tracking structure exerts a powerful constraint, limiting the potential of hard work for students in lower academic tracks and rewarding those who work hard in higher tracks. The lesson from these findings: we need to pay attention to students' effort while recognizing that the action students take is shaped by a tracking structure that influences their effort, expectations, and opportunities to learn.

Contemporary Educational Issues and Trends

Shifts in the economy, advances in digital technologies, an influx of immigrants, and political change have had an impact on the U.S. educational landscape. In this section, we look briefly at some educational challenges confronting citizens and policymakers.

Accountability for Basic Skills

The No Child Left Behind Act (NCLB), passed by the U.S. Congress in 2001, aimed to make schools more accountable for student performance. NCLB's best-known provision requires schools to test all children in reading and math each year from grades three through eight. Researchers refer to these examinations as high-stakes tests because student performance on them is tied to federal school funding. Low test scores over a multiyear period can have consequences for school systems: students may be sent to other public schools, teachers and administrators may be fired, or the school might be turned over to a private company for wholesale restructuring.

Supporters of NCLB argue that this kind of testing regime will push schools with low test scores to perform better and will help to address inequalities in academic achievement. Sociologists of education emphasize, however, that a successful approach to school reform must pay careful attention to outside social forces. Understanding differences in academic performance requires an examination of broader patterns of inequality affecting access to health care, housing, job opportunities, adequate income, and supportive communities (Karen 2005).

Bilingual Education

U.S. schools are home to students from diverse backgrounds, including a growing number of children for whom English is not their first language. For children in the early years of elementary school, school policies often emphasize English language acquisition with the expectation that younger students will quickly become fluent in English. However, English language instruction for new immigrant students in middle school or high school is often far more complex.

Since the 1970s, Americans have passionately debated the value of **bilingual education,** in which *students receive instruction in both their first language and English.* Although some organized immigrant groups have pressed for robust bilingual programs, opposition to bilingual education grew in the early 2000s. Voters in several states, including California, Arizona, and Massachusetts, supported ballot initiatives that largely eliminated bilingual education programs. At the same time, the number of English language learners, as students who are not proficient in English are called, was growing rapidly. The U.S. Department of Education (Aud et al. 2010) reports that, today, 21 percent of school-age children in the United States speak a language other than English at home, and 5 percent of five to seventeen year olds have difficulty speaking English.

Research points to the complexity of the questions raised by bilingual education advocates and critics. For example, in his study of children of immigrants in Florida and California, sociologist Alejandro Portes (2011) observed a "positive association between bilingualism and better academic performance" (p. 569). Portes also identified benefits of bilingualism beyond academic performance; bilingual high school students had higher self-esteem and higher educational aspirations than similarly situated monolingual children of immigrants. Despite these positive findings, however, other research indicates that immigrants who do not achieve English language proficiency are more likely to drop out of high school and to have lower incomes than their counterparts who learn English (Bleakley and Chin 2004; White and Kaufman 1997).

Much of the debate ultimately centers on whether bilingual programs help or hinder students' capacity to learn English and other subjects in school. One study of elementary school students in New York City (Conger 2010) found that students in bilingual programs may learn English less quickly than students in English as a Second Language (ESL) classes. At the same time, however, evidence indicates that non-English-speaking students learn science, math, and history more effectively in bilingual programs than in English-only classrooms. One five-year study of Spanish-speaking elementary school students in the United States found that bilingual and English-immersion classrooms were equally effective at teaching children to read English proficiently, concluding that the quality (rather than language) of instruction is what matters most (Slavin et al. 2010).

School Choice and the Debate Over Charter Schools

The vast majority of U.S. elementary and secondary school students (89 percent) go to public schools. In most such cases, place of residence limits families' options about which school their children can attend.

One longstanding school reform approach revolves around the concept of **school choice,** *various policies that give fami-*

lies options for deciding which school their children will attend. School choice advocates argue that granting parents the power to choose where their children are schooled will produce competition among public schools that creates incentives for positive reform. Critics of these policies argue that market-oriented school choice programs undermine the integrity of the public education system and further benefit already advantaged families who have access to better information about educational options for their children.

Perhaps the most talked-about school reform initiative in the early 2000s has been the development of **charter schools,** *public schools run by an organization independent from local school districts.* As part of their charter from state government, these schools are exempt from some rules and regulations that govern typical public schools. Charter schools have expanded dramatically since they first appeared in the 1990s. By 2010, charter schools were operating in forty states and Washington, D.C., and there are more than 4,400 charter schools in the United States, with a total of 1.3 million students (Aud et al. 2010). In light of these schools' autonomy from state regulations and school district authorities, some reformers believe that charter schools can develop innovative approaches to teaching and learning—and thus can genuinely offer families a local and public choice, especially in communities with low-performing public schools.

Large-scale research on learning outcomes of students enrolled in charter schools, however, presents a mixed picture. Some studies have found no difference in the academic performance of charter school and public school students, whereas other studies have reported that students admitted to charter schools performed better than public school students who applied to but did not attend charter schools (Renzulli and Roscigno 2011). The most comprehensive examination of charter schools, published by the U.S. Department of Education (Braun, Jenkins, and Grigg 2006), found that, on average, charter school students' test scores were *lower* than public school students' scores in both reading and math. In addition, one national study found that the creation of new charter schools is often associated with an increase in racial segregation among schools (Renzulli and Evans 2005).

The Online Classroom

Today's digital technologies mean that education no longer has to take place in the physical space of a school building. In recent years, higher education has moved online at a rapid pace. The largest private university in the United States is the University of Phoenix, a for-profit online institution with over 400,000 students. The *Chronicle of Higher Education* (2010) estimates that the number of college students enrolled in online-only programs jumped from 780,000 in 2004 to 2.14 million

EDUCATION **AND** **CHANGE**

U.S. schoolchildren in the mid- and late-twentieth century experienced their formal education in traditional classrooms. Students sat tall at desks arranged in neat rows and focused on the teacher at the front of the room. Today, with ongoing advances in computer and media technology, as well as in online teaching and learning resources, learners from grade-schoolers to graduate students have a world of information at their fingertips.

in 2009, and the *Chronicle* projects the size of the online-only college population to rise to nearly 4 million by 2014. By 2009, more than 5 million college students, representing 29 percent of the total population of U.S. college students, had taken at least one online course (Allen and Seaman 2010).

Online education has made it easier for working adults to earn a college credential by making travel to the school site unnecessary and providing scheduling flexibility. But proponents of online courses point to more than just the flexibility they offer working adult students—who are often juggling family obligations in addition to a job and school. These supporters say that online learning makes college more accessible to students from a wider range of backgrounds, saves students and universities money, allows students to earn a degree faster, and helps universities manage demand for limited classroom space (Parry 2010). Questions abound regarding the quality and rigor of online education, the degree of student effort required for online classes, and the training of faculty to use innovative online teaching tools effectively.

Even as online learning opportunities make a college education more widely accessible, the growth in online college programs may be producing a two-tier system of higher education. To date, little comparative research has examined the learning outcomes of online versus face-to-face education. Nonetheless, one highly regarded survey of academic leaders from more than 2,500 colleges and universities found that the academic reputation of online learning is improving. By 2010, almost two-thirds of the academic leaders rated online education as "at least as good" as a traditional classroom. Still, about one-third of academic leaders judge distance learning to be inferior to face-to-face instruction. Concern about the quality of online education is far greater at schools that offer exclusively traditional classroom instruction—and these schools disproportionately are highly selective private colleges (Allen and Seaman 2010). Elite private colleges are likely to retain their focus on traditional classroom instruction, providing one-on-one mentoring and academic guidance that is largely absent from online programs.

Workplace Structure and Power

Work experiences are incredibly diverse. Some people work at home; others go to an office, a factory, or a retail store; and still others report to a different job site every day. Some people work for large companies with staff all around the globe, others work for small businesses with only a handful of employees in one location, and still other people are self-employed.

Sociologists who study work examine both the specificity of individual work experiences and the shared features of diverse workplaces. As we will see, broad social and structural forces shape people's work lives, and work is a source of inequality in the distribution of both status and income. In addition, workplaces teach people profound lessons about how power works (see the Sociology Works box).

Occupational Structure and Status Attainment

Work and socioeconomic status are closely connected. Differences in pay help to produce, and to reinforce, inequalities of income and wealth. These financial disparities have far-reaching effects, since high earners are much more likely than low earners to live in upscale neighborhoods and to pass on the rewards of their pay to their children (see Table 13.3 on

SOCIOLOGY WORKS

Kimberly Jones and Educational Publishing

Kimberly Jones didn't plan to major in sociology, but she has found her sociological training and imagination to be a valuable resource in her job. The recipient of a bachelor's degree in sociology from Cornell University in 2006, Jones works in McGraw-Hill's Reading Department, where she collaborates with the editorial team that develops K–12 reading textbooks and creates online learning tools for elementary school teachers and students. Jones was unfamiliar with the sociological perspective until she took Sociology 101, through which she became intrigued by sociology's emphasis on the relationship between the individual and society.

Jones's sociology courses trained her to be a careful and critical reader, learning how to extract important information from articles and books, what she describes as an essential skill in her work. However, becoming a thoughtful reader was only the first step. As Jones gained confidence in talking with classmates and instructors in the sociology classroom about their readings, she developed vital communication skills, including the ability to present her own ideas about a text and to listen attentively to and absorb different perspectives on that same text. As for the discipline itself, Jones notes that sociology helped her open her eyes and ears to different ways of thinking about issues, a vital skill in all realms of public life. These various communication and critical thinking skills are essential components of a sociological imagination.

Sociology also gave Jones strong writing and analytical skills—valuable assets in *any* workplace. In describing the ways her sociology education has been helpful in her career, Jones stresses the importance of writing assignments that required her to examine sociological theory critically. As a sociology major, Jones explains, "you'll learn how to compose well-written essays in which you

Kimberly Jones

build and defend your arguments with an engaging style. Learning all of these skills will take you far as a student"—and in a future career.

Jones focused her study of sociology on business and organizations. Her courses taught her a great deal about what happens beneath the surface in the workplace. For example, Jones learned that there are often complex power dynamics in an office setting and that a person's official job title doesn't always align with his or her power on the job. The ability to recognize these dynamics and to respect the knowledge that low-ranking administrative staff often have in the day-to-day activities of the workplace has helped Jones successfully navigate a fast-paced and competitive work world. Ultimately, Jones observes, there are "endless possibilities as a sociology major."

> "With some creativity and courage, your sociology degree can take you wherever you want to go."

think about it

1. *How are strong communication skills—the ability to listen, speak, and write effectively—helpful in one's work life?*

2. *How do you think the ability to recognize the complex workplace power dynamics that Jones describes can be helpful in navigating the work world?*

---

page 364). As we saw earlier in this chapter, these rewards include the wider educational opportunities that are disproportionately more available to high-income families.

One of the oldest traditions in the sociology of work focuses on **status attainment,** *the process by which people come to occupy a certain level in a social hierarchy.* Status attainment research examines the economic and educational factors that shape an individual's life chances, particularly one's adult occupation. The classic work in this approach is Blau and Duncan's *The American Occupational Structure* (1967), which mapped the

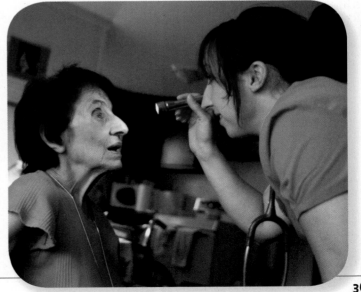

Elder care is a rapidly growing field. Some elder-care providers work in residential facilities such as nursing homes and assisted living facilities, whereas others are home health care aides who tend to senior citizens in their own residences. What kind of pay and benefits do you think is typical of jobs in the health care sector?

TABLE 13.3	AVERAGE HOURLY EARNINGS, U.S. CIVILIAN WORKERS, 2009

Job Category	Average Hourly Earnings (US$)
Management, business, and financial	37.77
Professional	32.14
Installation, maintenance, and repair	21.20
Construction and extraction	20.98
Sales	17.13
Production	16.16
Office and administrative support	16.01
Transportation and material moving	15.54
Service	12.01

Source: U.S. Bureau of Labor Statistics (2010b).

TABLE 13.4	MOST PRESTIGIOUS OCCUPATIONS, 2009

Rank	Occupation	Percentage of U.S. Adults Who Regard Occupation as Carrying "Very Great Prestige"
1	Firefighter	62
2	Scientist	57
3	Doctor	56
4	Nurse	54
5	Military officer	51
6	Teacher	51
7	Police officer	44
8	Priest/minister/clergy	41
9	Engineer	39
10	Farmer	36

Source: HarrisInteractive (2009).

SPOTLIGHT on social theory

According to the **conflict approach,** groups with more power in a society have an advantage in acquiring good jobs. Think of the job you eventually hope to obtain. What factors determine that job's prestige and earnings?

patterns in U.S. work life. Blau and Duncan found that the circumstances that lead some people into high-status or high-paying jobs, and others into lower-status or low-paying jobs, are not based primarily on merit. Instead, the two researchers found that factors such as parents' education, race, and community of residence were major determinants of a person's adult job and earnings.

Blau and Duncan's research was part of a broader trend within American sociology to understand the roots of socio-economic inequality and to evaluate the degree of social mobility in contemporary societies. Much of this research focuses on people's work lives because work plays such a significant role in shaping how—and often where—we live.

Occupational Prestige and Job Satisfaction

Work-related inequalities extend beyond income disparity. An individual's job is also a source of his or her social status, and some jobs are widely perceived to have higher status than others. Income and status levels of jobs do not always go together. Some jobs are high paying yet not high status; others are high status but not particularly high paying.

We are usually aware of these work-based status differences, and we may respond to people in ways that reflect their (or our) occupational status. For example, you probably are willing to wait patiently for a doctor who is running late to see you, even when you have an appointment for a specific time. But you are probably not going to be as patient if you must wait for help from a store clerk or an insurance agent. Because the profession of doctor is among the most prestigious jobs in the United States, you are more willing to wait for the doctor's attention than you are for that of people—such as store clerks and insurance agents—whose jobs do not carry the same high status.

Various surveys measure what researchers call **occupational prestige,** *collective attitudes about the status of various jobs.* The measure is based on surveys that ask people to rate their view of the prestige of different jobs. In 2009, respondents to one survey in the United States ranked scientist, doctor, and nurse among the most prestigious jobs (see Table 13.4).

Sociologists also study what makes people happy with their work. A key assumption of their research is that **job satisfaction**—*the degree to which a person is content in his or her job*—is an integral part of one's overall happiness or well-being. Research shows a connection between occupational prestige and job satisfaction, but the link is not as strong as you might expect. A recent study found that about one-third of people with low-prestige jobs are "very satisfied" with their work and that more than half of those with high-status jobs are "very satisfied" (Smith 2007). However, as Table 13.5 shows, the jobs with the highest levels of satisfaction are not the same as the ones with the highest status. So holding a high-status job is no guarantee of job satisfaction. Research on job satisfaction is more focused on *levels* of satisfaction than on the reasons why people are satisfied—or not—with their work. Still, recent survey research indicates that "the most satisfying jobs are mostly

TABLE 13.5 — JOB SATISFACTION IN THE UNITED STATES

Top Occupations in Job Satisfaction	Bottom Occupations in Job Satisfaction
1. Clergy	1. Roofers
2. Physical therapists	2. Waiters/servers
3. Firefighters	3. Laborers, except in construction
4. Education administrators	4. Bartenders
5. Painters, sculptors, and related artists	5. Hand packers and packagers
6. Teachers	6. Freight, stock, and material handlers
7. Authors	7. Apparel clothing salespersons
8. Psychologists	8. Cashiers
9. Special education teachers	9. Food preparers
10. Operating engineers	10. Expediters
11. Office supervisors	11. Butchers and meat cutters
12. Security and financial services salespersons	12. Furniture/home furnishing salespersons

Source: Smith (2007)

professions, especially those involving caring for, teaching, and protecting others and creative pursuits" (Smith 2007, 1).

The Gender Gap at Work

A central concern for sociologists who study work is the **gender division of labor,** *differences between men and women in access to jobs.* One result of the gender division of labor is that, historically, men have monopolized higher-paying jobs and have therefore earned more money than women. Although the pay gap between men and women in the United States has closed considerably since 1980, the difference between their earnings remains significant. In 2009 the median income for women who worked full time for a full year was 77 percent of men's median income (see Figure 13.5).

As we saw in Chapter 11, sociologists seek to understand the diverse sources and the dynamics of the gender wage gap. One underlying factor is gender socialization, which likely steers girls and young women toward often lower-paying jobs such as preschool teacher and receptionist while encouraging boys and young men to enter higher-paying occupations such as engineer and architect. After marriage, moreover, women are much more likely than men to leave the workforce to care for children, a pattern again reflecting a cultural value.

Another part of the explanation for the gender division of labor is discrimination. Peterson and Saporta (2004) identify three different types of discrimination that might explain the persistent inequality in earnings between men and women:

1. *Allocative discrimination:* Patterns in processes of hiring and promotion that place women in lower-paying jobs than men.
2. *Within-job wage discrimination:* The practice of giving women lower pay than men for doing the same job at the same firm.
3. *Valuative discrimination:* The devaluation and lower compensation of occupations dominated by women in comparison to those dominated by men, even though similar skills may be required.

Peterson and Saporta report that within-job wage discrimination is not a significant contributor to the gender wage gap but that valuative discrimination is. For this reason, advocacy groups working on behalf of equal pay for women emphasize the concept of **comparable worth,** *a commitment to setting salaries for different job titles based on their value to an employer, regardless of the typical gender of those working in such jobs.* In addition, Peterson and Saporta find that allocative discrimination is also a factor; the key moment that produces lower wages is the point of initial hiring, when women are typically offered jobs that are lower in pay and status than men.

The gender wage gap is not just a problem in low-wage or low-skill jobs. Even among the most highly trained workers, earning differences persist between men and women. A recent study of University of Michigan Law School graduates showed that male and female lawyers earn about the same in the first year out of law school (Noonan, Corcoran, and Courant 2005). But fifteen years later, the female lawyers earned far less than male lawyers with the same training—less than 65 percent of their male counterparts' earnings. The researchers noted that female lawyers work fewer hours than male lawyers and are far more likely to work part time or take time off for child care. However, the authors find little support for these as the reasons that women earn less. In fact, women *without* children earn about the same as women *with* children, and single women earn about the same as married women. Something else must explain the gender earnings gap for lawyers. Noonan and her colleagues concluded that the persistent earnings gap is a result, at least in part, of unequal treatment in the legal profession.

Power on the Job

For just about all of us, work is a place where we can see and experience power in action. Let's start with a simple premise: most people who work are not their own boss. They report to, are supervised by, or are accountable to someone else. But some workers operate in the middle of a workplace hierarchy, reporting to their boss while also supervising other employees. With

Women's earnings as a percentage of men's

FIGURE 13.5 | THE FEMALE EARNINGS GAP

Women's Median Annual Earnings as a Percentage of Men's Median Annual Earnings, Full-Time Workers, United States, 1960–2009. *Source:* Institute for Women's Policy Research (2011).

CORE CONCEPTS CHALLENGE

 What traditions in U.S. **culture** *have been factors in these income differences? As more and more women attain professional jobs in which they exercise* **power,** *do you anticipate that the pay gap will close more?*

this kind of complexity, how can we understand power in the workplace?

One useful approach, summarized in Table 13.6, is to analyze three key assets—ownership, control, and credentials—that are distinct sources of workplace power (Wright 1985). This approach provides a valuable framework for thinking about power at work and the individual and institutional forces that wield it—owners, managers, professionals, and labor unions.

OWNERS   One form of occupational power is the ability to influence broad decisions about the operation of a particular organization or company, including how the firm will operate, who will run the day-to-day operations, and what resources are invested in the company. This is the power of ownership.

TABLE 13.6	SOURCES OF WORKPLACE POWER
Key Assets	**Who Has Them**
Ownership of capital	Owners of companies
Control of organizations (employees, budgets, decision making)	Managers of companies
Possession of credentials	Highly skilled professionals

Owners may not be on the scene every day, but they have a distinctive form of power that is a result of their ownership status. For example, the late George Steinbrenner, the longtime owner of the New York Yankees baseball team, did not make day-to-day decisions about the game or even hire all the team personnel. But he established a budget, hired (and fired) senior management, and had the final say on major decisions, including those concerning large investments in players and the building of a new stadium.

In many instances, ownership lies in the hands of a large group of *shareholders*—individuals who own shares of stock in a company. Shareholders may not exercise power in the same way as an owner, but they can still significantly shape workplace dynamics, especially in the case of those with a large ownership stake. In the early 2000s, major newspapers throughout the United States were forced to terminate newsroom staff when shareholders demanded increased profits through cost cutting. In one notable case, the Knight-Ridder newspaper chain sold its prestigious newspapers in response to shareholders who were not satisfied with the company's financial performance.

MANAGERS   A second form of occupational power is the ability to make decisions about the day-to-day activities at a workplace. This is the domain of a company's managers. Managers have the power to direct other workers—to tell them what to do and how to do it. A given organization may have multiple layers of management, and some managers have more power and authority than others.

The source of managerial power is the organizational hierarchy. A given business or government agency will have formal guidelines that specify managers' roles within the organization and the degree of authority they have. Current New York Yankees owners Hal and Hank Steinbrenner, successors to their famous father, have a general manager who is responsible for acquiring players for the team, as well as a field manager who makes daily decisions about the line-up and game strategy.

The source of management's power can be very unstable. Managers, including general managers of baseball teams, are fired all the time; organizations are frequently restructured, and job titles change. That's why managers have sought a potentially more durable basis for power: credentials. Graduate schools of business—which confer the degree of MBA (master's in business administration)—provide managers with a specific credential that certifies their managerial training and differentiates those who hold a degree from those who do not.

The emergence of graduate degrees in business in the early twentieth century reflected a broader trend in U.S. business, as managers sought to develop new strategies for securing power. Many companies adopted engineer Frederick Taylor's philosophy of **scientific management** (also known as Taylorism), *the effort by trained managers to study workflow and develop precise procedures that governed the completion of work tasks.* Taylor's approach rested on time and motion studies that used a stopwatch to measure and examine the specific body motions involved in a given job. Taylor would then reconstruct the job—identifying the precise way employees should stand and move their arms and legs, and the exact number of seconds they should take in each of these motions—in an effort to improve efficiency. Often, more complex tasks performed by skilled workers were redesigned into separate steps requiring little skill or training.

In Taylor's method, only managers, not workers, understood the overall production process. Moreover, lower-skill workers could be hired, paid a lower wage, and easily replaced. The advent of scientific management marked a substantial change from earlier periods when skilled crafts and trades workers not only performed the labor but also held the knowledge about how to do a job.

Although scientific management claimed to focus on efficiency, it was also a strategy for asserting a particular form of managerial power over workers (Braverman 1974). Today's managers may use different strategies to wield power in the workplace, often relying on the credentials of a graduate degree to legitimize their authority.

PROFESSIONALS For some employees, workplace power derives almost entirely from having valued skills that are typically the result of a credentialing process that includes specialized training and an advanced degree. For example, physicians typically have an M.D., lawyers have a J.D., and most college professors hold a Ph.D. These are all examples of **professionals,** *a class of workers who are highly educated, hold degrees to certify their education, and have jobs that require a particular form of expertise.* Professionals make up about 15 percent of the U.S. workforce (Gilbert 2011).

Professionals typically have a great deal of control over the conditions of their own work. They are rarely subject to the kind of supervision that nonprofessional workers experience; instead, typical professionals are largely self-directed. Having control over one's own work is a significant form of workplace power.

The power of professionals is rooted in our collective belief in their expertise, which we trust because they have credentials. Perhaps that is why so many professionals—doctors, lawyers, engineers, architects, professors—display their framed diplomas on their office walls. Sociologist Charles Derber and his colleagues (1990) argue that professionals have learned how to "spin knowledge into gold" by turning their advanced degrees into jobs that generally pay substantial salaries and give them significant control over their own work lives.

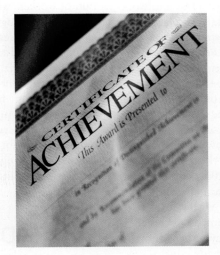

An official-sounding credential suggests expertise, usually expertise backed by a professional association that certifies the credential-holder's training. But not all credentials are equal. For example, a financial advisor might have any of the following credentials, and it can be difficult to know what kinds of training or experience are associated with any of the specific titles:

- Certified senior advisor
- Certified retirement financial advisor
- Registered financial gerontologist
- Certified retirement counselor
- Certified financial planner
- Chartered financial analyst

The first four credentials require very little training—less than one week of classroom instruction. In contrast, the final two credentials typically require years to complete and include significant work experience as part of the certification process (Duhigg 2007).

Some professionals are certified experts in management with a graduate degree in, for example, business administration, public administration, or arts administration. Sociologists sometimes refer to these experts as the *professional managerial class.* They typically have the power to supervise and direct other workers, but their power is legitimized further by their education and certification. For *management consultants,* the high-priced experts that companies hire to help them reorganize or solve problems, power comes largely from their credentials as specialists in how to manage an organization. The recommendations of management consultants have the mark of expert objectivity because they are outsiders who have no loyalties to any specific group within an organization. These outside experts have the power and autonomy in their work that comes from their education and claims to expertise.

LABOR UNIONS Most employees do not wield a great deal of individual power in their workplaces. In contrast to professionals, the majority of employees are subject to control by superiors or by organizational rules that specify when, where, and how to work. However, far from being passive actors, employees use various strategies to cope with, oppose, evade, or otherwise act in response to workplace power.

In a widely cited study, James Scott (1992) described the diverse ways that individual employees seek to assert their power. Some arrive late to work, steal supplies or food from an

thinking about power

Reflect on a job you have held. Did you have **power** in this workplace? How did you know?

What were some of the consequences of your status?

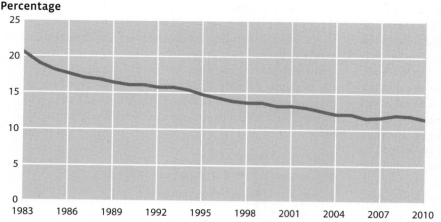

Percentage

employer, share information about a supervisor's whereabouts with other employees, and engage in nonwork activities during the work day. Greta Foff Paules (1991) studied how waitresses in a highway diner exercised power. Paules found that these waitresses were active agents who defined themselves as independent businesswomen trying to control the flow of people, food, and money or as soldiers fighting against both management and customers for control of the diner floor.

Individual acts of resistance often have little, if any, larger effect, however. When employees organize themselves and work together, they often have more power in the workplace than when they act alone. **Labor unions,** *associations of employees that join together for the purpose of improving their working conditions,* give workers the power to speak to their employers with a collective voice. By joining forces to address management, unions give employees power based on the group's solidarity.

The foundation for unions' power is the possibility that workers will act collectively and demand recognition for their grievances. If employers refuse to work toward a solution, unionized workers may strike to protest working conditions. A strike was the strategy adopted in May 2010 by employees at the Mott's apple juice factory in Williamson, New York. The workers had been unable to come to terms with Mott's parent company, Dr Pepper Snapple, over the company's threat of hourly pay cuts and a wage freeze. When they returned to the bargaining table in September, both sides made concessions. The president of the union local in Williamson commented, "Was it worth it? Yes, because we stood strong and the company knows we're a force to be reckoned with" (Greenhouse 2010, B6).

The basic power of union workers is that their employers need workers—perhaps not any individual worker but the group of employees as a whole. More highly skilled workers, or those in whom a company has invested by training them for specific jobs, often have more power when they organize because they may be more difficult to replace than less skilled workers.

Strikes or work slowdowns are relatively uncommon in the United States. The primary way contemporary labor unions try to exercise power is through collective bargaining. In **collective bargaining,** *unionized workers typically authorize union* representatives to negotiate with their employer on questions of pay, benefits, and working conditions. When union representatives reach an agreement with management, and union members approve the agreement, an employer and a union sign a contract that specifies the terms of the negotiated agreement. These contracts typically specify wage and benefit agreements over a multiyear period, as well as issues associated with work schedules and other working conditions.

The presence of a union generally means that workers receive higher wages and better working conditions, but employers can also benefit. Unionized workers tend to be a more stable workforce. This stability means a higher quality of work and lower employer costs for recruitment and training.

In recent years, though, employers have been exerting their own power in resisting unionization efforts, and the proportion of workers who are union members has declined (see Figure 13.6). Taking advantage of labor laws that generally favor employers, bosses at many companies have actively fought union efforts. Tactics commonly used include firing workers who lead organizing drives, intimidating workers sympathetic to unions in "one-on-one" meetings, hiring consultants from "union-busting" firms, and threatening to relocate a company abroad to avoid unionization. In the past, these anti-union tactics have been used mostly against private-sector unions, but in recent years, efforts to limit or eliminate unions in the public sector—including those of teachers, police, and government workers—have increased.

Workplace Culture

In the cartoon strip *Dilbert,* frustrated, powerless employees struggle for job survival in an environment in which clueless managers create pointless rules and preside over nasty office politics. Just as workers vary in the kind of power they hold (or, as in the case of the Dilbert workers, do not hold), each workplace has what sociologist Gary Alan Fine (2006) calls a **shop-floor culture**—*a distinctive set of norms and rules that shape daily behavior and interaction on the job.* Likewise, specific occupations have their own norms and rules that help to define how to be a baker, a teacher, an electrician, or an accountant.

Workplace and occupational cultures, however, are not always obvious to outsiders. When you begin a new job, you typically have to learn the ropes of the position. The task is far more complex than studying your job description and learning your specific responsibilities. In your first few weeks, you are

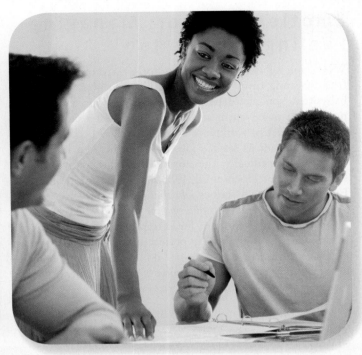

Clothing styles reflect trends in the larger culture. In the first half of the twentieth century—an era when formality and tradition prevailed—professional men and women dressed in a tailored, buttoned-down manner. In today's more relaxed business culture, a looser, more individualized corporate look is in vogue. With what broader social shifts—or changes in workplace culture—might these changing norms about appropriate business clothing be connected?

likely to be socialized, both formally and informally, into the norms of your new work environment and new job.

Formal and Informal Socialization

Job socialization occurs in both formal and informal settings. Many workplaces have an orientation session for new employees to discuss the company's formal expectations. Some workplaces establish formal peer-mentoring programs that pair new employees with experienced workers who can give newcomers tips on how to navigate an unfamiliar shopfloor culture.

More informally, in some work settings, new employees go through an initiation process that is usually organized by fellow employees and often not officially recognized by management. The seasoned employees' intent is to teach newcomers the work group's informal rules. For example, when Major League Baseball teams travel to away games, first-year players are typically expected to carry veteran ballplayers' luggage. Experienced coal miners, according to a classic study by Charles Vaught and David Smith (2003), subject new miners to beatings and humiliation in their first days in the underground mine, as a way of "making a miner" out of the new hires. In both examples, newcomers learn that they are expected to respect old-timers and that each individual employee is subject to the work group's demands.

Much workplace socialization occurs through informal interaction with other employees, supervisors, and clients during the workday. Think for a moment about all the questions you might have on the first day of a new job. For example,

- What should I wear?
- Do I refer to my bosses by their first names or as Mr. and Ms.?
- What tools, if any, should I bring with me to work?
- Is it okay to check my personal e-mail while I'm at work? Will anyone know?
- Do I really have to work overtime if my boss asks me to stay late?

You are not likely to ask these kinds of questions in a formal orientation session. Instead, you will learn the informal rules of your workplace by interacting with others. At first, you'll probably be keenly aware that you do not know the answers to these questions. However, once you are socialized into the norms of the work group, you will know when to show up, what to wear, how to address your bosses, and when it is okay to leave at the end of the day—all without having to think about these issues. If you move on to a different job within the same company or are promoted to a supervisory position, you might find that you have to learn the norms and expectations of your new job.

thinking about culture

What initiation processes into a workplace **culture** have you experienced? Was there a difference between what you learned through formal and informal socialization? Why?

Emotional Labor: Managing Feelings on the Job

When you sit down in a restaurant, you probably expect a friendly smile from your waiter. If you've ever worked as a babysitter, you may have recognized that your employer expected you to be warm and nurturing. These examples illustrate an aspect of workplace culture that has become increasingly important as service jobs have proliferated in the U.S. economy—specifically, the norms of jobs that involve what sociologist Arlie Hochschild (1983) has called emotional labor. **Emotional labor** describes *jobs that require employees to manage their feelings and to display specific feelings to their customers or clients.* Flight attendants, for example, are expected to smile throughout the flight and to project an attitude of calm reassurance. Those who are successful do not appear to be putting on an act. For service workers, bosses and customers typically expect displays of emotion to seem genuine.

It is very difficult for a company to formally teach service workers how to manage their emotions in encounters with customers. One study of a chain of British pubs found that workers had little training in "customer care" and typically laughed at the idea that the company could teach them specific techniques for interacting with customers. Instead, new pub employees learned how to deal with customers and the norms of emotional labor from "observing and copying more experienced colleagues, mentoring, 'trial and error,' and other informal on-the-job training techniques" (Seymour and Sandiford 2005, 555). A key source of socialization for new pub employees was after-work conversation with other staff. Informal gatherings with coworkers provided an opportunity for pub employees to share stories and experiences and to learn from their peers about the behavior and rules for customer-oriented emotional labor.

In Transition

UNCERTAINTY IN THE TWENTY-FIRST CENTURY WORKPLACE

Workplace trends are tightly connected to the sweeping social, technological, and economic changes of recent years. Globalization—the ongoing worldwide integration of social life, economies, cultures, political systems, and populations—is one noteworthy factor. The development and application of new technologies, and the emergence of new industries, are also contributing to dramatic changes in people's work experiences in the United States and around the world.

The nature of the U.S. workforce has been changing. Today only a small segment of the population works in agriculture, and the proportion of people in industrial jobs also has declined significantly. New kinds of work have emerged and grown in the past several decades. An increasing number of Americans work in jobs that provide services to other people and to businesses, such as health care, childcare, and financial and other support services. And many new jobs are in the information sector, where workers collect, analyze, and store data about individuals and organizations. While remarkable, the changing nature of work is also a source of uncertainty.

You will most likely change jobs several times during your adult life and work for different organizations. You probably will even change your career at least once. This employment path will stand in sharp contrast to the experiences of people in your grandparents'—and perhaps even your parents'—generation, who were much more likely to work for one organization for many years, maybe even their entire adult lives. Today, because large employers are far less loyal to their employees than they once were, many young workers assume that they will not be able to retain the same job over the long haul. Younger workers are changing their career expectations to fit contemporary work patterns. The sociological significance of this new orientation to work remains a matter of debate. As Richard Sennett (2007) observes, these changes pose a new challenge: "how to manage short term relationships, and oneself, while migrating from task to task, job to job, place to place" (p. 4).

Many workplaces now stress teamwork and flexibility—in contrast to more rigid and hierarchical management traditions. The work-team approach emphasizes employee participation and worker "empowerment." However, researchers have long debated the merits of team-oriented workplaces, with some arguing that teamwork is liberating for workers and others insisting that it is simply a new strategy for controlling workers (Hodson 2001).

The debate is likely to continue. It will be enriched by in-depth research in specific workplaces. Your understanding of structure and action should remind you, however, that as management imposes new work rules, employees will find ways to make sense of—and to respond to—shifting management strategies (Vallas 2007).

In recent years, U.S. corporations have increasingly relied on **outsourcing,** *moving jobs out of the country to take advantage of cheaper labor costs elsewhere.* In the case of the United States, Asia and Eastern Europe are the typical sites for outsourced jobs. A wide range of jobs—in manufacturing, information technology, telemarketing, tax preparation, market research, and pharmaceutical research, to name only a few—migrated from U.S. to overseas factories and offices, where wages are typically far lower.

Each year, the range of outsourced jobs increases. For example, more jobs in journalism are now going overseas.

Reuters has more than 100 journalists in Bangalore, India, who cover stories in the United States. The Columbus (Ohio) *Dispatch* is moving graphic design jobs to India, and California's Contra Costa *Times* is sending its ad production jobs to a U.S.-owned company in New Delhi, India, a city that markets itself as the "world's media back office" (Carvajal 2006). Sociologists who study work are paying careful attention to the significance of outsourcing beyond the workplace, looking at its impact on education, family life, and the changing ties that bind people together in our global economy.

With such change and uncertainty, the workplace of the future will surely be different than today's. However, examining the culture, structure, and power relations of tomorrow's workplaces will continue to be a useful approach to understanding these new environments.

THINKING SOCIOLOGICALLY ABOUT . . . Education and Work

culture

- Education plays a vital part in instructing children about the core values of their culture.
- Each workplace has its own distinctive culture, which shapes people's everyday experiences at work. When people begin a new job, they typically undergo a process of socialization, learning the norms and rules of a new workplace culture.

structure

- Schools reinforce social and economic inequality through various, often unintended, means. Since existing inequalities are built in to the structure of the educational system, schools reflect and reaffirm these inequalities.
- Mapping the patterns in work life reveals the contours of the occupational structure in the United States. Research shows that the circumstances that lead some people into high-status or high-paying jobs, and others into low-status or low-paying jobs, are not based primarily on merit but on factors such as parents' education, race, and community of residence.

power

- Education helps to reproduce social and economic inequality. Schooling can be a source of power for privileged students—those who have educational advantages, make beneficial social connections, build their self-esteem, and are encouraged to see themselves as future leaders.
- Workplace power is typically based on the possession of key organizational assets, which include ownership of capital (company owners), control of budgets and decision making (managers), and possession of valued credentials (professionals).

In Transition

Looking Back

1. Education is vital to the transmission of basic cultural knowledge from one generation to the next. The sociological study of education focuses foremost on schools—the primary arena of formal education—and on the process of schooling.

2. A sociological perspective highlights the various functions of schooling: transfer of knowledge, job preparation, occupational sorting, childcare, social integration, change and innovation, and socialization.

3. Schools are among the primary agents of socialization in contemporary societies, teaching broad lessons that extend well beyond specific academic skills.

4. Schools reinforce social and economic inequality through various, often unintended, means. Because existing social and economic inequalities are built in to the educational system, schools reflect and reaffirm these inequalities.

5. Schools are complex organizations that are shaped by policies and rules, their own organizational histories, and wider social forces.

6. With today's digital technologies, education no longer has to take place in the physical space of a school building. More and more high school and higher education classes are being held in virtual classrooms over the Internet.

7. Work and socioeconomic inequality are very closely connected because differences in work-related income help to produce, and to reinforce, inequalities of income and wealth.

8. To understand workplace power, we can analyze three key assets—which serve as sources of power—that people bring to their jobs. Company owners have capital assets, managers have control of organizational assets, and professionals possess credential assets. In addition, unions exercise a collective form of power that derives from their members' numbers and significance to a particular company's functioning.

9. Each workplace has its own culture—a distinctive set of norms and rules that shape daily behavior and interaction on the job. When an individual begins a new job, he or she typically has to learn the ropes of the job.

10. Globalization, the development of new technologies, and the emergence of new industries are contributing to change in and producing uncertainty about the work experiences of people in the United States and around the world.

Critical Thinking: Questions and Activities

1. Identify some socialization messages from your school experience. How have traditional and new messages coexisted in your own educational experience? Are the implicit socialization messages you are receiving in college consistent with those from high school? Explain.

2. Would making a college education available to all high school students reduce economic inequality? Why or why not? Consider what your response suggests about the relationship between education and inequality.

3. What do you think are the most important differences between online and face-to-face education? How would you evaluate the relative effectiveness of these two learning environments?

4. Consider the occupations that are ranked highest in job satisfaction. What, if anything, do these jobs have in common? What do you think are the qualities of a satisfying work experience?

5. How does an employee learn the shopfloor culture at a new job? What are some differences between formal and informal workplace socialization?

Key Terms

bilingual education (p. 360) instruction in both a student's first language and English.

charter schools (p. 361) public schools run by an organization that is independent from local school districts.

collective bargaining (p. 368) negotiations between union representatives and an employer on questions of pay, benefits, and working conditions.

comparable worth (p. 365) a commitment to setting salaries for different job titles based on their value to an employer, regardless of the typical gender of those working in such jobs.

credentialing (p. 357) the process whereby those with advanced educational degrees and formal certificates monopolize access to the most rewarding jobs.

cultural capital (p. 357) forms of knowledge, taste, preferences, and styles that high-status groups use to signal their status and to exclude others from their social circles.

education (p. 347), the social institution through which individuals acquire knowledge and skills and learn cultural norms and values.

emotional labor (p. 370) jobs that require employees to manage their feelings and to display specific feelings to their customers or clients.

gender division of labor (p. 365) differences between men and women in access to jobs.

hidden curriculum (p. 349) the lessons students learn simply by attending school, in contrast to the lessons from the formal subject-specific curriculum.

job satisfaction (p. 364) the degree to which a person is content in his or her job.

labor unions (p. 368) associations of employees that join together for the purpose of improving their working conditions.

literacy (p. 347) the ability to read and write.

moral education (p. 349) the role of schools in teaching children the central values and beliefs of their society.

occupational prestige (p. 364) collective attitudes about the status of various jobs.

outsourcing (p. 371) moving jobs out of the country to take advantage of cheaper labor costs elsewhere.

professionals (p. 367) a class of workers who are highly educated, hold degrees to certify their education, and have jobs that require a particular form of expertise.

racial school segregation (p. 358) the separation of students into exclusively white and exclusively black public schools.

school choice (p. 361) various policies that give families options for deciding which school their children will attend.

schooling (p. 347) organized instruction by trained teachers.

scientific management (p. 367) (also known as Taylorism) the effort by trained managers to study workflow and develop precise procedures that govern the completion of work tasks.

shopfloor culture (p. 368) a distinctive set of norms and rules that shape daily behavior and interaction on the job.

social reproduction theory (p. 354) theory that explores the ways that schools help to reproduce systems of inequality.

status attainment (p. 363) the process by which people come to occupy a certain level in a social hierarchy.

tracking (p. 360) placing students into different curricular paths intended to accommodate varying levels of academic work.

Media and Consumption

looking **AHEAD**

What role do media play in your life, and how might this be changing as the **structure** of media changes?

How do you experience the **power** of media in contemporary society?

How has the growth of consumer **culture** changed your social life and your community?

On September 21, 2005, fifteen minutes into JetBlue Airways flight 292 from Burbank, California, to New York City, the captain announced a problem. A light on the instrument panel indicated that the front landing gear may not have retracted properly. After a flyover at a local airport to get visual confirmation, the pilots learned that not only was the front gear stuck in the down position, but the wheels were turned 90-degrees sideways. The plane, carrying 146 people, would have to make an emergency landing at the nearby Los Angeles airport.

To reduce the threat of an explosion upon landing, the plane burned off extra fuel by flying in circles for more than two hours. During that time, news of the flight's situation spread, and local television stations rushed camera crews to the airport to cover the developing story.

The seats on the JetBlue aircraft were equipped with DirecTV satellite television, providing thirty-six channels of news and entertainment. Row after row of seat-back television sets were tuned to the news coverage of the impending landing. In a moment made possible by modern media, passengers could watch their own fate developing live on television. They described this situation to reporters as "surreal" and "eerie" (Mooney 2005; Yu 2005).

Upon landing, the jet's front wheels burst into flames, but the plane stopped safely and no one was injured. As one passenger later reflected, "now instant celebrities, we were greeted by the mayor, hundreds of McDonald's cheeseburgers, and dozens of TV and print reporters. . . . The ratings for our show, we were told, had been stellar" (Laventhol 2005). Passengers can relive the tense moments any time they want; video clips of the landing are on YouTube. ▪

The JetBlue incident is just a tiny example of the pervasiveness of media in social life. Media have proliferated in many different forms throughout society and become accessible twenty-four hours a day, virtually anywhere, even on planes. Electronic media, especially, have saturated our lives, making vast quantities of text, sounds, and images available to us instantly—sometimes even images of our own impending fate. As in the JetBlue incident, in which the passengers were rewarded with a moment in the media spotlight and the chance to consume a brand-name fast-food treat, media coverage produces instant celebrities.

Usually, our media consumption is much more mundane than that experienced by the JetBlue passengers, but it is no less significant. We learn about our world, our society, and ourselves through the media's delivery of news and information and through its fictional depiction of social life. The media's role makes them profoundly influential in shaping our understanding of reality and therefore a central concern to anyone wanting to understand social life.

Much of the media content that surrounds us is produced and delivered by an enormous multifaceted industry that both sells media products to audiences and sells audiences to advertisers. Consequently, most media are inextricably linked to advertising and the promotion of consumption. This connection, too, has had a deep impact on social life, influencing how we spend our time and money as well as how we see ourselves and others.

As a major part of our daily lives, media play a crucial role in socialization and are a central part of contemporary culture. The structure of the media industry shapes, to a large degree, the content of popular media. Media content also reflects broader inequalities in contemporary society. Media help to promote consumerism, which reflects differences in economic power in society.

In this chapter we consider both media and consumption in contemporary society. We apply a sociological framework to understand media as a social institution, looking at the interactions among the media industry, media content, audiences, and technology within the broader social context. We then consider the role of consumption in society, examining how it is promoted and the consequences of a consumer culture.

A Sociological Approach to Media

Karl Marx, Max Weber, Emile Durkheim, and other early sociologists never saw television, imagined the Internet, or conceived of a tweet. When they were writing more than a century ago, media played a very different and much more limited role. But as the variety and significance of media have grown, media's impact on society has become a central topic of sociological study (Croteau, Hoynes and Milan 2011). We begin by defining important terms and describing key characteristics of media, both old and new.

What Are Media?

Media is the plural of the word *medium*, derived from the Latin word *medius*, meaning "middle." **Media** are *the various technological processes that enable communication between (and are in the "middle" of) the sender of a message and the receiver of that message.* Radio is a medium; film is a medium; print is a medium. Collectively, we refer to these as the media. "The media" can also popularly refer to the companies that produce media content, not just to the mechanisms that deliver the content. It is important to remember that media are sociologically significant because they enable and influence communication. Some media are useful primarily for individual communication between users who know each other, such as the traditional telephone. You know specifically whom you are trying to reach; you don't typically dial a number randomly. In contrast, **mass media** *reach a relatively large and mostly anonymous audience.* Unlike personal communication, the content of mass media is publicly available. People who record music, create television programs, make films, or construct web sites usually hope to reach large numbers of people without knowing specifically who they are. But, as we will see, the emergence of new forms of digital media has helped to blur boundaries between mass media and interpersonal communication.

Characteristics of Mass Media and New Media

The pre-Internet years, from the invention of the printing press in the fifteenth century through the late twentieth century, can be characterized as an era of traditional mass media—including books, newspapers and magazines, radio, film, and television. Traditional mass media typically have four key features:

1. *One-to-many communication.* Mass media allow communication to be delivered from one source to a large audience; they have a *one-to-many* orientation. Television, film, magazines, newspapers, and music are centrally produced and distributed to many viewers, readers, or listeners.

2. *Anonymous receivers.* Mass media messages generally have a known sender and are directed at a group of anonymous receivers. For example, when we read a book or watch a television program, the names of the author or producer are displayed prominently, whereas the book readers and television viewers are anonymous.

3. *One-way communication.* Traditional forms of mass media are not interactive; they typically enable *one-way* communication that does not permit direct feedback from audiences. For example, when we watch television or listen to a song on a CD, we can't use those media to respond directly to their creators.

4. ***Distinction between producers and audiences.*** In the traditional mass media landscape, a clear distinction exists between producers and audiences. Producers of mass media content are generally commercial media companies, whereas audiences are generally individual viewers, readers, or listeners.

New forms of media represent a significant break with traditional mass media. Digital media—including text, video, and audio content—can be stored as the 0s and 1s of computer code. Digital media content can be distributed through various media channels, including DVD, CD, or digital broadcast signal. The emergence of digital media made it easier and less expensive to copy and store media content. Digital media hardware and software—from desktop computers to digital video cameras and design programs to sound editing tools—opened up new opportunities for low-cost production of media, from newsletters and magazines to films and music.

Linking digital media to the Internet was the key to the development of the new media landscape. The Internet can deliver digital media content to a potentially wide audience on a growing number of devices, such as laptops, tablet computers, and various mobile devices from MP3 players to smartphones. The Internet opens up the possibility of a "many-to-many" web of communication in place of the "one-to-many" model of mass media. At the same time, it is more difficult to distinguish between individual and mass audiences online. People use the Internet for individual communication with individual known recipients (e-mail), small group communication (social networking sites), and forms of mass communication with an unlimited number of unknown recipients (web sites, blogs). This weakening of the boundaries between personal communication and mass communication has encouraged a shift from the term *mass media* to *media* in everyday language.

The idea of known senders and anonymous receivers does not accurately describe the online media environment. Media producers may remain anonymous when posting material on a blog or web site. At the same time, online audiences are not always anonymous; when registration is required to post comments on a web site, producers can know specific details about individual receivers. Even if you do not register, you still leave a digital trace (in the form of your computer's IP address). As a result, online advertisers can know far more about the identity and behavior of their target audience than they ever could in the age of traditional mass media.

In the Internet age, communication is potentially interactive, rather than being one-way. For example, visitors to a news web site can post comments on a news story, upload their own video, and communicate with one another through various user tools on the web site.

Finally, new media challenge the distinction between producers and audiences. More people have the capacity to create media than ever before, especially in wealthier nations. Individuals can build web sites and write their own blogs, post

FIGURE 14.1 | SIMPLIFIED MODEL OF MEDIA AND SOCIETY

This model of media and society illustrates the complex relationships among media content, media industries, audiences, and technology. A sociological approach to media highlights the bidirectional influence shown in this graphic. For example, the specific content of media messages can influence audiences by shaping how people think; at the same time, audience preferences can have a powerful influence on media content.

photos or songs online, and upload films to video-sharing sites. Instead of being an *audience* that merely receives media, more people today are media *users,* acting simultaneously as producer and consumer of media content (Bruns 2008; Ritzer and Jurgenson 2010).

Figure 14.1 illustrates the dynamics of media (Croteau, Hoynes, and Milan 2011). The model shows that the media content and the technology used to deliver it are influenced by the actions of two groups—the media industry and audiences or users. Each of these elements is influenced, in turn, by broad social forces—including cultural norms, legal standards, and regulatory practices of different societies.

The two-way arrows connecting the elements of the model indicate that interactions occur in both directions. Each element of the model exerts influence on and is affected by other elements. New technologies, for example, can influence how audiences use media, but the media industry decides how to apply new technologies and audiences ultimately choose whether or not to adopt them. We will look at each element of this media model, beginning with the media industry and the structural trends affecting it.

The Structure of Media

Why have "reality" programs and game shows come to dominate prime-time network television? Do portrayals of violence in media encourage real-world violence? Why does the news so often seem to focus on trivial or sensational stories? Such questions can be answered by looking at how the structure of media affects industry trends, media content, and the interaction of media with audiences.

Trends in the Media Industries

Formal organizations that make up the media industry produce and deliver the vast bulk of media products. As we saw in Chapter 4 with the case of news reporters, the structure of media organizations influences how media workers do their jobs, helping to shape work routines within hierarchical media organizations.

In addition to looking at relationships within media organizations, sociologists also analyze relationships among them. Examining four significant industry trends—company growth, integration, ownership concentration, and globalization—helps us to understand how the media industries operate and reveals how industry structure shapes the content of popular media and our experience of it (Croteau and Hoynes 2006).

GROWTH IN COMPANY SIZE Along with an overall growth in the size of the media industry, media corporations have grown bigger because of mergers and acquisitions. *Advertising Age* compiles an annual list of the 100 largest U.S. media corporations based on their advertising revenue. In 1980 the magazine identified the American Broadcasting Company (ABC) as the nation's largest media company, with about $5.7 billion in revenues (when adjusted for inflation to 2009 dollars). In 2009 the largest media company was Comcast, with $32.1 billion in revenues (Johnson 2010). The largest U.S. media company today is more than five times the size of the largest company in 1980.

This growth in scale has significant consequences because larger companies are more influential, have more resources at their disposal, and, as we will see, own a broader range of media content, all factors that help to give them considerable power in society.

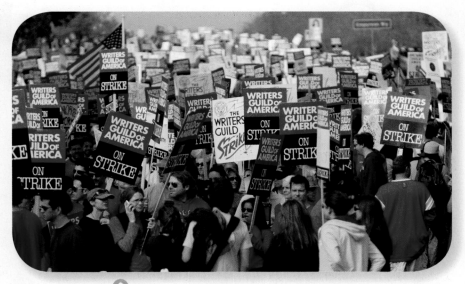

Hierarchy and conflict within media organizations erupted in a dispute between television writers and the television networks in 2007. The writers wanted to be paid for the use of their work in new media contexts, such as the Internet. Media owners opposed such compensation, arguing that the financial outlook for these new uses of content was unclear. In response, the television writers' union went on strike.

INTEGRATION OF MEDIA COMPANIES Much of this growth in scale has occurred through integration of media companies. In **vertical integration,** *a media company owns the different stages of production and distribution of a single media form.* For instance, in the book industry one company might own paper mills, printing firms, publishers, and bookstores. **Horizontal integration** occurs *when a media company owns different forms of media.* An example would be a corporation that owns television stations, radio outlets, and newspapers. Figure 14.2 illustrates these two forms of integration; many large media conglomerates are both vertically and horizontally integrated.

Large integrated media corporations have distinct advantages. Horizontally integrated companies can create and promote products that are sold in different media forms: a comic book can be transformed into a television cartoon series, and then made into a movie with an accompanying video game. Each form of media helps to promote the other. Consider the 2009 blockbuster film *Avatar*. Its revenues from box office sales were just the tip of the iceberg. DVD/Blu-ray, a video game, on-demand viewing, action figures, and other *Avatar* merchandise provided a wide range of additional revenue sources.

---

thinking about **power**

Commercial media are typically produced by hierarchical organizations, where **power** is concentrated in high-level executive positions. Decisions about what to make and how to produce media most efficiently are largely top-down processes. How do you think this top-down process influences media content?

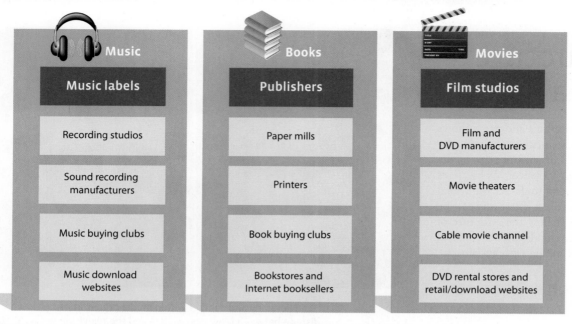

FIGURE 14.2 | VERTICAL AND HORIZONTAL INTEGRATION OF MEDIA COMPANIES

With vertical integration, illustrated in each column, a media company owns different stages of production and distribution of a single media form. Horizontal integration, illustrated by the blue boxes, occurs when one media company owns different forms of media.

CORE CONCEPTS CHALLENGE

How do media conglomerates gain forms of **power** *from having each type of integration?*

CONCENTRATION OF OWNERSHIP As the media become increasingly integrated, ownership of media is becoming increasingly concentrated. Media **ownership concentration** occurs when *more media outlets come to be owned by a diminishing number of media corporations.* Ben Bagdikian (2004) has tracked ownership patterns over the years in various editions of his book, *The Media Monopoly.* When the first edition of his book was published in 1983, Bagdikian determined that fifty media firms controlled the majority of all media products used by U.S. audiences. By the 2004 edition of his book, he found that just five global conglomerates—Time Warner, Disney, News Corporation, Viacom, and Bertelsmann—"own most of the newspapers, magazines, book publishers, motion picture studios, and radio and television stations in the United States" (p. 3). These information and entertainment conglomerates produce and distribute media across a range of media platforms: print, broadcasting, film, and online.

The major media conglomerates have the potential to wield a great deal of political power. Media owners can promote a specific political agenda or support their candidacies for public office through their media holdings. Silvio Berlusconi leveraged his extensive media ownership of television and radio to become prime minister of Italy four times (1994, 2001, 2005, and 2008) (Ginsborg 2005). In the United States, media entrepreneur Michael Bloomberg built on the name recognition of his Bloomberg business media products in his successful New York City mayoral campaigns in 2001, 2005, and 2009. Point-

ing to the vast and far-reaching media portfolios of the major media conglomerates, Bagdikian (2004) argues that the largest media companies have "more communication power than was exercised by any despot or dictatorship in history" (p. 3).

As chairman of News Corporation, Australian-born Rupert Murdoch has been known for conservative politics, daring business moves, and "tabloid journalism." Critics argue that Murdoch has used his vast media empire (see Figure 14.3) to influence elections in several countries and to produce journalism and programming that highlights sensational crime stories and endless celebrity coverage. In 2011, a phone hacking scandal at one of his British tabloids had international repercussions.

News Corporation
Select Holdings, 2011

Television	Satellite	Cable		Film	Newspapers	Books	Internet
Fox Broadcasting Company	BSkyB (partial)	FOX News Channel	FOX Business Network	20th Century Fox	New York Post	Harper Collins	Hulu.com
Fox Sports	FOXTEL (partial)	FOX Sports Net	Fuel TV	Fox Searchlight Pictures	The Wall Street Journal	More than 30 publishing imprints, including 12 that produce children's books	Fox.com
Fox Television Stations (27 stations)	Sky Network Television Limited (partial)	FX	National Geographic Channel	Fox Studios LA	Cape Cod Media Group		FoxSports.com
20th Century Fox Television	Sky Italia	Fox Movie Channel	Speed	Blue Sky Studios	Houdson Valley Media Group	Zondervan (Christian Books)	AmericanIdol.com
		Big Ten Network	STAR	Shine Group	Seacoast Media Group		Milkround.com
				20th Century Fox Home Entertainment	South Coast Media Group		Scout.com
				20th Century Fox International	Southern Oregon Media Group		Many newspaper websites
					4 National newspapers in the UK		
					More than 140 news brands in Australia		

 FIGURE 14.3 | NEWS CORPORATION, SELECT HOLDINGS

These are just some of the holdings of a single major media conglomerate, the News Corporation. *Sources:* News Corporation, and *Columbia Journalism Review.*

CORE CONCEPTS CHALLENGE

Do you think having such a vast portfolio of media holdings helps to give a single company too much **power** *in contemporary society? Explain.*

According to media scholar Herbert Schiller (1989), the major media conglomerates typically promote a "corporate voice" that is so pervasive most of us do not even think of it as a specifically corporate perspective. For example, news coverage of the 2008–2009 recession emphasized the perspectives of the business community, paying little attention to the views of everyday Americans (Project for Excellence in Journalism 2009).

GLOBALIZATION OF MEDIA CONGLOMERATES
To varying degrees, the major media conglomerates have become global entities, marketing their products worldwide. A single media conglomerate can own a vast array of media outlets that stretch around the globe. Consider News Corporation, best known for its Fox television network. News Corporation generates about half of its revenue from *outside* the United States (Wikinvest.com 2010). It owns satellite operations around the globe, as well as a variety of media that produce movies, television programs, magazines, newspapers, and books that are distributed around the world (see Figure 14.3).

The success of Hollywood movies was once measured by U.S. box office receipts alone. The *Sound of Music,* for ex-

ample, was a huge hit in the 1960s, earning more than $158 million in U.S. ticket sales (the equivalent of more than $1 billion in 2010 dollars). With the rise of integrated and globalized media conglomerates, however, the business model that studios use to make movies has changed. For example, *Avatar* made $760 million at the U.S. box office, but almost three times as much—more than $2 billion—in overseas ticket sales. To maximize their profit potential in markets outside the United States, major studios tend to look for films with content that will be well-received in other cultures. They reduce risk and maximize profit by following proven blockbuster formulas.

Media Content

The volume of media content is so vast that sociologists and other media scholars use several approaches to study it (McQuail 2005), including the following:

1. ***Compare content between two or more types of media.*** How does news reported on television compare with that found in newspapers?

Through a half-century of television, some of the best-known white, male, working-class television characters have shared strikingly similar stereotypical characteristics. Ralph Kramden (*The Honeymooners*, above), Archie Bunker (*All in the Family*, right), and Homer Simpson (*The Simpsons*, top right) are all generally lovable but ignorant and doltish.

2. ***Compare media depictions to social reality.*** How does the depiction of women in movies compare with their real-world roles in society?

3. ***Examine media content as an expression of broader cultural values and beliefs.*** How do music videos reflect contemporary values in the United States?

4. ***Evaluate the quality and performance of media based on certain criteria.*** How well did the news media perform in its coverage of the most recent election?

5. ***Examine the potential effects of media content on audiences.*** Do violent video games encourage real-world violence?

6. ***Study media content as a text, with its own structure, grammar, and syntax.*** How do entertainment "news" programs imitate the conventions of regular news broadcasts?

Because media play an important role in socialization, sociologists have been especially interested in how media content compares to social reality. Even content that is meant to be "just entertainment" and that does not claim to represent reality teaches us about our world. We use the example of class to illustrate this broader point.

IMAGES OF CLASS Society in the United States, as portrayed in the media, is wealthier than it is in real life. Entertainment media—especially television, films, and magazines—disproportionately feature upper- and middle-class characters and underrepresent working-class and poor people. Doctors and lawyers are common, and even shows that portray police—a working-class occupation—tend to focus on better-educated and more highly paid detectives.

The most extensive study of class representation in entertainment television remains Richard Butsch's (2005) comprehensive analysis of more than 300 domestic-based situation comedies that aired between 1946 and 2000. Butsch found that only 14 percent of such programs featured blue-collar, clerical, or service workers as heads of the household. In contrast, more than two-thirds of these programs featured middle-class families. The portrayals of working-class life that did appear were usually unflattering stereotypes, showing the blue-collar workers as bungling, incompetent buffoons.

The media also typically depict labor unions, most of which represent working-class people, in stereotyped ways. William Puette (1992) analyzed representations of labor in television, film, and newspapers and found that unions were often portrayed as protecting unproductive, lazy, and insubordinate workers and as outmoded. In general, union leaders were portrayed as more likely to be corrupted by power than the more educated or cultured business and political leaders. Christopher Martin (2004) found that news coverage of labor disputes tends to favor management. The news media often treat labor strikes as stories about inconvenience to consumers rather than as struggles over economic justice, and they rarely communicate the source and substance of the conflict, accepting often-inaccurate claims from management as fact.

More broadly, news organizations orient their coverage to middle- and upper-class audiences, and provide extensive economic and business news aimed at investors and managers. Other "hard news" usually focuses on people in positions of power, notably politicians, professionals, and corporate managers. Working-class and poor people tend to be featured in crime stories (Croteau, Hoynes, and Carragee 1996; Heider 2004).

CLASS, ADVERTISING, AND MEDIA CONTENT

Media content is connected to the economic aspects of the media process. Back in the 1970s, the ABC television network produced a profile of its audiences for potential advertisers that it titled, "Some People Are More Valuable Than Others" (Wilson, Gutierrez, and Chao 2003, 27). This unusually frank title summarizes a basic reality of commercial media: content is produced to attract audiences that are desirable to advertisers. This insight can help us to understand the nature of much media content.

Most media firms operate in what is called a **dual product market,** in which *a company sells two completely different types of "products" to two completely different sets of buyers.* One buyer is the consumer audience, who purchase media products such as books, cable services, movies, and music CDs and downloads. The other buyer is the advertiser, who buys space or time in web and print ads, television and radio commercials, and other media platforms. Most media companies try to attract audiences so that they can sell advertising.

Dual product markets are important because the way they are structured determines who has the power to influence media content. For example, if a television program with modest ratings reaches a demographic group that advertisers want, it may be renewed, whereas a program with higher ratings but demographics less appealing to advertisers might be dropped. Higher income viewers are typically more appealing than low-income viewers because they are more likely to be able to afford many advertisers' products. In fact, for many forms of media, their customer is really the advertiser, not the audience. As a result, audiences may not get the media content they want simply because advertisers want something different.

Media content is also shaped by the desire of media companies not to offend their corporate sponsors. These sponsors have little interest in advertising in media with content critical of them (Herman and Chomsky 1988/2002). Media without corporate sponsors, such as documentary films and books, can afford to present a broader range of critical views.

Media content also reflects the broader social inequality in society. Studies exploring media depictions of race, gender, and sexual orientation have found plenty of stereotypes but have also shown that the images of various groups improve as those groups gain more power in society. For example, for decades racial minorities were either excluded from mainstream media or relegated to marginal roles (Wilson, Gutierrez, and Chao 2003). As racial discrimination was tempered and as people of color became a target of advertisers, racial minorities became a more regular staple of media content. The same is true for the increasing inclusion of lesbian and gay characters in television and film. For example, recent hit programs such as *Glee* and

 HBO's critically acclaimed series *The Wire* was set on the gritty streets of Baltimore. Its predominantly African American cast portrayed a variety of characters, from drug addicts and dealers to high school students, police officers, and public officials, and the series also tackled major social issues. The character pictured here is a police officer whose complicated relationship with her lesbian domestic partner added another layer of diversity.

CORE CONCEPTS CHALLENGE

What does The Wire *suggest about the potential for media to portray* cultural *diversity? Why do you think such images are so rare on television?*

Modern Family have won acclaim for including diverse characters. The Sociology Matters box on page 384 explores the efforts of one advocacy group to combat media stereotypes.

The Interaction of Audiences and Media

Do images of rail-thin models contribute to eating disorders? Do antismoking public service announcements have any impact? Since the advent of mass media, researchers have examined the interaction between media content and audiences, exploring how audiences use media as well as how they are influenced by them. As the findings have accumulated, researchers have come to see audiences as active participants in the media process rather than passive recipients of media messages.

ACTIVE AUDIENCES **Active audiences** *make choices about how they use the media and actively interpret media content.* But how audiences use and interpret media varies depending on their social position and social characteristics, such as race, class, gender, age, and nationality. In a classic study, media scholars Jhally and Lewis (1992) studied how audiences interpreted the popular 1980s situation comedy, *The Cosby Show.* They found that white and black audiences liked the show for dramatically different reasons. Blacks appreciated the references to black culture and the positive portrayal of a *black* family. Whites, though, tended to see the show as evidence that

Combating Media Stereotypes

MTV's reality show *Jersey Shore* was a hit in 2010, with millions of viewers and cast members who became minor celebrities. But the program was also the source of significant controversy for its regular use of the term *Guido*—widely regarded as an ethnic slur—to describe the cast members and its stereotypical depiction of Italian Americans as lazy, beer-guzzling, tan- and hair-obsessed beach bums.

For decades, sociologists have been documenting how the media often stereotype groups of people, helping to perpetuate racism, sexism, classism, and homophobia. Influenced by the evidence compiled by such research, numerous advocacy groups now track and combat media stereotypes, sometimes using the latest sociological studies. One such group is the Media Action Network for Asian Americans (MANAA). Among other activities, MANAA works "to advocate and provide reinforcement for fair, accurate, sensitive, and balanced depictions of persons of Asian Pacific descent in all facets of the media." As part of that effort, the group has compiled a list of common media stereotypes of Asians and the "stereotype-busters" that the media could employ to combat inaccuracies. Some of these are listed below:

Media Stereotype	Stereotype-Buster
Asian Americans as foreigners who cannot be assimilated.	Portraying Asians as an integral part of the United States. More portrayals of acculturated Asian Americans speaking *without* foreign accents.
Asian Americans restricted to clichéd occupations (for example, grocers, martial artists, laundry workers).	Asian Americans in diverse, mainstream occupations: doctors, lawyers, therapists, educators, U.S. soldiers, etc.
Asian racial features, names, accents, or mannerisms as inherently comic or sinister.	Asian names or racial features as no more unusual than those of Whites.
Asians relegated to supporting roles in projects with Asian or Asian American content.	More Asian and Asian American lead roles.
Asian male sexuality as negative or nonexistent.	More Asian men as positive romantic leads.
Asian women as "China dolls."	Asian women as self-confident and self-respecting, pleasing themselves as well as their loved ones.
Asian women as "dragon ladies."	Whenever villains are Asian, it's important that their villainy not be attributed to their ethnicity.
Asian Americans as the "model minority."	Asian characters with flaws and foibles, with whom audiences can empathize.
"Asian-ness" as an explanation for the magical or supernatural.	Asian cultures as no more or less magical than other cultures.

Source: Media Action Network for Asian Americans.

The efforts of researchers who document media stereotyping and activists who advocate for more accurate and diverse portrayal can help make a difference. Media scholar Jack Shaheen has studied film and television images of Arabs for more than three decades. He explains the formula for successfully challenging media stereotypes: "People worked together, until finally they managed to become filmmakers themselves, producing, directing, and appearing in courageous movies that elevated their humanity" (Shaheen 2009, 6).

think about it

1. *What would you include in a list of media stereotypes about college students? What "stereotype-buster" would you suggest for each?*
2. *What TV programs have perpetuated stereotypes? What shows have "busted" them?*

successful African Americans could be just like Whites; they liked the portrayal because it was *nonracial*. In a dynamic observed in many audience studies, *Cosby* audiences were active interpreters of media content, but those interpretations were influenced by their social positions.

Media audiences are also active when they engage in various forms of audience participation, such as calling in to talk radio shows and casting a vote on *American Idol*. In addition, some members of media audiences are actively involved in fan communities where they share opinions on media personalities and media content. They may attend events with other fans or participate in online fan forums. In the digital age, new forms of audience activity have developed, as viewers, listeners, readers, and players post reviews, analysis, and criticism on their own blogs, web sites, and Twitter accounts. Increasingly, audiences are active as both interpreters and producers of media in an evolving media environment (Napoli 2010).

MEDIA'S SOCIAL EFFECTS Beginning in the 1940s, studies emphasized media's power to influence audiences. One theory, known as the hypodermic model of media influence, suggested that media could inject ideas into the public mind. Mass society theory argued that modern society has been marked by a decline in traditional social bonds, such as the family and neighborhood, leaving audiences susceptible to the influence of mass media.

Later studies, however, incorporated an appreciation for active audiences, leading to a more nuanced view of media effects. For example, **agenda-setting theory** *holds that media may not be able to tell people what to think, but they can significantly influence what people think about.* They do so through their emphasis (or silence) on various issues. This effect is especially true for the news media, but entertainment media, too, can raise or stifle awareness of specific social and political issues.

Through constant exposure, media can influence our view of reality. **Cultivation theory** *argues that by repeated and long-term exposure to the media's portrayal of the world (especially on television), people come to accept many of these depictions as reality.* Local broadcast news programs are notorious for emphasizing crime, fires, and accidents in their coverage. Such relentless media images inflame public anxiety and contribute to a "culture of fear," leading people in the United States to be "inordinately fearful of unlikely dangers" (Glassner 2009, xii). Over the long term, heavy viewers of such broadcasts are more likely than light or moderate viewers to believe that the world is a dangerous place, people cannot be trusted, and most people are selfishly looking out for themselves (Gerbner et al. 2008). In effect, by being exposed to constant images of danger and violence, people come to believe that this depiction accurately represents their community.

Media effects are difficult to prove definitively because we experience many influences at once in our complex social environment. Nevertheless, numerous studies using various methodologies have given us significant insight into the media's social influence.

The Explosive Growth of Media

Daneane Gallardo is located in Kitchener, Ontario, but she lives on the Internet. She coordinates web site development for a living, so she is online all day long. But her media use doesn't stop there. Reading the posts in her e-mail groups, exchanging instant messages, updating her blog—these take up more hours of her day. Her life is spent in the electronic cocoon of media. As she jokes, "If I didn't have to eat, pee, and have sex, probably I'd have no need for the 3-D world" (Hof 2005).

Media have become fully integrated into most waking moments of our daily lives. People in the United States spend more time producing and consuming media than any other single activity except breathing (Ransford 2005). Arguably no other change in contemporary life has been as far reaching and influential as the explosive growth of media.

Media Growth and Saturation

This media saturation has not only changed *what* we see and hear, but also *how* we interact with our world. As in Gallardo's case, more and more of our connection to the world is filtered through media, rather than generated through face-to-face personal contact. We often interact with our family and close friends through various communication media; some parents even wake up their school-age children via text message. Most of the music we hear is recorded rather than live. Increasingly, we learn about and discuss politics online rather than in our local communities. Students may contact professors via e-mail or even take entire courses online, rather than meet face-to-face. In whatever form, we spend increasing amounts of our life with media. Just ask yourself: how much time do you spend on Facebook?

How we use media varies, depending on the social context. Sometimes we focus closely on one form of media, as when we watch a movie in a theater. Other times, media are background to other activities, as when we drive with the radio on. Often, people use multiple forms of media simultaneously, such as listening to music while surfing the Internet. This multitasking makes it difficult for researchers to get a precise measure of media use.

The U.S. Census Bureau (2010i) reports that, in 2007, people in the United States used media an average of 9 hours and 35 minutes a day. This overall number counts simultaneous

Many people are surrounded by a number of media devices that enable multitasking. Fragmented attention to multiple media content has become a hallmark of contemporary life.

FIGURE 14.4 | **BREAKDOWN OF AVERAGE DAILY MEDIA USE**

This pie chart summarizes the results from the Middletown Media Studies II project, a study that tracked the different types of media people use on a typical day. *Source:* Holmes and Bloxham (2007).

media forms separately, and it does not count media use at work. However it is counted, time spent using media has grown significantly in recent years as more media, in more portable forms, have become available. Television continues to make up the bulk of media use, at an average of 4 hours and 25 minutes per person each day.

People dramatically underestimate the amount of time they spend with media (Papper, Holmes, and Popovich 2004). This tendency causes a problem for researchers who estimate media use based on surveys and individually kept records. To address this problem, some researchers followed nearly 400 individuals in Muncie, Indiana, for an entire day in 2005 to observe and record their media use at 15-second intervals. This approach enabled researchers to note whether individuals were using multiple forms of media simultaneously and whether they were carrying out other activities while they used media (Finberg 2005; Holmes and Bloxham 2007).

The study found that people used media an average of 8 hours and 41 minutes a day—about two-thirds of the time they were observed. During nearly a third of the time they spent with media, the research subjects used multiple forms of media simultaneously. Adding up the multitasking separately brought the total exposure to media to 12 hours and 2 minutes—significantly higher than the Census Bureau's estimate. As Figure 14.4 shows, television took up the largest share: just over 4 hours a day (33 percent). Overall, about 30 percent of the individuals' waking day was spent focused exclusively on using media. Another 39 percent of the time, they used media while engaged in some other activity.

The recent growth of media is due partly to the changing nature of media technology, which has made it possible for different forms of media to converge and has enabled the rise of portable media devices.

Media Convergence

Historically, different forms of media were marked by clear boundaries, and some still maintain distinct characteristics—for example, print newspapers do not have sound, and radio

has no images. But one of the most significant developments in recent years has been media **convergence,** *the merging of different media forms.* Digital technology that makes it easy to transfer information across different media platforms has accelerated this convergence. A digital image can easily be converted to print, television, the Internet, DVD, or a host of other media formats.

Individual types of media can also deliver multiple forms of media content. The Internet can be used for personal communication (e-mail) or for mass communication (web sites, e-blasts, and blogs). You can use it to send a message in the form of text, audio, or images. Even older forms of media, notably the telephone, have been reinvented as all-purpose media devices. Today's cell phones allow users to make personal calls, send text messages, listen to music, watch television, take photos and videos, and access the Internet, all while being completely portable.

User-Generated Content

Traditionally, formal organizations created mass media content. Today, however, **user-generated content** is *created by ordinary media users rather than by media organizations and is available to a potentially large audience.*

Users have always created media content. For decades, picture albums have housed family photos, home movies have starred wobbly toddlers, tapes have captured garage band performances, and yearbooks have immortalized high school se-

CHAPTER 14 Media and Consumption

niors. Today, however, user-generated content can potentially reach a mass audience, not just family and friends. Ordinary YouTube stars, relatively unknown bands with a cult following, and podcasts aimed at a niche audience are all possible with today's media technology. More than ever, media-based information and entertainment that sidestep the media industry are available for potentially widespread distribution. Most will never develop a large audience, but some will.

Among the many forms of user-generated content are the following:

- Personal web sites created and controlled by an individual or a small group working together can serve as a platform for other media forms such as music recordings, blogs, photos, and videos.

- Some commercial web sites allow users to create or upload content. Examples include YouTube and Facebook, as well as book publishing sites such as CreateSpace and Lulu.

- Individuals can create user-generated content by manipulating existing content (often illegally) by sampling, altering, and recombining to make mash-ups, parodies, and other hybrid creations. For example, well-known music is sometimes remixed into new forms and distributed online, a process made famous early on by Danger Mouse's *Grey Album*, combining lyrics from Jay-Z's *Black Album* with samples from the Beatles' *White Album*.

- More broadly collaborative user-generated content, such as a *wiki*, a web site, or other online resource, allows users to add and edit content. No single user is responsible for the content on such sites. Wikipedia, the collaborative online encyclopedia, is the most well-known form of wiki media.

Regardless of the type, user-generated content is an alternative to the traditional industry-generated media experience.

User-generated content is not without costs, however. This unfiltered and unregulated media environment can include disturbing material. Racist hate groups, for example, have flourished on the Internet. Their web sites can help link far-flung individuals who share a racist ideology. Child pornography, bomb-making instructions, and other forms of potentially dangerous content can also flourish. Terrorists have made good use of encrypted e-mail communications, voice-over-Internet audio, and web sites. Such user-generated sites can feature political analyses; instructions on how to carry out violent attacks; and videos of incendiary speeches, attacks on U.S. soldiers, and even ghastly beheadings of kidnap victims. It is possible to post this content while maintaining anonymity (*The Economist* 2007).

Functions of Media

Reading this book gives you access to information. Watching a movie or listening to the radio can entertain you. Creating a web page on a social networking site can enable you to meet people and stay in touch with friends. Clearly, the many hours we spend with media serve different functions for us personally. The media serve similarly varied functions for society as a whole.

 Because the Internet is unfiltered, it can serve as a platform for user-generated content—like this YouTube video of a German neo-Nazi band—produced by groups that promote hate and violence.

CORE CONCEPTS CHALLENGE

How might hate groups take advantage of the Internet to build and sustain a racist subculture? How might the Internet be used to combat such efforts?

SOURCES OF INFORMATION Media serve as the storehouse and conduit for a society's accumulated knowledge and information, from the mundane to the profound. By examining media content, we can learn everything from the latest sports scores and celebrity sightings to vital medical information and the policy positions of political candidates. In recent years, media have made information more accessible more quickly than ever before. This development has transformed human society. Whereas information once was scant and difficult to obtain, a central challenge now is to make sense of the glut of information at our fingertips.

AGENTS OF SOCIALIZATION When a man was stopped for a traffic violation in Virginia, he tossed a box from his car window. The police discovered that the box contained sixty rocks of crack cocaine. The jury at the subsequent drug possession trial found the man "not guilty," largely because the box was never tested for fingerprints.

This case was one of many in which juries have acquitted suspects on charges that, in the past, would have routinely resulted in guilty verdicts. Criminal prosecutors and police believe the primary reason for the rise in acquittals is that many jurors have watched a popular television police drama, *CSI: Crime Scene*

 SPOTLIGHT
on social theory

A **functionalist approach** emphasizes media's role in social integration through the construction of a national audience that shares a common culture. With so many media options available in the digital age, do you think media will continue to serve as a source of social integration in the United States?

Investigation, which highlights the extensive use of forensic evidence to solve crimes. They refer to jurors' increased and unrealistic expectation that detailed forensic evidence will be collected for all crimes as the "CSI effect" (Hooper 2005; Stockwell 2005).

The "CSI effect" is one example of how media can socialize us by telling stories and informing us about our culture and its norms. Even media content that is obviously "just entertainment" can influence how we interpret the world and alter how we see reality. The same is true for thousands of other aspects of social life that we learn about through the media filter. The media even provide models of appropriate behavior for the various social roles that are part of our lived experience, such as friend, parent, and citizen.

Our steady diet of media content informs and entertains us and, over time, influences how we come to understand ourselves, our society, and our world. Indeed, most of what we know about the world has reached us through the media. Media socialization can be especially influential for children. They have limited life experience and have not yet fully developed their own identity, and yet they are increasingly barraged with media messages on TV and the Internet. Children, in fact, spend more time with media than they do in the classroom, interacting with their parents, or engaged in physical activity (Rideout, Foehr, and Roberts 2010; Roberts, Foehr, and Rideout 2005). This constant media exposure shapes their understanding of the world.

PROMOTERS OF IDEOLOGY The contest to control the media's messages—and thus its ideological influence—does not take place on an even playing field. Those with more power in society generally have greater access to the mainstream media to promote their ideas. That access is one reason why the issue of who owns and controls the media is such an important topic. User-generated content cannot compete with the deluge of media messages emanating from commercial media sources.

In discussing stratification in previous chapters, we defined ideology as a system of beliefs that justifies the existence of social inequality. But ideology also helps us to define, explain, and make value judgments about the world more broadly. The dominant ideology promotes the interests and reflects the worldview of the powerful. As we will see, the media's ideological function is not carried out by a single depiction in a newspaper or movie, but through the cumulative effect of exposure to many such depictions—and to the persistent absence of other depictions.

For example, U.S. news media typically take for granted the desirability of free markets, downplaying their negative features. They raise few questions about the growing economic inequality discussed in Chapter 9 or about the exploitation of workers in a global economy. Instead, the vast bulk of economic news coverage is actually "business" news, presented from the perspective of investors and managers, not labor representatives (Kollmeyer 2004). As we will see, much media content is linked to the promotion of consumption, with little regard for the social or environmental consequences of consumer culture. Even the recent uptick in environmental news coverage is often accompanied by the call for more consumption—this time of "green" products. The end result is coverage that explains the economic world from a particular perspective and treats this perspective as if it were the only reality.

As the media carry out their various functions, they are enmeshed in a variety of social relationships that make the media a key social institution. To understand media as an institution, we need to look at how power influences the media and is used by them.

Power and Media

Some scholars have heralded the media's compression of time and space as a new stage of human history. Canadian media theorist Marshall McLuhan (1911–1980) famously argued that the "medium is the message," meaning that the most significant feature of contemporary media is their technological capabilities rather than any particular content. McLuhan (1964) wrote that, with the rise of electronic media, "We have extended our central nervous system itself in a global embrace" (p. 19). He foresaw the rise of a "global village" in which media would bring people across the planet closer together.

The Effect of Social Inequality on Media Use

In the years since McLuhan wrote, global communication has become a reality, but it is tempered sharply by social inequality. The **digital divide** refers to *the gap between those who have the knowledge and resources needed to use digital information technology, especially computers and the Internet, and those who do not.* Class is the primary determinant of this digital divide. For example, in 2009 more than 94 percent of respondents from U.S. households with incomes of at least $100,000 had a broadband (high-speed) Internet connection at home, but only 36 percent of households with an income below $25,000 had such a connection (U.S. Department of Commerce 2010; see Figure 14.5).

The biggest digital divide exists between wealthy and poor nations. Comparable figures can be difficult to obtain, but as of 2010 the percentage of the population with Internet access (known as the "penetration rate") ranged from a high of 78.3 percent in North America to a low of 11.4 percent in Africa (see Map 14.1). Global media expansion has developed very unevenly, following preexisting lines of economic inequality.

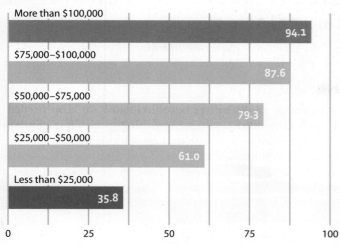

Household income

Percent of U.S. households with broadband

- More than $100,000: 94.1
- $75,000–$100,000: 87.6
- $50,000–$75,000: 79.3
- $25,000–$50,000: 61.0
- Less than $25,000: 35.8

(scale: 0, 25, 50, 75, 100)

FIGURE 14.5 | THE U.S. DIGITAL DIVIDE, 2009

Broadband Internet access increases with household income. Although the vast majority of higher income households have a high-speed connection, most low-income households do not. *Source:* U.S. Department of Commerce (2010).

Rather than being a "global village," the bulk of the world is still left out of the advances in media. To a large degree, the Internet is the preserve of the world's elites.

Inequities in media access vary by medium but include all forms of media. For example, television is far more prevalent than just a decade or so ago, but it is still rare in some poor and rural parts of the globe. As access to various forms of media expands to more of the earth's population, media's influence will continue to grow, playing an increasingly important role in social life. However, social inequality in the broader society will continue to create inequities in media access and use.

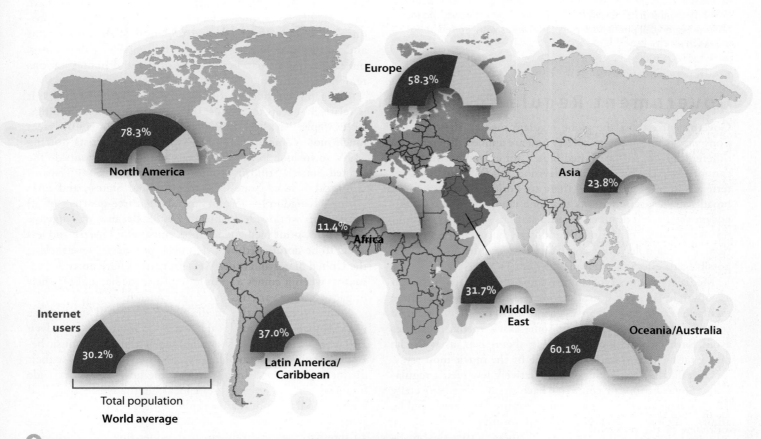

MAP 14.1 | GLOBAL DIGITAL DIVIDE: INTERNET PENETRATION RATES, MARCH 2011

Much of the world still lacks access to the Internet. Whereas 77 percent of U.S. residents can log on to the Internet, only 11 percent of Africans are able to do so. Such dramatic discrepancies in Internet access help to sustain substantial inequality in information access and communication capacity, which can have political and economic consequences. *Source:* Internet World Stats (2011).

CORE CONCEPTS CHALLENGE

In what ways can access to the Internet be a source of **power**? *How might the "digital divide" help perpetuate global inequalities?*

Power and Media

Economic inequality across the globe results in the world's poorest being locked out of access to media technology. However, cell phones have become the "poor person's computer" in many developing countries, providing access to the Internet, banking services in rural areas without banks, and texting services that deliver health information, weather forecasts, political news, and more. Solar-powered cell phones are popular in areas with limited or no access to electricity.

Government Regulations

Governments across the globe regulate media. These regulations vary from society to society and are applied differently to different media. In the United States, for example, companies cannot advertise cigarettes on television, but they can buy cigarette ads in print media, and there are limits on the number of broadcast television stations that one company can own but not on the overall number of radio stations. Many regulations restrict activities of the media industry, but some require action. For example, drug companies are required to disclose possible side effects of their medications in ads.

Media companies typically welcome some regulations, such as copyright laws and licenses to use the public airwaves. These regulations protect their investments and give them exclusive control over their products. In some cases, media industries avoid formal regulation by policing themselves, as with the movie rating system initiated in 1968 by the movie industry.

Overall, the United States has relatively few media regulations. Some European countries have many more, especially on children's media. Some nations require that news, public affairs, religious, and children's programming run for thirty minutes before a commercial break. Others restrict the broadcast of violent programming during hours when children might be watching.

Global Media and Cultural Imperialism

In mid-May 2008, the movie *Iron Man* topped that week's U.S. box office revenue. At the same time, it was also the number one movie in nineteen other countries. The number two U.S. movie that week, *What Happens in Vegas,* was the top movie in twenty other countries (see boxofficemojo.com). This particular week's box office results were nothing special; it is common for U.S. movies to dominate theaters worldwide.

This U.S. domination of the global film box office is one example of **cultural imperialism,** *the tendency of media corporations from wealthier nations—especially the United States—to export so many of their media products that they come to dominate the local cultures of other, especially poorer, nations.* But films—especially big-budget Hollywood films—are somewhat unique in that they are so expensive to produce. India has a massive film industry of its own, widely known as Bollywood, and there is a large movie industry in Nigeria, often referred to as "Nollywood," but few other countries have the scale of capital investment in facilities necessary to produce big-budget films. The introduction of digital cameras and editing programs is lowering the costs of filmmaking, but the economic gap between wealthier and poorer nations remains enormous.

The gap is considerably smaller for other forms of media. It is relatively cheap to produce high-quality music recordings, for example. As a result, Western and American music faces much more competition from local recording artists (forcing MTV to include local artists in its programming outside the United States). Still, just four conglomerates—Sony (Japan), Universal (United States), Warner (United States), and EMI (United Kingdom)—account for about three-quarters of all music sales worldwide (Sabbagh 2008). Because of language differences, print media tend to be much more diverse and less likely to be dominated by U.S. media products. Nevertheless, the United States and other Western nations have unrivaled resources when it comes to promoting their media, making their impact on other societies a very real concern.

Some critics argue that media globalization will homogenize world culture and erode local cultures (Hamm and Smandych 2005; Schiller 1992). As television, movies, film, and music become globally mass-produced, cultures may begin to lose their distinctive elements. In response, some governments provide financial support to nurture a local alternative to imported foreign media. More than seventy countries participate in an International Network on Cultural Policy that seeks to "create an international environment that values diversity, creativity, accessibility and freedom" (International Network on Cultural Policy 2010).

thinking about**structure**

Government regulations have an impact on the **structure** of media in the United States and in other countries. In what situations, if any, do you think the government has the right to regulate media structure and content? Explain.

The Impact of Technology on Society

What effects might the nonstop advances in media technology have on our society? New media have many widely celebrated advantages, including increased connectivity, easier access to information, and a democratization of content creation. But a variety of analysts argue that new media technologies also have negative social consequences.

Traditional print media are generally read in a linear fashion, which is ideal for contemplation and rational thought. Books store a great deal of information. But the creation of books is a slow process, and access to the information in them is limited to those who are both literate and sufficiently disciplined to stay focused on an extended linear presentation.

In contrast, media developed since the mid-twentieth century—particularly television and online media—are immediate, easy to access, and often emotionally engaging. These media lead to a preoccupation with the immediate, as with "live" news and entertainment, constantly updated web sites, and instant messaging. They also use fast-changing images that evoke emotions, or hyperlinks that connect—but also fragment—bits of information.

The result of these new technologies is content that can be fast, fleeting, fragmented, and often insubstantial. Maggie Jackson (2008) argues that our embrace of new media has produced a sort of attention-deficit culture—characterized by constant stimulation, interruption, and multitasking—that provides little intellectual nutritional value. This culture undermines our ability to focus, concentrate, and attend to the deeper and more substantive issues in life that are the bedrock of intimate social relationships, wisdom, and advances in culture.

Experimental evidence from neuroscience suggests that surfing the Internet develops different neural pathways in the brain than does reading a book. The constant stimulus that characterizes the contemporary media environment contributes to a decline in people's ability to focus, concentrate, and engage in serious thought (Carr 2010).

The ability of the Internet and mobile devices to connect people is typically celebrated as one of its greatest features. William Powers (2010) agrees but argues that wisdom, insight, and perspective are gained from being *disconnected;* by creating time and space for solitude and contemplative thought. A healthy and vibrant life in the digital age, he argues, needs to involve a balance between the advantages of connectivity and the benefits of solitude.

Some critics suggest that, despite the world of knowledge at their fingertips, the generation that has grown up with new media is less informed, less literate, and more self-absorbed than any that has preceded it (Bauerlein 2008; Twenge 2006). They point to the popularity of social networking as one source of the problem. The immediacy and personalized nature of social networking, these critics argue, emphasizes the value of newness and promotes an extreme focus on the self and an immediate network of friends. Information or news that isn't about this narrow world is often of little interest. The result is a worldview that promotes entitlement and self-centeredness, what Jean Twenge (2006) dubbed "Generation Me."

This all-encompassing world of fast, fragmented, fleeting images is a part of what some observers contend makes our postmodern period of history unique. Most famously, French scholar Jean Baudrillard (1988a) argued that in many ways we experience **hyperreality,** *the condition in which media depictions of the world replace the experience of the "real" world.* Increasingly, our lives are saturated by a near constant stream of media images that can create a reality all its own. A simple example of hyperreality is the familiar "photo opportunity"—an event created specifically for the purpose of being covered by the media. When the news becomes coverage of an event

When Gannett launched *USA Today* in the early 1980s, it became the symbol of how electronic media were changing the newspaper business. The paper relied on bright colorful graphics, kept stories very short, and highlighted entertainment topics over more substantial news. The vending machines designed to sell the papers, with rounded corners and a pedestal format, resembled television sets.

created precisely for media coverage, media reality supplants the "real" world.

As Neil Postman (1985/2005) argues, electronic media have shifted the emphasis so dramatically from matters of substance to fleeting entertainment that we are in danger of "amusing ourselves to death." He and other observers (Downie and Kaiser 2003; Henry 2007) contend that this emphasis on immediate, engaging visuals has contributed significantly to a loss of substance in our media culture.

As media have come to permeate society, they have been accompanied by relentless messages promoting consumption. These messages have contributed to the rise of consumer culture, a defining characteristic of contemporary society.

Consumer Culture

Twenty-five-year-old Reema Patel thinks that "the first class in college should be about credit cards." That's because by the time she was twenty-one she had accumulated $28,000 in credit card debt and has been working hard to pay it off ever since. Like many college students, Reema was sucked into the trap of easy credit and the allure of consumer culture, spending much more than she should have on travel, shopping, and

partying. More than 80 percent of college students have at least one credit card, and the average number of cards per student is 4.6. Upon graduation the average college student carries $4,100 in credit card debt (Sallie Mae 2009).

Easy credit is just one feature of a broader consumer culture that incessantly promotes **consumption,** *the process of choosing, purchasing, and using goods.* A sociological approach to consumer culture emphasizes its economic, political, cultural, and social dimensions (Zukin and Maguire 2004). To sociologists, consumption

- Is structured by the economic institutions, political regulations, and social norms that help organize the production and sale of consumer goods
- Is promoted through advertising and the media
- Involves the values, beliefs, and behaviors of consumers who, beyond meeting basic needs, use consumption to form and express their identities

Humans have consumed basic goods—such as clothing, tools, and simple household goods—for centuries. But modern technological advances—especially the rise of industrialization and capitalism—fundamentally changed the nature and significance of consumption as a social process. (The Sociology Works box explores an applied sociologist's efforts to better understand consumers.)

The Rise of Consumer Culture

Consumer culture in the United States and Europe emerged in the late nineteenth and early twentieth centuries, enabled by several key developments:

- *Industrialization made it possible to produce an unprecedented quantity of goods.* Factories could mass produce a surplus of common personal and household items.

- *Mass production greatly reduced the cost of many items, making them affordable to a much larger number of people.* More people became consumers of manufactured goods rather than producers of their own items. Fewer clothes, for example, were made in the home as more were purchased in stores.

- *The immense capital investments needed to create mass manufacturing facilities gave rise to larger, more centralized business firms.* Eventually, the production and sale of most consumer goods shifted from craftsmen and small merchants to large corporations and retail chain stores.

- *Over time, competition to produce and sell goods more cheaply came to dominate much of the consumer market.* As part of this process, manufacturers introduced **planned obsolescence,** *the intentional design and manufacture of consumer goods so as to ensure a loss of utility in a relatively short period of time.* Products made cheaply could sell for less but would also break or become outdated more quickly, fueling another round of profitable consumption.

Hy Mariampolski and Consumer Research

Hy Mariampolski has been hired by the likes of Nissan, Clorox, Citibank, Microsoft, McDonald's, and dozens of other well-known corporations as well as numerous not-for-profits, such as Business for Social Responsibility, San Francisco Unified School District, Liberty Science Center, and the New Victory Theater, to better understand their customers. Like many sociologists who end up conducting consumer research studies, he sometimes faces criticism from academic colleagues who disdain his work as doing the bidding of corporate America, "the devil incarnate" (Rice 2007). Such are the contradictions involved when sociologists use their understanding of human behavior to assist clients in creating and selling their products.

With a Ph.D. in sociology, Mariampolski moved into consumer behavior studies after trying out work in an academic setting. Mariampolski and his spouse and business partner, Sharon Wolf, run a firm that specializes in qualitative data on how consumers use everyday products. Although the company, QualiData, uses focus groups and interviewing to learn about some consumer needs, it is best known for pioneering the use of ethnographic research in marketing. This involves taking account of evolving cultural habits and observing consumers as they buy various brands and use products in their homes and workplaces. Mariampolski (2001, 2005) has written two books teaching these research methods. He also shares his tools and techniques and applies his academic training in workshops he conducts worldwide.

First-hand observations in natural settings can shed new light on how customers use products, on their frustrations with product design, and on how they may use products in ways that manufacturers never intended. Such insights help manufacturers design better products and market more effectively to consumers.

Mariampolski likes to think of himself as representing the "voice of the consumer," providing manufacturers with feedback on what people like and don't like. For example, one of his projects highlighted how working-class men avoid many pain relievers because they cause drowsiness, which can interfere with their ability to perform their jobs.

His firm was also involved in a variety of ad campaigns involving sexual health. He helped condom manufacturers find more "life-affirming" ways to advertise that encouraged consumers to integrate condoms into their "natural eroticism." "People are not necessarily motivated by ads threatening them with death," Mariampolski observed.

Mariampolski endorses the trend among consumers that demands more socially responsible business practices, such as caring about nutrition and the environment. Nevertheless, he sometimes gets criticized for "his enthusiastic endorsement of free-market capitalism" that runs counter to sociologists whose research documents the negative effects of consumer culture and corporate advertising. Mariampolski, though, is comfortable in his alliance with corporate America. "We help corporations implement their good intentions," he says. "We're not outside throwing bricks." (Rice 2007)

> "I use my [sociology] background and knowledge every day of the week when I explain to my clients how their products may have to be adapted for new or growing demographic categories, when I demonstrate how foundational ideas in societies undergo cross-cultural diffusion and drift and when I show them how technological changes stimulate modifications in social structures and beliefs."

Hy Mariampolski

think about it

1. *What do you think about sociologists using their knowledge and research techniques to help companies market their products effectively? What ethical issues, if any, might this form of research raise?*

2. *What insights might you gain from observational research that you might not learn from an interview or a focus group?*

■ *Excessive manufacturing capacity contributed to the rise of advertising as a way to promote more consumption.* Advertising also generated new kinds of consumer "needs" (Ewen 2001). As Stephanie Coontz (1992) notes, with the rise of consumer society, "The word consumption increasingly lost its earlier connotations of destroying, wasting, or using up, and came instead to refer in a positive way to the satisfying of human needs and desires" (p. 170).

Even when consumer culture was still in its infancy, it did not escape the notice of early sociologists. In the late nineteenth century, Karl Marx in particular considered the links between the changing methods of production and the new culture of consumption.

Alienated Labor and Commodity Fetishism

Have you ever experienced the satisfaction of doing it yourself—say, repairing a car, completing a craft project, or creating a web site? For Marx, work that we engage in to meet our human needs is, ideally, creative and satisfying. Growing food, building a home, or knitting a sweater are all inherently meaningful tasks that help to develop human potential. The rise of industrial capitalism, however, distorted our relationship to work so that it became separated from meeting basic needs. Rather than working for themselves to create useful things, wage laborers work at the discretion of employers for money to buy goods that will meet their needs. This system creates a distance between what we *do* (for money) and what we *use* (as consumers). One consequence of this distance, according to Marx, is **alienation,** *the separation and isolation of workers as a result of the structure of capitalist society.* Alienation under capitalism has several dimensions:

- *Workers are separated from their natural state as creative, autonomous beings.* They become largely interchangeable cogs in a productive machine.

- *Workers are separated from one another,* instead of working together toward a common good.

- *Workers are separated from what they produce.* Little or no connection exists between workers and the products of their labor, which are owned by their employers.

- *Workers are separated from the process of production.* For many, work is a meaningless, tedious activity with few, if any, intrinsic rewards.

Ironically, later researchers have found that the impersonal, isolating nature of work creates dissatisfaction and unhappiness that advertisers then exploit by encouraging consumption as a solution for this alienation. The beneficiaries of this system of production and consumption are capitalists, who gain, first, by exploiting workers—paying them less than the value of the goods they generate—and, second, by profiting from the sales of such goods back to workers.

When we no longer create or grow the goods we consume, the source of consumer products can seem obscure. Marx used the term **commodity fetishism** to describe *the failure of people to recognize the labor that created the value in the commodities they use.* In the study of primitive religions, *fetish* refers to objects that have magical powers. When we buy jeans or a t-shirt, they seem to appear magically at the local mall with a price tag, entirely separate from the workers who made them. We generally do not think about the labor process involved in an item's creation: the likely low-paid workers—perhaps even child laborers—who made the item, the extensive mark-up added to the price to create profit, or the natural resources consumed in its production and transportation. This disconnect between production of goods and their consumption has become a feature of our consumer culture.

Consumption and Identity

Your great grandparents probably had identities that reflected where they were born and lived and worked, their religious beliefs, and their strong ties to a particular community. Your identity is no doubt still forming as a result perhaps of various moves, changing schools and peer groups, and living on your own and considering future career choices while you attend college. The nature of our identities reflects, in large part, the nature of our society.

As sociologist Peter Berger (1963) once put it, "[T]raditional societies assign definite and permanent identities to their members" (p. 48). In such societies, identity is often rooted firmly in the family and community, with rigid and permanent roles that are recognized widely. With the rise of modernity, radical economic, social, and political changes contributed to the creation of modern identities, partially freed from the influences of family and place. "In modern society," Berger notes, "identity itself is uncertain and in flux." Since our family of origin and place of birth do not necessarily determine our future, our sense of self does not develop automatically.

Today's postmodern era requires us to choose who we will become. We have more freedom to choose or construct our own social roles, decide where to live and what to do, and much more. A paramount question—one nearly unthinkable in traditional societies—becomes "Who do we want to be?"

In a highly commercial society, where nearly everything is a product for sale, what you buy and where you buy it can take on great importance as an affirmation of your identity. **Consumerism** is *an emphasis on shopping and the possession of material goods as the route to personal happiness.* Advertisers sell an identity through products, and individuals express their identity through the choices they make as consumers (or by their rejection of consumerism).

In his aptly titled book, *The Conquest of Cool,* cultural historian Thomas Frank (1997) showed how advertisers in the 1960s tapped into the popular culture of the day by promoting consumption as a type of creative self-expression. A variety of consumer products were touted as the choice of nonconformists, rebels, and the "hip," such as Volkswagen vans, Old Gold cigarettes, Polaroid cameras, and Suzuki motorcycles. Ads encouraged consumers to reject conformity—by following the

Regardless of the product being sold or the audience being targeted, many advertisers sell their products by associating them with a particular image and lifestyle. Are these ads really about milk, MP3 players, watches, or big box stores?

ads' advice to buy a product. The result, of course, is conformity among all those who buy the product. The spectacle of major corporations selling mass consumption as a means of self-expression and individual rebellion—ironic though it may be—surfaces frequently in advertising campaigns. Apple Computer, for example, promoted the iPad "revolution" when it first released the new tablet computer in 2010. Its earlier "Think Different" Macintosh ad campaign featured rebels such as Mahatma Gandhi, John Lennon, and Martin Luther King, Jr.

Advertisers often promote their products to particular demographic groups, sometimes reinforcing differences based on gender, race, age, and class. Products not only do something, they *say* something about who we want to be and the group to which we belong. Far removed from Marx's notion that products meet human needs, today's consumer products are often about image and identity. This phenomenon is not entirely new. As we saw in Chapter 9, Thorstein Veblen explored the "conspicuous consumption" of the leisure class a century ago. However, this kind of consumption has expanded to include most of society. The brands we choose become infused with social meaning that go well beyond the practical use of the product. Prestigious commodities (such as cars, electronics, and clothes) are taken to be a reflection of our own social value (Baudrillard 1988b).

Promoting Consumption

Advertising is ubiquitous in contemporary society. Just think of the various places you've observed ads in the past week: On large highway billboards, on taxis and buses, at the airport, throughout your local mall, in the stalls in public restrooms, on a sticker on a piece of fruit—and in much of the media you consume. Advertising provides the primary source of revenue for most media. You don't have to pay for broadcast television and radio because advertisers foot the bill. The fees for cable television and print subscriptions are affordable because the majority of operating revenue typically comes from advertising. New media, such as Google and Facebook, have adopted the broadcast model—advertising-supported and free to users—for online sites. Most successful high-traffic web sites, from news and entertainment sites to medical advice and "how to" sites, are supported by advertisers willing to pay a premium for a targeted audience.

At its most basic level, advertising provides consumers with information about specific products and services. On the whole, however, advertising promotes more than just a particular product. As sociologist Michael Schudson (1986) has noted, advertising "fosters a consumer way of life" (p. 238).

A great deal of thought, money, and effort goes into encouraging people to be consumers. Advertisers must make people

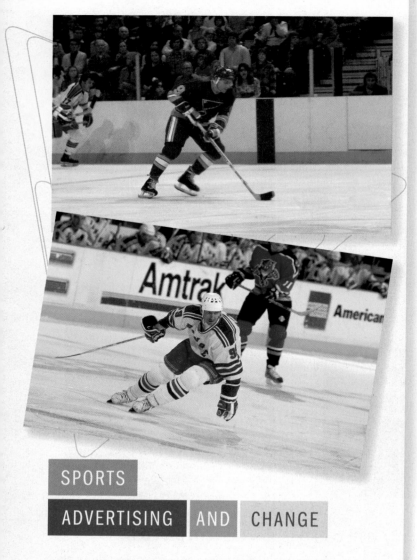

SPORTS ADVERTISING AND CHANGE

Until the mid-1980s, players in the National Hockey League skated on rinks with plain white ice and boards. When today's players take to the rink, they skate past countless commercial advertisements plastered on the boards and painted right into the ice on which they play. It is impossible to watch professional sports today without being forced to view the logos and other advertisements that cover and surround the playing surfaces and, sometimes, the players themselves. Even sports arenas and ballparks now carry the names of corporate sponsors and are designed to promote consumption.

unhappy with what they have and lead them to believe that a purchase will improve their condition. They cultivate dissatisfaction by encouraging consumers to feel insecure, bored, anxious, envious, or frustrated about the life they lead and then evoke an image or a lifestyle that consumers supposedly want to emulate, a process called "emotional obsolescence." The cycles of fashion, the new car models, the constant upgrades of media devices are all techniques designed to promote dissatisfaction with the older version of a product and plant the seed

of desire for the new product. This endless cycle of consumption, dissatisfaction, and consumption is an inherent part of consumer culture. Increasingly, advertisers are also exploiting the emotional vulnerabilities of children, as the Through a Sociological Lens box describes.

One problem for the advertising industry is that people generally do not like advertisements. As a result, the ad industry is constantly developing new ways to overcome audience resistance and promote consumption, including through advertising in public spaces, product integration, and stealth advertising.

PUBLIC SPACES AND CAPTIVE AUDIENCES

One way to overcome resistance to ads is simply to place them in public spaces that are difficult to avoid. In recent years, for example, ads have appeared on the exterior of airplanes, inside school classrooms, all around sports arenas, and just about everywhere on the Internet. Another strategy is to show ads in places where people are temporarily a captive audience: in elevators, taxicabs, airports, waiting rooms in doctors' offices, and rest rooms.

PRODUCT INTEGRATION
Today's television viewers can use their remote controls to change channels during commercials and fast forward past commercials in recorded programs. In response to audience resistance, advertisers in recent years have used the technique of **product placement,** in which *the product being advertised is integrated into media content,* making the ads unavoidable. For example, an entire episode of the television comedy *Arrested Development* was set in a Burger King restaurant. One report found that in a four-month period, Apple products—including Mac computers and iPods—were shown or mentioned over 250 times in television programs such as *The Office, 24,* and *CSI: NY* (Goo 2006).

Other media use product placement, as well. In movies, the car the hero drives, the computer the police detective uses, and the wristwatch the spy consults are all likely to be products provided to the movie producers and inserted into the film, sometimes for a fee. Movie producers keep costs down by using such free (or paid-for) props, advertisers get to associate their products with popular movie stars, and audiences experience a form of advertising that is woven seamlessly into the film.

Product placements show up regularly in just about every form of commercial media. Even many news programs incorporate advertising into their content. Companies distribute "video news releases" promoting their products that are broadcast by some local news programs, often without attribution. In addition, freelance "experts" appear on many local and national morning news shows offering reviews of new consumer products. Some of these experts are paid by advertisers for a positive mention of their products (Rainey 2010).

South Korean teen idol Lee Hyo Lee brought this form of advertising to its logical conclusion in her hit pop song "Anymotion." In the video for this song, Lee dances with Samsung's Anycall brand cell phone while she sings. The song, the video, even the choreographer were all paid for by Samsung, which crafted the lyrics to repeatedly include the word *any,*

Examining the Commercialization of Childhood

More than ever before, advertisers are using the media to target society's most vulnerable members: children. Today's ad campaigns are much more sophisticated than in the past. For example, children in laboratories are studied for their reactions to various kinds of advertising; marketers even measure their eye movements and physiological responses. Children fill out marketing surveys in schools, and sponsored classroom materials sometimes include brand-name acknowledgments that serve as advertisements for youth-oriented products. Marketers also employ psychologists who help craft messages to exploit the emotional vulnerabilities of children, especially their feelings that they are "uncool," a "loser," or simply "left out" if they don't have the latest product. Children are even being hired for "stealth advertising" efforts (described later), for example, by participating in slumber parties sponsored by the research and marketing firm Girls Intelligence Agency, at which the children try to learn about and influence their friends' tastes and habits.

Once a tiny portion of the advertising industry, children's advertising has grown dramatically in the past few years as corporations have found ways to tap parents' wallets through their kids. This barrage of ad messages, says sociologist Juliet Schor, is literally making children sick, contributing to obesity and causing an array of health and psychological problems. Schor has used sociological inquiry to study the inside operations of advertising agencies that target children, and she has explored the effects of advertising on children. What she found is alarming.

Today's children are being inundated with many more ads than any other generation has ever experienced. In the 1970s, children watched an estimated fifty-five television commercials a day. By the 1990s this figure had doubled to 110 (or 40,000 a year), and it continues to increase. In 2006 the medical journal *Pediatrics* noted, with concern, that children see ads everywhere—on television, online, in magazines, and on billboards—and that the average child in the United States views more than 3,000 advertisements per day. In recent years, ads have become increasingly prevalent in other youth-oriented media, including video games and social networking web sites.

Children have a keen awareness of themselves as consumers and are often the first to try new technology. As Schor points out, "Children have become conduits from the consumer marketplace into the household, the link between advertisers and the family purse." As such, children drive many forms of household consumption, often by nagging parents until they give in or using their own allowance to purchase products. Advertisers understand this process and target children accordingly.

All this exposure to advertising, says Schor, has led to a public health crisis. An epidemic in childhood obesity can be traced, in part, to a sedentary lifestyle (often spent watching television and playing video games) coupled with the dramatic increase in the consumption of high-fat and high-sugar junk food (advertised on children's programs). More broadly, Schor's research suggests that the more children are caught up in the consumer culture, the more likely they are to suffer from depression, anxiety, lower self-esteem, and a variety of physical complaints brought on by emotional distress. The ability of advertising to promote dissatisfaction and envy can take a toll on young psyches.

Surveys show that four out of five Americans think there should be more restrictions on children's advertising, and nearly nine out of ten think that our consumer culture makes it more difficult to instill positive values in children. Even many of the marketers that Schor interviewed for her study knew something was wrong; they spontaneously expressed ambivalence and guilt about what their work was doing to children.

Sources: American Academy of Pediatrics (2006); Babb (2004); Center for the New American Dream, http://newdream.org; Schor (2004); Strasburger and Wilson (2002); Strasburger, Wilson, and Jordan (2009).

think about it

1. *What sorts of regulations, if any, do you think should be placed on advertising to children? Did your parents restrict your access to media? What steps would you take as a parent to help shield your children from the effects of advertising?*

2. *List all the consequences for children who are overly commercialized. Think about the psychic as well as the economic consequences. What might these children be missing in their lives?*

reminding listeners over and over again of their Anycall brand (Fowler 2005).

In all of these cases, the line between content and advertisement has been erased, a development that has angered some actors and writers. Their unions have protested these practices, saying they force actors to make product endorsements for which they are not compensated and writers to write ad copy rather than program content. They also argue that the practice is inherently deceptive (Waxman 2005).

STEALTH ADVERTISING Another increasingly common practice is stealth advertising. Sometimes called "guerilla marketing," **stealth advertising** is *the creation of covert advertising in everyday real-life situations*. For example, many advertisers take advantage of social networking sites and consumer review features of online retail sites to plant surreptitious advertising for their products. Advertisers hire employees to pose as ordinary users of these sites and praise the attributes of their employer's products by posting enthusiastic reviews. In one high-profile 2010 case, the Federal Trade Commission (2010) charged a public relations firm with posting game reviews at the iTunes store without disclosing that the firm was hired to promote the games.

Advertisers also hire people to promote their products subtly by, for example, going to bars and ordering a particular brand of beer, in effect becoming a walking advertisement. Camera companies have hired people to pose as tourists and ask passersby to take their picture in front of a popular landmark. As this innocuous exchange takes place, the "tourists" praise the virtues of their new camera, creating another stealth ad. Such advertising techniques, which rely on people's trust and good will, are deceptive and insert commercial motivations into everyday social interactions.

The Social Impact of Consumer Culture

What happens to a culture in which consumption becomes the center of social life and citizens are subject to an endless stream of advertising? We note some of the social implications in the sections that follow.

INEQUALITY AND CONSUMPTION Social and economic inequality is important to keep in mind when considering the impact of consumer culture. The affluence necessary for consumer spending is not distributed evenly, and large segments of the world's population still endure poverty and subsistence living. The transformation to consumer culture came first to the more affluent Western societies in the nineteenth and early twentieth centuries, and only recently to parts of the developing world that are now integrated into the global economy. After the fall of communism in 1989, Eastern Europe saw a dramatic expansion in consumer culture. China, too, has recently instituted major economic changes, enabling growth in consumer spending.

Using data to measure purchasing power, a United Nations study found that 85 percent of Americans were classified as active consumers, but only 28 percent of the world's population qualified for this classification (Gardner, Assadourian, and Sarin 2004). The vast majority of the world's population is un-

TABLE 14.1	THE COST OF LUXURY CONSUMER PRODUCTS VERSUS HUMAN NEEDS		
Luxury Consumer Products		**Human Needs**	
Product	**Annual Expenditure**	**Social or Economic Goal**	**Annual Investment Needed to Achieve Goal**
Makeup (global)	$18 billion	Reproductive health care for all women	$12 billion
Pet food in the United States and Europe	$17 billion	Elimination of hunger and malnutrition	$19 billion
Perfumes (global)	$15 billion	Universal literacy	$5 billion
Ocean cruises (global)	$14 billion	Clean drinking water for all	$10 billion
Ice cream in Europe	$11 billion	Immunizing every child	$1.3 billion

 The table lists examples of the annual expenditure on luxury consumer items compared to the estimated annual expenditures needed to achieve key social and economic goals. As the authors who assembled the table note, the list debunks the idea that "many of the unmet basic needs of the world's poor are too costly to address" (Gardner, Assadourian, and Sarin 2004, 10).

CORE CONCEPTS CHALLENGE

What does the list in Table 14.1 suggest about the hidden costs of consumer culture?

able to participate in consumer culture because of their starkly limited resources. Those who are active consumers face some sobering choices about how they direct their wealth. Table 14.1 compares the annual expenditure on luxury items versus what might have been accomplished had those resources been allocated to more basic human needs.

DEBT AND DISSATISFACTION

As we saw in Chapter 12, Marx regarded religion as an "opiate" that gave temporary, but ultimately false, comfort to people suffering from society's injustices. Since the middle of the twentieth century, critical theorists have suggested that consumerism fills a similar role in modern society (Adorno and Horkheimer 1944/2000). Shopping is often touted as an escape from the drudgeries of daily life. "Treating yourself," "living for the weekend," and "splurging" because "you are worth it" are all popular notions that encourage guilt-free consumption. However, the fleeting comfort of consumption is often coupled with the accumulation of burdensome debt, producing more stress and anxiety in a person's life. Consumption and working to pay for it become a cyclical way of life (Schor 1999).

As far back as Durkheim, sociologists have understood that satisfaction in life comes from understanding and staying within limits and boundaries. Insofar as advertising and consumer culture encourage boundless desires that can never be

SPOTLIGHT on social theory

Marx and contemporary **conflict theorists** emphasize the inability of consumption ultimately to offer satisfaction. Has consumption helped give you a sense of satisfaction? Who has benefited from your participation in consumer culture?

satisfied, they can be a source of social instability and can undermine human happiness.

Excessive consumption cannot substitute for addressing the underlying social conditions that create unhappiness. Since the cycle of consumption is at bottom based on perpetual dissatisfaction (Ewen 2001), any comforting effects are likely to be temporary, leaving deep-seated troublesome issues unchanged. What is more likely to produce happiness and satisfaction? Scholars point to rewarding interpersonal relationships, meaningful employment, outlets for creative self-expression, and gratifying civic and community participation (Kasser 2003; Lane 1994).

COMMODIFICATION **Commodification** is *the process of transforming all things into a product to be bought and sold.* Social relationships that used to be based on, and promoted by, mutual aid and trust are often just commercial transactions today. For example, a variety of goods and services that were once produced and shared among family and friends—such as yard work, pet sitting, home repairs, and childcare—are now more likely to be paid services. Today we even shop for mates on the Internet.

Religious holidays and communal festivals that once promoted social solidarity are now celebrations of consumption. Beginning with "Black Friday's" middle-of-the-night sales immediately following Thanksgiving, we count the shopping days left until Christmas. Birthdays, Mother's Day and Father's Day, Valentine's Day, and other events are marked by the obligatory mass-produced greeting card and the purchase of a consumer item. Big sales are associated with President's Day, Labor Day, and Memorial Day. The newest civic holiday, the Super Bowl, is as notable for the unveiling of new advertisements as for the game played on the field. Shopping has been transformed from a necessary chore to America's favorite pastime.

With commodification, monetary terms increasingly measure social life. If carried to an extreme, such a development can undermine the social trust necessary for a healthy society. A society in which everything—and everyone—has a price is one in which emptiness and alienation are likely to thrive (Dunn 2000; Slater 1999).

ENVIRONMENTAL DEGRADATION Finally, the spread of the culture of consumption around the globe has taken a toll on the environment. For decades, affluent nations, especially the United States, have consumed the Earth's resources at a vastly disproportionate level. With about 5 percent of the Earth's population, Americans consume about 25 percent of the world's resources. Now, billions of residents of developing nations are seeing improvements in their standards of living and are themselves becoming consumers. For some, consumer culture is a step up from the grinding pain of poverty.

The more widespread availability of basic, affordable consumer goods has been a major positive development.

The overall expansion of consumer culture, however, has resulted in environmental destruction on a massive, unprecedented, and unsustainable scale—including slashed and burned forests, polluted air and water, toxic landfills, crippling carbon dioxide emission, holes in the atmosphere's protective ozone layer, and wholesale climate change. We explore some of these effects in Chapter 15.

In Transition

TARGETING CONSUMERS IN THE DIGITAL AGE

The Internet has taken advertising to a whole new level because it is the only medium that allows advertisers to track the activity of potential consumers (Story 2008), providing information about users' interests and habits.

In a 2010 investigative report about what it called "the business of spying on Internet users," the *Wall Street Journal* discovered that the "tracking of consumers has grown both far more pervasive and far more intrusive than is realized by all but a handful of people in the vanguard of the industry" (Angwin 2010). For example, the top fifty web sites in the United States each installed, on average, sixty-four different pieces of tracking technology on a visitor's computer—typically without giving users any warning. The top fifty youth sites installed a total of more than 4,000 tracking tools on users' computers. These new tracking tools are the foundation for a new promotional approach known as **behavioral targeting,** *advertising sent to online users based on their earlier Internet activities.*

The most well-known form of online tracking involves the installation of cookies. Many web sites install a tracking number, known as a cookie, on your computer when you visit the sites. Cookies initially facilitated online shopping by allowing consumers to place items in a virtual shopping cart until they checked out. Their use has since been expanded to link all of a consumer's online activity, including the sites you visit, the items you buy, and any personal information you supply. You may have noticed, for example, that on a visit to Amazon.com, the site recommends items related to your previous browsing. Cookies also help web sites to store important personal information such as your name, address, and payment preferences. This information can help users learn about new products that might match their interests and can make online shopping fast and easy.

In recent years, however, cookies have been installed primarily by companies that specialize in tracking and recording users' online activity and selling this information to advertisers. These companies pay web sites to permit them to install tracking tools on the computers of visitors to the site. In addition, tracking tools are sometimes hidden in banner ads or free downloadable apps, games, and ring tones.

By piecing together bits of information you leave behind as you browse the Internet, advertisers can anticipate your likely interests and pitch products to you based on your past online activity. Records of your searches on Google or other sites, the products you have viewed, the articles you have read, the zip code you entered to get local weather, your Facebook or MySpace likes and dislikes—all these pieces of information can be assembled to create a sophisticated consumer profile that allows marketers to create a targeted online consumer experience, steering you to advertisements tailor-made to your specific interests.

The principles of behavioral targeting are also visible in political campaigns. By mining data about your online activities, campaigns can customize the information you receive about a candidate. In this way, the campaign can personalize the candidate's message and target it to you based on your demographic and consumer profile. Different citizens can literally be getting different messages from the same candidate (Howard 2005; Panagopoulos 2009).

thinking about culture

As consumer **culture** spreads throughout the globe, environmental pollution is spreading, as well. What aspects of U.S. consumer culture might create these problems?

Research suggests there is substantial public concern about online tracking. One comprehensive national survey found that two-thirds of Internet users in the United States do not want to receive targeted advertising. Asked about the prospect of receiving targeted online ads based on their *offline* consumer activity, more than 85 percent of respondents indicated their disapproval (Turow et al. 2009).

Public opposition to behavioral targeting is connected to broader concerns about online privacy. For example, the practice of "scraping" involves copying material from online forums, career-oriented web sites, and social networking sites, on which users often discuss and post information about various aspects of their lives, from school, work, and relationships to health, exercise, and hobbies (Angwin and Stecklow 2010). In some cases, scrapers construct individual user profiles that connect people's online screen names to their real names, which they sell to advertisers, employers, and other web sites. Online scrapers also sell so-called "listening services," in which they report to clients what people are saying about a specific topic or product. Facebook and other social networking sites, which include personal information that users post voluntarily, are particularly valuable sources for information scrapers.

In the face of the growing sophistication of behavioral targeting and other data gathering techniques, consumer advocates have called for government regulations. The Federal Trade Commission proposed a "do not track" option in 2010, which would permit users to opt out of all tracking tools. In response, online data trackers and advertisers have come up with their own proposals to head off potential regulation. A group of online tracking companies started a service called the Open Data Partnership in 2011, which allows consumers to view and edit data that have been collected on them but does not permit users to opt out of tracking altogether (Steel 2010). In early 2011 Google and Mozilla announced software for their browsers that would allow consumers to opt out permanently. Whether the tracking companies would honor the opt-out requests is another worrisome question (*New York Times* 2011a).

The debate about online advertising techniques is sure to continue throughout the decade, as citizens and policymakers sort through the various arguments about consumer privacy and efficient marketing. In this new era of customized consumption, sociologists are likely to pay careful attention to the power associated with information tracking and the cultural consequences of the proliferation of personalized advertising (and political) messages.

THINKING SOCIOLOGICALLY ABOUT . . . Media and Consumption

culture
- Media reflect and promote cultural norms.
- Consumption has become central to our culture and is used to help form social identities.

structure
- The structure of the media industry shapes the content of popular media.
- Media organizations must operate within the structural constraints imposed by their legal, political, economic, and cultural environments.
- The widespread presence of advertising helps to structure consumer society.

power
- Major media ownership is highly concentrated; those who control the media wield considerable power in society.
- Consumerism is linked to inequality and reflects disparities in economic power in society.

Looking Back

1. As a social institution, media involve the interaction of several key elements: the media industry, media content, audiences, technology, and the broader social context.

2. The media industry has been expanding, integrating, and globalizing, while its ownership has become more concentrated.

3. Media content often reflects the broader social inequalities in society, sometimes perpetuating them through the socialization process.

4. Audiences consist of active readers, viewers, and listeners who make choices about their media use and interpret media content, often based on their social position. But extensive and long-term exposure to media does have an impact on audiences, influencing what they think about and how they view the world.

5. Converging media forms, technological advances, and the rise in user-generated content have been major contributors to the explosive growth of media.

6. Whatever their form, media act as sources of information, agents of socialization, and as a means for those in power to promote ideology.

7. The rise in electronic media technology in postmodern life is a significant change from modernity's reliance on print, introducing new ways of thinking about and seeing the world.

8. The rise of consumer culture was accompanied by an increase in advertising delivered through various media. Advertising has become a ubiquitous force, and advertisers use a variety of techniques to influence our identities and promote consumption.

9. Consumer culture has had a significant social impact on how we live, work, and value our lives. It has also been a key factor in the escalation of environmental degradation.

Critical Thinking: Questions and Activities

1. In what ways and for how long do you use media in a typical day? Keep a log for one or two days, noting every use of media. How would you summarize the role that media play in your life? How do you think your lifelong exposure to media has influenced how you understand the world? How does the influence of media extend beyond *what* you know to include *how* you relate to the social world?

2. If someone relied exclusively on popular media portrayals to understand the life of a college student today, would they get a reasonably accurate picture of your real-world experiences in college? What does this say about the role of media in teaching about aspects of the world we don't experience first-hand?

3. Note your exposure to advertising for one day. What techniques did advertisers use to get your attention? Is there any part of your life that is free from brand names, logos, and ads?

4. Would you agree to have a corporate advertiser pay for your wedding ceremony in exchange for incorporating the corporation's logo into the event (for example, printed on invitations and napkins, displayed on a banner at the reception, announced as part of the ceremony)? Why or why not? What issues does this "product placement" raise about the appropriate limits for advertising?

5. In what ways do you participate in consumer culture? Do you have any concerns about the role of consumption in your life?

Key Terms

active audiences (p. 383) audiences that make choices about how they use the media and actively interpret media content.

agenda-setting theory (p. 385) a theory that holds that media may not be able to tell people what to think but can significantly influence what people think about.

alienation (p. 394) the separation and isolation of workers as a result of the structure of capitalist society.

behavioral targeting (p. 400) advertising sent to online users based on their earlier Internet activities.

commodification (p. 399) the process of transforming all things into a product to be bought and sold.

commodity fetishism (p. 394) consumers' failure to recognize the labor that created the value in the commodities they use.

consumerism (p. 394) an emphasis on shopping and the possession of material goods as the route to personal happiness.

consumption (p. 392) the process of choosing, purchasing, and using goods.

convergence (p. 386) the merging of different media forms.

cultivation theory (p. 385) a theory that argues that, by repeated and long-term exposure to the media's portrayal of the world (especially on television), people come to accept many of these depictions as reality.

cultural imperialism (p. 390) the tendency of media corporations from wealthier nations—especially the United States—to export so many of their media products that they come to dominate the local cultures of other, especially poorer, nations.

digital divide (p. 388) the gap between those who have the knowledge and resources needed to use digital information technology, especially computers and the Internet, and those who do not.

dual product markets (p. 383) the situation that occurs when a company sells two completely different types of "products" to two completely different sets of buyers.

horizontal integration (p. 379) what occurs when a media company owns different forms of media.

hyperreality (p. 391) the condition in which media depictions of the world replace the experience of the "real" world.

mass media (p. 377) communications that reach a relatively large and mostly anonymous audience.

media (p. 377) the various technological processes that enable communication between (and are in the "middle" of) the sender of a message and the receiver of that message.

ownership concentration (p. 380) what occurs when more media outlets come to be owned by a diminishing number of media corporations.

planned obsolescence (p. 392) the intentional design and manufacture of consumer goods so as to ensure a loss of utility in a relatively short period of time.

product placement (p. 396) the integration into media content of a product that is being advertised.

stealth advertising (p. 398) the creation of covert advertising in everyday real-life situations.

user-generated content (p. 386) content that is created by ordinary media users, rather than by media organizations, and that is available to a potentially large audience.

vertical integration (p. 379) what occurs when a media company owns the different stages of production and distribution of a single media form.

Politics and
the Economy

looking AHEAD

How is "security" defined in our **culture** and what is the government's role in helping to achieve it?

How do politics **structure** the way our society operates?

Capitalism? Socialism? How do economies reflect different ways that **power** is distributed in society?

U.S. leaders have long gone to war in the name of national security. "Success in Iraq will mean that the American people are more secure at home," argued President George W. Bush, even after it was revealed that Iraqi weapons of mass destruction—the initial reason for war—did not exist (Bush 2008). "I am convinced that our security is at stake in Afghanistan and Pakistan," argued President Barack Obama, justifying an expanded war against the Taliban, which had sheltered the Al Qaeda leaders responsible for the 9/11 attacks (Obama 2009).

Staff Sgt. Daniel Escamilla was one of hundreds of thousands of U.S. troops who fought in Iraq. But during his third tour of duty he faced a new and unexpected threat: foreclosure on his Colorado home. Escamilla had been unable to keep up with rising mortgage payments, and his lender had piled on massive penalties, making the problem worse. While still in Iraq, Escamilla sought help in negotiating with the bank. "Not only do I have to worry about staying alive," he told a reporter, "but now I got to worry about whether or not my family's going to get kicked out of the house" (Zoroya 2008). He was not alone. In 2010, more than 20,000 active-duty troops and reservists lost their homes due to foreclosures (Zoroya 2011).

A majority of Americans initially supported military action in Iraq and Afghanistan, which so far has resulted in the loss of more than 6,000 U.S. lives, but about two-thirds came to believe these wars were not worth fighting (Agiesta 2008; Wilson and Cohen 2011). Instead, economic security became the new priority. Corporations recklessly—and sometimes fraudulently—pursuing high profits triggered a global financial crisis that led to home foreclosures, rising unemployment, and sharp declines in the stock market, and left the banking, financial, and auto industries teetering on the brink of collapse. Only government intervention in the form of controversial corporate bailouts and massive stimulus spending brought some semblance of stability. The global economic crisis reminded everyone, including Sgt. Escamilla, that security is not just a military matter. ■

How does a country ensure its national security while protecting its economic security? Will people be asked to put their lives in danger in a war? Will education funding be adequate to meet students' needs? Will young people be able to find jobs? Will Medicare be available for the health care of an aging population? Such questions involve both politics and the economy—the two social institutions on which we focus in this chapter. We begin by examining the role of politics and the government in society, including aspects of the military. Then we look at the structure of the economy and the government's role in relationship to it. We conclude by considering ways to define *security*.

The Structure of Politics

Politics is an especially important social institution because it structures the way a society operates, setting its ground rules and priorities.

Politics as a Social Institution

Politics is *the arena in which societies make collective decisions about priorities and policies.* We use politics to answer key questions about what type of society we will have. How much freedom will we as citizens have? How will our resources be used? Will we go to war? How will we address crime and respond to our health care, energy, and transportation needs?

You've probably heard people use the term *politics* in a negative way, as in, "It's all just politics." Because so much is at stake in politics, it is an arena often full of conflict, deception, hypocrisy, and self-interest. At its worst, politics can produce murderous regimes that oppress and terrorize their own people. But at its best, politics can produce many benefits for a society, such as a well-run, responsive government that protects the quality of people's lives through regulations that minimize environmental threats, promote food safety, ensure fair treatment of workers, and guard against fire hazards. Government

agencies can provide roads and public transportation; supply clean water; and offer social services, education, and health care. And through the military, police, and courts, government can help defend our physical safety and civil liberties. For better or worse, politics and governments are interwoven with the fabric of social life.

Systems of Government

German sociologist Max Weber (1919/1946a) noted that politics is about power—how it is maintained, distributed, challenged, and transferred. (As we have seen, **power** is *the ability to bring about an intended outcome, even when opposed by others.*) Weber stressed that the fundamental location for political activity is **government,** *the organization that exercises authority and steers decision making in a specific community.* He noted that governments ("the state") have one specific feature that distinguishes them from other powerful organizations: they hold a monopoly on the legitimate use of force in a given territory. A government can authorize military personnel to kill on its behalf in wars; its police can arrest and even shoot people in the line of duty; and its prison guards can keep people incarcerated, depriving them of their freedom.

Because political processes are socially constructed, governments around the world differ in the way they choose leaders and how politically engaged their citizens are. We can classify government structures into three basic types: monarchies, authoritarian governments, and democracies.

A **monarchy** is *a system of government headed by a single person, the monarch, who typically inherits the position as a member of a ruling family.* Monarchs' titles signify their royal status (king, queen, sultan, emir, or emperor) and are passed from one generation to the next. There are two broad types of monarchies. In *traditional* (or *absolute*) *monarchies,* a single royal leader enjoys essentially unconditional power. This form of government is very rare today, existing (as of 2012) only in Saudi Arabia (king), Qatar (emir), and Oman (sultan) in the Middle East; Brunei (sultan) in Southeast Asia; and Swaziland (king) in Southern Africa. Instead, most contemporary monarchies are *constitutional monarchies,* democracies that recognize a limited and often only symbolic role for the royal family. Queen Elizabeth II—the monarch of the United Kingdom of Britain and Northern Ireland—is the best-known constitutional monarch today. She plays a ceremonial role as head of state, while an elected parliament and a prime minister run the government.

Instead of monarchies, two broad types of government now predominate: authoritarian and democratic. An **authoritarian government** *typically features self-appointed leaders who exert great control over the lives of citizens that includes severely limiting their civil liberties.* Central ruling parties or the military usually run authoritarian governments. They do not rely on popular support from citizens or tolerate meaningful political

thinking about **power**
According to Weber and other sociologists, the legitimate use of force distinguishes governments from other powerful organizations. When might a government's use of force cease to be legitimate?

437

opposition, though authoritarian leaders may rig elections to try to legitimize their power. Disdainful of civil liberties, authoritarian governments often intrude in the lives of citizens, directing, for example, what people may read or publish, what religion they practice, or where they may travel. They often go to considerable expense to monitor the private lives of citizens through various forms of surveillance.

Democracy is *a political system in which the right to vote is widespread and government leaders are selected through multiparty elections.* In its literal definition, democracy is "rule by the people." However, the specific mechanisms by which "the people" rule can vary. In a *direct democracy,* citizens themselves participate in political decision-making in such venues as town hall meetings or in referendums to decide the fate of a proposed policy. More common is *representative democracy,* in which citizens elect delegates who carry out the policymaking processes of government. Democratic systems often include elements of both direct and representative democracy, as does the United States. Free and fair elections are a fundamental component of all representative democracies.

The widespread embrace of democracy is relatively recent in human history. Many nations have not yet adopted democracy, though some leaders use its rhetoric to help legitimize

their rule. The Democracy Index, published by the *Economist*'s Economist Intelligence Unit (2010), identifies five key components of a democratic government:

- Free and fair competitive elections
- Civil liberties, including freedom of speech, expression, and the press; freedom of religion; freedom of assembly and association; and the right to due judicial process
- A functioning government that can implement democratically based decisions
- Active political participation by citizens in public life
- A democratic political culture in which supporters of losing candidates accept the judgment of voters and permit the peaceful transition of power

In 2010, Economist Intelligence Unit researchers, awarding points in each of these categories, labeled only 15.6 percent of the world's countries as "full democracies" (including the United States), 31.7 percent as "flawed democracies," nearly one-third (32.9 percent) as authoritarian, and the remainder as hybrids (see Map 16.1). About half the world's population (49.5 percent) live in a democracy of some sort; the remainder do not.

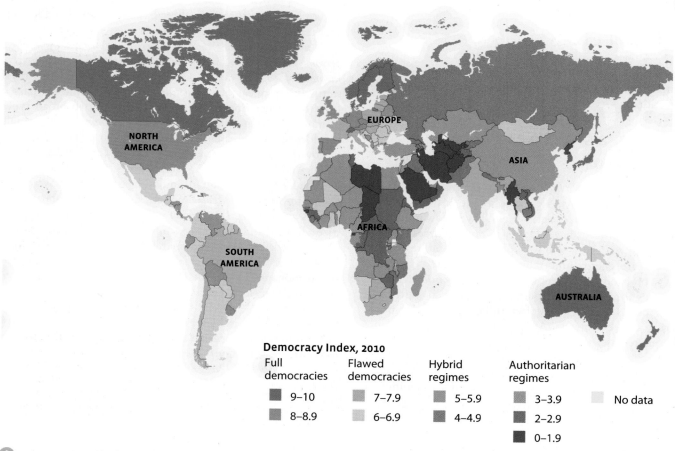

Democracy Index, 2010

Full democracies	Flawed democracies	Hybrid regimes	Authoritarian regimes	
■ 9–10	■ 7–7.9	■ 5–5.9	■ 3–3.9	No data
■ 8–8.9	■ 6–6.9	■ 4–4.9	■ 2–2.9	
			■ 0–1.9	

MAP 16.1 | 2010 DEMOCRACY INDEX

The degree of democratic rule varies considerably from country to country. On the scale used here, a higher number indicates a more democratic nation. *Source:* Economist Intelligence Unit (2010).

Political Structure and Political Action

The political structure of a society shapes the possibilities for political action, and political action can sometimes have a significant impact on the political structure.

An authoritarian society allows little opportunity for dissent, limiting the possibilities for political action. To oppose the ruling party by speaking out or joining an underground movement is to risk harsh consequences, including jail or execution. But even in an authoritarian society, actions matter. Compliance or cooperation may help reinforce the existing political structure. But with broad enough participation, as history has repeatedly shown, even small challenges can over time turn into public protests, demands for reform, or a revolution that changes the political structure.

Citizens in democracies, in contrast, have a wide range of options for political participation without fear of reprisal. In turn, how citizens use—or don't use—their rights helps to determine a democracy's future.

Democracies vary. For example, voters elect the head of government in *presidential* systems, whereas members of the legislature typically elect (and dismiss) the prime minister in a *parliamentary* system. Another major distinction between democratic systems is that some offer plurality voting whereas others feature proportional representation. **Plurality voting** is *a "winner-take-all" system in which the candidate with the most votes wins the office being contested.* For example, in U.S. federal elections each House and Senate seat is awarded to the candidate receiving the most votes in that seat's district. Even if a candidate loses by a single vote, his or her party goes unrepresented in that district. In **proportional representation** systems, *parties are awarded seats in government based on the percentage of votes they receive in an election.* A party that wins 20 percent of the vote might be awarded 20 percent of the seats in the legislature. Many countries, including Japan, Ireland, Brazil, Hungary, Canada, and South Africa, have some form of proportional representation.

In the United States, plurality voting has been a major factor in the emergence of a system dominated by two parties, the Republicans and the Democrats. Although small political parties such as the Libertarian Party and the Green Party do exist (see Figure 16.1), few voters know much about them. Debate organizers typically exclude third-party candidates, and news organizations rarely cover their campaigns, helping to ensure that small parties remain on the margins of political life.

Because of the structural limitations of the two-party system, major change to the system must often originate from outside the two major parties, often through social movements (see Chapter 17). In recent years, the Tea Party has received considerable media attention and influenced political debates. The Tea Party is neither a formal political party nor a social movement. It is supported by Republican Party funders, including some major corporations, and is a loosely organized collection of activists, about 80 percent of whom are from the conservative wing of the Republican Party (Mayer 2010; Newport 2010). As such, it works both inside and outside the Republican Party, pressuring the party to take more conservative positions on issues such as health care reform and government spending.

Many countries have a more diverse multiparty system, often due to their system of proportional representation.

Green Party

Libertarian Party

Independence Party

Reform Party

Socialist Party

FIGURE 16.1 | MINOR POLITICAL PARTIES IN THE UNITED STATES

Plurality voting has contributed to a two-party system that helps marginalize minor parties such as the ones listed here with their logos. (Some others, whose logos aren't shown, include the American First Party, the Constitution Party, the Labor Party, and the Working Families Party.) Do you think the United States would be better served by having more than two viable political parties? Why or why not?

thinking about structure

The **structure** of the two-party system in the United States effectively prevents most third-party candidates from winning elections. Have you voted for a third-party candidate? What was the outcome? What impact did that candidate have, regardless of the outcome?

(See Figure 16.2.) Citizens in multiparty systems are more likely to find a party that represents their views, thereby contributing to higher voter turnout than is typical in the United States. Such systems, though, can produce fragmented and unstable governments.

Political Culture

Like any social institution, politics features culturally specific norms and practices. The cultural norms we learn influence what issues we consider political and whether we speak out about them.

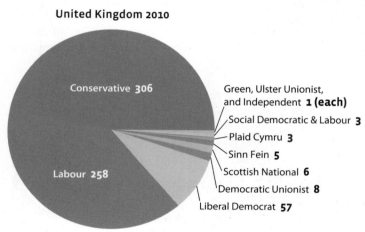

United Kingdom 2010

Conservative 306
Green, Ulster Unionist, and Independent **1 (each)**
Social Democratic & Labour **3**
Plaid Cymru **3**
Sinn Fein **5**
Scottish National **6**
Democratic Unionist **8**
Liberal Democrat **57**
Labour 258

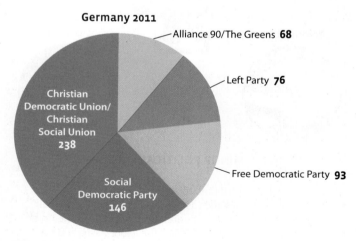

Germany 2011

Alliance 90/The Greens **68**
Left Party **76**
Christian Democratic Union/ Christian Social Union 238
Free Democratic Party **93**
Social Democratic Party 146

FIGURE 16.2 | MULTIPARTY LEGISLATURES: POLITICAL PARTIES IN THE UNITED KINGDOM AND GERMANY
Unlike in the United States, other democracies have legislatures with significant representation from more than two parties. *Sources:* German Bundestag (2011); U.K. Parliament (2010).

Political Socialization

Political socialization *teaches us basic norms and expectations about political life and attitudes toward involvement in politics.* Democratic political systems, like that of the United States, encourage citizens to participate in politics, at least to a degree. Schools typically teach students basic lessons about civics, including the significance of voting rights. (The Through a Sociological Lens box on page 441 explores another way schools can promote civic engagement.) During election season, news coverage regularly stresses the importance of voting as a basic act of citizenship. Freedom and democracy are celebrated through patriotic cultural events, from schoolchildren's recitation of the Pledge of Allegiance to sports fans' singing of the national anthem at the start of baseball games.

But the U.S. political process and citizens' relationship to politics are in fact more complicated than our celebrations suggest. For most of U.S. history, the majority of citizens were denied even the basic right to vote. Scholars have documented election fraud past and present, including voting by dead people, uncounted votes, and interference with registration as well as the possibility of tampering with electronic voting machines (Alvarez, Hall, and Hyde 2008). Allegations of voter manipulation and inaccurate counting periodically pro-

A girl watches her mother voting at a polling station. Did you receive any political socialization early in life that either encouraged or discouraged your participation in politics?

CHAPTER 16   Politics and the Economy

The Political Socialization of Teenagers

Sociological research on political socialization shows that schools can help connect young people with politics, activating their interest in political participation.

In one study, McFarland and Thomas (2006) examined the relationship between youth extracurricular activities and later adult political participation. Using two national surveys that followed respondents from high school through early adulthood, the authors examined the relationship between teenagers' involvement in voluntary organizations and their political participation as adults a decade later. They found that students active in specific types of voluntary organizations in high school, regardless of class background, were more likely to register to vote, to vote in an election, to participate in community service, to work on a political campaign, and to join a political party.

Not all extracurricular activities promote adult political involvement. For example, neither high school sports nor academic clubs enhance political socialization, whereas participation in student government, service organizations, debate teams, and drama and musical groups do. McFarland and Thomas (2006) explain, "Youth organizations that demand student time commitments and that concern service, political activity, and public performance have the most significant, positive relation to long-term political participation" (p. 416). These organizations encourage young people to develop valuable political knowledge, skills, and identities, including the ability to speak in public, knowledge of group processes, and a sense of community service.

think about it

1. Have you ever engaged in voluntary activities of the sort that appear to encourage political involvement?

2. What other early socialization experiences do you think either encouraged or discouraged you from becoming involved in political life?

---

duce election controversies, most notably the contested 2000 presidential election settled by the intervention of the Supreme Court. Further, some observers criticize the news media for failing to adequately serve their crucial democratic functions of being a watchdog on the powerful and effectively informing citizens about politics (McChesney and Nichols 2010). Others argue that cuts in spending for public education limit the teaching of critical thinking skills necessary for a well-informed citizenry in a democracy (Nussbaum 2010). In short, although the U.S. political system and broader political culture may be preferred to many others, it is far from the ideal portrayed in children's textbooks.

As a result, many Americans are at best highly skeptical of the political process and political figures. Millions simply avoid politics and decline to vote. Ironically, the United States—which often prides itself on being a global symbol of freedom and democracy—typically has one of the lowest voter turnouts of any Western industrialized democracy (see Table 16.1).

Public Opinion and the "Spiral of Silence"

In democratic political systems, the legitimacy of government is rooted in the idea that elected governments have public support. But elections are only one measure of public support, and long periods—four years for U.S. presidential elections—often separate one election from the next. If the literal meaning of democracy is government by the people, how do the people "govern" between elections?

One way is by expressing their opinions about the issues of the day. But talking about politics is not always easy, especially for those with unpopular views. The **spiral of silence** is *a theory that explains how people keep quiet about controversial issues when they think their opinions are not widely shared, in order to avoid social isolation* (Noelle-Neuman, 1974, 1993).

---

thinking about culture

In what ways might people with unpopular views become part of a **subculture**? Can you think of an example of such a subculture? How might this group make its views heard?

TABLE 16.1 — VOTER TURNOUT IN SELECT COUNTRIES

Country	Type (of election)	Year (of election)	Voter Turnout[1] (as a percentage of the voting-age population)
Greece	Parliamentary	2000	89%
Belgium	Parliamentary	2007	86%
Italy	Parliamentary	2001	85%
Denmark	Parliamentary	2001	84%
Australia	Parliamentary	2001	84%
Sweden	Parliamentary	2006	81%
Spain	Parliamentary	2004	80%
France	Presidential	2007	77%
Norway	Parliamentary	2005	77%
Turkey	Parliamentary	2007	74%
Germany	Parliamentary	2002	74%
Portugal	Parliamentary	2005	69%
Ireland	Parliamentary	2007	69%
Russian Federation	Presidential	2000	69%
Japan	Parliamentary	2005	67%
Mexico	Parliamentary	2006	64%
Poland	Presidential	2000	63%
India	Parliamentary	2004	61%
Canada	Parliamentary	2006	58%
United Kingdom	Parliamentary	2005	58%
United States	Presidential	2008	58%
Luxembourg	Parliamentary	2004	57%

What factors do you think contribute to the relatively low voter turnout in the United States? *Source:* Institute for Democracy and Electoral Assistance.

[1] Voter turnout is the highest reported turnout for a presidential or parliamentary election during the period 2000–2008.

Political activists speak out at a Tea Party event, vowing to hold elected officials accountable in the November elections.

One comprehensive review of spiral of silence theory and research summarizes the five key dynamics of this process (Scheufele and Moy 2000):

1. Societies require some degree of agreement about basic values and goals and exert social pressure on individuals to agree, including an implicit threat of isolation for those who do not.

2. As individuals develop their own opinions, they fear social isolation and seek to conform to what they see as the prevailing views in their community.

3. People monitor their environment, paying careful attention to the opinions of others as they try to decipher the most common opinions and future opinion trends.

4. People are likely to express their opinions when they believe their views are popular or rising in popularity. However, when people believe their views are unpopular or declining in popularity, they are likely to be guarded and remain silent.

5. "The tendency of the one to speak up and the other to be silent starts off a spiraling process which increasingly establishes one opinion as the prevailing one" (Noelle-Neuman 1974).

The spiral of silence narrows public discussion by squeezing out minority views and overstating the degree of political consensus. The media play an important role because people often look to media for indications of which views are currently popular. If they do not see their perspectives reflected there, they are likely to believe that their views are marginal, making it more likely they will be quiet.

Political Issues and Private Matters

If politics is the social institution whereby societies make collective decisions about priorities and policies, it matters a great deal what issues count as politics. A mixture of culture and power determines how a society defines politics. Feminist activists in the 1970s challenged traditional definitions of politics, arguing that "the personal is political" because power pervades all aspects of social life (Evans 1980). In other words, politics is not just about what happens in government but also includes many aspects of our daily and personal lives, such as the food we choose to buy and eat, the choices we make about the work we do, and the way we structure our personal relationships.

SPOTLIGHT on social theory

Feminist theory and activism have been important in advancing the notion that the "personal is political." How might actions in your personal life have political implications?

Social theorist Nancy Fraser (1992) points out that one consequential question that reflects our political culture is what gets defined as "private" and therefore inappropriate for public discussion. A variety of issues—including child abuse, domestic violence, sexual orientation, and mental illness—were, until quite recently, considered private matters and excluded from politics. Political and cultural changes have transformed these into political issues to which public policy is attuned and about which public discussion is permissible. On the other hand, asserting the right to have a private life—free of surveillance or intrusion—is itself a political position. Current debates about the government's right to use surveillance on citizens, conduct searches at airports, and legislate personal behavior illustrate that the relationship between public and private is always being contested and involves power struggles, to which we now turn.

Power and Politics

Whoever makes the rules for a society gets to influence the direction of that society. In the United States today, do "the people" rule? Do "special interests"? Does someone else? Sociologists have long examined such issues of power, considering who takes part in politics and how government policies reflect this participation.

Theories of Political Power: Pluralism, Elites, and Class Domination

Three broad classic approaches help us understand the distribution of political power in U.S. society. **Pluralist theory** *argues that political power is fragmented among many different competing groups.* Business owners, labor unions, teachers, retired people, gun owners, environmentalists, antiabortion advocates, and a host of other interests are represented by organizations that try to influence public policy by educating the public, lobbying elected officials, and supporting sympathetic candidates. Developed mostly by political scientists and adopted by some functionalist sociologists, pluralism suggests that politics is a constant negotiation among these various interests and that policies change as one or another group gains more influence (Dahl 1961).

In contrast, **power elite theory** *suggests that political power is concentrated in the hands of a small dominant group of business, government, and military leaders.* Developed by sociologist C. Wright Mills (1956), power elite theory is a form of conflict theory that argues power is heavily concentrated in the hands of those who head society's major bureaucratic institutions: the very wealthy who own or control big business, politicians and bureaucrats who run government, and the military brass who head the United States' military structure. Elites move back and forth among these three fields,

Masked women rally with male supporters in a demonstration against domestic violence in Madrid, Spain, during 2007's International Women's Day. Until recently, domestic violence in Spain was considered a "private" family affair, not the stuff of political action.

as when a military general leaves to become an executive for a defense contractor or when a banking executive becomes secretary of the Treasury. The flow of people among the three sectors helps solidify the power these elites have over the policies and budgets of their interlocking bureaucracies. According to power elite theory, ordinary citizens' influence is minimal in the face of such concentrated power, except when elites disagree among themselves, opening the door to possible citizen influence.

Class domination theory *suggests that political power is concentrated in the hands of the rich who own or control a large share of the nation's economic resources.* Based on the work of Karl Marx and adapted by modern interpreters (Domhoff 2009), class domination theory is a form of conflict theory that views the economic system as the ultimate source of power. Those who control this system—especially super-wealthy owners and executives of major corporate conglomerates—use their financial clout to influence government by funding lobbyists, financially supporting political campaigns, and bankrolling "astroturf" campaigns that advance corporate goals through what appear to be grassroots citizen efforts. Corporate-owned media outlets also help to limit the range of political debate on news and other programs. These uses of economic resources undermine the ability of ordinary citizens to significantly influence the political system. Although efforts to rein in the power of the rich—through higher taxes and limits on campaign contributions, for example—are sometimes criticized as promoting "class warfare," proponents of class domination theory say that it's actually the other way around—ordinary citizens are the real targets of class warfare. As investor Warren Buffett, one of the richest men in the country, once put it, disapprovingly, "There's class warfare, all right, but it's my class—the rich class—that's making war, and we're winning" (quoted in Stein 2006).

Many sociologists would likely agree that the United States follows some aspects of the pluralist model, especially on issues that are not fundamentally economic, such as abortion, gay marriage, and gun control, where lively debates are pursued by various groups. But there is little doubt that elites wield disproportionate influence on political life, particularly economic affairs, though the precise nature and degree of this influence is a topic of ongoing study and debate.

Class Differences in Political Participation

Societies with a healthy democratic political system have broad public participation in politics, even if only in elections. But more than in many other democracies, political participation

S P O T L I G H T
on social theory

Both **power elite** and **class domination theory**—forms of **conflict theory**—argue that political power is not really in the hands of ordinary citizens, as **pluralist theory** suggests. Can you think of an example that seems to support such claims? Can you think of a situation in which ordinary citizens seem to have prevailed over powerful interests?

in the United States is stratified by class. Working-class and poor people are less likely to vote in the United States than are middle-class people (Verba, Schlozman, and Brady 1995). As we saw in Chapter 9, one likely reason is the absence of a strong labor or socialist party that can speak on behalf of working-class voters. All other Western democracies have such a party, and the class gap in voter turnout is considerably less in those countries. In contrast, both major parties in the United States are closely aligned with major corporate interests and depend heavily on their financial contributions.

The political socialization of young people is another important influence on political participation. Informed political discussion benefits from self-confidence, education, knowledge, and a time commitment, and these resources are not distributed equally. Although a healthy democracy requires the inclusion of diverse perspectives from all sectors of society, research suggests that higher levels of education and income contribute significantly to a sense of political competence (Jacobs and Skocpol 2007). Children from highly educated, wealthier, and higher-status families enjoy numerous advantages that encourage and enable them to become involved in politics: their parents are more likely than working-class parents to participate in politics and to talk to their children about political activity; their teachers and school officials are more likely to encourage students to become involved in school and community activities; and their peer networks are more likely to support interest and involvement in politics. People from poor or working-class backgrounds are less likely to perceive themselves as adequately prepared for political discussions and are less likely to be active in an arena that seems to reward the affluent.

Campaign Contributions, Lobbying, and Policy Outcomes

Class differences in political participation are even more pronounced in activities beyond voting. Not surprisingly, financial contributions—the lifeblood of political campaigns—come disproportionately from more affluent voters. The rich have more money to contribute. For example, the 2008 Obama presidential campaign touted its ability to use the Internet to generate contributions from small donors. In fact, only 24 percent of contributors gave less than $200 (nearly the same percentage as in President George W. Bush's campaign four years earlier), and a full 47 percent gave $1,000 or more, suggesting that more affluent citizens bankrolled the campaign to a degree typical of recent presidential campaigns (Malbin 2008).

Once candidates are elected, money continues to be important. Officials must immediately begin fundraising for reelection while lobbyists encourage lawmakers to vote in their client's interests—often the same clients who make major campaign contributions. Although labor unions and single-issue groups engage in lobbying, the practice is dominated by the corporate sector (Figure 16.3).

Campaign donations give donors and lobbyists unique access to elected officials, which they often parlay into special

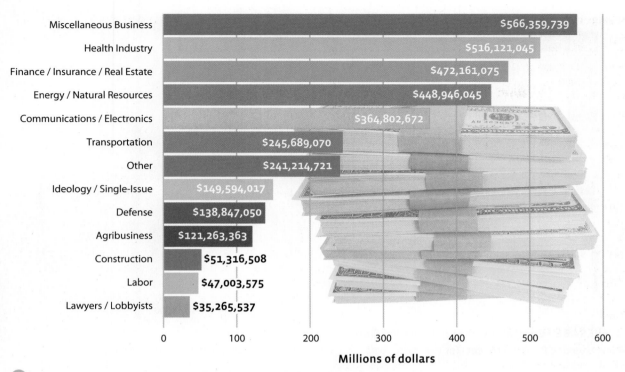

FIGURE 16.3 | LOBBYING EXPENDITURES BY SECTOR, 2010

Business-sector spending on lobbyists far surpasses that of labor groups or single-issue organizations such as environmental, gay rights, or gun rights groups. *Source:* OpenSecrets.Org: Center for Responsive Politics

assistance for projects that benefit them directly (Clawson et al 1998). Consider the following examples:

- Many industries, including oil, banking, and financial services industries, lobby for reduced government regulation. Inadequate regulation and lax enforcement contributed to both the BP gulf oil spill (Levitz 2010; National Commission 2011) and the global financial crisis (Financial Crisis Inquiry Commission 2011).

- Some observers see the taxpayer-funded bailout of big banks, financial institutions, and other companies as more evidence of the power of wealthy donors and lobbyists. Though the well-known TARP (Troubled Asset Relief Program) loans that bailed out banks were repaid, other lesser-known bailout programs will end up costing taxpayers many billions of dollars (ProPublica 2011; SourceWatch 2010).

- In response to pressure from lobbyists representing the health care and insurance industries, the 2009 health care reform law protected the interests of the health care and insurance industries by mandating that uninsured individuals buy insurance coverage from private companies rather than offering a government-run "public option" that advocates argued would have been more cost-effective (Eaton and Pell 2010).

In addition, wealthy corporations and individuals lobby for lower tax rates and tax loopholes (Johnston 2005, 2007). In one dramatic example, the Boeing Corporation made $10 billion in domestic pretax profits between 2008 and 2010 (and received tens of billions of dollars in government contracts) but paid no federal corporate income taxes over those three years (Citizens for Tax Justice 2011). The 2010–2012 Obama-supported tax deal that extended Bush-era tax cuts added billions to the deficit, sending a disproportionate share of the savings to the wealthy, even though most people opposed this deal, with 56 percent saying the bill did "too much for wealthy Americans" (CNN/Opinion Research Corporation 2010). (See Figure 16.4 on the following page.)

Considerable research suggests that the government is most responsive to the affluent classes. In one study of public opinion and government policy between 1981 and 2002, Martin Gilens (2005) focused on issues for which the policy preferences of high-income people differed from those of middle- and low-income citizens. The inheritance tax, government-funded health care, and affirmative action are supported substantially more by those with modest incomes than by those with higher incomes. Gilens concluded that "government policy appears to be fairly responsive to the well-off and virtually unrelated to the desires of the low- and middle-income citizens" (p. 789).

Inequality, Power, and Politics

Connecting the dots between economic inequality, campaign finances, lobbying, and legislation, some critics argue that concentrated wealth is undermining democratic institutions

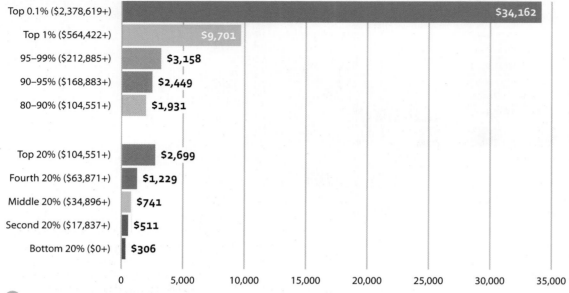

Average annual savings by income bracket, dollars

Income bracket	Savings
Top 0.1% ($2,378,619+)	$34,162
Top 1% ($564,422+)	$9,701
95–99% ($212,885+)	$3,158
90–95% ($168,883+)	$2,449
80–90% ($104,551+)	$1,931
Top 20% ($104,551+)	$2,699
Fourth 20% ($63,871+)	$1,229
Middle 20% ($34,896+)	$741
Second 20% ($17,837+)	$511
Bottom 20% ($0+)	$306

FIGURE 16.4 | AVERAGE FEDERAL TAX SAVINGS BY INCOME GROUP, 2011

The 2010 tax bill, which extended Bush-era tax cuts for two more years, gave the largest tax breaks (in dollars) to the wealthiest taxpayers. *Source:* Tax Policy Center (2011b).

(Collins and Yeskel 2005). (See Figure 16.5.) Those with money use their resources to influence the political system, while those struggling to earn a living have little time to take part in the political process and no money to contribute. Because political parties and politicians speak to and respond mostly to the more affluent, the less affluent often do not see political participation as a wise investment of time and energy. However, by opting out of the political process, the less affluent virtually guarantee that politicians and the government will continue to neglect their interests. The vacuum they leave makes it easier for powerful players to shape laws, rules, and regulations to benefit their own interests, some of which increase inequality.

FIGURE 16.5 | INEQUALITY, POWER, AND POLITICS: A MODEL

Economic inequality can endanger the health of a democracy—and unhealthy democracy can lead to greater inequality. *Source:* Adapted from Collins and Yeskel (2005). Reprinted by permission of The New Press, www.thenewpress.com.

CORE CONCEPTS CHALLENGE

*Do you think this model summarizes accurately the way political **power** works in contemporary U.S. politics? Why or why not?*

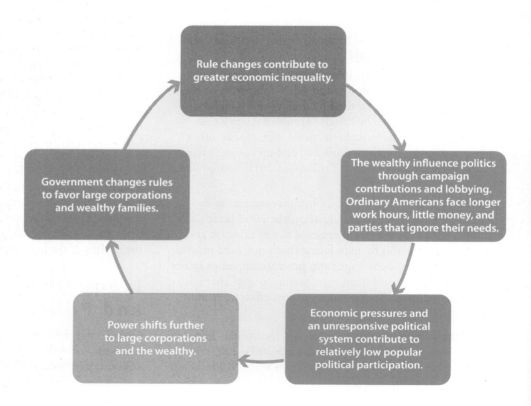

Rule changes contribute to greater economic inequality.

The wealthy influence politics through campaign contributions and lobbying. Ordinary Americans face longer work hours, little money, and parties that ignore their needs.

Economic pressures and an unresponsive political system contribute to relatively low popular political participation.

Power shifts further to large corporations and the wealthy.

Government changes rules to favor large corporations and wealthy families.

Democracies, however, always contain within them the possibility for reform. As long as basic civil rights, such as freedoms of speech and assembly and the right to vote, remain in place, citizens can promote change through the electoral process. If that process is not working properly, then social change can occur through the efforts of social movements that challenge authority outside the electoral system (Piven 2008). It remains to be seen whether and how citizens will act to reform our democracy in the coming years.

War and the Military

Mao Zedong (1936/2010), the leader of the Communist Revolution in China, famously justified armed insurrection with the slogan, "Political power grows out of the barrel of a gun" (p. 24). As Mao knew, **war**—*organized armed conflict among two or more specially trained military groups*—is often used to overcome opposition. Or as nineteenth-century German military theorist Carl von Clausewitz (1832/1976) put it, war is "the continuation of policy [or politics] by other means" (p. 87).

Some sociologists argue that war is a permanent feature of modern societies, since preparing for war is now a routine and perpetual government activity. A sociological approach to war and the military includes a consideration of the military's role in society and the socialization processes that create citizens who accept war and soldiers who fight it.

The Rise of the National Security State

During its first 125 years or so of existence—with the exception of the Civil War—the U.S. government kept a relatively small military force, even as it fought its way across the continent, acquiring new territories and subjugating indigenous peoples. At the end of the nineteenth century, when U.S. territory stretched from the Atlantic to the Pacific, some political leaders—most famously Theodore Roosevelt—wanted to continue expanding U.S. influence abroad. This goal required a much larger military, especially a modern navy that could project U.S. power overseas. The United States began building such a navy, and after its 1898 war with Spain, it quickly acquired colonies in the Philippines, Cuba, Guam, and Puerto Rico. Its time as a traditional colonial power was short, however; armed insurrections and resistance movements forced the United States to give up most of its newly acquired colonies. But the growing U.S. military continued to play an ever larger role in society, expanding dramatically during the two world wars.

After World War II ended, the United States maintained a military of unprecedented size as it engaged in the Cold War (1945–1989), an ongoing state of military tension among the

The distinctive Pentagon building, just outside of Washington, D.C., is the headquarters of the U.S. Department of Defense and the world's largest office building, with a daily workforce of 24,000 people. At the time of its construction at the start of World War II, it was widely assumed that the building would be converted after the war to some peacetime use, perhaps as an archive or a hospital. Instead, the military never left (Vogel 2007). Does the military have a visible presence in your community?

United States and the Soviet Union. Although these superpowers never directly engaged in war, the United States developed a **national security state,** *a government dominated by powerful military, foreign policy, and intelligence agencies.* The key moment in the development of the national security state was the passage of the National Security Act of 1947. The act created the National Security Council to advise the president on foreign policy and the Central Intelligence Agency, which collects and analyses security information and engages in covert operations abroad. It also consolidated the military under the newly formed Department of Defense, headquartered at the recently built Pentagon (Hogan 1998).

The national security state is not monolithic. Debates often exist within its circles about the proper priorities and allocation of resources. But as a whole it wields enough power to influence major economic and political policy decisions and priorities. In the eyes of critics, the national security state has an unhealthy preoccupation with foreign and domestic enemies that distorts economic and political policy decisions and priorities. For example, military spending receives priority well beyond the amount needed to ensure territorial security (Greider 1999, 2010). Intelligence-gathering capacities have been used in ways that critics contend violate basic democratic values, since they involve secrecy, surveillance, and limits on civil liberties at home and often occur without public knowledge or review (Cole and Dempsey 2006; Etzioni 2004).

The rise of the national security state was part of a broader change in which the U.S. military grew much more powerful, enjoying unprecedented peacetime funding, and the federal government increasingly defined international affairs in military terms. In his farewell speech to the nation in 1961, outgoing Republican president (and supreme commander of the Allied Forces during World War II) Dwight D. Eisenhower

War and the Military

warned of the growth of a military establishment and arms industry, cautioning that "in the councils of government, we must guard against the acquisition of unwarranted influence, whether sought or unsought, by the military-industrial complex. The potential for the disastrous rise of misplaced power exists and will persist."

Eisenhower's warnings were extraordinary, given that they came from an army general, but they were not new. C. Wright Mills (1956), in his analysis *The Power Elite,* had already documented the rise of military influence in political life, the declining influence of civilian diplomats, the growing impact of military spending on the economy, and the influential role of military money and priorities on research on university campuses. Mills observed that "the professional military believe firmly in the military definition of world reality and . . . are genuinely frightened for their country" (p. 202). With their growing influence, military leaders were able to promote these fears and definitions of reality, thereby helping to transform the United States into a more militarized society.

Military Funding

The United States is bounded by oceans on both the east and west coasts and shares its northern and southern borders with close allies, making it among the most geographically safe countries in the world. Yet, since the middle of the twentieth century, it has maintained the most powerful military in the world, on which it spends far more than any other country (See Figure 16.6.) The United States in 2010 accounted for about 43 percent of the world's $1.63 trillion in military spending (Stockholm International Peace Research Institute 2011) and devoted nearly 60 percent of its federal discretionary budget to military spending (Figure 16.7).

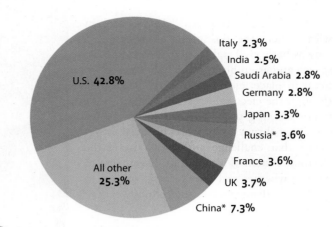

FIGURE 16.6 | GLOBAL MILITARY SPENDING, 2010

The United States spends as much on its military as almost all other countries combined spend on theirs. *Source:* Stockholm International Peace Research Institute [SIPRI] (2011).

* = SIPRI estimate.

Much of the United States' military spending is devoted to projecting power worldwide. In addition to military sites in all fifty states, the U.S. Department of Defense (2009) counts 121 sites in seven U.S. territories, and 737 sites in thirty-eight foreign countries, including Germany (235), Japan (123), and South Korea (87) (see Map 16.2). No other country comes close to maintaining this type of global military presence. What's more, the U.S. military owns so much property—more than 539,000 buildings and other structures on almost 30 million acres of land across the globe—that it may be the largest property owner on the planet (U.S. Department of Defense 2009).

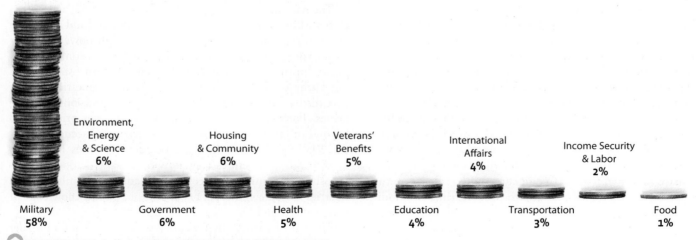

FIGURE 16.7 | U.S. DISCRETIONARY SPENDING, 2011

Most U.S. discretionary spending is used on the military, far surpassing the amount spent on education, the environment, and public welfare. Discretionary spending is the portion of the federal budget that must be allocated each year. It does not include dedicated trust funds, such as Social Security and Medicare, which are paid largely from payroll taxes, not income taxes. *Source:* National Priorities Project (2010).

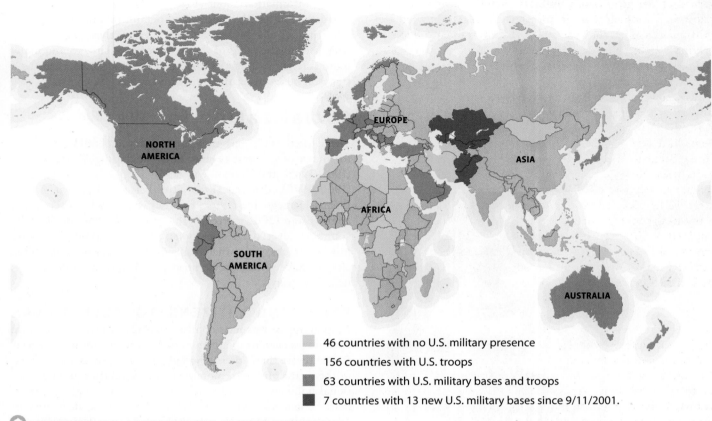

	46 countries with no U.S. military presence
	156 countries with U.S. troops
	63 countries with U.S. military bases and troops
	7 countries with 13 new U.S. military bases since 9/11/2001.

⌂ MAP 16.2 | U.S. ARMED FORCES AROUND THE WORLD
The U.S. has, by far, the greatest global military presence of any country. *Source:* U.S. Department of Defense (2009).

The Politics of Fear and Civil Liberties

Ironically, massive U.S. military spending intended to promote security has long been accompanied by a deep sense of fear and insecurity among many citizens. The postwar arms race between the United States and the former Soviet Union raised concern that nuclear annihilation could occur at any moment and that communism threatened U.S. democratic freedoms. With the collapse of the Soviet Union in 1991 and the 2001 attacks on 9/11, terrorists have replaced communists as the perceived threat to security.

Echoing some of the "spiral of silence" analysis, Altheide (2006) argues that a "politics of fear" characterizes contemporary life. People are often afraid to disagree publicly with authorities' views and policies. Instead they remain silent to avoid being labeled naïve, foolish, or unpatriotic. Altheide suggests that news coverage defining the world as dangerous and unpredictable intensifies this politics of fear.

News and the Politics of Fear

Fear can lead people to take actions that they otherwise would not consider, including accepting policies that threaten civil liberties and jeopardize basic democratic principles in the name of security. As we saw in Chapter 10, thousands of Asian Americans were sent to internment camps during World War II. During the Cold War, the FBI monitored the peaceful political activities of citizens; schools and other institutions demanded "loyalty oaths" as a condition of employment (some of which

"WE'LL BE BACK, AFTER THIS COMMERCIAL BREAK, WITH MORE REASONS WHY IT'S NOT SAFE TO LEAVE YOUR HOUSE."

War and the Military

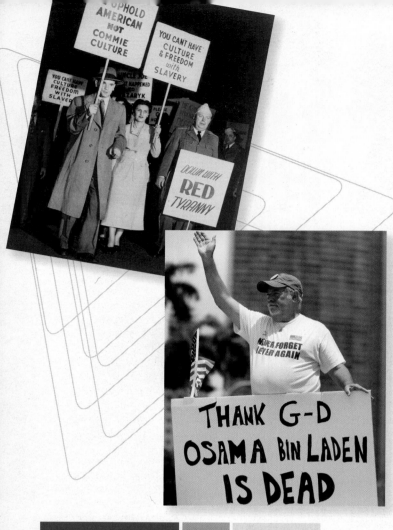

POLITICS AND CHANGE

Despite unrivaled spending on the military, U.S. citizens have long been plagued by a sense of fear and insecurity. In the 1950s and 1960s, fear of communism led to military action abroad and a clampdown on political freedom at home. In the 2000s, terrorism became the reason for wars abroad and surveillance at home.

lecting information about citizens' phone calls, e-mail, financial data, and health records; and detaining immigrants without criminal charges. In just a few years, these policies have been used against tens of thousands of U.S. citizens and many more foreign visitors. So far, most have accepted them as a trade-off between security and liberty.

Socialization for War

The United States has engaged in wars and military actions for much of the past seventy years, including World War II (1941–1945), the Korean War (1951–1953), the Vietnam War (1960–1975), Panama (1989), the Persian Gulf war (1991), Bosnia-Herzegovina (1999), the Iraq war (2003–current), and Afghanistan (2001–current). This partial list does not include countless covert CIA operations, smaller bombing runs and missile attacks, and other displays of military strength. U.S. citizens have grown accustomed to living in a nation that is usually at war.

PREPARING CITIZENS TO ACCEPT WAR

Responding to this near-continuous engagement, U.S. culture encourages citizens to affirm their support for military actions and to revere the soldiers who fight them. Soldiers are honored in the media and with monuments, memorials, museums, national holidays, and countless "Support our troops" car magnets. School textbooks often mark the progress of history in relationship to the start or end of a war. Socialization for war encourages citizens to accept, even actively support, military action. In many European nations, in contrast, after the devastations of two world wars fought partially on European soil, military values have much less appeal (Sheehan 2008). (For efforts to promote a culture of peace, see the Sociology Matters box.)

TRAINING CITIZENS TO FIGHT   Citizens may be socialized to support wars, but soldiers must learn how to fight them, typically beginning with "basic training" or "boot camp." In addition to developing physical fitness, intensive basic training resocializes young people to behave in ways that contradict much of what they have already learned (Dyer 2004). Raised in a culture that emphasizes freedom and individuality, recruits must learn to obey their commanding officers, follow orders unquestioningly, work as part of a unit, suppress their emotions, and kill as a normal job requirement.

To achieve this transformation, recruits, usually young, are taken away from mainstream society and kept in relative isolation for a number of weeks. Their individual identity is stripped away through the use of standardized close-cropped haircuts, identical clothing and gear, and collective barracks with no privacy. The recruits are then subjected to just enough physical and mental stress to wear them down, while—in the

are still required today); and a congressional committee—the House Un-American Activities Committee—questioned public figures about their political views and loyalty. Many of these activities are now recognized as misguided efforts that undermined basic civil liberties.

But the 2001 USA Patriot Act, adopted after 9/11, included a range of new government policies meant to fight terrorism, including wiretapping phone lines without a warrant; col-

thinking about culture

Have you or someone you know experienced basic training? What did the experience suggest about the differences between civilian and military culture?

Peace Studies

If peace is widely valued, then why do we so rarely study how to achieve and maintain it? That question animates peace studies, a multidisciplinary field that was founded with the significant input and insight of sociologists. In its various forms, peace studies seeks alternatives to violence and promotes conflict resolution and social justice. These efforts include many campus-based programs, collaborations between activists and academics through professional associations such as the Peace and Justice Studies Association in the United States and the International Peace Research Association, and real-world implementation of the ideas developed in peace studies through the United Nations and nongovernmental organizations.

Perhaps the best known founder of peace studies is Norwegian sociologist Johan Galtung, who has spent more than fifty years studying, teaching about, and promoting peace, becoming an internationally known advocate of innovative methods of nonviolent conflict resolution. Galtung helped to create the International Peace Research Institute in Oslo in 1959 and later started the *Journal of Peace Research,* which became an arena for an ongoing global conversation about the causes of war and violence, strategies of peace-building and nonviolence, and approaches to peace education.

Galtung's (1996, 2000) work reflects a sociological orientation to peace and conflict, incorporating a structural analysis of violence, considering the forms of inequality that often underlie war, and highlighting the capacity of human action to create a more just society. His work has included an emphasis on the importance of building a culture of peace, in which primary agents of socialization—parents, schools, media—promote values, attitudes, and behaviors that emphasize nonviolence, human rights, and social justice. Instructors in peace studies courses often teach military personnel and tackle these cultural issues, recognizing and respecting military experience, but questioning the idea of "defense" and assumptions that violence is the inevitable focus of defense policies (Page 2007).

For Galtung, violence is more than just acts of physical brutality; it includes what he calls "structural violence," the underlying social conditions of inequality and injustice that prevent people from achieving their full potential and that often lead to direct physical violence. Likewise, peace is more than just the absence of overt conflict (what he dubs "negative peace"); it is the existence of social justice ("positive peace").

Galtung's work, like that of many other peace researchers, extends beyond the university. He has been involved in over 120 mediations in dozens of countries, including Afghanistan, Colombia, Israel and the Palestinian Territories, Kashmir, Korea, Northern Ireland, Rwanda, and Sri Lanka, often with positive results. For example, his mediation was central to the resolution of a border conflict between Peru and Ecuador that had led to war three times previously. He has worked as a consultant to the United Nations on a wide range of peace-building and peacekeeping projects, and he even wrote the training manual *Conflict Transformation by Peaceful Means* for the UN Disaster Management Training Programme (Galtung 2000). Since 1993, Galtung has been director of TRANSCEND, a network of like-minded colleagues from more than eighty countries who work with him to mediate conflict and provide training in conflict resolution, nonviolence, and reconciliation (transcend.org).

In a recent book, dedicated "to a country I love, the United States of America," Galtung (2009) argues that the United States as a global power (what he calls the U.S. Empire), is unraveling, like other empires before it, as its reliance on the military to achieve economic and political ends proves increasingly economically burdensome and politically ineffective. But Galtung sees this as an opportunity for the United States as a nation (what he calls the U.S. Republic) to blossom, relieved from the burdens of empire.

think about it

1. *How might our culture give greater priority to promoting peace?*
2. *Do you agree with Galtung that the United States has an opportunity to blossom by refocusing from projecting power abroad toward caring for domestic needs? Why or why not?*

U.S. services—enabling about 90 percent to successfully complete basic training.

Adopting military culture can come at a cost, though. The traumatic events soldiers sometimes experience in combat, combined with the ongoing stress caused by lengthy deployments and separation from family, create enormous strains for many, resulting in mental health issues and suicides. The military lifestyle also tends to create distinct new identities for soldiers, some of whom find it difficult to reintegrate into civilian life after their service is over; substance abuse, posttraumatic stress disorders, and other psychological difficulties are persistent problems for some (Alvarez 2009b).

Social Inequality and the Military

The military is a social institution with its own traditions, values, norms and organizational structure (Siebold 2001). But it is also influenced by issues found in broader society, including social inequality.

RACE, GENDER, AND SEXUAL ORIENTATION IN THE MILITARY

The clash between the ideal of fighting for freedom and the reality of inequality in the United States has always been especially stark in the military. African American soldiers, for example, fought overseas in World War II against the ideology of racial supremacy in Nazi Germany, only to return home to racial segregation in the United States. Like other social institutions at the time, the military was a bastion of racist behaviors and policies. But the military is a unique institution in that authority within it is intensely enforced from the top down, and, as a consequence, it is able to introduce and enforce new ideas and behaviors.

In 1948—long before the peak of the civil rights movement—President Truman issued an executive order to begin a swift process of racial integration in the military. Since then, the military has often taken the lead in promoting progressive racial policies, making it a particularly attractive career choice for African Americans, Latinos, and other minorities who face continuing discrimination in civilian employment.

Women and gays and lesbians have had a more mixed experience. The military first excluded women and then grudgingly allowed them entry to an often hostile "macho" environment in which sexism and sexual violence remain major concerns to this day. The pressure to avoid being either too feminine (defined as soft and unprepared for military life) or too masculine (therefore not womanly) makes the military a site of ongoing negotiation for women (Herbert 2000).

The military has lagged behind changes in the broader society in its treatment of lesbian and gay soldiers. The military banned gays and lesbians until 1993, when it adopted a "don't ask, don't tell" policy that allowed them to serve as long as they kept their sexual orientation a secret. Studies in Canada (which changed its policy in 1992), Israel (1993), and Great Britain (2000) found that, contrary to some military leaders' beliefs, the inclusion of gay and lesbian soldiers does not undermine morale or degrade military performance (Belkin and Evans 2000; Belkin and Levitt 2001; Belkin and McNichol 2000). The "don't ask, don't tell" policy was repealed in 2010, and gays and lesbians may now serve openly.

CLASS AND MILITARY SERVICE

Class distinctions have long marked military service in the United States. The nation's first national mandatory service (known as *conscription* or *the draft*) was instituted—and fiercely resisted—during the Civil War when both North and South allowed wealthy citizens to avoid service by hiring substitutes. In World War I substitutes were not allowed, but biased local draft boards sent a disproportionate number of poor and working-class people to war (Keith 2003). In World War II a more equitable lottery system was used, but during Vietnam class bias returned in the form of exemptions for college students, who were disproportionately middle and upper class. In 1973 the U.S. government ended required military service and instituted an all-volunteer force (Janowitz and Moskos 1979).

The military does not keep data on the family income of its recruits, but some studies suggest that the all-volunteer military draws disproportionately from working-class and lower-middle-class families; the poor (who often cannot meet the entry requirements), the upper middle class, and especially the wealthy are underrepresented (National Priorities Project 2009). To attract recruits who have limited job prospects and cannot afford a college education, the military highlights its education and training programs. Recruitment is considerably easier in periods of economic recession (Alvarez 2009a). Thus class inequality continues to mark the all-volunteer force.

In its recruitment of labor, the military has also adopted a strategy from the civilian sector: outsourcing. Civilian employees of private companies are taking on an increasingly prominent role in military affairs. In 2007, for example, approximately 160,000 U.S. soldiers were in Iraq—but so were more than 180,000 civilian contractors (Miller 2007). Contractors in Iraq and Afghanistan carried out a variety of jobs, including building roads and training new Iraqi military and police forces. They were also hired to interrogate prisoners, linking them to cases of alleged torture and abuse of those prisoners, and to serve as "private security forces," protecting military installations, guarding prominent individuals, and escorting supply convoys. These contractors had immunity from Iraqi laws even when, as in one case, the Iraqi government accused a private security convoy of "deliberate murder" (Glanz and Rubin 2007). Such incidents produced considerable hostility from locals toward what were sometimes seen as mercenary troops-for-hire. Trouble continued once contractors returned home, because they were not eligible for the benefits or medical care that regular soldiers receive. As one injured contractor put it, "It's almost like we're this invisible, discardable military" (ProPublica 2010).

An all-volunteer military provides employment opportunities, especially for working-class and lower-middle-class people who have fewer options. Given this economic bias, do you think an all-volunteer system is fair?

Some sociologists have argued that the shift to an all-volunteer military has changed military service gradually from a widely shared experience to a specialized occupation isolated from civilian society (Siebold 2001). The reliance on a small "soldier class" to carry out military duties has also had political consequences. It makes troops less likely to actively oppose a war (as draftees during the Vietnam War commonly did) and, by eliminating the risk of being drafted, may reduce civilian opposition to wars. Perhaps most important, if children of the more affluent and powerful are not a major component of the military, government officials may be less hesitant to put troops in harm's way.

Terrorism as a Political Strategy

Today, the most widely discussed threat facing the military is terrorism. There is no universally accepted definition of terrorism, in part because it encompasses a wide range of activities, organizations, circumstances, and beliefs (Tilly 2004b).

The U.S. government, for instance, defines terrorism as "politically motivated violence perpetrated against noncombatant targets by subnational groups or clandestine agents" (Perl 2006, 5). Thus it reserves the *terrorism* label for political acts (not the random violence of a psychopath, for example) that direct violence at civilian (noncombatant) targets. But the government definition makes the highly contested claim that only "subnational groups" can be terrorists; governments cannot.

In reality, however, many governments throughout history—from the Soviet government under Joseph Stalin to Saddam Hussein's regime in Iraq—have used political violence against civilians at home and abroad. Even the United States has targeted civilian populations. For example, in World War II it tried to break the enemy's will to fight by targeting civilians in Germany (by firebombing cities) and in Japan (by dropping atomic bombs on two major cities). Indeed, political violence was first described as "terror" during the French Revolution (1789–1799), when the revolutionary government executed thousands of French civilians, often by guillotine, in what became known as the "reign of terror." **State terrorism,** then, is *political violence directed at civilians by governments.*

Sociologist Austin Turk (2004, 273) usefully defines terrorism as "the deliberate targeting of more or less randomly selected victims whose deaths and injuries are expected to weaken the opponent's will to persist in a political conflict." Combining this with the U.S. government's definition, we can say **terrorism** is *politically motivated violence that intentionally targets noncombatants.*

Labels are important. When we identify an act of violence as terrorism, we are providing a powerful interpretation of it. We typically apply the label *terrorist* to groups we oppose, while we fail to see that our allies and our own government have used strategies that could be labeled as terrorism.

Terrorism is neither new nor rare, but the technology available to inflict terrorist violence is now more readily available to more disparate parties. As a consequence, even the overwhelming conventional military might of the world's only superpower cannot guarantee the safety of its citizens. In this new era, conflict is likely to require diplomatic and political solutions, rather than just military ones.

While governments are clearly concerned about their citizens' physical security, they must help ensure their economic security, as well. We turn now to a consideration of the economy as a social institution and to the government's influence on economic life.

The Economy

We have already considered topics related to the economy, such as class inequality (Chapter 9), the world of work (Chapter 13), consumerism (Chapter 14), and the connection between types of communities and the economy (Chapter 15). Here we focus on the social nature of the economy and the role of government in relation to economic affairs.

The Economy as an Evolving Social Institution

The **economy** is *a social institution that includes a society's production, distribution, and consumption of goods and services.* Like other aspects of social life, economies are neither "natural" nor inevitable; they are created through human action and vary considerably over time and across cultures.

Because they are socially constructed, there are many types of economies. In Chapter 15, we traced the evolution of economies from those based on hunting and gathering to today's information-based economies. As the name suggests, *hunter-gatherer* societies obtained food and other materials by hunting animals and gathering seeds, roots, fruits, and other foodstuffs. Often these were collective efforts in which nearly the entire community took part, sharing resources and serving as a single economic unit. This arrangement was an economy, though it lacked many of the elements we associate with today's wage-based economies, such as markets, buyers, sellers, and wages. When a hunter's kill was divided among community members, or when coastal dwellers exchanged some of their fish catch for the skins of animals taken by hunters living inland, these transactions had as much to do with establishing and affirming social bonds as they did with gaining access to goods (Polyani 1977).

Later, when plants and livestock became domesticated, paving the way for agricultural and pastoral economies, the family became the primary economic unit. Family members, including children, typically worked together on land they owned, shared, or sharecropped for landowners to produce food and other goods for use, trade, or sale. The family was the center of both work and consumption, in a model that still dominates in many parts of the world today.

When industrialization expanded in the nineteenth century, economic life became increasingly separated—culturally and physically—from other aspects of social life. People left their homes and families to earn wages in workplaces where social relationships were not tied to family or personal links.

Home was now associated with consumption, and work with production.

Modern economies came increasingly to rely on the **corporation,** *a business that is treated legally as an entity separate from its owners.* Corporations have many of the rights of individuals—including the right to make contracts, incur debt, and engage in political speech—but their owners are not responsible for the corporation's obligations and liabilities and so corporations are able to take more risks. This has enabled corporations to grow substantially. Today, many are huge *multinational* (or *transnational) corporations* with facilities spread across the globe, rather than being in just one country.

The Social Economy

Regardless of the type of economy, politics and culture affect economic life just as economic conditions influence politics and culture (Holton 1992). Economic activities are inherently *social* activities requiring interaction, cooperation, coordination, and exchanges among individuals, organizations, and even governments. Max Weber (1949/2011) coined the term *social economics* to emphasize this connection between social and economic life, a connection we can view in relation to social cohesion, to culture, and to other social institutions.

ECONOMIES AND SOCIAL COHESION First, economic life is social because economic relationships can take place only with a level of trust. As we saw in Chapter 1, Durkheim argued that social cohesion is necessary for the maintenance of a well-functioning society, and this applies to economic life. Economic agreements—to purchase something, to provide a service, to pay for labor—will succeed only if the parties can trust each other to follow through. That is, a *social* relationship must exist prior to the economic relationship. Generalized trust—sometimes called *precontractual solidarity*—assures us that obligations will be honored and disputes resolved to allow economic life to proceed smoothly. Thus when social relationships collapse, as in war and civil unrest, economies often collapse, as well.

ECONOMIES AND CULTURE A second reason economic life is social is that economies are embedded within and reflect the cultural values of a society (Granovetter 1985). For example, our society discourages the marketing of crack cocaine and child pornography, even though they are often profitable ventures, because cultural values outweigh the opportunity for economic gain. Different cultures also value different features of economic life. In recent years, the United States has emphasized "free trade" and "free market" principles that encourage the relative autonomy of the economic sphere and a highly individualistic competitive economy. Other societies focus more on freedom from want, directing the economy toward meeting collective human needs such as more equal access to good schools, housing, and health care. In either case, economic priorities and policies are being filtered through broader cultural values. (A sociologist whose work focuses on freedom from want is featured in the Sociology Works box.)

ECONOMIES AND OTHER SOCIAL INSTITUTIONS A third reason economic life is social is that the economy is intertwined with other social institutions. We saw in Chapter 13 how education and work are often closely connected. Another especially important relationship exists between the government and the economy.

Here is a simple example. Imagine you and some friends start a small business making accessories for cell phones and MP3 players. Being independent-minded entrepreneurs, you want to run your business your own way, without government interference. However, ironically, the very existence of your business and its success depend on government intervention and assistance at every step of the way:

- The government produces deeds and titles certifying the ownership of your building and the land it is on. (If you rent, your lease agreement complies with government regulations protecting both landlord and tenant.)
- A police force monitors and enforces your property rights, and firefighters help lower your risk of loss due to fire.
- A legal system provides a mechanism (courts) for settling disputes and enforcing your contracts.
- The government issues and enforces trademark protection for your company's name and logo. Copyright law protects some of the designs you use on your merchandise, and patents protect your innovative products.
- Public utilities commissions manage access to rights-of-way for power lines, water pipes, and fiber optic cables through public spaces, making available the power you purchase from the electric company and other services.
- A government-financed system of roads and airports enables you to ship products anywhere.
- Government-issued currency enables you to carry out your business.

Because all contemporary economies depend on government intervention of one sort or another, the real question isn't *whether* the government will be involved in the economy but rather *how* and *to what extent*. Different societies answer these questions in ways that result in different economic systems.

Major Economic Systems

Capitalism and socialism have been the modern world's two dominant economic systems. Here we take a basic look at the idealized theory behind each system (see Table 16.2 on page 456 for a summary); then, following this section, we consider the more complex economic conditions that exist in the real world.

SOCIOLOGY WORKS

Mark Nord and Food Security

Mark Nord

As an undergraduate, Mark Nord studied electronics and aviation, topics far removed from sociology. But after being a bush pilot in Indonesia and Central America, where he observed the impact of technology on local cultures and people, he went to graduate school to study rural sociology. Nord brought his new training to the U.S. Department of Agriculture (USDA), where he and his colleagues study the degree to which households have consistent access to adequate food, the economic and social condition scholars describe as food security. The USDA defines *food insecurity* as "limited or uncertain availability of nutritionally adequate and safe foods or limited or uncertain ability to acquire acceptable foods in socially acceptable ways." Each year, working with data from the Census Bureau, Nord and his colleagues analyze the results of a national survey of about 50,000 households that asks a range of questions on household access to food and spending on food. Their analysis appears as an annual report, "Household Food Security in the United States." Nord and his colleagues found that, in 2009, 14.7 percent of U.S. households (17.4 million) experienced food insecurity (Nord et al. 2010).

Nord's work serves as a helpful tool for the development of social policy aimed at combating food insecurity. Nord once learned that a congressional committee working on a bill related to nutrition programs cited his new data just a few hours after they were released. As he says, "It makes a researcher want to be really sure that the numbers are right and that their meaning is correctly explained and understood!"

Although his focus is food security, Nord sees the applicability of sociology everywhere. "The sociological insight—that reality is, to a large extent, socially created—has proved useful for

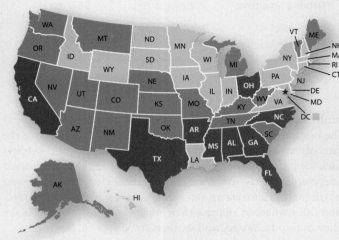

- ☐ Food insecurity below U.S. average
- ■ Food insecurity near U.S. average
- ■ Food insecurity above U.S. average

MAP 16.3 | FOOD INSECURITY IN THE UNITED STATES, 2008–2010

Source: U.S. Department of Agriculture Economic Research Service (2011).

"Watch. Listen," he advises. "You will see reality being created right before your eyes."

understanding human interactions ranging from family get-togethers to policy debates in the halls of Congress."

think about it

1. *Have you or has anyone you know experienced food insecurity?*

2. *How is food insecurity related to economic security?*

Capitalism in Theory

Capitalism is *an economic system that emphasizes private ownership of the means of production, which are operated for profit.* Under capitalism, businesses and industries that produce and sell goods and services are owned privately, either directly or indirectly (through stock ownership). These businesses seek to generate profit for their owners by selling goods and services at

a price higher than the cost of producing them. Profits are the incentive for companies to be innovative and efficient. By providing a product or service many consumers want and keeping costs as low as possible, owners can maximize their profit. The profit incentive drives the capitalist system; profit is the yardstick by which success is measured.

Capitalism relies on competitive markets to operate successfully. Ideally, informed consumers get to choose between

TABLE 16.2 IDEAL CHARACTERISTICS OF MAJOR ECONOMIC SYSTEMS

	Capitalism	Socialism
Major means of production	Owned privately	Owned publicly
Driving incentive	Personal profit	Public good
Economic structure	Markets	Government planning

communism, but no modern economies have been truly communist. Politically, communism is a system associated with Russian revolutionary Vladimir Lenin, in which an elite political party supposedly leads the nation toward an egalitarian (thus communist) future. The Soviet Union and China were communist societies in the political sense—led by a communist party—but not in the economic sense—a classless society with collective ownership of the means of production.

The reality of capitalism and socialism is more complicated than the simple economic theories we have just outlined. Neither system has worked in the way economic theory suggests, in part because economies are affected by broad social forces, especially inequalities in power.

Capitalism in Reality

Capitalism has proven very successful at unleashing productivity and innovation. A competitive marketplace motivates producers to search constantly for new goods and services to offer consumers, promoting innovation and reacting quickly to new market conditions and needs. Pursuing higher profits by lowering costs motivates producers to look constantly for ways to be more efficient and productive.

"Free-market" capitalist theory argues that governments should ensure the conditions necessary for businesses to operate and then leave them free to function as they see fit (which is why it is also called *laissez-faire* capitalism (*laissez-faire* is French for "leave alone"). Free-market adherents often oppose labor, environmental, and consumer protections, all of which add to the cost of doing business.

Nineteenth-century industrial capitalism is probably the closest we have come to a fully free-market system, and in many ways it was a disaster. One problem is that without government intervention and regulation, unfettered capitalism tends to produce a concentration of enormous wealth and power in the hands of a small elite who can then use that power to prevent others from competing fairly, thus undermining the very premise of a capitalist system. Shrewd late-nineteenth-century U.S. industrialists—"captains of industry" to their admirers— became more commonly known as "robber barons" for their unscrupulous business behavior. They used their early success to build "trusts," powerful companies that unfairly forced out competitors and monopolized key industries, including railroads (Cornelius Vanderbilt), steel making (Andrew Carnegie), and oil (John D. Rockefeller). These industrialists then used their resources to help undermine democracy by financing political campaigns and improperly influencing government decision-making. As a result, government provided them with special favors and enormous giveaways of public resources such as vast tracts of land for building commercial railroads.

While producing great wealth for a few in a period during the late nineteenth century known as the Gilded Age, this system also produced enormous hardship and poverty for many. Powerful industrialists often subjected their workers to grueling working conditions, including twelve-hour workdays, six days a week, for poverty wages. Exhaustion coupled with inadequate safety equipment often made work deadly. Steel mill workers were sometimes roasted alive in spills of molten

multiple providers who compete to offer the best product at the best price. Collectively, these purchasing choices decide the fate of various products and businesses. Meanwhile, workers look for jobs that offer the best wages, benefits, and conditions, and employers try to attract the talent they need at the lowest possible cost. The system as a whole emphasizes individual freedom: of owners to operate their business, consumers to make choices in purchasing, and workers to choose employment.

Socialism in Theory

Socialism is *an economic system that emphasizes public ownership of the major means of production, which are operated to meet human needs and promote social justice.* Major industries— energy production, communications, banking, health care, and the like—are publicly owned through the government. (Smaller businesses providing retail consumer goods and services may be privately owned.) Ideally, instead of focusing on generating profits for owners, these state-owned industries meet basic human needs by making essential goods and services available to all citizens. Free or subsidized public goods and services can include health care, education, housing, day care, public transportation, and other essentials. These are paid for, in part, through a system of progressive taxation (which taxes higher incomes at a higher rate), thereby limiting economic inequality.

A socialist system relies on government to coordinate key economic functions. Since they are nonprofit and able to eliminate the wasteful costs of marketplace competition (advertising, duplication of services and administrative bureaucracy, excessive executive salaries, and so on), well-functioning socialist governments can help to meet basic needs efficiently. Because they make major economic decisions in the name of the public good to promote social justice, they can take into account the collective benefits of labor rights and environmental protection, for example, rather than just their costs for individual private firms. The system as a whole emphasizes the collective good by directing resources to meet basic human needs.

Often confused with socialism, *communism* can refer to both an economic and a political system. Economically, communism is an egalitarian system in which property is owned collectively and class inequality is nonexistent. Some simple hunter-gatherer societies can be considered a form of primitive metal. Workers—sometimes children—were decapitated or had limbs torn from their bodies by rapidly moving machinery. Early reformers documented thousands of such cases (MacLaury 2011). Meanwhile, the advantages of early industrial activity were passed from generation to generation, fueling a cycle of inequality. To this day, the names Vanderbilt, Carnegie, and Rockefeller are icons of inherited wealth and power.

A variety of social movements of the late 1800s and early 1900s pressed for more government intervention in the economy. In the United States, these included the early labor movement, the Populist Movement (which included farmers and small business owners oppressed by the large business trusts), and the Progressive Movement (which advocated various economic, political, and social reforms, including workplace safety). These movements pressured federal and state governments to introduce reforms, including outlawing anticompetitive monopolies and cartels, setting wage and safety standards, and protecting the right of workers to form unions. Eventually, government intervention limited the power of industrialists, protected the basic rights of workers, and, many historians argue, helped save capitalism from itself.

Reforming Capitalism

Governments around the world have repeatedly intervened since then to address the excesses of capitalism and to shore up unstable capitalist economies subject to cycles of "boom and bust," or rapid growth followed by collapse. The second period of major government intervention in the United States took place in the wake of the Great Depression of the 1930s. A variety of causes contributed to this worst economic depression, or deep economic slump, of the twentieth century, including the 1929 stock market crash that followed a boom in speculation (high-risk investment in stocks or other ventures in the pursuit of high profits). Other factors were the collapse of thousands of U.S. banks that cost millions of workers their savings, and high levels of economic inequality that helped undermine the economy.

Elected in 1932 following this calamity, President Franklin Roosevelt responded not by implementing socialism in the form of a government takeover of banks and major industry. The New Deal policies he introduced in 1933 were instead intended to revive the economy and help stabilize capitalism. Though business leaders opposed many of his reforms, they were extremely popular and included the following:

■ New spending for public works programs that created jobs by building roads, dams, and national parks. (Later, massive military spending for World War II created even more jobs and an endless demand for military supplies.)

■ New social programs, notably Social Security, that helped create a social safety net to protect modest- and low-income workers from economic setbacks.

■ New government regulation and intervention in the financial system, such as the creation of the Federal Deposit Insurance Corporation (FDIC) that insures bank deposits.

■ New worker protections through the Wagner Act, which recognized the right to form unions in the workplace and to strike for better wages and working conditions.

These reforms became a central feature of the U.S. economic system during the period of post–World War II prosperity.

By the 1980s, though, the global economy had enabled large businesses to move production to foreign countries and flee government regulation, giving them greater leverage in negotiations with government. Employers aggressively opposed labor unions, undermining their political power. In this new climate, conservatives called for the deregulation of business, financial institutions, and the economy. In the 1980s, deregulation of savings and loan institutions (S&Ls), which had been limited to providing savings accounts and mortgage loans, allowed them to operate more like banks, but without any of the regulations that governed banks. This deregulation contributed to a new financial crisis in which over 700 S&Ls failed, requiring government action to clean up the mess and stabilize the industry through new regulations. The S&L scandal costs taxpayers at least $125 billion dollars and led to some bank executives serving time in prison (Pizzo, Fricker, and Muolo 1989).

The Housing Bubble and Global Economic Crisis

The S&L crisis was small compared to the global financial meltdown, rooted in the housing industry, that occurred in 2007–2009 with effects that continue today (Das 2010; Financial Crisis Inquiry Commission 2011; Foster and Magdoff 2009; Friedman and Posner 2009; Glass 2008; Rajan 2010; Sorkin 2010; U.S. Senate Permanent Subcommittee on Investigations 2011). A closer look at this most recent crisis illustrates the economy as an integrated social system—from micro-level consumers to macro-level global investors—that can sometimes be dysfunctional.

SOURCES OF THE CRISIS The global economic crisis—sometimes referred to as the Great Recession—stemmed from several factors:

■ Facing stagnant wages, many ordinary U.S. households relied increasingly on credit. Meanwhile the world's richest investors searched for investments that would yield steady profits, eventually buying much of this consumer debt.

■ Deregulation in the financial services industry enabled commercial banks to engage in high-risk speculation, which had been prohibited before.

- The financial services industry developed new forms of complex and unregulated investment devices (known as *derivatives*) that led to massive high-risk speculation.
- Corporations engaged in misleading and fraudulent behavior. Some of the world's largest financial firms—including JP Morgan, Citibank, and Merrill Lynch—often had been caught laundering money, defrauding customers, and committing accounting fraud. In most such cases, the firms agreed to pay large fines—sometimes well over $100 million dollars—but did not have to admit to any wrongdoing. But when fraudulent tactics were used in the housing market, the impact was much more widespread.

When these factors combined, the result was disastrous.

THE HOUSING BUBBLE AND BURST

A "bubble" occurs when the price of something is overinflated. The recent housing crisis involved social relationships between various parties in a chain that connected individual homeowners to global investors, linking micro-level economic decisions with macro-level economic forces:

- Homebuyers acquired cheap mortgages that often featured low rates in the early months that increased dramatically over the life of the loan. Some borrowers used poor judgment in entering these contracts; others were greedy and bought more expensive houses than they should have. Many, though, either did not understand the conditions of their mortgage or were defrauded by unscrupulous lenders who misled applicants and approved high-risk mortgages to clearly unqualified borrowers.
- Some lenders used deceptive or fraudulent sales tactics to entice borrowers into mortgages they could not afford. Lenders had an incentive to make as many loans as possible, regardless of people's ability to pay, because they sold these individual loans to investment banks that preferred risky subprime loans because they carried higher interest rates and, thus, the potential for more profits.
- Investment banks bought a large number of mortgages from lenders, combined these with other debt, such as student loans and credit card debt, and then sold pieces of this debt as a type of derivative called *collateralized debt obligations* (CDO). Major investment firms such as Goldman Sachs were selling CDOs to investors as a safe investment, while simultaneously betting that CDOs they didn't own would fail.
- Ratings agencies (Standard & Poor's, Moody's, Fitch)—paid by the investment banks—evaluated CDOs and

often gave them the highest possible grade, AAA, obscuring their actual high-risk nature.

- Investors from around the world in search of steady profits purchased CDOs, believing them to be safe investments, thereby generating massive profits for the investment banks that sold them.

In the short term, everyone in the chain benefitted. Homebuyers had a chance to experience the American Dream of homeownership. Lenders, rating agencies, investment banks, and investors made money. Wall Street executives and traders, especially, became enormously rich on bonuses they had generated from these often-tainted deals. For example, between 2000 and 2007, the CEO of the Lehman Brothers investment firm, Richard Fuld, took home about $529 million dollars (Sterngold 2010).

Since almost anyone could get a mortgage in this system, the housing market boomed, creating an artificial bubble in which housing prices nearly doubled in less than ten years. The FBI and some leading economists warned of massive and widespread mortgage fraud, but those warnings went unheeded and the government failed to step in to regulate the industry. In fact, many of the major government regulators and economic advisors were former finance industry executives. Henry Paulson, for example, was paid $35 million in 2005 as CEO of investment firm Goldman Sachs while it was issuing billions of dollars in high-risk CDOs, and in 2006 he was appointed secretary of the U.S. Treasury (Sloan 2007).

By 2007 the housing bubble had burst. Homebuyers could not keep up with mortgage payments and families lost their homes. Investment banks found themselves still holding tens of thousands of mortgages whose values were plummeting and that could not be sold. Investors began losing their money. The impact of these failures rippled through the economy as banks and the insurance companies that insured them teetered on the brink of bankruptcy. The stock market plunged, and everyone from major institutional investors to individuals with retirement accounts invested in stocks suffered major losses. Unemployment increased as firms facing financial trouble began laying off workers.

At the height of the crisis, the federal government responded with massive spending to bail out major commercial firms and stimulate the economy. As of this writing, though, the government has not prosecuted any of the corporate executives who helped destroy their companies, wreck the economy, and walk away with the fortunes they accumulated carrying out these actions. After the crisis, U.S. banks are bigger, more concentrated, and more powerful than

Long before the collapse of the housing market, investigators were examining the fraudulent business practices of some Wall Street investment firms. Without reform, some of these practices contributed to the global financial crisis.

ever before. They were able to use their political clout to successfully resist any significant reform of Wall Street.

Periodic crises lead many observers to conclude that capitalist markets seem to operate best when they are well regulated to prevent fraud and abuse by powerful economic players. Canada, for example, had much stronger regulation of its banking industry and largely avoided the economic crisis that affected the U.S. banking industry. In addition, capitalism seems to require a robust social safety net to assist those left behind in the competitive marketplace. Critics of these measures, however, see such developments as an abandonment of capitalist ideals and the encroachment of socialism.

Socialism in Reality

By prioritizing social needs over personal profit, a socialist economy can effectively reduce inequality and drastically reduce or even eliminate some social problems commonly found in capitalist economies, such as homelessness, lack of health care, and lack of affordable access to higher education (Lebowitz 2010). But as the most prominent experiment with socialism—the former Soviet Union—has illustrated, this system can also lead to disaster.

SOVIET-STYLE SOCIALISM Russia was an agricultural society, lagging far behind Western industrialized nations in economic development, when the Russian Revolution of 1917 ended its monarchy and eventually brought an authoritarian communist government into power. This government began a massive transformation of the economy that introduced gigantic industrialization campaigns, dramatically raised living standards, and catapulted the newly formed Soviet Union into a global superpower in a single generation. But, especially under the leadership of Joseph Stalin, the authoritarian government used its power to ruthlessly suppress political dissent, condemning those accused of anti-Soviet or anticommunist activity to remote penal labor camps (*gulags*), where prisoners often died or disappeared. These camps played a key economic function for the then-industrializing Soviet Union, which exploited the labor of millions of imprisoned criminals and political dissidents to work in mines, on infrastructure projects like roads and bridges, and on other development efforts.

By the 1960s, the economic role of the gulags had declined dramatically. However, the government's significant expenditures on a large military to compete with its Cold War adversary, the United States, worsened the bureaucratic inefficiencies of centralized economic planning right up to the country's formal dissolution in 1991. Economic inequality in the Soviet Union and the Soviet-dominated countries of Eastern Europe was very low by Western standards, but so too was the standard of living.

Under the leadership of Mikhail Gorbachev in the late 1980s, the Soviet Union sought to simultaneously reform its economic structure (*perestroika*) while introducing more democratic freedoms (*glasnost*). The changes proved too radical, and the Soviet Union disintegrated into separate nation-states.

Since the collapse of Soviet-style socialism, Russia and other Eastern European nations formerly under Soviet control have experienced widely divergent fates. With the privatization of public resources, capitalism has created enormous wealth and even some billionaires (sometimes due to rampant fraud and corruption). However, rising unemployment has pushed millions of other people into poverty and created a vast new set of social problems, including skyrocketing alcoholism and a resurgence of tuberculosis, a disease typically associated with poverty.

A basic problem with Soviet-style socialism was that it was administered by an authoritarian government with no accountability. Socialism coupled with democracy, however, has achieved greater success.

DEMOCRATIC SOCIALISM Whereas capitalism needs government intervention to curb the excesses of concentrated economic power, socialism needs a democratic political system to curb the excesses of concentrated government power. Scandinavian countries that feature both democratic political systems and socialist economies are among the most affluent and democratic countries in the world.

One example is Norway, a constitutional monarchy in which real power rests in a parliamentary system where a half-dozen major political parties regularly compete for power. In the three decades following World War II, the country developed a system that features state ownership of major industrial, financial, and communications firms and a major role for labor unions in deciding workplace issues. It also includes free universal health care, nearly free higher education, and a generous lifelong social welfare system that includes twelve months of paid leave for new parents. Combined, these programs make up about half the country's goods and services. Since the 1970s, Norway has maintained its programs in part because the government, rather than private corporations, controls its major oil and natural gas resources. But during this period it has decentralized control of its government assets, allowing local and regional authorities to adapt social and economic programs to their own particular needs. It has also introduced more market-based competition as it has become a significant participant in the global economy. While the global economic crises has caused much of the industrialized world to stagger, close regulation of its financial sector, large public-sector employment, astute management of natural resources, and a culture of financial thrift have largely insulated Norway from the worst effects.

The Rise of Mixed Economies

Our brief survey of economies shows that four ideal types of political-economic systems exist. They differ based on the degree of government intervention in the economy and the presence or absence of a democratic political system (see Table 16.3). We have already considered capitalist democracies, state socialism, and democratic socialism. The final form of political-economic system is authoritarian capitalism.

TABLE 16.3 — BASIC POLITICAL AND ECONOMIC SYSTEMS

Economic System	Political System: Democratic	Political System: Authoritarian
Capitalist	**Capitalist democracies** have democratic political systems and private ownership of industry with modest state intervention in the economy. Example: United States	**Authoritarian capitalism** is found in countries that have considerable private ownership of industry and market-based economies but few civil rights or political freedoms. Example: China
Socialist	**Democratic socialism** is found in countries that have democratic political systems, public ownership of some key industries, and significant state intervention in the economy. Example: Norway	**State socialism** involves an authoritarian government that dominates a largely centralized economy. Example: North Korea

China is an authoritarian capitalist system. Over the past several decades, China has allowed many aspects of market capitalism and encouraged foreign investment, though state-run enterprises still play a major role in the economy. However, China's leaders maintain strict political control by suppressing dissent, most famously during the 1989 uprisings in Beijing's Tiananmen Square, which unsuccessfully called for democratic reforms.

Today, the world's largest and most vibrant economies are all mixed economies to varying degrees, and the line between socialism and capitalism is becoming murkier every year. **Mixed economies** *contain elements of both market-based capitalism and the significant government intervention associated with socialism.* Successful socialist nations have learned to harness the power of markets to spur innovation and respond to consumer needs, while still directing key industries to meet social needs, guarding public resources for the common good, and providing a broad social safety net for citizens. Successful capitalist nations have learned that reasonable government regulation of business and markets can help protect against abuses of concentrated economic power, that a social safety net blunts the excesses of capitalist inequality, and that government intervention can help limit capitalism's characteristic boom-and-bust cycles.

Convergence theory *suggests that capitalist and socialist economies are becoming increasingly similar.* Globalization appears to have accelerated the process, introducing competitive markets to economies around the world and making them more capitalistic. Globalization has also made many capitalist economies more volatile and vulnerable to the pressures of competition from other nations. This is in large part the reason for the decline of manufacturing industries in the United States and the global financial crisis. Governments in capitalist economies have responded to such economic difficulties by intervening more actively in economic affairs, a tendency typically associated with socialist economies. The result has been the global rise of mixed economies.

In Transition

WHAT IS SECURITY?

As we saw in this chapter's opening vignette, military action abroad in the name of national security can seem inadequate when threats to economic security loom at home. A defeat in Vietnam, a protracted engagement in Iraq with mixed results, and the ongoing fighting in Afghanistan highlight the limits of both conventional military power and the traditional notion of security. While most discussion about "security" in the United States still focus on the military and "national security," the idea of what security is has been undergoing some changes.

"Economic security" is the most prominent alternative to "national security." **Economic security** is *the condition of having a stable means of financial support adequate to maintain a given standard of living.* Economic security can include access to good employment and assistance during times of sickness or disability. For example, the Social Security Act of 1935 aimed to provide government support for the elderly, the disabled, mothers and children, and the unemployed, as well as to promote public health. Although we typically think of Social Security as a benefit program for retired persons, the original act implied a government commitment to the general welfare. Other countries have an even stronger focus on economic security.

As the public has become more aware of the dangers of environmental degradation, concern has grown about **environmental security,** *the safe management of natural resources* to protect social stability. Policymakers worry that environmental problems such as drought, erosion, toxic waste, and air pollution could become a consistent source of conflict that might escalate into military confrontation. Environmental security also takes into account how threats to the natural environment may imperil the foundations of our society. The effects of climate change, for example, can threaten people's homes and their health, uproot communities, and compromise food supplies, endangering individual and collective security. Climate change will likely increase the number of short-term refugees, as people flee worsening natural disasters, and the scale of long-term migration, as people move to where water is more plentiful and crops can be grown more easily. With the world's attention focused more intensely than ever on environmental degradation and protection, the environmental dimensions of security are becoming ever clearer (Eddy 2004).

The United Nations has developed an even broader definition of security: **human security,** which *emphasizes the health and rights of individual human beings rather than the security of nations*. The UN Commission on Human Security, created in 2001, has worked both to clarify the concept of human security and to support projects that make a real contribution to advancing this cause. Instead of focusing exclusively on military threats, those who advance the human security concept define poverty and illiteracy, HIV and drug abuse, the displacement of populations into refugee camps, and the trafficking of women and children into forced prostitution as threats to the security and dignity of individuals and communities. The UN Commission on Human Security (2004) identifies two interrelated approaches to advancing human security: *protecting* people's basic rights and freedoms and *empowering* people to act on their own behalf.

The breadth of the human security concept makes it a challenge for advocates to define concrete goals and measure the success of human security projects (MacFarlane and Khong 2006). Still, by articulating a new nonmilitary vision of security, and connecting that to the ability of ordinary people to take control of their own lives, advocates of the human security concept have challenged governments—and all of us—to address many of the threats and indignities that people experience every day.

THINKING SOCIOLOGICALLY ABOUT . . .

Politics and the Economy

culture

- Cultural values help shape both political and economic systems.
- A broad sense of insecurity and a culture of fear help support a large investment in the military.
- Differing cultural approaches to individual freedom or social justice inform capitalist and socialist economies.

structure

- The political structure of a society shapes the possibilities for political action, creating specific constraints and opportunities for individuals and groups to engage in political action.
- Similarly, economic structures help shape the opportunities people have.

power

- Politics involves the exercise of power to decide priorities and policies for society.
- The type of government helps determine who has power in society.
- The decisions governments make can have a profound impact on levels of inequality, especially since the way in which economies are organized can either increase or decrease economic inequality.
- Socialist economies make reducing inequality a priority, whereas capitalist economies accept greater levels of inequality and prioritize the free pursuit of profit.

Looking Back

1. Politics is the arena in which societies make collective decisions about priorities and policies and government is the focus of political activity. Governments claim a monopoly on the legitimate use of force in a given territory. Contemporary forms of government include democracies, authoritarian governments, and monarchies. Political culture influences whether and how we become involved in politics.

2. Pluralism, power elite theory, and class domination theory each explain power and politics in a different way. Political involvement in the United States reflects class inequality: people in the middle class are more active than those in the working class, and the political system responds most readily to concerns of the affluent.

3. As part of the national security state, the size, reach, and financial resources of the U.S. military are unrivaled. But a politics of fear continues to shape how we think about the world, leading to policies that would otherwise be unlikely to be adopted. People are socialized to accept war, and recruits are resocialized to become soldiers. The military reflects some of the social inequality that exists in society. Terrorism, which is perhaps the biggest threat faced by today's military, has no universally accepted definition.

4. The economy is a social institution that includes a society's production, distribution, and consumption of goods and services. Economies reflect the cultural values and political priorities of the societies in which they exist.

5. Capitalism and socialism have been the modern world's two dominant economic systems. The ideals of both these systems contrast with complicated realities that expose each of their shortcomings, including the periodic crisis of capitalism and the repressive nature of state socialism. Capitalist and socialist economies have become more similar to each other, producing mixed economies that incorporate elements of each system.

6. As governments cope with providing security, new notions of security have emerged, including economic security, environmental security, and human security.

Critical Thinking: Questions and Activities

1. Do you feel prepared to participate in politics? Do you vote? How can you explain your specific engagement with—or disengagement from—the world of politics?

2. Why do you think the United States spends so much more on the military than any other country? Do you think this is a wise investment of resources for the country? Why or why not?

3. What are the basic differences between capitalist and socialist economies? Do you think the U.S. economic system is best described as capitalist, socialist, or mixed? Why?

4. What do you think is the best way to define security? What, if anything, should the government do to help achieve this security?

Key Terms

authoritarian government (p. 437) a government that typically features self-appointed leaders who exert great control over the lives of citizens, which includes severely limiting their civil liberties.

capitalism (p. 455) an economic system that emphasizes private ownership of the means of production, which are operated for profit.

class domination theory (p. 444) a theory that suggests that political power is concentrated in the hands of the rich, who own or control a large share of the nation's economic resources.

convergence theory (p. 460) a theory that suggests capitalist and socialist economies are becoming increasingly similar.

corporation (p. 454) a business that is treated legally as an entity separate from its owners.

democracy (p. 438) a political system in which the right to vote is widespread and government leaders are selected through multiparty elections.

economic security (p. 460) the condition of having a stable means of financial support adequate to maintain a given standard of living.

economy (p. 453) a social institution that includes a society's production, distribution, and consumption of goods and services.

environmental security (p. 460) the safe management of natural resources to protect social stability.

government (p. 437) the organization that exercises authority and steers decision making in a specific community.

human security (p. 461) concern for the health and rights of individual human beings rather than the security of nations.

mixed economies (p. 460) economies that combine elements of both market-based capitalism with the significant government intervention associated with socialism.

monarchy (p. 437) a system of government headed by a single person, the monarch, who typically inherits the position as a member of a ruling family.

national security state (p. 447) a government dominated by powerful military, foreign policy, and intelligence agencies.

pluralist theory (p. 443) a theory that argues that political power is fragmented among many different competing groups.

plurality voting (p. 439) a "winner-take-all" electoral system in which the candidate with the most votes wins the office being contested.

political socialization (p. 440) the inculcation of basic norms and expectations about political life and attitudes toward involvement in politics.

politics (p. 437) the arena in which societies make collective decisions about priorities and policies.

power (p. 437) the ability to bring about an intended outcome, even when opposed by others.

power elite theory (p. 443) a theory that suggests that political power is concentrated in the hands of a small dominant group of business, government, and military leaders.

proportional representation (p. 439) an electoral system in which parties are awarded seats in government based on the percentage of votes they receive in an election.

socialism (p. 456) an economic system that emphasizes public ownership of the major means of production, which are operated to meet human needs and promote social justice.

spiral of silence (p. 441) a theory that explains how people keep quiet about controversial issues when they think their opinions are not widely shared, in order to avoid social isolation.

state terrorism (p. 453) political violence directed at civilians by governments.

terrorism (p. 453) politically motivated violence that intentionally targets noncombatants.

war (p. 447) organized armed conflict among two or more specially trained military groups.

A

absolute poverty (p. 233) a scarcity of resources so severe that it is life-threatening.

achieved status (p. 90) a position in a social system that a person attains voluntarily, to a considerable degree, as the result of his or her own efforts.

action (p. 87) the ability to operate independent of social constraints.

active audiences (p. 383) audiences that make choices about how they use the media and actively interpret media content.

affective action (p. 99) behavior guided by emotions and feelings.

affirmative action (p. 273) a variety of policies and programs that aim to avoid discrimination and redress past discrimination through the active recruitment of qualified minorities for jobs, promotions, and educational opportunities.

agenda-setting theory (p. 385) a theory that holds that media may not be able to tell people what to think, but they can significantly influence what people think about.

agents of social control (p. 206) the authorities and social institutions that enforce norms and rules, attempt to prevent rule violations, and identify and punish rule violators.

agents of socialization (p. 137) people and groups who teach us about our culture.

alienation (p. 394) the separation and isolation of workers as a result of the structure of capitalist society.

amalgamation (p. 259) the process by which a majority and a minority group blend or mix to form a new group.

anomie (p. 14) social normlessness, without moral guidance or standards.

anticipatory socialization (p. 144) the process by which individuals practice for a future social role by adopting the norms or behaviors associated with a position they have not yet achieved.

applied research (p. 33) the primary goal of this type of research is to directly address some social problem or need.

ascribed status (p. 90) a position in a social system, assigned to a person from birth, regardless of his or her wishes.

asexual (p. 305) people who experience no sexual attraction for anyone.

assimilation (p. 259) the process by which members of a minority group come to adopt the culture of the majority group.

authoritarian government (p. 437) a government that typically features self-appointed leaders who exert great control over the lives of citizens, which includes severely limiting their civil liberties.

B

basic research (p. 33) the primary goal of this type of research is to describe some aspect of society and advance our understanding of it.

behavioral targeting (p. 400) advertising sent to online users based on their earlier Internet activities.

behaviors (p. 68) the actions associated with a group that help to reproduce a distinct way of life.

beliefs (p. 63) the specific convictions or opinions that a people generally accept as being true.

bilingual education (p. 360) instruction in both a student's first language and English.

biological determinism (p. 149) a theory that contends that biology, specifically our genetic makeup, almost completely shapes human behavior.

bisexual (p. 305) people who are attracted to others of both sexes.

breaching experiments (p. 91) controlled social situations that intentionally break social rules, violating basic norms and patterns of behavior.

built environment (p. 407) the physical surroundings that humans create, including the buildings, roads, dams, homes, and consumer products we use every day.

bureaucracy (p. 177) a hierarchical administrative system with formal rules and procedures used to manage organizations.

C

capital (p. 222) money to invest in factories, real estate, and other businesses.

capital punishment (p. 210) the death penalty.

capitalism (p. 455) an economic system that emphasizes private ownership of the means of production, which are operated for profit.

capitalist class (or **bourgeoisie**) (p. 222) those who control major capital and own the means of production.

caste system (p. 126) stratification based on various ascribed characteristics determined at birth.

charismatic authority (p. 120) power whose legitimacy is derived from the extraordinary personal characteristics of an individual leader, which inspire loyalty and devotion.

charter schools (p. 361) public schools run by an organization that is independent from local school districts.

church (p. 330) formal religious organization with broad mainstream acceptance.

civil religion (p. 337) a set of common beliefs and ritual practices that bind people in a predominantly secular society.

class (p. 123) a group of people who share a roughly similar economic position and lifestyle.

class mobility (p. 228) the ability to move from one social class to another.

class domination theory (p. 444) a theory that suggests that political power is concentrated in the hands of the rich, who own or control a large share of the nation's economic resources.

class system (p. 128) stratification determined by economic position, which results from a combination of individual achievement and family of birth.

classism (p. 232) prejudice or discrimination based on social class.

coerce (p. 114) to force people's compliance by threatening, intimidating, pressuring, or harming them.

cohabitation (p. 319) a social relationship that can create family ties and typically involves sexual intimacy, in which people live together as unmarried partners.

collective bargaining (p. 368) negotiations between union representatives and an employer on questions of pay, benefits, and working conditions.

collective conscience (p. 14) the shared norms, beliefs, and values in a community.

colonialism (p. 244) the use of military, political, and economic power by one society to dominate the people of another society, usually for economic benefit.

color-blind racism (p. 276) a form of bias in which the promotion of race neutrality helps to maintain existing racial and ethnic inequality.

commodification (p. 399) the process of transforming all things into a product to be bought and sold.

commodity fetishism (p. 394) consumers' failure to recognize the labor that created the value in the commodities they use.

community (p. 407) a set of social relationships, typically arising from living in a particular place, that give people a sense of identity and belonging.

community studies (p. 413) a field that typically looks at groups of people who share some common tie and engage in social interaction within a particular geographic area.

comparable worth (p. 365) a commitment to setting salaries for different job titles based on their value to an employer, regardless of the typical gender of those working in such jobs.

conflict theories (p. 19) social theories that focus on issues of contention, power, and inequality, highlighting the competition for scarce resources.

conspicuous consumption (p. 232) lavish spending, done to compete for status with others.

consumerism (p. 394) an emphasis on shopping and the possession of material goods as the route to personal happiness.

consumption (p. 392) the process of choosing, purchasing, and using goods.

content analysis (p. 44) a variety of techniques that enable researchers to systematically summarize and analyze the content of various forms of communication—written, spoken, or pictorial.

contextual analyses (p. 470) analyses that take into account the particular historical and social context within which change is occurring and do not assume that a single factor is the most important in all situations.

control theory (p. 206) a theory that suggests that our behavior is regulated by the strength of our connection to major social institutions, including family, school, and religion.

convention (p. 93) a practice or technique that is widely used in a particular social setting.

convergence (p. 386) the merging of different media forms.

convergence theory (p. 460) a theory that suggests capitalist and socialist economies are becoming increasingly similar.

conversation analysis (p. 92) a method of analyzing the patterns in face-to-face conversation that produce the smooth, back-and-forth turn-taking of such exchanges.

corporation (p. 454) a business that is treated legally as an entity separate from its owners.

correlation (p. 36) a relationship in which change in one variable is connected to change in another variable.

counterculture (p. 74) a subculture that champions values and lifestyles distinctly opposed to those of the dominant culture.

credentialing (p. 357) the process whereby those with advanced educational degrees and formal certificates monopolize access to the most rewarding jobs.

crime (p. 206) deviant behavior that violates a law.

crime rates (p. 207) statistics that measure the incidence of crime in relation to population size.

critical social science (p. 49) research carried out explicitly to create knowledge that can be used to bring about social change.

crude birth rate (p. 480) the number of live births per 1,000 people in a population.

crude death rate (p. 480) the number of deaths per 1,000 people in a population.

cult (p. 331) small religious communities whose beliefs and practices are at odds with the dominant culture.

cultivation theory (p. 385) a theory that argues that, by repeated and long-term exposure to the media's portrayal of the world (especially on television), people come to accept many of these depictions as reality.

cultural capital (p. 235) forms of knowledge, taste, preferences, and styles that high-status groups use to signal their status and to exclude others from their social circles.

cultural imperialism (p. 390) the tendency of media corporations from wealthier nations—especially the United States—to export so many of their media products that they come to dominate the local cultures of other, especially poorer, nations.

cultural lag (p. 65) the ways that new technological developments often outpace the norms that govern our collective experiences with these new technologies.

cultural object (p. 70) a physical item that is created by and associated with people who share a culture.

cultural relativism (p. 77) the practice of understanding a culture by its own standards.

culture (p. 21) the collection of values, beliefs, knowledge, norms, language, behaviors, and material objects shared by a people and socially transmitted from generation to generation.

culture shock (p. 64) the experience of being disoriented because of a lack of knowledge about an unfamiliar social situation.

culture war (p. 62) an intense disagreement about core values and moral positions.

D

decriminalization (p. 207) the process of making an illegal action legal.

deindustrialization (p. 247) the process by which investment in the nation's manufacturing capacity decreased.

democracy (p. 438) a political system in which the right to vote is widespread and government leaders are selected through multiparty elections.

demographic divide (p. 479) the inequality in population and health conditions between rich and poor countries.

demographic transition theory (p. 483) the view that a society's population patterns are influenced decisively by its level of affluence and its adoption of new technology.

demography (p. 478) the study of human population trends.

dependency theory (p. 244) a theory that attributes global inequality to the exploitation of weaker, poor nations by wealthy, more powerful ones.

dependent variable (p. 36) the entity that changes in response to the independent variable.

deviance (p. 191) behavior that does not conform to basic cultural norms and expectations.

deviant subculture (p. 198) a group in which membership is based on a shared commitment to specific nonconformist beliefs or behaviors.

dialect (p. 68) a variant of a language with its own distinctive accent, vocabulary, and in some cases grammatical characteristics.

differential association theory (p. 197) according to this theory, deviance is learned through interaction with other people involved in deviant behavior.

digital divide (p. 388) the gap between those who have the knowledge and resources needed to use digital information technology, especially computers and the Internet, and those who do not.

discrimination (p. 124) unequal treatment that gives advantages to one group of people over another without justifiable cause.

division of labor (p. 13) the way people specialize in different tasks, each requiring specific skills.

doing gender (p. 291) creating gender through interactions in particular social settings.

domestic violence (or **intimate partner violence**) (p. 301) a pattern of abusive behavior in any relationship that is used by one partner to gain or maintain power and control over another intimate partner.

dominant culture (p. 71) a culture that permeates a society and that represents the ideas and practices of those in positions of power.

dominant ideology (p. 70) a widely held and regularly reinforced set of assumptions that generally support the current social system and serve the interests of authorities.

dramaturgy (p. 170) an approach to the study of social interaction that uses the metaphor of social life as a theater.

dual product markets (p. 383) the situation that occurs when a company sells two completely different types of "products" to two completely different sets of buyers.

dysfunctional (p. 19) inhibiting or disrupting the working of a system as a whole.

E

economic security (p. 460) the condition of having a stable means of financial support adequate to maintain a given standard of living.

economy (p. 453) a social institution that includes a society's production, distribution, and consumption of goods and services.

education (p. 347) the social institution through which individuals acquire knowledge and skills and learn cultural norms and values.

emotional labor (p. 370) jobs that require employees to manage their feelings and to display specific feelings to their customers or clients.

empirical evidence (p. 36) data that can be observed or documented using the human senses.

empowerment (p. 111) an increase in the capacity of people to bring about an intended outcome.

endogamy (p. 319) legal restrictions or customs that limit marriage to people within the same social category.

environmental health (p. 429) the aspects of health, illness, and disease that result from environmental factors.

environmental justice (p. 424) the prevention of harmful practices that unfairly burden low-income people and racial minorities with disproportionate exposure to environmental hazards.

environmental security (p. 460) the safe management of natural resources to protect social stability.

environmental sociology (p. 421) the study of the interaction between social life and the natural environment.

equal opportunity (p. 234) the idea that all people should have the same chance to achieve success.

ethic of reciprocity (p. 331) the "golden rule" that encourages people to treat others as they would like to be treated.

ethnicity (p. 253) shared cultural heritage often deriving from a common ancestry and homeland.

ethnocentrism (p. 76) the practice of judging another culture by the standards of one's own.

ethnomethodology (p. 91) an approach that examines the methods people use to make sense of their daily activities, emphasizing the ways in which we collectively create social structure in our everyday activities.

exogamy (p. 319) marriage between people from different social categories.

experiment (p. 44) a data gathering technique in which the researcher manipulates an independent variable under controlled conditions to determine if change in an independent variable produces change in a dependent variable, thereby establishing a cause-and-effect relationship.

extended family (p. 319) nuclear family plus other relatives who commonly live together.

F

faith (p. 329) belief grounded in personal conviction or divine revelation rather than scientific evidence.

family (p. 317) two or more people, related either by birth or through social commitment, who share resources, care for any dependents, and often maintain a close emotional relationship.

feminism (p. 309) a philosophy that advocates social, political, and economic equality for women and men.

feminization of poverty (p. 234) a trend in which women made up an increasingly large share of the poor.

fertility rate (p. 326) the average number of births per female.

field research (p. 44) a data collection technique in which the researcher systematically observes some aspect of social life in its natural setting.

folkways (p. 66) group habits or customs that are common in a given culture.

framing (p. 488) interpreting and assigning meaning to events and conditions in order to shape a movement's message and the collective identity that develops among members.

functionalist theories (p. 18) see "structural-functionalist theories."

fundamentalism (p. 338) a religious movement that advocates strict adherence to traditional principles in all aspects of social life, usually based on literal interpretation of a religion's infallible sacred texts.

G

Gemeinschaft (p. 411) social organization in which most relationships are based on the long-term personal ties of collective kinship, common tradition, and shared values.

gender (p. 285) the socially constructed cultural expectations associated with women and men.

gender convergence (p. 310) a trend toward increasing similarity in how women and men live.

gender division of labor (p. 365) differences between men and women in access to jobs.

gender expression (p. 287) the way a person communicates gender identity to others, through behavior, clothing, hairstyle, and other means.

gender identity (p. 287) a person's identification as a woman, a man, or some combination of the two.

gender role (p. 290) a set of social expectations regarding behavior and attitudes based on a person's sex.

gender stratification (p. 295) the systematic and unequal distribution of power and resources in society between women and men.

generalize (p. 42) the ability to describe patterns of behavior of a larger population based on findings from a sample.

generalized other (p. 154) the values and orientations of one's overall community rather than those of specific individuals.

genocide (p. 259) the systematic killing of a group of people, based on their race, ethnicity, nationality, or religion.

gentrification (p. 416) the process of rehabilitating older housing stock and investing in neighborhood development in a way that typically attracts new higher-income residents and displaces current middle- and low-income residents.

Gesellschaft (p. 411) social organization in which most social relationships are impersonal, temporary, and based primarily on the pursuit of individual rational self-interest.

glass ceiling (p. 299) the often invisible barrier created by individual and institutional sexism that prevents qualified women from advancing to higher levels of leadership and management.

global inequality (p. 241) the differences in wealth and power among the countries of the world.

globalization (p. 471) the interaction or integration among various aspects of social life, including economies, cultures, political systems, and populations.

government (p. 437) the organization that exercises authority and steers decision making in a specific community.

groupthink (p. 182) a form of uncritical thinking in which people reinforce a consensus rather than ask serious questions or thoroughly analyze the issue at hand.

growth machines (p. 415) a label for cities that highlights how powerful businesses and politicians work together to promote urban development, often while ignoring the interests of ordinary citizens.

growth rate (p. 479) the indicator that measures how quickly a country's population is increasing.

H

Hawthorne effect (p. 38) the fact that human beings will react differently because they know they are in a study.

health disparities (p. 427) persistent patterns of inequality in health.

hegemony (p. 119) a condition that exists when those in power have successfully spread their ideas—and marginalized alternative viewpoints—so that their perspectives and interests are accepted widely as being universal and true.

heterosexism (p. 306) attitudes and behavior that indicate an assumption that everyone is heterosexual.

heterosexual (p. 305) people who are attracted to people of a different sex.

hidden curriculum (p. 139) the lessons students learn simply by attending school, in contrast to the lessons from the formal subject-specific curriculum.

high culture (p. 74) cultural forms associated with elites that are widely recognized as valuable and legitimate.

historical materialism (p. 469) the part of Marx's work suggesting that the economic base of a society is the primary force driving change in other aspects of social life.

homophily (p. 173) the idea that social contact occurs at a higher rate between people who are similar than it does between people who are different.

homophobia (p. 307) the disapproval and fear of LGBT people.

homosexual (p. 305) people who are attracted to people of the same sex.

horizontal integration (p. 379) what occurs when a media company owns different forms of media.

human ecology (p. 413) the study of the links between the physical environment—natural and built—and social life.

human security (p. 461) concern for the health and rights of individual human beings rather than the security of nations.

hyperreality (p. 391) the condition in which media depictions of the world replace the experience of the "real" world.

hypothesis (p. 36) a statement about the relationship between variables that is to be investigated.

I

ideal culture (p. 68) what the members of a culture report to be their values, beliefs, and norms.

ideology (p. 70) a system of meaning that helps define and explain the world and that makes value judgments about that world.

illegitimate power (p. 119) a form of authority that relies on force or coercion to generate obedience.

incest taboo (p. 304) a norm restricting sexual relations between certain relatives.

income (p. 225) money received from sources such as wages, interest on savings, and dividends from stocks and bonds.

independent variable (p. 36) the entity that is associated with and/or causes change in the value of the dependent variable.

individual mobility (p. 229) a change in a person's class position that occurs without any change in the larger class structure.

individualism (p. 234) a system of beliefs that highlights the importance of the single person over any social group.

industrialization (p. 10) the use of large-scale machinery for the mass manufacture of consumer goods.

inequality (p. 123) the unequal distribution of resources among groups of people.

infant mortality rate (p. 479) the number of infants less than a year old who die per 1,000 live births.

informed consent (p. 46) the principle that subjects in any study must know about the nature of the research project, any potential benefits or risks that they may face, and that they have the right to stop participating at any time, for any reason.

in-group (p. 180) a social group with which a person identifies and toward which he or she feels positively; members have a collective sense of "us."

institutional discrimination (p. 273) unequal treatment that results from the structural organization, policies, and procedures of social institutions such as the government, businesses, and schools.

intensive interview (p. 42) a data gathering technique that uses open-ended questions during somewhat lengthy face-to-face sessions.

interpretive social science (p. 48) an approach that focuses on understanding the meaning that people ascribe to their social world.

intersectionality theory (p. 124) a perspective that highlights the connections and interactions between various forms of inequality, especially race, class, and gender.

intersexual people (p. 285) individuals born with ambiguous reproductive or sexual anatomy.

intersubjectivity (p. 163) a common understanding between people about knowledge, reality, or an experience.

iron law of oligarchy (p. 183) the eventual and inevitable consolidation of power at the top of bureaucratic organizations.

J

job satisfaction (p. 364) the degree to which a person is content in his or her job.

K

kinship (p. 317) the bonds of family relationships.

knowledge (cultural) (p. 64) the range of information, awareness, and understanding that helps us navigate our world.

L

labeling theory (p. 192) the theory that deviance is the result of how others interpret a behavior and that individuals who are labeled deviant often internalize this judgment as part of their self-identity.

labor unions (p. 368) associations of employees that join together for the purpose of improving their working conditions.

language (p. 66) an elaborate system of symbols that allows people to communicate with one another in complex ways.

latent function (p. 19) the largely unrecognized and unintended consequences of social phenomena.

legitimate power (p. 119) authority that is voluntarily accepted by those who are affected.

liberation theology (p. 332) a form of Christian belief dedicated to combating poverty and other forms of social injustice.

life chances (p. 123) the opportunities offered by a person's economic position.

life-course perspective (p. 142) looks at how age, time, and place shape social identities and experiences over a lifetime.

life expectancy (p. 479) the median number of years a person is likely to live given the current conditions.

literacy (p. 347) the ability to read and write.

loner deviance (p. 199) the activities of individuals who commit deviant acts without the social support of other participants.

looking glass self (p. 153) the idea that our sense of self develops as a reflection of the way we think others see us.

M

macro level of analysis (p. 18) a focus on large-scale social systems and processes such as the economy, politics, and population trends.

majority group (p. 258) a collection of people who enjoy privileges and have more access to power because of identifiable physical or cultural characteristics.

manifest functions (p. 19) the recognized and intended consequences of social phenomena.

marriage (p. 319) a social relationship that creates family ties, typically involves sexual relations, and is formalized by legal contract, religious ceremony, or both.

mass media (p. 377) communications that reach a relatively large and mostly anonymous audience.

master status (p. 169) a social position that is overwhelmingly significant, powerfully influences a person's social experience, and typically overshadows all the other social positions that person may occupy.

material culture (p. 59) the physical objects produced by people in a particular culture, including tools, clothing, toys, works of art, and housing.

matriarchy (p. 295) a social system dominated by women.

matrix of domination (p. 125) the interlocking systems of oppression associated with race, class, and gender.

Mead's "I" (p. 153) the part of the self that is spontaneous, impulsive, creative, and unpredictable.

Mead's "me" (p. 153) the sense of self that has been learned from interaction with others.

media (p. 377) the various technological processes that enable communication between (and are in the "middle" of) the sender of a message and the receiver of that message.

medicalization of deviance (p. 195) the designation of a deviant behavior as an illness that can be treated by medical professionals.

meritocracy (p. 234) the notion that people are rewarded and are able to advance because of their abilities.

meso level of analysis (p. 18) a focus somewhere between very large and very small social phenomena—on organizations or institutions, for example.

micro level of analysis (p. 18) a focus on small-scale, usually face-to-face social interaction.

middle class (p. 226) a group that is distinctive for its contribution of specialized knowledge and expertise to the economy.

migration (p. 481) the movement of people from one place to another.

minority group (p. 258) a collection of people who suffer disadvantages and have less power because of identifiable physical or cultural characteristics.

mixed economies (p. 460) economies that combine elements of both market-based capitalism with the significant government intervention associated with socialism.

modernity (p. 7) a historical era beginning in the 1700s characterized by the growth of democracy and personal freedom, increased reliance on reason and science to explain the natural and social worlds, and a shift toward an urban industrial economy.

modernization theory (p. 244) a theory that attributes global inequality to cultural differences between countries.

monarchy (p. 437) a system of government headed by a single person, the monarch, who typically inherits the position as a member of a ruling family.

monogamy (p. 319) the practice of restricting sexual relations to one partner.

moral education (p. 349) the role of schools in teaching children the central values and beliefs of their society.

mores (p. 66) norms that are strictly enforced, with potentially severe penalties for violating them.

multiculturalism (p. 75) the recognition, valuing, and protection of the distinct cultures that make up a society.

N

national security state (p. 447) a government dominated by powerful military, foreign policy, and intelligence agencies.

natural environment (p. 407) the land, water, air, vegetation, and organisms that make up the physical world.

nature versus nurture debate (p. 149) a disagreement about the relative importance of biology ("nature") and the social environment ("nurture") in influencing human behavior.

neocolonialism (p. 245) a system of economic domination of poorer nations by wealthier ones without the use of formal political control or military occupation.

neoliberalism (p. 476) a set of economic policies that aim to allow private markets to operate with little or no government oversight or intervention.

neo-Malthusian perspective (p. 482) the view, derived from Malthus's thought, warning that overpopulation is threatening the planet.

new urban sociology (p. 415) an approach to studying cities that focuses on the interactions of politics and economics and locates them in the larger context of the global economy.

nonmaterial culture (p. 59) the ideas of a culture, including values and beliefs, accumulated knowledge about how to understand and navigate the world, and standards or "norms" about appropriate behavior.

normalization (p. 202) a shift in which previously deviant behaviors become accepted as conventional.

norms (p. 65) a culture's rules and expectations for "appropriate" behavior.

nuclear (or **conjugal**) **family** (p. 319) parent(s) and their children.

O

occupational prestige (p. 364) collective attitudes about the status of various jobs.

occupational socialization (p. 141) the learning of the informal norms associated with a type of employment.

operationalize (p. 47) to define the variables you are interested in studying.

organizational environment (p. 178) factors that exist outside the organization but that potentially affect its operation.

organizational structure (p. 93) the rules and routines, both formal and informal, that shape daily activity within organizations.

organizations (p. 176) secondary groups that have a degree of formal structure and are formed to accomplish particular tasks.

organizing (p. 487) coordinating and directing the efforts of many individuals to work for a cause.

out-group (p. 180) a social group toward which a person feels negatively, considering its members to be inferiors, or "them."

outsourcing (p. 371) moving jobs out of the country to take advantage of cheaper labor costs elsewhere.

overconformity (p. 202) following cultural expectations to an excessive degree.

ownership concentration (p. 380) what occurs when more media outlets come to be owned by a diminishing number of media corporations.

P

patriarchy (p. 129) male domination through social institutions and cultural practices.

peer group (p. 140) a group of people, usually of comparable age, who share similar interests and social status.

peer-review process (p. 50) a way in which scholars evaluate research manuscripts before they are published in order to ensure their quality.

persuade (p. 113) to obtain people's compliance by convincing them of the correctness of your position and goals.

planned obsolescence (p. 392) the intentional design and manufacture of consumer goods so as to ensure a loss of utility in a relatively short period of time.

pluralism (p. 258) a situation in which distinct ethnic and racial groups coexist on equal terms and have equal social standing.

pluralist theory (p. 443) a theory that argues that political power is fragmented among many different competing groups.

plurality voting (p. 439) a "winner-take-all" electoral system in which the candidate with the most votes wins the office being contested.

political opportunities (p. 489) factors outside a social movement that can influence whether it emerges and is successful.

political socialization (p. 440) the inculcation of basic norms and expectations about political life and attitudes toward involvement in politics.

politics (p. 437) the arena in which societies make collective decisions about priorities and policies.

polygamy (p. 319) a marriage system in which an individual is allowed multiple spouses.

popular culture (p. 74) cultural forms that are widespread and commonly embraced within a society.

population pyramid (p. 479) a bar chart showing the distribution of a population by age and sex.

positive deviance (p. 202) overconformity that gets a favorable response.

positivism (p. 11) a belief that accurate knowledge must be based on the scientific method.

positivist social science (p. 48) an approach that assumes that the social world, like the natural world, is characterized by laws that can be identified through research and used to predict and control human affairs.

postmodernity (p. 25) a historical period beginning in the mid-twentieth century characterized by the rise of information-based economies and the fragmentation of political beliefs and ways of knowing.

poverty line (U.S.) (p. 233) a measure of scarcity determined by figuring the cost of a minimal food budget and multiplying it by three.

poverty rate (p. 233) the percentage of the population that falls below the poverty line.

power (p. 24) the ability to bring about an intended outcome, even when opposed by others.

power elite theory (p. 443) a theory that suggests that political power is concentrated in the hands of a small dominant group of business, government, and military leaders.

power tactics (p. 115) the specific strategies people use to influence others in everyday life.

prejudice (p. 258) to "pre-judge" someone or some group negatively based on inadequate information.

primary groups (p. 175) people who have regular contact, enduring relationships, and a significant emotional attachment to each other.

privilege (p. 122) a special advantage or benefit that is not enjoyed by everyone.

product placement (p. 396) the integration into media content of a product that is being advertised.

profane (p. 330) the ordinary world of everyday life.

professional authority (p. 426) legitimate power to define the terms of discussion within a specific field.

professionals (p. 367) a class of workers who are highly educated, hold degrees to certify their education, and have jobs that require a particular form of expertise.

progressive taxation (p. 238) tax policy in which those with higher incomes pay a higher rate.

proportional representation (p. 439) an electoral system in which parties are awarded seats in government based on the percentage of votes they receive in an election.

public assistance (p. 240) either tax credits or actual payments and benefits provided to citizens by the government.

public sociology (p. 33) the effort to bring the findings of both basic and applied sociological research to a broader nonacademic audience.

Q

qualitative data (p. 36) any kind of evidence that is not numerical in nature, including evidence gathered from interviews, direct observation, and written or visual documents.

quantitative data (p. 36) evidence that can be summarized numerically.

R

race (p. 253) a category of people widely perceived as sharing socially significant physical characteristics such as skin color.

racial essentialism (p. 256) the idea that supposedly natural and immutable differences separate the races.

racial school segregation (p. 358) separating students into exclusively white and exclusively black public schools.

racialization of the state (p. 273) the implementation of government and private-sector policies that discriminated against minorities and provided Whites with numerous advantages.

racism (p. 256) the belief that one race is inherently superior to another.

random sample (p. 42) a sample in which every element of the population has an equal chance of being chosen.

rational action (p. 99) behavior motivated by calculations of efficiency.

rationalization of society (p. 15) the long-term historical process by which rationality replaced tradition as the basis for organizing social and economic life.

rational-legal authority (p. 119) power that has legitimacy because it is based on established laws, rules, and procedures.

real culture (p. 68) what members of a culture actually do, which may or may not reflect the ideal.

recidivism (p. 209) a relapse into criminal behavior.

redlining (p. 417) the use of discriminatory practices in the sale or rental of housing to minorities.

reference groups (p. 175) the groups against which we choose to measure ourselves.

regressive taxation (p. 239) taxes that disproportionately affect those with lower incomes.

relative poverty (p. 233) situation that exists when people do not have the basic resources to maintain a standard of living considered acceptable in their society.

religion (p. 331) a unified system of beliefs and ritual practices relating to the sacred that bond people into a moral community.

research methods (p. 41) the procedures used by a researcher to collect and analyze data.

resocialization (p. 142) the process by which individuals replace old norms and behaviors with new ones as they move from one role or life stage to another.

resource mobilization (p. 488) the process by which social movements generate the assets necessary to build and sustain a movement.

reward (p. 113) to encourage people's compliance by offering some compensation as a positive incentive.

rites of passage (p. 143) activities that mark and celebrate a change in a person's social status.

rituals (p. 330) symbolic actions, typically performed at specified times, that help evoke an emotional bond among participants.

role conflict (p. 170) the problem that occurs when the expectations associated with different roles clash.

role strain (p. 170) the problem that occurs when the expectations associated with a single role compete with each other.

roles (p. 90) the sets of expected behaviors that are associated with particular statuses.

S

sacred (p. 330) something extraordinary, to be treated respectfully, with reverence and awe.

sample (p. 42) part of the population a researcher is studying that represents the whole.

Sapir-Whorf hypothesis (p. 68) the idea that because of their different cultural content and structure, languages affect how their speakers think and behave.

scapegoat (p. 275) an individual or a group of people falsely blamed for a negative situation.

school choice (p. 361) various policies that give families options for deciding which school their children will attend.

schooling (p. 347), organized instruction by trained teachers.

science (p. 9) a method of inquiry that uses logic and the systematic collection of evidence to support knowledge claims.

scientific management (p. 183) (also known as Taylorism) the effort by trained managers to study workflow and develop precise procedures that govern the completion of work tasks.

second shift (p. 299) the phenomenon of employed women still having primary responsibility for housework and childcare.

secondary data analysis (p. 44) a type of research using data previously collected by other researchers.

secondary deviance (p. 192) deviant behavior that is a response to the negative consequences of labeling.

secondary groups (p. 175) people who interact in a relatively impersonal way, usually to carry out some specific task.

sect (p. 330) a small dissenting faction of a church that promotes new beliefs or practices.

secular humanism (p. 337) a belief system that emphasizes morality and decision making based on reason, ethics, and social justice rather than religious doctrine or the supernatural.

secularization (p. 336) the decline in the social significance of religious beliefs, practices, and institutions.

secularization thesis (p. 336) the argument that, in the face of modernity, the social significance of religion has declined.

segregation (p. 259) keeping distinct social groups physically and socially separate and unequal.

sense of self (p. 153) the collection of thoughts and feelings you have when considering yourself as an object.

sex (p. 285) the biological distinction between females and males.

sexism (p. 290) the ideology that one sex is superior to the other.

sexual harassment (p. 300) unwelcome sexual advances, requests for sexual favors, and other verbal or physical harassment of a sexual nature.

sexual identity (or **orientation**) (p. 305) our sense of self as it relates to the type of sexual attraction we have for others.

sexuality (p. 304) a person's sexual desires, behaviors, and identity.

shopfloor culture (p. 368) a distinctive set of norms and rules that shape daily behavior and interaction on the job.

social capital (p. 236) relationships that are potentially economically valuable resulting from membership in a group.

social change (p. 467) the modification of structural or cultural patterns over time.

social closure (p. 124) the process whereby a status group maximizes its own advantages by restricting access to rewards only to members of the group.

social control (p. 205) the incentives and punishments that promote conformity in social life.

social determinism (p. 149) a theory that contends that culture and the social environment almost completely shape human behavior.

social environment (p. 407) the cultural context and patterns of relationships within which humans live.

social groups (p. 174) collections of people who interact regularly with one another and who are aware of their status as a group.

social institutions (p. 87) the major arenas of social life in which durable routines and patterns of behavior take place.

social integration (p. 96) the social structures that bind people together and the values that link people to the broader society.

social mobility (p. 126) movement from one stratum of a stratification system to another.

social movements (p. 485) organized, ongoing collective efforts by relatively powerless people engaging in extrainstitutional action to promote or resist change.

social networks (p. 172) the collection of social ties that connect people to each other.

social reproduction theory (p. 354) theory that explores the ways that schools help to reproduce systems of inequality.

social solidarity (p. 13) the collective bonds that connect individuals.

social structure (p. 87) recurring patterns of behavior.

social theory (p. 17) a set of principles and propositions that explains the relationships among social phenomena.

social trend (p. 469) the direction a society takes when many individuals act independently but similarly.

socialism (p. 456) an economic system that emphasizes public ownership of the major means of production, which are operated to meet human needs and promote social justice.

socialization (p. 137) the process through which people learn their culture's basic norms, values, beliefs, and behaviors.

society (p. 59) a group of people who live together in a specific territory and share a culture.

sociological imagination (p. 5) see "sociological perspective."

sociological perspective (p. 5) a view of the social world that focuses on discovering and understanding the connections between individuals and the broader social contexts in which they live; what C. Wright Mills called the *sociological imagination.*

sociology (p. 5) the systematic study of the relationship between individuals and society.

spiral of silence (p. 441) a theory that explains how people keep quiet about controversial issues when they think their opinions are not widely shared, in order to avoid social isolation.

spirituality (p. 340) an inner sense of meaning or purpose, especially as it involves a person's relationship to something greater than the self.

split labor market theory (p. 275) the theory that ethnic and racial conflicts often emerge when two racial or ethnic groups compete for the same jobs.

sprawl (p. 418) low-density development that disperses people over a wide area, separates homes from workplaces and stores, and depends heavily on cars for transportation.

standpoint theory (p. 122) a theory that questions taken-for-granted assumptions about society by looking at it from multiple viewpoints, especially from the perspective of people in subordinate positions.

state terrorism (p. 453) political violence directed at civilians by governments.

status (p. 90) a position in a social system that can be occupied by an individual.

status attainment (p. 363) the process by which people come to occupy a certain level in a social hierarchy.

status category (p. 168) a status that people can hold in common.

status hierarchy (p. 169) a ranking of social positions according to their perceived prestige or honor.

status set (p. 168) the collection of statuses that an individual holds.

stealth advertising (p. 398) the creation of covert advertising in everyday real-life situations.

stereotypes (p. 166) exaggerated, distorted, or untrue generalizations about categories of people that do not acknowledge individual variation.

stigma (p. 192) the shame attached to a behavior or status that is considered socially unacceptable or discrediting.

strain theory (p. 199) a theory that emphasizes that the strain or pressure on those who lack the means to achieve culturally defined goals leads them to pursue deviant routes to success.

stratification systems (p. 125) social structures and cultural norms that create and maintain inequality by ranking people into a hierarchy of groups that receive unequal resources.

structural mobility (p. 228) a change in class position that occurs when a shift in available occupations changes the class system as a whole.

structural-functionalist theories (p. 18) theories that focus on consensus and cooperative interaction in social life, emphasizing how different elements that make up a society's structure contribute to its overall operation.

structure (p. 22) the recurring patterns of behavior in social life.

subculture (p. 71) cultures associated with smaller groups in society that have distinct norms, values, and lifestyles setting them apart from the dominant culture.

surveillance (p. 206) monitoring by authorities who police the boundaries of what's normal.

survey (p. 41) a data collection technique that involves asking someone a series of questions.

sustainability (p. 423) a balance between resource protection and consumption that can be maintained indefinitely.

symbol (p. 66) anything—a sound, a gesture, an image, an object—that represents something else.

symbolic interactionist theories (p. 19) social theories that focus on how people use shared symbols and construct society as a result of their everyday interactions.

T

terrorism (p. 453) politically motivated violence that intentionally targets noncombatants.

theism (p. 331) a belief in the existence of a god or gods.

Thomas theorem (p. 165) the idea that if people define situations as real, they are real in their consequences.

total institution (p. 142) confining social settings in which an authority regulates all aspects of a person's life.

tracking (p. 360) placing students into different curricular paths intended to accommodate varying levels of academic work.

traditional action (p. 99) behavior motivated by custom.

traditional authority (p. 119) power that has legitimacy because of compliance with well-established cultural practices.

transgender people (p. 287) individuals who identify with a gender different from the one associated with their sex.

transnational migrants (p. 269) immigrants who retain strong personal, cultural, and economic ties to both their country of birth and their newly adopted home.

transparency (p. 37) the requirement that researchers explain how they collected and analyzed their evidence and how they reached their conclusions.

transsexuals (p. 289) people who have sex reassignment surgery to change their physical appearance.

treadmill of production (p. 424) a term that refers to the way capital-intensive industries and the modern state, in pursuit of continual growth as a central good, have led to increasing resource depletion and worsening pollution.

U

underclass (p. 226) chronically unemployed people who have no ongoing relationship to the mainstream economy.

unintended consequences (p. 469) results that are unplanned and unforeseen.

urbanization (p. 10) the growth of cities.

user-generated content (p. 386) content that is created by ordinary media users, rather than by media organizations, and that is available to a potentially large audience.

V

value (p. 60) a deeply held principle or standard that people use to make judgments about the world, especially in deciding what is desirable or worthwhile.

value-neutrality (p. 48) the goal of removing any personal views from the research process; part of positivist social science.

variables (p. 36) measures that can change (or vary) and thus have different values.

vertical integration (p. 379) what occurs when a media company owns the different stages of production and distribution of a single media form.

W

war (p. 447) organized armed conflict among two or more specially trained military groups.

wealth (p. 225) financial assets, such as savings, real estate, and stocks.

white-collar crime (p. 204) crime committed by people of high social status in the course of their occupation.

working class (p. 222) (or proletariat), those who survive on the wages they earn.

world systems analysis (p. 245) an approach that focuses on the interdependence among the countries that make up a single global economic system.

X

xenophobia (p. 77) an unreasonable fear or hatred of foreigners or people of a different culture.

Z

zero population growth (p. 483) a balance between birth rates and death rates, which maintains stable population numbers.

References

Aboud, Frances E. 1988. *Children and prejudice.* Cambridge, MA: Basil Blackwell.

Adams, Michele, and Scott Coltrane. 2005. Boys and men in families: The domestic production of gender, power, and privilege. In *Handbook of studies on men & masculinities,* ed. Michael S. Kimmel, Jeff Hearn, and R. W. Connell, pp. 230–48. Thousand Oaks, CA: Sage.

Addams, Jane. 1895/2007. *Hull House maps and papers.* Chicago: University of Illinois Press.

Addams, Jane. 1902/2002. *Democracy and Social Ethics.* Urbana and Chicago: University of Illinois Press.

Adler, Nancy E., and Katherine Newman. 2002. Socioeconomic disparities in health. *Health Affairs* 21 (2): 60–76.

Adler, Patricia A., and Peter Adler. 2005. Self-injurers as loners: The social organization of solitary deviance. *Deviant Behavior* 26 (4): 345–78.

Adorno, Theodor W., and Max Horkheimer. 1944/2000. The culture industry: Enlightenment as mass deception. In *The consumer society reader,* ed. Juliet B. Schor and Douglas B. Holt, pp. 3–19. New York: New Press.

Agiesta, Jennifer. 2008. Iraq: Public opinion five years in. *Washington Post,* March 19. Retrieved from http://voices.washingtonpost.com/behind-the-numbers/2008/03/iraq_public_opinion_five_years_1.html.

Akpabio, Eno, and Kayode Mustapha-Lambe. 2008. *Nollywood* films and the cultural imperialism hypothesis. *Perspectives on Global Development and Technology* 7 (3): 259–70.

Alexander, Jeffrey, ed. 1985. *Neofunctionalism.* Beverly Hills, CA: Sage.

Alinsky, Saul. 1971/1989. *Rules for radicals.* New York: Vintage.

Allen, Amy. 2000. *The power of feminist theory.* Boulder, CO: Westview.

Allen, Amy. 2005. Feminist perspectives on power. *Stanford Encyclopedia of Philosophy,* ed. Edward N. Zalta. Retrieved from http://plato.stanford.edu/archives/fall2008/entries/feminist-power.

Allen, Amy. 2008. *The politics of our selves: Politics, autonomy, and gender in contemporary political theory.* New York: Columbia University Press.

Allen, I. Elaine, and Jeff Seaman. 2010. *Class differences: Online education in the United States, 2010.* Babson Survey Research Group. Retrieved from http://sloanconsortium.org/publications/survey/class_differences.

Allen, James, Jon Lewis, Leon F. Litwack, and Hilton Als. 2000. *Without sanctuary: Lynching photography in America.* Santa Fe, NM: Twin Palms Publishers.

Allport, Gordon. 1954. *The nature of prejudice.* Cambridge, MA: Addison-Wesley.

Alon, Sigal. 2009. The evolution of class inequality in higher education: Competition, exclusion, and adaptation. *American Sociological Review* 74 (October): 731–755.

Alon, Sigal, and Marta Tienda. 2007. Diversity, opportunity, and the shifting meritocracy in higher education. *American Sociological Review* 72 (August): 487–511.

Alper, Joseph. S. 2002. Genetic complexity in human disease and behavior. In *The double-edged helix: Social implications of genetics in a diverse society,* ed. Joseph S. Alper, Catherine Ard, Adrienne Asch, John Beckwith, Peter Conrad, and Lisa N. Geller, 17–38. Baltimore, MD: Johns Hopkins University Press.

Alsop, Ruth, and Nina Heinsohn. 2005. Measuring empowerment in practice: Structuring analysis and framing indicators. World Bank Policy Research Working Paper 3510. Washington, DC: World Bank.

Altheid, David. 2006. *Terrorism and the politics of fear.* Lanham, MD: AltaMira Press.

Altonji, Joseph G., and Rebecca M. Blank. 1999. Race and gender in the labor market. In *Handbook of labor economics,* Vol. 3C, ed. Orley Ashenfelter and David Card, pp. 3143–259. New York: Elsevier Science.

Alvarez, Lizette. 2009a. More Americans joining military as jobs dwindle. *New York Times,* January 18, p. A1. Retrieved from www.nytimes.com/2009/01/19/us/19recruits.html.

Alvarez, Lizette. 2009b. Suicides of soldiers reach high of nearly 3 decades. *New York Times,* January 30, p. A19. Retrieved from www.nytimes.com/2009/01/30/us/30suicide.html.

Alvarez, R. Michael, Thad E. Hall, and Susan D. Hyde, eds. 2008. *Election fraud.* Washington, DC: Brookings Institution Press.

Amato, Paul R., and Alan Booth. 2000. *A generation at risk.* Cambridge, MA: Harvard University Press.

American Academy of Pediatrics. 2006. Children, adolescents, and advertising. Policy statement. *Pediatrics* 118 (6): 2563–69. Retrieved from http://pediatrics.aappublications.org/cgi/content/full/118/6/2563#R2.

American Anthropological Association. 2011. *Race: Are we so different?* Retrieved from http://understandingrace.org/lived/global_census.html.

American Civil Liberties Union. 2010. LGBT rights: Lesbian, gay, bisexual, and transgender project. Retrieved from www.aclu.org/lgbt-rights.

American Crossroads. 2011. About us. Retrieved from www.americancrossroads.org/about-us.

American National Election Studies. 2007. *The ANES guide to public opinion and electoral behavior.* Ann Arbor: University of Michigan, Center for Political Studies. Retrieved from www.electionstudies.org.

American Social History Project. 2007. *Who built America?* New York: Bedford/St. Martin's.

American Society for Aesthetic Plastic Surgery. 2010. *2010 Cosmetic Surgery National Data Bank: Statistics.* New York: American Society for Aesthetic Plastic Surgery.

American Society of Newspaper Editors. 2011. ASNE newsroom census 2011. Retrieved from http://asne.org/key_initiatives/diversity/newsroom_census/table_l.aspx.

American Society of Plastic Surgeons. 2006. Abdominoplasty: Tummy tuck. Retrieved from www.plasticsurgery.org/public_education/procedures/Abdominoplasty.cfm.

American Sociological Association. 1999. Code of ethics. Retrieved from www.asanet.org/page.ww?section=Ethics&name=Code+of+Ethics+Table+of+Contents.

Americans for Campaign Reform. 2010. Money in politics: Who gives? Retrieved from www.acrreform.org/research/money-in-politics-who-gives/.

Anderson, Barbara A., Chris Provis, and Shirley J. Chappel, 2003. The selection and training of workers in the tourism and hospitality industries for the performance of emotional labour. *Journal of Hospitality and Tourism Management* 10 (1): 1–12.

Anderson, Elijah. 1999. *Code of the street.* New York: Norton.

Anderson, Jenny. 2011. Push for A's at private schools is keeping costly tutors busy. *New York Times,* June 7. Retrieved from www.nytimes.com/2011/06/08/education/08tutors.html?pagewanted=1&_r=1.

Anderson, Margaret, and Patricia Hill Collins, eds. 2009. *Race, class & gender.* Belmont, CA: Wadsworth.

Anderson, Margaret, and Dana Hysock Witham. 2008. *Thinking about women: Sociological perspectives on sex and gender.* Boston, MA: Allyn & Bacon.

Andersson, Hilary. 2005. Born to be a slave in Niger. BBC, February 12. Retrieved from http://news.bbc.co.uk/1/hi/programmes/from_our_own_correspondent/4250709.stm.

Angwin, Julia. 2010. The web's new gold mine: Your secrets. *Wall Street Journal,* July 30. Retrieved from http://online.wsj.com/article/SB10001424052748703940904575395073512989404.html.

Angwin, Julia, and Steve Stecklow. 2010. "Scrapers" dig deep for data on the web. *Wall Street Journal,* October 12. Retrieved from http://online.wsj.com/article/SB10001424052748703358504575544381288117888.html.

Appold, Stephen. 2007. Human ecology. In *21st Century sociology: A reference handbook,* ed. Clifton D. Bryant and Dennis L. Peck, pp. 444–54. Thousand Oaks, CA: Sage.

AP-Univsion. 2010. The AP-Univision poll, May 7–12. Retrieved from http://surveys.ap.org/data%5CGfK%5CAP-Univision%20Poll%20May%202010%20Hispanic%20Topline_ALL_updated.pdf.

Arab American Institute. 2010. Demographics. Retrieved from www.aaiusa.org/pages/demographics/.

Aries, Philippe. 1965. *Centuries of childhood: A social history of family life,* trans. Robert Baldick. New York: Vintage.

Arnason, Johann P. 2001. History of civilizational analysis. In *International encyclopedia of the social and behavioral sciences,* ed. Neil J. Smelser and Paul B. Baltes. Oxford and New York: Elsevier.

Arnett, Jeffrey Jensen. 2004. *Emerging adulthood.* New York: Oxford University Press.

Arum, Richard. 2003. *Judging school discipline.* Cambridge: Harvard University Press.

Asch, Solomon E. 1952. *Social psychology.* Englewood Cliffs, NJ: Prentice Hall.

Asch, Solomon E. 1955. Opinions and social pressures. *Scientific American* 193 (5): 31–35.

Ashmawey, Rogaya. 2010. A write-in campaign. *Newsweek,* March 1. Retrieved from www.newsweek.com/2010/02/28/a-write-in-campaign.html.

Astin, Alexander W. 1998. The changing American college student: Thirty-year trends, 1966–1996. *Review of Higher Education* 21 (2): 115–35.

Attewell, Paul, David Lavin, Thurston Domina, and Tania Levey. 2007. *Passing the torch: Does higher education for the disadvantaged pay off across the generations?* New York: Russell Sage Foundation.

Aud, S., W. Hussar, M. Planty, T. Snyder, K. Bianco, K., M. Fox, et al. 2010. *The condition of education 2010* (NCES 2010-028). Washington, DC: National Center for Education Statistics, Institute of Education Sciences, U.S. Department of Education.

Auletta, Ken. 2011. Annals of communication: The dictator index. *New Yorker,* March 7, pp. 44–55.

Austin, Andrew. 2002. Advancing accumulation and managing its discontents: The U.S. anti-environmental countermovement. *Sociological Spectrum* 22: 71–105.

Babb, Sarah. 2004. Born to buy: Sarah Babb interviews Juliet Schor. In *Sociology speaks 2003–2004.* Chestnut Hill, MA: Boston College Department of Sociology.

Babbie, Earl. 2006. *The practice of social research,* 11th ed. Belmont, CA: Wadsworth.

Bagdikian, Ben. 2004. *The new media monopoly.* Boston: Beacon Press.

Bahrampour, Tara. 2010. Students raise the stakes against immigration's status quo. *Washington Post,* July 21, p. A3.

Baisnee, Olivier, and Dominique Marchetti. 2006. The economy of just-in-time television newscasting, trans. Fredline Laryea. *Ethnography* 7 (1): 99–123.

Bajaj, Vikas, and Ford Fessenden. 2007. What's behind the race gap? *New York Times,* November 4, 2007. Retrieved from www.nytimes.com/2007/11/04/weekinreview/04bajaj.html?_r=2&ref=business&oref=slogin&oref=slogin.

Baker Miller, Jean. 1991. Women and power. In *Women's growth in connection: Writings from the Stone Center,* ed. Judith V. Jordan, Alexandra G. Kaplan, Jean Baker Miller, Irene P. Stiver, and Janet L. Surrey, 197–205. New York: Guilford Press.

Baker, Wayne E. 2005. *America's crisis of values: Reality and perception.* Princeton, NJ: Princeton University Press.

Barabási, Albert-László. 2010. Limits of predictability FAQ. Retrieved from http://barabasilab.neu.edu/projects/predictability/FAQ.

Baron-Cohen, Simon. 1999. *Mindblindness: An essay on autism and theory of mind.* Cambridge, MA: MIT Press.

Barres, Ben A. 2006. Does gender matter? *Nature,* July 13, pp. 133–36.

Barstow, Anne Llewellyn, ed. 2001. *War's dirty secret: Rape, prostitution, and other crimes against women.* Cleveland, OH: Pilgrim Press.

Baudrillard, Jean. 1988a. For a critique of the political economy of the sign. In *Selected writings,* ed. Mark Poster, pp. 57–97. Stanford, CA: Stanford University Press.

Baudrillard, Jean. 1988b. Consumer society. In *Selected writings,* ed. Mark Poster, pp. 29–56. Stanford, CA: Stanford University Press.

Bauerlein, Mark. 2008. *The dumbest generation.* New York: Tarcher/Penguin.

Bauman, Zygmunt. 2001. *Community: Seeking safety in an insecure world.* Cambridge, U.K.: Polity Press.

Bawden, Tom. 2007. Buffett blasts system that lets him pay less tax than secretary. *Times (U.K.),* June 28. Retrieved from www.timesonline.co.uk/tol/money/tax/article1996735.ece.

Baxter, Janeen, and Erik Olin Wright. 2000. The glass ceiling hypothesis: A comparative study of the United States, Sweden, and Australia. *Gender and Society* 14 (2): 275–94.

Bayat, Asef. 2007. *Making Islam democratic.* Stanford, CA: Stanford University Press.

BBC. 2010a. Suicide-hit Foxconn factory to increase wages. Retrieved from http://news.bbc.co.uk/2/hi/business/10184186.stm.

BBC. 2010b. Taiwan iPhone-maker Foxconn suffers another death. Retrieved from http://news.bbc.co.uk/2/hi/world/asia_pacific/10182824.stm.

Beaglehole, Robert. 1990. International trends in coronary heart disease mortality, morbidity, and risk factors. *Epidemiologic Reviews* 12: 1–16.

Becker, Howard. 1973. *Outsiders: Studies in the sociology of deviance.* New York: Free Press.

Beeghley, Leonard. 2008. *The structure of social stratification in the United States.* Boston: Allyn & Bacon.

Belkin, Aaron, and R. L. Evans. 2000. *The effects of including gay and lesbian soldiers in the British armed forces: Appraising the evidence.* Santa Barbara: Center for the Study of Sexual Minorities in the Military, University of California at Santa Barbara.

Belkin, Aaron, and Melissa Levitt. 2001. Homosexuality and the Israel defense forces: Did lifting the gay ban undermine military performance? *Armed Forces and Society* 27 (4): 541–565.

Belkin, Aaron, and Jason McNichol. 2000. Homosexual personnel policy in the Canadian forces: Did lifting the gay ban undermine military performance? *International Journal* 56 (1): 73–88.

Belknap, Joanne, and Heather Melton. 2005. *Are heterosexual men also victims of intimate partner abuse?* Harrisburg, PA: National Resource Center on Domestic Violence. Retrieved from http://new.vawnet.org/Assoc_Files_VAWnet/AR_MaleVictims.pdf.

Bell, Nathan. 2010. Graduate enrollment and degrees: 1999–2009. Washington, DC: Council of Graduate Schools. Retrieved from www.cgsnet.org/portals/0/pdf/R_ED2009.pdf.

Bellah, Robert N., Richard Madsen, William M. Sullivan, Ann Swidler, and Steven M. Tipton. 2007. *Habits of the heart: Individualism and commitment in American Life,* 3rd ed. Berkeley: University of California Press.

Benhabib, Seyla. 2002. *The claims of culture: Equality and diversity in a global era.* Princeton, NJ: Princeton University Press.

Benokraitis, Nijole V., ed. 2000. *Feuds about families: Conservative, centrist, liberal and feminist perspectives.* Upper Saddle River, NJ: Prentice Hall.

Benton, Ted. 1977. *Philosophical foundations of the three sociologies.* Boston: Routledge.

Berardo, Felix M., and Constance L. Shehan. 2004. Family problems in global perspective. In *Handbook of social problems: A comparative international perspective,* ed. George Ritzer, pp. 246–60. Thousand Oaks, CA: Sage.

Berbrier, Mitch. 1998. Being deaf has very little to do with one's ears: Boundary-work in the Deaf Culture movement. *Perspectives on Social Problems* 10: 79–100.

Berger, Joseph. 2006. For Hispanic parents, lessons on helping with the homework. *New York Times,* November 1, p. 11.

Berger, Peter. 1963. *Invitation to sociology.* New York: Doubleday.

Berger, Peter. 1967. *The sacred canopy.* Garden City, NY: Doubleday.

Berger, Peter. 1997. Four faces of global culture. *National Interest* 49 (Fall): 23–29.

Berger, Peter L., and Thomas Luckmann. 1966. *The social construction of reality.* New York: Doubleday.

Best, Joel, and David F. Luckenbill. 1982. *Organizing deviance.* Englewood Cliffs, NJ: Prentice Hall.

Bianchi, Suzanne M., John P. Robinson, and Melissa A. Milkie. 2007. *Changing rhythms of American family life.* New York: Russell Sage Foundation.

Bielby, Denise D. 1999. Gender and family relations. In *Handbook of the sociology of gender,* ed. Janet Saltzman Chafetz, pp. 391–406. New York: Kluwer Academic/Plenum Publishers.

Bish, Connie L., Heide Michels Blanck, Mary K. Serdula, Michele Marcus, Harold W. Kohn III, and Laura Kettel Khan. 2005. Diet and physical activity behavior among Americans trying to lose weight. *Obesity Research* 13 (3): 596–607.

Black, Dan, Gary Gates, Seth Sanders, and Lowell Taylor. 2000. Demographics of the gay and lesbian population in the United States: Evidence from available systematic data sources. *Demography* 37 (2): 139–54.

Black, Edwin. 2003. *War against the weak: Eugenics and America's campaign to create a master race.* New York: Four Walls Eight Windows.

Blackledge, Adrian. 2001. The wrong sort of capital? *International Journal of Bilingualism* 5 (3): 345–69.

Blackless, Melanie, Anthony Charuvastra, Amanda Derryck, Anne Fausto-Sterling, Karl Lauzanne, and Ellen Lee. 2000. How sexually dimorphic are we? Review and synthesis. *American Journal of Human Biology* 12: 151–66.

Blake, Mariah. 2005. Stations of the cross. *Columbia Journalism Review* (May/June): 32–39.

Blalock, Hubert M. 1989. *Power and conflict: Toward a general theory.* Newbury Park, CA: Sage.

Blanton, Hart, and James Jaccard. 2008. Unconscious racism: A concept in pursuit of a measure. *Annual Review of Sociology* 34: 277–97.

Blau, Joel, and Mimi Abramovitz. 2007. *The dynamics of social welfare policy.* New York: Oxford University Press.

Blau, Peter, and Otis D. Duncan. 1967. *The American occupational structure.* New York: Wiley.

Bleakley, Hoyt, and Aimee Chin. 2004. Language skills and earnings: Evidence from childhood immigrants. *Review of Economics and Statistics* 86: 481–96.

Bloom, Barbara, Barbara Owen, and Stephanie Covington. 2005. *Gender-responsive strategies for women offenders.* Washington, DC: National Institute of Corrections, U.S. Department of Justice.

Bluestone, Barry, and Bennett Harrison. 1982. *The deindustrialization of America.* New York: Basic Books.

Blumer, Herbert. 1969/1986. *Symbolic interactionism: Perspective and method.* Berkeley: University of California Press.

Bobo, Kim, Jackie Kendall, and Steve Max. 2001. *Organizing for social change: Midwest Academy manual for activists.* Santa Ana, CA: Seven Locks Press.

Bobo, Lawrence, James R. Kluegel, and Ryan A. Smith. 1997. Laissez-faire racism: The crystallization of a kinder, gentler, antiblack ideology. In *Racial attitudes in the 1990s: Continuity and change,* ed. Jack K. Martin and Steven A. Tuch, pp. 15–42. Westport, CT: Praeger.

Boff, Leonardo, and Clodovis Boff. 1987. *Introducing liberation theology.* Maryknoll, NY: Orbis Books.

Bogaert, Anthony F. 2004. Asexuality: Prevalence and associated factors in a national probability sample. *Journal of Sex Research* 41 (August): 279–87.

Bogardus, Emory S. 1967. *A forty-year racial distance study.* Los Angeles: University of Southern California Press.

Boisjoly, Johanne, Greg J. Duncan, Michael Kremer, Dan M. Levy, and Jacque Eccles. 2006. Empathy or antipathy? The impact of diversity. *American Economic Review* 96: 1890–905.

Bonacich, Edna. 1972. A theory of ethnic antagonism: The split labor market. *American Sociological Review* 37 (5): 547–59.

Bonacich, Edna. 1976. Advanced capitalism and black/white relations in the United States: A split labor market interpretation. *American Sociological Review* 41 (1): 34–51.

Bond, Rod, and Peter B. Smith. 1996. Culture and conformity: A meta-analysis of studies using Asch's line judgment task. *Psychological Bulletin* 119: 111–37.

Bonilla-Silva, Eduardo. 2001. *White supremacy and racism in the post-civil rights era.* Boulder, CO: Lynne Rienner Publishers.

Bonilla-Silva, Eduardo. 2009. *Race without racists.* Lanham, MD: Rowman & Littlefield.

Bordo, Susan. 1998. *Unbearable weight.* Berkeley: University of California Press.

Bosso, Christopher J. 2005. *Environment Inc.: From grassroots to beltway.* Lawrence: University of Kansas Press.

Boulding, Kenneth. 1989. *Three faces of power.* Newbury Park, CA: Sage.

Bourdieu, Pierre. 1986. The forms of capital. In *Handbook for theory and research for the sociology of education,* ed. J. G. Richardson, 241–58. Westport, CT: Greenwood Press.

Bourdieu, Pierre, and Jean Claude Passeron. 1977. *Reproduction in education, society, and culture.* Thousand Oaks, CA: Sage.

Bourgois, Philippe. 2003. *In search of respect,* 2nd ed. New York: Cambridge University Press.

Bowen, William G., and Derek Bok. 1998. *The shape of the river.* Princeton, NJ: Princeton University Press.

Bowles, Samuel, and Herbert Gintis. 1976. *Schooling in capitalist America.* New York: Basic Books.

Bowles, Samuel, Herbert Gintis, and Melissa Osbourne Groves, eds. 2005. *Unequal chances: Family background and economic success.* Princeton, NJ: Princeton University Press.

BRAC. 2010a. Community empowerment: Community rights awareness & legal literacy. Retrieved from www.brac.net/content/legal -empowerment-community-rights-awareness -legal-literacy.

BRAC. 2010b. Who we are. Retrieved from www .brac.net/content/who-we-are-0.

Braithwaite, John. 1989. *Crime, shame, and reintegration.* New York: Cambridge University Press.

Braun, Henry, Frank Jenkins, and Wendy Grigg. 2006. *A closer look at charter schools using hierarchical linear modeling (NCES 2006-460).* Washington, DC: U.S. Government Printing Office.

Braverman, Harry. 1974. *Labor and monopoly capital.* New York: Monthly Review Press.

Braverman, Harry. 1974/1998. *Labor and monopoly capital.* New York: Monthly Review Press.

Brenner, Philip. 2011. Exceptional behavior or exceptional identity? Overreporting of church attendance in the U.S. *Public Opinion Quarterly* 75 (1): 19–41.

Bridges, J. S. 1993. Pink or blue: Gender-stereotypic perceptions of infants as conveyed by birth congratulations cards. *Psychology of Women Quarterly* 17: 193–205.

Brint, Steven, Mary F. Contreras, and Michael T. Matthews. 2001. Socialization messages in primary schools. *Sociology of Education* 74 (July): 157–80.

Brint, Steven. 2006. *Schools and societies,* 2nd ed. Palo Alto, CA: Stanford University Press.

Brooks, Abigail. 2004. Under the knife and proud of it: An analysis of the normalization of cosmetic surgery. *Critical Sociology* 30 (2): 207–39.

Brothers, Leslie. 1997. *Friday's footprint: How society shapes the human mind.* New York: Oxford University Press.

Brown, Callum G. 2009. *The death of Christian Britain: Understanding secularisation, 1800–2000.* New York: Routledge.

Brown, M. Christopher, II, and James Earl Davis. 2001. The historically black college as social contract, social capital, and social equalizer. *Peabody Journal of Education* 76 (1): 31–49.

Brown, Patricia Leigh. 2006. Supporting Boys or girls when the line isn't clear. *New York Times,* December 2. Retrieved from www .nytimes.com/2006/12/02/us/02child .html?pagewanted=1&_r=1.

Brown, Susan I. 2005. How cohabitation is reshaping American families. *Contexts* 4 (3): 33–37.

Bruce, Steve. 2000. *Fundamentalism.* Malden, MA: Blackwell.

Bruce, Steve. 2002. *God is dead: Secularization in the West.* Malden, MA: Wiley-Blackwell.

Bruce, Steve. 2011. *Secularization: In defense of an unfashionable theory.* New York: Oxford University Press.

Bruinius, Harry. 2006. *Better for all the world: The secret history of forced sterilization and America's quest for racial purity.* New York: Knopf.

Bruns, Axel. 2005. *Gatewatching: Collaborative online news production.* New York: Peter Lang.

Bruns, Axel. 2008. *Blogs, Wikipedia, Second Life, and beyond: From production to produsage.* New York: Peter Lang.

Budig, Michelle J., and Paula England. 2001. The wage penalty for motherhood. *American Sociological Review* 66 (2): 204–25.

Buell, Frederick. 2004. *From apocalypse to way of life: Environmental crisis in the American century.* New York: Routledge.

Bugental, D. B., & Lewis, Jeffrey C. 1999. "The paradoxical misuse of power by those who see themselves as powerless: How does it happen?" *Journal of Social Issues* 55 (1): 51–64.

Bullard, Robert. 2000. *Dumping in Dixie: Race, class and environmental quality.* Boulder, CO: Westview Press.

Bumpass, Larry, and Hsien-Hen Lu. 2000. Trends in cohabitation and implications for children's family contexts in the U.S. *Population Studies* 54: 29–41.

Burawoy, Michael, William Gamson, Charlotte Ryan, Stephen Pfohl, Diane Vaughan, Charles Derber, and Juliet Schor. 2004. Public sociologies: A symposium from Boston College. *Social Problems* 51 (1): 103–30.

Bush, George W. 2008. President Bush visits Fort Campbell, discusses Iraq and Afghanistan. November 25. Office of the Press Secretary, White House. Retrieved from http:// georgewbush-whitehouse.archives.gov/news/ releases/2008/11/20081125-1.html.

Butsch, Richard. 2005. Five decades and three hundred sitcoms about class and gender. In *Thinking outside the box: A contemporary television genre reader,* ed. Gary R. Edgerton and Brian G. Rose, pp. 111–35. Lexington: University Press of Kentucky.

Buttel, Frederick H. 2003. Environmental sociology and the explanation of environmental reform. *Organization & Environment* 16 (3): 306–44.

Buttel, Frederick H. 2004. The treadmill of production: An appreciation, assessment, and agenda for research. *Organization & Environment* 17 (3): 323–36.

Caldera, Y. M., A. C. Huston, and M. O'Brien. 1989. Social interaction and play patterns of parents and toddlers with feminine, masculine, and neutral toys. *Child Development* 60: 70–76.

Caldera, Y. M., and M. A. Sciaraffa. 1998. Parent-toddler play with feminine toys: Are all dolls the same? *Sex Roles* 39: 657–62.

Calhoun, Craig. 2007. *Classical sociological theory.* Malden, MA: Blackwell Publishing.

Callero, Peter. 2003. The sociology of the self. *Annual Review of Sociology* 29: 115–33.

Campbell, Donald, and Julian Stanley. 1963. *Experimental and quasi-experimental design for the social sciences.* Chicago: Rand McNally.

Carbonaro, William. 2005. Tracking, students' effort, and academic achievement. *Sociology of Education* 78 (1): 27–49.

Carli, Linda L. 1999. Gender, interpersonal power, and social influence. *Journal of Social Issues* 55 (1): 81–99.

Carlson, Marcia, and Paula England, eds. 2011. *Social class and changing families in an unequal America.* Stanford, CA: Stanford University Press.

Carnvale, Anthony P., and Stephen J. Rose. 2004. Socioeconomic status, race/ethnicity, and selective college admissions. In *America's untapped resource: Low-income students in higher education,* ed. Richard D. Kahlenberg. Washington, DC: Century Foundation Press.

Carr, Deborah, and Michael A. Friedman. 2005. Is obesity stigmatizing? Body weight, perceived discrimination, and psychological well-being in the United States. *Journal of Health and Social Behavior* 46 (3): 244–59.

Carr, Nicholas. 2010. *The shallows.* New York: Norton.

Carvajal, Doreen. 2006. Outsourcing hits a new class of workers. *International Herald Tribune,* November 20. Retrieved from www.iht.com/articles/2006/11/19/business/outsource.php.

Casanova, Jose. 1994. *Public religions in the modern world.* Chicago: University of Chicago Press.

Caspi, Avshalom, Joseph McClay, Terrie E. Moffitt, Jonathan Mill, Judy Martin, Ian W. Craig, Alan Taylor, and Richie Poulton. 2002. Role of genotype in the cycle of violence in maltreated children. *Science* 297: 851–54.

Castells, Manuel. 1983. *The city and the grass roots.* Berkeley: University of California Press.

Castells, Manuel. 1996. *The Rise of network society.* Oxford, U.K.: Blackwell.

Catalano, Shannon. 2007. Intimate partner violence in the United States. U.S. Bureau of Justice Statistics. Retrieved from www.ojp.usdoj.gov/bjs/intimate/ipv.htm.

Catalyst. 2010. 2010 Catalyst census: *Fortune* 500 women board directors. Retrieved from http://catalyst.org/publication/460/2010-catalyst-census-fortune-500-women-board-directors.

Center for American Women and Politics. 2011. Current numbers of women officeholders. Rutgers University. Retrieved from www.cawp.rutgers.edu/fast_facts/levels_of_office/Current_Numbers.php.

Center for Media and Public Affairs. 2007. 2006 Year in review. *Media Monitor* 21 (1): 1–8.

Cesari, Jocelyne. 2004. *When Islam and democracy meet.* New York: Palgrave Macmillan.

Cha, Ariana Eunjung. 2008. China's cars, accelerating a global demand for fuel. *Washington Post,* July 28, pp. A1, A6–A7.

Chafetz, Janet Saltzman, ed. 1999. *Handbook of the sociology of gender.* New York: Kluwer Academic/Plenum Publishers.

Chandola, Tarani, Eric Brunner, and Michael Marmot. 2006. Chronic stress at work and the metabolic syndrome: Prospective study. *British Journal of Medicine* 332: 521.

Changemakers. 2009. Barefoot . . . and speaking up for her rights. Ashoka. Retrieved from www.changemakers.com/node/30060.

Chaves, Mark. 1994. Secularization as declining religious authority. *Social Forces* 72 (3): 749–44.

Chazan, David. 2010. Row over "torture" on French TV. BBC News, March 18, Retrieved from http://news.bbc.co.uk/2/hi/europe/8573755.stm.

Chazan, Guy, Benoit Faucon, and Ben Casselman. 2010. As CEO Hayward remade BP, safety, cost drives clashed. *Wall Street Journal,* June 29. Retrieved from http://online.wsj.com/article/SB10001424052748703964104575335154126721876.html.

Chen, Henglien Lisa. 2010. Welfare and long-term care in the East and West. *International Journal of Sociology and Social Policy* 30 (3/4): 167–81.

Chen, Kathy. 2005. China's growth places strains on a family's ties. *Wall Street Journal,* April 13, pp. A1, A15.

Cherlin, Andrew J. 2005. American marriage in the early twenty-first century. *The Future of Children* 15 (2): 33–55.

Cherlin, Andrew J. 2008. *Public and private families.* New York: McGraw-Hill.

Cheshire, Tamara. 2006. American Indian families: Strength and answers from our past. In *Families in global and multicultural perspective,* 2nd ed., ed. Bron B. Ingoldsby and Suzanna D. Smith, 315–27. Thousand Oaks, CA: Sage.

Chesler, Naomi C., and Mark A. Chesler. 2002. Gender-informed mentoring strategies for women engineering scholars: On establishing a caring community. *Journal of Engineering Education* 91 (9): 49–55.

Chinn, Sarah. 2008. *Inventing modern adolescence.* Rutgers, NJ: Rutgers University Press.

Chomsky, Noam. 1989. *Necessary illusions: Thought control in democratic societies.* Cambridge, MA: South End Press.

Christopher, Karen. 2002. Family-friendly Europe. *American Prospect* 13 (7): 60–64.

Chronicle of Higher Education. 2010. Online learning: By the numbers. *Chronicle of Higher Education,* October 31. Retrieved from http://chronicle.com/article/Online-Learning-Enrollment/125202/.

Chun, Jennifer Jihye. 2009. *Organizing at the margins: The symbolic politics of labor in South Korea and the United States.* Ithaca, NY: ILR/Cornell University Press.

Cialdini, Robert B., and Noah H. Goldstein. 2004. Social influence: Compliance and conformity. *Annual Review of Psychology* 55: 591–621.

Citizens for Tax Justice. 2011. Boeing's reward for paying no federal taxes over last three years?

A \$35 billion federal contract. Retrieved from www.ctj.org/pdf/boeing0211.pdf.

Clarke, Lee. 2006. Worst case Katrina. In *Understanding Katrina: Perspectives from the social sciences.* Retrieved from http://understanding katrina.ssrc.org/Clarke/.

Clawson, Dan. 2003. *The next upsurge: Labor and the new social movements.* Ithaca, NY: ILR/Cornell University Press.

Clawson, Dan, Alan Neustadtl, and Mark Weller. 1998. *Dollars and votes: How business campaign contributions subvert democracy.* Philadelphia, PA: Temple University Press.

Clayman, Steven, and John Heritage. 2002. *The news interview.* New York: Cambridge University Press.

Clearfield, Melissa W., and Naree M. Nelson. 2006. Sex differences in mothers' speech and play behavior with 6-, 9-, and 14-month-old infants. *Sex Roles: A Journal of Research* 54 (1–2): 127–37.

Clendinen, D., and A. Nagourney. 1999. *Out for good: The struggle to build a gay rights movement in America.* New York: Simon & Schuster.

Cloward, Richard A., and Lloyd E. Ohlin. 1960. *Delinquency and opportunity.* New York: Free Press.

CNN/Opinion Research Corporation. 2010. CNN/opinion research poll. December 20. Retrieved from http://i2.cdn.turner.com/cnn/2010/images/12/20/rel17a.pdf.

Cochran, John K., and Mitchell B. Chamlin. 2006. The enduring racial divide in death penalty support. *Journal of Criminal Justice* 34: 85–99.

Cohen, Patricia. 2010. Indian tribes go in search of their lost languages. *New York Times,* April 5, p. C1.

Cole, David, and James X. Dempsey. 2006. *Terrorism and the Constitution: Sacrificing civil liberties in the name of national security.* New York: New Press.

Collins, Chuck, and Sam Pizzigati. 2010. *Resurrect the estate tax.* Washington, DC: Institute for Policy Studies. Retrieved from www.ips-dc.org/articles/resurrect_the_estate_tax.

Collins, Chuck, and Felice Yeskel. 2005. *Economic apartheid in America.* New York: New Press.

Collins, Patricia Hill. 1990. *Black feminist thought.* New York: Routledge.

Collins, Patricia Hill. 2000. *Black feminist thought.* New York: Routledge.

Collins, Randall. 1979. *Credential society.* New York: Academic Press.

Collins, Randall, Janet Saltzman Chafetz, Rae Lesser Blumberg, Scott Coltrane, and Jonathan H. Turner. 1993. Toward an integrated theory of gender stratification. *Sociological Perspectives* 36 (3): 185–216.

Coltrane, Scott. 1989. Household labor and the routine production of gender. *Social Problems* 36 (5): 473–90.

Commission on Social Determinants of Health. (2008). *Closing the gap in a generation: Health equity through action on the social determinants of health. (Final report of the Commission on Social Determinants of Health.)* Geneva: World Health Organization.

Compa, Lance. 2004. *Unfair advantage: Workers' freedom of association in the United States under international human rights standards.* Ithaca, NY: ILR Press/Cornell University Press.

Conger, Dylan. 2010. Does bilingual education interfere with English-language acquisition? *Social Science Quarterly* 91 (4): 1103–22.

Conklin, John E. 2010. *Criminology,* 10th ed. Boston: Allyn & Bacon.

Conlin, Michelle. 2008. In the land of plenty, why pay? *Business Week,* October 20, p. 56.

Connell, R. W. 2000. *The men and the boys.* Berkeley: University of California Press.

Connell, R. W. 2005. *Masculinities.* Berkeley: University of California Press.

Connell, Raewyn. 1987. *Gender and power.* Stanford, CA: Stanford University Press.

Conrad, Peter. 2005. General introduction. In *The sociology of health and illness,* 7th ed., ed. Peter Conrad. New York: Worth Publishers.

Conrad, Peter. 2005. The shifting engines of medicalization. *Journal of Health and Social Behavior* 46 (March): 3–14.

Conrad, Peter, and Joseph Schneider. 1980. *Deviance and medicalization.* St. Louis, MO: Mosby.

Conway, Oliver. 2004. Congo word "most untranslatable." BBC News, June 22. Retrieved from http://news.bbc.co.uk/2/hi/africa/3830521.stm.

Cookson, Peter, and Caroline Persell. 1985. *Preparing for power: America's elite boarding schools.* New York: Basic Books.

Cooley, Charles Horton. 1902/1964. *Human nature and the social order.* New York: Schocken Books.

Coontz, Stephanie. 1992. *The way we never were: American families and the nostalgia trap.* New York: Basic Books.

Coontz, Stephanie. 2000. Historical perspectives on family studies. *Journal of Marriage and the Family* 62: 283–97.

Coontz, Stephanie. 2006. *Marriage, a history: How love conquered marriage.* New York: Penguin.

Cornell, Stephen, and Douglas Hartmann. 2007. *Ethnicity and race: Making identities in a changing world.* Thousand Oaks, CA: Pine Forge Press.

Cose, Ellis. 1995. *The rage of a privileged class.* New York: Harper Perennial.

Coser, Lewis. 1956. *The functions of social conflict.* New York: Free Press.

Costa-Font, Joan, David Elvira, and Oscar Mascarilla-Miro. 2009 "Ageing in place?" Exploring elderly people's housing preferences in Spain. *Urban Studies* 46 (2): 295–316.

Cottle, Simon. 2007. Ethnography and news production: New(s) developments in the field. *Sociology Compass* 1 (1): 1–16.

Cowie, Jefferson, and Joseph Heathcott, eds. 2003. *Beyond the ruins: The meanings of deindustrialization.* Ithaca, NY: Cornell University Press.

Cowley, Geoffrey, and Karen Springen. 2005. Designing heart-healthy communities. *Newsweek,* October 3, pp. 60–66.

Crockett, Alasdair, and David Voas. 2006. Generations of decline: Religious change in 20th-century Britain. *Journal for the Scientific Study of Religion* 45 (4): 567–84.

Cromartie, John, and Shawn Bucholtz. 2008. Defining the "rural" in rural America. *Amber Waves,* June. Retrieved from www.ers.usda.gov/AmberWaves/June08/Features/RuralAmerica.htm.

Croteau, David, and William Hoynes. 1994a. All the usual suspects: *MacNeil/Lehrer* and *Nightline.* In *By Invitation Only: How the Media Limit Political Debate,* pp. 105–37. Monroe, ME: Common Courage Press.

Croteau, David, and William Hoynes. 1994b. *By invitation only: How the media limit political debate.* Monroe, ME: Common Courage Press.

Croteau, David, and William Hoynes. 2006. *The business of media: Corporate media and the public interest.* Thousand Oaks, CA: Pine Forge Press.

Croteau, David, William Hoynes, and Kevin Carragee. 1996. The political diversity of public television. *Journalism and Mass Communication Monographs* 157: 1–55.

Croteau, David, William Hoynes, and Stefania Milan. 2011. *Media/society: Industries, images, and audiences,* 4th ed. Thousand Oaks, CA: Pine Forge Press.

Crothers, Lane. 2009. *Globalization and American popular culture,* 2nd ed. Lanham, MD: Rowman & Littlefield.

Crumley, Bruce. 2009. Will France impose a ban on the burqa? *Time,* June 19.

Czaja, Ronald, and Johnny Blair. 2004. *Designing surveys,* 2nd ed. Thousand Oaks, CA: Pine Forge Press.

Dahl, Robert. 1957. The concept of power. *Behavioral Science* 2: 201–15.

Dahl, Robert. 1961. *Who governs? Democracy and power in an American city.* New Haven, CT: Yale University Press.

Dahrendorf, Ralf. 1959. *Class and class conflict in industrial society.* Stanford, CA: Stanford University Press.

Danaher, Kevin, and Anuradha Mittal. 2004. *10 Reasons to abolish the IMF and World Bank.* Westminster, MD: Seven Stories Press.

Daniels, Roger. 1997. *Not like us: Immigrants and minorities in America, 1890–1924.* Chicago: Ivan R. Dee Publishers.

Das, Satyajit. 2010. *Traders, guns, and money.* New York: Financial Times/Prentice Hall.

Davidov, Eldad, Bart Meuleman, Jaak Billiet and Peter Schmidt. 2008. Values and support for immigration: A cross-country comparison. *European Sociological Review* 24 (5): 583–99.

Davidov, Eldad, Peter Schmidt, and Shalom H. Schwartz. 2008. Bringing values back in. *Public Opinion Quarterly* 72: 420–45.

Davie, Grace. 1994. *Religion in Britain since 1945: Believing without belonging.* Oxford: Blackwell.

Davies, Karen. 2003. The body and doing gender: The relations between doctors and nurses in hospital work. *Sociology of Health & Illness* 25 (7): 720–42.

Davies, Scott, and Julian Tanner. 2003. The long arm of the law: Effects of labeling on employment. *Sociological Quarterly* 44 (3): 385–404.

Davis, Kathy, Monique Leijenaar, and Jantine Oldersma. 1991. *The gender of power.* Thousand Oaks, CA: Sage.

Davis, Kingsley. 1947. Final note on a case of extreme isolation. *American Journal of Sociology* 52 (5): 432–37.

Davis, Kingsley, and Wilbert Moore. 1945. Some principles of stratification. *American Sociological Review* 10: 242–49.

Davis, Shannon N., and Theodore N. Greenstein. 2004. Cross national variations in the division of household labor. *Journal of Marriage and the Family* 66 (5).

Day, Dorothy. 1952. *The long loneliness.* New York: Harper & Row.

Death Penalty Information Center. 2011. Facts about the death penalty. Retrieved from www.deathpenaltyinfo.org.

Deegan, Mary Jo. 1988. *Jane Addams and the men of the Chicago School, 1892–1918.* New Brunswick, NJ: Transaction Books.

Della Porta, Donatella, and Mario Diani. 2006. *Social movements: An introduction.* Malden, MA: Blackwell.

Demo, David H., Katherine R. Allen, and Mark A. Fine, eds. 2000. *Handbook of family diversity.* New York: Oxford University Press.

Denvir, Daniel. 2011. The 10 most segregated urban areas in America. Retrieved from http://politics.salon.com/2011/03/29/most_segregated_cities/slide_show/10/.

Derber, Charles, William A. Schwartz, and Yale Magrass. 1990. *Power in the highest degree.* New York: Oxford University Press.

Devlin, Bernie, Stephen E. Fienberg, Daniel P. Resnick, Kathryn Roeder, eds. 1997. *Intelligence, genes, and success: Scientists respond to the bell curve.* New York: Springer-Verlag.

Dey, Judy Goldberg, and Catherine Hill. 2007. *Behind the pay gap.* Washington, DC: American Association of University Women Educational Foundation.

Dill, Karen E., and Kathryn P. Thill. 2007. Video game characters and the socialization of gender roles. *Sex Roles* 57: 851–64.

Do, D. Phuong, Brian Karl Finch, Ricardo Basurto-Davila, Chloe Bird, Jose Escarce, and Nicole Lurie. 2008. Does place explain racial health disparities. *Social Science & Medicine* 67: 1258–68.

Dobbelaere, Karel. 1999. Towards an integrated perspective of the processes related to the descriptive concept of secularization. *Sociology of Religion* 60 (3): 229–47.

Domhoff, G. William. 2009. *Who rules America?* New York: McGraw-Hill.

Douglass, Frederick. 2003. *Frederick Douglass on slavery and the Civil War: Selections from his writings,* ed. Joslyn T. Pine. Mineola, NY: Dover.

Dowd, Timothy J. Concentration and diversity revisited: Production logics and the U.S. mainstream recording market, 1940 to 1990. *Social Forces* 82 (4): 1411–55.

Downes, David, and Paul Rock. 2011. *Understanding deviance,* 6th ed. New York: Oxford University Press.

Downie, Leonard, Jr., and Robert G. Kaiser. 2003. *The news about the news: American journalism in peril.* New York, Vintage.

Doyle, Thomas P., A. W. Richard Sipe, and Patrick J. Wall. 2006. *Sex, priests, and secret codes: The Catholic Church's 2,000 year paper trail of sexual abuse.* Los Angeles: Bonus Books.

Draper, Elaine. 2003. *The company doctor.* New York: Russell Sage Foundation.

Dreher, Axel. 2006. Does globalization affect growth? Empirical evidence from a new index. *Applied Economics* 38 (10): 1091–110.

Dreher, Axel, Noel Gaston, and Pim Marens. 2008. *Measuring globalization, gauging its consequences.* New York: Springer.

Dreifus, Claudia. 2005. A sociologist confronts "the messy stuff" of race, genes and disease. *New York Times,* October 18, p. 2.

Du Bois, W.E.B. 1899/1996. *The Philadelphia negro: A social study.* Philadelphia: University of Pennsylvania Press.

Du Bois, W.E.B. 1903/2005. *The souls of black folk.* New York: Simon & Schuster.

Dubois, W.E.B. 1935/1998. *Black reconstruction in the United States, 1860–1880.* New York: Free Press.

Duchrow, Ulrich. 2011. A European revival of liberation theology. *Tikkun* 26 (1): 74. Retrieved from www.tikkun.org/article.php/jan2011duchrow.

Dudley, Kathryn Marie. 1997. *The end of the line: Lost jobs, new lives in postindustrial America.* Chicago: University of Chicago Press.

Dugan, Máire A. 2003. Empowerment. In *Beyond intractability,* ed. Guy Burgess and Heidi Burgess. Boulder, CO: Conflict Research Consortium, University of Colorado. Retrieved from www.beyondintractability.org/essay/empowerment.

Dugsin, R. 2001. Conflict and healing in the family experience of second-generation emigrants from Indian living in North America. *Family Process* 40 (2): 233–41.

Duhigg, Charles. 2007. For elderly investors, instant experts abound. *New York Times,* July 8, pp. 1, 14.

Dunlap, Riley E., and William R. Catton, Jr. 1994. Struggling with human exceptionalism: The rise, decline and revitalization of environmental sociology. *American Sociologist* 25: 5–30.

Dunlap, Riley E., and Brent K. Marshall. 2007. Environmental sociology. In *21st Century sociology: A reference handbook,* ed. Clifton D. Bryant and Dennis L. Peck, pp. 329–40. Thousand Oaks, CA: Sage.

Dunn, Robert G. 2000. Identity, commodification, and consumer culture. In *Identity and social change,* ed. Joseph E. Davis, pp. 109–34. New Brunswick, NJ: Transaction.

Durand, Jorge, Douglas S. Massey, and Rene Zenteno. 2001. Mexican immigration to the United States: Continuities and changes. *Latin American Research Review* 36 (1): 107–11.

Durkheim, Emile. 1893/1997. *The division of labor in society.* New York: Free Press.

Durkheim, Emile. 1895/1982. *The rules of sociological method,* trans. Sarah A. Solovay and John H. Mueller. New York: Free Press.

Durkheim, Emile. 1897/1951. *Suicide,* trans. John A. Spaulding and George Simpson. New York: Free Press.

Durkheim, Emile. 1915/2001. *Elementary forms of the religious life,* trans. Carol Cosman. New York: Oxford University Press.

Durkheim, Emile. 1922/1956. *Education and sociology,* trans. D. F. Pocock. Glencoe, IL: Free Press.

Durkheim, Emile. 1925/1961. *Moral education,* trans. Everett K. Wilson. Glencoe, IL: Free Press.

Durkheim, Emile. 1938/1977. *The evolution of educational thought,* trans. Peter Collins. Boston, MA: Routledge/Kegan Paul.

Duster, Troy. 1991/2003. *Backdoor to eugenics.* New York: Routledge.

Dvorak, Petula. 2010. For bullied gay teens, the world is still far from accepting. *Washington Post,* October 4.

Dyer, Gwynne. 2004. *War: The lethal custom,* revised ed. New York: Carol & Graf Publishers.

Dyson, Michael Eric. 2000. *I may not get there with you: The true Martin Luther King Jr.* New York: Free Press.

Eaton, Joe, and M. B. Pell. 2010. Analysis: Health lobbyists' powerful impact on reform bills. Kaiser Health News. Retrieved from www.kaiserhealthnews.org/Stories/2010/February/24/CPI-health-lobbying.aspx.

The Economist. 2007. A world wide web of terror. July 14, pp. 28–30.

Economist Intelligence Unit. 2010. Democracy Index 2010: Democracy in retreat. *The Economist.* Retrieved from http://graphics.eiu.com/PDF/Democracy_Index_2010_web.pdf.

Eddy, Elizabeth. 2004. Environmental security: Securing what for whom? *Social Alternatives* 23 (4): 23–28.

Edelman, Laren B., and Mark C. Suchman. 1997. The legal environments of organizations. *Annual Review of Sociology* 23: 479–515.

Edin, Kathryn, and Maria Kefalas. 2005. *Promises I can keep: Why poor women put motherhood before marriage.* New York: Basic Books.

Editorial Projects in Education Research Center. 2009. *Cities in crisis 2009: Closing the graduation gap.* Retrieved from www.edweek.org/rc/articles/2009/04/22/cities_in_crisis.html.

Education for All Global Monitoring Report. 2010. *Reaching the marginalized.* UNESCO Publishing. Retrieved from www.unesco.org/new/en/education/themes/leading-the-international-agenda/efareport/reports/2010-marginalization/.

Edwards, Richard. 1982. *Contested terrain: The transformation of the workplace in the twentieth century.* New York: Basic Books.

Ehrlich, Paul R. 1968/1986. *The population bomb.* New York: Ballantine Books.

Einstein, Albert. 1946/1999. Quoted in *The Oxford Dictionary of Quotations,* ed. Elizabeth Knowles, p. 290. New York: Oxford University Press.

Elder, Glen H., Jr. 2006. Life course perspective. In *The Blackwell encyclopedia of sociology,* ed. George Ritzer, 2634–39. Boston: Blackwell.

Elder, Glen. 1974/1999. *Children of the Great Depression.* Boulder, CO: Westview Press.

Eller, Cynthia. 2001. *The myth of patriarchal prehistory.* Boston: Beacon.

Elson, Diane, and Hanke Keklik. 2003. *Progress of the world's women, 2002,* Vol. 2. New York: UN Development Fund for Women.

Emerson, Michael O., and David Hartman. 2006. The rise of religious fundamentalism. *Annual Review of Sociology* 32: 127–44.

Engels, Frederick. 1884/1972. *The origin of the family, private property and the state.* New York: International Publishers.

Entman, Robert, and Andrew Rojecki. 2001. *The black image in the white mind.* Chicago: University of Chicago Press.

Erickson, Kai. 1966. *Wayward puritans: A study in the sociology of deviance.* New York: Wiley.

Erlanger, Steven. 2010. France: Senate passes bill on facial veils. *New York Times,* September 15, p. A6.

Espenshade, Thomas J., Chang Y. Chung, and Joan L. Walling. 2004. Admission preferences for minority students, athletes, and legacies at elite universities. *Social Science Quarterly* 85 (5): 1422–46.

Esping-Andersen, Eosta, ed. 2007. *Family formation and family dilemmas in contemporary Europe.* Madrid, Spain: BBVA Foundation.

Esposito, John L., and John Voll. 2001. *Makers of contemporary Islam.* New York: Oxford University Press.

Etzioni, Amitai. 2004. *How patriotic is the Patriot Act? Freedom versus security in the age of terrorism.* New York: Routledge.

European Audiovisual Observatory. 2010. *Focus 2010: World film market trends.* Retrieved from www.obs.coe.int/oea_publ/market/focus.html.

Evangelical Climate Initiative. 2006. Climate change: An evangelical call to action. Retrieved from http://christiansandclimate.org/learn/call-to-action.

Evans, Peter. 1997. Review of *The clash of civilizations and the remaking of the world order. Contemporary Sociology* 26 (6): 691–93.

Evans, Sarah. 1980. *Personal politics.* New York: Vintage.

Ewen, Stuart. 2001. *Captains of consciousness: Advertising and the social roots of consumer culture.* New York: McGraw-Hill.

Fadiman, Anne. 1998. *The spirit catches you and you fall down.* New York: Farrar, Strauss, & Giroux.

Fan, Maureen. 2008. A fresh face for the Olympics. *Washington Post,* July 21, p. A7.

Farkas, Steve, Jean Johnson, and Tony Foleno with Ann Duffett and Patrick Foley. 2001. For goodness' sake: Why so many want religion to play a greater role in American life. New York: Public Agenda. Retrieved from www.publicagenda.org/files/pdf/for_goodness_sake.pdf.

Fass, Paula, and Mary Mason, eds. 2000. *Childhood in America.* New York: New York University Press.

Fastenberg, Dan. 2010. A brief history of international gay marriage. *Time,* July 22. Retrieved from www.time.com/time/world/article/0,8599,2005678,00.html.

Fausto-Sterling, Anne. 2000. *Sexing the body.* New York: Basic Books.

Feagin, Joe R., and Eileen O'Brien. 2003. *White men on race power, privilege, and the shaping of cultural consciousness.* Boston: Beacon Press.

Feagin, Joe R., and Melvin P. Sikes. 1994. *Living with racism: The black middle class experience.* Boston: Beacon Press.

Feagin, Joe, and Hernan Vera. 2001. *Liberation sociology.* Boulder, CO: Westview Press.

Federal Interagency Forum on Aging-Related Statistics. 2010. *Older Americans 2010: Key indicators of well-being.* Washington, DC: Federal Interagency Forum on Aging-Related Statistics.

Federal Trade Commission. 2010. FTC approves final order settling charges that public relations firm used misleading online endorsements to market gaming apps. November 26. Retrieved from www.ftc.gov/opa/2010/11/reverb.shtm.

Fels, Anna. 2005. *Necessary dreams: Ambition in women's changing lives.* New York: Anchor.

Feng, Jing, Ian Spence, and Jay Pratt. 2007. Playing an action video game reduces gender differences in spatial cognition. *Psychological Science* 18 (10): 850–55.

Ferree, Myra Marx. 1990. Beyond separate spheres: Feminism and family research. *Journal of Marriage and the Family* 52: 866–84.

Ferriss, Susan. 2003. Free trade's broken promises. (Austin) *American-Statesman,* November 5. Retrieved from www.statesman.com/specialreports/content/specialreports/mexico_farms/1102mexfactory.html.

Field, Kelly. 2010. Senators vow to crack down on 'bad actors' in the for-profit sector. *Chronicle of Higher Education,* June 24. Retrieved from http://chronicle.com/article/Senators-Vow-to-Crack-Down-on/66058/.

Filson, Jennifer, Emilio Ulloa, Cristin Runfola, and Audrey Hokoda. 2010. Does powerlessness explain the relationship between partner violence and depression? *Journal of Interpersonal Violence* 25 (3): 400–15.

Financial Crisis Inquiry Commission. 2011. *The financial crisis inquiry report.* New York: Public Affairs.

Finberg, Howard I. 2005. Our complex media day. Retrieved from www.poynter.org/content/content_view.asp?id=89510.

Fine, Gary Alan. 2006. Shopfloor cultures. *Sociological Quarterly* 47: 1–19.

Fiorina, Morris. 2011. *Culture war? The myth of a polarized America,* 3rd ed. Boston: Longman.

Fischer, Claude. 1992. *America calling: A social history of the telephone to 1940.* Berkeley: University of California Press.

Fischer, Claude, and Michael Hout. 2006. *Century of difference: How America changed in the last one hundred years.* New York: Russell Sage Foundation.

Fischer, Claude, Micheal Hout, Martin Sanchez Jankowski, Samuel R. Lucas, Ann Swidler, and Kim Voss. 1996. *Inequality by design: Cracking the bell curve myth.* Princeton, NJ: Princeton University Press.

Fischer, Claude, Martin Sanchez Jankowski, Samuel R. Lucas, Ann Swidler, and Kim Voss. 1996. *Inequality by design: Cracking the bell curve myth.* Princeton, NJ: Princeton University Press.

Fischer, Kimberly, Muriel Egerton, Jonathan I. Gershuny, and John P. Robinson. 2007. Gender convergence in the American Heritage time use study. *Social Indicators Research* 82: 1–33.

Fishman, Mark. 1980. *Manufacturing the news.* Austin: University of Texas Press.

Flacks, Richard. 1988. *Making history.* New York: Columbia University Press.

Fletcher, Colin. 1974. *Beneath the surface.* Boston: Routledge.

Flew, Terry. 2007. *Understanding global media.* New York: Palgrave Macmillan.

Flint, Anthony. 2006. *This land: The battle over sprawl and the future of America.* Baltimore, MD: Johns Hopkins University Press.

Flora, Cornelia Butler, and Jan L. Flora. 2008. *Rural communities,* 3rd ed. Boulder, CO: Westview Press.

Floyd-Thomas, Stacy M., and Anthony B. Pinn, eds. 2010. *Liberation theologies in the United States.* New York: New York University Press.

Forsyth, Donelson. 2010. *Group dynamics.* Belmont, CA: Wadsworth.

Foster, John Bellamy, and Fred Magdoff. 2009. *The great financial crisis: Causes and consequences.* New York: Monthly Review Press.

Foucault, Michel. 1975/1995. *Discipline and punish: The birth of the prison,* transl. Alan Sheridan. New York: Vintage.

Foucault, Michel. 1977/1979. *Discipline and punish,* trans. Alan Sheridan. New York: Vintage.

Foucault, Michel. 1978/1980. *The history of sexuality,* vol. 1. New York: Vintage.

Fowler, Geoffrey A. 2005. In Asia, it's nearly impossible to tell a song from an ad. *Wall Street Journal,* May 31, pp. A1, A10.

Fox, Greer Litton, and Velma McBride Murray. 2000. Gender and families: Feminist perspectives and family research. *Journal of Marriage and the Family* 62: 1160–72.

Frank, Thomas. 1997. *The conquest of cool.* Chicago: University of Chicago Press.

Frankowski, Barbara L. 2004. Sexual orientation and adolescents. *Pediatrics* 113 (6): 1827–32.

Fraser, Nancy. 1992. Rethinking the public sphere: A contribution to the critique of actually existing democracy. In *Habermas and the Public Sphere,* ed. Craig Calhoun, pp. 109–42. Cambridge, MA: MIT Press.

Fraser, Steve, ed. 1995. *The bell curve wars.* New York: Basic Books.

Freedman, Robert. 2009. *Noise wars: Compulsory media and our loss of autonomy.* New York: Algora Publishing.

Freire, Paulo. 1970. *Pedagogy of the oppressed,* transl. Myra Bergman Ramos. New York: Seabury Press.

French, John R. P. Jr., and Bertram Raven. 1959/2001. The bases of social power. In *The negotiation sourcebook,* ed. Ira G. Asherman and Sandra Vance Asherman, 61–73. Amherst, MA: HRD Press.

Fried, Mindy. 2008. The evaluator in the field as an outsider within. *Footnotes* 36 (3). Retrieved from www.asanet.org/footnotes/mar08_R/fn6.html.

Friedland, Lewis A., and Shauna Morimoto. 2005. The changing lifeworld of young people: Risk, resume-padding, and civic engagement. CIRCLE Working Paper 40. Medford, MA: Center for Information and Research on Civic Learning and Engagement.

Friedland, N. 1976. Social influence via threats. *Journal of Experimental Social Psychology* 12: 552–63.

Friedman, Jeffrey, and Richard A. Posner, eds. 2009. *What caused the financial crisis.* Philadelphia: University of Pennsylvania Press.

Friedrichs, David O. 2009. *Trusted criminals: White collar crime in contemporary society,* 4th ed. Belmont, CA: Wadsworth.

Friese, Bettina, and Karen Bogenschneider. 2009. The voice of experience: How social scientists communicate family research to policymakers. *Family Relations* 58 (April): 229–43.

Frumkin, Howard. 2003. Healthy places: Exploring the evidence. *American Journal of Public Health* 93 (9): 1451–56.

Fussell, Elizabeth. 2006. Leaving New Orleans: Social stratification, networks, and hurricane evacuation. In *Understanding Katrina: Perspectives from the social sciences.* Retrieved from http://understandingkatrina.ssrc.org/Fussell/.

Futrell, Robert, and Pete Simi. 2004. Free spaces, collective identity, and the persistence of U.S. white power activism. *Social Problems* 51 (1): 16–42.

Fuwa, Makiko. 2004. Macro-level gender inequality and the division of household labor in 22 countries. *American Sociological Review* 69 (6): 751–67.

Gaines, Donna. 1991. *Teenage wasteland.* New York: Pantheon.

Gaines, Donna. 2003. *A misfit's manifesto: The spiritual journey of a rock-and-roll heart.* New York: Villard.

Gallian, Joseph A. 2004. A conversation with Melanie Wood. *Math Horizons* (September): 13–14, 31.

Gallup Organization. 2007. Racial disagreement over death penalty has varied historically. July 30. Retrieved from www.gallup.com/poll/28243/Racial-Disagreement-Over-Death-Penalty-Has-Varied-Historically.aspx.

Galtung, Johan. 1996. *Peace by peaceful means.* London: Sage.

Galtung, Johan. 2000. *Conflict transformation by peaceful means.* New York: United Nations.

Galtung, Johan. 2009. *The fall of the US empire—and then what?* TRANSCEND University Press.

Gamson, William A., Bruce Fireman, and Steven Rytina. 1982. *Encounters with unjust authority.* Homewood, IL: Dorsey Press.

Gans, Herbert J. 1999. *Popular culture & high culture,* rev. ed. New York: Basic Books.

Gans, Herbert J. 2004. *Deciding what's news.* New York: Random House.

Gans, Herbert J. 2005. *Deciding what's news,* 25th anniversary ed. Chicago: Northwestern University Press.

Ganz, Marshall. 2009. *Why David sometimes wins: Leadership, organization, and strategy in the California farm worker movement.* New York: Oxford University Press.

Garcia, Marlen. 2009. At some schools, budget cuts put the kibosh on sports. *USA Today,* September 2. Retrieved from www.usatoday.com/sports/preps/2009-09-02-budget_sports_cuts_N.htm.

Gardner, Gary, Erik Assadourian, and Radhia Sarin. 2004. The state of consumption today. In *The state of the world, 2004* by the Worldwatch Institute, pp. 3–23 New York: Norton.

Garfinkel, Harold. 1967. *Studies in ethnomethodology.* New York: Prentice-Hall.

Garland, David. 1993. *Punishment and modern society.* Chicago: University of Chicago Press.

Gates, Gary J. 2010. New Census Bureau data shows growth in same-sex couples outpacing population. Los Angeles: Williams Institute, UCLA School of Law.

Gates, Gary J. 2011. How many people are lesbian, gay, bisexual and transgender? Los Angeles: Williams Institute, UCLA School of Law.

Gauchet, M. 1997. *The disenchantment of the world.* Princeton, NJ: Princeton University Press.

Gauntlett, David. 2002. *Media, gender and identity.* New York: Routledge.

Gaventa, John. 1982. *Power and powerlessness.* Urbana: University of Illinois Press.

Gazzaniga, Michael. 1998. *The mind's past.* Berkeley: University of California Press. Goffman, Erving. 1961. *Asylums.* New York: Anchor.

Gecas, Viktor. 2008. The ebb and flow of sociological interest in values. *Sociological Forum* 23 (June): 344–50.

Gelder, Ken, ed. 2005. *The subcultures reader,* 2nd ed. New York: Routledge.

Gerbner, George, Larry Gross, Michael Morgan, and Nancy Signorielli. 2008. Growing up with television: Cultivation processes. In *Media effects: Advances in theory and research,* ed. Jennings Bryant and Dolf Zillmann. Hillsdale, NJ: Lawrence Erlbaum.

German Bundestag. 2011. Parliamentary groups, as of 3 March 2011. Retrieved from www.bundestag.de/htdocs_e/bundestag/groups/index.html.

Gerson, Kathleen. 1987. *Hard choices: How women decide about work, career, and motherhood.* Berkeley: University of California Press.

Gibson, Campbell. 1998. Population of the 100 largest cities and other urban places in the United States: 1790 to 1990. Retrieved from www.census.gov/population/www/documentation/twps0027/twps0027.html.

Gibson, Campbell, and Kay Jung. 2002. Historical census statistics on population totals by race, 1790 to 1990, Table 1. Washington, DC: U.S. Census Bureau. Retrieved from www.census.gov/population/www/documentation/twps0056/twps0056.html.

Gibson, Margaret. 1988. *Accommodation without assimilation: Sikh immigrants in an American high school.* Ithaca, NY: Cornell University Press.

Gieryn, Thomas F. 2000. A space for place in sociology. *Annual Review of Sociology* 26: 463–96.

Gilbert, Dennis. 2008. *The American class structure in an age of growing inequality.* Belmont, CA: Thomson Wadsworth.

Gilbert, Dennis. 2011. *The American class structure in an age of growing inequality,* 8th ed. Thousand Oaks, CA: Pine Forge Press.

Gilens, Martin. 1996. Race and poverty in America: Public misperceptions and the American news media. *Public Opinion Quarterly* 60 (4): 515–41.

Gilens, Martin. 2005. Inequality and democratic responsiveness. *Public Opinion Quarterly* 69 (5): 778–96.

Gill, Rosiland. 2007. *Gender and the media.* Malden, MA: Polity Press.

Gilley, Brian Joseph. 2006. *Becoming two-spirit: Gay identity and social acceptance in Indian country.* Omaha: University of Nebraska Press.

Ginsborg, Paul. 2005. *Silvio Berlusconi: Television, power and patrimony.* London: Verso.

Gladwell, Malcolm. 1997. The coolhunt. *The New Yorker,* March 17.

Glanz, James, and Alissa Rubin. 2007. Blackwater shooting was "deliberate murder," Iraq says. *New York Times,* October 8. Retrieved from www.nytimes.com/2007/10/08/news/08iht-iraq.4.7803511.html.

Glass, Ira. 2008. The giant pool of money. *This American Life,* May 9. Retrieved from www.thisamericanlife.org/radio-archives/episode/355/the-giant-pool-of-money.

Glassner, Barry. 2009. *The culture of fear,* 10th anniversary ed. New York: Basic Books.

Goe, W. Richard, and Sean Noonan. 2007. The sociology of community. In *21st Century sociology: A reference handbook,* ed. Clifton D. Bryant and Dennis L. Peck, pp. 455–64. Thousand Oaks, CA: Sage.

Goffman, Erving. 1959. *The presentation of self in everyday life.* Garden City, NY: Doubleday Anchor Books.

Goffman, Erving. 1963. *Stigma: Notes on the management of spoiled identity.* New York: Simon & Schuster.

Goffman, Erving. 1974. *Frame analysis.* New York: Harper & Row.

Goldsmith, Marshall. 2004. Why even thinking about retirement can be a bad idea. *Fast Company* 78 (January).

Goldsmith, Pat Antonio. 2004. Schools' racial mix, students' optimism, and the black-white and Latino-white achievement gaps. *Sociology of Education* 77 (2): 121–47.

Göle, Nilüfer. 2011. *Islam in Europe.* Princeton, NJ: Markus Weiner.

Gonzalez, Juan. 2000. *Harvest of empire: A history of Latinos in America.* New York: Penguin.

Goo, Sara Kehaulini. 2006. Apple gets a big slice of product-placement pie. *Washington Post,* April 15, p. D1.

Goodman, Amy. 2007. Egyptian human rights activist Saad Eddin Ibrahim defies threats, arrests to challenge U.S.-backed Mubarak government. Retrieved from www.democracynow.org/2007/10/10/egyptian_human_rights_activist_saad_eddin.

Gordon, David M., Richard Edwards, and Michael Reich. 1982. *Segmented work, divided workers.* New York: Cambridge University Press.

Gottdiener, Mark, and Ray Hutchison. 2010. *The new urban sociology,* 4th ed. Boulder, CO: Westview Press.

Gould, Kenneth A., David N. Pellow, and Allen Schnaiberg. 2008. *The treadmill of production: Injustice and unsustainability in the global economy.* Boulder, CO: Paradigm Publishers.

Government Accountability Office. 2008. Tax administration: Comparison of the reported tax liabilities of foreign- and U.S.-controlled corporations, 1998–2005. Retrieved from www.gao.gov/new.items/d08957.pdf.

Gramsci, Antonio. 1929–1935/1971. *Selections from the prison notebooks,* ed. and trans. Quintin Hoare and Geoffrey Nowell Smith. New York: International Publishers.

Granfield, Robert. 1992. *Making elite lawyers.* New York: Routledge.

Granfield, Robert, and Thomas Koenig. 1990. From activism to pro bono. *Critical Sociology* 17 (1): 57–80.

Granovetter, Mark S. 1973. The strength of weak ties. *American Journal of Sociology* 78 (6): 1360–80.

Granovetter, Mark S. 1974. *Getting a job.* Cambridge, MA: Harvard University Press.

Granovetter, Mark. 1985. Economic action and social structure: The problem of embeddedness. *American Journal of Sociology* 91 (3): 481–510.

Gray, Herman. 2004. *Watching race.* Minneapolis: University of Minnesota.

Gray, John. 2004. *Men are from Mars, women from Venus.* New York: Harper.

Greeley, Andrew. 2004. *Religion in Europe at the end of the second millennium: A sociological profile.* Edison, NJ: Transaction.

Green, Sara, Christine Davis, Elana Karshmer, Pete Marsh, and Benjamin Straight. 2005. Living stigma: The impact of labeling, stereotyping, separation, status loss, and discrimination in the lives of individuals with disabilities and their families. *Sociological Inquiry* 75 (2): 197–215.

Greenhouse, Steven. 2010. Ending strike, Mott's plant union accepts deal. *New York Times,* September 14, 2010, p. B6.

Greider, William. 1999. *Fortress America.* New York: Public Affairs/Perseus.

Greider, William. 2010. *Come home, America.* New York: Rodale Press.

Griffin, Larry J. 2004. "Generations and collective memory" revisited. *American Sociological Review* 69 (4): 544–57.

Griswold, Daniel T. 2009. *Mad about trade: Why main street America should embrace globalization.* Washington, DC: Cato Institute.

Gross, Michael B. 2004. *The war against Catholicism.* Ann Arbor: University of Michigan Press.

Grossman, Lev. 2006. *Time*'s person of the year: You. *Time,* December 13. Retrieved from www.time.com/time/magazine/article/0,9171,1569514,00.html.

Grusky, David B. 2001. The past, present, and future of social inequality. In *Social stratification,* ed. David B. Grusky, 3–51. Boulder, CO: Westview Press.

Guba, Egon, and Yvonna Lincoln. 1994. Competing paradigms in qualitative research. In *Handbook of Qualitative Research,* ed. N. Denzin and Yvonna Lincoln, 105–17. Thousand Oaks, CA: Sage.

Guo, Guang. 2005. Twin studies: What can they tell us about nature and nurture? *Contexts* 4 (3): 43–47.

Gusfield, Joseph. 1996. *Contested meanings: The construction of alcohol problems.* Madison: University of Wisconsin Press.

Haas, Mark L. 2008. Pax Americana Geriatrica. *Miller-McCune,* August, pp. 31–39.

Habermas, Jurgen. 2002. *Religion and rationality,* trans. E. Mendieta. Cambridge, MA: MIT Press.

Hadaway, C. Kirk, Penny Long Marler, and Mark Chavez. 1993. What the polls don't show: A closer look at U.S. church attendance. *American Sociological Review* 58: 741–52.

Hadaway, C. Kirk, Penny Long Marler, and Mark Chavez. 1998. Overreporting church attendance in America. *American Sociological Review* 63: 122–30.

Hall, Richard, and Pamela Tolbert. 2004. *Organizations,* 9th ed. Englwood Cliffs, NJ: Prentice Hall.

Hamburger, Philip. 2002. *Separation of church and state.* Cambridge, MA: Harvard University Press.

Hamilton, Emily A., Laurie Mintz, and Susan Kashubeck-West. 2007. Predictors of media effects on body dissatisfaction in European American women. *Sex Roles* 56 (5–6): 397–402.

Hamm, Bernd, and Russell Smandych, eds. 2005. *Cultural imperialism.* Toronto, Ontario: University of Toronto Press.

Hannigan, John. 2006. *Environmental sociology: A social constructionist perspective.* London: Routledge.

Haq, Naimul. 2011. "Women find a way out of poverty." *Inter Press Service,* February 24. Retrieved from www.ipsnews.net/news.asp?idnews=54599.

Harding, Sandra. 1991. *Whose science? Whose knowledge?: Thinking from women's lives.* Ithaca, NY: Cornell University Press.

Harding, Sandra, ed. 2004. *The feminist standpoint theory reader.* New York: Routledge.

Hardisty, Jean. 1999. *Mobilizing resentment.* Boston: Beacon.

Harper, Charles L., and Kevin T. Leicht. 2007. *Exploring social change.* Upper Saddle River, NJ: Pearson.

Harper, Tim. 2007. Think you have it bad? Try a 240-km commute. *Toronto Star,* December 8. Retrieved from www.thestar.com/article/283771.

Hartsock, Nancy. 1983. *Money, sex, and power: Toward a feminist historical materialism.* Boston: Northeastern University Press.

Hartsock, Nancy. 1996. Community/sexuality/gender: Rethinking power. In *Revisioning the political: Feminist reconstructions of traditional concepts in Western political theory,* ed. Nancy J. Hirschmann and Christine Di Stefano, pp. 27–50. Boulder, CO: Westview Press.

Harvey, David. 1985. *The urban experience.* Baltimore, MD: Johns Hopkins University Press.

Harvey, David. 1990. *The condition of postmodernity.* Oxford: Blackwell.

Harvey, David. 2007. *A brief history of neoliberalism.* New York: Oxford University Press.

Harwood, Paul G., and Wayne V. McIntosh. 2004. Virtual communities and America's changing sense of community. In *Democracy online,* ed. Peter M. Shane, 209–28. London: Routledge.

Hayim, Gila. 1980. *The existential sociology of Jean-Paul Sartre.* Amherst: University of Massachusetts.

Heckert, Alex, and Druann Maria Heckert. 2004. Using an integrated typology of deviance to analyze ten common norms of the U.S. middle class. *Sociological Quarterly* 45 (2): 209–28.

Heckert, Druann Maria, Carina Michelle Heckert, and Daniel Alex Heckert. 2005. Labeling theory and creative/alternative hair. *Sociological Imagination* 41 (2): 83–103.

Heclo, Hugh, Theda Skocpol, Mary Jo Bane, and Alan Wolfe. 2007. *Christianity and American democracy.* Cambridge, MA: Harvard University Press.

Heelas, Paul, and Linda Woodhead. 2005. *The spiritual revolution.* Malden, MA: Blackwell.

Heider, Don, ed. 2004. *Class and news.* Lanham, MD: Rowman & Littlefield.

Heiland, Frank, and Shirley H. Liu. 2006. Family structure and wellbeing of out-of-wedlock children: The significance of biological parents' relationship. *Demographic Research* 15 (September): 61–104.

Held, David, Anthony McGrew, David Goldblatt, and Jonathan Perreton. 1999. *Global transformations: Politics, economics, and culture.* Stanford, CA: Stanford University Press.

Held, Virginia. 1993. *Feminist morality: Transforming culture, society, and politics.* Chicago: University of Chicago Press.

Helft, Miguel, and Ashlee Vance. 2010. Apple passes Microsoft as no. 1 in tech. *New York Times,* May 27, p. B1. Retrieved from www.nytimes.com/2010/05/27/technology/27apple.html.

Henig, Robin Marantz. 2010. What is it about 20-somethings? *New York Times Magazine,* August 22. Retrieved from www.nytimes.com/2010/08/22/magazine/22Adulthood.

Henneck, Rachel. 2003. Family policy in the US, Japan, Germany, Italy and France: Parental leave, child benefits/family allowances, child care, marriage/cohabitation, and divorce. Council on Contemporary Families. Retrieved from www.contemporaryfamilies.org/work-family/fampolicy.html.

Henry, Neil. 2007. *American carnival: Journalism under siege in an age of new media.* Berkeley: University of California Press.

Herbenick, Debby, Michael Reece, Vanessa Schick, Stephanie A. Sanders, Brian Dodge, and J. Dennis Fortenberry. 2010. Sexual behavior in the United States: Results from a national probability sample of men and women ages 14–94. *Journal of Sexual Medicine* 7 (Suppl. 5): 255–65.

Herbert, Melissa. 2000. *Camouflage isn't only for combat: Gender, sexuality, and women in the military.* New York: New York University Press.

Herman, Edward S., and Noam Chomsky. 1988/2002. *Manufacturing consent: The political economy of the mass media.* New York: Pantheon Books.

Herrnstein, Richard, and Charles Murray. 1996. *The bell curve: Intelligence and class structure in American life.* New York: Free Press.

Hertz, Tom. 2005. Rags, riches and race: The intergenerational economic mobility of black and white families in the United States. In *Unequal chances: Family background and economic success,* ed. Samuel Bowles, Herbert Gintis, and Melissa Osborne, 165–91. Princeton, NJ: Princeton University Press.

Heuveline, Patrick, and Matthew Weinshenker. 2008. The international child poverty gap: Does demography matter? *Demography* 45 (1): 173–91.

Hirsch, Barry T., and David A. Macpherson. 2003. Union membership and coverage database from the Current Population Survey: Note. *Industrial and Labor Relations Review* 56 (2): 349–54.

Hirschfield, Paul. 2008. Preparing for prison? The criminalization of school discipline in the USA. *Theoretical Criminology* 12 (1): 79–101.

Hirschi, Travis. 1969. *Causes of delinquency.* Berkeley: University of California Press.

Hochschild, Arlie. 1979. Emotion work, feeling rules, and social structure. *American Journal of Sociology* 85: 551–75.

Hochschild, Arlie. 1983. *The managed heart.* Berkeley: University of California Press.

Hochschild, Arlie, with Anne Machung. 1989. *The second shift: Working parents and the revolution at home.* New York: Viking.

Hodson, Randy. 2001. *Dignity at work.* New York: Cambridge University Press.

Hoefer, Michael, Nancy Rytina, and Bryan C. Baker. 2011. Estimates of the unauthorized immigrant population residing in the United States: January 2010. Washington, DC: Department of Homeland Security, Office of Immigration Statistics. Retrieved from www.dhs.gov/xlibrary/assets/statistics/publications/ois_ill_pe_2010.pdf.

Hof, Robert. 2005. It's a whole new web. *Businessweek,* September 26, pp. 76–79.

Hoffman, Lisa, and Brian Coffey. 2008. Dignity and indignation: How people experiencing homelessness view services and providers. *The Social Science Journal* 45: 207–22.

Hofstede, Geert. 1980. *Culture's consequences: International differences in work-related values.* Beverly Hills, CA: Sage.

Hogan, Dennis P. 1978. The variable order of events in the life course. *American Sociological Review* 43 (August): 573–86.

Hogan, Dennis P., and Nan Marie Astone. 1986. The transition to adulthood. *Annual Review of Sociology* 12: 109–130.

Hogan, Michael H. 1998. *A cross of iron: Harry S Truman and the origins of the national security state, 1945–1954.* New York: Cambridge University Press.

Hohler, Bob. 2009. Ill-equipped to compete. *Boston Globe,* June 24. Retrieved from www.boston.com/sports/schools/articles/2009/06/24/ill_equipped_to_compete/?page=1.

Hollander, Justin B. 2011. *Sunburnt cities: The Great Recession, depopulation and urban planning in the American Sunbelt.* New York, NY: Routledge.

Holmes, Michael, and Mike Bloxham. 2007. An observational method for time use research: Advantages, disadvantages, and lessons learned from the Middletown Media Studies. Paper presented at the 2007 conference of the International Association of Time Use Researchers, Washington, DC.

Holsti, Ole. 1968. *Content analysis for the social sciences and humanities.* Reading, MA: Addison-Wesley.

Holton, Robert J. 1992. *Economy and society.* New York: Routledge.

Holyfield, Lori, Matthew Ryan Moltz, and Mindy S. Bradley. 2009. Race discourse and the U.S. Confederate flag. *Race, Ethnicity, and Education* 12 (December): 517–37.

Hook, Jennifer L. 2010. Gender inequality in the welfare state: Sex segregation in housework, 1965–2003. *American Journal of Sociology* 115 (5): 1480–523.

hooks, bell. 2000. *Feminist theory: From margin to center.* Boston: South End Press.

Hooper, Rowan. 2005. Television show scrambles forensic evidence. *New Scientist.* Retrieved from http://technology.newscientist.com/article/mg18725163.800.

Hoover, Kenneth, and Todd Donovan. 2007. *The elements of social scientific thinking,* 9th ed. Belmont, CA: Wadsworth.

Horsman, Reginald. 1981. *Race and manifest destiny: The origins of American Anglo-Saxonism.* Cambridge, MA: Harvard University Press.

Horton, James Oliver, and Lois Horton. 2005. *Slavery and the making of America.* New York: Oxford University Press.

Hougham, Victoria. 2005. Sociological skills used in the capture of Saddam Hussein. *Footnotes* 33 (6): 3.

Howard, Philip N. 2005. *New media campaigns and the managed citizen.* New York: Cambridge University Press.

Hsieh, Elaine. 2007. Interpreters as co-diagnosticians. *Social Science & Medicine* 64: 924–37.

Hua, C. 2001. *A society without fathers or husbands: The Na of China.* New York: Zone Books.

Huber, Joan. 2007. *On the origins of gender inequality.* Boulder, CO: Paradigm Publishers.

Hughes, Everett C. 1945. Dilemmas and contradictions of status. *American Journal of Sociology* 50: 353–59.

Human Rights Campaign. 2011a. LGBT equality at the Fortune 500. Retrieved from www.hrc.org/issues/fortune500.htm.

Human Rights Campaign. 2011b. Marriage equality & other relationship recognition laws. Retrieved from www.hrc.org/issues/marriage.asp.

Hunter, James Davison. 1991. *Culture wars: The struggle to define America.* New York: Basic Books.

Hunter, James Davison. 1994. *Before the shooting begins: Searching for democracy in America's culture war.* New York: Free Press.

Hunter, James Davison, and Alan Wolfe. 2006. *Is there a culture war?* Washington, DC: Brookings Institution Press.

Huntington, Samuel. 1993. The clash of civilizations? *Foreign Affairs* 72 (3): 22–49.

Huntington, Samuel. 1996. *The clash of civilizations and the remaking of world order.* New York: Simon & Schuster.

Huntington, Samuel. 1998. *The clash of civilizations and the remaking of world order.* New York: Simon & Schuster.

Huntington, Samuel. 2005. *Who are we? The challenges to America's national identity.* New York: Simon & Schuster.

Hurlbert, Jeanne S., Valerie A. Haines, and John J. Beggs. 2000. Core networks and tie activation: What kinds of routine networks allocate resources in nonroutine situations? *American Sociological Review* 65: 598–618.

Hutchison, William R. 2003. *Religious pluralism in America.* New Haven, CT: Yale University Press.

Hyde, Janet Shibley. 2005. Gender similarities hypothesis. *American Psychologist* 40 (6): 581–92.

Iceland, John, et al. 2010. Racial and ethnic residential segregation in the United States: Comparisons across racial and ethnic groups, 1970–2009. Retrieved from http://projects.pop.psu.edu/canc/segregation/Cross-group-report-12-19-2010.pdf.

Ignatiev, Noel. 1996. *How the Irish became white.* New York: Routledge.

Inglehart, Ronald, and Pippa Norris. 2003. The true clash of civilizations. *Foreign Policy* 135: 62–70.

Institute of Medicine. 2003. *Unequal treatment: Confronting racial and ethnic disparities of healthcare.* Washington, DC: National Academies Press.

Inter-Parliamentary Union. 2011. Women in national parliaments. Situation as of July 31, 2011. Retrieved from www.ipu.org/wmn-e/classif.htmon.

Interfaith Worker Justice. 2010. *A worker justice reader: Essential writings on religion and labor.* Maryknoll, NY: Orbis Books.

International Network on Cultural Policy. 2010. About us. Retrieved from www.incp-ripc.org/about/index_e.shtml.

Internet Crime Complaint Center. 2008. Internet crime report. Retrieved from www.ic3.gov/media/annualreports.aspx.

Internet World Stats. 2011. World internet usage and population statistics. Retrieved from http://internetworldstats.com/stats.htm.

Irwin, Douglas A. 2009. *Free trade under fire.* Princeton, NJ: Princeton University Press.

Irwin, Rachel. 2007. Culture shock: Negotiating feelings in the field. *Anthropology Matters* 9 (1): 1–11.

Jablonski, Nina G., and George Chaplin. 2002. Skin deep. *Scientific American* 287 (4): 74–82.

Jackson, Maggie. 2008. *Distracted.* Amherst, NY: Prometheus Books.

Jackson, Pamela Braboy, and Alexandra Berkowitz. 2005. The structure of the life course: Gender and racioethnic variation in the occurrence and sequencing of role transitions. *Advances in Life Course Research* 9: 55–90.

Jackson, Philip. 1968. *Life in classrooms.* New York: Holt, Rinehart, and Winston.

Jacobs, Alexandra. 2010. Fashion democracy. *The New Yorker,* March 29, pp. 52–57.

Jacobs, Lawrence R., and Theda Skocpol. 2007. *Inequality and American democracy.* New York: Russell Sage Foundation.

Jacobs, Sue Ellen, Wesley Thomas, and Sabine Lang, eds. 1997. *Two-spirit people: Native American gender identity, sexuality, and spirituality.* Urbana: University of Illinois Press.

Janis, Irving L. 1972. *Victims of groupthink: A psychological study of foreign-policy decisions and fiascoes.* Boston: Houghton Mifflin.

Janis, Irving L. 1989. *Crucial decisions.* New York: Free Press.

Janowitz, Morris, and Charles C. Moskos, Jr. 1979. Five years of the all-volunteer force: 1973–1978. *Armed Forces and Society* 5 (2): 171–218.

Jaschik, Scott. 2007. Momentum for gender neutrality. Inside Higher Ed, August 27. Retrieved from http://insidehighered.com/layout/set/pring/news/2007/08/27/gender.

Jasper, James M. 1997. *The art of moral protest.* Chicago: University of Chicago.

Jasper, James M., and Jeff Goodwin. 2011. *Contention in context: Political opportunities and the emergence of protest.* Stanford, CA: Stanford University Press.

Jensen, Per, Kirsten Fenger, Tom G. Bolwig, and Sven Asger Sorensen. 1998. Crime in Huntington's disease: A study of registered offences among patients, relatives, and controls. *Journal of Neurology, Neurosurgery, and Psychiatry* 65: 467–71.

Jhally, Sut, and Justin Lewis. 1992. *Enlightened racism.* Boulder, CO: Westview.

Johnson, Alan. 2007. A politics of inclusion: An interview with Saad Eddin Ibrahim. *Democratiya* 8 (Spring): 154–170. Retrieved from http://dissentmagazine.org/democratiya/article_pdfs/d8Interview.pdf.

Johnson, Allan G. 2001. *Privilege, power and difference.* New York: McGraw-Hill.

Johnson, Allen, and Timothy Earle. 2000. *The evolution of human societies: From foraging groups to agrarian state.* Stanford, CA: Stanford University Press.

Johnson, Bradley. 2007. 100 Leading media companies. *Advertising Age.* Retrieved from http://adage.com/article/mediaworks/100-leading-media-companies-report/120726/.

Johnson, Bradley. 2010. 100 Leading media companies. *Advertising Age,* September 27, p. 34.

Johnson, Carolyn Y. 2008. Study finds culture a factor in female math achievement. *Boston Globe,* October 10, p. A4.

Johnson, Charles, and Patricia Smith. 1999. *Africans in America: America's journey through slavery.* New York: Harvest Books.

Johnson, Stephen. 2004. *Mind wide open: Your brain and the neuroscience of everyday life.* New York: Scribner.

Johnston, David Cay. 2003. *Perfectly legal: The covert campaign to rig our tax system to benefit the super rich—and cheat everybody else.* New York: Portfolio/Penguin.

Johnston, David Cay. 2005. *Perfectly legal: The covert campaign to rig our tax system to benefit the super rich—and cheat everybody else.* New York: Penguin.

Johnston, David Cay. 2007. *Free lunch: How the wealthiest Americans enrich themselves at government expense.* New York: Penguin.

Johnston, Hank, and John A. Noakes, eds. 2005. *Frames of protest.* Lanham, MD: Rowman & Littlefield.

Jones, Stephanie J., ed. 2007. *The state of black America, 2007.* Silver Spring, MD: Beckham Publications Group.

Jordan, Don, and Michael Walsh. 2008. *White cargo: The forgotten history of white slaves in America.* New York: New York University Press.

Jordan, Tim, and Steve Pile. 2002. *Social change.* Cambridge, MA: Blackwell Publishers.

Juergensmeyer, Mark. 2003. *Terror in the mind of God: The global rise of religious violence.* Berkeley: University of California Press.

Jung, Moon-Kie. 2006. *Reworking race: The making of Hawaii's interracial labor movement.* New York: Columbia University Press.

Jutte, Robert. 2008. *Contraception: A history.* Malden, MA: Polity Press.

Jylha, Marja, and Marja Saarenheimo. 2010. Loneliness and aging: Comparative perspectives. In *The Sage handbook of social gerontology,* ed. Dale Danaher and Chris Phillipson, 317–28. Los Angeles: Sage.

Kahlenberg, Richard D. 1997. *The remedy: Class, race, and affirmative action.* New York: Basic Books.

Kahlenberg, Richard D., ed. 2010a. *Affirmative action for the rich: Legacy preferences in college admissions.* New York: Century Foundation Press.

Kahlenberg, Richard D. 2010b. Introduction. In *Rewarding strivers: Helping low-income students succeed in college,* 1–16. New York: Century Foundation Press.

Kahlenberg, Richard D., ed. 2010c. *Rewarding strivers: Helping low-income students succeed in college.* New York: Century Foundation Press.

Kandal, T. R. 1988. *The woman question in classical sociological theory.* Miami: Florida International University Press.

Kane, Emily W. 2000. Racial and ethnic variations in gender-related attitudes. *Annual Review of Sociology* 26: 419–39.

Kang, Cecilia. 2010. For the poor, cellphones can offer lifeline. *Washington Post,* September 8, p. A16.

Kant, Immanuel. 1784/1999. An answer to the question: What is enlightenment? In *Practical Philosophy,* ed. Mary J. Gregor, pp. 11–22. Cambridge: Cambridge University Press.

Kaplinsky, Raphael. 2007. *Globalization, poverty and inequality.* Malden, MA: Polity Press.

Karabel, Jerome. 2005. *The chosen: The hidden history of admissions and exclusion at Harvard, Yale, and Princeton.* New York: Houghton Mifflin.

Karen, David. 2005. No child left behind? Sociology ignored! *Sociology of Education* 78 (2): 165–69.

Karner, Christian, and Alan Aldridge. 2004. Theorizing religion in a globalizing world. *International Journal of Politics, Culture, and Society* 18 (1/2): 5–32.

Karp, David. 1996. *Speaking of sadness.* New York: Oxford University Press.

Karp, David. 2000. A decade of reminders: Changing age consciousness between fifty and sixty years old. In *Aging and everyday life,* ed. J. F. Grubium and J. A. Holstein, 65–86. Malden, MA: Blackwell.

Karraker, Katherine Hildebrandt, Dena Ann Vogel, and Margaret Ann Lake. 1995. Parents' gender-stereotyped perceptions of newborns: The eye of the beholder revisited. *Sex Roles* 33 (9–10): 687–702.

Kasser, Tim. 2003. *The high price of materialism.* Cambridge, MA: MIT Press.

Kaufman, Jason, and Jay Gabler. 2004. Cultural capital and the extracurricular activities of girls and boys in the college attainment process. *Poetics* 32: 145–68.

Kaufman, Joan, Bao-Zhi Yang, Heather Douglas-Palumberi, Shadi Houshyar, Deborah Lipschitz, John H. Krystal, and Joel Gelernter. 2004. Social supports and serotonin transporter gene moderate depression in maltreated children. *Proceedings of the National Academy of Sciences* 101 (5): 17316–21.

Kay, Paul, and Willett Kempton. 1984. What is the Sapir-Whorf hypothesis? *American Anthropologist* 86 (1): 65–79.

Keaten, Jamey. 2010. French polemic over fake game show electrocutions. Associated Press, March 17.

Keeter, Scott. 2011. Who's winning the fight over public sector unions? Pew Research Center for People and the Press. Retrieved from http://pewresearch.org/pubs/1915/polls-winning-losing-fight-over-public-employee-unions-wisconsin.

Keith, Jannette. 2003. *Rich man's war, poor man's fight*. Durham: University of North Carolina Press.

Kelly, Sanja, and Sarah Cook. 2011. Freedom on the Internet 2011. Washington, DC: Freedom House.

Kennicott, Philip. 2008. Sizing up a mega-city. *Washington Post,* August 4, pp. C1–C2.

Kephart, Ronald. 2003. Latin America and the Caribbean. In *Race and ethnicity: An anthropological focus on the United States and the world,* ed. Raymond Scupin, pp. 288–308. Upper Saddle River, NJ: Prentice Hall.

Kerbo, Harold. 2008. *Social stratification and inequality.* New York: McGraw-Hill.

Kerrey, Bob, and Larry Pressler. 2010. The biggest election winner: Big money. *USA Today,* November 6. Retrieved from www.usatoday.com/news/opinion/forum/2010-11-06-kerrey05_ST_N.htm.

Keshavarz, Somayeh, and Rozumah Baharudin. 2009. Parenting style in a collective culture of Malaysia. *European Journal of Social Sciences* 10 (1): 66–73.

Khandelwal, M. S. 2002. *Becoming American being Indian: An immigrant community in New York City.* Ithaca, NY: Cornell University Press.

Kiel, Paul. 2011. Behind administration spin: Bailout still $123 billion in the red. March 17. *ProPublica.* Retrieved from www.propublica.org/ion/bailout.

Kiernan, Ben. 2007. *Blood and soil: A world history of genocide and extermination from Sparta to Darfur.* New Haven, CT: Yale University Press.

Kim, Eunjung. 2005. Korean American parental control: Acceptance or rejection? *Ethos* 33 (3): 347–66.

Kim, Heejung, and Hazel Rose Markus. 1999. Deviance or uniqueness, harmony or conformity? A cultural analysis. *Journal of Personality and Social Psychology* 77 (4): 785–800.

Kim, Julia C., Charlotte H. Watts, James R. Hargreaves, Luceth X. Ndhlovu, Godfrey Phetla, Linda A. Morison, et al. 2007. Understanding the impact of a microfinance-based intervention on women's empowerment and the reduction of intimate partner violence in South Africa. *American Journal of Public Health* 97 (10): 1–9.

Kimmel, Michael. 1996. *Manhood in America.* New York: Free Press.

Kimmel, Michael. 2007. *The gendered society.* New York: Oxford University Press.

Kimmel, Michael, and Michael Messner, eds. 2009. *Men's lives.* Boston: Allyn & Bacon.

Kinder, Donald R., and Lynn M. Sanders. 1996. *Divided by color: Racial politics and democratic ideals.* Chicago: University of Chicago Press.

Kinsey, Alfred C., Wardell B. Pomeroy, and Clyde E. Martin. 1948/1998. *Sexual behavior in the human male.* Bloomington: Indiana University Press.

Kinsey, Alfred C., Wardell B. Pomeroy, Clyde E. Martin, and Paul H. Gebhard. 1953/1998. *Sexual behavior in the human female.* Bloomington: Indiana University Press.

Klein, Alec. 2003. *Stealing Time: Steve Case, Jerry Levin, and the collapse of AOL Time Warner.* New York: Simon & Schuster.

Klinenberg, Eric. 2003. *Heat wave.* Chicago: University of Chicago Press.

Klinenberg, Eric. 2005. Convergence: News production in a digital age. *Annals of the American Academy of Political and Social Science* 597: 48–63.

Kluckhohn, Clyde. 1968. *Mirror for man.* New York: Fawcett Crest.

Koch, Pamela Ray, and Lala Carr Steelman. 2009. From molehills mountains made: An examination of red and blue state cultural stereotypes. *Cultural Sociology* 3 (1): 165–89.

KOF Swiss Economic Institute. 2011. KOF index of globalization 2011: Economic crisis slows down globalization. Retrieved from http://globalization.kof.ethz.ch/static/pdf/press_release_2011_en.pdf.

Kohn, Melvin L. 1977. *Class and conformity: A study in values,* 2nd ed. Chicago: University of Chicago Press.

Kohn, Melvin L., Kazimierz M. Slomczynski, and Carrie Schoenbach. 1986. Social stratification and the transmission of values in the family: A cross-national assessment. *Sociological Forum* 1 (1): 73–102.

Kohut, Andrew. n.d. *Andrew Kohut on polling at the Pew Research Center.* Retrieved from www.pewtrusts.org/expert_qa_detail.aspx?id=29046.

Kollmeyer, Christopher. 2004. Corporate interests: How the news media portrays the economy. *Social Problems* 51 (3): 432–52.

Konieczny, Piotr. 2009. Governance, organization, and democracy on the Internet: The iron law and the evolution of Wikipedia. *Sociological Forum* 24 (1): 162–92.

Kosfeld, Michael, Markus Henrichs, Paul J. Zak, Urs Fischbacher, and Ernst Fehr. 2005. Oxytocin increases trust in humans. *Nature* 435 (2): 673–76.

Kovach, Bill, and Tom Rosenstiel. 1999. *Warp speed: America in the age of mixed media.* New York: Century Foundation Press.

Kozol, Jonathan. 1991. *Savage inequalities.* New York: Crown Publishers.

Kozol, Jonathan. 2005. *The shame of the nation.* New York: Crown.

Kreider, Marilyn. 2007. Young adults living in their parents' home. Paper presented at the American Sociological Meeting, New York, NY, August 12. Retrieved from www.census.gov/population/www/socdemo/hh-fam/young-adults-in-parents-home.pdf.

Kreider, Rose M., and Diana B. Elliot. 2009. America's families and living arrangements: 2007. U.S. Census Bureau, Department of Commerce. Retrieved from www.census.gov/population/www/socdemo/hh-fam/p20-561.pdf.

Kriesberg, Louis. 1982. *Social conflicts.* Englewood Cliffs, NJ: Prentice-Hall.

Kurutz, Steven. 2007. Not buying it. *New York Times,* June 21, p. F1.

LaFraniere, Sharon. 2005. Cellphones catapult rural Africa to 21st century. *New York Times,* August 25, p. A1.

LaFree, Gary. 1999. Declining violent crime rates in the 1990s: Predicting crime booms and busts. *Annual Review of Sociology* 25: 145–68.

LaFree, Gary, and Richard Arum. 2006. The impact of racially inclusive schooling on adult incarceration rates among U.S. cohorts of African Americans and whites since 1930. *Criminology* 44 (1): 73–103.

Lammers, J., A. D. Galinsky, E. H. Gordijn, and S. Otten. 2008. Illegitimacy moderates the effects of power on approach. *Psychological Science* 19: 558–64.

Lane, Robert E. 1994. The road not taken: Friendship, consumerism, and happiness. *Critical Review* 8 (4): 521–54.

Lang, Molly Monahan, and Barbara J. Risman. 2007. Blending into equality: Family diversity and gender convergence. In *Handbook of gender and women's studies,* ed. Kathy Davis, Mary Evans, and Judith Lorber, pp. 287–303. Thousand Oaks, CA: Sage.

Lareau, Annette. 2003. *Unequal childhoods: Class, race, and family life.* Berkeley: University of California Press.

Lareau, Annette, and Elliot B. Weininger. 2003. Cultural capital in educational research. *Theory and Society* 32 (5–6): 567–606.

Laumann, Edward O., John H. Gagnon, Robert T. Michael, and Stuart Michaels. 2000. *The social organization of sexuality.* Chicago: University of Chicago Press.

Laventhol, David. 2005. That soothing blue glow. *Columbia Journalism Review* November/December, p. 71.

Layton, Lyndsey, and Spencer S. Hsu. 2008. Letting the market drive transportation; Bush officials criticized for privatization. *Washington Post,* March 17, p. A1.

Lebowitz, Michael. 2010. *The socialist alternative.* New York: Monthly Review Press.

Lechner, Frank J. 1991. The case against secularization: A rebuttal. *Social Forces* 69 (4): 1103–19.

Lee, Jennifer, and Frank D. Bean. 2004. America's changing color lines: Immigration, race/ethnicity, and multiracial identification. *Annual Review of Sociology* 30: 221–42.

Lee, Valerie E., and Julia B. Smith. 1995. Effects of high school restructuring and size on early gains in achievement and engagement. *Sociology of Education* 68 (4): 241–70.

Leeland, John. 2006. A spirit of belonging, inside and out. *New York Times,* October 8. Retrieved from www.nytimes.com/2006/10/08/fashion/08SPIRIT.html?pagewanted=1&_r=1&ref=fashion.

Lemert, Edwin M. 1951. *Social pathology.* New York: McGraw-Hill.

Lenski, Gerhard. 1966. *Power and privilege: A theory of social stratification.* New York: McGraw-Hill.

Leondar-Wright, Betsy. 2005. *Class matters.* Gabriola Island, B.C.: New Society Publishers.

Lethbridge-Cejku, Margaret, Jeannine S. Schiller, and Luther Bernadel. 2004. *Summary health statistics for U.S. adults: National Health Interview Survey, 2002.* Washington, DC: National Center for Health Statistics.

Levitt, Martin Jay. 1993. *Confessions of a union buster.* New York: Crown Publishers.

Levitt, Peggy. 2004. Salsa and ketchup: Transnational migrants straddle two worlds. *Contexts* 3 (2): 20-26.

Levitz, Jennifer. 2010. BP didn't provide failsafe requirements. *Wall Street Journal,* May 12. Retrieved from http://online.wsj.com/article/SB 10001424052748703393045752408536172 29196.html.

Levy, Frank. 1998. *The new dollars and dreams.* New York: Russell Sage Foundation.

Lewis, Bernard. 2004. *The crisis of Islam: Holy war and unholy terror.* New York: Random House.

Licoppe, Christian, and Zbigniew Smoreda. 2005. Are social networks technologically embedded? How networks are changing today with changes in communication technology. *Social Networks* 27: 317–25.

Lindberg, David C., and Ronald L. Numbers. 2008. *When science and Christianity meet.* Chicago: University of Chicago Press.

Linden, Greg, Kenneth L. Kraemer, and Jason Dedrick. 2007. Who captures value in a global innovation system? The case of Apple's iPod. Irvine, CA: Personal Computing Industry Center, UC Irvine.

Ling, Rich. 2008. *New tech, new ties.* Cambridge, MA: MIT Press.

Link, Bruce G., and Jo C. Phelan. 2001. Conceptualizing stigma. *Annual Review of Sociology* 27: 363–85.

Liptak, Adam. 2010. Justices, 5-4, reject corporate spending limit. *New York Times,* January 21. Retrieved from www.nytimes.com/2010/01/22/us/politics/22scotus.html.

Lobao, Linda. 2007. Rural sociology. In *21st Century sociology: A reference handbook,* ed. Clifton D. Bryant and Dennis L. Peck, pp. 465–75. Thousand Oaks, CA: Sage.

Loeb, Paul Rogat. 1999. *Soul of a citizen.* New York: St. Martin's.

Logan, John. 2006. The union avoidance industry in the United States. *British Journal of Industrial Relations* 44 (4): 651–675.

Logan, John R., and Harvey L. Molotch. 1987. *Urban fortunes: The political economy of place.* Berkeley: University of California Press.

Logan, John R., and Brian J. Stults. 2011. The persistence of segregation in the metropolis: New findings from the 2010 Census. Census brief prepared for Project US2010. Retrieved from www.s4.brown.edu/us2010/Data/Report/report2.pdf.

Logan, John R., Brian J. Stults, and Reynolds Farley. 2004. Segregation of minorities in the metropolis: Two decades of change. *Demography* 41 (1): 1–22.

Lonergan, Raymond. 1941. A steadfast friend of labor. In *Mr. Justice Brandeis, great American,* ed. Irving Dillard, 42+. St. Louis, MO: Modern View Press.

Long, Elizabeth. 2003. *Book clubs: Women and the uses of reading in everyday life.* Chicago: University of Chicago Press.

Lopes, Paul D. 1992. Innovation and diversity in the popular music industry, 1969–1990. *American Sociological Review* 57: 56–71.

Lorber, Judith, and Lisa Jean Moore. 2010. *Gendered bodies: Feminist perspectives.* New York: Oxford University Press.

Lubrano, Alfred. 2004. *Limbo: Blue-collar roots, white-collar dreams.* Hoboken, NJ: Wiley.

Lucas, Samuel. 1999. *Tracking inequality.* New York: Teachers College Press.

Lucy, William H. 2003. Mortality risk associated with leaving home: Recognizing the relevance of the built environment. *American Journal of Public Health* 93 (9): 1564–69.

Lucy, William, and Raphael Rabalais. 2002. Traffic fatalities and homicides by strangers: Danger of leaving home in cities, inner suburbs, and outer suburbs. Retrieved from http://urban.arch.virginia.edu/exurbia/death-in-exurbia.pdf.

Lukes, Stephen. 2006. Questions about power: Lessons from the Louisiana hurricane. In *Understanding Katrina: Perspectives from the social sciences.* Retrieved from http://understanding katrina.ssrc.org/Lukes/.

Lukes, Steven. 2005. *Power: A radical view,* 2nd ed. Palgrave Macmillan.

Lustgarten, Abrahm. 2010. Furious growth and cost cuts led to BP accidents past and present. Retrieved from www.propublica.org/article/bp-accidents-past-and-present.

Lutendo, Malisha, Pranitha Maharaj, and Michael Rogan. 2008. Rites of passage to adulthood: Traditional initiation schools in the context of HIV/AIDS in the Limpopo Province, South Africa. *Health, Risk and Society* 10 (6): 585–98.

Lynch, Kevin. 1960. *The image of the city.* Cambridge, MA: MIT Press.

Lynch, Thomas. 2001. We should witness the death of McVeigh. *New York Times,* February 20, p. A21.

MacFarlane, S. Neil, and Yuen Foong Khong. 2006. *Human security and the UN.* Bloomington: Indiana University Press.

Macgregor, G. H. C. 1954. *The New Testament basis of pacifism.* Nyack, NY: Fellowship Publications.

MacLaury, Judson. 2011. *Government regulation of workers' safety and health, 1877–1917.* Washington, DC: U.S. Department of Labor. Retrieved from www.dol.gov/oasam/programs/history/mono-regsafeintrotoc.htm.

MacLeod, Jay. 1995. *Ain't no makin' it: Aspirations and attainment in a low-income neighborhood.* Boulder, CO: Westview Press.

MacMillan, Ross. 2005. The structure of the life course: Classic issues and current controversies. *Advances in Life Course Research* 9: 3–24.

Macoby, Eleanor E. 2007. Historical overview of socialization research and theory. In *Handbook of socialization: Theory and research,* ed. Joan E. Grusse and Paul D. Hasting, pp. 13–41. New York: Guilford Press.

Malbin, Michael. 2008. Reality check: Obama received about the same percentage from small donors in 2008 as Bush in 2004. Washington, DC: Campaign Finance Institute. Retrieved from www.cfinst.org/pr/prRelease.aspx?ReleaseID=216.

Mann, Michael. 1986. *The sources of social power,* vol. 1. Cambridge, U.K.: University of Cambridge.

Mannheim, Karl. 1928/1952. The problem of generations. In *Essays on the sociology of knowledge,* 276–322. London: Routledge/Kegan Paul.

Manohar, Namita. 2008. "Sshh...!! Don't tell my parents": Dating among second generation Patels in Florida. *Journal of Comparative Family Studies* 39 (4): 571–88.

Mao Zedong. 1936/2010. *Quotations from Chairman Mao Zedong during the Cultural Revolution.* Fairfax, CA: Intercultural Publishing.

Marcus, Mary Brophy. 2011. Bin Laden's death a turning point for Millennials. *USA Today,* May 4. Retrieved from http://yourlife.usatoday.com/mind-soul/story/2011/05/Bin-Ladens-death-a-turning-point-for-Millennials-/46778218/1.

Marger, Martin N. 2007. *Social inequality.* New York: McGraw-Hill.

Mariampolski, Hy. 2001. *Qualitative market research: A comprehensive guide.* Thousand Oaks, CA: Sage.

Mariampolski, Hy. 2005. *Ethnography for marketers: A guide to consumer immersion.* Thousand Oaks, CA: Sage.

Marini, Margaret Mooney. 1984. The order of events in the transition to adulthood. *Sociology of Education* 57 (2): 63–84.

Marler, Penny Long, and C. Kirk Hadaway. 2002. "Being religious" or "being spiritual" in America: A zero-sum proposition? *Journal for the Scientific Study of Religion* 41 (2): 289–300.

Marquart James W., Sheldon Ekland-Olson, and Janathan R. Sorensen. 1994. *The rope, the chair, & the needle.* Austin: University of Texas Press.

Marsh, Charles. 2006. *The beloved community: How faith shapes social justice from the civil rights movement to today.* New York: Basic Books.

Marsh, Robert. 2009. How similar are the values of the people of China and Taiwan? *Comparative Sociology* 8: 39–75.

Martin, Christopher R. 2004. *Framed! Labor and the corporate media.* Ithaca, NY: ILR Press/Cornell University Press.

Martin, Karin A. 1998. Becoming a gendered body: Practices of preschools. *American Sociological Review* 63(4): 494–511.

Martin, Steven P. 2004. Women's education and family timing: Outcomes and trends associated with age at marriage and first birth. In *Social inequality,* ed. Kathryn Neckerman, pp. 79–118. New York: Russell Sage Foundation.

Martin, Steven P. 2006. Trends in marital dissolution by women's education in the United States. *Demographic Research* 15: 537–60.

Martineau, Harriet. 1837/2009. *Society in America.* New York: Cambridge University Press.

Martineau, Harriet. 1838/2009. *How to observe morals and manners.* Charleston, SC: BiblioLife.

Marx, Karl. 1844/1978. Contribution to the critique of Hegel's *Philosophy of Right*: Introduction. In *The Marx-Engels reader,* ed. Robert C. Tucker, pp. 53–65. New York: Norton.

Marx, Karl. 1845/1978. Theses on Feuerbach. In *The Marx-Engels Reader,* 2nd ed., ed. Robert C. Tucker. New York: Norton.

Marx, Karl. 1852/1978. The eighteenth Brumaire of Louis Bonaparte. In *The Marx-Engels Reader,* 2nd ed., ed. Robert C. Tucker. New York: Norton.

Marx, Karl. 1859/1978. Preface to *A contribution to the critique of political economy.* In *The Marx-Engels reader,* 2nd ed., ed. Robert C. Tucker, pp. 3–6. New York: Norton.

Marx, Karl. 1867/1976. *Capital,* trans. Ben Fowkes. New York: Vintage.

Marx, Karl, and Friedrich Engels. 2008. *On religion.* Mineola, NY: Dover.

Massey, Douglas S., and Mary J. Fischer. 2006. The effect of childhood segregation on minority academic performance at selective colleges. *Ethnic and Racial Studies* 29 (1): 1–26.

Matsueda, Ross. L. 1992. Reflected appraisals, parental labeling, and delinquency. *American Journal of Sociology* 97 (6): 1577–611.

Maurer, Lora. 2009. Naomi Chesler: Teacher, researcher, mentor, mom. *The Connector* 23 (1): 8–9. Harvard-MIT Division of Health Sciences and Technology. Retrieved from http://hst.mit .edu/images/upload/Connector_Winter09.pdf.

Mayer, Jane. 2010. Covert operations. *The New Yorker,* August 30. Retrieved from www .newyorker.com/reporting/2010/08/30/ 100830fa_fact_mayer.

McAdam, Doug. 1989. The biographical consequences of activism. *American Sociological Review* 54 (5): 744–60.

McAdam, Doug, John D. McCarthy, and Mayer N. Zald, eds. 1996. *Comparative perspectives on social movements.* New York: Cambridge University Press.

McCarthey, John D., and Mayer N. Zald. 1977. Resource mobilization and social movements: A partial theory. *American Journal of Sociology* 82 (6): 1212–41.

McChesney, Robert, and John Nichols. 2010. *The death and life of American journalism.* Philadelphia, PA: Nation Books.

McConahay, John B. 1986. Modern racism, ambivalence, and the modern racism scale. In *Prejudice, discrimination and racism,* ed. John F. Dovidio and Samuel L. Gaertner, pp. 91–125. Orlando, FL: Academic Press.

McConkey, Dale. 2001. Whither Hunter's culture war? *Sociology of Religion* 62 (2): 149–74.

McCright, Aaron M., and Riley E. Dunlap. 2003. Defeating Kyoto: The conservative movement's impact on U.S. climate change policy. *Social Problems* 50: 348–73.

McCrummen, Stephanie. 2005a. Building unity in subdivisions. *Washington Post,* February 27, pp. A1, A13.

McCrummen, Stephanie. 2005b. Subdivisions impose social divide. *Washington Post,* May 1, pp. A1, A16.

McDonald, Michael. 2010a. 2008 General election turnout rates. George Mason University. Retrieved from http://elections.gmu.edu/ Turnout_2008G.html.

McDonald, Michael. 2010b. 2010 General election turnout rates. George Mason University. Retrieved from http://elections.gmu.edu/ Turnout_2010G.html.

McFarland, Daniel A., and Reuben J. Thomas. 2006. Bowling young: How youth voluntary associations influence adult political participation. *American Sociological Review* 71 (3): 401–25.

McGray, Douglas. 2007. Pop up cities: China builds a bright green metropolis. *Wired Magazine,* May, pp. 160–165, 180–185.

McGregor, Richard. 2010. *The party: The secret world of China's communist rulers.* New York: HarperCollins.

McGrew, Anthony, and David Held, eds. 2007. *Globalization theory.* Malden, MA: Polity.

McHale, Susan M., and Ann C. Crouter. 2003. How do children exert an impact on family life? In *Children's influence on family dynamics,* ed. Ann C. Crouter and Allan Booth, pp. 207–20. Mahway, NJ: Lawrence Erlbaum Associates.

McIntosh, Peggy. 1988. *White privilege and male privilege: A personal account of coming to see correspondences through work in women's studies.* Wellesley, MA: Center for Research on Women.

McIntyre, Robert S., and T. D. Coo Nguyen. 2004. Corporate income taxes in the Bush years. Washington, DC: Citizens for Tax Justice and the Institute on Taxation and Economic Policy. Retrieved from www.ctj.org/corpfed04an.pdf.

McKinlay, John B., and Lisa D. Marceau. 2002. The end of the golden age of doctoring. *International Journal of Health Services* 32 (2): 379–416.

McLanahan, Sarah, and Gary Sandefur. 2006. *Growing up with a single parent.* Cambridge, MA: Harvard University Press.

McLeod, Hugh. 2000. *Secularisation in Western Europe, 1848–1914.* New York: Palgrave Macmillan.

McLeod, Hugh. 2010. *The religious crisis of the 1960s.* New York: Oxford University Press.

McLeod, Hugh, and Werner Ustorf, eds. 2011. *The decline of Christendom in Western Europe, 1750–2000.* New York: Cambridge University Press.

McLuhan, Marshall. 1964. *Understanding media: The extensions of man.* New York: New American Library.

McPherson, Miller, Lynn Smith-Lovin, and Matthew E. Brashears. 2006. Social isolation in America: Changes in core discussion networks over two decades. *American Sociological Review* 71: 353–75.

McPherson, Miller, Lynn Smith-Lovin, and James M. Cook. 2001. Birds of a feather: Homophily in social networks. *Annual Review of Sociology* 27: 415–44.

McQuail, Denis. 2005. *Mass communication theory,* 5th ed. Thousand Oaks, CA: Sage.

Mead, George Herbert. 1934/1962. *Mind, self, and society,* ed. Charles W. Morris. Chicago: Chicago University Press.

Mehta, Chirag, and Nik Theodore. 2005. Undermining the right to organize: Employer behavior during union representation campaigns. Chicago: Center for Urban Economic Development, University of Illinois at Chicago.

Merton, Robert K. 1938. Social structure and anomie. *American Sociological Review* 3: 672–82.

Merton, Robert. 1949. Discrimination and the American creed. In *Discrimination and the national welfare,* ed. R. M. MacIver, pp. 99–126. New York: Harper & Row.

Merton, Robert K. 1968a. The bearing of empirical research on sociological theory. In *Social Theory and Social Structure,* 156–71. New York: Free Press.

Merton, Robert K. 1968b. *Social theory and social structure.* New York: Free Press.

Meyer, David. 2006. *The politics of protest.* New York: Oxford University Press.

Meyer, John W., David Tyack, Joane Nagel, and Audri Gordon. 1979. Public education as nation-building in America: Enrollments and bureaucratization in the American states, 1870–1930. *American Journal of Sociology,* 85 (3): 591–613.

Meyrowitz, Joshua. 1985. *No sense of place: The impact of electronic media on social behavior.* New York: Oxford University Press.

Michener, H. A., and E. J. Lawler. 1975. The endorsement of formal leaders: An integrative model. *Journal of Personality and Social Psychology* 31: 216–33.

Milgram, Stanley. 1963. Behavioral study of obedience. *Journal of Abnormal and Social Psychology* 67 (4): 371–78.

Milgram, Stanley. 1965. Some conditions of obedience and disobedience to authority. *Human Relations* 18 (1): 57–76.

Milgram, Stanley. 1969. *Obedience to authority.* New York: Harper Collins.

Milkman, Ruth. 1997. *Farewell to the factory: Auto workers in the late twentieth century.* Berkeley: University of California Press.

Milkman, Ruth. 2006. *L.A. story: Immigrant workers and the future of the U.S. labor movement.* New York: Russell Sage Foundation.

Miller, Alan S., and Tmoko Mitamura. 2003. Are surveys on trust trustworthy? *Social Psychology Quarterly* 66 (1): 62–70.

Miller, Neil. 2006. *Out of the past: Gay and lesbian history from 1869 to the present.* Los Angeles, CA: Advocate Books.

Miller, T. Christian. 2007. Private contractors outnumber U.S. troops in Iraq. *Los Angeles Times,* July 4.

Mills, C. Wright. 1948. *The new men of power.* New York: Harcourt.

Mills, C. Wright. 1952. *White collar.* New York: Oxford University Press.

Mills, C. Wright. 1956. *The power elite.* New York: Oxford University Press.

Mills, C. Wright. 1959. *The sociological imagination.* New York: Oxford University Press.

Miranda, Candice. 2003. In Kenya, television opens window mainly in the west. *Washington Post,* April 28, p. A19.

Mishel, Lawrence, Jared Bernstein, and Heidi Shierholz. 2009. *The state of working America 2008/2009.* Ithaca, NY: ILR Press/Cornell University Press.

Mohanty, Chandra Talpade, ed. 2003. *Feminism without borders: Decolonizing theory, practicing solidarity.* Durham, NC: Duke University Press.

Molm, L. D. 1997. Risk and power use: Constraints on the use of coercion in exchange. *American Sociological Review* 62: 113–33.

Molotch, Harvey L. 1976. The city as a growth machine. *American Journal of Sociology* 82 (2): 309–30.

Montejano, David. 1987. *Anglos and Mexicans in the making of Texas, 1836–1986.* Austin: University of Texas Press.

Moody, Harry R. 2010. *Aging: Concepts and controversies,* 6th ed. Thousand Oaks, CA: Pine Forge Press.

Mooney, Mark. 2005. Passengers tuned in to nightmare TV. *The Daily News,* September 22, p. 2.

Moore, Christopher J. 2004. *In other words.* Walker.

Moore, Ryan. 2005. Alternative to what? Subcultural capital and the commercialization of a music scene. *Deviant Behavior* 26 (3): 229–52.

Morin, Rich, and D'Vera Cohn. 2008. Women call the shots at home; public mixed on gender roles in jobs. Pew Research Center. Retrieved from http://pewresearch.org/pubs/967/gender-power.

Morin, Richard. 1994. That misleading Holocaust survey; A flawed poll overstated the public's skepticism. *New York Times,* March 20, p. C3.

Morrill, Calvin, Mayer N. Zald, and Hayagreeva Rao. 2003. Covert political conflict in organizations: Challenges from below. *Annual Review of Sociology* 29: 391–415.

Morris, Aldon. 1984. *The origins of the civil rights movement.* New York: Free Press.

Morris, Allison, and Gabrielle Maxwell. 1998. Restorative justice in New Zealand: Family group conferences as a case study. *Western Criminology Review* 1 (1).

Mosco, Vincent. 2009. *The political economy of communication,* 2nd ed. Thousand Oaks, CA: Sage.

Motz, Lotte. 1997. *The faces of the goddess.* New York: Oxford University Press.

Mouw, Ted, and Barbara Entwisle. 2006. Residential segregation and interracial friendship in schools. *American Journal of Sociology* 112 (2): 394–441.

Mukhopadhyay, Carol C., Rosemary Henze, and Yolanda T. Moses. 2007. *How real is race?* Lanham, MD: Rowman & Littlefield.

Muller-Hill, B. 1988. *Murderous science: Elimination by scientific selection of Jews, Gypsies, and others, Germany, 1933–1945.* Oxford: Oxford University Press.

Mumford, Lewis. 1968. *The city in history.* New York: Harvest.

Munnell, Alicia H., and Steven Sass. 2008. *Working longer: The solution to the retirement income challenge.* Washington, DC: Brookings Institution Press.

Murray, Pauli, ed. 1997. *States' laws on race and color.* Athens: University of Georgia Press.

Naff, Alixa. 1985. *Becoming American: The early Arab immigrant experience.* Cannondale: Southern Illinois University Press.

Napoli, Philip M. 2010. *Audience evolution.* New York: Columbia University Press.

National CASA (Court Appointed Special Advocates). 2005. Cultural perspectives on child rearing Retrieved from www.casanet.org/program-management/diversity/cultural-child.htm.

National Center for Education Statistics. 2010. What is the price of college? Retrieved from http://nces.ed.gov/pubsearch/pubsinfo.asp?pubid=2011175.

National Center for Health Statistics. 2011. *Health, United States, 2010.* Hyattsville, MD: National Center for Health Statistics.

National Commission on the BP Deepwater Horizon Oil Spill and Offshore Drilling. 2011. *Deep Water: The gulf oil disaster and the future of offshore drilling recommendations.* Washington, DC: National Commission on the BP Deepwater Horizon Oil Spill and Offshore Drilling.

National Gay and Lesbian Task Force. 2011. Relationship recognition for same-sex couples in the U.S. Retrieved from www.thetaskforce.org/downloads/reports/issue_maps/rel_recog_6_28_11_color.pdf.

National Opinion Research Center. 2010. *General Social Survey, 2010.* Retrieved from www3.norc.org/GSS+Website/.

National Priorities Project. 2009. Army recruitment in FY 2008: A look at age, race, income, and education of new soldiers. Retrieved from www.nationalpriorities.org/militaryrecruiting2008/a_look_at_race_ethnicity_and_income_of_new_soldiers.

Neff, Gina, and David Stark. 2004. Permanently beta: Responsive organizations in the Internet era. In *Society online: The Internet in context,* ed. Philip N. Howard and Steve Jones, 173–88. Thousand Oaks, CA: Sage.

Nelson, Margaret K. 2010. *Parenting out of control.* New York: New York University Press.

Neuman, W. Lawrence. 2005. *Social research methods,* 6th ed. Boston: Allyn & Bacon.

Neumark-Sztainer, Dianne. 2005. *I'm, like, so fat!* New York: Guilford Press.

New York Times. 2011a. Netizens gain some privacy. January 29. Retrieved from www.nytimes.com/2011/01/30/opinion/30sun3.html.

New York Times. 2011b. Rich district, poor district. March 26. Retrieved from www.nytimes.com/2011/03/27/opinion/27sun1.html?_r=2.

Newman, Katherine. 1988. *Falling from grace: The experience of downward mobility in the American middle class.* New York: Free Press.

Newman, Katherine S. 2004. *Rampage: The social roots of school shootings.* New York: Basic Books.

Newport, Frank. 2010. Tea Party supporters overlap Republican base. Gallup, July 2. Retrieved from www.gallup.com/poll/141098/Tea-Party-Supporters-Overlap-Republican-Base.aspx?version=print.

Ng, Sik H., and James J. Bradac. 1993. *Power in language.* Newbury Park, CA: Sage.

Ngowi, Rodrique. 2005. Africans adapt cell phone technology to suit continent's harsh realities. Associated Press Worldstream, September 16.

Nimrod, Galit. 2009. Seniors' online communities. *Gerontologist* 50 (3): 382–92.

Noelle-Neuman, Elisabeth. 1993. *The spiral of silence.* Chicago: University of Chicago Press.

Noelle-Neuman, Elisabeth. 1974. The spiral of silence: A theory of public opinion. *Journal of Communication* 24 (2): 43–51.

Noonan, Mary C., Mary E. Corcoran, and Paul N. Courant. 2005. Pay differences among the highly trained. *Social Forces* 84 (2): 853–72.

Nord, Mark, Alisha Coleman-Jensen, Margaret Andrews, and Steven Carlson. 2010. *Household food security in the United States, 2009.* Economic Research Report No. (ERR-108). Washington, DC: U.S. Department of Agriculture, Economic Research Service.

Norris, Pippa, and Ronald Inglehart. 2004. *Sacred and secular: Religion and politics worldwide.* New York: Cambridge University Press.

Nussbaum, Martha C. 2010. *Not for profit: Why democracy needs the humanities.* Princeton, NJ: Princeton University Press.

Nyberg, Renee Smith, and Trine C. Jensen. 2009. Honoring the Kun Lun way: Cross-cultural organization development consulting to a hospitality company in Datong, China. *Journal of Applied Behavioral Science* 45: 305–37.

O'Connell, Martin, Daphne Lofquist, Tavia Simmons, and Terry Lugaila. 2010. New estimates of same-sex couple households from the American Community Survey. Presented at the annual meeting of the Population Association of America, Dallas, Texas, April 15–17. Retrieved from www.census.gov/population/www/socdemo/hh-fam/SS_new-estimates.pdf.

Obama, Barack. 2009. Remarks by the president in address to the nation on the way forward in Afghanistan and Pakistan. Washington, DC: The White House. Retrieved from www.whitehouse.gov/the-press-office/remarks-president-address-nation-way-forward-afghanistan-and-pakistan.

Ogburn, William. 1922. *Social change.* New York: Huebsch.

Okin, Susan Moller. 1999. *Is multiculturalism bad for women?* Princeton, NJ: Princeton University Press.

Oliver, Melvin L., and Thomas M Shapiro. 2006. *Black wealth, white wealth: A new perspective on racial inequality.* New York: Routledge.

Orfield, Gary, and Chungmei Lee. 2006. *Racial transformation and the changing nature of segregation.* The Civil Rights Project. Cambridge, MA: Harvard University.

Organization for Economic Cooperation and Development (OECD). 2010. *OECD factbook 2010: Economic, environmental and social statistics.* Paris: OECD Publishing.

Orme, Nicholas. 2003. *Medieval children.* New Haven, CT: Yale University Press.

Ortiz, Isabel, and Matthew Cummins. 2011. Global inequality: Beyond the bottom million. UNICEF. Retrieved from www.networkideas.org/featart/apr2011/Ortiz_Cummins.pdf.

Otto, Mary. 2007. For want of a dentist; Prince George's boy dies after bacteria from tooth spread to brain. *Washington Post,* February 28, p. B1.

Ovide, Shira. 2010. Watch Warren Buffet say "raise my taxes." *Wall Street Journal,* November 22. Retrieved from http://blogs.wsj.com/deals/2010/11/22/watch-warren-buffett-say-raise-my-taxes/.

Ozment, Steven. 2001. *Ancestors: The loving family in Old Europe.* Cambridge MA: Harvard University Press.

Page, James S. 2007. Teaching peace to the military. *Peace Review* 19 (4): 571–77.

Pager, Devah. 2003. The mark of a criminal record. *American Journal of Sociology* 108 (5): 937–75.

Pager, Devah. 2007. *Marked: Race, crime, and finding work in an era of mass incarceration.* Chicago: University of Chicago Press.

Panagopoulos, Costas, ed. 2009. *Politicking online: The transformation of election campaign communications.* New Brunswick, NJ: Rutgers University Press.

Papper, Robert A., Michael E. Holmes, and Mark N. Popovich. 2004. Middletown Media Studies. *International Digital Media and Arts Association Journal* 1 (1)

Parker, Susan W., and Charles A. Nelson. 2005. The impact of institutional rearing on the ability to discriminate facial expressions of emotion: An event-related potential study. *Child Development* 76 (1): 54–72.

Parrillo, Vincent N., and Christopher Donoghue. 2005. Updating the Bogardus social distance studies: A new national survey. *Social Science Journal* 42 (2): 257–72.

Parry, Marc. 2010. Tomorrow's college. *Chronicle of Higher Education,* October 31. Retrieved from http://chronicle.com/article/Tomorrows-College/125120/.

Parsons, Talcott. 1940/1954. An analytical approach to the theory of social stratification. In

Essays in sociological theory, pp. 69–88. New York: Free Press.

Parsons, Talcott. 1949. The social structure of the family. In *The family: Its function and destiny,* ed. R. N. Asher, 173–201. New York: Harper.

Parsons, Talcott. 1951. *The social system.* Glencoe, IL: Free Press.

Parsons, Talcott. 1960. The distribution of power in American society. In *Structure and process in modern societies.* New York: Free Press.

Parsons, Talcott, and Robert F. Bales. 1955. *Family: Socialization and interaction process.* New York: Free Press.

Pascoe, C. J. 2007. *Dude, you're a fag: Masculinity and sexuality in high school.* Berkeley: University of California Press.

Passel, Jeffrey S., and D'Vera Cohn. 2008. *U.S. population projections: 2005–2050.* Washington, DC: Pew Research Center.

Passel, Jeffrey S., Wendy Wang, and Paul Taylor. 2010. *Marrying out.* Washington, DC: Pew Research Center.

Patterson, Charlotte J. 2000. Family relationships of lesbians and gay men. *Journal of Marriage and the Family* 62 (November): 1052–69.

Paules, Greta Foff. 1992. *Dishing it out.* Philadelphia: Temple University Press.

Pavlik, John V. 2008. *Media in the digital age.* New York: Columbia University Press.

Pearson, Jo. 2003. "Witchcraft will not soon vanish from this Earth": Wicca in the 21st century. In *Predicting religion: Christian, secular and alternative futures,* ed. Grace Davie, Paul Heelas, and Linda Woodhead, pp. 170–92. Burlington, VT: Ashgate.

Peet, Richard. 2009. *Unholy trinity: The IMF, World Bank, and WTO.* New York: Zed Books.

Pellow, David Naguib, and Robert J. Brulle, eds. 2005. *Power, justice, and the environment: A critical appraisal of the environmental justice movement.* Cambridge, MA: MIT Press.

Perl, Raphael F. 2006. *Terrorism and national security: Issues and trends.* CRS Issue Brief for Congress. Retrieved from http://fpc.state.gov/c17547.htm.

Peterson, Richard A., and David G. Berger. 1975. Cycles in symbol production: The case of popular music. *American Sociological Review* 40: 158–73.

Peterson, Trond, and Ishak Saporta. 2004. The opportunity structure for discrimination. *American Journal of Sociology* 109 (4): 852–901.

Pettigrew, T., and M. Taylor. 2000. Discrimination. In *Encyclopedia of sociology,* Vol. 1, ed. Edgar F. Borgatta, Rhonda J. V. Montgomery, pp. 688–95. New York: Macmillan.

Pew Center on the States. 2008. *One in 100: Behind bars in America 2008.* Washington, DC: Pew Charitable Trusts.

Pew Center on the States. 2009. *One in 31: The long reach of American corrections.* Washington, DC: Pew Charitable Trusts.

Pew Forum on Religion and Public Life. 2008a. *U.S. Religious Landscape Survey.* Washington, DC: Pew Research Center.

Pew Forum on Religion and Public Life. 2008b. Many Americans say other faiths can lead to eternal life. Washington, DC: Pew Research Center. Retrieved from http://pewforum.org/Many-Americans-Say-Other-Faiths-Can-Lead-to-Eternal-Life.aspx#1.

Pew Forum on Religion and Public Life. 2010a. *Religion among the millennials.* Washington, DC: Pew Research Center.

Pew Forum on Religion and Public Life. 2010b. U.S. religious knowledge survey. Washington, DC: Pew Research Center.

Pew Global Attitudes Project. 2008, September 17. Unfavorable views of Jews and Muslims on the increase in Europe. Washington, DC: Pew Research Center. Retrieved from http://pewglobal.org/2008/09/17/unfavorable-views-of-jews-and-muslims-on-the-increase-in-europe/.

Pew Research Center. 2005. Huge racial divide over Katrina and its consequences. Washington, DC: Pew Research Center for People and the Press. Retrieved from http://people-press.org/reports/pdf/255.pdf.

Pew Research Center. 2007a. *Blacks see growing values gap between poor and middle class.* Washington, DC: Pew Research Center.

Pew Research Center. 2007b. *Muslim Americans: Middle class and mostly mainstream.* Washington, DC: Pew Research Center.

Pew Research Center. 2010a. The decline of marriage and the rise of new families. Washington, DC: Pew Research Center. Retrieved from http://pewresearch.org/pubs/1802/decline-marriage-rise-new-families.

Pew Research Center. 2010b. Support for same-sex marriage edges upward; majority continues to favor gays serving openly in military. Retrieved from http://people-press.org/report/662/same-sex-marriage.

Pew Research Center for the People and the Press. 2010. Americans spend more time following the news. September 12. Retrieved from http://people-press.org/2010/09/12/americans-spending-more-time-following-the-news/.

Pfohl, Stephen. 1994. *Images of deviance and social control,* 2nd ed. New York: McGraw Hill.

Phelan, Jo C. 2005. Geneticization of deviant behavior and consequences for stigma: The case of mental illness. *Journal of Health and Social Behavior* 46: 307–22.

Phillips, D. R. 2000. *Ageing in the Asia-Pacific region: Issues, policies, and future trends.* New York: Routledge.

Picca, Leslie Houts, and Joe Feagin. 2007. *Two-faced racism: Whites in the backstage and frontstage.* New York: Routledge.

Pierce, Glenn L., and Michael L. Radelet. 2005. The impact of legally inappropriate factors on death sentencing for California homicides, 1990–1999. *Santa Clara Law Review* 46: 1–41.

Piketty, Thomas, and Emmanuel Saez. 2010. Income inequality in the United States. Supplemental updated data retrieved from http://elsa.berkeley.edu/~saez/TabFig2008.xls.

Pinker, Steven. 2007. *The language instinct: How the mind creates language.* New York: Harper Perennial Modern Classics.

Piven, Frances Fox. 2008. *Challenging authority.* Lanham, MD: Rowman & Littlefield.

Pizzo, Stephen, Mary Fricker, and Paul Muolo. 1989. *Inside job: The looting of America's savings and loans.* New York: McGraw-Hill.

Poggi, Gianfranco. 2001. *Forms of power.* Malden, MA: Blackwell Publishers.

Polivka, Anne E., and Jennifer M. Rothgeb. 1993. Redesigning the CPS Questionnaire. *Monthly Labor Review* 116 (9): 10–28.

Pollin, Robert, and Stephanie Luce. 1998. *The living wage.* New York: New Press.

Polyani, Karl. 1977. *The livelihood of man.* New York: Academic Press.

Pompper, Donnalyn, Jorge Soto, and Laren Piel. 2007. Male body image and magazine standards: Considering dimensions of age and ethnicity. *Journalism and Mass Communication Quarterly* 83: 3 (Autumn): 525–45.

Popenoe, David. 2007. *The state of our unions: The social health of marriage in America.* Piscataway, NJ: The National Marriage Project.

Popenoe, David. 2009. *Families without fathers.* Piscataway, NJ: Transaction Publishers.

Population Reference Bureau. 2008. *2008 World population data sheet.* Washington, DC: Population Reference Bureau.

Portes, Alejandro. 2002. NAFTA and Mexican immigration. Working Paper, No. 351. Princeton University, Woodrow Wilson School of Public and International Affairs, Center for Migration and Development. Retrieved from http://cmd.princeton.edu/papers/NAFTA%20and%20Mexican%20Immigration.pdf.

Portes, Alejandro. 2011. English-only triumphs, but the costs are high. In *The Structure of schooling: Readings in the sociology of education,* ed. Richard Arum, Irenee R. Beattie, and Karly Ford, pp. 567–71. Los Angeles: Sage.

Portes, Alejandro, and Rubin G. Rumbaut. 2001. *Legacies: The story of the immigrant second generation.* Berkeley: University of California Press.

Postman, Neil. 1985/2005. *Amusing ourselves to death.* New York: Penguin.

Potok, Mark. 2007. FAIR: Crossing the rubicon of hate. Southern Poverty Law Center: Hatewatch. Retrieved from www.splcenter.org/blog/2007/12/11/fair-crossing-the-rubicon-of-hate/.

Power, Matthew. 2006. The magic mountain: Trickle-down economics in a Philippine garbage dump. *Harper's,* September, pp. 57–68.

Powers, William. 2010. *Hamlet's BlackBerry.* New York: Harper.

Pressley, Sue Anne, Karin Brulliard, and Ernesto Londono. 2006. Marchers flood Mall with passion, pride; many take their first political step. *Washington Post,* April 11, p. A1.

Project for Excellence in Journalism. 2009. Covering the Great Recession. Retrieved from www.journalism.org/analysis_report/covering_great_recession.

The Project on Student Debt. 2010. Quick facts about student debt. Retrieved from http://projectonstudentdebt.org/fact_sheets.vp.html.

ProPublica. 2010. Disposable army: Civilian contractors in Iraq and Afghanistan. Retrieved from www.propublica.org/article/civilian-contractors-the-story-so-far.

Prothero, Stephen. 2007. *Religious literacy.* New York: HarperCollins.

Pryor, John H., Sylvia Hurtado, Victor B. Saenz, José Luis Santos, and William S. Korn. 2007. *The American freshman: Forty year trends.* Los Angeles: University of California, Higher Education Research Institute.

Public Citizen. 2011. 12 Months after: The effects of Citizens United on elections and the integrity of the legislative process. Retrieved from www.citizen.org/documents/Citizens-United-20110113.pdf.

References

Puette, William. 1992. *Through jaundiced eyes: How the media view organized labor.* Ithaca, NY: ILR Press.

Pugh, Allison J. 2009. *Longing and belonging: Parents, children and consumer culture.* Berkeley: University of California Press.

Puhl, Rebecca, and Kelly D. Brownell. 2001. Bias, discrimination, and obesity. *Obesity Research* 9 (12): 788–805.

Putnam, Robert D. 2000. *Bowling alone: The collapse and revival of American community.* New York: Simon & Schuster.

Putnam, Robert, and David E. Campbell. 2010. *American grace: How religion divides and unites us.* New York: Simon & Schuster.

Quillian, Lincoln. 2006. New approaches to understanding racial prejudice and discrimination. *Annual Review of Sociology* 32: 299–328.

Quillian, Lincoln, and Mary E. Campbell. 2003. Beyond black and white: The present and future of multiracial friendship segregation. *American Sociological Review* 68: 540–66.

Radelet, Michael L., and Marian J. Borg. 2000. The changing nature of death penalty debates. *Annual Review of Sociology* 26: 43–61.

Radelet Michael L., and Traci L. Lacock. 2009. Do executions lower homicide rates? The views of leading criminologists. *Journal of Criminal Law and Criminology* 99 (2): 489–508.

Radtke, Lorraine H., and Henderikus J. Stam. 1994. *Power/gender: Social relations in theory and practice.* Thousand Oaks, CA: Sage.

Rainey, James. 2006. Aiming for a more subtle fighting force. *Los Angeles Times,* May 9, p. A1.

Rainey, James. 2010. The news is, that pitch was paid for. *Los Angeles Times,* September 15. Retrieved from www.latimes.com/entertainment/news/la-et-onthemedia-20100915,0,370372.column.

Rajan, Raghuram G. 2010. *Fault Lines: How Hidden Fractures Still Threaten the World Economy.* Princeton, NJ: Princeton University Press.

Raley, R. Kelly, and Larry Bumpass. 2003. The topography of the divorce plateau: Levels and trends in union stability in the United States after 1980. *Demographic Research* 8: 245–59.

Rank, Mark R., and Thomas A. Hirschl. 2001. The occurrence of poverty across the life cycle: Evidence from the PSID. *Journal of Policy Analysis and Management* 20 (4): 737–55.

Ransford, Marc. 2005. Average person spends more time using media than anything else. Ball State University Center for Media Design. Middletown Media Studies II. Retrieved from www.bsu.edu/news/article/0,1370,--36658,00.html.

Rasinski, Kenneth. 1989. The effect of question wording on public support for government spending. *Public Opinion Quarterly* 53: 388–94.

Raven, Bertram H. 1965. Social influence and power. In *Current studies in social psychology,* ed. I. D. Stainer and M. Fishbein, 399–444. New York: Wiley.

Ray, Rebecca, and John Schmitt. 2007. No-vacation nation. Washington, DC: Center for Economic Policy and Research.

Ray, Rebecca, Janet C. Gornick, and John Schmitt. 2009. Parental leave policies in 21 countries: Assessing generosity and gender equality. Washington, DC: Center for Economic and Policy

Research. Retrieved from www.cepr.net/documents/publications/parental_2008_09.pdf.

Rectanus, Mark. 2002. *Culture incorporated: Museums, artists, and corporate sponsorships.* Minneapolis: University of Minnesota Press.

Redmon, David. 2003. Playful deviance as an urban leisure activity. *Deviant Behavior* 24 (1): 27–51.

Reed, Brian J., and David R. Segal. 2006. Social network analysis and counter-insurgency operations: The capture of Saddam Hussein. *Sociological Focus* 39 (4): 251–64.

Rees, Courtney, and Sonia Ruiz. 2003. Compendium of cultural competent initiatives in health care. Menlo Park, CA: Henry J. Kaiser Family Foundation. Retrieved from www.kff.org/uninsured/loader.cfm?url=/commonspot/security/getfile.cfm&PageID=14365.

Reese, William J. 2005. *America's public schools: From the common school to "No Child Left Behind."* Baltimore, MD: Johns Hopkins University Press.

Reiman, Jeffrey, and Paul Leighton. 2009. *The rich get richer and the poor get prison,* 9th ed. Boston: Allyn & Bacon.

Reinharz, Shulamit. 1992. *Feminist methods in social research.* New York: Oxford University Press.

Relationships Foundation. 2011. The family pressure gauge: A measurement of progress towards the goal of making Britain the "most family friendly" country in Europe. Cambridge, U.K.: Relationships Foundation.

Rendall, Steve, and Julie Hollar. 2006. Are you on the *NewsHour*'s guest list? Fairness and Accuracy in Reporting (FAIR). Retrieved from www.fair.org/index.php?page=2967.

Rendall, Steve, and Michael Morel. 2010. Does *NewsHour* "Help Us See America Whole"? Fairness and Accuracy in Reporting (FAIR). Retrieved from www.fair.org/index.php?page=4177.

Renkema, Lennart J., Diederik A. Stapel, and Nico W. Van Yperen. 2008. Go with the flow: Conforming to others in the face of existential threat. *European Journal of Social Psychology* 38: 747–56.

Renzulli, Linda A., and Lorraine Evans. 2005. School choice, charter schools, and white flight. *Social Problems* 52: 398–418.

Renzulli, Linda A., and Vincent J. Roscigno. 2011. Charter schools and the public good. In *The structure of schooling: Readings in the sociology of education,* ed. Richard Arum, Irenee R. Beattie, and Karly Ford, pp. 572–57. Los Angeles: Sage.

Reuben, Julie A. 1996. *The making of the modern university: Intellectual transformation and the marginalization of morality.* Chicago: University of Chicago Press.

Rheingold, Howard. 2003. *Smart mobs: The next social revolution.* New York: Basic Books.

Rhode Island Coalition Against Domestic Violence. 2000. *Domestic violence: A handbook for journalists.* Warwick, RI: RICADV.

Rice, LaVon. 2007. Shameless lackey or consumer advocate? *Footnotes* (January): 7.

Richeson, Jennifer A., Abigail A. Baird, Heather L. Gordon, et al., 2003. An fMRI investigation of the impact of interracial contact on executive function. *Nature Neuroscience* 6 (12): 1323–28.

Rideout, Victoria J., Ulla G. Foehr, and Donald F. Roberts. 2010. *Generation M2: Media in the lives of 8- to 18-year olds.* Menlo Park, CA: Kaiser Family Foundation.

Riesebrodt, Martin. 2000. Fundamentalism and the resurgence of religion. *Numen* 47: 266–87.

Risman, Barbara, and Pepper Schwartz. 2002. After the sexual revolution: Gender politics in teen dating. *Contexts* 1 (1): 16–24.

Ritzer, George. 1975. *Sociology: A multiple paradigm science.* Boston: Allyn & Bacon.

Ritzer, George. 1993. *The McDonaldization of society,* 1st ed. Thousand Oaks, CA: Pine Forge Press.

Ritzer, George. 2007. *Sociological theory,* 6th ed. New York: McGraw-Hill.

Ritzer, George. 2011. *The McDonaldization of society,* 6th ed. Thousand Oaks, CA: Pine Forge Press.

Ritzer, George, and Nathan Jurgenson. 2010. Production, consumption, prosumption. *Journal of Consumer Culture* 10 (1): 13–36.

Robert Wood Johnson Foundation. 2008. *Where we live matters for our health: The links between housing and health.* Issue Brief 2, September.

Roberts, Donald, Ulla Foehr, and Victoria Rideout. 2005. *Generation M: Media in the lives of 8 to 18 year olds.* Menlo Park, CA: Kaiser Family Foundation.

Roberts, Sam, and Peter Baker. 2010. Asked to declare his race, Obama checks "black." *New York Times,* April 3, p. A9.

Rodriguez, Nestor. 2004. Workers wanted: Employer recruitment of immigrant labor. *Work and Occupations* 31 (4): 453–73.

Roediger, David R. 1999. *The wages of whiteness.* London: Verso.

Roethlisberger, Fritz Jules. 1939. *Management and the worker.* Cambridge, MA: Harvard University Press.

Rohter, Larry. 2006. Billboard ban in São Paulo angers advertisers. *New York Times,* December 12. Retrieved from www.nytimes.com/2006/12/12/world/americas/12iht-brazil.html.

Roscigno, Vincent J., Sherry Mong, Reginald Byron, and Griff Tester. 2007. Age discrimination, social closure and employment. *Social Forces* 86 (1): 313–34.

Roscoe, Will. 1992. *The Zuni woman-man.* Albuquerque: University of New Mexico Press.

Rose, Mike. 2004. *The mind at work.* New York: Penguin.

Ross, Robert J. S. 2004. *Slaves to fashion: Poverty and abuse in the new sweatshops.* Ann Arbor: University of Michigan Press.

Ross, Robert, and Kent Trachte. 1983. Global cites and global classes: The peripheralization of labor in New York City. *Review* 6 (3): 393–431.

Rothenberg, Paula S., ed. 2004. *White privilege: Essential readings on the other side of racism.* Boston: Worth Publishers.

Rothenberg, Paula S. 2009. *Race, class, and gender in the United States.* New York: Worth Publishers.

Roy, Olivier. 1994. *The failure of political islam.* Cambridge, MA: Harvard University Press.

Roy, Olivier. 2004. *Globalized Islam.* New York: Columbia University Press.

Roy, Olivier. 2007. *Secularism confronts Islam.* New York: Columbia University Press.

Rubin, Herbert J., and Irene S. Rubin. 2004. *Qualitative interviewing.* Thousand Oaks, CA: Sage.

Rubin, J. Z., F. J. Provenzano, and Z. Luria. 1974. The eye of the beholder: Parents' views on sex of newborns. *American Journal of Orthopsychiatry* 44: 512–19.

Rupp, Deborah E., and Sharmin Spencer. 2006. When customers lash out: The effects of customer interactional injustice on emotional labor and the mediating role of discrete emotions. *Journal of Applied Psychology* 91 (4): 971–78.

Russell, Bertrand. 1938/2004. *Power: A new social analysis.* New York: Routledge.

Sabbagh, Dan. 2008. Tough year leaves EMI trailing the music majors. *Sunday Times,* April 4. Retrieved from http://business.timesonline.co.uk/tol/business/industry_sectors/media/article3683398.ece.

Sabia, Joseph J. 2008. There's no place like home: A hazard model analysis of aging in place among older homeowners in the PSID. *Research on Aging* 30 (1): 3–35.

Saez, Emmanuel. 2010. Striking it richer: The evolution of top incomes in the United States. Retrieved from http://elsa.berkeley.edu/~saez/saez-UStopincomes-2008.pdf.

Sallie Mae. 2009. Study finds rising number of college students using credit cards for tuition. April 13. Retrieved from https://www1.salliemae.com/about/news_info/newsreleases/041309.htm.

Sassen, Saskia. 1991. *The global city: New York, London, Tokyo.* Princeton, NJ: Princeton University Press.

Sassen, Saskia. 2006. *Cities in a global economy,* 3rd ed. Thousand Oaks, CA: Pine Forge Press.

Sassen, Saskia. 2007. *A sociology of globalization.* New York: Norton.

Scharf, Deepti. 2003. *Melanie Wood: The making of a mathematician.* Durham, NC: Duke University Office of News and Communications. Retrieved from www.dukenews.duke.edu/2003/05/melaniewood0503.html.

Schatzman, Leonard, and Anselm Strauss. 1973. *Field research.* Englewood Cliffs, NJ: Prentice Hall.

Scheufele, Dietram A., and Patricia Moy. 2000. Twenty-five years of the spiral of silence: A conceptual review and empirical outlook. *International Journal of Public Opinion Research* 12 (1): 3–28.

Schiller, Herbert I. 1989. *Culture, Inc.: The corporate takeover of expression.* New York: Oxford University Press.

Schiller, Herbert I. 1992. *Mass communications and American empire,* 2nd ed. Boulder, CO: Westview Press.

Schlesinger, Arthur. 1998. *The disuniting of America.* New York: Norton.

Schlozman, Kay, Benjamin Page, Sidney Verba, and Morris Fiorina. 2005. Inequalities of political voice. American Political Science Association Task Force on Inequality and American Democracy. Retrieved from www.apsanet.org/imgtest/voicememo.pdf.

Schmidt, Alvin. 1997. *The menace of multiculturalism.* Westport, CT: Praeger.

Schnaiberg, Allan. 1980. *The environment.* New York: Oxford University Press.

Schneiberg, Marc, Marissa King, and Thomas Smith. 2008. Social movements and organizational form: Cooperative alternatives to corporations in the American insurance, dairy, and grain industries. *American Sociological Review* 73: 635–67.

Schneider, Joseph. 1978. Deviant drinking as a disease: Alcoholism as a social accomplishment. *Social Problems* 25 (4): 361–72.

Scholte, Jan Aart. 2005. *Globalization: A critical introduction,* 2nd ed. (New York: Palgrave McMillan).

Schor, Juliet. 1999. *The overspent American.* New York: Basic Books.

Schor, Juliet. 2004. *Born to buy: The commercialized child and the new consumer culture.* New York: Scribner.

Schudson, Michael. 1986. *Advertising: The uneasy persuasion.* New York: Basic Books.

Schulz, Amy J., and Leith Mullings, eds. 2005. *Gender, race, class and health: Intersectional approaches.* San Francisco: Jossey-Bass.

Schutz, Alfred. 1962. *Collected papers: The problem of social reality,* ed. Maurice Natanson. The Hague: Martinus Nijhoff.

Schwartz, Shalom H. 1992. Universals in the content and structure of values. *Advances in Experimental Social Psychology* 19: 255–65.

Schwartz, Shalom H. 1994. Are there universals in the content and structure of values? *Journal of Social Issues* 50: 19–45.

Schwartz, Shalom H., Gila Melech, Arielle Lehmann, Steven Burgess, Mari Harris, and Vicki Owens. 2001. Extending the cross-cultural validity of the theory of basic human values with a different method of measurement. *Journal of Cross-Cultural Psychology* 32: 519–42.

Schwedler, Jillian. 2006. *Faith in moderation.* New York: Cambridge University Press.

Scott, James. 1987. *Weapons of the weak.* New Haven, CT: Yale University Press.

Scott, James C. 1992. *Domination and the arts of resistance.* New Haven, CT: Yale University Press.

Scott, Joan Wallach. 2010. *The politics of the veil.* Princeton, NJ: Princeton University Press.

Scott, John P. 2000. *Social network analysis: A handbook.* London: Sage.

Seidman, Steven, ed. 1996. *Queer theory/sociology.* Malden, MA: Blackwell Publishers.

Sengupta, Somini. 2007. Careers give India's women new independence. *New York Times,* November 23.

Sennett, Richard. 2000. *The corrosion of character: The personal consequences of work in the new capitalism.* New York: Norton.

Sennett, Richard. 2007. *The culture of the new capitalism.* New Haven, CT: Yale University Press.

Settersten, Richard A., Jr. 2002. Socialization and the life course. *Advances in Life Course Research* 7: 13–40.

Seymour, Diane, and Peter Sandiford. 2005. Learning emotion rules in service organizations. *Work, Employment and Society* 19 (3): 547–64.

Shaheen, Jack. G. 2009. *Reel bad Arabs: How Hollywood vilifies a people.* Northhampton, MA: Olive Branch Press.

Shanahan, Michael J. 2000. Pathways to adulthood in changing societies: Variability and mechanisms in life course perspective. *Annual Review of Sociology* 26: 667–92.

Shanahan, Michael J., and Scott M. Hofer. 2005. Social context in gene-environment interactions: Retrospect and prospect. *Journals of Gerontology, Series B* 60 (March): 65 (12).

Sharp, Gene. 1973. *Power and struggle.* Boston: Porter Sargent.

Sharp, Gene. 1993/2010. *From dictatorship to democracy.* Boston: Albert Einstein Institute. Retrieved from www.aeinstein.org/organizations/org/fdtd.pdf.

Sheehan, James. 2008. *Where have all the soldiers gone?* New York: Houghton Mifflin.

Shierholz, Heidi. 2009. *Fix it and forget it: Index the minimum wage to growth in average wages.* Washington, DC: Economic Policy Institute. Retrieved from http://epi.3cdn.net/91fd33f4e013307415_rum6iydua.pdf.

Shimberg, Elaine Fantle. 1999. *Blending families.* New York: Berkeley Publishing.

Shulman, Kevin A., et al. 1999. The effect of race and sex on physicians' recommendations for cardiac catheterization. *New England Journal of Medicine* 340 (8): 618–26.

Shweder, Richard A., Martha Minow, and Hazel Rose Marcus, eds. 2002. *Engaging cultural differences: The multicultural challenge in liberal democracies.* New York: Russell Sage Foundation.

Siebold, Guy L. 2001. Core issues and theory in military sociology. *Journal of Political and Military Sociology* 29 (1): 140–59.

Silver, Catherine B. 2002. Japanese and American identities: Values and their transmission in the family. *Sociological Inquiry* 72 (2): 195–219.

Simmel, Georg. 1964. *The sociology of Georg Simmel,* trans. Kurt H. Wolff. New York: Free Press.

Simon, Clea. 1997. Haunted by my family's madness. *Washington Post,* March 9, p. C1.

Simon, Clea. 1998. *Mad house: Growing up in the shadow of mentally ill siblings.* New York: Penguin.

Simpson, Miles. 1990. Political rights and income inequality: A cross-national test. *American Sociological Review* 55 (October): 682–93.

Sischo, Lacey, John Taylor, and Patricia Yancey Martin. 2006. Carrying the weight of self-derogation? Disordered eating practices as social deviance in young adults. *Deviant Behavior* 27 (1): 1–30.

Skocpol, Theda. 2003. *Diminished democracy: From membership to management in American life.* Norman: University of Oklahoma Press.

Slater, Don. 1999. *Consumer culture and modernity.* Malden, MA: Polity/Blackwell.

Slavin, Robert E., Nancy Madden, Margarita Calderon, Anne Chamberlain, and Megan Hennessy. 2010. *Reading and language outcomes of a five-year randomized evaluation of transitional bilingual education.* Baltimore, MD: Johns Hopkins University.

Slivinski, Stephen. 2007. The corporate welfare state. *Policy Analysis* No. 542. Washington, DC: Cato Institute. Retrieved from www.cato.org/pubs/pas/pa592.pdf.

Sloan, Allan. 2007. House of junk: Junk mortgages under the microscope. *Fortune,* July 29.

Small, Meredith. 2005. Dare to bare. *New York Times,* October 11, p. A23.

Smedley, Audrey. 2007. *Race in North America: Origin and evolution of a worldview.* Boulder, CO: Westview Press.

Smith, Christian, ed. 2003. *The secular revolution.* Berkeley: University of California Press.

Smith, Dorothy. 1974. Women's perspective as a radical critique of sociology. *Sociological Inquiry* 44: 7–14.

Smith, Dorothy. 1987. *The everyday world is problematic: A feminist sociology.* Boston, MA: Northeastern University Press.

Smith, Dorothy. 1989. *The everyday world as problematic: A feminist sociology.* Boston: Northeastern University Press.

Smith, Dorothy. 1990. *The conceptual practices of power.* Boston: Northeastern University Press.

Smith, Eliot R., and James R. Kluegel. 1986. *Beliefs about inequality.* Hawthorne, NY: Aldine Transaction.

Smith, Jackie, and Hank Johnston. 2002. *Globalization and resistance: Transnational dimensions of social movements.* Lanham, MD: Rowman & Littlefield.

Smith, Michael Peter, and Luis Gurnizo, eds. 1998. *Transnationalism from below: Comparative urban and community research,* vol. 6. Brunswick, NJ: Transaction Publishers.

Smith, Thomas S., and David D. Franks. 1999. Emergence, reduction and levels of analyses in the neurosociological paradigm. In *Mind, brain, and society: Toward a neurosociology of emotion,* ed. David D. Franks and Thomas S. Smith, 3–17. Stamford, CT: JAI Press.

Smith, Tom W. 2007. *Job satisfaction in the United States.* Chicago: NORC/University of Chicago.

Smith-Lovin, Lynn, and Miller McPherson. 1993. You are who you know: A network perspective on gender. In *Theory on gender. feminism on theory,* ed. Paula England, 223–51. New York: Aldine.

Smock, Pamela, Wendy Manning, and Meredith Porter. 2005. "Everything's there except money": How money shapes decisions to marry among cohabitors. *Journal of Marriage and Family* 67 (3): 680–96.

Snow, David A., and Robert D. Benford. 1988. Ideology, frame resonance, and participant mobilization. In *International social movement research,* pp. 197–217. Greenwich, CT: JAI Press.

Snow, David A., E. Burke Rochford, Jr., Steven K. Worden, and Robert D. Benford. 1986. Frame alignment processes, micromobilization, and movement participation. *American Sociological Review* 51: 464–81.

Song, Chaoming, Zehui Qu, Nicholas Blumm, and Albert-László Barabási. 2010. Limits of predictability in human mobility. *Science* 327 (5968): 1018–21.

Sorkin, Andrew. 2010. *Too big to fail: The inside story of how Wall Street and Washington fought to save the financial system—and themselves.* New York: Viking.

SourceWatch. 2010. Total Wall Street bailout cost. Retrieved from www.sourcewatch.org/index .php?title=Total_Wall_Street_Bailout_Cost.

SourceWatch. 2011. American Crossroads. Retrieved from www.sourcewatch.org/index .php?title=American_Crossroads.

Spaargaren, Gert, and Arthur P. J. Mol. 1992. Sociology, environment, and modernity: Ecological modernization as a theory of social change. *Society and Natural Resources* 5: 323–44.

Spalter-Roth, Roberta, and Nicole Van Vooren. 2008. *What are they doing with a bachelor's degree in sociology?* Washington, DC: American Sociological Association.

Spalter-Roth, Roberta, and Nicole Van Vooren. 2009. *Idealists versus careerists: Graduate school choices of sociology majors.* Washington, DC: American Sociological Association.

Spalter-Roth, Roberta, and Nicole Van Vooren. 2010. *Mixed success: Four years of experiences of 2005 sociology graduates.* Washington, DC: American Sociological Association.

Span, Paula. 2003. Marriage at first sight. *Washington Post Magazine,* February 23, p. 16+.

Spencer, Wayne. 2003. Are the stars coming out? Secularization and the future of astrology. In *Predicting religion: Christian, secular and alternative futures,* ed. Grace Davie, Paul Heelas, and Linda Woodhead, pp. 214–28. Burlington, VT: Ashgate.

Squires, Gregory D., Samantha Friedman, and Catherine E. Saidat. 2002. Experiencing residential segregation: A contemporary study of Washington, DC. *Urban Affairs Review* 38 (2): 155–84.

Squires, Gregory, and Chester Hartman. 2006. *There is no such thing as a natural disaster: Race, class and Katrina.* New York: Routledge.

Srinivasan, Shobha, Liam R. O'Fallon, and Allen Dearry. 2003. Creating health communities, healthy homes, and healthy people. *American Journal of Public Health* 93 (9): 1446–50.

Stanton, Elizabeth Cady. 1889. *A history of woman suffrage,* Vol. 1. Rochester, NY: Fowler and Wells. Retrieved from www.fordham.edu/ halsall/mod/Senecafalls.html.

Stapinski, Helene. 1998. Let's talk dirty. *American Demographics* 20 (11): 50–56.

Stark, Rodney. 1999. Secularization RIP. *Sociology of Religion.* 60: 249–273.

Stark, Rodney, and William Sims Bainbridge. 1985. *The future of religion: Secularization, revival, and cult formation.* Berkeley: University of California Press.

Starr, Paul. 1983. *The social transformation of American medicine.* New York: Basic Books.

Stearns, Elizabeth, Claudia Buchmann, and Kara Bonneau. 2009. Interracial friendships in the transition to college. *Sociology of Education* 82: 173–95.

Steel, Emily. 2010. Some data-miners ready to reveal what they know. *Wall Street Journal,* December 3. Retrieved from http://online.wsj .com/article/SB1000142405274870437700457 5650802136721966.html.

Stein, Ben. 2006. In class warfare, guess which class is winning. *New York Times,* November 26. Retrieved from www.nytimes.com/2006/11/26/ business/yourmoney/26every.html.

Sterngold, James. 2010. How much did Lehman CEO Dick Fuld really make? *Bloomberg Businessweek,* April 29. Retrieved from www .businessweek.com/print/magazine/content/ 10_19/b4177056214833.htm.

Stevens, Mitchell. 2007. *Creating a class: College admissions and the education of elites.* Cambridge, MA: Harvard University Press.

Stewart, David W., Prem N. Shamdasani, and Dennis Rook. 2006. *Focus groups: Theory and practice,* 2nd ed. Thousand Oaks, CA: Sage.

Stiglitz, Joseph, and Andrew Charlton. 2007. *Fair trade for all.* New York: Oxford University Press.

Stockholm International Peace Research Institute (SIPRI). 2011. *SIPRI yearbook 2011.* New York: Oxford University Press. Retrieved from www .sipri.org/yearbook.

Stockman, Farah. 2011. Bush program helped lay the groundwork in Egypt. *Boston Globe,* February 11. Retrieved from www.boston.com/news/ nation/articles/2011/02/13/bush_program _helped_lay_the_groundwork_in_egypt/?rss _id=Boston.com+--+Top+political+stories.

Stockwell, Jamie. 2005. Defense, prosecution play to new "CSI" savvy. *Washington Post,* May 22, pp. A1, A10.

Stohlberg, Carol Gay. 2011. Shy U.S. intellectual created playbook used in a revolution. *New York Times,* February 16. Retrieved from www.nytimes.com/2011/02/17/world/ middleeast/17sharp.html.

Stoller, Robert. 1968. *Sex and gender: On the development of masculinity and femininity.* New York: Science House.

Story, Louise. 2008. To aim ads, web is keeping closer eye on you. *New York Times,* March 10. Retrieved from www.nytimes.com/2008/03/10/ technology/10privacy.html.

Strasburger, Victor C., and Barbara J. Wilson. 2002. *Children, adolescents, and the media.* Thousand Oaks, CA: Sage.

Strasburger, Victor C., Barbara J. Wilson, and Amy B. Jordan. 2009. *Children, adolescents, and the media,* 2nd ed. Thousand Oaks, CA: Sage.

Straus, Murray A. 2004. Prevalence of violence against dating partners by male and female university students worldwide. *Violence Against Women* 10 (7): 790–811.

Sulik, Gayle. 2007. The balancing act: Care work for the self and coping with breast cancer. *Gender & Society* 21 (6): 857–77.

Sullivan, Dennis, and Larry Tifft. 2006. *Handbook of restorative justice: A global perspective.* New York: Routledge.

Sumner, William Graham. 1906. *Folkways.* Boston: Ginn.

Sutherland, Edwin H. 1947. *Principles of criminology,* 4th ed. Philadelphia: Lippincott.

Sutherland, Edwin H. 1949. *White collar crime.* New York: Dryden Press.

Sutherland, Edwin H., Donald R. Cressey, and David F. Luckenbill. 1992. *Principles of criminology,* 11th ed. Lanham, MD: General Hall.

Swanson, Christopher B. 2009. Cities in crisis 2009: Closing the graduation gap. Editorial Projects in Education Research Center. Retrieved from www.edweek.org/rc/articles/ 2009/04/22/cities_in_crisis.html.

Swarns, Rachel L. 2006. Immigrants rally in scores of cities for legal status. *New York Times,* April 11, p. 1.

Sweeney, Brigid. 2010. Luxury retailers cash in as affluent shoppers step up holiday buying. *Chicago Business,* November 15. Retrieved from www.chicagobusiness.com/article/20101113/ ISSUE01/311139970/luxury-retailers-cash-in-as -affluent-shoppers-step-up-holiday-buying.

Switzer, Kathrine. 2007. *Marathon woman.* New York: Carroll & Graf.

Syme, S. Leonard, and Lisa F. Berkman. 1976. Social class, susceptibility, and sickness. *American Journal of Epidemiology* 104: 1–8.

Szasz, Andrew. 2007. *Shopping our way to safety: How we changed from protecting the environment to protecting ourselves.* Minneapolis: University of Minnesota Press.

Sztompka, Piotr. 1993. *The sociology of social change.* Malden, MA: Blackwell.

Tahirih Justice Center. 2011. About us. Retrieved from www.tahirih.org/about-us/.

Takaki, Ronald. 2008. *A different mirror: A history of multicultural America.* New York: Back Bay Books.

Taley, Margaret. 2006. When nature calls, women in House hike. *Denver Post,* December 12. Retrieved from www.denverpost.com/rockies/ci_4911077.

Tarrow, Sidney. 2011. *Power in movement.* New York: Cambridge University Press.

Tavernise, Sabrina. 2005. Middle-class family life in Iraq withers amid the chaos of war. *New York Times,* October 2, p. A1.

Tavernise, Sabrina. 2006. Young lives on hold: Nearly four years after the U.S.-led invasion, the relentless violence is freezing the lives of young Iraqis, and leaving their futures in doubt. *New York Times Upfront,* December 11, p. 10.

Tavernise, Sabrina, and Robert Gebeloff. 2010. Immigrants make paths to suburbia, not cities. *New York Times,* December 14. Retrieved from www.nytimes.com/2010/12/15/us/15census.html?ref=nyregion.

Tax Policy Center. 2011a. Tax facts. Retrieved from www.taxpolicycenter.org/taxfacts/listdocs.cfm?topic2id=20.

Tax Policy Center. 2011b. Table T11-0005: Current law against baseline of pre-2009-stimulus law plus AMT patch, evaluated in 2011; distribution of federal tax change by cash income percentile, 2011. Urban Institute and Brookings Institution. Retrieved from www.taxpolicycenter.org/numbers/displayatab.cfm?DocID=2883&topic2ID=40&topic3ID=41&DocTypeID=2.

Taylor, Alan. 2001. *American colonies: The settling of North America.* New York: Penguin.

Taylor, Frederick Winslow. 1911. *The principles of scientific management.* New York: Harper Brothers.

Taylor, Verta. 1989. Social movement continuity: The women's movement in abeyance. *American Sociological Review* 54 (5): 761–75.

Taylor, Verta, Leila Rupp, and Nancy Whittier, eds. 2008. *Feminist frontiers.* New York: McGraw-Hill.

TenHouten, Warren D. 1980. Social dominance and cerebral hemisphericity: Discriminating social groups by performance on two lateralized tests. *International Journal of Neuroscience* 10: 223–32.

TenHouten, Warren D. 1999. Text and temporality: Patterned-cyclical and ordinary-linear forms of time consciousness, inferred from a corpus of Australian Aboriginal and Euro-Australian life-historical interviews. *Symbolic Interaction* 22: 121–37.

Tewksbury, Richard, and George E. Higgins. 2006. Examining the effect of emotional dissonance on work stress and satisfaction with supervisors among correctional staff. *Criminal Justice Policy Review* 17 (3): 290–301.

Thomas, Sarah. 2010. Students, teachers agog at New Newton North High School. Retrieved from www.boston.com/yourtown/news/newton/2010/08/students_leaders_agog_at_new_n.html.

Thomas, William I. 1923. *The unadjusted girl.* Boston: Little, Brown.

Thomas, William I., and Dorothy Swain Thomas. 1928. *The child in America: Behavior problems and programs.* New York: Knopf.

Thomson, Irene Taviss. 2010. *Culture wars and enduring American dilemmas.* Ann Arbor: University of Michigan Press.

Thorne, Barrie, and Marilyn Yalom, eds. 1992. *Rethinking the family: Some feminist questions.* Boston, MA: Northeastern University Press.

Thrasher, Frederick Milton. 1927. *The gang.* Chicago: University of Chicago Press.

Tilly, Charles. 2004a. *Social movements 1768–2004.* Boulder, CO: Paradigm.

Tilly, Charles. 2004b. Terror, terrorism, terrorists. *Sociological Theory* 22 (1): 5–13.

Timberg, Craig. 2005. The rise of a market mentality means many go hungry in Niger. *Washington Post,* August 11, p. A17.

Timiraos, Nick. 2009. Mortgage deductions look less sacred. *Wall Street Journal,* February 27. Retrieved from http://online.wsj.com/article/SB123569898005989291.html.

Tjaden, Patricia, and Nancy Thoennes. 2000. *Full report of the prevalence, incidence, and consequences of violence against women.* Washington, DC: U.S. Department of Justice.

Tjaden, Patricia, and Nancy Thoennes. 2006. *Extent, nature, and consequences of rape victimization: Findings from the National Violence Against Women Survey.* Washington, DC: U.S. Department of Justice.

Tolson, A. 1977. *The limits of masculinity.* London: Tavistock.

Tomlinson, John. 2008. *Cultural imperialism: A critical introduction.* London: Continuum.

Tönnies, Ferdinand. 1887/2001. *Community and civil society,* trans. Margaret Hollis. Cambridge, U.K.: University of Cambridge Press.

Toussaint, Eric, and Damien Millet. 2010. *Debt, the IMF, and the World Bank.* New York: Monthly Review Press.

Trescott, Jacqueline. 2010. Ant-covered Jesus video removed from Smithsonian after Catholic League complains. *Washington Post,* December 1.

Tschannen, Oliver. 1991. The secularization paradigm: A systematization. *Journal for the Scientific Study of Religion* 30 (4): 395–415.

Tuchman, Gaye. 1978. *Making the news.* New York: Free Press.

Tumin, Melvin. 1953. Some principles of stratification: A critical analysis. *American Sociological Review* 18: 387–94.

Turk, Austin T. 2004. Sociology of terrorism. *Annual Review of Sociology* 30: 271–86.

Turkle, Sherry. 1985. *The second self.* New York: Simon & Schuster.

Turkle, Sherry. 1995. *Life on the screen.* New York: Simon & Schuster.

Turkle, Sherry. 2008. Always-on/always-on-you: The tethered self. In *Handbook of mobile communication studies,* ed. James E. Katz, 121–37. Cambridge, MA: MIT Press.

Turner, Darrell J. 2011. Religion: Year in review 2009. In *Britannica Book of the Year, 2010.* Retrieved from www.britannica.com/EBchecked/topic/1581715/religion-Year-In-Review-2009.

Turner, Jonathon. 1999. The neurology of emotion: Implications for sociological theories of interpersonal behavior. In *Mind, brain, and society: Toward a neurosociology of emotion,* ed. David D. Franks and Thomas S. Smith, 81–108. Stamford, CT: JAI Press.

Turner, Jonathon. 2000. *On the origins of human emotions: A sociological inquiry into the evolution of human affect.* Stanford, CA: Stanford University Press.

Turner, Margery Austin, and Stephen L. Ross. 2005. How racial discrimination affects the search for housing. In *The geography of opportunity,* ed. Xaviar de Souza Briggs, pp. 81–100. Washington, DC: Brookings Institution Press.

Turow, Joseph, Jennifer King, Chris Jay Hoofnagle, Amy Bleakley, and Michael Hennessy. 2009. Contrary to what marketers say, Americans reject tailored advertising and three activities that enable it. Retrieved from http://papers.ssrn.com/sol3/papers.cfm?abstract_id=1478214.

Twenge, Jean M. 2006. *Generation me.* New York: Free Press.

Tyler, T. R. 2005. Introduction: Legitimating ideologies. *Social Justice Research* 18: 211–15.

Tyler, T. R., and S. L. Blader. 2003. The group engagement model: Procedural justice, social identity, and cooperative behavior. *Personality and Social Psychology Review* 7: 349–61.

Tyron, Maida. 2007. Killed by a cavity. *Washington Post,* March 3, p. A14.

U.S. Bureau of Labor Statistics. 2009. Table 1.4: Occupations With the Largest Job Growth, 2008, and Projected, 2018. Retrieved from www.bls.gov/emp/emptab3.htm.

U.S. Bureau of Labor Statistics. 2010a. Current Population Survey: Education pays. Retrieved from www.bls.gov/emp/ep_chart_001.htm.

U.S. Bureau of Labor Statistics. 2010b. National Compensation Survey: Occupational earnings in the United States. Retrieved from www.bls.gov/ncs/ncswage2009.htm#Wage_Tables.

U.S. Bureau of Labor Statistics. 2010c. Occupational employment and wages by ownership—May 2009. BLS news release USDL-10-1045, July 27.

U.S. Bureau of Labor Statistics. 2011a. Union membership declines in 2010. Retrieved from www.bls.gov/opub/ted/2011/ted_20110125.htm.

U.S. Bureau of Labor Statistics. 2011b. Women in the labor force, 1970–2009. Retrieved from www.bls.gov/opub/ted/2011/ted_20110105.htm.

U.S. Census Bureau. 2000. Urban/rural and metropolitan/nonmetropolitan population: 2000. Table GCT-P1. Retrieved from http://factfinder2.census.gov/faces/tableservices/jsf/pages/productview.xhtml?pid=DEC_00_SF2_GCTP1.US93&prodType=table.

U.S. Census Bureau. 2004. U.S. interim projections by age, sex, race, and Hispanic origin. Retrieved from www.census.gov/ipc/www/usinterimproj/.

U.S. Census Bureau. 2005a. Americans spend more than 100 hours commuting to work each year, Census Bureau reports. Retrieved from www.census.gov/Press-Release/www/releases/archives/american_community_survey_acs/004489.html.

U.S. Census Bureau. 2005b. Fertility of American women: June 2004. Washington, DC: U.S. Department of Commerce.

U.S. Census Bureau. 2006. Current Population Survey, March and annual social and economic supplements. Retrieved from www.census.gov/population/socdemo/hh-fam/fm1.xls.

U.S. Census Bureau. 2008. Table 1: Full-time, year-round civilian employed workers and median earnings in the past 12 months by sex and detailed occupation: 2008. Retrieved from www.census.gov/hhes/www/ioindex/reports.html.

U.S. Census Bureau. 2009a. American Community Survey. Tables B02001, B03001, and

B04006. Retrieved from http://factfinder.census.gov.

U.S. Census Bureau. 2009b. American Community Survey. Table S1501: Educational attainment. Retrieved from http://factfinder.census.gov/servlet/STTable?_bm=y&-geo_id=01000US&-qr_name=ACS_2009_5YR_G00_S1501&-ds_name=ACS_2009_5YR_G00_.

U.S. Census Bureau. 2009c. Voting and registration in the election of 2008, Table 8. Retrieved from www.census.gov/hhes/www/socdemo/voting/publications/p20/2008/Table%2008.xls.

U.S. Census Bureau. 2010a. America's families and living arrangements. Retrieved from www.census.gov/population/www/socdemo/hh-fam/cps2010.html.

U.S. Census Bureau. 2010b. American Community Survey, 2009. Retrieved from http://factfinder.census.gov/servlet/DatasetMainPageServlet?_program=ACS&_submenuId=&_lang=en&_ts=.

U.S. Census Bureau. 2010c. CPS historical time series tables, Table A-3. Retrieved from www.census.gov/hhes/socdemo/education/data/cps/historical/index.html.

U.S. Census Bureau. 2010d. *Current Population Survey, 2009: Annual social and economic supplement.* Retrieved from www.census.gov/hhes/socdemo/education/data/cps/2009/tables.html.

U.S. Census Bureau. 2010e. *Current Population Survey, 2010: Annual social and economic supplement.* Retrieved from www.census.gov/hhes/www/cpstables/032010/hhinc/new05_000.htm.

U.S. Census Bureau. 2010f. Income, poverty, and health insurance coverage in the United States: 2009. Retrieved from www.census.gov/prod/2010pubs/p60-238.pdf.

U.S. Census Bureau. 2010g. Observations from the Interagency Technical Working Group on Developing a Supplemental Poverty Measure. Washington, DC: U.S. Department of Commerce. Retrieved from www.census.gov/hhes/www/poverty/SPM_TWGObservations.pdf.

U.S. Census Bureau. 2010h. Race and Hispanic origin of the foreign-born population in the United States: 2007. Retrieved from www.census.gov/prod/2010pubs/acs-11.pdf.

U.S. Census Bureau. 2010i. *Statistical abstract of the United States: 2010.* Retrieved from www.census.gov/compendia/statab/2010edition.html.

U.S. Census Bureau. 2010j. *Statistical abstract of the United States: 2010.* Table 1112: Cellular telecommunications industry: 1990 to 2008. Retrieved from www.census.gov/compendia/statab/cats/information_communications.html.

U.S. Census Bureau. 2010k. Table H-2: Share of aggregate income received by each fifth and top 5 percent of households. Washington, DC: U.S. Department of Commerce. Retrieved from www.census.gov/hhes/www/income/data/historical/household/index.html.

U.S. Census Bureau. 2010l. Families and living arrangements. Table HH-1: Households, by type: 1940 to present; Table HH-4: Households, by size: 1960 to present; and Table FM-1: Families, by presence of own children under 18: 1950 to present. Retrieved from www.census.gov/population/www/socdemo/hh-fam.html.

U.S. Census Bureau. 2010m. Years of school completed by people 25 years and over, by age and sex: Selected years 1940 to 2009. Current Population Survey. Washington, DC: U.S.

Department of Commerce. Retrieved from www.census.gov/population/www/socdemo/educ-attn.html.

U.S. Census Bureau. 2011a. *Current Population Survey, 2011: Annual social and economic supplement.* Retrieved from www.census.gov/hhes/www/cpstables/032011/hhinc/new05_000.htm.

U.S. Census Bureau. 2011b. Current Population Survey, March and annual social and economic supplements, 2010 and earlier, Table AD-1. Retrieved from www.census.gov/population/www/socdemo/hh-fam.html#ht.

U.S. Census Bureau. 2011c. The Hispanic population: 2010. Retrieved from www.census.gov/prod/cen2010/briefs/c2010br-04.pdf.

U.S. Census Bureau. 2011d. Income, Poverty, and Health Insurance Coverage in the United States: 2010. Retrieved from www.census.gov/prod/2011pubs/p60-239.pdf.

U.S. Census Bureau. 2011e. Overview of race and Hispanic origin: 2010. Retrieved from www.census.gov/prod/cen2010/briefs/c2010br-02.pdf.

U.S. Census Bureau. 2011f. *Statistical abstract of the United States: 2011.* Table 225: Educational attainment by race and Hispanic origin. Retrieved from www.census.gov/compendia/statab/cats/education/educational_attainment.html.

U.S. Department of Agriculture Economic Research Service. 2011. Food security in the United States: Key statistics and graphics. Retrieved from www.ers.usda.gov/Briefing/FoodSecurity/stats_graphs.htm.

U.S. Department of Commerce. 2010. *Exploring the digital nation: Home broadband internet adoption in the United States.* Economics and Statistics Administration and National Telecommunications and Information Administration. Retrieved from www.ntia.doc.gov/reports.html.

U.S. Department of Defense. 2009. Base structure report. Retrieved from www.acq.osd.mil/ie/download/bsr/BSR2008Baseline.pdf.

U.S. Department of Defense. 2010. Report of the comprehensive review of the issues associated with a repeal of "don't ask, don't tell." November 30. Retrieved from www.defense.gov/home/features/2010/0610_gatesdadt/DADTReport_FINAL_20101130%28secure-hires%29.pdf.

U.S. Department of Health and Human Services. 2010. *Healthy people 2020.* Retrieved from www.healthypeople.gov/2020/topicsobjectives2020/overview.aspx?topicid=12.

U.S. Department of Housing and Urban Development. 2005. Discrimination in metropolitan housing markets: National results from phase I of HDS2000. Retrieved from www.huduser.org/portal/publications/hsgfin/phase1.html.

U.S. Department of Justice. 2008. About domestic violence. Retrieved from www.ovw.usdoj.gov/domviolence.htm.

U.S. Department of Labor, Bureau of Labor Statistics. 2008. Older workers. Retrieved from www.bls.gov/spotlight/2008/older_workers/.

U.S. Department of Labor, Women's Bureau. 2010. 20 Leading occupations of employed women, 2010 annual averages. Retrieved from www.dol.gov/wb/factsheets/20lead2010.htm.

U.S. Department of State. 2004. Saudi Arabia: Country reports on human rights practices. Retrieved from www.state.gov/g/drl/rls/hrrpt/2003/27937.htm.

U.S. Equal Employment Opportunity Commission. 2010. Sexual harassment. Retrieved from

www.eeoc.gov/laws/types/sexual_harassment.cfm.

U.S. Senate Permanent Subcommittee on Investigations. 2011. *Wall Street and the financial crisis.* April 13. Washington, DC. Retrieved from http://hsgac.senate.gov/public/_files/financial_crisis/financialcrisisreport.pdf.

Ugochukwu, Chioma. 2008. Cultural resistance and resilience amid imported TV programming in Nigeria. *Africa Today* 55 (1): 35–58.

UN Commission on Human Security. 2004. *Human security now.* New York: United Nations.

UN Department of Economic and Social Affairs, Population Division. 2010. *World population prospects: The 2009 revision.* Retrieved from esa.un.org/unpd/wup/index.htm.

UN Department of Economic and Social Affairs, Population Division. 2011. *World population prospects: The 2010 revision.* Retrieved from esa.un.org/unpd/wpp/.

UN Development Fund for Women. 2007. Violence against women—facts and figures. Retrieved from www.unifem.org/attachments/gender_issues/violence_against_women/facts_figures_violence_against_women_2007.pdf.

UN Development Programme. 2005. *Human development report 2005.* New York: UN Development Programme.

UN Development Programme. 2010. *Human development report 2010.* New York: Palgrave Macmillan.

UN Human Settlements Programme. 2003a. *Slums of the world.* Nairobi, Kenya: UN Settlements Programme.

UN Human Settlements Programme. 2003b. *The challenge of slums.* Sterling, VA: Earthscan Publications.

UN Office on Drugs and Crime. 2006. *Trafficking in persons: Global patterns.* Retrieved from www.unodc.org/documents/human-trafficking/HT-globalpatterns-en.pdf.

UN Population Fund. 2008. State of the world's population, 2007. Retrieved from www.unfpa.org/swp/2007/presskit/pdf/sowp2007_eng.pdf.

Underwood, Anne, and Jerry Adler. 2005. When cultures clash. *Newsweek,* April 25, pp. 68–72.

UNESCO-Institute for Statistics. 2005. *International flow of selected cultural goods and services, 1994–2003.* Montreal, Quebec: UNESCO Institute for Statistics.

Union of Concerned Scientists. 2008. UCS satellite database. Retrieved from www.ucsusa.org/nuclear_weapons_and_global_security/space_weapons/technical_issues/ucs-satellite-database.html.

Unitarian Universalist Association of Congregations. 2008. Web pages: www.uua.org/visitors/index.shtml and www.uua.org/visitors/beliefswithin/6677.shtml.

United Nations. 2005. *The inequality predicament*: Report on the world situation 2005. New York: United Nations. Retrieved from http://daccessdds.un.org/doc/UNDOC/GEN/N05/418/73/PDF/N0541873.pdf?OpenElement.

Unnever, James D., and Francis T. Cullen. 2007. The racial divide in support for the death penalty. Does white racism matter? *Social Forces* 85 (3): 1281–301.

Unnever, James D., and Frances T. Cullen. 2010. Racial-ethnic intolerance and support for capital punishment: A cross-national comparison. *Criminology* 48 (3): 831–64.

Urban, Wayne J., and Jennings L. Wagoner, Jr. 2009. *American education: A history,* 4th ed. New York: Routledge.

Valian, Virginia. 1999. *Why so slow? The advancement of women.* Cambridge, MA: MIT Press.

Vallas, Steven Peter. 2007. Theorizing teamwork under contemporary capitalism. *Research in the Sociology of Work* 16: 3–24.

van Gennep, Arnold. 1909/1961. *The rites of passage,* trans. Monika B. Vizedom and Gabrielle L. Caffee. Chicago: University of Chicago Press.

Varian, Hal R. 2007. An iPod has global value. Ask the (many) countries that make it. *New York Times,* June 28. Retrieved from www.nytimes.com/2007/06/28/business/worldbusiness/28scene.html.

Vartabedian, Ralph, and Ken Bensinger. 2010. Toyota's structure may be an issue. *Los Angeles Times,* February 23, p. A1.

Vaughan, Diane. 1996. *The Challenger launch decision.* Chicago: University of Chicago Press.

Vaughn, Diane. 2003. History as cause: *Columbia* and *Challenger. Report, Columbia Accident Investigation Board,* vol. 1, ch. 8.

Vaught, Charles, and David L. Smith. 2003. Incorporation and mechanical solidarity in an underground coal mine. In *The cultural study of work,* ed. Douglas Harper and Helene M. Lawson, pp. 96–115. Lanham, MD: Rowman & Littlefield.

Veblen, Thorstein. 1899/1973. *The theory of the leisure class.* Boston: Houghton Mifflin.

Vedantam, Shankar. 2005. See no bias. *Washington Post Magazine,* January 23, pp. 12–17, 38.

Verba, Sidney, Kay Schlozman, and Henry Brady. 1995. *Voice and equality.* Cambridge, MA: Harvard University Press.

Vertovec, Steven. 2009. *Transnationalism.* New York: Routledge.

Vigil, James Diego. 1996. Street baptism: Chicano gang initiation. *Human Organization* 55 (Summer): 149–54.

Vogel, Joachim, and Töres Theorell. 2005. Social welfare models, labor markets, and health outcomes. In *Healthier societies: From analysis to action,* ed. Jody Heymann, Clyde Hertzman, Morris L. Barer, and Robert G. Evans, pp. 267–95. New York: Oxford University Press.

Vogel, Steve. 2007. *The Pentagon: A history.* New York: Random House.

von Clausewitz, Carl. 1832/1976. *On war,* ed. and trans., Michael Howard and Peter Paret. Princeton, NJ: Princeton University Press.

Wainright, Jennifer, Stephen Russell, and Charlotte Patterson. 2004. Psychosocial adjustment, school outcomes and romantic relationships of adolescents with same-sex parents. *Child Development* 75 (6): 1886–98.

Wajcman, Judy. 2008. Life in the fast lane? Toward a sociology of technology and time. *British Journal of Sociology* 59 (1): 59–77.

Wakefield, Sara, and Christopher Uggen. 2010. Incarceration and stratification. *Annual Review of Sociology* 36: 387–406.

Waldfogel, Jane. 1997. The effect of children on women's wages. *American Sociological Review* 62 (2): 209–17.

Waldinger, Roger, ed. 2001. *Strangers at the gates: New immigrants in urban America.* Berkeley: University of California.

Walker, Pat, ed. 1979. *Between labor and capital.* Boston: South End Press.

Wallerstein, Immanuel. 1974. *The modern world-system.* New York: Academic Press.

Wallerstein, Immanuel. 1979. *The capitalist world-economy.* New York: Cambridge University Press.

Wallerstein, Immanual. 2004. *World systems analysis: An introduction.* Durham, NC: Duke University Press.

Wang, Marian. 2011. Magnetar deal prompts SEC settlement with JPMorgan Chase. June 21. ProPublica. Retrieved from www.propublica.org/blog/item/magnetar-deal-prompts-sec-settlement-with-jpmorgan-chase.

Ward, John T. 2010. Dissident in exile. *Drew Magazine.* Drew University. Retrieved from www.drewmagazine.com/2009/12/dissident-in-exile/.

Warner, Stephen. 1993. Work in progress toward a new paradigm for the sociological study of religion in the United States. *American Journal of Sociology* 98 (5): 1044–93.

Wartenberg, Thomas. 1990. *The forms of power: From domination to transformation.* Philadelphia: Temple University Press.

Waskul, Dennis D., and Justin A. Martin. 2010. Now the orgy is over. *Symbolic Interaction* 33 (2): 297–318.

Wasserman, Stanley, Katherine Faust, and Dawn Iacobucci. 1994. *Social network analysis: Methods and applications.* Cambridge, U.K.: Cambridge University Press.

Watts, Duncan. 2004. The "new" science of networks. *Annual Review of Sociology* 30: 243–70.

Waxman, Sharon. 2005. Hollywood unions object to product placement on TV. *New York Times,* November 14. Retrieved from www.nytimes.com/2005/11/14/business/14guild.html.

Weber, Max. 1905/1958. *The Protestant ethic and the spirit of capitalism,* trans. Talcott Parsons. New York: Scribner's.

Weber, Max. 1915/1946a. Religious rejections of the world and their directions. In *From Max Weber: Essays in sociology,* ed. H. H. Gerth and C. Wright Mills, pp. 323–59. New York: Oxford University Press.

Weber, Max. 1915/1946b. The social psychology of world religions. In *From Max Weber: Essays in sociology,* ed. Hans Gerth and C. Wright Mills, 267–301. New York: Oxford University Press.

Weber, Max. 1919/1946a. Politics as a vocation. In *From Max Weber: Essays in sociology,* ed. H. H. Gerth and C. Wright Mills, pp. 77–128. New York: Oxford University Press.

Weber, Max. 1919/1946b. Science as a vocation. In *From Max Weber: Essays in sociology,* ed. H. H. Gerth and C. Wright Mills, pp. 129–56. New York: Oxford University Press.

Weber, Max. 1922/1978. *Economy and society,* ed. Guenther Rother and Claus Wittich. Berkeley: University of California Press.

Weber, Max. 1946. *From Max Weber: Essays in sociology,* trans. Hans Gerth and C. Wright Mills. New York: Oxford University Press.

Weber, Max. 1949/2011. *Methodology of social sciences,* trans. Edward A. Shils and Henry A. Finch. New Brunswick, NJ: Transaction Publishers.

Wechsler Henry, Tobin F. Nelson, Jae Eun Lee, Mark Seibring, Catherine Lewis, and Richard P. Keeling. 2003. Perception and reality: A national evaluation of social norms marketing interventions to reduce college students' heavy alcohol use. *Journal of Studies on Alcohol* 64 (4): 484–94.

Weiss, Bari. 2011. A Democrat's triumphant return to Cairo. *Wall Street Journal,* February 26. Retrieved from online.wsj.com/article/SB10001424052748703408604576164482658051692.html.

Weiss, Jessica. 2000. *To have and to hold: Marriage, the baby boom and social change.* Chicago: University of Chicago Press.

Wellman, Barry. 2001. Physical place and cyberplace: The rise of personalized networking. *International Journal of Urban and Regional Research* 25 (2): 227–52.

Wellman, Barry, and Caroline Haythornthwaite. 2002. *The internet in everyday life.* Oxford, U.K.: Blackwell.

Wellman, Barry, and Scot Wortley. 1990. Different strokes from different folks: Community ties and social support. *American Journal of Sociology* 96 (3): 558–88.

Welzel, Christian, and Ronald Inglehart. 2010. Agency, values, and well-being: A human development model. *Social Indicators Research* 97: 43–63.

West, Candace, and Don H. Zimmerman. 1987. Doing gender. *Gender & Society* 1 (2): 125–51.

Western, Bruce. 2007. *Punishment and inequality in America.* New York: Russell Sage Foundation Publications.

Wharton, Amy S. 2009. The sociology of emotional labor. *Annual Review of Sociology* 35: 147–65.

White, Michael J., and Gayle Kaufman. 1997. Language usage, social capital, and school completion among immigrants and native-born ethnic groups. *Social Science Quarterly* 78: 385–98.

Whyte, William Foote. 1943/1993. *Street corner society,* 4th ed. Chicago: University of Chicago Press.

Wikinvest.com. 2010. News Corporation. Retrieved from www.wikinvest.com/stock/News_Corporation_%28NWS%29.

Williams, Krissah. 2005. In hip-hop, making name-dropping pay. *Washington Post,* August 29, pp. D1, D9.

Williams, Robin M. 1970. *American society: A sociological interpretation.* New York: Knopf.

Williams, Terry. 1990. *The cocaine kids.* Boston: Addison Wesley.

Willis, Paul. 1977. *Learning to labor.* New York: Columbia University Press.

Wilson, Clint C., Felix Gutierrez, and Lena Chao. 2003. *Racism, sexism, and the media.* Thousand Oaks, CA: Sage.

Wilson, James Q. 2002. *The marriage problem.* New York: Harper.

Wilson, Scott, and Jon Cohen. 2011. Poll: Nearly two-thirds of Americans say Afghan war isn't worth fighting. *Washington Post,* March 15. Retrieved from www.washingtonpost.com/world/poll-nearly-two-thirds-of-americans-say-afghan-war-isnt-worth-fighting/2011/03/14/ABRbeEW_story.html.

Wilson, William Julius. 1973. *Power, racism, and privilege: Race relations in theoretical and sociohistorical perspectives.* New York: Free Press.

Wilson, William Julius. 1980. *The declining significance of race.* Chicago: University of Chicago Press.

Wilson, William Julius. 1996. *When work disappears: The world of the new urban poor.* New York: Knopf.

Wolfe, Allan. 2005. *The transformation of American religion.* Chicago: University of Chicago Press.

Wolff, Edward N. 2010. Recent trends in household wealth in the United States: Rising debt and the middle-class squeeze—An update to 2007. Annandale-on-Hudson, NY: Levy Economics Institute of Bard College. Retrieved from www.levyinstitute.org/pubs/wp_589.pdf.

Wolfinger, Nichaolas H. 2003. Family structure homogamy: The effects of parental divorce on partner selection and marital stability. *Social Sciences Research* 32 (1): 80–97.

Women's Prison Association Institute on Women & Criminal Justice. 2006. *Hard hit: The growth in the imprisonment of women, 1977–2004.* Retrieved from www.wpaonline.org/institute/hardhit/HardHitReport4.pdf.

Women's Prison Association. n.d. Luz's story. Retrieved from www.wpaonline.org/press/luz.htm.

Woodward, Bob. 2006. *State of denial: Bush at war, part III.* New York: Simon & Schuster.

World Bank. 2011. World development indicators: Literacy rate, adult total. Retrieved from http://data.worldbank.org/indicator/SE.ADT.LITR.ZS.

World Health Organization. 2004. *The global burden of disease.* Geneva, Switzerland: World Health Organization.

World Health Organization. 2005a. *WHO multicountry study on women's health and domestic violence against women.* Geneva: World Health Organization. Retrieved from www.who.int/gender/violence/who_multicountry_study/summary_report/summary_report_English2.pdf.

World Health Organization. 2005b. *World health report, 2005.* Geneva, Switzerland: World Health Organization.

World Health Organization. 2006. *Preventing disease through healthy environments.* Geneva, Switzerland: World Health Organization.

World Health Organization. 2007a. *Deaths and DALYs attributable to water, sanitation & hygiene (2002).* Retrieved from www.who.int/quantifying_ehimpacts/national/countryprofile/mapwsh/en/index.html.

World Health Organization. 2007b. *Male circumcision: Global trends and determinants of prevalence, safety and acceptability.* Retrieved from http://whqlibdoc.who.int/publications/2007/9789241596169_eng.pdf.

World Health Organization. 2010. Female genital mutilation. Retrieved from www.who.int/mediacentre/factsheets/fs241/en/.

World Values Survey. 2005–2008. Online data analysis. Retrieved from www.wvsevsdb.com/wvs/WVSAnalizeSample.jsp.

Worldwatch Institute. 2006. *State of the world, 2006.* New York: Norton.

Wray, Harry. 2008. *Japanese and American education: Attitudes and practices.* Charlotte, NC: Information Age Publishing.

Wray, John. 2010. Lives: Acquired taste. *New York Times Magazine,* February 25, p. 50.

Wright, Daniel, Gail Self, and Chris Justice. 2000. Memory conformity: Exploring misinformation effects when presented by another person. *British Journal of Psychology* 91: 189–202.

Wright, Erik Olin. 1985. *Classes.* London: Verso Press.

Wrong, Dennis. 1979. *Power: Its forms, bases and uses.* New York: Oxford University Press.

Wuthnow, Robert. 2008. The sociological study of values. *Sociological Forum* 23 (June): 333–43.

Yamagata, Hisashi, Kuang S. Yeh, Shelby Stewman, and Hiroko Dodge. 1997. Sex segregation and glass ceilings: A comparative statics model of women's career opportunities in the federal government over a quarter century. *American Journal of Sociology* 103 (3): 566–632.

Yamane, David. 1997. Secularization on trial: In defense of a neosecularization paradigm. *Journal for the Scientific Study of Religion* 36 (1): 109–22.

Yeatmann, Anna. 1997. Feminism and power. In *Reconstructing political theory: Feminist perspectives,* ed. Mary Lyndon Shanley and Uma Narayan, pp. 144–57. University Park: Pennsylvania State University Press.

Young, Iris Marion. 1992. Five faces of oppression. In *Rethinking power,* ed. Thomas Wartenberg, pp. 174–95. Albany: State University of New York Press.

Yu, Roger. 2005. JetBlue passengers watched their own ordeal on live TV. *USA Today,* September 23, p. 3B.

Yukl, G., H. Kim, and C. Falbe. 1996. Antecedents of influence outcomes. *Journal of Applied Psychology* 81: 309–17.

Yunker, John. 2008. The best global web designs of 2008. Retrieved from www.globalbydesign.com/blog/2008/02/28/the-best-global-web-sites-of-2008/.

Zimmerman, Jonathan. 2002. *Whose America? Culture wars in the public schools.* Cambridge, MA: Harvard University Press.

Zinn, Maxinne Baca, and Bonnie Thornton Dill, eds. 1994. *Women of color in U.S. society.* Philadelphia, PA: Temple University Press.

Zoroya, Gregg. 2008. More U.S. troops battle foreclosure. *USA Today,* April 25. Retrieved from www.usatoday.com/news/military/2008-04-24-foreclosure_N.htm.

Zoroya, Gregg. 2011. 20,000 military members, vets faced foreclosure in 2010. *USA Today,* February 4. Retrieved from www.usatoday.com/news/military/2011-02-04-1Avetforeclosures04_ST_N.htm.

Zukin, Sharon, and Jennifer Smith Maguire. 2004. Consumers and consumption. *Annual Review of Sociology,* 30: 173–97.

Zweig, Michael. 2000. *The working class majority.* Ithaca, NY: Cornell University Press.

Credits

Text and Line Art Credits

Chapter 1

p. 6: C. Wright Mills, *The Sociological Imagination.* New York: Oxford University Press. Copyright © 1959 Oxford University Press. Used with permission; **p. 13:** Quotation from *The Marx-Engels Reader,* 2nd edition by Karl Marx and Friedrich Engels, edited by Robert C. Tucker. Copyright © 1978, 1972 by W.W. Norton & Company. Reprinted by permission of W.W. Norton & Company, Inc.

Chapter 2

p. 34: *The Rhode Island Media Study, 1996–1999.* Copyright © 2000 Rhode Island Coalition Against Domestic Violence. www.ricadv.org; **p. 43:** Kohut, Andrew. N.D. Andrew Kohut on Polling at the Pew Research Center. Online at: http://www.pewtrusts.org/expert_qa_detail.aspx?id=29046. Accessed December 1, 2008. Copyright © 2008. Reprinted with permission; **p. 44:** Dill, Karen E. and Kathryn P. Thill. 2007. "Video Game Characters and the Socialization of Gender Roles." *Sex Roles* 57: 851–864. Copyright © 2007, Springer Science+Business Media, LLC; **p. 49:** Marx, Karl. [1845] 1978. "Theses on Feuerbach." In Robert C. Tucker, ed. The Marx-Engels Reader, 2nd edition. New York: W.W. Norton & Company.

Chapter 3

p. 51: Robin Williams, *American Society: A Sociological Interpretation.* Copyright © 1951, 1970; **p. 62:** Schwartz, Shalom H., Gila Melech, Arielle Lehmann, Steven Burgess, Mari Harris, and Vicki Owens, "Extending the Cross-Cultural Validity of the Theory of Basic Human Values with a Different Method of Measurement," *Journal of Cross-Cultural Psychology* 32: 519–542. Copyright © 2001 Sage Publications. Used with permission; **p. 63, Maps 3.1, 3.2:** Created by Mark Newman, Department of Physics and Center for the Study of Complex Systems, University of Michigan; **p. 64, Figure 3.2:** Pew Global Attitudes Project. 2008. "Unfavorable Views of Jews and Muslims on the Increase in Europe." Washington, DC: Pew Research Center, September 17. http://pewglobal.org/2008/09/17/unfavorable-views-of-jews-and-muslims-on-the-increase-in-europe/. Copyright © 2008 Pew Research Center. Used with permission; **p. 81:** Miranda, Candice. 2003. "In Kenya, Television Opens Window Mainly on the West." *Washington Post,* April 28, p. A19. Copyright © 2003 Candice Miranda.

Chapter 4

p. 93: Excerpt of transcript from Crossfire, October 19, 2004. Copyright © 2004 CNN, Inc.; **p. 99, Table 4.1:** George Ritzer. *The McDonaldization of Society,* 5th edition. Thousand Oaks: Sage Publications. Copyright © 2007 Sage Publications. Used with permission; **p. 102, Map 4.1:** Central Intelligence Agency, The World Factbook, https://www.cia.gov/library/publications/the-world-factbook/rankorder/rankorderguide.html; calculations by authors.

Chapter 5

p. 111: Max Weber, *Essays in Sociology,* translated by Hans Gerth and C. Wright Mills. Copyright © 1946 Oxford University Press. Used with permission; **p. 112:** "Organize" fish graphic from http://www.Yesrthernsun.com/n/s/Organize-TShirt-%281016%29.html; **p. 115:** Reprinted by permission of The Institute for Social Research from Studies in Social Power, "The Bases of Social Power" by John R.P. French Jr. and Bertram Raven. Copyright © 1959 Institute for Social Research, University of Michigan, pp. 150–167; **p. 115:** Forsyth, Group Dynamics 5/e. Copyright © 2010 Wadsworth, a part of Cengage Learning, Inc. Reproduced by permission. www.cengage.com/permissions; **p. 116, Table 5.1:** Adapted from Forsyth, *Group Dynamics* 5/e. Copyright © 2010 Wadsworth, a part of Cengage Learning, Inc. Reproduced by permission. www.cengage.com/permissions; **p. 119:** Max Weber, *Essays in Sociology,* translated by Hans Gerth and C. Wright Mills. Copyright © 1946 Oxford University Press. Used with permission; **p. 119-120:** Quotation from "Monty Python and the Holy Grail" Written by Graham Chapman, John Cleese, Terry Gilliam, Eric Idle, Terry Jones and Michael Palin © 1974 National Film Trustee Company Ltd. Krypton International Corp. RCA/Columbia Python Pictures in association with Michael White; **p. 126:** Grusky, David B., "The Past, Present, and Future of Social Inequality." Pp. 3–51 in David B. Grusky, ed. *Social Stratification.* Copyright © 2001 Westview Press. Reprinted with permission; **p. 131, Figure 5.1:** Copyright © Center for Responsive Politics (Opensecrets.org). Used with permission.

Chapter 6

p. 136: Joseph A. Gallian, "A Conversation with Melanie Wood." *Math Horizons.* Sept., pp. 13–14, 31, 2004. Copyright © The Mathematical Association of America, 2010. All rights reserved; **p. 138:** Friedland, Lewis A. and Shauna Morimoto. 2005. "The Changing Lifeworld of Young People: Risk, Resume-Padding, and Civic Engagement." *CIRCLE*

Working Paper 40, The Center for Information and Research on Civic Learning and Engagement. Copyright © 2005. Reprinted by permission; **p. 142:** *Asylums: Essays on the Social Situation of Mental Patients and Other Inmates* by Erving Goffman. Copyright © 1961 by Erving Goffman. Used by permission of Doubleday, a division of Random House, Inc.; **p. 153:** Cooley, Charles Horton. 1902. *Human Nature and the Social Order.* New York: Schocken Books; **p. 153:** Mead, George Herbert. 1934/1962. *Mind, Self, and Society.* Edited by Charles W. Morris. Chicago: Chicago University Press. Copyright 1934, renewed © 1962. Reprinted by permission of the University of Chicago Press.

Chapter 7

p. 162: Tavernise, Sabrina. 2005. "Middle-class family life in Iraq withers amid the chaos of war." *New York Times.* October 2, p. A1; **p. 162:** Tavernise, Sabrina. 2006. "Young lives on hold: nearly four years after the U.S.-led invasion, the relentless violence is freezing the lives of young Iraqis, and leaving their futures in doubt." *New York Times Upfront.* December 11, p. 10; **p. 166, Maps 7.1, 7.2:** http://www.radicalcartography.net/?projectionref; **p. 167:** Quotation from Betsy Leondar-Wright, *Class Matters.* Copyright © 2005 New Society Publishers. Used with permission; **p. 167:** *The Social Construction of Reality* by Peter L. Berger and Thomas Luckmann. Copyright © 1966 by Peter L. Berger and Thomas Luckmann. Used by permission of Doubleday, a division of Random House, Inc.; **p. 172, Figure 7.3:** Valdis Krebs http://www.orgnet.com/hijackers.html; **p. 175, Figure 7.4:** http://www.orgnet.com/steroids.html; **p. 177:** Quotation from Max Weber, *Essays in Sociology,* translated by Hans Gerth and C. Wright Mills. Copyright © 1946 Oxford University Press. Used with permission; **p. 177, Figure 7.5:** http://www.miami.edu/index.php/about_us/leadership/how_the_university_is_organized/; **p. 179:** Fried, Mindy. 2008. *The Evaluator in the Field as an Outsider Within.* FootNotes. 36 (3), March. American Sociological Association. Online at: http://www.asanet.org/footNotes/mar08_R/fn6.html. Retrieved May 24, 2010. Copyright © 2010 Mindy Fried. Used with permission.

Chapter 8

p. 192, Figure 8.1: Link, Bruce G. and Jo C. Phelan, "Conceptualizing Stigma," *Annual Review of Sociology* 27: 363–385. Copyright © 2001 Annual Reviews, Inc. Used with permission; **p. 194:** Erikson, Kai T., Wayward Puritans: *A Study in the Sociology of Deviance,* Classic Edition, 1st. © 2005. Printed and electronically reproduced by permission of Pearson education, Inc., Upper Saddle River, New Jersey; **p. 196:** Conrad, Peter and Joseph Schneider, *Deviance and Medicalization.* Copyright © 1980. Reprinted by permission of Temple University Press; **pp. 198, 199:** Copyright © Donna Gaines. Used with permission. http://www.donnagaines.com/shrine/shrine2.htm; **p. 205:** Map of cameras in downtown Boston from http://www.notbored.com/boston.html; **p. 211:** Women's Prison Association, Wpaonline.org. http://66.29.139.159/press/luz.htm; **p. 212, Map 8.1:** http://www.amnestyusa.org/death-penalty/death-penalty-in-states/page.do?id=1101153 © Amnesty International.

Chapter 9

p. 220: Quotation from Lubrano, Alfred. 2004. *Limbo: Blue-Collar Roots, White-Collar Dreams.* Hoboken, NJ: John Wiley & Sons. Reprinted with permission of John Wiley & Sons, Inc.; **p. 231, Figure 9.3:** Hertz, Thomas, "Rags, Riches and Race: The Intergenerational Economic Mobility of Black and White Families in the United States," 2005. Used with permission; **p. 238, Figure 9.7:** Ray, Rebecca and John Schmitt. 2007. "Yes-Vacation Nation." Washington, DC: Center for Economic Policy and Research. Copyright © 2007. Used with permission; **p. 240, Figure 9.8:** "Shifting Responsibility: How 50 Years of Tax Cuts Benefited the Wealthiest Americans," by Chuck Collins, Alison Goldberg and Sam Pizzigati, April 7, 2010. Copyright © 2010 Institute for Policy Studies. Used with permission; **p. 241, Map 9.1:** The World Bank; **p. 242, Figure 9.9:** World Development Indicators database, World Bank, 2010, http://siteresources.worldbank org/DATASTATISTICS/Resources/GNIPC.pdf; **p. 243, Figure 9.10:** Human Development report. Copyright © 1992. Used by permission of Oxford University Press; **p. 244, Map 9.2:** © World Sites Atlas (sitesatlas.com); **p. 245:** *The Capitalist World-Economy* by Immanuel Wallerstein. Copyright © 1979 Cambridge University Press. Used with permission; **p. 246:** Figure 9.11 *Analysis of US Census Bureau data in Economic Policy Institute, The State of Working America 1994–95,* p. 37 Copyright © 1995 M.E. Sharpe.

Chapter 10

p. 255, Map 10.1: Map of global distribution of skin tone produced by Dennis O'Neil from "Distribuzione della Varia Intensitá del Colore della Pelle" in Renato Biasutti, Le Razze e I Popoli della Terra: Volume Primo—Razze, Popoli e Culture (1959); **p. 257, Figure 10.2:** Reproduced by permission of the American Anthropological Association from the web site RACE Are We So Different?, Lived Experience Global Census section; **p. 260, Map 10.2:** James West Davidson et al., *Experience History* (New York: McGraw-Hill, 2011), p. 485.

Copyright © 2011 McGraw-Hill Companies, Inc. Used with permission; **p. 273:** Oliver, Melvin L. and Thomas M Shapiro, *Black Wealth, White Wealth: A New Perspective on Racial Inequality.* Copyright © 1995, 2006 Taylor & Francis Group LLC. Used with permission; **p. 278, Figure 10.6:** Jeffrey S. Passel, Wendy Wang and Paul Taylor, "Marrying Out: One-in-Seven New U.S. Marriages is Interracial or Interethnic," Pew Research Center, June 2010. http://pewsocialtrends.org/2010/06/04/marrying-out.

Chapter 11

p. 292: Davies, Karen, "The body and doing gender: the relations between doctors and nurses in hospital work." *Sociology of Health & Illness* 25(7):720–742. Copyright © 2003. Reprinted by permission of John Wiley & Sons, Inc.; **p. 300, Table 11.2:** Inter-Parliamentary Union, "Women in National Parliament" October 2010. Used with permission; **p. 300:** Quotation from The Holy Bible, New International Version®, NIV® Copyright © 1973, 1978, 1984, 2010 by Biblica, Inc.™ Used by permission. All rights reserved worldwide; **p. 300:** Koran (4.34) from the University of Michigan Library's Digital Collections. This is an electronic version of The Holy Qur'an, translated by M.H. Shakir and published by Tahrike Tarsile Qur'an, Inc., in 1983. The text was provided by the Online Book Initiative and subsequently marked up at the HTI in SGML http://quod.lib.umich.edu/k/koran/; **p. 302, Figure 11.4:** World Health Organization. 2005. "WHO Multi-country Study on Women's Health and Domestic Violence against Women" Geneva: World Health Organization. Copyright © 2005. Used with permission; **p. 302,** World Health Organization. 2005. "WHO Multi-country Study on Women's Health and Domestic Violence against Women" Geneva: World Health Organization. http://www.who.int/gender/violence/who _multicountry_study/summary_report/summary_report_English2.pdf

Chapter 12

p. 312: Coontz, Stephanie. 1992. *The Way We Never Were: American Families and the Nostalgia Trap;* Copyright © 1992 Perseus Books. Used with permission; **p. 325, Figure 12.2:** Popenoe, David. 2007. *The State of Our Unions: The Social Health of Marriage in America.* Piscataway, NJ: The National Marriage Project; **p. 332:** Marx, Karl. 1844/1978. "Contribution to the Critique of Hegel's Philosophy of Right: Introduction." Pp. 53–65 in Robert C. Tucker, ed. *The Marx-Engels Reader.* New York: W. W. Norton & Company; **pp. 332, 333:** H.H. Gerth and C. Wright Mills, *From Max Weber: Essays in Sociology.* New York: Oxford; University Press. Used by permission; **p. 338, Map 12.1:** U.S. Religious Landscape Survey, Pew Research Center's Forum on Religion & Public Life, © 2008, Pew Research Center. http://religions.pewforum.org/; **p. 339:** Emerson, Michael O. and David Hartman. 2006. "The Rise of Religious Fundamentalism." *Annual Review of Sociology* 32:127–144. Copyright © 2006 Annual Reviews, Inc.; **p. 339:** © beliefnet.com

Chapter 13

p. 348, Table 13.1: *Organisation for Economic Cooperation and Development, Education at a Glance 2009: OECD Indicators,* OECD Publishing. http://dx.doi.org/10.1787/eag-2009-en; **p. 350:** Brint, Steven, Mary F. Contreras, and Michael T. Matthews. 2001. Socialization Messages in Primary Schools. *Sociology of Education* 74 (July): 157–180. Copyright © 2001 Sage Publications, Inc. Used with permission; **p. 351:** Brint, Steven. 2006. *Schools and Societies,* second edition. Copyright © 1998 Pine Forge Press; 2006 by the Board of Trustees of the Leland Stanford Jr. University. All right reserved. Used with the permission of Stanford University Press. www.sp.org; **p. 355, Figure 13.3:** original data from *Cities in Crisis 2009: Closing the Graduation Gap,* Editorial Projects in Education Research Center (April 2009); **p. 359, Map 13.1:** Segregation in US Schools adapted from NYT 4/2/2000, p. A5 by http://www.umich.edu/~lawrace/schoolsegregation1.htm Courtesy of Elizabeth Anderson, University of Michigan; **p. 364, Table 13.4:** HarrisInteractive, "Firefighters, Scientists and Doctors Seen as Most Prestigious Occupations." August 4, 2009. Copyright © 2009 HarrisInteractive. Used with permission; **p. 365:** Smith, Tom W. 2007. Job Satisfaction in the United States. NORC/University of Chicago, April 17; **p. 365, Table 13.5:** "Job Satisfaction in the United States." NORC/University of Chicago, April 17. Available www.news .uchicago.edu/releases/07/pdf/070417.jobs.pdf; **p. 365:** Peterson, Trond and Ishak Saporta. 2004. The Opportunity Structure for Discrimination. *American Journal of Sociology* 109 (4): 852–901. Copyright © 2004 the University of Chicago Press. Used with permission; **p. 366, Figure 13.5:** Institute for Women's Policy Research. www.iwpr.org/publications/pubs/the-gender-wage-gap-2010-updated-march-2011. Copyright © 2011. Used with permission.

Chapter 14

p. 381, Figure 14.3: NewsCorp holdings flow chart from News Corporation, Annual Report, 2007; Columbia Journalism Review (http://cjrarchives.org/tools/owners/newscorp .asp; **p. 384:** Table from Media Action Network for Asian Americans (http://www.manaa .org/asian_stereotypes.html) Copyright © Media Action Network for Asian Americans. Used with permission; **p. 386, Figure 14.4:** Holmes and Bloxham, 2007. Holmes, Michael and MikeBloxham. 2007. "An Observational Method for Time Use Research: Advantages, Disadvantages, and Lessons Learned from the Middletown Media Studies." October. Paper presented at the 2007 Conference of the International Association of Time Use Researchers, Washington, DC.; **p. 393:** Quotations from Mariampolski, Hy, 2001. *Qualitative Market Research: A Comprehensive Guide.* Thousand Oaks, CA: Sage Mariampolski, Hy. 2005. *Ethnography for Marketers: A Guide to Consumer Immersion.* Thousand Oaks, CA: Sage; **p. 393:** Coontz, Stephanie. 1992. *The Way We Never Were: American Families and the Nostalgia Trap.* Copyright © 1992 Perseus Books. Used with permission; **p. 398, Table 14.1:** Gardner, Gary, Erik Assadourian, and Radhia Sarin. 2004. "The State of Consumption Today." Pp. 3–23 in *The State of the World, 2004: Worldwatch Institute Report on Progress towards a Sustainable Society,* edited by Linda Starke. Copyright © 2004 by Worldwatch Institute. Used by permission of W.W. Norton & Company, Inc.; **p. 400:** Angwin, Julia. 2010. "The Web's New Gold Mine: Your Secrets." *The Wall Street Journal.* July 30, 2010. Copyright © 2010 Dow Jones Co., Inc. Used with permission.

Chapter 15

p. 411, Table 15.2: UN Department of Economic and Social Affairs, "World Urbanization Prospects: The 2009 Revision." Retrieved from http://esa.un.org/unpd/wup/index .htm; **p. 416, Figure 15.3:** www.salon.com/news/politics/war_room/2011/03/29/most _segregated_cities/slideshow.html; **p. 417, Figure 15.4:** John R. Logan and Brian Stults. 2011. "The Persistence of Segregation in the Metropolis: New Findings from the 2010

Census" Census Brief prepared for Project US2010. http://www.s4.brown.edu/us2010; **p. 430, Map 15.1:** Global death rates map © 2007 http://gamapserver.who.int/mapLibrary/app/searchResults.aspx

Chapter 16

p. 436: Zoroya, Gregg. 2008. "More U.S. Troops Battle Foreclosure." *USA Today.* April 25. On-line: http://www.usatoday.com/news/military/2008-04-24-foreclosure_N.htm.; **p. 438:** The Democracy Index, published by the *Economist* magazine's Economist Intelligence Unit (2010), identifies five key components of a democratic government; **p. 438, Map 16.1:** Economist Intelligence Unit 2010; **p. 439, Figure 16.1a** © Green Party. Used with permission. Figure 16.1b © Libertarian Party. Used with permission. Figure 16.1c © Independence Party. Used with permission. Figure 16.1d © Reform Party USA. Used with permission. Figure 16.e © Socialist Party. Used with permission; **p. 440, Figure 16.2:** © German Bundestag/Klimpel; **p. 442, Table 16.1:** Institute for Democracy and Electoral Assistance, www.idea.int/vt/; **p. 442:** Scheufele, Dietram A. and Patricia Moy. 2000. Twenty-five years of the spiral of silence: A conceptual review and empirical outlook. *International Journal of Public Opinion Research.* 12 (1): 3 28. Copyright © 2000, Oxford University Press. Used with permission; **p. 444, Figure 16.3:** Lobbying expenditures by sectors 2010 http://www.opensecrets.org/lobby/top.php?showYear=2010&indexType=c; **p. 446, Figure 16.4:** Tax cuts for the wealthy graph taxpolicycenter.org, February 9, 2011.http://www .taxpolicycenter.org/numbers/displayatab.cfm?DocID=2883&topic2ID=40&topic3ID=4 1&DocTypeID=2; **p. 446, Figure 16.5:** Adapted from *Economic Apartheid in America: A Primer on Economic Inequality & Insecurity,* Revised and Updated Editions. Copyright © 2005 by Chuck Collins and Felice Yeskel, United for a Fair Economy, and Class Action. Reprinted by permission of The New Press. www.thenewpress.com; **p. 448, Figure 16.6:** Copyright © 2010 SIPRI. Used with permission; **p. 448, Figure 16.7:** National Priorities Project http://nationalpriorities.org/en/resources/federal-budget-101/charts/discretionary spending/discretionary-budget-fy2011/; **p. 453:** Turk, Austin T. 2004. Sociology of Terrorism. *Annual Review of Sociology* 30: 271–286. Copyright © 2004 Annual Reviews, Inc.

Chapter 17

p. 468: Table copyright © American Sociological Association Research and Development Department, What can I do with a bachelor's degree in sociology? Wave I and Wave II; **p. 476:** Table 17.1: Dreher, Axel (2006): Does Globalization Affect Growth? Evidence from a new Index of Globalization, *Applied Economics* 38, 10: 1091–1110; **p. 472:** Map 17.1: Map of British Empire in 1920. Based on archival maps at www.probertencyclopaedia .com and www.britishempire.co.uk; **p. 479, Figure 17.1:** *World Population Prospects: The 2010 Revision.* Copyright © 2010 United Nations; **p. 480, Figure 17.2:** *World Population Prospects: The 2010 Revision.* Copyright © 2010 United Nations; **p. 480, Figure 17.3:** World Population Prospects: The 2010 Revision. Copyright © 2010 United Nations; **p. 481, Table 17.1:** *World Population Prospects: The 2010 Revision.* Copyright © 2010 United Nations; **p. 490, Figure 17.5:** "Ten Years of Changing Attitudes on Gay Marriage," Pew Research Center's Forum on Religion & Public Life, © 2011, Pew Research Center. http:// www.pewforum.org/.

Photo Credits:

Subject Index

Applying Sociological Theory

Theory is integral to the discipline of sociology and is covered in every chapter of *Experience Sociology*. This list provides a sample of the application of sociology's major theoretical perspectives to key sociological issues. The numbers in parentheses indicate chapters.

OVERVIEW OF SOCIOLOGICAL THEORY

Role of theory in sociological research (2)
Sociology's common ground: culture, structure, and power (1)
Sociology's major theoretical perspectives (1)

STRUCTURAL FUNCTIONALISM

Addams and urban sociology (15)
And culture, structure, power (1)
Cultural lag (17)
Culture and prejudice (10)
Culture wars (3)
Debt and dissatisfaction (14)
Demography and population change (17)
Deviance: boundaries, solidarity, and innovation (8)
Durkheim (1)
Durkheim on deviance (8)
Economy and social cohesion (16)
Functions of class (9)
Functions of religion (12)
Functions of schooling (13)
Functions of the family (12)
Functions of the media (14)
Gender stratification (11)
Global culture, structure, and power (17)
Government regulation of media (14)
Groups and organizations (7)
Herbert Spencer (1)
Human ecology (15)
Ideas and change (17)
Institutional interrelationships (4)
Moral education (13)
Multiculturalism's critics (3)
Nature of work (4)
Organic and mechanical solidarity (15)
Organizations and structure (4)
Parsons and power (5)
Place, people, relationships (15)
Promoting values via socialization (6)
Religion (3)
Rituals (2)
Sacred/Profane (12)
Social cohesiveness (3)
Socialization (11)
Socialization and social control (8)
Solidarity and team success (2)
Statuses and roles (4)
Strain theory (8)
Tönnies (15)
Traditional gender roles (4)

CONFLICT THEORY

Addams and urban sociology (15)
Alienation and consumption (14)
And culture, structure, power (1)
Anti-corporate activism (3)
Arab societies (1)
Authority (5)
Bureaucracy (7)
Class inequality (5)
Competition for jobs (10)
Cultural capital (9, 13)
Cultural imperialism (14)
Culture wars (3)
Debt and dissatisfaction (14)
Demographic divide (17)
Digital divide (14)
Disenchantment (12)
Dominant ideology (3)
Domination and "power over" (5)
DuBois (1)
Educational inequality (13)
Eliminating sweatshops (4)
Environmental destruction (14)
Ethnocentrism (3)
Gender gap and division of labor (13)
Gender stratification (11)
Gender, power, and the family (12)
Global culture, structure, and power (17)
Globalization and colonialism (17)
Globalization of culture (3)
Globalization of work (4)
Hegemony and cultural power (5)
Historical materialism (17)
Ideas and change (17)
Inequality (1)
Inequality and consumption (14)
Institutional discrimination (10)
Leadership and oligarchy (7)
Marx (1)
Marx on class (9)
Marx on religion (12)
Media consolidation (14)
Multiculturalism (3)
New urban sociology (15)
Occupational status and prestige (13)
Organizations and structure (4)
Organizing for power (17)
Political power (5)
Politics of fear (16)
Power and crime (8)
Power and deviance (8)
Power and government (16)
Power and privilege (5)
Power in groups and organizations (7)

Power of disobedience (5)
Power on the job (13)
Promoting values via socialization (6)
Rationalization (4)
Sexual identities and inequality (11)
Social economy (16)
Socialization (11)
Socialization in school (13)
Status (5)
Stratification systems (5)
Sustainability and inequality (15)
Treadmill of production (15)
Urban growth machine (15)
Weber (1)
Weber and power (5)
Weber's concept of "life chances" (9)
Workplace control (7)

SYMBOLIC INTERACTIONISM

Addams and urban sociology (15)
And culture, structure, power (1)
Binge drinking (2)
Consumption and identity (14)
Conversation analysis (4)
Cooley and Mead (6)
Cultural capital (9, 13)
Culture and prejudice (10)
Developing a self (6)
Deviance: boundaries, solidarity, and innovation (8)
Differential association theory (8)
Doing gender (11)
Emotional labor (13)
Framing messages (17)
Humans without culture (6)
Individual prejudice (10)
Interaction and intersubjectivity (7)
Internet norms (3)
Learning gender (11)
Navigating communities (15)
Neurosociology (6)
Occupational status and prestige (13)
Online identity (6)
Peer group socialization (6)
Political socialization (16)
Power in groups and organizations (7)
Power tactics (5)
Religious symbols and interaction (12)
Rites of passage (6)
Sacred canopy (12)
Social construction of environmental problems (15)
Social construction of reality (7)
Socialization (11)
Socialization for war (16)
Socialization in school (13)
Status (5)
Statuses and roles (4, 7)
Subcultures and countercultures (3)

Symbols and language (3)
Team success (2)
Thomas theorem (7)
Transnational identities (17)
Workplace culture (13)

FEMINIST THEORIES

Addams (1)
Addams and urban sociology (15)
Breast cancer (2)
Defining political issues (16)
Doing gender (11)
Emotion work (7)
Emotional labor (13)
Empowerment and "power to" (5)
Feminist scholarship and activism (11)
Gender gap and division of labor (
Gender, power, and the family (12)
Inequality (11)
Intersectionality theory (5)
Learning gender (11)
Martineau (1)
Patriarchy (5)
Power and privilege (5)
Sexual identities and inequality (1
Socialization (11)
Standpoint theory (5)
Team success (2)

OTHER THEORETICAL PERSPECTIV

DEPENDENCY THEORY
Exploitation and global inequality (

DRAMATURGICAL THEORY
Racist "back-stage" behavior (10)
Role expectations and impression management (7)

ETHNOMETHODOLOGY
Conversation analysis (4)
Ethnomethodology (4)

FOUCAULT
Categorizing sexualities (11)
Foucault and power (5)
Power and the self (6)
Surveillance and social control (8)

LABELING THEORY
Deviance and stigma (8)

PLURALIST THEORY
Political power (5)

POSTMODERNISM
Postmodernism (1, 14)

RATIONAL CHOICE THEORY
Deviance as rational choice (8)
Religious marketplace (12)

WORLD SYSTEMS THEORY
Global economy (15, 17)